NETWORKING WITH
MICROSOFT TCP/IP

THIRD EDITION

BY DREW HEYWOOD

New Riders

201 West 103rd Street, Indianapolis, Indiana 46290

Networking with Microsoft TCP/IP, Third Edition

Copyright © 1998 by New Riders Publishing

International Standard Book Number: 0-7357-0014-1

Library of Congress Catalog Card Number: 98-86324

Printed in the United States of America

First Printing: October, 1998

00 99 98   4 3 2 1

Warning and Disclaimer

EXECUTIVE EDITOR:
Jeff Koch

ACQUISITIONS EDITOR
Jane Brownlow

DEVELOPMENT EDITOR
Jeff Koch

MANAGING EDITOR
Brice Gosnell

PROJECT EDITOR
Katie Purdum

COPY EDITOR
Pamela Woolf

INDEXER
Tina Trettin

PROOFREADER
Benjamin Berg

TECHNICAL EDITOR
Walter Glenn

INTERIOR DESIGN
Louisa Klucznik

LAYOUT TECHNICIANS
Michael Dietsch
Ayanna Lacey
Heather Hiatt Miller

Trademarks

Dedication

For Woody from his proud father

– Drew Heywood

Acknowledgments

My sincere thanks go out to:

Blythe, for her patience, support, and business expertise that support me every day.

My mother, for always helping out in a crisis.

New Riders Publishing for giving me yet another opportunity. To everyone at New Riders, many thanks.

Jane Brownlow for keeping the project on track.

About the Author

Drew Heywood first became involved with computers when he was ensnared by the come-hither look of an Apple II 1978, and they've been eating up large parts of his paychecks ever since. He started conversing with the ether in 1985 when a LAN crossed his path, and has spent so much time with networks that he's not good for much of anything else. After several years of running networks he fell into book development at New Riders publishing, where he launched many of the best-selling network books in the industry. While at New Riders a dormant writing bug—squashed by a couple of flops in the early 1980s—reasserted itself, and Drew once again started pounding the keys late into the night as he authored and co-authored a variety of popular network titles. In 1984, he left New Riders to try writing full time. Now with three successful books, Drew is well on the way to enjoying the occupational benefits of the writing profession: failing eyesight, pallid skin, and deadline stress. And, thankfully, the kind comments of a number of readers, for which he is extremely grateful. Drew is a Microsoft Certified Systems Engineer (MCSE) and a Certified NetWare Engineer (CNE).

On the rare occasions when he is not in his office staring at a monitor, Drew enjoys activities with his wife Blythe. A seasoned computer professional herself, Blythe keeps Drew honest and keeps the business running smoothly. Together they enjoy music and dance concerts and travel to historic areas.

Contents at a Glance

Table of Contents

Tell Us What You Think!

As the reader of this book, *you* are our most important critic and commentator. We value your opinion and want to know what we're doing right, what we could do better, what areas you'd like to see us publish in, and any other words of wisdom you're willing to pass our way.

As the Executive Editor for the Operating Systems team at Macmillan Computer Publishing, I welcome your comments. You can fax, email, or write me directly to let me know what you did or didn't like about this book—as well as what we can do to make our books stronger.

Please note that I cannot help you with technical problems related to the topic of this book, and that due to the high volume of mail I receive, I might not be able to reply to every message.

When you write, please be sure to include this book's title and author as well as your name and phone or fax number. I will carefully review your comments and share them with the author and editors who worked on the book.

Fax:[317-581-4663]

E-mail: [opsys@mcp.com]

Jeff Koch
Executive Editor
Macmillan Computer Publishing
201 West 103rd Street
Indianapolis, IN 46290 USA

Introduction

INTRODUCTION

When I wrote the first edition of this book, Microsoft had barely made a move toward the Internet. To add a World Wide Web server to Windows NT you had to use a third-party product such as the EMWAC software that was included with the Windows NT Resource Kit.

But Microsoft was already on the move, and before the ink was dry on the first edition it was becoming apparent that Microsoft intended to be a major player in the Internet arena. First came Internet Explorer, which has grown into a world-class Web browser. Then came the Internet Information Server, which was already at version 2.0 when it was bundled with Windows NT Server 4 in August 1996. Now Microsoft has too many Internet products to keep track of; just try to keep up with the announcements and new products on their Web site. Internet Information Server is now at version 4, and several new products such as Microsoft Proxy Server have been added to Microsoft's Internet product line.

The Internet was hot when I wrote the first edition, but now, as I put the third edition to bed, it is on fire. If you are a LAN administrator who has been sitting on the sidelines you can't stay there any longer. It is time to learn TCP/IP and get cooking on Internet and intranet technologies.

In today's world, as IS managers seek to base their systems on standards and as everyone wants to connect to the Internet, TCP/IP has become unavoidable for anyone working with LANs. That doesn't make TCP/IP any less imposing, however. If you're among the many LAN administrators who need to get up to speed on TCP/IP this book is for you.

TCP/IP is an extremely rich set of network protocols, probably the richest. After all, no other protocols implement the Internet as TCP/IP does. Many of the millions of Internet users are bent on making the Internet do more, which often means adding to TCP/IP. As a result, the family of TCP/IP protocols can become a professional preoccupation and has for many in the networking community. The vastness of TCP/IP forces any author addressing the subject to select a subset of the field—a subset that will meet the needs of the book's readers.

In selecting material for this book, I have tried to meet two goals: To tell you what you must know without overwhelming you, and to tell you everything you are ever likely to need to know. Although there is a lot of information is in this book, I have tried to organize it so that you can focus on the topics that are most relevant to your current needs. Later as your experience grows and your responsibilities expand, you should find it profitable to return to this book to round out your knowledge. In short, this isn't a book you will read just once.

So, What's New In This Edition?

I've gone on and on about what's changed in Microsoft's approach to the Internet, so it's fair to ask how I have responded to those changes in this edition of the book. I've made small additions and changes throughout the book, weaving in material I've gathered from Microsoft and other publications, but there are big changes as well, including whole new chapters. Here are some things you can look for:

- Naming support on Microsoft TCP/IP networks is quite complex. In this edition, I've added a new chapter that enhances discussion of the various ways Microsoft supports NetBIOS and TCP/IP naming. The new chapter on naming is Chapter 11.

- Another new chapter addresses network management with SNMP. Look in Chapter 15 for that material.

- Troubleshooting now has its own chapter. Management and troubleshooting are covered in Chapter 16.

- Coverage of the routing and remote access service (RAS), which greatly enhances Microsoft's routing and connectivity support. Now you can set up Windows NT routers with RIP version 2 or OSPF for example. Look for coverage of routing and (RAS) in Chapter 18.

- Microsoft Exchange Server has good hooks into Internet email. Although Exchange is too complex to cover in a chapter, I asked Bruce Hallberg to do his best to introduce you to Exchange and its connectivity to TCP/IP mail systems. You'll find Bruce's material in Chapter 19.

- Internet Information Server has grown in complexity and capability. I've updated the IIS chapter to cover version 4, and I've worked with Bob Willsey to address the full range of IIS features. IIS is covered in Chapter 20.

- Microsoft Proxy Server is a dandy program that improves the efficiency of your access to the Internet while enhancing security with several firewall features. Proxy Server is covered in Chapter 21.

With these new or expanded chapters I've tried to keep pace with Microsoft's frequent product announcements. The enhanced scope of this book reflects the enhanced scope of TCP/IP, which grows in complexity with each passing month.

How This Book Is Organized

Part I, "TCP/IP Concepts," provides background information about the TCP/IP family of protocols. The information in these chapters applies to all implementations of TCP/IP. Although it may seem like the information goes overboard, you'll find a use for nearly all of it in Part II, "Implementing Microsoft TCP/IP," which examines in detail how TCP/IP is implemented on Microsoft networking products.

The first time you read Part I don't get caught up in the details. Try to get the gist of the information and remember what the main topics are and where they are discussed. Then you can return to these basic chapters when you need more theory to bolster your understanding of the more practical chapters in Part II. Don't try to understand every word you read, just keep going back and each time your understanding will improve.

Part I takes the classic approach of discussing protocol stacks in layers. Both the OSI and the TCP/IP models are addressed because both are evident in Microsoft networking products. Here is what happens in Part I:

Chapter 1, "Introduction to TCP/IP," is a general overview. You will learn how TCP/IP protocols are developed, how standards are set, and how to obtain information.

Chapter 2, "TCP/IP Architecture," introduces the structures of the OSI reference model as well as the TCP/IP protocol stack architecture. You are introduced to the four layers of the TCP/IP architecture, which are the subjects of the next four chapters.

Chapters 3 through 6 discuss each layer of the TCP/IP protocol model in turn. You will learn how each layer functions and, more importantly, how the layers relate to each other.

With the theory of Part I behind you, you are ready to look at implementing specific features of Microsoft's TCP/IP implementation. Essentially, after a chapter of introduction, each TCP/IP subsystem gets its own chapter.

Chapter 7, "Introducing Microsoft TCP/IP," is just what the title implies. Here you will learn how Microsoft TCP/IP is organized and what the general features are.

Chapter 8, "Installing TCP/IP on Windows NT Computers," describes the details of installing and configuring TCP/IP on Windows NT servers and clients.

Chapter 9, "Routing Basics," explores how Windows NT can be configured to handle traffic in routed internetworks.

Chapter 10, "Managing DHCP," shows you how to implement the Dynamic Host Configuration Protocol, one of the most time-saving administrative tools included with Microsoft TCP/IP.

Chapter 11, "Host Naming in the Microsoft TCP/IP World," discusses the complexities of naming on a Microsoft TCP/IP network. NetBIOS and TCP/IP naming schemes are examined along with the ways they come together on Microsoft networks.

Chapter 12, "Managing WINS," explains how to use the Windows Internet Naming Service to provide name resolution for Microsoft TCP/IP clients.

Chapter 13, "Managing the Microsoft DNS Server," shows how to set up a domain name service (DNS) name server on your network, enabling your hosts to participate in the DNS name service on the Internet.

Chapter 14, "Installing TCP/IP on Microsoft Clients," covers installation of TCP/IP on MS-DOS, Windows 3.x, and Windows 95/98 clients.

Chapter 15, "Managing TCP/IP with SNMP," describes SNMP and shows you how to set up SNMP monitoring agents on your Microsoft clients.

Chapter 16, "Troubleshooting," shows how to use various troubleshooting utilities that are included with NT, how to collect statistics using Performance Monitor, and how to examine network traffic with Network Monitor.

Chapter 17, "Enabling a Secure Connection to the Internet," shows you how to connect to the Internet and explores RAS an Internet connectivity tool.

Chapter 18, "Routing and Remote Access Server," explores Microsoft's powerful router enhancements for NT. In this chapter you learn how to add RIP version 2 or OSPF routing support to your network and how to enhance the capabilities of RAS.

Chapter 19, "Email and Microsoft Exchange Server," introduces you to Microsoft Exchange and shows how Exchange can be used to establish a mail system with connections to TCP/IP mail servers and clients.

Chapter 20, "Internet Information Server," shows you how easy it is to build servers for the World Wide Web and FTP. It also examines some advanced IIS capabilities such as the use of digital certificates to ensure communication security.

Chapter 21, "Microsoft Proxy Server," shows you how to set up Microsoft's Proxy Server as an Internet firewall and as an intelligent proxy server that dramatically improves Internet access performance for your network clients.

Appendix A describes binary, decimal, and hexadecimal numbers, which you will encounter if you are working with TCP/IP.

Keep in Touch

No book is perfect. I am sure that I have missed topics readers want to know about, and I haven't seen a computer book yet that hasn't had an error or two. So I would like to hear from you, whether your words are blessings or curses. What questions have I left unanswered? What tips have I left unmentioned? How can I make the next edition of the book better? Please let me know. Write to NRP and they will get the word to me. Please include an email address if you have one. I'm sorry to have to ask you to use snail mail! Unfortunately, as I write this I am moving, and my future email address is unknown.

Thank you for buying my book. Thank you for reading it. And thank you in advance for letting me know what you think.

New Riders Publishing

The staff of New Riders Publishing is committed to bringing you the very best in computer reference material. Each New Riders book is the result of months of work by authors and staff who research and refine the information contained within its covers.

As part of this commitment to you, the NRP reader, New Riders invites your input. Please let us know if you enjoy this book, if you have trouble with the information and examples presented, or if you have a suggestion for the next edition.

Please note, though: New Riders staff cannot serve as a technical resource for Microsoft TCP/IP or for questions about software- or hardware-related problems. Please refer to the documentation that accompanies Microsoft products.

If you have a question or comment about any New Riders book there are several ways to contact New Riders Publishing. We will respond to as many readers as we can. Your name, address, and phone number will never become part of a mailing list or be used for any purpose other than to help us continue to bring you the best books possible. You can write us at the following address:

New Riders Publishing
Attn: Publishing Manager—Networking
201 W. 103rd Street
Indianapolis, IN 46290

If you prefer, you can fax New Riders Publishing at (317) 581-4670.

You can also send email to New Riders at the following Internet address:

`edulaney@newriders.mcp.com`

New Riders is an imprint of Macmillan Computer Publishing. To obtain a catalog or information, or to purchase any Macmillan Computer Publishing book, call (800) 428-5331.

Thank you for selecting *Networking with Microsoft TCP/IP*, Third Edition!

Part I

PART I: TCP/IP CONCEPTS

Chapter 1

INTRODUCTION TO TCP/IP

This chapter introduces several different aspects of TCP/IP, including its evolution and its standardization. The chapter covers the following topics:

- A brief history of TCP/IP

- The need for open computing standards

- Administration of the Internet

- The Internet standards process

- Obtaining RFCs and other Internet information

Until recently, computer systems were islands that communicated with one another only with difficulty (with one significant exception—as you will discover). When you bought a computer, you bought a network communication system with it. IBM mainframes, for example, networked using the System Network Architecture. SNA is a robust network architecture that's well-suited to the terminal-host environment of the mainframe computer, but IBM developed SNA to meet the needs of IBM computers, not the needs of the networking community as a whole. Consequently, few other vendors developed network equipment for SNA, preferring instead to develop their own network architectures to meet their visions of networking.

Dozens of network architectures populated the computers of the 1970s and 1980s. Equipment from the mainframe companies IBM, Digital, Sperry, Burroughs, Honeywell, and others frequently were virtual islands, unable to communicate with one another because each company had designed a proprietary network architecture. At that time, the computer vendors made most of their money by selling hardware, so they tended to view a proprietary network architecture as a way to bind their customers to specific brands of computer and network equipment.

When LANs became more common in the late 1980s, they, too, tended to utilize proprietary protocols. To consider only a few examples, Novell promoted their IPX/SPX protocol suite, Apple had AppleTalk, and IBM and Microsoft focused on NetBEUI. Enabling computers on one brand of LAN to communicate with computers on a competing LAN architecture presented a daunting task. Getting a PC to talk to a mainframe required specialized technologies that would turn a smart PC into a dumb terminal that could be permitted within the mainframe's sphere of influence. Often, moving data from one computer environment to another meant dumping the files to a data tape or disk that could be loaded on the destination computer. Enabling different computer systems to transparently share files and data was practically unknown.

As the end of the 1980s approached, this isolation of computer systems was becoming unacceptable. Companies that once viewed LANs as noncritical began to realize that their LANs were now serving vital business needs. Moreover, LANs were used to produce more than word processing documents and spreadsheets. LANs were becoming the repositories of critical company data that often needed to be shared with programs running on the mainframe. Left to their own resources, computer manufacturers likely would still be fighting over the design of a common network architecture. Fortunately for the user community, however, a grass-roots movement has accomplished what commercial enterprise has not. Thanks to a serendipitous chain of events, an architecture for internetworking various types of computers emerged.

That architecture was found on the Internet, the exception mentioned in the first sentence of this chapter. One group of users has been doing what everyone else wanted to do, and that group has been doing it for a long time. For more than 20 years, the Internet has provided a context for internetworking thousands of computers spread throughout the world. And TCP/IP is the language of the Internet.

This chapter introduces you to several aspects of TCP/IP. Because TCP/IP is best understood in its historical context, the first topic of discussion is the evolution of TCP/IP, starting with its early roots in the United States Department of Defense. That discussion introduces you to many of the networking problems that have stimulated the design and redesign of TCP/IP.

Finally, this chapter examines the TCP/IP standardization process. Unlike vendor proprietary protocols, which tend to evolve in manufacturers' laboratories, TCP/IP standardization is open and public. As you become involved with TCP/IP, you need to know about the standardization process so that you can monitor changes that might affect you.

A Brief History of TCP/IP

Perhaps no organization has more complex networking requirements than the United States Department of Defense (DoD). Simply enabling communication among the wide variety of computers found in the various services is not enough. DoD computers often need to communicate with contractors and organizations (such as many universities) that do defense-related research. Defense-related network components must be able to withstand considerable damage if the nation's defenses are to remain operable during a disaster.

That the DoD initiated research into networking protocols (investigating the technology now known as *packet switching*), therefore, is not surprising. In fact, research on the protocols that eventually became the TCP/IP protocol suite began in 1969. Among the goals for this research were the following:

- **Common protocols.** The DoD required a common set of protocols that could be specified for all networks. Common protocols would greatly simplify the procurement process.

- **Interoperability.** If equipment from various vendors could interoperate, development efficiency could be improved, and competition among vendors would be promoted.

- **Robust communication.** A particularly dependable network standard was required to meet the nation's defense needs. These protocols needed to provide reliable, high-performance networking with the relatively primitive wide-area network technologies then available.

- **Ease of reconfiguration.** Because the DoD would depend on the network, the capability to reconfigure the network and add and remove computers without disrupting communication was a necessity.

In 1968, the DoD Advanced Research Project Agency (then called ARPA but since redubbed DARPA) initiated research into networks using the technology now called packet switching. The first experimental network connected four sites: the University of California at Los Angeles (UCLA), the University of California at Santa Barbara (UCSB), the University of Utah, and SRI International. Early tests were encouraging, and additional sites were connected to the network. The ARPAnet, as it came to be called, incorporated 20 hosts by 1972.

Although it was originally intended to facilitate communication among the DoD, commercial research firms, and universities, the ARPAnet gradually became a medium for non-DoD communication as well. By the mid-1980s, the ARPAnet had become the backbone of an internetwork that connected large numbers of educational institutions and defense contractors, as well as the military network called MILnet. This extended network, of which ARPAnet was the backbone, became known as the Internet.

NOTE

You will encounter the terms "Internet" and "internet," and should be aware of an important distinction between them. An internet (short for internetwork) is any network comprised of multiple interconnected networks. The Internet is the global internetwork that traces its lineage back to the ARPAnet.

In 1986, groundwork was laid for the commercialization of the ARPAnet. At that time, work to isolate military networks from the ARPAnet commenced. The ARPAnet backbone was dismantled, replaced by a network funded by the National Science Foundation. NSFnet, which now functions as the Internet backbone, is managed by Advanced Network Services (ANS).

The evolutionary approach of the ARPAnet produced a community of users that became involved in debating and setting standards for the network. Most network protocols are developed under the control of the companies that develop them. Debate on the Internet protocols, however, has long taken place on a public forum. Consequently, these protocols are not "owned" by any particular company. Responsibility for setting Internet standards rests with an *Internet Activity Board*.

The initial set of TCP/IP protocols was developed in the early 1980s and became the standard protocols for the ARPAnet in 1983. The protocols gained popularity in the user community when TCP/IP was incorporated into version 4.2 of the BSD (Berkeley Standard Distribution) UNIX. This version of UNIX is used widely in educational and research institutions and was used as the foundation of several commercial UNIX implementations, including Sun's SunOS and Digital's Ultrix. Because BSD UNIX established a relationship between TCP/IP and the UNIX operating system, the vast majority of UNIX implementations now incorporate TCP/IP.

Evolution of the TCP/IP protocol suite continues in response to the evolution of the Internet. In recent years, access to the Internet has extended beyond the original community and is available to virtually anyone who has a computer. This dramatic growth has stressed the Internet and has pushed the design limitations of several protocols. On the Internet, nothing is permanent except change.

The Need for Open Computing Standards

As computing has escaped the MIS department and found a home on the desktop, the communication boundaries imposed by proprietary protocols have become less and less tolerable. The user community has come to demand more open standards: standards that are open to public debate, not controlled by a single commercial interest, and are free to be used by all. Vendor-controlled proprietary standards, however, present two disadvantages. Vendors who want to use the protocols must license them, often at considerable cost. Also, the controlling vendor can be unresponsive to requests from other vendors for changes in the protocols.

Given those requirements, the protocols used on the Internet are the only fully functioning protocols that can be regarded as truly open. Only TCP/IP is available freely and is defined in an environment of public review.

NOTE

For several years, the International Organization for Standardization (ISO) attempted to define an open protocol suite called Open Systems Interconnection (OSI). As work on the OSI protocols progressed, it was widely assumed that they would supplant TCP/IP as the open protocol solution. The United States government announced that future computer purchases would conform to a government subset of the OSI protocols, called GOSIP, and the DoD indicated that GOSIP would replace TCP/IP on military networks.

As often happens with international bodies, negotiations on the OSI protocol suite have become bogged down. In part because the designers attempted to make the protocols everything for everyone, the OSI protocols have been slow to emerge. In fact, development appears to be stalled, and interest in OSI has waned, even as the fortunes of TCP/IP have prospered. Many industry analysts argue that OSI was not needed because a functional open protocol suite already is available in TCP/IP. The DoD has backed off from its declaration that future procurements would require GOSIP. Although OSI might yet be resurrected, the immediate future of TCP/IP appears to be secure. Given the growth of the Internet into a worldwide entity, it is difficult to see how TCP/IP could be dislodged.

One consequence of this openness is that TCP/IP has evolved into an extremely rich suite of protocols and applications. The name by which the protocol suite is most commonly known is misleading because TCP and IP are only two of dozens of protocols that constitute the protocol suite. Some refer to the suite as the *Internet protocol suite* or the *DoD protocol suite* to emphasize the fact that TCP/IP is much more than just TCP and IP.

The following are but a few examples of protocols and services associated with TCP/IP:

- **Telnet.** A remote terminal emulation protocol that enables clients to log in to remote hosts on the network.

- **FTP.** A file transfer application that enables users to transfer files between hosts.

- **NFS (Network File System).** A more sophisticated remote file access service that enables clients to access files on remote hosts as though the files were stored locally.

- **SNMP (Simple Network Management Protocol).** Used to remotely manage network devices.

- **SMTP (Simple Mail Transfer Protocol).** Used to implement electronic mail systems.

- **DNS (Domain Name Service).** Puts a friendly face on the network by assigning meaningful names to computers.

- **HTTP (Hypertext Transfer Protocol).** This protocol, the core of the World Wide Web, facilitates retrieval and transfer of hypertext (mixed media) documents.

Later chapters in this book describe these applications in greater detail. Chapter 6, "The Process-Application Layer," discusses Telnet, FTP, NFS, and SMTP. SNMP is one of several subjects addressed in Chapter 14, "Installing TCP/IP on Microsoft Clients." Chapter 13, "Managing the Microsoft DNS Server," shows you how to set up a DNS server. In Chapter 20, "Internet Information Server," you will see how the Internet Information Server can be used to set up a World Wide Web server.

Besides protocol proliferation, another consequence of this openness is that TCP/IP has been implemented on virtually all hardware and operating system platforms. No other protocol suite is available on all the following systems:

- Novell NetWare

- IBM mainframes

- Digital VMS systems

- Microsoft Windows NT Server

- UNIX workstations

- DOS personal computers

Administration of the Internet

The Internet Activities Board (IAB), established in 1983 and described as "an independent committee of researchers and professionals with a technical interest in the health and evolution of the Internet system," coordinates design, engineering, and management of the Internet. Figure 1.1 illustrates the organization of the IAB, along with its relationship to related groups. The IAB has two task forces: the Internet Engineering Task Force (IETF) and the Internet Research Task Force (IRTF).

FIGURE 1.1

Organizations involved with the Internet.

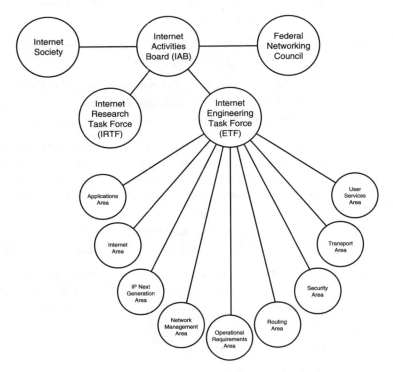

Two organizations serve a liaison function with the IAB. The *Federal Networking Council* represents all agencies of the United States federal government involved with the Internet. The *Internet Society* is a public organization that takes its membership from the entire Internet community. Both organizations provide input on Internet policy and standards.

The IETF is responsible for specifying the Internet protocols and architecture. By its own description, the IETF is not a traditional standards organization, although many specifications are produced that become standards. The IETF is made up of volunteers who meet three times a year to fulfill the IETF mission. RFC 1718, "The Tao of IETF," is an excellent introduction to the IETF.

NOTE

The IAB makes most information public in the form of Request for Comments (RFC) memos. Nearly 2,000 RFCs have been published since 1969. Some RFCs describe Internet standards. Most are posted to promote discussion. A few are sheer whimsy. For a taste of the latter, check out RFC 968, "Twas the night before start-up," by Vint Cerf.

Work of the IETF is organized into areas that change over time. The directors for the technical areas comprise the *Internet Engineering Steering Group*, which is responsible for recommending protocol standards. The current IETF areas include the following:

- Applications
- Internet
- IP: Next Generation Area
- Network Management
- Operational Requirements
- Routing
- Security
- Transport
- User Services

The IRTF is the research organization of the IAB. Membership of the IETF and the IRTF overlap considerably to promote technology transfer.

Figure 1.1 mentions two organizations that influence the IAB. The *Federal Networking Council* is the federal government's body for coordinating agencies that support the Internet.

The *Internet Society* is an open membership organization that involves educators, industry, users, and government in promoting use of the Internet. The Internet Society has a supporting role in the Internet standards process and has been delegated some responsibilities by the IETF. For membership information, contact the Internet Society using regular or electronic mail at either of the following addresses:

Internet Society
Suite 100
1895 Preston White Drive
Reston, VA 22091
U.S.A.

http://www.isoc.org
email: isoc@isoc.org
phone: (703) 648-9888

The Internet Standards Process

As you review the documentation for the TCP/IP component of Windows NT, you will see a list of RFCs that the product supports. Request for Comment (RFC) documents are the means for developing and publishing standards for use on the Internet. Because the vast majority of TCP/IP systems connect to the Internet, a standard for the Internet is a standard for the TCP/IP protocol suite.

On its way to becoming a standard, a protocol passes through stages as a Proposed Standard, which the IESG might promote to a Draft Standard and finally to a full-fledged Standard. At each stage, the proposed standard is subject to review, debate, implementation, and testing. Proposed Standards, for example, are subject to at least six months of review before IESG might promote them to a Draft Standard. In general, promoting a standard requires two independent implementations of the protocol.

A memo titled "Internet Official Protocol Standards" describes the standards for protocols to be used on the Internet. It also includes a thorough discussion of the standards process, which has been simplified considerably here. The memo is updated quarterly and is RFC 2200 as of this writing.

Note that not all RFCs are standards—many represent work in progress. Many RFCs, for example, have been posted to provide industry input to the process of updating the IP standard. Although not all RFCs are standards, all Internet standards are defined in RFCs and are assigned a standard number.

Not all protocols in common use on the Internet are defined as Internet standards. A protocol developed outside the Internet review process occasionally achieves widespread acceptance in the TCP/IP community; for example, the Network File System (NFS) protocol developed by Sun Microsystems. NFS is a crucial TCP/IP protocol in extremely wide use, but it is not an Internet standard. A protocol cannot be described as a standard in an RFC unless the IAG engineering study group approves its status.

NOTE

After a document has been assigned an RFC number and is published, it can never be revised using the same RFC number. Any published revisions are assigned new RFC numbers. If a new RFC obsoletes older RFCs, the obsolete RFCs are identified on the title page. Also, the old RFC is labeled as obsolete and classified as historical. Some Internet standards have been updated many times in this manner.

You don't need to concern yourself, therefore, about having the latest version of an RFC; only one version of a given RFC ever exists. You do need to ensure, however, that you have the current RFC for a given standard.

Internet protocols can be assigned several designations, depending on their state in the standards process:

- **Standard.** An official standard protocol for the Internet.

- **Draft Standard.** A protocol in the final stages of study prior to approval as a standard.

- **Proposed Standard.** A protocol under consideration for standardization in the future.

- **Experimental.** Protocols undergoing experimentation but not on the standards track.

- **Historic.** Protocols that have been superseded or are otherwise no longer under consideration for standardization.

You also see protocols identified as "informational." These are protocols that interest the Internet community but have not been through the IAG standards review process. RFC 1813 is an informational specification that describes the NFS Version 3 protocol.

Internet standards are categorized into these varying requirement levels:

- **Required.** Must be implemented by all systems connected to the Internet.

- **Recommended.** Should be implemented.

- **Elective.** Can be implemented if desired.

- **Limited.** Might be useful in some systems. Experimental, specialized, and historic protocols might receive this classification.

- **Not Recommended.** Historical, specialized, or experimental protocols not recommended for use on the Internet.

The matrix in Figure 1.2 summarizes the various possible classifications that can be assigned to a protocol.

FIGURE 1.2
Classifications of Internet protocols.

	Required	Recommended	Elective	Limited Use	Not Recommended
Standard	●	●	●		
Draft Standard	●	●	●		
Proposed Standard		●	●		
Informational					
Experimental				●	
Historic					●

NOTE

In recent years, new technologies have appeared on the Internet with staccato rapidity. A case in point is the World Wide Web, which depends on the Hypertext Transfer Protocol (HTTP). The Web and HTTP were in wide use long before RFC 1945 established an Internet standard for HTTP version 1.0. Increasingly, evolution of the Internet is being lead by network heavy hitters such as Microsoft and Netscape, and the standards process is too slow to satisfy vendors who want to establish themselves as leaders on the Net.

Internet-Drafts

At any time, IETF working groups are involved in a variety of projects that have not matured to the point of producing RFCs. These projects are frequently documented in *Internet-Drafts*, which are available from the same sources as RFCs. Internet-Drafts are subject to modification at any time.

A useful document to obtain is 1ID-ABSTRACTS.TXT, which contains abstracts of the various Internet-Drafts.

Obtaining RFCs and Other Internet Information

Information about the Internet abounds and is most readily available through—guess what—the Internet. RFCs and other information are available through FTP, WAIS, electronic mail, and the World Wide Web (WWW). A primary Internet resource is the InterNIC Directory and Database Services, which has two components:

- **Directory & Database Services, provided by AT&T.** This service is a source of information about the Internet, including RFCs. Another resource is the WHOIS server providing a white pages directory of Internet users. A Gopher database provides access to numerous Internet documents.

- **Registration Services, provided by Network Solutions.** This service is used to register Internet addresses and domain names.RFCs can be obtained in printed form, but the most expedient approach is to use one of the available techniques for using the Internet to obtain them. Recent information about obtaining RFCs is published in the "Internet Official Protocol Standards" document, discussed earlier in this chapter. Several access options, however, are not explained in the RFC.

RFCs can be obtained by way of FTP, WAIS, electronic mail, or the World Wide Web. To get up-to-date information about sources of RFCs, send an electronic mail message to **rfc-info@ISI.EDU** and include **help: ways_to_get_rfcs** as the body text. The response message you receive will include a variety of options not included here.

The most recent guidelines for retrieving RFCs are given in the file RFC-RETRIEVAL.TXT, which is available from many sources including the InterNIC FTP server rs.internic.net and the RFC Editor's Web site (http://www.isi.edu/rfc-editor/). This Web site includes a list of secondary repositories that would be useful if you want to obtain RFCs from a host that is close to home.

The InterNIC Directory and Database Service is a primary depository that offers many options for information retrieval. Not all the options discussed are available from all servers.

Unless you are looking for a specific RFC by number, you should first retrieve a file named RFC-INDEX.TXT, which lists all the RFCs. A typical entry is as follows:

```
1800 S  J. Postel, "INTERNET OFFICIAL PROTOCOL STANDARDS",
07/11/1995.
            (Pages=36) (Format=.txt) (Obsoletes RFC1780) (STD 1)
```

One of the following letters follows the RFC number to indicate the status of the RFC:

S   Standard

DS   Draft Standard

PS   Proposed Standard

I   Informational

E   Experimental

H   Historic

Standards are assigned standard numbers. The preceding RFC is Standard 1. A list of Internet standards is published in RFC 1800.

In many cases, RFCs are obsolete or are rendered obsolete by other RFCs, as is clearly indicated in the index listing and on the title page of the document.

Anonymous FTP

FTP (File Transfer Protocol) provides a mechanism for transferring files between TCP/IP hosts. Chapter 6, "The Process/Application Layer," describes FTP. Anonymous FTP permits users to log in and access FTP files even if they don't have an account on the server. Enter **anonymous** as the login and your email address as the password. In Chapter 6, FTP is used to perform an anonymous transfer of an RFC from the InterNIC server.

RFCs can be obtained via FTP from these servers:

DS.INTERNIC.NET (InterNIC Directory and Database Services)

NIS.NSF.NET

NISC.JVNC.NET

FTP.ISI.EDU

WUARCHIVE.WUSTL.EDU

SRC.DOC.IC.AC.UK

FTP.NCREN.NET

FTP.SESQUI.NET

NIS.GARR.IT

These hosts are primary depositories that are updated when an RFC is first announced. Several secondary depositories also are available, although it sometimes takes a few days for them to receive the most recent updates.

In most cases, such as the InterNIC server, RFCs are stored using the path rfc/rfc*nnnn*.txt, where *nnnn* is the number of the RFC.

NOTE

RFCs can also be obtained in PostScript format by replacing "txt" with "ps" in the path.

WAIS

WAIS (Wide Area Information Servers) enables you to search a database for specific documents. Users can use their own WAIS clients or can telnet to DS.INTERNIC.NET to access a WAIS client. Log in as **wais** (no password is necessary). Help and a tutorial are available online. WAIS searches also can be conducted by using the WWW.

Gopher

The indexed document database can be searched using Gopher. To access the InterNIC Gopher server from a remote Gopher client, connect to `inter-nic.net` using port 70. To access a Gopher client on the server, telnet to `DS.INTERNIC.NET` and log in as **gopher** (no password is required).

Archie

An Archie database is also maintained, and Archie searches can be performed using Telnet login or electronic mail. To access Archie, telnet to `DS.INTERNIC.NET` and log in as **archie** (no password is required). Online help is available.

To receive instructions through email about accessing Archie, send a message to `archie@ds.internic.net`. Include the command **help** in the body of the message.

Finally, users who do not have FTP or Telnet access can obtain RFCs through electronic mail. To obtain an RFC from InterNIC, send a message to `mailserv@ds.internic.net`. Include the message **file /ftp/rfc/rfc*nnnn*.txt**, where *nnnn* is the number of the RFC.

World Wide Web

Certainly, the easiest way to access these resources is to use the World Wide Web. The RFC Editor maintains a Web-based index at the following URL:

```
http://www.isi.edu/rfc-editor/
```

Another interesting Web site is maintained by the InterNIC. Starting from the following URL, you can reach nearly every site that offers information or resources related to the Internet:

```
http://www.internic.net/
```

The IETF also maintains a Web server, which can be reached with the following URL:

```
http://www.ietf.org/
```

Now You're Ready to Start

As the old saying goes, "If you give a man a fish, you will feed him for a day, but if you teach a man to fish, you will feed him for the rest of his life." In this chapter, I have tried to teach you how to fish for information about TCP/IP. The information sources are many and are readily accessible. I hope that you will avail yourself of the many opportunities to educate yourself about TCP/IP.

I also attempted to put TCP/IP in its place, describing the Internet and the standardization process for the Internet protocols. If you understand this process, you can put the many protocols in their places as standards, non-standards, and standards-to-be. The Internet is a big world with many protocols, and the information in this chapter should give you a sense of perspective.

Now the time has come to grapple with the technologies of TCP/IP. You will start out slowly, beginning in Chapter 2, "TCP/IP Architecture," by examining some concepts that underlie data communication. By the end of the chapter, you will have a better idea of how networks transmit data and of how TCP/IP provides an answer to the problems of network communication.

Chapter 2

TCP/IP ARCHITECTURE

The architecture of a computer system refers to overall system design. Microsoft designs its networking products using a fairly elaborate networking architecture that enables the products to support several popular networking protocols: NetBEUI, Novell's IPX/SPX, and TCP/IP. Chapter 7, "Introducing Microsoft TCP/IP," discusses the full scope of the Microsoft protocol architecture. This chapter focuses on the characteristics of network protocol architectures in general and on the specific characteristics of the TCP/IP protocol architecture.

As Chapter 1 mentioned, despite its name, *TCP/IP* comprises much more than the TCP and IP protocols. TCP/IP is a suite of protocols in which each protocol performs a subset of overall network communication tasks. Network implementors select from these protocols to achieve a desired network functionality. The TCP/IP protocol suite architecture defines the way the various TCP/IP protocols fit together.

Microsoft networks can involve multiple protocol suites, so establishing a model that clarifies the relations between the various protocols is essential. The conventional model for comparing protocol suites is the OSI reference model, which is the first topic this chapter covers. The discussion uses the OSI reference model to illustrate common characteristics all network protocol suites share. Chapter 7 also discusses the OSI reference model, using it to illustrate the way Microsoft products support multiple protocols concurrently.

After discussing the OSI reference model, this chapter examines TCP/IP architecture.

Understanding the Communication Process

The communication process is surprisingly complicated. People tend to take communication for granted because they are immersed in many forms of it every day of their lives. Even in the simplest of situations, however, communication can be quite involved. Data communication is a highly technical topic, one in which it can be difficult to not get bogged down in the details. Before things get too formal, it is illuminating to look at some examples of communication in which humans engage.

Dialogs

Humans and computers both exchange information in orderly conversations called *dialogs*. Consider the everyday event of meeting a friend on the street and holding a conversation, illustrated in Figure 2.1. Even this simple situation has rules:

1. One person initiates communication by greeting the other person. They might need to negotiate some details, such as what language to use.

2. The other person acknowledges the greeting. This exchange initiates a conversation, which in data communication terminology is called a *session*.

3. The individuals undertake an orderly exchange of information. Generally, one person talks while another listens, then the parties exchange roles. A complex set of rules helps the speakers exchange roles without interfering with one another's utterances. Without these rules, orderly conversation breaks down, and information exchange grinds to a halt. An example of failed communication is a shouting match in which both parties are talking at once and receive little information.

4. Rules are observed for ending the conversation. Polite exchanges take place when both parties feel they have completed their messages. If the conversation breaks down mid-message, communication errors can occur. Data communication often requires a session termination procedure.

FIGURE 2.1

An example of a dialog.

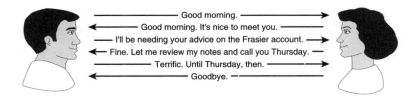

Human communication is not always so formal. If you need to warn someone about a falling brick, you do not need to establish a conversation. A single shouted warning might be the only communication that takes place. In such instances, however, the two parties must be in reasonable agreement about the rules of communication. A warning shout works if both parties speak the same language, for example, but it might be useless if the warning is in Japanese and the potential victim speaks only German.

Computers establish communication in much the same way as humans. They exchange greetings and negotiate the rules under which communication takes place. The result is a *connection* between the devices that ensures an orderly dialog. After the need for the connection ceases, another orderly procedure closes it. In that way, neither device is left hanging with incomplete information.

Communication Protocols

Data communication is surprisingly similar to human conversation. People and computers both utilize formal communication for complex data exchanges and informal processes for special purposes, such as warnings. Both follow *protocols*, rules that enable the subjects to exchange information in an orderly, error-free manner. Protocols are obeyed to establish and end communication, so that neither party is left hanging in an undesirable state. Just as the rude interruption of a conversation can offend a person, so too can the interruption of data communication without an orderly termination process confuse a computer.

The first characteristic to notice about the communication process, therefore, is that error-free communication can be achieved only by following communication protocols.

The inability of two entities to communicate directly complicates communication. Consider what happens when one person mails another person a letter:

1. Sender writes or types the letter on paper.

2. Sender inserts the paper in an envelope and labels that envelope with both his address and the intended receiver's address.

3. Sender places the envelope at a specific location, where the letter carrier picks it up and places it in a mail bag for transport.

4. The letter carrier takes the mail bag to the local post office branch, where yet another person or persons remove the letter from the bag, sort it, and place it in a mail bag destined for the city specified by the receiver's address.

5. Someone else transports the mail bag to the receiver's city.

6. After the mail bag arrives in the receiver's city, a person sorts the letters in the bag so that the letters can be given to the appropriate letter carriers for the regions in the city.

7. The letter carrier transports the letter to the receiver's address.

8. Finally, the receiver removes the letter from its envelope to recover the original message from the sender.

This scenario illustrates several important characteristics of communication. The diagram of this scenario, shown in Figure 2.2, closely resembles the architecture models that this chapter examines later.

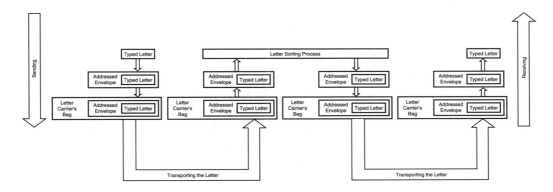

FIGURE 2.2

A model for communicating by letter.

One feature of the model shown in Figure 2.2 is that communication takes place in layers, each of which has a specifically defined area of responsibility. When you want a letter delivered, you need only place it in an envelope and address the envelope. You need not be concerned with the other layers of the process. You don't need to worry about whether the letter is transported by truck or by plane—another layer is responsible for that decision.

This approach to designing a communication system is known as a *layered architecture*. Each layer has specific responsibilities and specific rules for carrying out those responsibilities and knows nothing about the procedures the other layers follow. The layer carries out its tasks and delivers the message to the next layer in the process—and that is enough. Quite a few characteristics of layered architectures can be teased out of the preceding example:

■ Layers break the communication process into manageable chunks. Designing a small part of a process is much easier than designing the entire process, and it simplifies engineering. A postal customer must establish local mailroom procedures but does not need to devise a complete mechanism for delivering mail to remote sites.

- A change at one layer does not affect the other layers. The process of addressing an envelope does not change, whether the letter is being shipped by truck, train, or carrier pigeon. New delivery technologies can be introduced without affecting other layers. (This is the chief reason, in fact, for implementing protocols in layers.)

- When a layer receives a message from an upper layer, the lower layer frequently encloses the message in a distinct package. Letters are placed in mail bags when they are sent across the country, for example. In data communication terms, lower-layer protocols frequently treat upper-layer messages in a similar way, enclosing them in a "data envelope." The technical term for this process is *encapsulation*.

- The protocols at the various layers have the appearance of a stack, and a complete model of a data communication architecture is often called a *protocol stack*.

- Layers can be mixed and matched to achieve different requirements. By adding an overnight label to the envelope, the sender of a letter can have the letter routed through an overnight delivery service instead of being sent by standard first-class delivery.

- Layers follow specific procedures for communicating with adjacent layers. The interfaces between layers must be clearly defined.

- An *address mechanism* is the common element that allows letters to be routed through the various layers until it reaches its destination. Sometimes, layers add their own address information. The postal service often adds a bar code to letters, which enables letters to be routed more efficiently within the postal system. Postal addresses have two parts: a city and zip code that enable the postal service to deliver the message to the correct letter carrier, and a street address that enables the letter carrier to deliver the message to the correct recipient.

- Essentially, each layer at the sender's end communicates with the corresponding layer at the receiver's end. The process of putting the letter in an envelope, for example, has a matching process of opening the envelope in the destination city. The contents of the envelope are examined only by the sender and the receiver, and the contents have no significance at other layers.

■ Errors can occur at any of the layers. For critical messages, error-detecting mechanisms should be in place to either correct errors or notify the sender when they occur.

Each of these characteristics has its counterpart in data communication, and the time has come to examine some real data communication models. The first model this chapter considers is the OSI reference model, which is generic enough that it can serve to illustrate general characteristics of data communication models.

The OSI Reference Model

The International Organization for Standardization (ISO) developed the OSI reference model as a guide for defining a set of open protocols. Although interest in the OSI protocols has waned, the OSI reference model remains the most common standard for describing and comparing protocol suites.

NOTE

If only TCP/IP was being discussed, bypassing the OSI model would be possible. Microsoft networks can be implemented with protocols other than TCP/IP, however, including NWLink (Microsoft's implementation of Novell's IPX/SPX) and NetBEUI. The architecture for integrating these protocols is best illustrated using the OSI model.

Figure 2.3 shows the seven-layer OSI reference model. Each layer provides a specific type of network service. This chapter describes each of these layers.

FIGURE 2.3
The layers of the OSI reference model.

Application
Presentation
Session
Transport
Network
Data Link
Physical

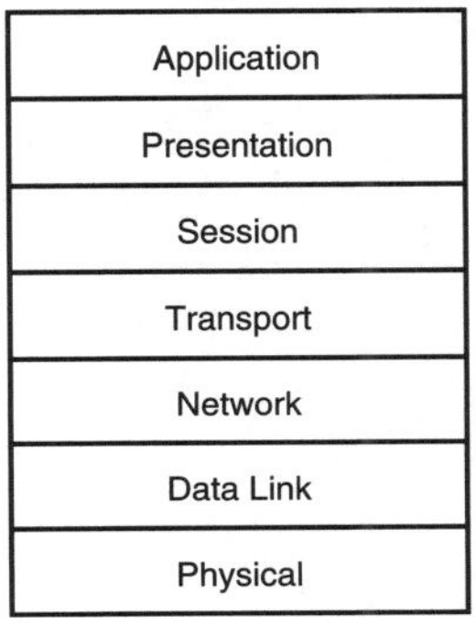

Figure 2.3 illustrates why groups of related protocols are frequently called *protocol stacks*. To an extent, network designers can build a protocol stack that meets their specific requirements by choosing an appropriate protocol for each layer and stacking them like digital Lego blocks. Layering makes changing the physical network easy (for example, changing from Ethernet to token ring), without the need for changes at other layers.

The layers are numbered from the bottom of the protocol stack to the top. The following sections discuss the layers in turn, from the bottom up.

The Physical Layer

The Physical layer communicates directly with the communication medium and has two responsibilities: sending bits and receiving bits. A *binary digit*, or *bit*, is the basic unit of information in data communication. A bit can have only two values, 1 or 0, which are represented by different states on the communication medium. Other communication layers are responsible for collecting these bits into groups that represent message data.

Bits are represented by changes in signals on the network medium. Some wire media represent 1s and 0s with different voltages, some use distinct audio tones, and yet others use more sophisticated methods, such as *state transitions* (changes from high-to-low or low-to-high voltages).

A wide variety of media are used for data communication, including electric cables, fiber optics, light waves, radio waves, and microwaves. The medium used can vary; a different medium simply necessitates substituting a different set of Physical layer protocols. Thus, the upper layers are completely independent from the particular process used to deliver bits through the network medium.

An important distinction is that the OSI Physical layer does not, strictly speaking, describe the media themselves. Physical layer specifications describe how data are encoded into media signals and the characteristics of the media attachment interface, but the specifications do not describe the medium itself. In actual practice, however, many Physical layer standards cover characteristics of the OSI Physical layer as well as characteristics of the medium.

The Data Link Layer

Devices that can communicate on a network are frequently called *nodes*. (Other names include *station* and *device*.) The Data Link layer is responsible for providing node-to-node communication on a single, local network. To provide this service, the Data Link layer must perform two functions. It must provide an address mechanism that enables messages to be delivered to the correct nodes. Also, it must translate messages from upper layers into bits that the Physical layer can transmit.

When the Data Link layer receives a message to transmit, it formats the message into a *data frame*. (You also hear data frames referred to as *packets*.) Figure 2.4 illustrates the format of a typical frame. Chapter 3, "The Network Access Layer," presents actual frame formats in the context of Ethernet and token ring protocols. The sections of a frame are called *fields*. The following fields appear in the given example:

- **Start Indicator.** A specific bit pattern indicates the start of a data frame.

- **Source Address.** The address of the sending node is also included so that replies to messages can be addressed properly.

- **Destination Address.** Each node is identified by an address. The Data Link layer of the sender adds the destination address to the frame. The Data Link layer of the receiver looks at the destination address to identify messages it should receive.

- **Control.** In many cases, additional control information must be included. The specific information is determined by each protocol.

- **Data.** This field contains all data that were forwarded to the Data Link layer from upper protocol layers.

- **Error Control.** This field contains information that enables the receiving node to determine whether an error occurred during transmission. A common approach is *cyclic redundancy checksum (CRC)*, which is a calculated value that summarizes all the data in the frame. The sending node calculates a checksum and stores it in the frame. The receiver recalculates the checksum. If the receiver's calculated CRC matches the CRC value in the frame, it can safely be assumed that the frame was transmitted without error.

Start Indicator	Source Address	Destination Address	Control	Data	Error Control

FIGURE 2.4
An example of a data frame.

Frame delivery on a local network is extremely simple. A sending node simply transmits the frame. Each node on the network sees every frame and examines the destination address. When the destination address of a frame matches the node's address, the Data Link layer at the node receives the frame and sends it up the protocol stack.

The Network Layer

Only the smallest networks consist of a single, local network. Most networks must be subdivided, as shown in Figure 2.5. A network that consists of several network segments is frequently called an *internetwork*, or an internet (not to be confused with *the* Internet).

FIGURE 2.5
An internetwork consists of several networks.

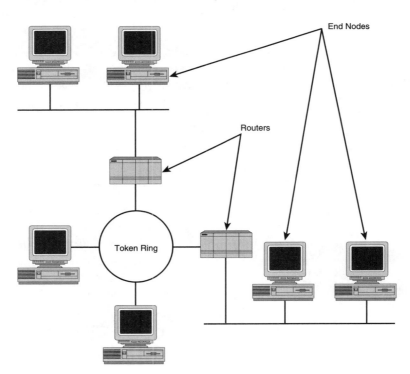

These subdivisions can be planned to reduce traffic on network segments or to isolate remote networks connected by slower communication media. When networks are subdivided, it can no longer be assumed that messages will be delivered on the local network. A mechanism must be put in place to route messages from one network to another.

For messages to be delivered on an internetwork, each network must be uniquely identified by a *network address*. When it receives a message from upper layers, the Network layer adds a header to the message that includes the source and destination network addresses. This combination of data plus the Network layer is called a *packet*. The network address information is used to deliver a message to the correct network. After the message arrives on the correct network, the receiving Data Link layer can use the node address to deliver the message to a specific node.

Forwarding packets to the correct network is called *routing*, and the devices that route packets are called *routers*. As you can see in Figure 2.5, an internetwork has two types of nodes:

- **End nodes** provide user services. End nodes do use the Network layer to add network address information to packets, but they do not perform routing. End nodes are sometimes called *end systems* (the OSI term) or *hosts* (the TCP/IP term).

- **Routers** incorporate special mechanisms that perform routing. Because routing is a complex task, routers usually are dedicated devices that do not provide services to end users. Routers sometimes are called *intermediate systems* (the OSI term) or *gateways* (the historic TCP/IP term).

The Network layer operates independently of the physical medium, which is a concern of the Physical layer. Because routers are Network layer devices, they can be used to forward packets between physically different networks. A router can join an Ethernet to a token ring network, for example. Routers also are often used to connect a local area network, such as Ethernet, to a wide area network, such as ATM.

The Transport Layer

All network technologies set a maximum size for frames that can be sent on the network. Ethernet, for example, limits the size of the data field to 1,500 bytes. This limit is necessary for the following two reasons:

- Small frames improve network efficiency when many devices must share the network. If a device could transmit frames of unlimited size, it might monopolize the network for an excessive period of time. With small frames, devices take turns at shorter intervals, and devices are more likely to have ready access to the network.

- With small frames, less data must be retransmitted to correct an error. If a 100KB message encounters an error of a single byte, the entire 100KB message must be retransmitted. However, if the message is divided into one hundred frames, each limited in size to 1KB, a one-byte error requires the retransmission of merely a single 1KB frame.

One responsibility of the Transport layer is to divide messages into fragments that fit within the size limitations established by the network. At the receiving end, the Transport layer reassembles the fragments to recover the original message.

When messages are divided into multiple fragments, the possibility that segments might not be received in the order they are sent increases. Figure 2.6 illustrates how the network can route packets differently as routers attempt to send each packet by the most efficient available route. When the packets are received, the Transport layer must reassemble the message fragments in the correct order. To enable packets to be reassembled in their original order, the Transport layer includes a message sequence number in its header.

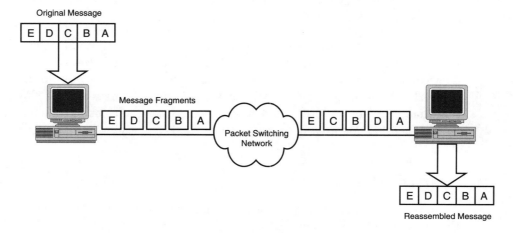

FIGURE 2.6

The fragmentation and reassembling of a message on a packet switching network.

Most computers are multitasking, running several programs at once. A user's workstation might, for example, be running simultaneous processes to transfer files to another computer, retrieve email, and access a network database. The Transport layer is responsible for delivering messages from a specific process on one computer to the corresponding process on the destination computer.

Under the OSI model, the Transport layer assigns a *service access point (SAP) ID* to each packet. (The TCP/IP term for a service access point is *port*.) The SAP ID is an address that identifies the process that originated the message. The SAP ID enables the Transport layer of the receiving node to route the message to the appropriate process.

Identifying messages from several processes so that the messages can be transmitted through the same network medium is called *multiplexing*. The procedure of recovering messages and directing them to the correct process is called *demultiplexing*. Figure 2.7 illustrates how message multiplexing and demultiplexing work. Multiplexing is a common occurrence on networks that are designed to enable many dialogs to share the same network medium.

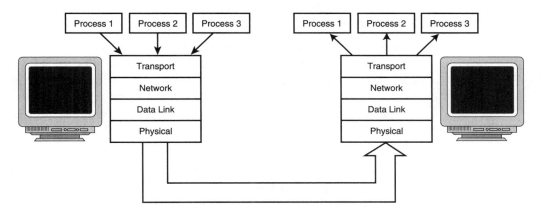

FIGURE 2.7
Message multiplexing and demultiplexing.

NOTE

Because multiple protocols can be supported for any given layer, multiplexing and demultiplexing can occur at many layers. Some examples of multiplexing include the following:

■ Transport of different Ethernet frame types over the same medium (Data Link layer).

■ Simultaneous support for NWLink and TCP/IP on Windows NT computers (Data Link layer).

■ Messages for multiple transport protocols, such as TCP and UDP on TCP/IP systems (Transport layer).

■ Messages for multiple application protocols (such as Telnet, FTP, and SMTP) on a UNIX host (Session and higher layers).

As subsequent chapters discuss layers of the TCP/IP protocol suite, the methods of multiplexing messages at each level are examined.

One more responsibility of the Transport layer must be examined. Although the Data Link and Network layers can be assigned responsibility for detecting errors in transmitting data, that responsibility generally is dedicated to the Transport layer. Two general categories of error detection can be performed by the Transport layer:

■ **Reliable delivery.** Reliable delivery does not mean that errors cannot occur, only that errors are detected if they do occur. Recovery from a detected error can take the form of simply notifying upper-layer processes that the error occurred. Often, however, the Transport layer can request the retransmission of a packet for which an error was detected.

■ **Unreliable delivery.** Unreliable delivery does not mean that errors are likely to occur, only that the Transport layer does not check for errors. Because error checking takes time and reduces network performance, unreliable delivery often is preferred when a network is known to be highly reliable, which is the case with the majority of local area networks. Unreliable delivery generally is used when each packet contains a complete message, whereas reliable delivery is preferred when messages consist of large numbers of packets. Unreliable delivery is often called *datagram delivery*, and independent packets transmitted in this way frequently are called *datagrams*.

Assuming that reliable delivery is always preferable is a common mistake among new students of network protocols. Unreliable delivery actually is preferable in at least two cases: when the network is fairly reliable and performance must be optimized, and when entire messages are contained in individual packets and loss of a packet is not critical.

The Session Layer

The Session layer is responsible for dialog control between nodes. A *dialog* is a formal conversation in which two nodes agree to exchange data.

Communication can take place in three dialog modes, as illustrated in Figure 2.8:

- **Simplex.** One node transmits exclusively, while another receives exclusively.

- **Half-duplex.** Only one node can send at a given time, and nodes take turns transmitting.

- **Full-duplex.** Nodes can transmit and receive simultaneously. Full-duplex communication typically requires some form of *flow control* to ensure that neither device sends faster than the other device can receive.

Sessions enable nodes to communicate in an organized manner. Each session has three phases:

1. *Connection establishment.* The nodes establish contact. They negotiate the rules of communication, including the protocols to be used and communication parameters.

2. *Data transfer.* The nodes engage in a dialog to exchange data.

3. *Connection release.* When the nodes no longer need to communicate, they engage in an orderly release of the session.

Steps 1 and 3 represent extra overhead for the communication process. This extra overhead might be undesirable for brief communication. Consider, for example, the communication associated with network management. When devices are managed on a network, they periodically send out brief status reports that generally consist of single frame messages. If all such messages were sent as part of a formal session, the connection establishment and release phases would transfer far more data than the message itself.

FIGURE 2.8
Communication dialog modes.

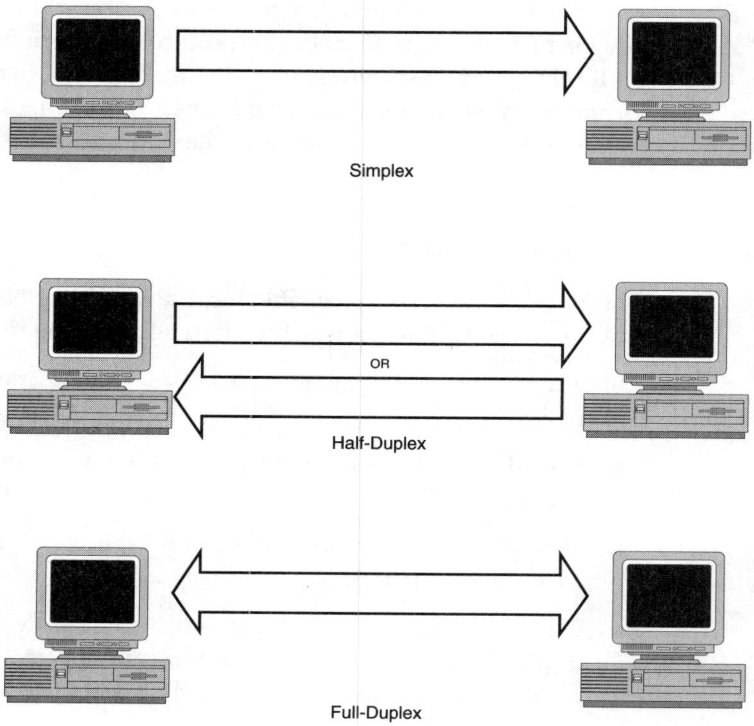

Simplex

Half-Duplex

OR

Full-Duplex

In such situations, communicating using a *connectionless* approach is common. The sending node simply transmits its data and assumes availability of the desired receiver.

A connection-oriented session approach is desirable for complex communication. Consider the task of transmitting a large amount of data to another node. Without formal controls, a single error that occurred anytime during the transfer would require the entire file to be resent. After establishing a session, the sending and receiving nodes can agree on a checkpoint procedure. If an error occurs, the sending node must retransmit only the data sent since the previous checkpoint. The process of managing a complex activity is called *activity management*.

The Presentation Layer

The Presentation layer is responsible for presenting data to the Application layer. In some cases, the Presentation layer directly translates data from one format to another. IBM mainframe computers use a character encoding scheme called *EBCDIC*, whereas virtually all other computers use the ASCII encoding scheme. If data are being transmitted from an EBCDIC computer to an ASCII computer, for example, the Presentation layer might be responsible for translating between the different character sets. Numeric data is also represented quite differently on different computer architectures and must be converted when transferred between different machine times.

A common technique used to improve data transfer is to convert all data to a standard format before transmission. This standard format probably is not the native data format of any computer. All computers can be configured to retrieve standard format data, however, and convert it into their native data formats. The OSI protocol standards define Abstract Syntax Representation, Revision 1 (ASN.1) as a standard data syntax for use at the Presentation layer. Although the TCP/IP protocol suite does not formally define a Presentation layer, a protocol that serves a similar function is External Data Representation (XDR), which is used with the Network File System (NFS). Chapter 6, "The Process-Application Layer," discusses NFS.

Other functions that may fall to the Presentation layer are data encryption/decryption and compression/decompression.

The Presentation layer is the least-frequently implemented of the OSI layers. Few protocols have been formally defined for this layer. In most cases, network applications perform the functions that might be associated with the Presentation layer.

The Application Layer

The Application layer provides the services user applications need to communicate through the network. Here are several examples of user Application layer services:

- **Electronic mail transport.** A protocol for handling electronic mail can be used by a variety of applications. Application designers who use the email protocols do not need to invent their own email handlers.

Also, applications that share a common email interface can exchange messages through the email message handler.

- **Remote file access.** Local applications can be given the capability to access files on remote nodes.

- **Remote job execution.** Local applications can be given the capability to start and control processes on other nodes.

- **Directories.** The network can offer a directory of network resources, including logical node names. This directory enables applications to access network sources by logical names instead of by abstract numeric node IDs.

- **Network management.** Network management protocols can enable various applications to access network management information.

You frequently encounter the term *application program interface (API)* used in conjunction with Application layer services. An API is a set of rules that enables user-written applications to access the services of a software system. Developers of program products and protocols frequently provide APIs, which enable programmers to easily adapt their applications to use the services the products provide. A common UNIX API is Berkeley Sockets, which Microsoft has implemented as Windows Sockets.

Characteristics of Layered Protocols

The OSI reference model illustrates several characteristics of layered protocol stacks. When a device transmits data to the network, each protocol layer processes the data in turn. Figure 2.9 illustrates the steps involved for the sending and receiving devices.

Consider the Network layer for the sending device. Data to be transmitted are received from the Transport layer. The Network layer is responsible for routing and must add its routing information to the data. The Network layer information is added in the form of a header, which is appended to the beginning of the data.

OSI terminology uses the term *protocol data unit (PDU)* to describe the combination of the control information for a layer with the data from the next higher layer. As Figure 2.9 shows, each layer appends a header to the PDU that it receives from the next higher layer. The data field for each layer consists of the PDU for the next higher layer. (The Data Link layer also adds a trailer that consists of the error control data.) The Physical layer does not encapsulate in this manner because the Physical layer manages data in bit form.

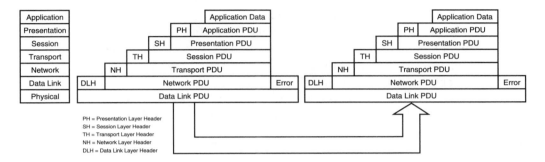

FIGURE 2.9

Headers and the OSI protocol layers.

When a layer adds its header to the data from a higher layer, the process resembles placing mail in an envelope. The envelope can be used to deliver the data to the correct location, where the envelope is opened and the data is recovered. When a protocol uses headers or trailers to package the data from another protocol, the process is called *encapsulation*. It is said that the Network layer *encapsulates* the data from the Transport layer.

As received data pass up the protocol stack, each layer strips its corresponding header from the data unit. The process of removing headers from data is called *decapsulation*. This mechanism enables each layer in the transmitting device to communicate with the corresponding layer in the receiver. Each layer in the transmitting device communicates with its *peer* layer in the receiving device, in a process called *peer-to-peer communication*.

NOTE

As a consequence of the encapsulation/decapsulation process, the identical PDU is present at corresponding layers in the sending and receiving protocol stacks. That is to say, the Network layer PDU at the sending node is identical to the Network layer PDU at the receiving node.

The Internet Model

As discussed in Chapter 1, the protocol architecture for TCP/IP currently is defined by the IETF, which is responsible for establishing the protocols and architecture for the Internet. The model dates back to the ARPANET and often is called the *DoD model*. The DoD protocol architecture predates the OSI reference model, which was first described in 1979. As such, unambiguous mapping of the DoD model to the OSI reference model is impossible to achieve. Figure 2.10 illustrates the four-layer Internet model, mapping the Internet model layers as closely as possible to the OSI reference model. Each of the layers is discussed in a separate chapter (see Chapters 3 through 6), but a brief description is in order here.

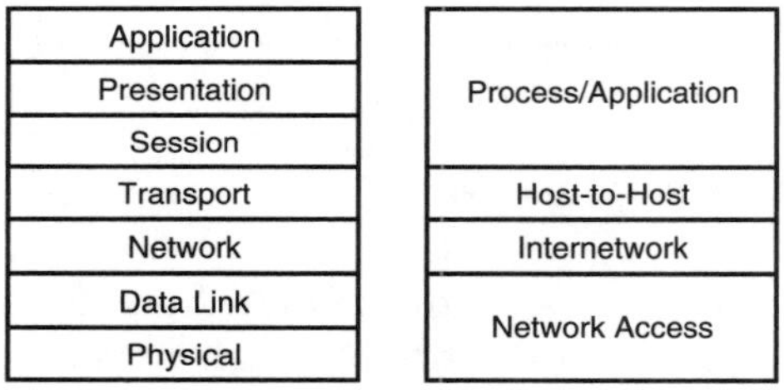

FIGURE 2.10

A comparison of the Internet protocol model and the OSI reference model.

Application	Process/Application
Presentation	
Session	
Transport	Host-to-Host
Network	Internetwork
Data Link	Network Access
Physical	

The *Network Access layer* is responsible for exchanging data between a host and the network and for delivering data between two devices on the same network. Node physical addresses are used to accomplish delivery on the local network. The DoD architecture was designed with the intent of using prevailing network standards, and TCP/IP has been adapted to a wide variety of network types, including circuit switching (for example, X.21), packet switching (such as X.25), Ethernet, the IEEE 802.x protocols, ATM, and frame relay. Data in the network access layer encode EtherType information that is used to demultiplex data associated with specific upper-layer protocol stacks.

The *Internet layer* corresponds to the OSI Network layer and is responsible for routing messages through internetworks. Devices responsible for routing messages between networks are called *gateways* in TCP/IP terminology, although the term router is also used with increasing frequency. The TCP/IP protocol at this layer is the *internet protocol (IP)*. In addition to the physical node addresses utilized at the Network Access layer, the IP protocol implements a system of logical host addresses called IP addresses.

The IP addresses are used by the internet and higher layers to identify devices and to perform internetwork routing. The *address resolution protocol (ARP)* enables IP to identify the physical address that matches a given IP address.

The *Host-to-Host layer* compares closely to the OSI Transport layer and is responsible for end-to-end data integrity. Two protocols are employed at this layer: *transmission control protocol (TCP)* and *user datagram protocol (UDP)*. TCP provides reliable full-duplex connections and reliable service by ensuring that data is present when transmission results in an error. Also, TCP enables hosts to maintain multiple simultaneous connections. UDP provides unreliable (datagram) service that enhances network throughput when error correction is not required at the Host-to-Host layer.

The *Process-Application layer* spans the functions of three layers of the OSI reference model: Session, Presentation, and Application. Not surprisingly, therefore, a wide variety of protocols are included in this layer of the DoD model. Examples of protocols at this layer include the following:

- **File Transfer Protocol (FTP).** Performs basic file transfers between hosts.

- **Telnet.** Enables users to execute terminal sessions with remote hosts.

- **Simple Mail Transfer Protocol (SMTP).** Supports basic message delivery services.

- **Simple Network Management Protocol (SNMP).** A protocol that is used to collect management information from network devices.

- **Network File System (NFS).** A system developed by Sun Microsystems that enables computers to mount drives on remote hosts and operate them as if they were local drives.

Some of these applications encompass functions from several layers of the OSI reference model. NFS, for example, enables hosts to maintain a session (Session layer), agree on a data representation (Presentation layer), and operate a network file system (Application layer).

Delivering Data Through Internetworks

In the discussion of protocols in the following chapters, you will encounter a variety of network concepts that are explained here. The way data are delivered through internetworks is involved—enough that it deserves more thorough discussion. It involves several topics:

- Methods for carrying multiple data streams on common media, a technique called *multiplexing*

- Methods for switching data through paths on the network

- Methods for determining the path to be used

Multiplexing

LANs typically operate in *baseband* mode, which means that a given cable is carrying a single data signal at any one time. The various devices on the LAN must take turns using the medium. This generally is a workable approach for LANs because LAN media offer high performance at low cost.

Long-distance data communications media are expensive to install and maintain, and it would be inefficient if each media path could support only a single data stream. Imagine the expense if it was necessary to equip each telephone with its own communication satellite or transatlantic cable to enable it to connect to Europe. WANs, therefore, tend to use *broadband* media, which can support two or more simultaneous data streams. Increasingly, as LANs are expected to carry more and different kinds of data, broadband media are being considered for LANs as well.

To enable many data streams to share a high-bandwidth medium, a technique called *multiplexing* is employed. Figure 2.11 illustrates one method of multiplexing digital signals. The signal-carrying capacity of the medium is divided into time slots, with a time slot assigned to each signal, a technique called *time-division multiplexing (TDM)*. Because the sending and receiving devices are synchronized to recognize the same time slots, the receiver can identify each data stream and recreate the original signals.

The sending device, which places data into the time slots, is called a *multiplexer* or mux. The receiving device is called a *demultiplexer* or demux.

TDM can be inefficient. If a data stream falls silent, its time slots are not used, and the media bandwidth is underutilized. Figure 2.12 depicts a more advanced technique called *statistical time-division multiplexing (stat-TDM)*. Time slots still are used, but some data streams are allocated more time slots than others. An idle channel is allocated no time slots at all. A device that performs statistical TDM is often called a *stat-MUX*.

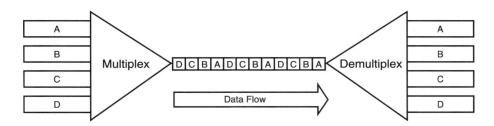

FIGURE 2.11
Time-division multiplexing.

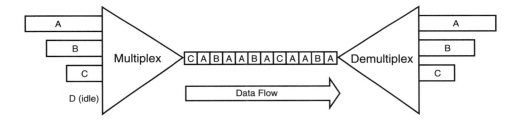

FIGURE 2.12
Statistical time-division multiplexing.

Switching Data

On an internetwork, data units must be switched through the various intermediate devices until they are delivered to their destinations. Two contrasting methods of switching data are commonly used: circuit switching and packet switching. Both are used in some form by protocols in common use. (A third, message switching, is useful in some situations but is not applicable to this book.)

Circuit Switching

Circuit switching is illustrated in Figure 2.13. When two devices negotiate the start of a dialog, they establish a path—called a *circuit*—through the network, along with a dedicated bandwidth through the circuit. After they establish the circuit, all data for the dialog flow through that circuit. This approach resembles a telephone connection in which a voice circuit is established to enable the telephones at the end-points to communicate. The chief disadvantage of circuit switching is that when communication takes place at less than the assigned circuit capacity, bandwidth is wasted. Also, communicating devices cannot take advantage of other less busy paths through the network unless the circuit is reconfigured.

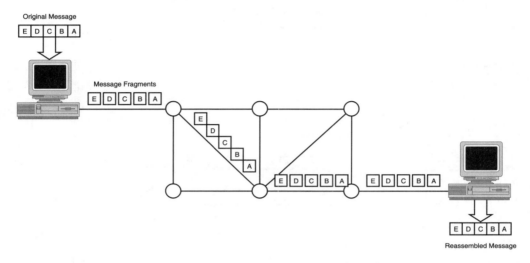

FIGURE 2.13
Circuit switching.

Circuit switching does not necessarily mean that a continuous physical pathway exists for the sole use of the circuit. The message stream might be multiplexed with other message streams in a broadband circuit. In fact, sharing of media is the more likely case with modern telecommunications. To the end devices, however, it appears that the network has configured a circuit dedicated to their use.

End devices benefit greatly from circuit switching. Because the path is pre-established, data travel through the network with little processing in transit. And because multipart messages travel sequentially through the same path, message segments arrive in order, so little effort is required to reconstruct the original message. For that reason, a form of circuit switching was used to design the new leading-edge technology ATM. The next chapter, "The Network Access Layer," shows you how ATM uses a form of circuit switching without the inefficiencies just described.

Packet Switching

Packet switching takes a different and generally more efficient approach to switching data through networks. In the late 1960s, packet switching was a new concept that the DoD sought to investigate in the early ARPA network research. As shown in Figure 2.14, messages are broken into sections called *packets*, which are routed individually through the network. At the receiving device, the packets are reassembled to construct the complete message. Messages are divided into packets to ensure that large messages do not monopolize the network. Packets from several messages can be multiplexed through the same communication channel. Thus, packet switching enables devices to share the total network bandwidth efficiently.

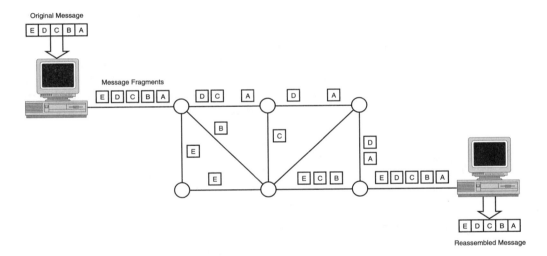

FIGURE 2.14
Packet switching.

Two variations of packet switching can be employed:

- **Datagram** services treat each packet as an independent message. The packets (also called *datagrams*) are routed through the network using the most efficient route currently available, enabling the switches to bypass busy segments and use underutilized segments. Datagrams frequently are employed on LANs, and Network layer protocols are responsible for routing the datagrams to the appropriate destination. Datagram service is called *unreliable*, not because it is inherently flawed but because it does not guarantee delivery of data. Recovery of errors is left to upper-layer protocols. Also, if several messages are required to construct a complete message, upper-layer protocols are responsible for reassembling the datagrams in order. Protocols that provide datagram service are called *connectionless* protocols.

- **Virtual circuits** establish a formal connection between two devices, giving the appearance of a dedicated circuit between the devices. When the connection is established, issues such as message sizes, buffer capacities, and network paths are considered, and mutually agreeable communication parameters are selected. A virtual circuit defines a *connection*, a communication path through the network, and remains in effect as long as the devices remain in communication. This path functions as a logical connection between the devices. When communication is over, a formal procedure releases the virtual circuit. Because virtual circuit service guarantees delivery of data, it provides reliable delivery service. Upper-layer protocols need not be concerned with error detection and recovery. Protocols associated with virtual circuits are called *connection-oriented*.

For the TCP/IP protocol suite, datagram service is provided by the User Datagram Protocol (UDP). The vast majority of systems rely on the Transmission Control Protocol (TCP) to provide reliable delivery.

Bridges, Routers, and Switches

Data can be routed through an internetwork using the following three types of information:

- **The physical address of the destination device, found at the Data Link layer.** Devices that forward messages based on physical addresses are generally called *bridges*.

- **The address of the destination network, found at the Network layer.** Devices that use network addresses to forward messages are usually called *routers*, although the original name—still commonly used in the TCP/IP world—is *gateway*.

- **The circuit that has been established for a particular connection.** Devices that route messages based on assigned circuits are called *switches*.

The following sections discuss each of these devices respectively.

Bridges

A bridge builds and maintains a database that lists known addresses of devices and how to reach those devices. When it receives a frame, the bridge consults its database to determine which of its connections should be used to forward the frame. Figure 2.15 illustrates the process in terms of the OSI reference model. A bridge makes use of only the Physical and Data Link layers of the protocol stack.

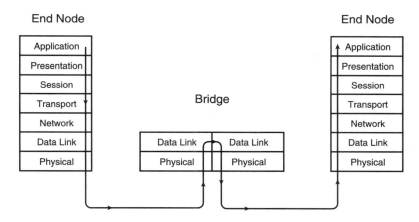

FIGURE 2.15

The protocol stack model for bridging.

Bridges are fairly simple devices. They receive frames from one connection and forward them to other connections known to be *en route* to the destinations. When more than one route is possible, bridges ordinarily cannot determine which route is most efficient. In fact, when multiple routes are available, bridging can result in frames simply traveling in circles. Having multiple paths available on the network is desirable, however, so that a failure of one path does not stop the network. With Ethernet, a technique called the *spanning-tree algorithm* enables bridged networks to contain redundant paths.

Token ring uses a different approach to bridging. When a device needs to send to another device, it goes through a discovery process to determine a route to the destination. The routing information is stored in each frame transmitted and is used by bridges to forward the frames to the appropriate networks. Although this actually is a Data Link layer function, the technique token ring uses is called *source routing*.

Notice in Figure 2.15 that the bridge must implement two protocol stacks, one for each connection. Theoretically, these stacks could belong to different protocols, enabling a bridge to connect different types of networks. Chapter 3, however, illustrates that each type of network, such as Ethernet and token ring, has its own protocols at the Data Link layer. Translating data from the Data Link layer of an Ethernet to the Data Link layer of a token ring is difficult (but not impossible). Bridges, therefore, which operate at the Data Link layer, generally can join only networks of the same type. You see bridges employed most often in networks that are all Ethernet or all token ring. A few bridges have been marketed that can bridge networks which have different Data Link layers.

Because bridges ignore network addresses, they cannot be used to create large internetworks consisting of multiple distinctly identified networks. In many cases, network technologies impose limits on the sizes of networks. TCP/IP, for example, organizes addresses into classes, each of which can support a specific maximum number of nodes. A class C address, for example, can support only 254 nodes on a given network. To expand beyond that limit, additional class C networks must be established in an internetwork. Therefore, there is always a limit on the extent to which a bridged network can expand.

NOTE

In recent years, new LAN devices dubbed *switches* have been strategically deployed to improve network bandwidth. A LAN switch is essentially a bridge that is equipped with large numbers of ports. Additionally, LAN switches use techniques that improve the rapidity with which frames can be forwarded. They often, for example, do not bother to buffer the entire packet before forwarding. Rather, as soon as the destination physical address is identified, a LAN switch can begin to forward the packet immediately without waiting for the end of the frame. Consequently, a LAN switch cannot use the error control field to determine whether the frame has been scrambled. In relatively error-free LAN environments, this lack of an integrity check is typically an acceptable tradeoff for greater efficiency. Because they rely on Data Link layer addresses, LAN switches, like bridges, cannot be used to establish internetworks.

Routing

A different method of path determination can be employed using data found at the Network layer. At that layer, networks are identified by logical network identifiers. This information can be used to build a picture of the network. This picture can be used to improve the efficiency of the paths that are chosen. Devices that forward data units based on network addresses are called routers. Figure 2.16 illustrates a protocol stack model for routing.

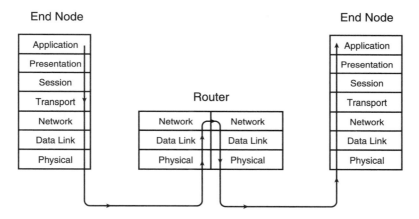

FIGURE 2.16

A protocol stack model for routing.

With TCP/IP, routing is a function of the Internet layer, which is discussed more thoroughly in Chapter 4, "The Internet Layer." Discussion here is limited to briefly illustrating one technique. Figure 2.17 shows an example network. The hop count defines the number of networks that must be crossed between two communication end nodes. A number of paths could be identified between A and E:

- A–B–C–E (five hops)

- A–E (three hops)

- A–D–E (four hops)

By this method, A–E is the most efficient route. This assumes that all the paths between the routers provide the same rate of service. A simple hop-count algorithm would be misleading, though, if A–D and D–E were 1.5Mbps lines while A—E was a 56Kbps line. Apart from such extreme cases, however, hop-count routing is a definite improvement over no route planning at all.

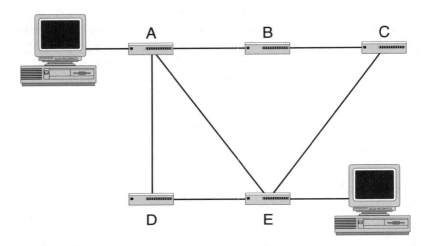

Figure 2.17
Hop-count routing.

Routing operates at the Network layer. By the time data reach that layer, all evidence of the physical network has been shorn away. In Figure 2.16, therefore, both protocol stacks in the router can share a common Network layer protocol. The Network layer does not know or care if the network is Ethernet or token ring. Therefore, the two stacks can support different Data Link and Physical layers. Consequently, routers possess a capability—fairly rare in bridges—to forward traffic between dissimilar types of networks. Owing to that capability, routers often are used to connect LANs to WANs.

Routers can be built around the same protocol stacks that are used at the end nodes. TCP/IP networks can use routers based on the same IP protocol employed at the workstation. It is not required, however, that routers and end nodes use the same routing protocol. Because Network layer protocols need not communicate with upper-layer protocols, different protocols can be used in routers than are used in the end nodes. Commercial routers (such as Cisco and Wellfleet) employ proprietary Network layer protocols to perform routing. These custom protocols are among the keys to the improved routing performance provided by the best routers.

Switching

Circuit-based networks operate with high efficiency because the path is established once, when the circuit is established. In Figure 2.18, each switch maintains a table that records how data from different circuits should be switched. Switching is typically performed by lower-level protocols to enhance efficiency and is associated most closely with the Data Link layer.

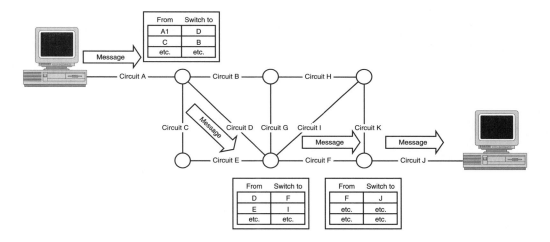

FIGURE 2.18

Switching.

Very seldom do real circuits resemble Figure 2.18, with one cable dedicated to each communication circuit. More commonly, many circuits are multiplexed onto a single media channel, and the multiplexing is hidden from the end nodes. Such circuits may then be referred to as *virtual circuits*, for they appear to the end nodes to be physical channels even though they actually share network bandwidth with many other virtual circuits.

NOTE

When data are routed through internetworks using protocols higher than the Network layer, the intermediate devices commonly are called gateways. This commonly confuses newcomers to TCP/IP because historically the TCP/IP term for router has been gateway. You can expect to see the term router used increasingly in discussions of TCP/IP networks, but gateway remains in widespread use as a name for devices that perform routing with the IP protocol.

Enough Basics, Already

This chapter showed you the overall organization of the TCP/IP protocol stack and covered many of the technologies that enable TCP/IP networks to function. But that's enough background. It's time for the real stuff. You should now be prepared to delve into the details of the various layers of the DoD protocol model.

In Chapter 3, you will start at the bottom of the protocol stack, where data meet the network. In subsequent chapters, you will proceed up through the layers until, in Chapter 5, you encounter applications in the Host-to-Host layer. When you complete this detailed tour, you will possess the theory required to set up and manage a TCP/IP network.

Chapter 3

THE NETWORK ACCESS LAYER

The planners of TCP/IP intended the protocols to operate with existing physical network architectures. Over the years, the popularity of TCP/IP has inspired network designers to adapt TCP/IP to virtually all types of networks, too many to discuss in one chapter. This chapter focuses on the following protocol standards:

- *Ethernet II*

- *IEEE 802.3 (IEEE Ethernet)*

- *IEEE 802.5 (IEEE token ring)*

- *X.25*

- *Frame Relay*

- *ATM*

It is not the purpose of this chapter to exhaustively examine these standards. If you require more detailed information about the standards, please consult *Windows NT Server 4 Professional Reference*, by Karanjit S. Siyan, Ph.D. (New Riders, 1996).

Ethernet II

Ethernet evolved from work by Robert Metcalf, David Boggs, and others at the Xerox Palo Alto Research Center (Xerox PARC). This early work laid the foundation for all networks that use the carrier-sensing access control method. The early network was named Ethernet, after the mythical substance once assumed to permit light to travel through space.

The first Ethernet standard, released in September 1980, was named DIX 1.0. The DIX acronym was derived from the names of the three companies that collaborated on the standard: Digital Equipment Corporation, Intel, and Xerox. A revised standard, released in November 1982, was called DIX 2.0 and is most commonly referred to as Ethernet II.

Ethernet II became available at much the same time TCP/IP was being widely deployed. The two have become closely associated, and Ethernet II remains the dominant LAN for TCP/IP networks.

How Ethernet Works

Typically, local area networks do not permit more than one node to transmit at a given time. This presents a problem because all nodes at times need to transmit. *Access control methods* are systems that enable many nodes to have access to a shared network medium by granting access to the medium in an organized manner.

Ethernet uses an elegant access control method, called *carrier sensing*. When a node has data to transmit, it senses the medium, essentially listening to see if any other node is transmitting. If the medium is busy, the node waits a few microseconds and tries again. If the medium is quiet, the node begins to transmit. The full name for this approach is *carrier sensing multiple access (CSMA)*, permitting multiple nodes to access the medium through a carrier sensing method. CSMA often is called the "listen before talking" method.

A brief period of time must expire before a transmitted electrical signal reaches the furthest extents of the medium on which it is sent. Figure 3.1 shows how two nodes can sense a quiet network and begin to transmit at the same time. As the two signals flow through the medium, eventually they overlap in an event called a *collision*. Collisions always damage data, and it is of paramount importance to have a mechanism for dealing with collisions.

FIGURE 3.1
An Ethernet collision.

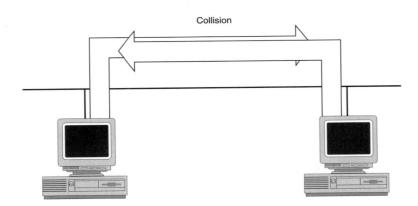

Ethernet nodes detect collisions by continuing to listen as they transmit. If a collision takes place, the nodes measure a signal voltage that is twice as high as expected. After detecting a collision, the nodes transmit a jamming signal that notifies all nodes on the network that a collision has occurred and the current frame should be disregarded. Then the nodes wait a random amount of time before attempting to retransmit. Because each node delays for a different time, the likelihood of a new collision is reduced. This technique of managing collisions is called *collision detection (CD)*, making the complete abbreviation for the Ethernet access control method *CSMA/CD*.

NOTE

Ethernet nodes detect collisions only when they are themselves transmitting. A potential collision detection problem is illustrated in Figure 3.2. Nodes A and B have sent frames that have not yet reached each other. When the frames collide, neither node is transmitting and the collisions will not be detected. This situation arises because the frames were not long enough to reach other transmitting nodes during the time the frames were being sent.

The maximum diameter of an Ethernet is 2,500 meters. Given the speed with which signals propagate (travel) through the medium, 576 bit-times are required to enable the first bits of a transmission to fully propagate through the network. As will be shown, Ethernet specifications require a 576-bit minimum frame size, ensuring that transmitting nodes will see all other transmissions that cause collisions.

FIGURE 3.2

How a collision may go undetected.

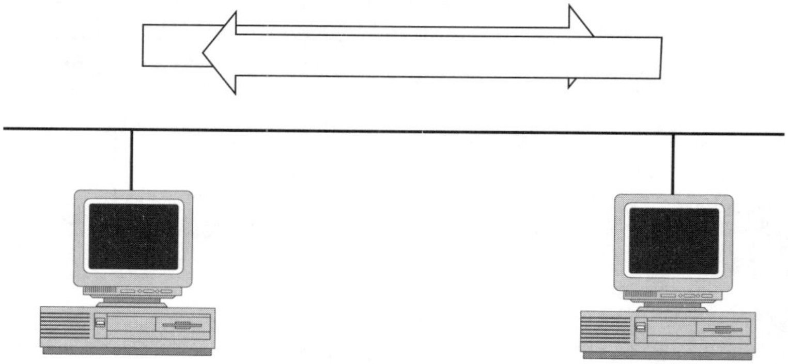

Collisions are part of the normal operation of an Ethernet. Because CSMA/CD is an exceptionally efficient access control method, normal collision activity does not seriously impair network performance. At some point, however, a heavily loaded network can experience high levels of collisions that seriously degrade network performance, possibly resulting in network gridlock. This disastrous condition seldom is seen on a properly designed Ethernet that has a reasonable number of nodes.

The CSMA/CD access method is elegant in its simplicity. Some networks, such as token ring, require elaborate mechanisms to maintain network access procedures. Ethernet requires few such mechanisms and consequently devotes a high proportion of network bandwidth to useful data transmission. The majority of networks are well-served by Ethernet. The simplicity of CSMA/CD has enabled the manufacture of extremely low-cost Ethernet hardware, and in most cases, Ethernet is the least expensive network media option. Engineers have been able to extend the scope of CSMA/CD, supporting its use on newer media options, such as unshielded twisted-pair (UTP).

Ethernet Media

Ethernet II is nearly 100 percent compatible with media specified by the IEEE 802.3 standard. Because the majority of developments in Ethernet media have been standardized by the IEEE, discussion of Ethernet media falls within the examination of the IEEE 802.3 standard. See the section "IEEE 802.3 Media" later in the chapter.

Ethernet II Frames

All protocol standards define a data structure used to transmit and receive data. Ethernet II data structures are called frames. The Ethernet II frame format is shown in Figure 3.3. The *preamble* consists of a series of 64 bits in a specific pattern that notifies receiving nodes that a frame is beginning. The preamble begins with seven *octets* (8-bit groups, frequently referred to as *bytes*) of the pattern 10101010. The final octet of the preamble has the bit pattern 10101011. The purpose of the preamble is to signal the beginning of a frame, and the preamble is not formally part of the frame. Therefore, the octets in the preamble are not counted as part of the length of the frame.

Preamble (8 octets)	Destination Address (6 octets)	Source Address (6 octets)	Type (2 octets)	Data (46-1500 octets)	FCS (4 octets)

FIGURE 3.3
Structure of an Ethernet II frame.

The *destination* and *source addresses* each consist of 48 bits (six octets). Each node on the network is assigned a unique 48-bit address. This information enables receiving nodes to identify frames that are addressed to them, and also enables the receiver of a message to reply to the sender. Ethernet addresses are discussed in the next section.

NOTE

Ethernet frame delivery is accomplished using a simple mechanism, illustrated in Figure 3.4. The sending node includes the Ethernet address of the destination node in the destination address field of the frame. The frame is transmitted to the network medium, where each node on the network examines it. Each node decodes the destination address field of each frame. If the destination address in the frame matches the node's own Ethernet address, the frame is received. If the addresses do not match, the frame is discarded.

To make this delivery mechanism work, the sending node must be able to determine the Ethernet address of the intended recipient. Chapter 4, "The Internet Layer," includes a discussion of how this is accomplished for TCP/IP.

FIGURE 3.4
Delivery of an Ethernet frame.

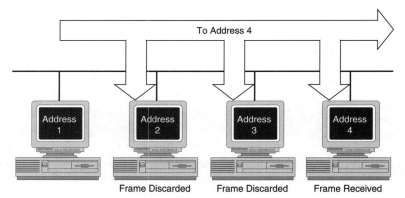

The *type* field (also called the *EtherType*) is a 16-bit (two octet) field that designates the data type of the data field. The EtherType enables the network drivers to demultiplex the packets and direct data to the proper protocol stack. The type mechanism enables Ethernet networks to support multiple protocol stacks. Table 3.1 lists some common Ethernet type values, taken from the RFC titled "Assigned Numbers" (currently RFC 1700). All EtherType values are 5DDh (1501 decimal) or greater. Values of 5DCh or below are used to specify the data length for IEEE 802.3 frames.

TABLE 3.1

Examples of EtherType Values

EtherType (decimal)	EtherType (hex)	Type of Data
2048	0800	Internet IP (IPv4)
2053	0805	X.25 Level 3
2054	0806	ARP
24579	6003	DEC DECNET Phase IV Route

EtherType (decimal)	EtherType (hex)	Type of Data
24580	6004	DEC LAT
24581	6005	DEC Diagnostic Protocol
32923	809B	AppleTalk
32981	80D5	IBM SNA Service on Ethernet
33079	8137-8138	Novell, Inc.

The *data* field contains the protocol data unit received from upper-layer protocols. The length of the data field can be from 46 to 1500 octets, inclusive. If the data field is less than 46 octets in length, upper-layer protocols must pad the data to the minimum length.

The *frame check sequence (FCS)* is a 32-bit code that enables the receiving node to determine if transmission errors have altered the frame. This code is derived through a *cyclic redundancy checksum (CRC)* calculation, which processes all fields except the preamble and the frame check sequence. This CRC value is recalculated by the receiving node. If the CRC calculated by the receiver matches the value in the FCS, it is assumed that transmission errors did not occur.

The minimum length of an Ethernet frame is 6+6+2+46+4=64 octets, and the maximum length is 6+6+2+1500+4=1518 octets. Frames shorter than 64 octets are not permitted, and the data field must be padded to achieve the minimum length. The 64-octet size minimum, combined with the 8-octet preamble, results in a minimum 576-bit transmission length required to ensure proper operation of the collision detection mechanism.

Ethernet II Node Addresses

Ethernet II node addresses consist of 48 bits, organized in three fields, as shown in Figure 3.5. The bits are numbered from bit 0 (the right-most or low-order bit) to bit 47 (the left-most or high-order bit). As these bits are discussed, they are examined both in binary and in hexadecimal notation. If you need a refresher on binary, decimal, and hexadecimal numbers, consult Appendix A.

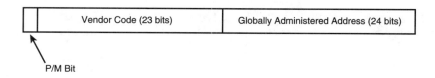

P/M Bit

FIGURE 3.5

Structure of an Ethernet address.

The 48-bit Ethernet address is commonly organized in six octets. (Many LAN standards use the term octet instead of byte to refer to eight bits.) To make it easier for humans to scan Ethernet addresses, the octet values are generally represented in hexadecimal notation. Each octet is represented by two hex digits. Pairs of digits are usually separated by periods, spaces, colons, or hyphens—there is no universal standard for the punctuation mark used. An example of an Ethernet address expressed in hexadecimal notation is 08–00–09–3A–20–1B.

Bit 47 (the high-order bit) is the Physical/Multicast (P/M) bit. If this bit is 0, the address specifies the physical address of one device on the network. If the bit is 1, it specifies a multicast address that identifies a group of devices. Multicasts are messages that are sent to predefined groups of nodes, as opposed to broadcasts, which are sent to all nodes on a local network.

The remainder of the first three octets comprise a vendor code. Through a registration system formerly administered by Xerox and now by the IEEE, vendors are assigned unique vendor codes that are used to identify their adapters. This registration system ensures that each Ethernet device that is manufactured has a physical address that is unique in the entire world. Burned addresses are called *physical addresses*. They are also referred to as *globally administered addresses* because all Ethernet addresses for the world are administered by the IEEE, but were formerly administered by Xerox.

Table 3.2 lists a few of the vendor codes, which are documented in RFC 1700.

TABLE 3.2

Sample Ethernet Vendor Codes

Vendor ID	Vendor
0080C2	IEEE 802.1 Committee
00AA00	Intel
080008	BBN
080009	Hewlett-Packard
080014	Novell
080020	Sun
08002B	DEC
080056	Stanford University
08005A	IBM
080069	Silicon Graphics

The value of the remaining three octets is designated by the manufacturer of the Ethernet equipment. Because each manufacturer is assigned a unique vendor ID, and the manufacturers assign a different identification number to each piece of equipment produced, the complete Ethernet ID for each Ethernet device is unique.

NOTE

In some cases, network administrators might override the physical address with a locally administered address configured in the computer's network software.

Three general categories of Ethernet addresses can be identified, as follows:

- **Physical (globally administered) addresses.** Identified by a 0 value of the first bit (bit 47). Only nodes having the specified address will receive a message identified by a globally administered address.

- **Multicast addresses.** Identified by a 1 value of the first bit (bit 47). The devices that will receive a message sent to a multicast address are defined by the network implementation. Some multicast addresses are specified in RFC 1700.

- **Broadcast address.** All bits are 1. Expressed in hexadecimal notation, the broadcast address is FF:FF:FF:FF:FF:FF. All nodes receive a message with the broadcast address in the destination address field.

IEEE LANs

The Institute of Electrical and Electronics Engineers (IEEE), the largest professional organization in the world, has been the major force in defining international standards for local area networks. The IEEE standards for LANs are defined by the 802 committee, so called because it first met in February, the second month of 1980.

The 802 committee has defined a wide variety of network standards, only a few of which are discussed in this book. This section focuses on examining the overall architecture of the 802 standards, along with the most widely implemented physical layer standards. International LAN standards have been established by the ISO, by adopting the IEEE 802 standards as the ISO 8802 standard.

Architecture of the IEEE 802 Standards

As a group, the IEEE 802 standards correspond to the OSI data link and physical layers. The architecture of the IEEE standards, however, does not match the organization of the OSI layers. As you can see in Figure 3.6, the IEEE architecture defines two sublayers that together correspond to the OSI data link layer:

- **Logical link control (LLC).** The *LLC* sublayer provides a network interface to upper-layer protocols and is concerned with transmitting data between two stations on the same network segment.

- **Medium access control (MAC).** The *MAC* sublayer provides the method by which devices access the shared network transmission medium.

Figure 3.6 illustrates how the 802 family of standards relates to the OSI reference model.

FIGURE 3.6

IEEE 802 standards related to the OSI reference model.

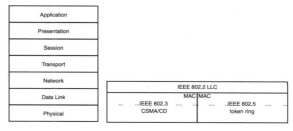

The work of the 802 committee is organized into subcommittees, designated as 802.x committees. Some committees directly define standards. Others serve an advisory function. The following 802.x standards are examined in this chapter:

- **802.2.** Defines the LLC sublayer protocol.

- **802.3.** Defines the MAC and physical layers for CSMA/CD (802.3 Ethernet) networks.

- **802.5.** Defines the MAC and physical layers for a token ring network based on IBM's Token Ring technology.

The relationships of these standards are shown in Figure 3.6. This figure illustrates an important design feature of the 802 standards—the 802.2 LLC protocol is used by all 802 LAN standards that define network physical layers. This approach to protocol layering simplifies the task of designing systems that can be easily adapted to different physical networks. A system can be converted from 802.3 Ethernet to 802.5 token ring with relative ease and without modification to upper protocol layers.

Another feature is that the 802.3 and 802.5 network standards span the functionality of the OSI physical layer, as well as the MAC sublayer for the data link layer.

802 LAN Physical Addresses

The 802 standards were designed to achieve as much uniformity as possible among the various LAN standards. The use of a common LLC layer for all LAN protocols has been discussed. Another area of uniformity is that all LAN protocols use the same address scheme.

Under the 802 model, physical device addresses are defined at the MAC protocol sublevel. Physical addresses, therefore, frequently are referred to as MAC addresses. MAC addresses can have 16-bit or 48-bit formats. All devices on the network must be configured to use the same address format. Because 48-bit addresses are used most commonly, only that format is examined in detail.

The format of a 48-bit MAC address was adopted from Ethernet and has been accepted for IEEE 802, ISO 8802, and other LAN standards. The 48-bit address format is shown in Figure 3.7. This format is similar to the format discussed earlier for Ethernet II addresses.

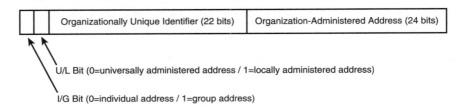

Figure 3.7
Format of IEEE 802 MAC addresses.

The first bit of the address (bit 47, the high-order bit) is the I/G bit. If the I/G bit value is 0, the address designates an individual address. If the I/G bit value is 1, the address designates a group address, which designates a multicast. An address of all 1s designates a broadcast. Apart from the different terminology, the I/G bit operates in the same manner as the Ethernet II Physical/Multicast bit.

Bit 46 is the U/L bit and indicates whether the address is universally or locally administered. When the U/L bit value is 0, the address follows a universal address format, consisting of a 22-bit *organizationally unique identifier* and a 24-bit address assigned by the organization. When the U/L bit value is 1, the 46-bit address is locally administered, often by software running on the networked device.

Organizations that apply to the IEEE are assigned a 22-bit organizationally unique identifier, a function that was transferred from Xerox to the IEEE. When the organization combines its unique identifier with a 24-bit address assigned individually for each device made, a unique address is assigned to each piece of network equipment that is manufactured to conform with IEEE 802 LAN standards.

IEEE 802.2 Logical Link Control

LLC performs a variety of functions. Some of these functions are optional and can be provided by upper-layer protocols.

Multiplexing and Demultiplexing

The LLC function most significant to this book is to multiplex and demultiplex data for multiple upper-layer protocols. Discussion of Ethernet II mentioned that the EtherType field is used to identify data that is associated with various upper-layer protocols. The mechanism used with IEEE 802 LANs differs significantly from that used with Ethernet II.

An interface between the LLC sublayer and upper-layer protocols is a *link service access point (LSAP)*. An LSAP is a logical address that identifies the upper-layer protocol from which the data originated or to which the data should be delivered. LSAPs serve a function similar to EtherType numbers with Ethernet II.

LLC Delivery Services

LLC was designed to provide a variety of delivery services, which determine the level of communication integrity established between devices. Three types of LLC delivery services provide various combinations of features.

Devices have a limited number of receive buffers, used to store frames that have been received but not processed. If the sending device continues to transmit while the destination receive buffers are full, frames not received are lost. *Flow control* ensures that frames are not sent at a rate faster than the receiving device can accept them. A variety of mechanisms can be used to provide flow control.

The simple *stop-and-wait* method requires the receiver to acknowledge received frames, signaling a readiness to accept more data. This simple mechanism is suitable to a connectionless, datagram service.

If the sender must wait for an acknowledgment of each frame, multiframe transmissions are handled inefficiently. The more sophisticated *sliding-window* technique enables the sender to transmit multiple frames without waiting for an acknowledgment. The receiver can acknowledge several frames at one time. A *window* determines the number of frames that can be outstanding at a given time, ensuring that the receiver's buffers do not over-flow. The complexity of sliding-window flow control requires a connection-oriented LLC service.

Error detection is performed at the MAC layer, but error recovery, when performed at the data link layer, is a function of LLC. An *automatic repeat request (ARQ)* approach can be employed by the LLC, whereby a positive acknowledgment of each correctly received frame is sent. *Stop-and-wait ARQ* requires an acknowledgment for each frame and functions with acknowledged connectionless service; unacknowledged frames are retrans-mitted. *Go-back-N ARQ* enables the receiver to request retransmission of specific frames and requires a connection-mode service.

LLC supports the following three types of delivery service:

- **Unacknowledged datagram service (Type 1 service).** This con-nectionless-mode service supports point-to-point, multipoint, and broadcast transmission. This service does not perform error detection and recovery or flow control.

- **Virtual circuit service (Type 2 service).** This connection-mode provides frame sequencing, flow control, and error detection and recovery.

- **Acknowledged datagram service (Type 3 service).** This mode implements point-to-point datagram service with message acknowl-edgments, and functions somewhere between Type 1 and Type 2 ser-vice.

To keep the lower-layer protocols trim and efficient, LLC is most commonly implemented with Type 1 service. Flow control and error recovery, if required, can be performed by a suitable transport protocol (such as TCP).

LLC Data Format

As with other protocol layers, the LLC layer constructs a *protocol data unit (PDU)* by appending LLC-specific fields to data received from upper layers. Figure 3.8 illustrates the format of the LLC PDU.

FIGURE 3.8

Format of the LLC protocol data unit.

DSAP	SSAP	Control	Data

The LLC PDU contains the following fields:

- **Destination Service Access Point (DSAP).** The LSAP address that identifies the required protocol stack on the destination computer.

- **Source Service Access Point (SSAP).** The LSAP address associated with the protocol stack that originated the data on the source computer.

- **Control.** Control information that varies with the function of the PDU.

- **Data.** Data received from upper-layer protocols in the form of the network layer PDU.

IEEE 802.3 Networks

Digital, Intel, and Xerox submitted their jointly developed Ethernet technology to the IEEE for standardization, resulting in the 802.3 standard for CSMA/CD LANs. The most significant changes required in adapting DIX Ethernet to the 802 architecture resulted from the decision to implement the 802.2 LLC layer as a common protocol for all 802.x LANs.

IEEE 802.3 networks utilize the same CSMA/CD access control mechanism that was developed for Ethernet II. The same media-signaling techniques are employed, and 802.3 and Ethernet II network hardware are interchangeable. 802.3 and Ethernet II frames can be multiplexed on the same media. The primary difference between the 802.3 and the Ethernet II standards has to do with frame formats.

NOTE

Xerox surrendered its trademark for Ethernet long ago, and no one owns the term any longer. Whether Ethernet should be used for Ethernet II or for IEEE 802.3 is a constant source of confusion. Unless Ethernet II disappears, however, the confusion seems likely to remain, so this book uses the term Ethernet fairly loosely when remarks apply to both network versions. When a distinction is necessary, the terms Ethernet II and IEEE 802.3 are used.

IEEE 802.3 Media

The 802.3 committee adopted cabling systems that were in use for Ethernet II, which were based on coaxial cable and data rates of 10 megabits per second. The committee has since developed a variety of newer media configurations. TCP/IP operates independently of the physical medium. Discussing the media options in detail, therefore, is unnecessary; however, a brief summary is appropriate. More detail can be found in NRP's books *Inside Windows NT Server* and *Windows NT Server 4 Professional Reference*.

Each of the 802.3 cable standards has a three-part name, for example, 10BASE5. The first number indicates the data rate, with 10 indicating 10 megabit-per-second operation. BASE specifies baseband operation, and BROAD indicates a broadband network. The final designation suggests the cable type. For example, 5 indicates a configuration that can support cables up to 500 meters in length.

- **10BASE5.** This is the original Ethernet network configuration and employs a thick, 50-ohm coaxial cable. Cables can extend up to 500 meters without repeaters, and each cable section can support up to 100 station attachments. The cable for 10BASE5 is expensive and difficult to work with, and now is used less frequently than other cable options.

- **10BASE2.** This cable system was designed as a lower-cost alternative to 10BASE5. It uses a thinner coaxial cable that supports segment lengths up to 185 meters. (The 2 indicates a segment length of about 200 meters.) 10BASE2 is economical and easier to install than 10BASE5 but does not adapt well to structured wiring systems, which are configured by running a cable from each device to a central hub. Structured wiring now is preferred in most cable installations of medium-to-large size.

- **10BASE-T.** The general trend in cabling is to use fewer coaxial and other shielded cables. Network designers increasingly rely on *unshielded twisted-pair cable (UTP)*, which costs somewhat less than coaxial cable. The T in the standard name indicates use of twisted-pair cable. 10BASE-T uses a hub-based wiring system and adapts readily to a structured wiring approach.

- **10BROAD36.** A broadband cable system that enables multiple 10Mbps channels to be carried by the same coaxial cable medium.

- **100BASE-TX.** A variety of 100Mbps standards are being considered by various IEEE 802 committees. All utilize UTP cable, but they differ in the grade of cable and number of wire pairs required. 100BASE-TX utilizes two pairs of high-grade (category 5) UTP cable. Other 100Mbps standards include 100 BASE-T4, which operates on four pairs of standard data-grade (category 3)UTP, and 100BASE-FX for optical fiber.

NOTE

The death of Ethernet has been predicted many times, as pundits have anticipated Ethernet's eclipse by token ring, FDDI, ATM, and other newer technologies. Ethernet survives in part because 10Mbps Ethernet offers adequate service for many applications, costs little, and is easy to administer. Additionally, a variety of clever strategies have extended Ethernet's viability in more demanding situations. Ethernet switching can be used to reduce traffic congestion by segmenting the network. Fast (100Mbps) Ethernet is the low-cost leader among fast LAN technologies, with connections costing significantly less than FDDI or ATM alternatives. Many modern Ethernet switches enable networks to marry 10Mbps and 100Mbps segments, enabling designers to deploy appropriate amounts of bandwith for different groups of users. Although it might someday be superceded by ATM, Ethernet will remain useful and popular for many more years.

IEEE 802.3 Frames

Figure 3.9 illustrates the format of an IEEE 802.3 frame. The frame format is derived from Ethernet II and is similar to the format of an Ethernet II frame in most respects.

Preamble (7 octets)	Start Frame Delimiter (1 octet)	Destination Address (6 octets)	Source Address (6 octets)	Length (2 octets)	LLC Data (46-1500 octets)	FCS (3 octets)

FIGURE 3.9

Format of an IEEE 802.3 frame.

The 802.3 preamble consists of seven octets having the bit pattern 10101010. Following the preamble is a one octet start frame delimiter (SFD) with the bit pattern 10101011.

The *destination address* and *source address* have the same functions as the corresponding fields in an Ethernet II frame. Both 16-bit and 48-bit addresses are supported for IEEE 802.3. The format for 802 physical addresses is discussed in the prior section, "802 LAN Physical Addresses."

The *length* field consists of two octets that specify the number of octets in the LLC data field. This value must be in the range of 46 through 1500, inclusive.

The *LLC data* field contains the protocol data unit received from the LLC sublayer, consisting of the LLC header and data. The size of this field is 46 to 1500 octets. If the data field falls short of the minimum 46 octets, octets with a value of 00000000 are appended to pad the field to the minimum length.

The *frame check sequence (FCS)* field stores a 32-bit checksum value that is used to detect transmission errors.

Assuming that 48-bit (6 octet) addresses are used, the minimum and maximum lengths of an 802.3 frame are the same as for Ethernet II frames: 64 and 1518 octets.

Comparison of IEEE 802.3 and Ethernet II Frames

Network equipment manufactured to IEEE 802.3 specifications is compatible with Ethernet II frames and with much of the equipment manufactured to the Ethernet II standard. It also is, in many cases, compatible with older equipment designed to the DIX specification. Hardware designed to the DIX 1.0 specification, however, might not interoperate with hardware designed to the Ethernet II and IEEE 802.3 standards.

NOTE

Older Ethernet equipment implements a feature called signal quality error (SQE) testing. The SQE circuitry sends a heartbeat signal that simulates a collision. The SQE signal interferes with the operation of devices designed according to 802.3 specifications, particularly repeaters. Therefore, SQE operation should be disabled on Ethernet devices being connected to an 802.3 network.

Figure 3.10 compares the frame formats of 802.3 and Ethernet II frames. Notice that the 802.3 preamble and SFD combined have the same bit pattern as the Ethernet II preamble.

FIGURE 3.10

Comparison of IEEE 802.3 and Ethernet II frames.

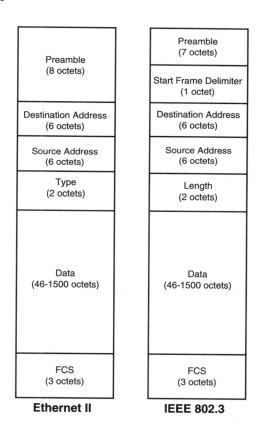

Ethernet II   IEEE 802.3

The organization identifiers used in Ethernet hardware addresses were originally administered by Xerox, but this responsibility has been handed over to the IEEE. A coherent catalog of identifiers has been maintained throughout the history of Ethernet, permitting Ethernet II and IEEE 802.3 devices to coexist without risk of address conflict.

The IEEE 802 standards permit two-octet MAC addresses, but these are seldom used. More commonly, six-octet addresses are used, a format that is compatible with Ethernet II. As discussed, the body of Ethernet II addresses coexists seamlessly with 802.3 addresses assigned by the IEEE.

The most significant difference in frame formats is that the 802.3 format has a two-octet length field in place of the EtherType field found in Ethernet II frames. Distinguishing Ethernet II and 802.3 frames is possible by examining this field. EtherType values are restricted to decimal values of 1501 and greater. If the decimal value of this field is 1500 or less, therefore, the field identifies an 802.3 length field. With IEEE 802.3, type information must be supplied by the LSAP fields in the 802.2 LLC frame.

Implementing TCP/IP over IEEE 802.3

As you have seen, the original implementations of TCP/IP on Ethernet networks were based on Ethernet II and used the EtherType data field, which is not supported by the IEEE 802 standards. When TCP/IP is run over an IEEE physical layer, the EtherType information is encoded in the frame using the *Sub-Network Access Protocol (SNAP)*, which is an extension to the LLC header. SNAP is described in RFC 1042.

Figure 3.11 illustrates the format of the LLC and SNAP header data as they relate to an 802.2 frame. The presence of a SNAP header is indicated by DSAP and SSAP values of 170, a control value of 3 (unnumbered information), and an organization code of 0.

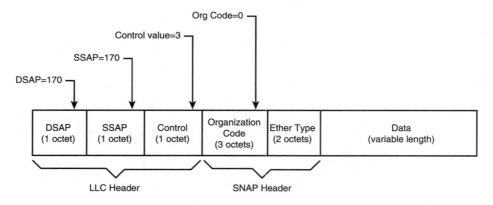

Note: maximum data size for 802.3 networks is 1492 octets.

FIGURE 3.11
Format of the SNAP header.

SNAP encapsulation increases the header overhead. On networks that specify maximum frame sizes, SNAP encapsulation necessarily reduces the number of octets available for upper-layer data. An IEEE 802.3 Ethernet frame has a maximum size of 1518 octets. Taking into account 18 octets for the MAC header and trailer and 8 octets for the LLC and SNAP headers, an IEEE 802.3 frame with SNAP encapsulation can accommodate 1492 octets of data. This compares to 1500 octets of data available with Ethernet II.

SNAP is an extension to the 802.2 LLC sublayer and, therefore, is compatible with all IEEE 802.x LANs. The SNAP mechanism is frequently used to implement TCP/IP over IEEE 802.5 token ring physical layers. SNAP is general enough to be adapted to other networks as well.

NOTE

Windows NT uses Ethernet II frames by default, as do most TCP/IP systems, but you may encounter an occasional installation that uses IEE 802.3 frames. A Registry parameter enables administrators to configure Microsoft TCP/IP to use Ethernet 802.3 frames.

IEEE 802.5 Networks

IBM developed the token ring network and submitted it to the IEEE for standardization, a task performed by the 802.5 subcommittee. IEEE 802.5 token ring is the second most commonly employed LAN physical layer, trailing significantly behind Ethernet. Several reasons can be cited for token ring's lower popularity:

- It was developed as an IBM technology. Although token ring technology is now offered by many vendors, many in the user community perceive it as proprietary.

- Ethernet is simple, reliable, and effective for the majority of networks, and, at the same time, costs significantly less than token ring.

- TCP/IP has traditionally been wed to Ethernet II. Growing industry demand for TCP/IP has accompanied a recent surge in Ethernet popularity.

Nevertheless, token ring is an effective physical layer technology with features that make it preferable under some circumstances.

How Token Ring Works

Token ring was developed by IBM to circumvent a perceived shortcoming of the CSMA/CD access method. Each time a device needs to transmit, some probability exists that the network will be busy. And, even when the device successfully begins to transmit, some probability exists that another device will also transmit and cause a collision, forcing both devices to back off and try again. These probabilities increase as the network becomes busier, and in extreme cases, a point might be reached at which a device needing to transmit data becomes extremely unlikely to receive the opportunity to do so. Because network access on a CSMA/CD network is uncertain, CSMA/CD is described as a probabilistic access method.

The mere probability of access is unacceptable in certain critical situations, such as industrial control. Suppose that an overheat sensor urgently needs to send a warning to the factory operators. If even a possibility exists that the sensor cannot access the network, the factory designers will not take the situation lightly.

access guarantees that every device on the network receives a periodic opportunity to transmit. The token access method chosen by IBM was implemented in a ring, as shown in Figure 3.12.

The token consists of a special frame that circulates from device to device around the ring. Only the device that possesses the token is permitted to transmit. After transmitting, the device restarts the token, enabling other devices the opportunity to transmit.

IBM's initial 4Mbps implementation of token ring permitted a single token to circulate on the network. Before releasing a token on the network that enabled other devices to transmit, a device that transmitted a frame waited for the frame to return after circulating the ring. A new feature, called *early token release*, introduced with the newer 16Mbps token ring, enables a sending device to release a token immediately after it completes transmission of a frame. Thus, a token can circulate at the same time as a data frame.

Although token access control appears simple, numerous problems lie beneath the surface.

- How does the network discover if the token frame is damaged or lost?

- How is a new token created?

- How does the network know when a device has malfunctioned and is no longer forwarding frames to the next device?

- How can the network recover from such a problem?

- How can the network identify a frame that is endlessly circulating the ring, destined for a node that does not exist?

- How can a frame be removed and a new token started?

FIGURE 3.12
The token access method in a ring network.

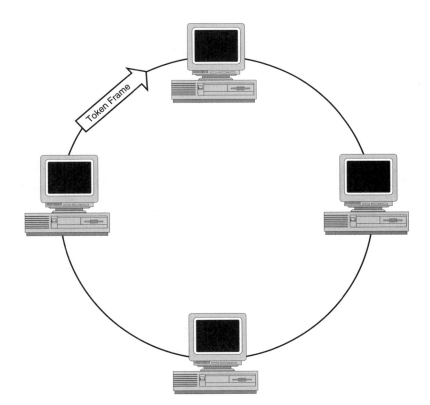

The causes and solutions for these and other token ring errors are beyond the scope of this book. The point of introducing them is to illustrate that the control mechanisms token ring uses are significantly more complicated than those required for CSMA/CD. These control mechanisms take up network bandwidth, reducing the efficiency of token ring.

To compensate for this added complexity, token ring offers significant benefits. Data throughput of a token ring can never reach zero, as is theoretically possible with an Ethernet experiencing excessive collisions. Although network performance slows as demand increases, every device on the network receives a periodic opportunity to transmit.

Token ring possesses a capability to set network access priorities, which is unavailable in Ethernet. High-priority devices can request preferred network access. This capability enables a critical device to gain greater access to the network.

Token ring was also designed to provide a higher level of diagnostic and management capability than is available with Ethernet. The mechanisms that compensate for token ring errors provide a capability for diagnosing other network problems, as well. Detecting devices causing network errors and forcing those devices to disconnect from the network, for example, is possible. Also, in the cabling system IBM designed, the network is serviced by two rings of cable. In the event of a cable break, it is possible to use the extra media ring to reconfigure the network and keep it operating.

Nevertheless, Ethernet—whether Ethernet II or IEEE 802.3—remains the most popular network physical layer. Ethernet works well in the majority of networks and costs considerably less than token ring. Equipment for token ring costs two-to-three times as much as corresponding Ethernet components.

NOTE

Although frames can be routed through token ring networks using conventional TCP/IP routing techniques, another form of routing is often used on token ring. With token ring *source routing*, when a host needs to communicate, it sends out a message that queries the network for the best route to the destination. When the query message reaches the destination, a message is returned that describes each router that should be used to reach the destination. The source host appends this routing information to each frame that it sends. Because each frame includes a complete route description, routers do not need to make routing decisions as they forward frames. They simply retrieve the next router from the routing list and forward the frame.

Although source routing is not used by default on Microsoft routers, it can be enabled through a Registry parameter. See the section "NBT Configuration Parameters" in Chapter 8, "Installing TCP/IP on Windows NT Computers," for more information on Registry parameters that configure TCP/IP operation.

Token Ring Media

IEEE 802.5 does not describe a cabling system for token ring, stopping with specifications for data rates, signaling, and the network interface. In most cases, manufacturers design their equipment around the IBM Cabling System, introduced in the early 1980s. The most popular cable type has been Type 1, a fairly heavy shielded twisted-pair cable, which has excellent electrical characteristics but is a bit bulky and expensive. Type 3 cable is a data-grade UTP cable. IBM provided early support for a data rate of 4Mbps over Type 1 and Type 3 cable. Although IBM engineers later sanctioned 16Mbps operation with Type 1 cable, they were slow to change their early position that operation faster than 4Mbps required Type 1 shielded cable.

Competing manufacturers were not so reticent, however, and introduced 16Mbps token ring for UTP cable well in advance of any IBM or IEEE standard. IBM finally yielded and offered a standard for 16Mbps token ring over UTP cable. IBM has now announced a revised cable system that supports operation at up to 100Mbps.

Although token ring networks operate logically as rings, they are cabled as physical stars so that each device is connected to a central hub through an individual cable. Figure 3.13 illustrates how the token ring is wired in a star configuration. Thus, token ring adapts naturally to a structured cabling plan.

A token ring can support up to 260 devices but generally accommodates fewer than that number. Token ring networks are somewhat difficult to plan because the number of devices allowed on the ring varies with the size of the ring and the data rate.

IEEE 802.5 Frames

The token ring frame format is shown in Figure 3.14. Three major sections can be identified, as follows:

- **Start-of-frame sequence (SFS).** This section signals to network devices that a frame is beginning.

- **Data section.** This section contains control information, upper-layer data, and the frame check sequence used for error checking.

- **End-of-frame sequence (EFS).** This section indicates the end of the frame and includes several control bits.

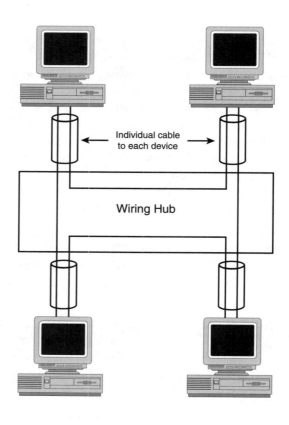

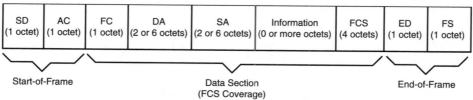

Start-of-Frame | Data Section (FCS Coverage) | End-of-Frame

SD = Starting Delimiter   SA = Source Address
AC = Access Control   FCS = Frame Check Sequence
FC = Frame Control   ED = Ending Delimiter
DA = Destination Address   FS = Frame Status

FIGURE 3.14
Format of a token ring frame.

The *starting delimiter (SD)* field is a single octet that consists of electrical signals that cannot appear elsewhere in the frame. The SD violates the rules for encoding data in the frame and contains nondata signals.

The *access control (AC)* field includes priority and reservation bits used to set network priorities. It also includes a monitor bit, used for network management. A token bit indicates whether the frame is a token or a data frame.

The *frame control (FC)* field indicates whether the frame contains LLC data or is a MAC control frame. Several types of MAC control frames are used to control network functions.

The *destination address (DA)* specifies the station or stations to which the frame is directed. Multicasts and broadcasts are possible in addition to transmission to a single device. 16-bit and 48-bit addresses are supported.

The *source address (SA)* specifies the device that originated the frame. The DA and SA addresses must utilize the same format.

The *information* field contains LLC data or control information if it appears in a MAC control frame.

The *frame check sequence (FCS)* is a 32-bit cyclic redundancy check that is applied to the FC, DA, SA, and information fields.

The *ending delimiter (ED)*, like the starting delimiter, violates the network data format and signals the end of the frame. This field includes two control bits. The intermediate bit indicates whether this is an intermediate frame or the final frame in a transmission. The error bit is set by any device that detects an error, such as in the FCS.

The *frame status (FS)* field contains other control bits that indicate that a station has recognized its address and that a frame has been copied by a receiving device.

NOTE

As with IEEE 802.3 networks, token ring networks must encode EtherType information using the SNAP protocol.

Digital Data Services

When networks must span more than a few kilometers, new categories of technology come into play. Before considering WAN standards, it is useful to take a look at options that might be used by an organization that wants to build a private WAN. Not all options are examined.

Dedicated Leased Lines

Communication providers offer dedicated, leased lines at a variety of capacities. A dedicated line is a communication channel between two points that is leased by an organization for its exclusive use. The dedicated line almost certainly does not consist of a pair of wires that stretches continuously between the end-points, and a customer's signal can pass through any combination of copper and optical fiber cables as well as terrestrial and satellite microwaves. The appearance to the customer, however, is of a directly wired channel.

Dedicated lines can be analog or digital in nature. At one time, dedicated 56Kbps analog lines were a common way to interconnect mainframe computers. Increasingly, however, dedicated lines are digital, and 56Kbps digital data service (DDS) lines are among the available options.

T1 is an example of a digital leased-line technology. T1 supports full-duplex communication between two points. Originally intended for digital voice communication, T1 adapts well to data communication, supporting data rates up to 1.544Mbps in the United States. T1 circuits can utilize combinations of cables and microwave links.

A T1 line supports 24 multiplexed 56Kbps digital channels (with some bandwidth utilized for control purposes). In some areas, *fractional T1* enables organizations to lease part of a T1 line in 56Kbps increments, paying only for the bandwidth they require. Other standards include T2, T3, and T4 support data rates of 6.312, 44.736, and 274.176Mbps respectively.

An organization that wants to connect remote computers might choose to do so using a dedicated line, employing a configuration similar to that shown in Figure 3.15. The interface to the leased line consists of the following components:

- A bridge or router to forward frames to the leased circuit

- A channel service unit/digital service unit (CSU/DSU) to translate between LAN and DDS signal formats

- A network interface provided by the communication service vendor

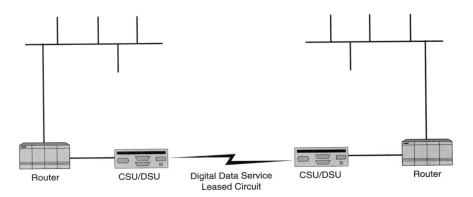

FIGURE 3.15
Connecting remote sites with a digital leased circuit.

Leased lines can be used to construct quite large networks. The Internet is a world-wide network that consists of thousands of hosts, most connected by leased lines. The participants in the Internet share the cost of operating the Internet by bearing the costs of one or more leased lines to connect to other host sites.

The downside of leased lines is that an organization bears the full cost of the capacity they have leased. Some allowance must be made for peak traffic periods, and a portion of the channel capacity being paid for might be idle a great deal of the time. Dedicated lines ensure an organization of a specified communication capacity but come at a high cost.

Switched Digital Lines

Switched lines provide an alternative to dedicated lines. When remote hosts need to communicate, one dials the other to establish a temporary connection. Switched connections can be configured using conventional modems and voice-grade lines, enabling organizations that have very limited band-width needs to avoid the cost of a digital service. Switched digital services are offered as well, and switched 56Kbps CSU/DSUs are available.

A technology that promises to lower the cost of switched digital communication is the Integrated Services Digital Network (ISDN). A variety of ISDN services is possible, providing different amounts of bandwidth. A common basic rate service consists of two 64Kbps digital channels. Although the potential bandwidth of this service is 128Kbps, the 64Kbps channels function separately. Equipment at the customer site must be capable of aggregating the separate 64Kbps channels into a 128Kbps logical channel. ISDN has the potential to make switched digital communication widely available at low cost. Service providers, however, have been slow to offer ISDN services. Only recently have the major providers committed to making ISDN available in their service areas. Smaller providers remain reluctant to jump on the bandwagon, and ISDN is less frequently an option away from larger metropolitan areas.

X.25

Dedicated leased circuits present a number of disadvantages. They are costly to operate, and high setup costs are incurred when the circuit is configured or moved. They also are inflexible so that moving a host site can be a big deal. Often, buying data services the way you buy telephone services, by obtaining them from a network provider, makes more sense.

A network provider constructs a data network that covers a geographic area, with the capacity to support large amounts of customer traffic. Customers who need to connect hosts within that area connect into the existing network and pay for only a portion of the network bandwidth.

X.25 is one of the oldest WAN technologies and remains widely available. X.25 is a recommendation of the International Telecommunications Union (ITU), formerly the International Telegraph and Telephone Consultative Committee (CCITT). The ITU is an agency of the United Nations that establishes international communication standards.

X.25 is a packet-switching network. Devices communicate through the network by establishing virtual circuits. Much like dialing a telephone call, devices can set up switched virtual circuits to serve a short-term communication need. Permanent virtual circuits, which function much like dedicated circuits offered by telecommunication providers, also can be established.

NOTE

Although X.25 has a long history with TCP/IP, the fit between them is not without problems. X.25 is connection-oriented, and connection-oriented networks do not support broadcasts and multicasts because all communication takes place between connected pairs of devices. However, many services supported by TCP/IP are dependent on broadcasts—the address resolution protocol (ARP), described in Chapter 4, uses broadcast messages to discover the physical addresses of destination nodes. For such protocols, extra work might be required to enable them to function via a connection-oriented networking infrastructure.

As illustrated in Figure 3.16, the X.25 standard uses three protocols, which correspond to the network, data link, and physical layers of the OSI model. Physical layer functionality is provided by X.21 for digital circuits and by X.21 *bis* for analog circuits. At the data link layer, full-duplex, synchronous communication is provided by the Link Access Procedures-Balanced (LAPB) protocol. Finally, the X.25 protocol provides for reliable service and flow control at the network layer.

FIGURE 3.16

The X.25 protocol stack.

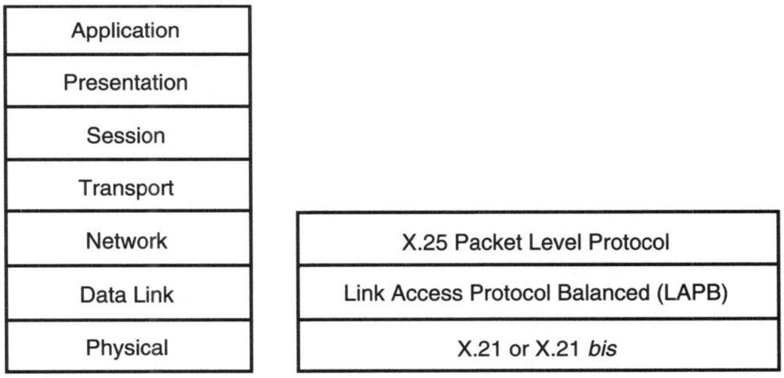

| Application |
| Presentation |
| Session |
| Transport |
| Network |
| Data Link |
| Physical |

| X.25 Packet Level Protocol |
| Link Access Protocol Balanced (LAPB) |
| X.21 or X.21 *bis* |

X.25 originated at a time when communication lines were slow and unreliable. The upper data rate for X.25 is 64Kbps, adequate for character-based terminal-to-host communication and most mainframe host communications, but far too limited for today's more demanding real-time applications that demand LAN speeds.

Because X.25 was designed to provide reliable communication over unreliable lines, the X.25 protocol is responsible for both detecting errors and correcting them by requesting retransmission of damaged packets. Modern digital communication options are highly reliable, and the reliability features of X.25 simply add overhead and inefficiency to the communication process. With X.25, error checks are performed by each switch along the route of a packet. The modern preference, implemented in the TCP protocol, is to perform data integrity checks at the final destination node only, eliminating redundant checks.

Figure 3.17 illustrates an X.25 network. The network itself consists of several X.25 switches that route frames through the network. The mechanics of the switching mechanism are hidden from the user, and WANs such as X.25 are frequently drawn as clouds to highlight the hidden nature of the switching process. Packets enter the network at one point and emerge at another, but the details do not concern the user.

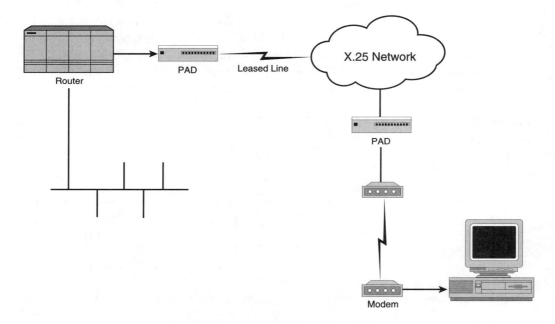

FIGURE 3.17
Example of an X.25 network.

NOTE

When remote computers communicate through a public network such as X.25, the public network operates independently of the protocols running on the end devices. If the end nodes are running TCP/IP, the IP datagrams are encapsulated in X.25 frames for transmission on the WAN. Decapsulation at the destination site recovers the original IP datagram.

Devices interface with the X.25 network through a *packet assembler-disassembler (PAD)*. The PAD can be located at the customer site, communicating with the X.25 network through a leased or dial-access line, or at a dial-in site with users accessing the network through dial-up modems.

Public X.25 networks are widely available and can be a cost-effective way to build a WAN to support moderate traffic. Private X.25 networks also can be constructed using leased circuits. For these reasons, X.25 is the WAN option Windows NT supports out of the box.

X.25 is a fairly rusty technology with many shortcomings. Because X.25 cannot be adapted to support the speed and reliability improvements available with modern WAN media, it has become necessary to develop a newer packet switching standard that rises above the shortcomings of X.25. That standard is frame relay.

Frame Relay

Frame relay is a packet switching, broadband, wide area network standard that is a streamlined update of X.25. The ITU (CCITT) is the body responsible for frame relay standardization. As shown in Figure 3.18, the services provided by frame relay correspond to the data link and physical layers of the OSI reference model. Frame relay was designed with the assumption that communication channels would be reliable. Therefore, frame relay is relieved of the responsibility to provide flow control and error correction. Frame relay performs error checking, discards frames with errors, and informs upper-layer protocols when errors occur. It is the responsibility of upper layers to recover from errors by requesting retransmission of frames. By moving error recovery to upper-layer protocols at end-nodes, processing at the switches is streamlined. X.25 networks must perform error detection and recovery at each switch.

Frame relay can operate over T1, T3, and other high-speed networks at speeds of 56Kbps to 44.6Mbps, sufficient to support most LAN-to-LAN communications. Frame relay network services can be obtained from a public data network, or private networks can be established.

Frame relay offers bandwidth-on-demand and better accommodates the bursty characteristics of LAN communication than does X.25. Terminal traffic, for which X.25 was designed, is limited in volume and fairly regular in nature. By contrast, LAN traffic demand tends to vary wildly between quiet periods and busy periods associated with high-traffic activities such as file transfers.

Figure 3.18

Relationship of frame relay to the OSI reference model.

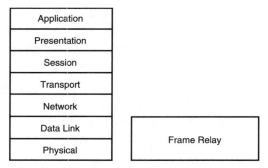

Subscribers to a public frame relay network service typically purchase a guaranteed amount of bandwidth called a *committed information rate (CIR)*. Some services permit customers to exceed the CIR temporarily on a pay-per-use basis. As a result, customers can purchase frame relay services that are closely tailored to their requirements without the risk that a temporary high demand will be unsupported.

Figure 3.19 illustrates a frame relay network. LANs are connected to frame relay through a *frame relay interface (FRI)*, generally incorporated into a router.

The data field of a frame relay frame is called the payload. The size of the payload field may be defined by the network implementation. Frame relay networks may thus be tuned to user requirements. TCP/IP protocol support utilizes SNAP encapsulation.

Frame relay is connection-oriented, supporting switched virtual circuits and *permanent virtual circuits (PVC)*. A PVC establishes a fixed network path that enables devices to communicate efficiently. Up to 1,024 logical connections can be multiplexed through a PVC. Little processing is required as frames pass through the network. Consequently, frame relay operates at high speeds with little transmission delay.

FIGURE 3.19

A frame relay network.

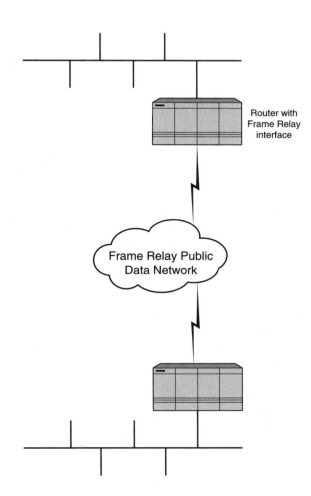

ATM

The nature of network data is changing. Imaging is a commonplace technology, associated with large data files that often are many megabytes in size. Transfer of imaging data alone can stress a network, but even more demanding applications are evolving from state-of-the-art to everyday technologies. Networks must often cope with digitized video and audio, which not only demand high bandwidth but require data packets to arrive synchronized in real-time.

Both video and audio data can be represented in digital form, but the data requirements exceed those commonly encountered with computer data. A single, digitized full-motion video signal can require 6Mbps or more of network bandwidth, but that is only one problem with networking video data. The picture and audio signals for a video signal constitute two separate data streams that must remain synchronized in real-time.

Asynchronous transfer mode (ATM) is an emerging technology that promises to solve these technical problems. ATM is flexible to an unprecedented degree and has been designed to integrate data, video, and voice support in a high-performance network.

A variety of organizations are involved in the ATM standards process. Much of ATM is derived from Broadband ISDN (B-ISDN), an extension of narrowband ISDN, a technology developed in 1988 by the CCITT. Standards from CCITT define the basic B-ISDN architecture but do not address many aspects of implementing ATM on LANs.

The ATM Forum is an industry consortium that formed to address problems of interfacing ATM to LANs. This group has developed the basic ATM-LAN architecture. The IETF is also addressing the problem of carrying LAN traffic over ATM. An Internet-draft document addressing these issues is Multiprotocol Interconnect over ATM Adaptation Layer 5.

Architecture of ATM LANs

ATM networks consist of two types of devices: endstations and switches (see Figure 3.20). The ATM Forum has designated two network interfaces. A *User-Network Interface (UNI)* connects an endstation to a switch. A *Network-Network Interface (NNI)* connects a switch to another switch.

LANs can interface with an ATM network through a router equipped with an ATM interface.

Transfer Modes: STM, PTM, and ATM

Synchronous Transfer Mode (STM) uses time-division multiplexing, assigning time slots to data channels. Use of fixed time slots guarantees dedicated bandwidth and synchronous transmission of data. It is, for example, possible to ensure that voice and picture data remain synchronized for a video transmission. STM is best suited to voice and video data.

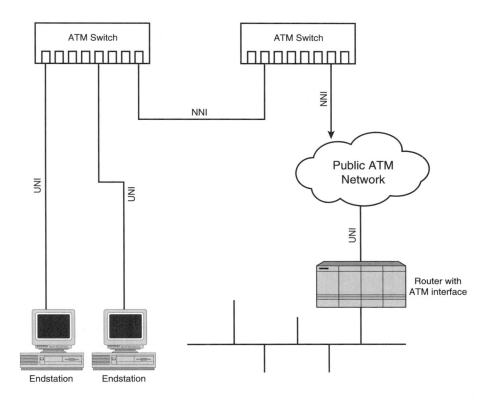

FIGURE 3.20

An ATM network.

Packet Transfer Mode (PTM) uses packet switching to provide flexible services well-suited to computer data. PTM adapts to packets of varying formats and sizes and provides flexible bandwidth.

Asynchronous Transfer Mode (ATM) provides a flexible transport method that is adaptable to voice, video, and computer data. Like X.25 and frame relay, ATM provides a mechanism for switching data units through networks. Unlike those packet switching protocols, which transmit data units of varying size, ATM operates with a fixed-size data unit called a *cell*. By standardizing on a data unit size, switch efficiency is greatly enhanced.

To satisfy the voice and video industries, ATM provides *cell synchronous* service, enabling ATM to provide guaranteed data rates and to synchronize data channels. ATM can provide *constant bit rate* service, compensating for any time irregularities encountered when transferring cells.

ATM cells are 53 bytes in length, incorporating a 5-byte header and a 48-byte payload, shown in Figure 3.21. Clearly, a 5-byte header cannot accommodate two 48-bit addresses, as was the case with other protocols discussed in this chapter. The short header is possible because of the strategy used to define routes through ATM networks.

FIGURE 3.21

Format of an ATM cell.

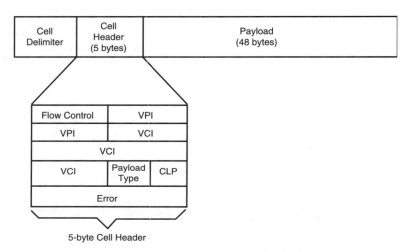

ATM is connection-oriented. Devices that communicate obtain a virtual circuit defining the route cells will follow through the network. Between any two ATM devices, a route is defined by two specifications. A specific *virtual channel (VC)* is assigned to the virtual circuit. A virtual channel functions on *a virtual path (VP)*. Virtual paths simply are collections of virtual channels.

Between ATM devices, one or more *virtual paths* are established. A T1 link between ATM switches might correspond to a virtual path. A path is virtual in the sense that a *physical path* is not dedicated to a given connection except during transference of a cell for that connection. At other times, the virtual path is available to service cells for other connections. Each virtual path can accommodate many *virtual channels*. An ATM virtual circuit is defined by a specific virtual channel on a specific virtual path.

The cell's virtual path between two given switches is represented by an 8-bit *virtual path identifier (VPI)* in the ATM cell header. A 16-bit *virtual channel identifier (VCI)* encodes the virtual channel information. Together, the VPI and VCI uniquely identify the virtual circuit associated with a given cell. With 24 bits to work with, ATM has the potential to support over 16 million virtual channels per switch, although most hardware supports fewer.

Each switch stores VPI and VCI information in a local connection database. For any given connection, it is likely that different VPI and VCI values will be selected between each pair of switches on the cell path. Switches consult their databases to determine the VPI and VCI to be used for the next step in forwarding a given cell. Figure 3.22 illustrates how VPIs and VCIs are used to route cells through a network.

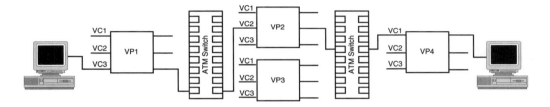

FIGURE 3.22
ATM switches and virtual circuits.

ATM Protocols

The CCITT has defined a three-level model for B-ISDN, shown in Figure 3.23. This model corresponds to the lower three layers of the OSI model. To improve efficiency, all switching (the ATM equivalent of routing) is performed by protocols below the network layer.

FIGURE 3.23
Relationship of ATM to the OSI reference model.

| Application |
| Presentation |
| Session |
| Transport |
| Network |
| Data Link |
| Physical |

| ATM Adaptation Layer |
| ATM Layer |
| ATM Physical Layer |

The *ATM adaptation layer (AAL)* provides an interface to upper-layer protocols and performs message fragmentation and reassembly. IEEE 802.2 LLC encapsulation is employed when it is necessary to support multiple protocols over the same VC. The AAL provides a variety of services, including connection and connectionless, variable and constant bit rate.

The ATM layer defines cell formats and performs. Support is provided for *permanent virtual channels (PVC)* and *switched virtual channels (SVC)*.

The ATM physical layer defines how cells are transported on the network and defines signaling for various media types. Data rates, however, are not specified. ATM can be adapted to virtually any data rate and medium.

ATM Media

ATM can operate over a wide variety of media, limited only by the physical transport. A common carrier is *Synchronous Optical Network (SONET)*, developed by BellCore. SONET data rates are specified by *optical carrier (OC)* levels ranging from OC-1 (52Mbps) to OC-48 (2.5 Gbps). Current SONET implementations provide OC-9 service, 466Mbps.

The ATM Forum has defined four types of interfaces:

- 45Mbps DS3 WAN interface

- 155Mbps OC-3 SONET

- 155Mbps multimode optical fiber based on Fiber Channel

- 100Mbps multimode optical fiber based on FDDI

Of these, two are likely to have an impact on LANs. The 100Mbps option based on FDDI is designed to take advantage of newer FDDI developments, such as FDDI over copper (UTP and STP) cable. DS3 service supports copper and optical fiber media as a means of interfacing the LAN to telecommunications networks.

Other data rates seem likely. In an effort to lower cost, IBM has introduced a 25Mbps ATM system intended to provide ATM service to the desktop.

One of the most intriguing characteristics of ATM is its capability to incorporate many data rates in an extended network. 25Mbps ATM desktop connections could switch into a 100Mbps ATM backbone, which would in turn connect to a 455Mbps public data network. Of available technologies, only ATM offers this level of flexibility to provide bandwidth as required for a specific environment.

An Emerging Technology

ATM has been voted the technology most likely to succeed by the majority of LAN pundits. At present, ATM costs hover at approximately $1,000 per connection, a figure that considerably exceeds the costs for competing technologies such as 100 Mbps Ethernet. Naturally, the price for ATM can be expected to decrease as the technology matures, and it might be that the technical advantages of ATM will win out when price becomes less an issue.

One potential drawback is that ATM is a connection-oriented network, requiring a connection between each pair of communicating nodes. Connection-oriented networks do not provide direct support for the broadcast (one-to-many) transmissions that are broadly employed by TCP/IP and other protocol stacks. To get around this problem, the ATM industry has developed *LAN emulation*, which makes it unnecessary for TCP/IP to be modified to function without broadcast messages by giving the ATM network the appearance of a conventional LAN such as Ethernet or token ring. LAN emulation is not without a price, in that considerable network bandwidth is lost to the emulation process. Nevertheless, it may help bring the benefits of ATM to the everyday LAN environment.

Nevertheless, ATM remains an emerging technology. A variety of LAN-related issues remain unresolved, and most standards are under development. At present, ATM is a technology for organizations that require its unique capabilities, and it is likely to coexist with current LAN and WAN technologies for quite some time.

Beyond the Physical Network

This chapter initiated our tour of the TCP/IP protocol stack by examining some of the network protocols that commonly support physical TCP/IP networks. Because some of the distinctive characteristics of these network protocols give rise to differences in TCP/IP administration, you need to have some familiarity with the network technologies that provide connectivity on your network.

With that background behind you, you can now take your first look at some details about TCP/IP itself. The next chapter moves up the protocol stack to the internetwork layer. There you will take a detailed look at IP and at several of the protocols that enable IP to do its job.

Chapter 4

THE INTERNET LAYER

The internet layer is responsible for delivering data through an internetwork. The primary internet layer protocol is the Internet Protocol (IP), which bears the bulk of the responsibility for the layer. The current standard for IP is specified in RFC 791, as amended by RFCs 919, 922, and 950.

IP uses other protocols for special tasks. The Internet Control Messaging Protocol (ICMP) is used to deliver messages to the host-to-host layer. Also, routing protocols may be implemented to improve the IP's routing efficiency. This chapter discusses certain protocols, despite the fact that they do not function at the internet layer, because they are closely related to IP.

IP is a required Internet protocol that has the following primary functions:

- Addressing

- Datagram fragmentation and reassembly

- Delivery of datagrams on the internetwork

Of these, the function that most concerns network administrators is addressing. IP has a unique addressing scheme that takes some getting used to. Consequently, the bulk of discussion about IP will focus on IP addressing.

IP Addressing

The groundwork for TCP/IP was laid before LANs existed. No broadly accepted standards were in place for network protocol layering, and particularly, no standards existed for assigning physical addresses to devices. The approach chosen for TCP/IP utilizes an address that the IP protocol uses, following a scheme that uniquely identifies each node on an internetwork. (Recall from Chapter 2, "TCP/IP Architecture," that identifying a node on an internetwork requires two pieces of information: the specific network to which the node is attached and the node's ID on that network.)

Upper-layer TCP/IP protocols do not directly use network hardware addresses. Instead, it was decided to use a system of logical addresses for identifying hosts (the official name for an end station on a TCP/IP network is *host*). The logical IDs, called IP addresses, provide several benefits. Routing is greatly simplified because network address information is encoded in the IP address. And logical addresses make TCP/IP resistant to changes in network hardware. If the network interface card is exchanged, its hardware address changes; even if the network changes to a completely new technology, while the device remains on the same network, the IP address the upper-layer protocols use can remain the same.

You will appreciate this stability when you configure TCP/IP hosts because a host configuration includes information about several other hosts, all expressed in the form of an IP address. Each host, for example, is configured with a default gateway. If the gateway address changed due to a hardware upgrade, every host on the network would require manual reconfiguration. The IP address scheme makes network configuration much simpler.

This capability is particularly important on the Internet because users and applications frequently access other hosts on the network. If host addresses were to change frequently, disseminating those changes to the network community would be difficult. The availability of the Domain Name Service significantly reduces the severity of this problem because it enables users to use names rather than numbers to identify hosts. At one time, however, host names and their related IP addresses were stored in manually maintained text files. A constant flux of new addresses would have made network administration impossible.

NOTE

On TCP/IP networks, routers traditionally have been called gateways. That usage is gradually fading, and recent RFCs employ the term *router*, which is the term used in this chapter. Default routers continue to often be referred to as default gateways, however, a convention that this book observes as well.

Today you will most commonly encounter the term gateway as the name of a device that translates data between two very different networks or systems. An SNA gateway, for example, enables computers on a LAN to communicate with IBM mainframe computers using IBM's System Network Architecture networks. Email gateways enable different electronic mail systems to communicate despite different message formats. But in the TCP/IP world, the term gateway is still frequently used to describe a router, so be prepared for a bit of confusion.

IP Address Format

IP addresses are 32 bits in length and are divided into two fields:

- A *netid* field identifies the network to which the host is attached.

- A *hostid* field assigns each host on a given network a unique identifier.

In TCP/IP terminology, a network consists of a group of hosts that can communicate directly without the use of routers. All TCP/IP hosts that occupy the same network must be assigned the same netid. Hosts that have different netids must communicate through a router. A TCP/IP internetwork is a network of networks and can incorporate many networks, interconnected by routers. Each network on the internetwork must be assigned a unique netid.

Address Classes

When the IP address scheme was conceived, it was assumed that the following varieties of networks would exist:

- A few networks that had a very large number of hosts

- A moderate number of networks that had an intermediate number of hosts

- A large number of networks that would have a small number of hosts

Consequently, it was decided to define classes of IP addresses tailored to each of these situations. This was achieved by assigning different numbers of bits to the netids for different classes.

Figure 4.1 illustrates the five classes of IP addresses. Notice that the bits in the addresses are organized into four octets.

- *Class A* addresses begin with a high-order bit of 0. The first octet of the IP address comprises the netid, and the remaining three octets are the hostid.

- *Class B* addresses begin with high-order bits of 10. The first two octets are the netid, and the remaining two octets are the hostid.

- *Class C* addresses begin with high-order bits of 110. The first three octets are allocated for the netid, and only one octet is available for the hostid.

- *Class D* addresses begin with the high-order bits 1110. Class D addresses are used to support multicasts.

- *Class E* addresses begin with the high-order bits 11110. These addresses are used for experimental purposes.

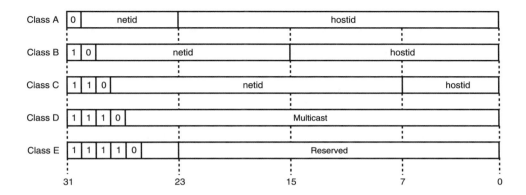

FIGURE 4.1
IP address classes.

Internet Address Registration

All networks that connect with the Internet must be configured with InterNIC-assigned IP addresses. The address registration service is managed by Network Solutions. Registration forms are available from several sources:

- Via FTP from DS.INTERNIC.NET or RS.INTERNIC.NET

- On the World Wide Web, from the URL http://ds.internic.net/

- By mail from the following address

Applications can be submitted by mail or email to the following addresses:

Network Solutions
InterNIC Registration Services
505 Huntmar Park Drive
Herndon, VA 22070

HOSTMASTER@INTERNIC.NET

At this point, only class C addresses are available. All class A addresses were assigned long ago. The very few class B addresses are available only to industry heavy hitters. Unfortunately, available class C addresses are dwindling. The designers of IP, working before the PC revolution, expected that a few thousand addresses would be sufficient for any foreseeable future. Work is proceeding on IP version 6, also called IP Next Generation (IPNG). A primary motivation for IPNG is to resolve the current address crunch.

NOTE

If you use a commercial Internet provider to connect to the Internet, your IP addresses must be obtained through the provider. Network providers are assigned blocks of addresses for that purpose.

Dotted-Decimal Notation

As mentioned earlier, an IP address is 32-bits long. Humans cannot reliably scan and remember 32-bit addresses, so the convention was developed of representing each octet as a decimal number ranging from 0 through 255. Consider this IP address:

```
11000001 00001010 00011110 00000010
```

Expressed in dotted-decimal form, the address would be 193.10.30.2.

By convention, when the hostid fields are 0, the address refers to the network. For example, 135.8.0.0 refers to the network with the netid 135.8.

NOTE

Although dotted-decimal representation is the rule, be sure to remember that IP addresses have a binary form. The majority of IP address configuration errors result because a network administrator fails to consider the binary address when setting up the network.

IP Address Restrictions

A few IP addresses have special uses and cannot be used to identify networks or hosts.

- Netids and hostids of 0 (binary 00000000) are not permitted because ids of 0 means "this network." An IP address 155.123.0.0 identifies the network with the netid 155.123. An address of 0.0.0.35 identifies the host with hostid 35 on the local network.

- The netid 127 (binary 01111111) has a special use. It is a loopback address, used for testing host network configurations. Messages addressed to netid 127 are not sent to the network but are simply reflected back.

- Hostids of 255 (binary 11111111) are restricted to use in broadcasts. A message sent to 255.255.255.255 is sent to every host on this network. A message sent to 183.20.255.255 is broadcast to every host on network 183.20.

- The last octet of an IP address cannot be 0 or 255.

Another way of expressing these rules is to examine IP addresses in terms of two fields, as in (netid, hostid). The following special cases can be noted:

- **(netid, hostid).** This address identifies a specific host on the internetwork and can be used as a source or destination address. Example: 172.16.5.143.

- **(all 0, all 0).** This address is used only to identify the network and host that originates a message and is equivalent to "this host on this network." This IP address can only be used to identify a host that is the source of a message, that is, as a "from" address. Example: 0.0.0.0.

- **(all 0, hostid).** This address identifies a specific host on "this network" and can only be used to identify the host that is the source of message, that is, as a "from" address. Example: 0.0.0.0.

- **(netid, all 0).** This address identifies the host that originates a message along with the host's network number. This type of address can be used only to identify the host that is the source of a message. Example: 172.16.0.0.

- **(all 1, all 1).** This is a local broadcast address. Messages with this "from" address are received by all hosts on the local network. Messages with this address must not be forwarded by routers. This address can be used only to identify the destination host of a message, that is, as a "to" address. Example: 255.255.255.255.

- **(netid, all 1).** This is a broadcast address for a specific network. Messages with this type of address will be forwarded to the appropriate destination network. This address can be used only to identify the destination network for a broadcast message. Example: 172.16.255.255.

NOTE

These rules ignore subnetworking. When you study subnetwork addresses later in this chapter, remember that the subnet id functions as an extension of the netid address. Consequently, the concept of an all 1 or all 0 netid can be expanded to include an all 1 or all 0 netid-subnetid combination.

Taking these restrictions into account, Table 4.1 summarizes the available class A, B, and C addresses.

TABLE 4.1

Available IP Addresses

Class	From	To	Netids	Hostids
A	1	126	126	16,777,214
B	128	191	16,384	65,534
C	192	223	2,097,152	254

NOTE

The InterNIC has reserved three ranges of IP addresses that are not supported on the Internet. These "nonroutable" addresses are not forwarded by Internet routers. Nonroutable addresses have been designated in each IP address class:

- Class A: 10.0.0.0 through 10.255.255.255

- Class B: 172.16.0.0 through 172.31.255.255

- Class C: 192.168.0.0 through 192.168.255.255

You can use these addresses on your network without fear of conflicting with other hosts on the Internet, so they are good for internal messaging and for experimentation. In Chapter 21, "Microsoft Proxy Server," you will see how the nonroutable IP addresses can be put to good use when setting up an Internet proxy server.

Transmission Modes and IP addresses

IP transmissions can take place in three modes, each of which is associated with a distinct type of IP address. These transmission modes have distinct behavioral characteristics with which you should be familiar.

Unicast Messages

The majority of IP messages are sent in *unicast* mode. That is to say, they are sent from one host to one specific destination host. Also referred to as *directed* messages, unicast frames can be routed. They can, therefore, reach any destination on an internetwork. Figure 4.2 illustrates the delivery of a unicast message. Notice that it is ignored by all hosts other than the desired recipient. Notice also that the example message experiences no difficulty crossing a router.

FIGURE 4.2

Unicast messages can be routed.

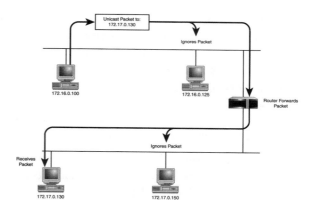

Broadcast Messages

Broadcast messages are received by all hosts that are active on a network segment, much like broadcast television can be received by anyone who installs a TV antenna and turns on his TV. Broadcast messages are easy to distinguish. They will either be all 1s (255.255.255.255) or will have all 1s in the hostid field. To understand the need for broadcast messages, look at an example in human communication. Suppose you need to speak to someone you have never met. All you know is that the person is somewhere in the room. How do you get her attention in a hurry? You shout, of course. Yes, everyone else hears the message, forcing them to stop what they are doing for a moment. But at least you get the attention of the person you need to speak to.

Broadcast messages are necessary, but they border on bad manners, particularly when they are overused. Just as conversation stops when you shout in a crowded room, every host on the network must pause for a moment to determine if it is the intended recipient for the message. Thus every host loses a bit of processing time although only one host is the target of the message. Thus it is good practice to minimize levels of broadcast messages.

Because broadcast messages can degrade network performance, they are not forwarded by IP routers. If IP broadcasts were routed, they could cross and recross routers, generating more broadcast traffic each time they returned to a network segment. The result would be *broadcast storms* that tied up increasing amounts of host processing.

Broadcast messages are used in two circumstances: when a host must send a message to everyone, or when a host must reach a particular host whose identity is unknown. A protocol that uses broadcast messages is ARP, the address resolution protocol, which is discussed later in this chapter. A host uses ARP to learn the MAC address of a host to which it wants to transmit a message. Because the MAC address is not known, a message cannot be sent directly to the target host, so a broadcast message is sent instead. Yes, every other host sees the message as well, but, like shouting in a room, it's the only way to reach your audience.

The most commonly used broadcast address is 255.255.255.255, the address of a broadcast directed to all hosts connected to the network segment on which the broadcast frame originates. As Figure 4.3 illustrates, broadcast messages are not forwarded through routers.

FIGURE 4.3

Broadcast frames are not forwarded by routers.

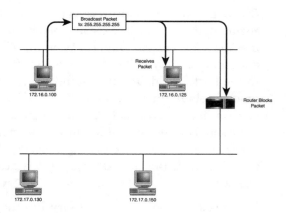

Less frequently encountered are broadcast addresses that specify a particular network. Here is a sample network-specific IP address for each address class:

- Class A: 10.255.255.255 (three all-1s fields)

- Class B: 172.16.255.255 (two all-1s fields)

- Class C: 192.168.45.255 (one all-1s field)

If subnet addressing is employed (as described a few sections later in this chapter), the bits of the hostid portion of the broadcast address must be all-1s. The subnetid portion will reflect the subnetid.

Multicast Messages

Multicast messages are directed to groups of hosts, which may be on local or remote network segments. Multicast messages use a special range of IP addresses with netids that begin with the bits 1110, as depicted in Figure 4.1. Referred to as Class D addresses, the decimal address range is from 224.0.0.0 through 239.255.255.255.

Suppose that you had to repeatedly send messages to twelve hosts on a network that contains hundreds of devices. You could send twelve messages to each of the target machines, but doing that repeatedly would waste bandwidth. In human terms, you might want to construct a "mail list" that names each recipient. You can send the message once, with the mail list addresses attached, and it's up to the recipients to recognize messages they should pull from the network.

Figure 4.4 illustrates the behavior of multicast messages. Some of the hosts have registered themselves to receive the multicast. Other hosts ignore the message as soon as they have examined the multicast IP address. Notice that multicast messages will be forwarded by routers that are configured to do so.

Figure 4.4

Multicast frames can be forwarded by routers.

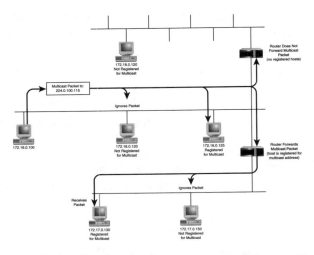

You will seldom explicitly configure services that use multicasts. But network software occasionally uses multicast messaging in the background.

You are most likely to have encountered the term multicast in connection with the MBone, the experimental Multicast Backbone that is being developed to support audio-video multicasts on the Internet. Two good sources of information about the MBone are the following Web sites:

```
http://www.serpentine.com/bos/tech/mbone/
```

```
http://www.mediadesign.co.at/newmedia/more/mbone-faq.html
```

Addressing in a TCP/IP Internetwork

Figure 4.5 illustrates a TCP/IP internetwork that consists of three networks connected with routers. This internet incorporates networks with class A, B, and C addresses.

The following list describes a number of reasons for segmenting a network:

- **Different LAN technologies might be used in different places.** An organization might have token ring in manufacturing and Ethernet in engineering, for example. Routers can interconnect different network technologies.

- **LAN connection limits.** A given network cable can support a limited number of attached devices. If these limits are exceeded, additional networks can be connected with routers.

- **Congestion.** If a network is overwhelmed, performance quickly falls apart. Internetworks may be created to reduce traffic on individual network segments.

- **Wide area networking.** If the distance between two LANs exceeds the size limits of the cabling technology, they may be interconnected through a point-to-point link.

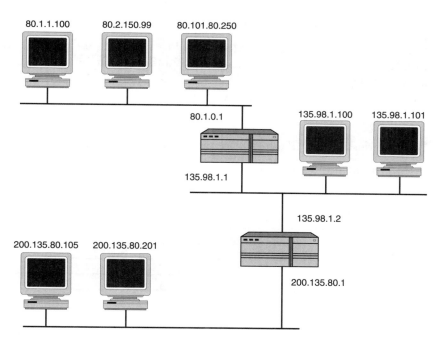

FIGURE 4.5
Example of a TCP/IP internetwork.

Subnet Addressing

If a network will never be connected to the Internet, network administrators might employ any of the available IP address classes. It is difficult to imagine any single organization that can run out of IP addresses on its own.

When a network is connected to the Internet, however, assigned addresses must be used. Unfortunately, the pool of available Internet addresses is dwindling, and even class C addresses are doled out reluctantly. As a result, many organizations find themselves with too few assigned IP addresses to assign a separate netid to each network.

To cope with this situation, a subnetting procedure was developed (RFC 950). Subnetting enables network administrators to distribute the hostids for a given netid to several subnetworks.

Figure 4.6 illustrates the formats of IP addresses with and without subnetting. The IP address always consists of 32 bits. Subnetting is a mechanism for using some bits in the hostid octets as a subnetid. Without subnetting, an IP address is interpreted in two fields:

netid + hostid

With subnetting, an IP address is interpreted in three fields:

netid + subnetid + hostid

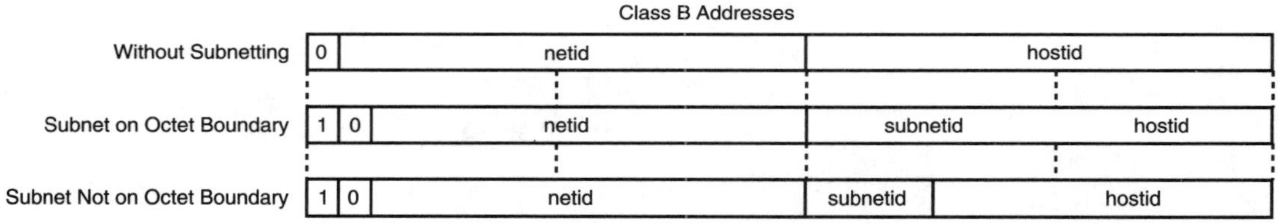

FIGURE 4.6
IP addresses with and without subnetting.

Subnet Masking

The subnetid is created by borrowing bits from the hostid field using a technique called subnet masking. Consider the following class B address:

```
10100001 01110101 10110111 10000111
```

The right-most two octets of a class B address are the hostid. To encode a subnetid, some of the hostid bits can be reserved for the subnetid by using a subnet mask. Figure 4.7 shows how a subnet mask might be used to reserve the first four bits of the hostid for the subnetid.

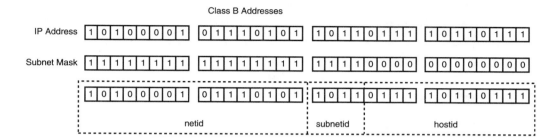

FIGURE 4.7

Subnet masking.

The subnet mask is a 32-bit number. A 1 in the subnet mask indicates that the corresponding bit in the IP address is part of the netid. A 0 in the subnet mask designates the bit as a part of the hostid.

NOTE

Subnet masks nearly always consist of adjacent, high-order bits. As a result, you need to remember only eight decimal numbers to recognize the vast majority of subnet masks. The nine common subnet masks are as follows:

Binary	Decimal
00000000	0
10000000	128
11000000	192
11100000	224
11110000	240
11111000	248
11111100	252
11111110	254
11111111	255

The RFCs permit subnet masks with nonadjacent (noncontiguous) bits and even provide an example. It is difficult to imagine a case where a noncontiguous mask would provide an advantage.

The number of bits in the subnet mask is adjusted depending on the number of subnets required. With a class B address, the subnet mask 255.255.255.0 allocates the third octet for subnet addressing, yielding 254 possible subnetids.

NOTE

Like netids, subnetids cannot consist entirely of 0s or 1s. That is why, with a class B address, a subnet mask of 255.255.255.0 makes 254 subnetids available rather than 256.

Default Subnet Masks

When a network is configured to support subnet addressing, a subnet mask must be designated, even if no subnetting actually is in use. The default subnet masks are as follows:

- Class A: 255.0.0.0
- Class B: 255.255.0.0
- Class C: 255.255.255.0

The subnet mask must be configured with 1s for bits corresponding to the netid field of the address class. A subnet mask of 255.255.0.0 is invalid for a class C address, for example.

Example of Subnet Addressing

The advantages, disadvantages, and caveats of subnet addressing can be illustrated most clearly with an example based on a class C address. Figure 4.8 illustrates the example.

The network will be based on the network address 195.100.205.0, which in binary is as follows:

```
11000011 01100100 11001101 00000000
```

The subnet mask used for the example is 255.255.255.224, which has the following binary equivalent:

```
11111111 11111111 11111111 11100000
```

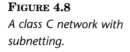

FIGURE 4.8

A class C network with subnetting.

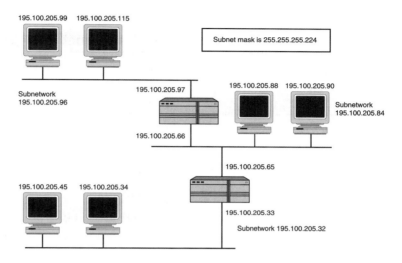

Three bits of the hostid are set aside for subnetids. Because subnetids cannot be all 0s or all 1s, six subnetids are made available: 001, 010, 011, 100, 101, and 110. With five hostid bits available, each subnet can support 30 hosts (hostids 00000 and 11111 are not available).

Consider the IP address 195.100.205.175. The binary form of the address is as follows:

```
11000011 01100100 11001101 10101111
```

Applying the subnet mask, the three bits allocated for the subnetid result in a subnetid of 10100000, which is 160 in decimal. The hostid is 01111, which is 15 in decimal.

Table 4.2 summarizes the values that are valid for the fourth octet when using a subnet mask of 255.255.255.224. The table illustrates, among other things, that subnetting a class C address wastes many potential hostids. (Subnetting isn't nearly as costly with class A and B addresses.) If you have a budget of one class C address and you must segment your network, however, you don't have much choice. But NT offers the capability to help minimize the impact of subnetting because NT can have one NIC represent several subnets. This helps overcome the problem of losing host IDs when subnetting with few subnets.

TABLE 4.2

Class C Host Addresses Available with a Subnet Mask 255.255.255.224

Subnet (Binary)	Subnet (Decimal)	Fourth Octet Available Values (Binary)	Fourth Octet Available Values (Decimal)
001	32	00100001–00111110	33–62
010	64	01000001–01011110	65–94
011	96	01100001–01111110	97–126
100	128	10000001–10011110	129–158
101	160	10100001–10111110	161–190
110	192	11000001–11011110	193–222

NOTE

It is essential to take the binary forms of addresses into account when planning subnets. Otherwise, selecting an invalid address becomes too easy. Another thing—if subnet masking is used on a subnet, all hosts must be configured with the same subnet mask.

Subnet Calculation Shortcuts

A few shortcuts make it easy to determine how many subnets will result from a given subnet mask, and what the host IDs will be for each subnet.

Calculating the number of subnets. If the number of 1 bits in the subnet portion of the subnet mask is n, the number of subnets the mask will create is 2^n-2. For example, if there are four 1 bits in the subnet portion of the subnet mask, there can be 2^4-2 (16-2) subnets.

Calculating the netids. This requires several steps:

1. Isolate the right-most bit in the subnet mask and convert its value to decimal notation. The number you obtain from this step is know as *Delta*.

2. Add Delta to the original network ID to obtain the first subnet ID.

3. Repeatedly add the Delta to the last subnet ID you obtained to determine the next subnet ID.

Look at an example, using the class C network 200.100.50.0 with a subnet mask of 255.255.255.196.

1. To obtain Delta, examine the subnet mask, which in binary is 11111111 11111111 11111111 11100000. The decimal equivalent of the rightmost bit is 32, which is the Delta you seek.

2. Add the Delta to the network ID 200.100.50.0 to determine that the first subnetwork ID is 200.100.50.32.

3. Repeatedly add the Delta as follows to determine the remaining subnetwork IDs, as follows:

200.100.50.32 + 32 = 200.100.50.64

200.100.50.64 + 32 = 200.100.50.96

200.100.50.96 + 32 = 200.100.50.128

200.100.50.128 + 32 = 200.100.50.160

200.100.50.160 + 32 = 200.100.50.192

200.100.50.192 + 32 = 200.100.50.224

As you can see, this calculation generates the same network IDs that you saw in Table 4.2. Compare the results to become familiar with the technique.

Subnetting Tables

Tables 4.3, 4.4, and 4.5 put a different complexion on subnetwork calculation. Assuming subnetids of eight bits or less, these tables help you quickly determine how subnets play out for each address class.

TABLE 4.3

Class A Subnetting

Additional Bits Req'd (n)	Maximum Subnets (2^n-2)	Maximum Number of Hosts per Subnet ($2^{24-n}-2$)	Subnet Mask
0	0	16,777,214	255.0.0.0
1	invalid	invalid	invalid

continues

Table 4.3, Continued

Class A Subnetting

Additional Bits Req'd (n)	Maximum Subnets (2^n-2)	Maximum Number of Hosts per Subnet ($2^{24-n}-2$)	Subnet Mask
2	2	4,194,302	255.192.0.0
3	6	2,097,150	255.224.0.0
4	14	1,048,574	255.240.0.0
5	30	524,286	255.248.0.0
6	62	262,142	255.252.0.0
7	126	131,070	255.254.0.0
8	254	65,534	255.255.0.0

Table 4.4

Class B Subnetting

Additional Bits Req'd (n)	Maximum Subnets (2^n-2)	Maximum Number of Hosts per Subnet ($2^{16-n}-2$)	Subnet Mask
0	0	65,534	255.255.0.0
1	invalid	invalid	invalid
2	2	16,382	255.255.192.0
3	6	8,190	255.255.224.0
4	14	4,094	255.255.240.0
5	30	2,046	255.255.248.0
6	62	1,022	255.255.252.0
7	126	510	255.255.254.0
8	254	254	255.255.255.0

TABLE 4.5

Class C Subnetting

Additional Bits Req'd (n)	Maximum Subnets (2^n-2)	Maximum Number of Hosts per Subnet ($2^{8-n}-2$)	Subnet Mask Subnet
0	0	254	255.255.255.0
1	invalid	invalid	invalid
2	2	62	255.255.255.192
3	6	30	255.255.255.224
4	14	14	255.255.255.240
5	30	6	255.255.255.248
6	62	2	255.255.255.252
7	invalid	invalid	255.255.255.254
8	invalid	invalid	255.255.255.255

The All-Zeros Subnet

Table 4.2 assumes that RFC 950 is strictly adhered to, and RFC 950 does not permit use of a subnetid that is all 0s. Therefore, the table lists only six subnets that are made available when three bits are set aside for the subnetid.

An all 1s subnetid is not possible because an all 1s network address is used for broadcast addressing. There is, however, no predefined use for an all 0s subnetid, and many consider the prohibition of the all 0s subnetid to be a waste of resources. Therefore, some vendors have chosen to permit the use of the all 0s subnet in their TCP/IP implementations. Although Microsoft documentation does not explicitly permit the all 0s subnetid, my tests indicate that the all 0s subnetid is supported by Windows NT.

If you choose to use the all 0s subnet, test all devices that participate in the network and proceed with caution. You are on *terra incognita*, and it is your responsibility to ensure that the network can operate properly.

Preserving Your Options

When an address scheme starts to go into place on a network, it becomes difficult to change because some changes require manual intervention on each affected host. Unless you work to preserve your options, changes can be quite difficult. Let's look at an example.

Suppose that you begin your network with the class B address 155.80.0.0 and decide that you need six subnets. Therefore, you elect to use the subnet mask 255.255.224.0.

As you begin to number hosts, you don't pay much attention to how you use the 13 available bits. As a result, you might have a host with the IP address 155.80.210.55.

Your company expands and now has a need to add some more subnets, forcing you to change the subnet mask. No problem. You can change the mask to 255.255.240.0, giving you four subnet bits to work with. Or can you?

If you look back two paragraphs and examine the bit pattern for the IP address 155.80.210.55, you will see that you have a problem because this address uses the fourth bit of the third byte, the bit that you want to add to the subnet mask. If a large number of hosts use this bit, you are faced with reconfiguring not only the subnet mask but the IP addresses of those hosts as well. And reconfiguring large numbers of IP addresses means planning, visiting the machines, and updating your records.

To avoid hassles like this, consider two guidelines:

- Always use subnetid bits starting from the high-order (left-most) bits. Assign subnets in the following order: 1, 01, 11, 001, 011, 101, 111, 0001, and so forth.

- Always assign hostid bits starting from the low-order (right-most) bits. Assign hostids in the following order: 1, 10, 11, 100, 101, 110, 111, 1000, and so forth.

By doing this, you maintain a buffer zone of zeros in the middle that gives you wiggle room when you need to change your subnetting. You can add bits to the subnet mask without affecting the hostids that have already been assigned.

Subnets Are Invisible to Outside Networks

An interesting thing about subnets is that they are visible only to routers that are immediately adjacent to the subnets. If this were not the case, if you connected a subnetted network to the Internet, you would need to notify the entire Internet routing community of your subnet mask. That isn't the case, as you can see in Figure 4.9. In this network, netid 128.0.0.0 has been subnetted and is currently represented by three subnets.

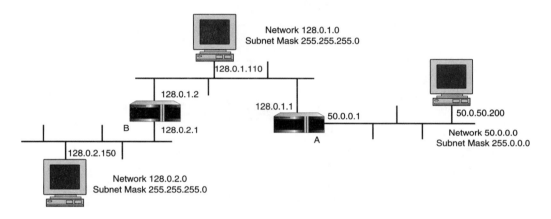

FIGURE 4.9
Subnets and external networks.

Suppose host 50.0.50.200 needs to send a datagram to host 128.0.3.50. Must 50.0.50.200 be aware of which subnet the destination is on? No, as far as hosts on network 50.0.0.0 are concerned, the router is connected to network 128.0.0.0. The other side of the router appears to be a single network, and the subnets are invisible.

Routing is this simple only if the subnets of 128.0.0.0 are configured to enable Router A to route all datagrams for that network through the same interface.

But Routing with Subnets Can Be Tricky

A small change to the network in Figure 4.9 introduces a complication. Consider the network in Figure 4.10. Suppose that router A does not understand subnetids. It will be confused by two things. One is the fact that it is connected to network 128.0.0.0 through two interfaces. Which interface should be used to route traffic for that network?

The other source of confusion is that subnet 128.0.3.0 is invisible to router A. Datagrams destined for host 128.0.3.50 could be misrouted to subnet 128.0.2.0. Router A must understand subnets to properly route in this network.

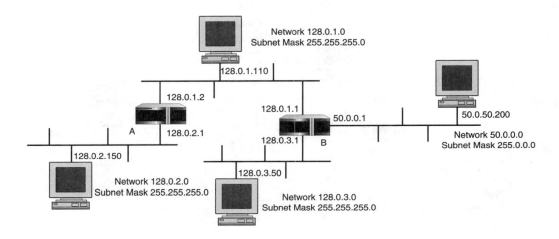

FIGURE 4.10

A router that must understand subnetids.

From the examples in Figures 4.9 and 4.10, it should be clear that care must be taken when planning the architecture of a network that includes subnets. You must be sure of one of two things:

- Either the subnets should be arranged to present the appearance to routers of a single network

- Or the routers should utilize protocols that understand the use of subnet masks

As you will see later in this chapter, the most common TCP/IP routing protocol, RIP, comes in two versions—version 1, which does not understand subnets and version 2, which does understand subnets. Many routers you will encounter support RIP version 1 only, placing the burden on network designers to ensure proper network design.

Classless Inter-Domain Routing

The systems of IP addresses and subnetting were arrived at long before the Internet's explosive growth in the 1990s. In recent years, two trends have complicated Internet address assignment:

- Class B addresses have been exhausted, requiring large organizations to obtain (and juggle) many class C addresses.

- Class C addresses are at risk of exhaustion, and small organizations that don't need a full class C allocation should receive only what they require.

Classless inter-domain routing (CIDR; RFC 1519) is a technique for assigning blocks of class C addresses to accommodate organizations larger and smaller than 254 hosts.

If your organization is small, you might be allocated a portion of a class C address. If you require 50 addresses, for example, you might be assigned addresses 220.185.8.64 through 220.185.8.127 to be used with the subnet mask 255.255.255.192. This arrangement gives you 6 bits for host IDs and results in 62 usable addresses.

Recall the rule stated earlier that subnet masks must include 1s corresponding to all bits in the netid portion of the address. Many rules have exceptions, and an exception called *supernet addressing* permits subnet masks to define a shorter network mask than the default mask for a given network class. Supernet addressing provides a means for large organizations to aggregate multiple class C addresses so that they can be managed as a larger address space.

Suppose you want to attach a network with 800 nodes to the Internet. At this time, the organization must accommodate this many nodes by registering four class-C addresses. Unfortunately, with standard addressing, these four class-C addresses define four distinct networks, and routing is required to enable data to be transferred between the networks.

If the class C addresses are carefully chosen, however, supernet addressing permits an administrator to treat four class C addresses as one network. To see how this works, apply the net mask 255.255.252.0 to the following addresses, shown with their binary equivalents:

```
200.5.180.0 (11001000 00000101 10110100 00000000)
200.5.181.0 (11001000 00000101 10110101 00000000)
```

```
200.5.182.0  (11001000  00000101  10110110  00000000)
200.5.183.0  (11001000  00000101  10110111  00000000)
```

In the list, the hostid portions are set in bold type. You will see that the supernet mask enables the administrator to use 10 bits for hostids, supporting a total of 1,046 hosts. Because sequential class C addresses are being used, all hosts share a common netid.

Supernet masks are not supported under all TCP/IP implementations. Be sure to check your system specifications for all affected devices before attempting an implementation.

CIDR is at best a workaround for our present IP address woes. Internet access providers are allocated large chunks of Internet address space, and CIDR enables them to allocate address blocks that are sized to meet their customers' needs. But suppose a customer relocates and begins connecting to the Internet through a different provider. Two disturbing choices are possible. The provider can retain the addresses for use by future customers, in which case the organization must readdress its entire network. Or the provider can generously permit the organization to retain its assigned addresses, in which case the customer has "punched a hole" in the provider's CIDR block, complicating future address allocations. Clearly, CIDR has not eliminated the need for a revised IP addressing scheme.

Datagram Fragmentation and Reassembly

An IP datagram can be as large as 65,535 octets. Many networks, however, cannot support data units of that size. An Ethernet frame, for example, can support only 1,500 octets of upper-layer data, and other network types are further restricted in the message sizes that can be accommodated. The *maximum transfer unit* (MTU) describes the number of octets in the maximum frame size that a network can deliver without fragmentation.

In internetworks, different network segments can have different MTU specifications. Consider the internet in Figure 4.11. The token ring has an MTU of 3,000, the Ethernet network has an MTU of 1,500, and the intermediate WAN has an MTU of 520 (allowing for a 20 octet IP header and 500 octets of data). If host 1 sends a 3,000 octet datagram to host 2, router A must fragment the original datagram for transfer through the WAN. Router B must reassemble the fragments to recover the original datagram and then refragment it for delivery to host 2.

FIGURE 4.11

An internetwork with varying MTU restrictions.

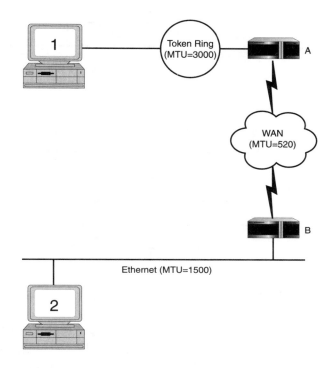

The IP protocol specification states that all hosts must be prepared to accept and reassemble datagrams of at least 576 octets. All routers must be able to manage datagrams up to the maximum message size of the networks to which they are attached, and must always be able to handle datagrams of up to 576 octets.

IP has the task of fragmenting large datagrams into datagrams that are compatible with the physical layer being used. The header for each fragment includes information that enables IP at the receiving host to identify the position of the fragment and to reassemble the original datagram.

When an oversize datagram must be fragmented, the header for each fragment includes an *offset* parameter that specifies where the first octet in the fragment is located in the overall datagram. In Figure 4.12, an original datagram, containing 1,300 octets in its data field, must be fragmented to accommodate a network with an MTU of 520. Allowing for the header, each fragment can contain 500 octets of data, and three fragments are generated with offsets of 0, 500, and 1,000 respectively.

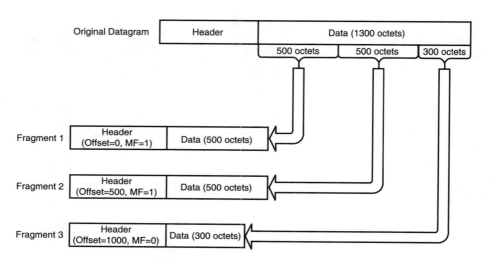

FIGURE 4.12

Fragmentation of a datagram.

Note that each of the fragments is a standard IP datagram. The headers of the fragments are nearly identical to the header of the original datagram except that the MF bit in the *flags* field is used to indicate whether the datagram is an intermediate fragment or the last fragment in a datagram. (The IP datagram header format is discussed later in this chapter.)

No error detection and recovery mechanisms are implemented in the IP protocol. If a fragment of an overall datagram is damaged or lost, IP cannot request retransmission of the fragment. Instead, IP is forced to report an error to the upper-layer protocol, which must then retransmit the entire datagram. This can be highly inefficient, requiring a large datagram to be retransmitted because a small fragment was lost.

When TCP is the upper-layer protocol, it is preferable to prevent fragmentation by IP. Ideally, the TCP should incorporate a mechanism to identify the minimum MTU between the source and destination host. This enables TCP to construct datagrams sized so that they need not be fragmented as they are routed through the internet.

IP Routing

IP is responsible for delivering datagrams on the internetwork. When IP datagrams must travel to a network other than the local one, IP performs routing for the network, ensuring that the datagram reaches the destination network.

Actual delivery to the destination host, however, is a function of the data link layer. Before examining how routing is performed, the process of delivering packets on a network must be understood.

Delivering Data on the Local Network

When two hosts communicate on the same local network, delivery of a datagram is a simple process. Actual delivery is performed by lower-level protocols. On IEEE 802.x LANs, frames are delivered under control of the medium access control (MAC) sublayer.

Recall from Chapter 2 that the MAC sublayer is responsible for node addressing. In fact, node hardware addresses are called MAC addresses in IEEE 802 terminology.

Figure 4.13 shows how simple it is to deliver a frame on a local network. The source node simply builds a frame that includes the recipient's *destination address (DA)*. The sender's responsibility ends when the addressed frame is placed on the network. On LANs, each node examines each frame that is sent on the network, looking for frames with a destination address that matches its own MAC address. Frames that match are received. Frames that do not match are discarded (Ethernet) or forwarded to the next node (token ring). The only bit of information needed to send a frame to a node on the same network is the recipient's MAC address.

FIGURE 4.13

Delivering a frame on a local network.

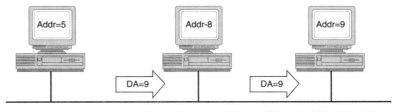

Addr=5   Addr-8   Addr=9

DA=9   DA=9

DA is not Hardware Address   DA matches Hardware Address
Frame is discarded   Frame is received

At first, incoming frames are examined only to the point that the destination address can be determined. If a node determines that its MAC address matches the destination address in the frame, it receives the remainder of the frame. If the addresses don't match, the node ignores the subsequent data in the frame.

In other words, a node will examine only the data portions of frames for which it is the addressee. This is typically desirable for two reasons. To preserve security, you do not want nodes listening in on each other's messages. Also, if nodes fully received every frame on the network, they would be doing lots of extra and unnecessary work.

In certain cases, such as network protocol analysis, it is necessary to have network interfaces that operate in *promiscuous* mode, receiving in full all frames on the network. On some networks, such as token ring, special network interface adapters are required to operate in promiscuous mode. On some networks, promiscuous mode is enabled through software driver settings.

Address Resolution Protocol

The simple scenario previously described ignores the fact that IP uses its own address scheme, consisting of logical IP addresses. To deliver a datagram on the local network, IP must provide the MAC layer with the physical address of the receiving host.

The Address Resolution Protocol (ARP) provides that information. IP calls ARP with the IP address of the destination host, and ARP returns the physical address for that node. Figure 4.14 shows the method ARP uses to obtain address information.

FIGURE 4.14
Operation of ARP.

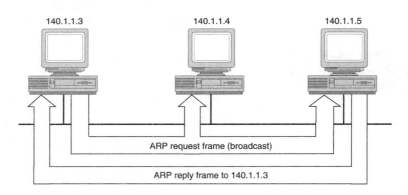

To identify a hardware address, the following steps take place:

1. ARP on host 140.1.1.3 sends an ARP request frame, which is broadcast to the local network. (On Ethernet, this is accomplished by sending the message to the address FF:FF:FF:FF:FF:FF.) The ARP request frame includes the sender's IP and MAC addresses, as well as the destination IP address.

2. All hosts on the network receive the ARP request frame and compare the destination IP address in the frame to their own addresses.

3. If a host finds that the addresses match, it creates an ARP response frame by placing its physical address in a field in the ARP request frame and returning the frame to the host that sent it.

4. When ARP on 140.1.1.3 receives the completed ARP response frame, the information is passed on to IP.

If ARP on each host were to broadcast an ARP request frame each time a datagram was to be sent, the traffic would overwhelm the network. To reduce the frequency of address requests, ARP maintains a cache table with recently received addresses. This cache table can be consulted in the future before broadcasting an ARP request. Information in the cache table has a limited life, and ARP reacquires an address after the cache table entry expires. (The system administrator determines the lifetime of a cache entry.) As an extra traffic saver, the ARP request frame includes address information for the host originating the frame. On the assumption that the originating and responding hosts will be corresponding in the near future, the responding host updates its address cache with the originator's address information.

NOTE

A Reverse Address Resolution Protocol (RARP) compliments ARP, enabling a host to determine the IP address associated with a hardware address. RARP is particularly useful on diskless workstations that must boot from the network. When the diskless workstation boots, it generates a RARP request to determine its IP address.

Preventing Duplicate IP Addresses

Microsoft and other TCP/IP clients use ARP to prevent duplicate IP addresses from being established on the network. When a host first enters a network, it broadcasts an ARP request frame with its own IP address to announce its presence. If another host responds to the ARP request frame, the new host knows that its address is already in use. The result is that the new host is prevented from using the IP address and is barred from entering the network. Error messages notify the new and established host that a potential address conflict has been prevented.

Local Delivery of IP Datagrams

To deliver a datagram, IP must determine whether it can be delivered on the local network or be routed to a remote network. Before examining routing, the local delivery process must be understood.

1. IP receives a frame from a higher-level protocol.

2. IP compares the destination netid of the frame to the netid of the local network (taking subnet masks into account if subnetting is employed). If the netids match, the frame can be sent directly to the hardware address of the destination host.

3. IP obtains the destination hardware address from ARP.

4. IP constructs a datagram that contains, among other things, the source and destination IP addresses.

5. IP passes the datagram to the network access layer protocol (for example, Ethernet II or IEEE 802.2 LLC) along with the source and destination hardware addresses.

6. The network access layer constructs a frame that incorporates the source and destination hardware addresses. The IP datagram is stored in the frame's data field. (See Chapter 3, "The Network Access Layer," for frame formats of various protocols.)

7. The destination host examines the frame, recognizes its hardware address, and receives the frame.

Delivering Data to Remote Networks

The previous section assumed that the datagram to be transmitted had source and destination addresses for hosts attached to the same network. On an internetwork, however, data must frequently be sent to remote hosts, hosts on other networks. On TCP/IP networks, delivery is performed through IP routing.

Simple IP Routing

When a datagram is to be routed to an adjacent network, as shown in Figure 4.15, the procedure is straightforward. Each host on the network is configured with the address of a default gateway, which specifies the host to which frames should be sent if they are directed to a host on a remote network.

An IP router (or gateway) is essentially a TCP/IP host equipped with two or more network connections. Such hosts are called multihomed hosts. A router can be a designated computer or a workstation host configured to perform routing.

In Figure 4.15, host 128.1.0.3 must route a frame to host 128.2.0.2. The routing procedure illustrated in Figure 4.15 is as follows:

1. Host 128.1.0.3 determines that the destination host is not on the local network by comparing the destination netid to its own netid. The frame must be routed.

2. To route the frame, host 128.1.0.3 performs an ARP request to determine the hardware address of its default gateway. IP then addresses the frame with the destination hardware address of its default router. The destination IP address, however, is the address of the ultimate destination 128.2.0.2. The address information used to address the frame is as follows:

   - Source hardware address 1
   - Source IP address 128.1.0.3
   - Destination hardware address 4
   - Destination IP address 128.2.0.2

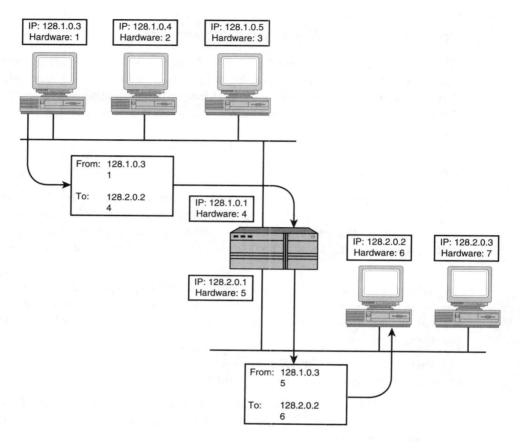

FIGURE 4.15

Routing to an adjacent network.

3. IP on the router receives the frame from network 128.1.0.0. By examining the destination IP address, the router determines that it is not the final recipient of the datagram, which must be forwarded to network 128.2.0.0. Because the router is attached directly to the destination network, routing is a simple task.

4. IP on the router calls ARP to determine the hardware address for 128.2.0.2.

5. The router sends the packet on network 128.2.0.0 with the following address information:

- Source hardware address 5

- Source IP address 128.1.0.3

- Destination hardware address 6

- Destination IP address 128.2.0.2

The source IP address is that of the host that originated the datagram. The source hardware address corresponds to the router's network connection on network 128.2.0.0.

6. Host 128.2.0.2 recognizes its hardware address and receives the packet. Two things should be emphasized in this scenario:

- The source and destination IP addresses do not change as the datagram traverses the network.

- The source and destination hardware addresses change each time the frame is sent.

Complex IP Routing

The simple routing scenario just presented falls apart if the destination network is not directly attached to a router on the delivery path. Consider the example shown in Figure 4.16. Router A is unaware of the existence of network 128.3.0.0 and has no information that enables it to forward a datagram from host 128.1.0.100 to host 128.3.0.50.

For that reason, routing tables are maintained on IP routers. IP consults the routing tables to determine where to route a datagram for a particular destination network. On a complex internetwork, routing tables should offer all the available routes, along with an estimate of the efficiency for each route.

Routing tables can take the following two forms:

- **Static tables.** Maintained by the network administrator.

- **Dynamic tables.** Maintained automatically by a routing protocol.

Even though static routing tables are fairly archaic, they are the only routing supported by Windows NT as it ships. Taking a look at static tables before examining routing protocols, therefore, should prove worthwhile.

FIGURE 4.16
A network with more complex routing.

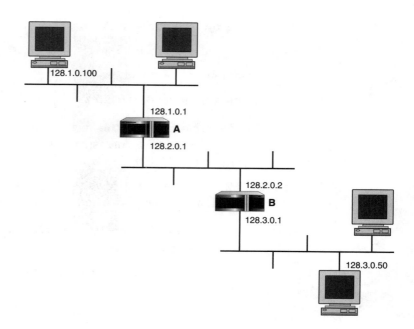

Static Routing Tables

Static routing tables are not automatically updated, but rather, must be manually maintained. On a dynamic network, router table maintenance can be tedious, but Windows NT administrators must face up to the task or buy commercial routers.

Figure 4.17 shows an example of a Windows NT routing table. Static routing tables are maintained by the route utility, which also was used to produce this listing.

The routing table lists known networks, along with the IP address that should be used to reach the networks. The entries in the table are as follows:

- **Network Address.** This column lists addresses of known networks. Notice that entries are included for the local network 0.0.0.0 and for broadcasts, 255.255.255.255. (A table entry for network 0.0.0.0 describes a *default gateway*, which is used whenever a destination is not explicitly described in the routing table.)

- **Netmask.** This column lists the subnet mask in effect for each network.

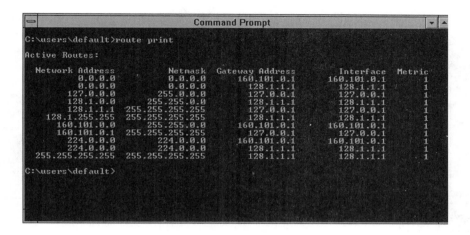

```
─                              Command Prompt                      ▼ ▲
C:\users\default>route print

Active Routes:
Network Address          Netmask  Gateway Address        Interface  Metric
        0.0.0.0          0.0.0.0      160.101.0.1      160.101.0.1       1
        0.0.0.0          0.0.0.0        128.1.1.1        128.1.1.1       1
      127.0.0.0        255.0.0.0        127.0.0.1        127.0.0.1       1
      128.1.0.0      255.255.0.0        128.1.1.1        128.1.1.1       1
      128.1.1.1  255.255.255.255        127.0.0.1        127.0.0.1       1
  128.1.255.255  255.255.255.255        128.1.1.1        128.1.1.1       1
    160.101.0.0      255.255.0.0      160.101.0.1      160.101.0.1       1
    160.101.0.1  255.255.255.255        127.0.0.1        127.0.0.1       1
      224.0.0.0        224.0.0.0      160.101.0.1      160.101.0.1       1
      224.0.0.0        224.0.0.0        128.1.1.1        128.1.1.1       1
255.255.255.255  255.255.255.255        128.1.1.1        128.1.1.1       1

C:\users\default>
```

FIGURE 4.17

A Windows NT routing table.

- **Gateway Address.** This column lists the IP addresses that should receive datagrams destined for each network.

- **Metric.** This column is an estimate of the cost of the route in hops. A hop occurs each time a datagram crosses a router.

Clearly, maintaining such a table would be quite tedious. That is why the majority of networks rely on routers that employ a routing protocol to maintain routing tables.

Another problem with static routing is that it does not enable routers to automatically identify alternative routes. Figure 4.18 illustrates a situation involving three routers. If the link between A and 128.2.0.0 fails, router A cannot take advantage of the route A-C-B unless an entry for router C has been stored in A's router table.

Routing Information Protocol

The Internet Routing Information Protocol (RIP; RFC 1058) is the protocol most commonly used to maintain routing tables on TCP/IP internets. If you have experience on Novell networks, you probably are familiar with the Novell RIP protocol, which is similar in function to Internet RIP (both were derived from the XNS protocol Xerox originated) but not interchangeable with it.

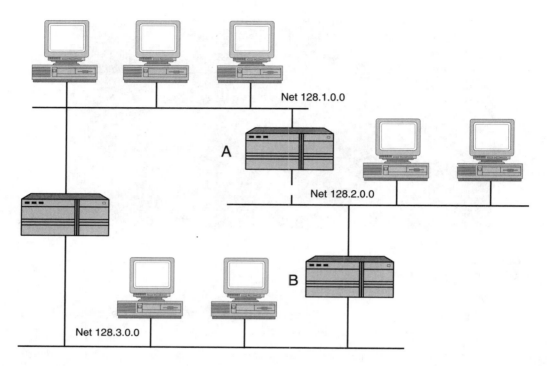

Net 128.1.0.0

A

Net 128.2.0.0

B

Net 128.3.0.0

FIGURE 4.18

A network path failure.

RIP is a distance vector routing protocol. As Chapter 2 explains, distance vector routing protocols represent routing information in terms of the cost of reaching destination networks. Cost is a fairly simple metric (measure) that represents the cost of using a route using a number from 1 through 15. In general, each network that a route must traverse is represented by a cost of 1. RIP is used to discover the costs of various routes to destination networks and store that information in a routing table, enabling IP to select the lowest-cost route.

A RIP routing table entry contains at least the following information:

- The IP address of the destination
- A metric that represents the sum of the costs to reach the destination
- The IP address of the next router on the path to the destination

- A flag indicating a recent change to the route

- Timers

In a router, RIP builds and maintains its routing table using a mechanism that is at its heart quite simple: Each router periodically broadcasts its routing table, which other routers use to update their route information.

NOTE

In a routing table, the special address 0.0.0.0 describes a default route, which can be used if maintaining a complete network routing table is inconvenient.

Route Convergence

Figure 4.19 illustrates an internetwork with four routers. Assume that the entire internet has just come up and that all router tables have been newly initialized. The following steps describe how A initializes its routing table and how its information propagates through the internet.

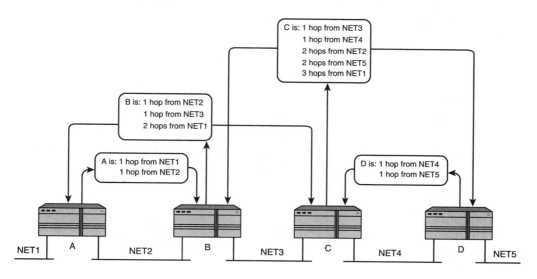

FIGURE 4.19

Route convergence on a simple internetwork.

1. After initialization, A knows only of the directly attached networks. A is 1 hop from NET1 and 1 hop from NET2 (1 is the minimum cost metric). A broadcasts a RIP response packet containing this information to its attached networks.

2. B receives A's broadcast. B is directly attached to NET2 at a cost of 1 and discards the route learned from A. Because B is attached to a network that is attached to A, B learns that it is 1 hop from A. B determines the cost to reach NET1 by adding its cost to reach A (1) to A's cost to reach NET1 (1). Consequently, B's cost to reach NET1 is 2.

3. B broadcasts a RIP response packet using its routing table, including its attached networks. A learns from this table that it has a route to NET3 at a cost of 2. C learns that it has routes to NET1 (cost 3) and to NET2 (cost 2).

Meanwhile, other routers have not been idle. D has broadcast its routing table as well, informing the other routers of routes to NET5. In this way, routers arrive on a complete picture of the network in terms of the costs to each destination and the routers through which a message should next be routed to reach a given destination. The process of bringing all routers up-to-date on the state of the network is called *convergence*.

Each router broadcasts a route response packet to its neighbors at 30-second intervals. The general rule is that a router updates its route tables after it discovers a route that has a lower cost. Routers eventually converge on the lowest-cost routes.

When a new router is started on an established network, the new router can solicit routing information from nearby routers by issuing a RIP request packet, which reduces the time required to converge the new router and informs other routers of new routes the new router makes available.

Potential Convergence Problems with RIP

The RIP algorithm, as described to this point, has some potential for problems. Before examining techniques for alleviating the problems, the problems themselves must be examined.

Figure 4.20 illustrates an internetwork. Each of the networks shown is associated with a cost of 1, with one exception. The cost from C to D is 10, which might be the result of crossing many routers. Or it might result because the link is a low-speed link that should be used only in emergencies, and the network administrator has manually assigned a high cost to it.

Figure 4.20

Example of a fully converged network.

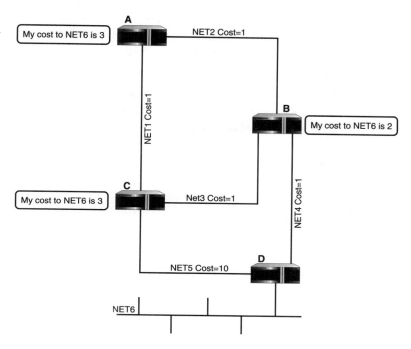

When the network is working properly, the routing information for the routers with respect to NET6 is as follows:

- A can reach NET6 through B at a cost of 3.

- B can reach NET6 through D at a cost of 2.

- C can reach NET6 through B at a cost of 3.

- D can reach NET6 directly at a cost of 1.

If NET4 fails between B and D, current routes are invalidated on A, B, and C. It takes some time, however, for the routers to converge on a new route. B rids itself of the old route fairly quickly by using a time out mechanism. If B fails to receive a route response packet from D after 90 seconds (three 30-second intervals), B times out the entries in its tables that route through D.

Timing out solves the immediate problem for B. But RIP routers have specific route knowledge only of the networks to which they are directly attached, causing problems in this instance because neither A nor C is aware that NET4 has failed and that B's route is invalid. A and C advertise that they have a route to NET6 with a cost of 3 but do not specify that the route requires the link between B and D. Therefore, C assumes it can use A's route, and A assumes it can use C's route.

After B advertises that its route is gone, C looks for the least costly route available and discovers that A offers a route with a cost of 3. Similarly, A selects the route advertised by C, with a cost of 3. When A and C forward their routing tables, B sees routes to D through A or C with a cost of 4 and makes those entries in its routing table. Figure 4.21 shows the new routing status.

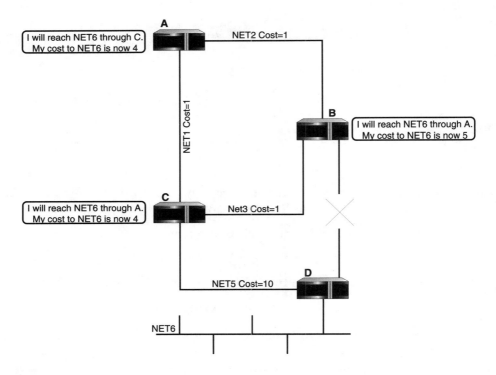

FIGURE 4.21
Reconverging after a network failure.

B's routing information causes A and C to update their costs to reach NET6, revising the costs to 6. This information, when received by B, prompts B to assign a cost of 7 to the routes through A and C. In this way, the cost metrics in the routing tables gradually ratchet up until the direct route from C to D, through NET5, becomes the low-cost route. Because RIP updates occur at 30-second intervals, considerable time might elapse before the network reconverges on the new route.

The Count to Infinity Problem

A more sinister scenario can take place if a network becomes inaccessible. In Figure 4.22, the connection between router B and NET1 has failed. B has been advertising itself as a router to A, with a cost of 1 to reach NET1. Also, because A advertises its entire routing table, A advertises that it can reach NET1 at a cost of 2.

When B loses its route to NET1, it examines incoming RIP advertisements to determine if another route exists. Because A is advertising a route to NET1 at a cost of 2, B assumes that it can route through A to reach NET1 at a cost of 3. Because NET1 is no longer connected, a suitable route never becomes available, and the counting process can proceed indefinitely—hence, the count to infinity problem.

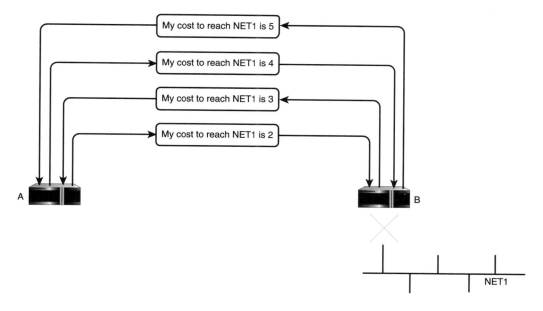

FIGURE 4.22
Counting to infinity.

The technique for breaking this loop is to make "infinity" a suitably low number that is reached fairly rapidly. For RIP, the number chosen to represent infinity is 16. Any network that has a cost of 16 is considered unreachable. Any counting loop stops feeding itself when the metrics reach 16. Only when the metric reaches 16 do A and B realize that NET1 is not reachable.

Convergence is simplified by making a simple change in B's behavior when a route times out. When B's table entry for NET1 times out, B is aware that the route is invalid. Rather than simply discarding the table entries, B assigns a cost of 16 to its routes to NET1. When A does its next route update, A arrives at a cost of 17 to reach NET1 through B. Consequently, all routers quickly become aware that NET1 cannot be reached through B.

With distance-vector algorithms, the value used for "infinity" is a compromise between the capability to support a reasonably complex network and the need to promote speedy convergence. RIP's designers did not feel that diameters larger than 15 were appropriate for networks using the RIP protocol.

Split Horizon and Poison Reverse

Although setting infinity to 16 eventually stops hop counts from incrementing, eliminating the count to infinity problem altogether would be better. One technique for doing so is called *split horizon*. Examining the preceding scenarios reveals one source of problems: A relies on routes advertised by C, while C uses routes advertised by A. The self-referential nature of this relationship generates loops. Split horizon is a technique that helps routers be a bit more careful about the routing information they send.

If A advertises to B a route, it is never beneficial for B to advertise that route back to A. The split horizon technique prevents a router from advertising routes through the interface from which it has learned the routes, thereby keeping two routers from getting into a self-referential loop. Figure 4.23 illustrates the split horizon in action. In the figure, B learns that A is 1 hop from NET1. After adding this information to its routing table, B passes the route along to C. However, B does not advertise the route back to A.

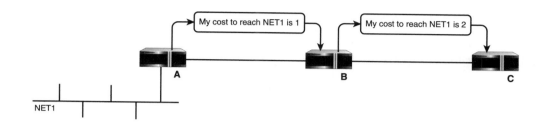

FIGURE 4.23
Split horizon.

A technique called *poison reverse* (see Figure 4.24) amplifies the safeguard provided by split horizon. If B can reach D through A, A's route cannot go back to B without forming a self-referential loop. Therefore, when A advertises its routes to B, B advertises that NET1 is unreachable by advertising to A a metric of 16 to reach NET1. A, thus, cannot attempt to route to NET1 through B because the distance through B is infinite. Poison reverse informs attached routers that a route is invalid immediately, without the delay required for the route entries to time out. Poison reverse is useful on many complex internetworks and generally is safer than split horizon. A cost is associated with poison reverse, however, in the form of increased network traffic.

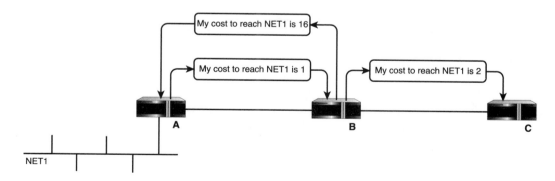

FIGURE 4.24
Poison reverse.

Routing Loops

Split horizon and poison reverse can prevent self-referential loops from being created between any pair of routers. But even with those safeguards, RIP remains vulnerable to loops that are formed by three or more routers. Consider the situation in Figure 4.25.

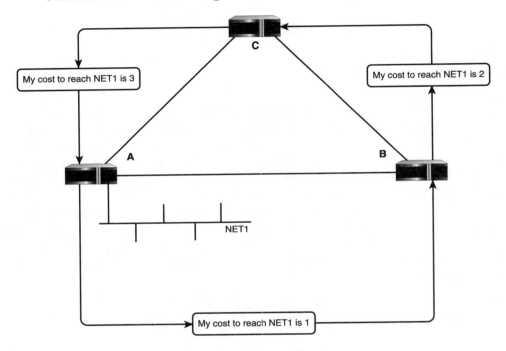

FIGURE 4.25
A multirouter RIP routing loop.

A advertises to B that it can reach NET1 in 1 hop. Split horizon prevents B from advertising the route back to A, but B does advertise to C that it can reach NET1 at a cost of 2. C is unaware that the route originates with A, and C has no inhibitions about advertising to A that it can reach NET1 in 3 hops. Now, if A loses its connection to NET1, a loop has been established involving all three routers, and it will be necessary for the loop to count to 16 before all routers become aware that NET1 is unavailable.

Redundant paths are desirable in internetworks, providing fault tolerance and alternate routes should certain paths become overburdened with traffic. RIP has great difficulty, however, dealing with the loops that can be established when redundant paths are present. RIP's inability to cope with redundant paths is one of the reasons OSPF—which cannot develop self-referential loops—is viewed as a superior routing protocol.

RIP-1 and RIP-2

RIP version 1 (RIP-1), as specified in RFC 1058, has some significant limitations; the most critical limitation is that it does not comprehend subnets and subnet masks. If all the non-netid bits in an address are 0, RIP-1 can determine that the address is a network address and that the default subnet mask is in effect. If, however, any of the non-netid bits are 1, RIP cannot determine whether it is the address of a subnet or a host.

As you observed in the discussion of subnetting earlier in this chapter, careful design can conceal the structures of subnets from outside hosts and routers. In these circumstances, RIP1 can function adequately as a router. If, however, routers must comprehend subnets to facilitate routing, RIP-1 is inadequate.

RIP version 2 (RIP-2) is specified in RFC 1723, a standards track document that updates RFC 1058. RIP-2 adds several enhancements to RIP-1:

- The message format is updated to include subnet masks.

- Authentication enables network managers to configure password authentication of messages exchanged by RIP routers.

- Route tags enable RIP to interface more smoothly with routing protocols outside a RIP autonomous area (a routing region using the RIP protocol). Route tags determine which routes should be advertised to external autonomous areas.

Not all routers support RIP-2. In particular, the Multiprotocol Router included with Windows NT Server 4 supports RFC 1058 but does not support the extensions proposed by RFC 1723. However, some routers, such as Novell's Multiprotocol Router, support RIP-1 and RIP-2 simultaneously. If RIP-2 will be deployed on your network, you must examine the specifications for each router to determine compliance with RFC 1723.

Limitations of RIP

RIP functions reliably and provides reasonably rapid route convergence. RIP does, however, have some undesirable traits.

The necessity for declaring some hop count to represent infinity places a size limitation on networks. RIP cannot provide routing on networks that have diameters of greater than 15 hops. Without declaring a metric to signify infinity, however, loops can develop that prevent routers from reaching convergence in the event of a network change.

RIP's method of advertising routes results in slow convergence and high traffic. RIP requires routers to advertise their routing tables every 30 seconds. When many routers are present on a network, a significant amount of network bandwidth can be monopolized to send the many RIP response packets required.

For these reasons, the network community is gradually moving toward routing based on link-state algorithms. The protocol being developed for the Internet community is open shortest path first (OSPF).

Open Shortest Path First

OSPF (RFC 1583) is a protocol on the Internet Standards track that is becoming increasingly popular for routing in autonomous systems. An autonomous system (AS) is a group of routers that share a common routing protocol. An entire TCP/IP internetwork does not have to use a common routing protocol.

OSPF is a link-state routing protocol, meaning that each router maintains a database that describes the topology of the local autonomous system. This topological database takes the form of a tree, with each router placed at the root of its own tree. Data to construct the database come from link-state advertisements sent by the routers in the AS.

To illustrate this process, consider the network illustrated in Figure 4.26. As shown, link-state algorithms can use more flexible metrics than RIP. The network administrator can assign the cost of any given link, and the total cost for a path does not necessarily have a limit, which enables link-state routing to model ASs that are indefinitely large. The upper limit for the metric used with OSPF is 65,535, which is sufficient to support networks of considerable scope.

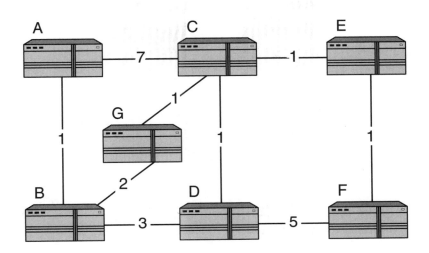

FIGURE 4.26
Network illustrating the OSPF algorithm.

Each node places itself at the root of its tree. The tree constructed for router B in Figure 4.26 is shown in Figure 4.27. The link state database contains information about the most efficient route available to each destination. The tree shown in Figure 4.25 contains the route B-G-C (cost 3) but has discarded the route B-A-C (cost 6).

NOTE

When multiple routes of the same cost are available to a destination, OSPF routers can perform load balancing by distributing traffic across the available routes. RIP lacks this capability.

OSPF routers have the following two relationships:

- Neighboring routers connect to a common network.

- Adjacencies are relationships among selected neighboring routers used to share routing information. Not all neighboring routers become adjacent.

A router that starts up uses the OSPF Hello Protocol to acquire neighbors. On networks that support broadcasts, routers can dynamically discover neighbors; Hello packets are multicast to all routers on the local network. If a network does not support broadcast messaging, some level of configuration is required before the router can identify its neighbors.

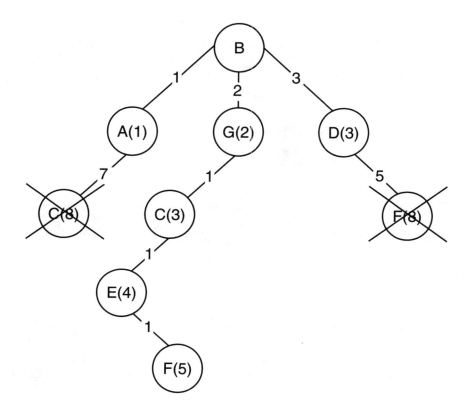

FIGURE 4.27
A router's link state database tree.

Routers attempt to form adjacencies with newly acquired neighbors. Adjacent routers synchronize their topological databases. Adjacencies then are used to distribute routing protocol packets. A router advertises its state by transmitting a link state update packet to its adjacencies.

Link-state advertisements flood the routing area. Reliable delivery is used to ensure that each router in the area has identical information. Each router uses this information to calculate its own shortest-path tree.

OSPF operates directly above IP, unlike RIP, which utilizes UDP as a transport. When the fragmentation of OSPF protocol packets is necessary, the responsibility falls to IP.

OSPF uses several techniques to reduce the amount of messaging required to maintain the routing database:

- Although routers periodically transmit link-state advertisements, this is done at infrequent intervals. This contrasts sharply with RIP, which requires each router to send its entire routing table every 30 seconds.

- Apart from those infrequent updates, a router advertises its state only when it detects a change in the network.

- Link-state update packets can contain routing information for multiple routers.

- Link-state update packets are sent only to adjacencies. Adjacencies are responsible for forwarding the information until it has been flooded throughout the AS. Consequently, each OSPF packet travels a single IP hop.

This overview of OSPF has been necessarily brief. A full description in the RFC requires over 200 pages. The goal has been to illuminate the areas in which OSPF improves on RIP. In particular, OSPF eliminates incidents of self-referential routing information by enabling each router to build an unambiguous routing database. Also, maintenance of OSPF routing places more modest demands on network bandwidth than RIP, a capability of special importance on WAN links of limited bandwidth. Finally, OSPF does not impose an artificial size limit on the network, as with the 15-hop limit specified for RIP.

Exterior Routing Protocols

RIP and OSPF are classified as *interior routing protocols*, protocols designed to support routing within an autonomous system. These are the routing protocols that LAN and private network administrators are most likely to encounter.

To route among autonomous systems, *external routing protocols* are employed. Figure 4.28 illustrates how an exterior routing protocol can be used to link autonomous systems running different interior routing protocols. This section briefly discusses two exterior router protocols that are mentioned in the RFCs.

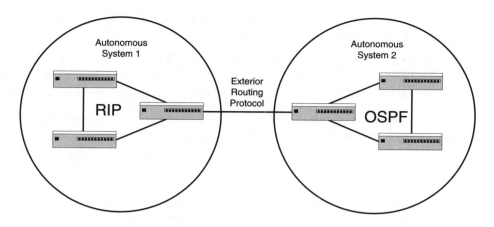

FIGURE 4.28

An exterior routing protocol linking two autonomous systems.

Exterior Gateway Protocol (EGP; RFC 827/904), introduced in 1982, performs exterior routing in a very rudimentary fashion. First EGP establishes other directly connected external routers as neighbors. Then EGP determines which networks are available through a given exterior router. Finally, EGP advertises route availability. Route information is limited to which destinations are available through which router. Therefore, no load balancing or route optimization is possible.

The more recent Border Gateway Protocol (BGP; RFC 1267) is an improved protocol that advertises full path information to BGP routers. This information enables BGP routers to select the best path between two autonomous systems.

Summary of Routing Decisions

When a host is required to transmit a datagram, it can obtain routing information from the following sources:

- Routes to specific host IP addresses
- Routes to remote networks
- Network numbers to which the host is attached
- A default gateway specification

Figure 4.29 presents a flow chart that illustrates the algorithm that governs how the available routing information will be used.

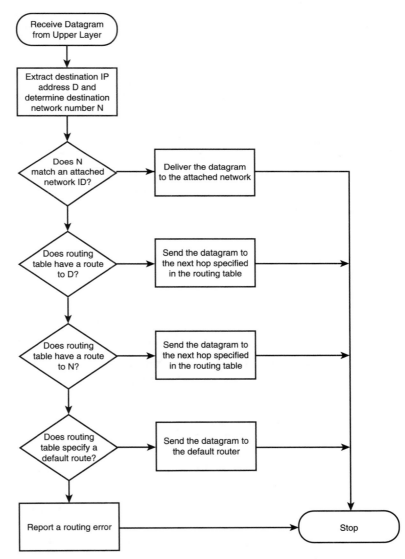

FIGURE 4.29

Algorithm for routing a datagram.

IP Datagram Header Format

Figure 4.30 shows the format of the IP header. Operation of the IP protocol can be tailored with a variety of parameters that appear in the IP header, many of which can be managed in Windows NT TCP/IP.

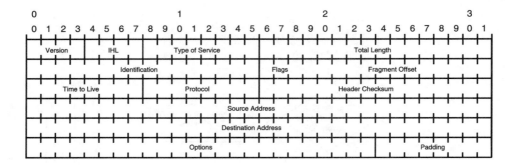

Figure 4.30
Format of the IP datagram header.

The IP header contains the following fields:

- **Version (4 bits).** Indicates the format of the internet header. The current version as described in RFC 791 is version 4.

- **Internet Header Length (IHL; 4 bits).** Describes the length of the header in 32-bit words. The minimum size for a correct header is five words.

- **Type of Service (8 bits).** Data in this field indicate the quality of service desired. The field is dissected in Figure 4.31.

The effects of values in the precedence fields depend on the network technology employed, and values must be configured accordingly.

Not all options in this field are compatible. When special service is desired, a choice must be made among options of low delay, high reliability, and high throughput. Better performance in one area often degrades performance in another. Few cases call for setting all three flags.

FIGURE 4.31

Format of the Type of Service field.

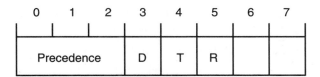

Legend:

Bits	0-2:	Precedence		
Bit	3:	Delay	(0=Normal Delay	1=Low Delay)
Bit	4:	Throughput	(0=Normal Throughout	1=High Throughout)
Bit	5:	Reliability	(0=Normal Reliability	1=High Reliability)
Bits	6-7:	Reserved		

Legend:

111	Network Control
110	Internetwork Control
101	CRITIC/ECP
100	Flash Override
011	Flash
010	Immediate
001	Priority
000	Routine

- **Total length (16 bits).** The length of the datagram in octets, including the IP header and data. This field enables datagrams to consist of up to 65,535 octets. The standard recommends that all hosts be prepared to receive datagrams of at least 576 octets in length.

- **Identification (16 bits).** An identification field used to aid reassembly of the fragments of a datagram.

- **Flags (3 bits).** This field contains three control flags:

    - **Bit 0.** Reserved; must be 0

    - **Bit 1 (DF).** 0=May fragment; 1=Do not fragment

    - **Bit 2 (MF).** 0=Last fragment; 1=More fragments

If a datagram is fragmented, the MF bit is 1 in all fragments but the last.

- **Fragment Offset (13 bits).** For fragmented datagrams, indicates the position in the datagram of this fragment.

- **Time to Live (8 bits).** Indicates the maximum time the datagram can remain on the network. If this field has a value of 0, the datagram is discarded. The field is modified during IP header processing and generally is measured in seconds. Each IP module that handles the datagram, however, must decrement Time to Live by 1. This mechanism ensures that undeliverable datagrams eventually are removed.

- **Protocol (8 bits).** The upper-layer protocol associated with the data portion of the datagram. Consult Assigned Numbers (currently RFC 1700) for values assigned for many protocols.

- **Header Checksum (16 bits).** A checksum for the header only. This value must be recalculated each time the header is modified.

- **Source Address (32 bits).** The IP address of the host that originated the datagram.

- **Destination Address (32 bits).** The IP address of the host that is the final destination of the datagram.

- **Options (0 to 11 32-bit words).** Can contain 0 or more options. Options are described in RFC 791.

IP Version 6

Internet protocol version 4 has demonstrated remarkable durability. RFC 791 was published in 1981 and remains the standard specification for IP. New demands placed on the Internet, however, have stimulated the effort to define a new internet protocol.

The effort to develop IP version 6 (IPv6) is the responsibility of the IP Next Generation (IPNG) Working Group of the IETF. IPv6 is currently in the draft standards process, and numerous relevant Internet-Drafts have been published. At the time of this writing, the draft standard is available in the file `draft-ietf-ipngwg-ipv6-spec-02.txt` from sources mentioned in Chapter 1, "Introduction to TCP/IP."

Changes from IPv4 are concentrated in the following areas:

- Extending the IP address size from 32 to 128 bits. The new scheme will support more levels of addressing hierarchy, many more address-able nodes, and simpler auto-configuration of addresses.

- To simplify the header format, some fields have been dropped or made optional.

- Support for extensions and options will be improved.

- Greater support is provided for authentication, data integrity, and privacy. IPv4 is not a secure protocol, an obstruction to doing business on the Internet.

Don't strain yourself waiting for IPv6. The Internet infrastructure isn't ready for it. An experimental IPv6 network is being constructed. But large-scale deployment of IPv6 is unlikely to begin before the 21st century and is unlikely to be complete for ten years or more after that.

Internet Control Message Protocol (ICMP)

IP was not designed as a reliable protocol, and numerous potential problems can arise. ICMP (RFC 792) is a standard protocol that provides a messaging capability for IP. Although ICMP is described separately from IP, ICMP is an integral part of the internet protocol, and ICMP messages are carried as data in IP datagrams.

For a complete list of messages, consult RFC 792. A glance at some of the potential messages is sufficient for this discussion.

- **Destination Unreachable.** These messages provide information when a host, net, port, or protocol is unreachable.

- **Time Exceeded.** These messages notify the source if a datagram is undeliverable because its time to live expired.

- **Parameter Problem.** These messages report a parameter problem and the octet in which the error was detected.

- **Source Quench.** These messages can be sent by destination routers or hosts that are forced to discard datagrams due to limitations in available buffer space or if for any reason a datagram cannot be processed.

- **Redirect.** These messages are sent to a host when a router receives a datagram that could be routed more directly through another gateway. The message advises the host that was the source of the datagram of a more appropriate router to receive the datagram.

- **Echo Request and Echo Reply Messages.** These messages exchange data between hosts.

- **Timestamp Request and Timestamp Reply.** These messages exchange timestamp data between hosts.

- **Information Request and Information Reply.** These messages can be used to enable a host to discover the network to which it is attached.

ICMP provides a mechanism for reporting errors to the host that originated an IP datagram, but ICMP has no capability of correcting the error. The original host must associate the error message with the application that produced the datagram and take steps to correct the problem.

ICMP Router Discovery Messages (RFC 1256) are an extension to ICMP that extend the capabilities of hosts to discover routes to gateways. Router Advertisements are multicast at periodic intervals, announcing IP addresses for its interfaces to networks. Hosts obtain route information by listening for these announcements. When a host starts up, it might send a Router Solicitation to request immediate advertisements. This technique provides information about available routers but cannot provide best-path information.

Unfortunately, Router Discovery Messages cannot substitute for a routing protocol such as RIP and OSPF. All ICMP messages are sent to the host that originated the datagram inspiring the message. Intermediate routers do not learn of a routing error and do not have the opportunity to update their routing tables. Therefore, you can rely on ICMP as a routing protocol only on very simple networks.

NOTE

RFC 1256 is not listed as a standard that is supported by Windows NT. Therefore, the Router Discovery Messages extensions cannot be used to support routing in a Windows NT environment.

IP Is the Foundation

IP is the foundation protocol of the TCP/IP protocol infrastructure and is required as part of every TCP/IP implementation. As you have seen, IP performs many essential network tasks such as delivering data between hosts and routing through internetworks. But by itself, IP isn't enough. If applications interfaced directly with IP, they would need to know quite a bit about how the network works, including the maximum message size for the network being used. Applications needing to send large messages would need to fragment those messages to match the network and reassemble the fragments they receive. In other words, every application would need to solve part of the network communication problem for itself.

That is inefficient. Far better is to isolate the applications from the network as much as possible, so that the application works much as though it is communicating with the local hardware. And that is the function of the host-to-host layer, which provides applications with two levels of network service, prepackaged and ready to go. The host-to-host layer is the home of the other quintessential Internet protocol, TCP. So, without further ado, let's move up a layer and see how applications communicate with the network.

Chapter 5

THE HOST-TO-HOST LAYER

The network layer, as you have seen, has responsibilities limited to delivering datagrams between hosts connected to a local network. Network layer datagrams are very limited message structures that will not meet the communication needs of most applications. It is the responsibility of the host-to-host layer to ease the process whereby applications interact with the network.

The host-to-host layer has the following two primary areas of responsibility:

■ Providing upper-layer processes and applications with a convenient interface to the network.

■ Delivering upper-layer messages between hosts.

Because upper-layer processes have different needs, two host-to-host protocols have been implemented.

Transmission Control Protocol (TCP) is a reliable protocol. It makes a concerted effort to deliver data to its destination, testing for errors, resending if required, and reporting errors to upper layers only if TCP cannot achieve a successful transmission. TCP was designed to meet a DoD requirement for robust network transmission in the days when wide area networks were not very reliable, and remains well-suited to applications that require a reliable transport. The robustness of TCP is provided, however, at the cost of high network overhead. When high reliability is not required, a lower-overhead transport is preferable.

User Datagram Protocol (UDP) is an unreliable protocol that makes a best-effort attempt to deliver data. *Datagrams* are independent messages that are transmitted independently from other datagrams. UDP makes no attempt to discover lost datagrams, and upper-layer processes must take responsibility for detecting missing or damaged data and retransmitting data if required. UDP operates with less overhead than TCP and is used by a variety of prominent protocols.

The host-to-host layer is the middle layer in the TCP/IP protocol suite. Figure 5.1 displays protocols associated with the layers of the TCP/IP protocol stack, including some of the many process/application layer protocols. Data multiplexing for processes and applications uses ports, which identify data transmitted between two end-protocols on communicating hosts.

The remainder of this chapter examines more closely the features and operation of TCP and UDP.

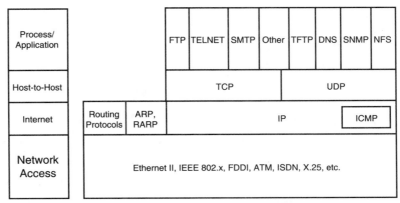

FIGURE 5.1

Protocols in the TCP/IP protocol stack.

Transmission Control Protocol

TCP (RFC 793) provides reliable communication between processes that run on interconnected hosts. This host-to-host communication functions independently of the network structure. TCP is not concerned with routing data through the internetwork; the network infrastructure is IP's responsibility. At the host-to-host layer, TCP on one host communicates directly with TCP on another host, regardless of whether the hosts are on the same network or remote from each other. TCP is not implemented on routers unless the router function is performed on a host that runs upper-layer processes. (Windows NT can perform routing on a computer being used as a workstation, for example.)

In fact, TCP is oblivious to the network. A wide variety of network technologies can be accommodated, including circuit switching and packet switching on local and wide area networks. TCP identifies hosts using IP addresses and does not concern itself with physical addresses.

The following sections discuss several characteristics and functions of TCP:

- Maintenance of data streams with upper-layer processes and applications

- Provisions for reliable communication

- Connection maintenance

- TCP data communication

- Provisions for precedence and security

Following those discussions, the TCP header format is examined.

Data Stream Maintenance

From their perspectives, processes and applications in hosts communicate by transmitting streams of data. They are unconcerned with the underlying mechanisms that provide data fragmentation and flow control.

The interface between TCP and a local process is a *port*, which is a mechanism that enables the process to call TCP and in turn enables TCP to deliver data streams to the appropriate process.

Ports are identified by a port number. Implementors of TCP are permitted considerable freedom in assigning port numbers to processes, but specific port numbers have been assigned to a number of common processes by the Internet Assigned Numbers Authority (IANA). These port assignments, called *well-known ports*, are described in the Assigned Number RFC (currently RFC 1700). Well-known ports provide a convenient means for establishing connections between common processes. The Telnet-Server process, for example, is assigned a well-known port, easing the difficulty of initiating a Telnet session with a host.

To fully specify a connection, the host IP address is appended to the port number. This combination of IP address and port number is called a *socket*. Consequently, a given socket number is unique on the internetwork. A connection between two hosts is fully described by the sockets assigned to each end of the connection. The connection between two sockets provides a bidirectional (full-duplex) communication path between the end processes. Figure 5.2 depicts process-to-process communication through a connection.

Two types of sockets are used in TCP/IP:

- **Stream sockets** are used with TCP to provide reliable, sequential, bidirectional exchange of data.

- **Datagram sockets** are used with UDP to provide unreliable, bidirectional data transfer.

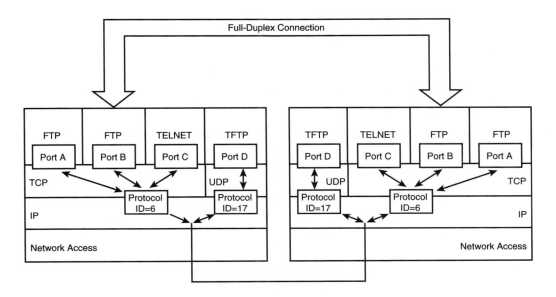

FIGURE 5.2

Process-to-process communication.

Sockets provide an *Application Program Interface (API)* between TCP and processes and applications. This API provides programmers with a clean interface between their applications and TCP.

NOTE

The most common process API for UNIX is Berkeley (or BSD) Sockets, which is incorporated in Berkeley Standard Distribution UNIX. Microsoft Windows products utilize a Windows Sockets API, which is derived from Berkeley Sockets.

Managing Connections

From the perspective of the process, communication with the network involves sending and receiving continuous streams of data. The process is not responsible for fragmenting the data to fit lower-layer protocols. Figure 5.3 illustrates how data are processed as they travel down the protocol stack, through the network, and up the protocol stack of the receiver.

1. TCP receives a stream of data from the upper-layer process.

2. TCP may fragment the data stream into *segments* that meet the maximum datagram size of IP.

3. IP may fragment segments as it prepares datagrams that are sized to conform to restrictions of the network.

4. Network protocols transmit the datagram in the form of bits.

5. Network protocols at the receiving host reconstruct datagrams from the bits they receive.

6. IP receives datagrams from the network. Where necessary, datagram fragments are reassembled to reconstruct the original segment.

7. TCP presents data in segments to upper-layer protocols in the form of data streams.

FIGURE 5.3
Processing data during transmission and receipt.

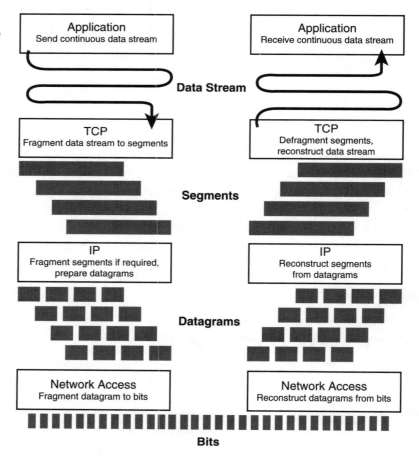

Windowing

TCP has the responsibility of managing flow control between the hosts. The essential goal of flow control is to ensure that the sending host does not transmit faster than the receiving host can receive. A simple form of flow control is illustrated in Figure 5.4. Here every message unit must be acknowledged before another message unit can be sent. This start-and-stop approach obviously makes inefficient use of the network because the sending host stops transmitting after each message segment and spends half its time awaiting acknowledgments. Because of all the waiting, the hosts cannot take advantage of the full-duplex nature of the transmission medium.

FIGURE 5.4

A start-and-stop approach to flow control.

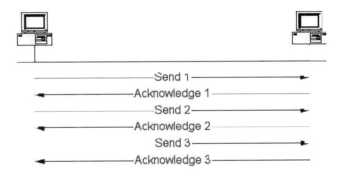

TCP uses a more efficient approach called *windowing*. The receiving host reports a window to the sending host, which specifies the number of octets that the receiving TCP is prepared to accept. The sending TCP does not transmit past the window unless it receives acknowledgments that verify the receipt of data.

The *TCP receive window size* designates the amount of data a receiving host can hold in its receive buffer. This is the maximum amount of data a host can have outstanding at a given time. Figure 5.5 illustrates how windowing works. In this example, the receiving host's buffer will accommodate three message segments at a given time. If more than three message segments are outstanding at a given time, the sending host ceases transmission until part or all of the outstanding segments are acknowledged.

Windowing is very efficient. If the receiving host can process incoming data promptly, windowing enables the sending host to transmit continually. Transmission and acknowledgment take place seamlessly, controlled by a smooth, full-duplex dialog.

FIGURE 5.5
Flow control using windowing.

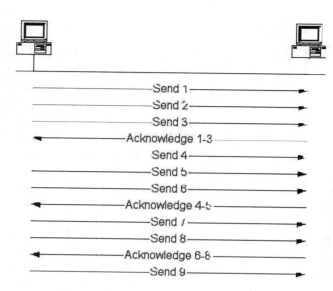

Message transmission is most efficient when messages are fragmented to match the *maximum transfer unit* (MTU), the largest message size that can be accommodated along a given network route. When a connection is established, the MTU of the intervening network is used by TCP to adjust to the *maximum segment size* (MSS). Typically, the MSS is the MTU minus 40 bytes to allow for the TCP and IP headers.

PMTU discovery is the process that establishes the MTU when a connection is being established, and it is defined in RFC 1191. TCP transmits segments with the *don't fragment* bit set. If a router attempts to send the segment through a network with a smaller MTU, an ICMP error informs the sender that the destination cannot be reached because the segment would require fragmentation. In most cases, the router will specify the MTU that is permitted for the network segment. The sender adjusts its MSS to the MTU of the intervening network and continues to try until the MTU for the path is discovered.

Some routers, referred to as "black hole" routers, do not comply with RFC 1191 and simply drop segments that have the *don't fragment* flag set and that exceed the MTU of the next hop. By default, Microsoft TCP/IP detects black hole routers.

The receive window is adjusted to match even increments of the MSS. Under Microsoft TCP/IP, on an Ethernet network an MSS of 1460 bytes is used, and the window will typically be 8,760 bytes (8,192 rounded up to six

1,460-byte segments). On token ring networks, the window will be about 16K bytes. Upper-layer processes request data transmissions by issuing SEND calls to TCP. Ordinarily, TCP queues data to be sent, but the process can specify an immediate send by setting a PUSH flag, which forces TCP to send queued data to its destination. A push also forces the receiver to flush its buffers and send outstanding data to upper-layer processes.

Opening and Closing Connections

Processes can open, close, and obtain the status of a connection. Connections must be explicitly opened and closed. When TCP issues an *open* call, it specifies the local port and the remote socket. Upper-layer processes receive a name used to identify the connection. Connections can be active or passive:

- An *active open* is an attempt to open a connection with a remote TCP.

- A *passive open* sets up TCP to accept incoming connection requests, enabling the process that requested the passive open to accept connections from remote processes. Passive opens enable processes to make services available to outside requesters, which can make active open requests to form connections. Well-known ports are a convenient mechanism for enabling remote hosts to request connections with specific services.

When a process originates an open request, TCP prepares a segment in which the SYN (synchronize) control bit is set. Control bits are discussed in the section "TCP Header Format." The TCP receiving this segment matches the remote socket to a local socket to establish a connection. The connection is completed when the TCP modules exchange sockets and synchronize segment sequence numbers, which are described in the next section.

When a process requests closing of a connection, TCP sends a segment in which the FIN control bit is set. A connection must be closed from both ends. A TCP that sends a close can continue to receive until it receives a close from the TCP at the other end of the connection. This enables both ends of the connection to flush any untransmitted data. A TCP reliably receives all data sent before the connection was closed, and the process that receives the close should remain capable of receiving until it receives all data.

Providing Reliable Communication

TCP is a reliable protocol and is responsible for delivering data streams to its destinations reliably and in order. To verify receipt of data, TCP uses *segment sequence numbers* and *acknowledgments*.

Every octet in a segment is assigned a sequence number, enabling every octet sent to be acknowledged. The TCP header specifies the segment sequence number for the first octet in the data field, and each segment also incorporates an acknowledgment number. When TCP sends a segment, it retains a copy of the segment in a queue, where it remains until an acknowledgment is received. Segments that are not acknowledged are retransmitted.

When TCP acknowledges receipt of an octet with segment sequence number *n*, it relieves the sending TCP of responsibility for all octets preceding the specified octet. The receiving TCP then becomes responsible for delivering the data in the segment to the appropriate upper-layer process. As is shown in the preceding section, acknowledgments also are part of the windowing mechanism, determining the amount of transmitted data that can be outstanding at any given time.

Precedence and Security

The IP header provides a type of service field and a security option field, which TCP can use to implement precedence and security. TCP modules operating in a security environment must identify segments with required security information. TCP also enables upper-layer processes to specify required security.

 NOTE

TCP is intended to be highly robust and it is worth quoting this robustness principle from RFC 793: "Be conservative in what you do, be liberal in what you accept from others."

TCP Header Format

TCP formats a header for each segment transmitted to IP. When IP constructs an IP datagram, the TCP header follows the IP header in the datagram. Figure 5.6 shows the format of the TCP header.

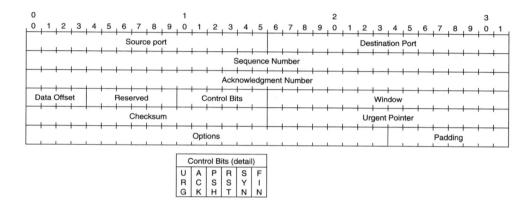

FIGURE 5.6

The format of the TCP header.

TCP segments are organized into 16-bit words. If a segment contains an odd number of octets, it is padded with a final octet that consists of zeros.

Fields in the TCP header are as follows:

■ **Source port (16 bits).** Specifies the port on the sending TCP module.

■ **Destination port (16 bits).** Specifies the port on the receiving TCP module.

■ **Sequence number (32 bits).** Specifies the sequence position of the first data octet in the segment.

When the segment opens a connection (the SYN bit is set; see discussion about Control Bits later in this list), the sequence number is the initial sequence number (ISN), and the first octet in the data field is at sequence ISN+1.

- **Acknowledgment Number (32 bits).** Specifies the next sequence number that is expected by the sender of the segment. TCP indicates that this field is active by setting the ACK bit (see discussion about Control Bits), which is always set after a connection is established.

- **Data Offset (4 bits).** Specifies the number of 32-bit words in the TCP header. Options are padded with 0-value octets to complete a 32-bit word when necessary.

- **Reserved (6 bits).** Must be zero. Reserved for future use.

- **Control Bits (6 bits).** The six control bits are as follows:

  - **URG.** When set (1), the Urgent Pointer field is significant. When cleared (0), the field is ignored.

  - **ACK.** When set, the Acknowledgment Number field is significant.

  - **PSH.** Initiates a push function.

  - **RST.** Forces a reset of the connection.

  - **SYN.** Synchronizes sequencing counters for the connection. This bit is set when a segment requests opening of a connection.

  - **FIN.** No more data. Closes the connection.

- **Window (16 bits).** Specifies the number of octets, starting with the octet specified in the acknowledgment number field, which the sender of the segment can currently accept.

- **Checksum (16 bits).** An error control checksum that covers the header and data fields. It does not cover any padding required to have the segment consist of an even number of octets. The checksum also covers a 96-bit pseudoheader. The pseudoheader is discussed immediately following this list.

- **Urgent Pointer (16 bits).** Identifies the sequence number of the octet following urgent data. The urgent pointer is a positive offset from the sequence number of the segment.

- **Options (variable).** Options are available for a variety of functions, including the following: end of options list, no operation, maximum segment size, and maximum segment size option data.

- **Padding (variable).** 0-value octets are appended to the header to ensure that the header ends on a 32-bit word boundary.

A 12-octet TCP *pseudoheader* (see Figure 5.7) includes source and destination addresses, the protocol, and the segment length. This information is forwarded with the segment to IP to protect TCP from misrouted segments. The value of the segment length field includes the TCP header and data but does not include the length of the pseudoheader.

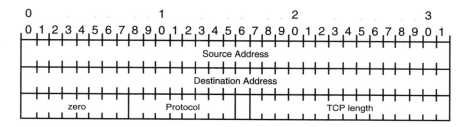

FIGURE 5.7
The format of the TCP pseudoheader.

User Datagram Protocol

TCP is a formal protocol that requires hosts to establish a connection that is maintained for the duration of a conversation, after which the connection is formally closed. The overhead required to maintain connections is justified when bulletproof reliability is required, but often proves to be misspent effort.

User Datagram Protocol (UDP; RFC 768) provides an alternative transport for processes that do not require reliable delivery. UDP is a datagram protocol that does not guarantee data delivery or duplicate protection. As a datagram protocol, UDP need not be concerned with receiving streams of data and developing segments suitable for IP. Consequently, UDP is an uncomplicated protocol that functions with far less overhead than TCP.

Here are several situations in which UDP might be preferred over TCP as a host-to-host protocol:

- **Messages that require no acknowledgment.** Network overhead can be reduced by using UDP. Simple Network Management Protocol (SNMP) alerts fall into this category. On a large network, considerable

SNMP alerts are generated as every SNMP device transmits status updates. Seldom, however, is loss of an SNMP message critical. Running SNMP over UDP, therefore, reduces network overhead.

- **Messages between hosts are sporadic.** SNMP again serves as a good example. SNMP messages are sent at irregular intervals. The overhead required to open and close a TCP connection for each message would delay messages and bog down performance.

- **Reliability is implemented at the process level.** Network File System (NFS) is an example of a process that performs its own reliability function and runs over UDP to enhance network performance.

Figure 5.8 illustrates the header format for UDP, which consists of two 32-bit words. Here are the fields in the UDP header:

- **Source port (16 bits).** This field is optional and specifies the source port when enabling the receiver of the datagram to send a response is necessary. Otherwise, the source port value is 0.

- **Destination port (16 bits).** The port destination at the destination IP host.

- **Length (16 bits).** The length in octets of the datagram, including the header and data. The minimum value is 8 to allow for a header. Consequently, a UDP datagram is limited to a maximum length of 65,535 octets, making 65,527 octets available for data.

- **Checksum (16 bits).** A checksum value that covers data in the pseudoheader, the UDP header, and data.

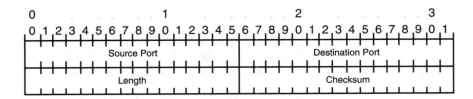

FIGURE 5.8
UDP header format.

Like TCP, UDP generates a pseudoheader that is passed with the UDP datagram to IP. The UDP pseudoheader guards against misrouted datagrams. Figure 5.9 depicts the UDP pseudoheader.

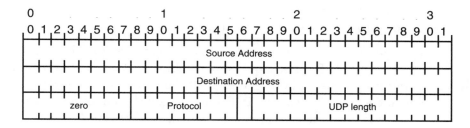

FIGURE 5.9
UDP pseudoheader format.

Now You're Ready for Applications

The internet and host-to-host layers provide the infrastructure that enables communication to take place on TCP/IP networks. The key point to notice at the host-to-host layer is that TCP and UDP provide a choice for network designers, enabling them to select reliability or efficiency as needed. The key distinctions between TCP and UDP are summarized in Table 5.1.

TABLE 5.1

Feature Comparison of TCP and UDP

TCP	UDP
Reliable	Unreliable
Connection-oriented	Connectionless
Virtual circuit	Datagrams
Higher overhead	Low overhead
Message segmentation	No message segmentation and reassembly
Sequenced message segments	Unsequenced

TCP is an interesting protocol because of the degree to which it isolates upper-layer processes from the network. Processes do not need to be concerned with message sizes because TCP takes responsibility for message fragmentation and reassembly. And processes need not worry about network reliability because TCP fanatically ensures the end-to-end integrity of the messages with which it is entrusted.

UDP, however, is a more casual protocol that does its job with little fuss. Unlike TCP, UDP is not required to establish virtual circuits between communicating hosts, resulting in high efficiency when messages are informal and independent. Because TCP must establish connections between two hosts, it is unsuitable for broadcast messages where one host must transmit to many. UDP, however, can support multicast and broadcast messaging.

Now that the infrastructure of the information superhighway is in place, it is time to put it to work. That is the function of the process/application layer, the topic of the next chapter.

Chapter 6

THE PROCESS-APPLICATION LAYER

This chapter focuses on the process-application layer and

covers the following topics:

- *Naming hosts on the Internet*

- *Mapping addresses to names*

- *TCP/IP applications*

The process-application layer is why the other network layers exist. The lower protocol layers simply deliver messages. The process-application layer is where real work gets done. On it, you find programs that provide network services, such as mail servers, file transfer servers, remote terminal, and system management servers, as well as programs that interface with the end user, such as FTP and Telnet.

Keep in mind that other layers might exist above the process-application layer, consisting of applications that use services that certain processes provide.

The *Simple Mail Transfer Protocol (SMTP)*, for example, is a protocol that users could operate directly to send and receive mail. More commonly, however, users interface with SMTP by way of an email program, which generates messages in the SMTP protocol.

This section introduces several processes and applications commonly seen on TCP/IP networks. Before embarking on those discussions, however, examining the use of host names is necessary.

Naming Hosts on the Internet

Because users interface with the process-application layer, putting a friendly face on the network is desirable for this layer. Imagine using a network as vast as the Internet if you had to use IP addresses to address all messages and users. How many IP addresses could you remember?

Therefore, long ago the Internet community began to use *host names* as a convenient way to identify hosts. Most users agree that remembering ds.internic.net is much easier than 198.49.45.10.

To provide host names requires a system that can match host names to their IP addresses. Historically, two technologies have been employed on the Internet:

- Static naming using hosts files
- Domain Name System

Static Naming with *Hosts* Files

In the early days, the ARPAnet consisted of a few hundred hosts and was, by today's standards, relatively stable. Growth was measured in terms of a

few hosts per year, not thousands of hosts per day. Host names were cata-
logued in a file named HOSTS.TXT, which was maintained on a host at the
Network Information Center and then maintained by Stanford Research
Institute, dubbed the SRI-NIC. Every few days, the contents of HOSTS.TXT
would be compiled into a table in a file named hosts.

The HOSTS.TXT and hosts files were maintained manually. ARPAnet
administrators would email their changes to the NIC, where they would be
recorded in HOSTS.TXT and compiled to build a new hosts file, which
would then be FTP'd to all hosts in the ARPAnet to update the local copies.

The UNIX convention is to store a host table as a file named hosts in the
directory /etc. Processes and applications consult /etc/hosts to obtain mappings between host names and IP addresses. Here is a sample of a hosts file:

```
#IP Address     Aliases
127.0.0.1       localhost loopback lb    #this host
200.235.80.1    x                        #x client host
200.235.80.5    sales1
200.235.80.6    sales2
```

Each entry in hosts consists of an IP address and one or more spaces, followed by one or more aliases that can be used to name the host. Characters
following the # character are regarded as comments.

The hosts file remains an effective means of making host names available
to users. It worked best in the days of timeshared host computers, when a
single copy of hosts was sufficient for an entire site. By the early 1980s,
however, the character of the ARPAnet was changing. Increasingly, time-
share hosts were being supplemented or replaced by local area networks
populated by single-user workstations. This produced several consequences:
the number of host names was dramatically increasing, change was accelerating, but it took longer for changes to make their way through the
ARPAnet, and local administrators were frustrated because their local
names could not be locally administered. Moreover, the network traffic
required to distribute the hosts file to all hosts via FTP was becoming a burden on the ARPAnet.

NOTE

Many administrators of moderate-sized LANs still rely on hosts files to provide naming on
their networks. A naming service such as DNS can be time-consuming to maintain and generates some extra network traffic. If a LAN is fairly stable, hosts files might be the only naming support that is required.

Domain Name Service

Clearly, a better host-naming mechanism was required for the ARPAnet. Several proposals were evaluated before the Domain Name System (DNS; currently standardized in RFC 1034/1035) was introduced as a standard in 1983. DNS indexes host names in a hierarchical database that can be managed in a distributed fashion. Before examining DNS in any detail, looking at the characteristics of hierarchies in general and at the DNS hierarchy in particular should prove useful.

Hierarchies

You are already familiar with a common form of hierarchical organization: the hierarchical directory structure used by virtually all operating systems, including UNIX, DOS, and Windows. Figure 6.1 illustrates a Windows NT directory hierarchy, more commonly called a *directory tree.* Even though real trees and family trees—perhaps the oldest hierarchical databases— frequently place their roots at the bottom, database trees are always upended (see Figure 6.1). The upside-down trees commonly used to depict computer data structures are called *inverted trees.*

Data in a tree is represented by the intersections, or end points, of the lines that describe the tree structure. These points are called *nodes;* here are three kinds of nodes:

- **Root.** Every tree has exactly one root node. On a file system, this is called the *root directory*, represented by a \ (DOS and Windows) or a / (UNIX).

- **Intermediate nodes.** An indefinite number of nodes can be made subordinate to the root node. Intermediate nodes might themselves have subordinate nodes. On file systems, intermediate nodes are called subdirectories and are assigned logical identifiers, such as WINNT35.

- **Leaf nodes.** A leaf node is the end of a branch in the tree.

Nodes frequently are referred to as *parent* and *child* nodes. Leaf nodes are always children. Intermediate nodes are parents of their child (subordinate) nodes and children of their parent nodes. The root node is a parent to all first-level intermediate nodes. Nodes that are children of the same parent are known as *siblings.*

Any given node on the tree can be fully described by listing the nodes between itself and the root. Figure 6.1 shows an example identifying the node (in this case a subdirectory) \WINNT\system32\Repl\Export. Names that list all nodes between a node and the root are called *fully qualified names*. Note that fully qualified names for file systems begin with the root and proceed down the tree to the node in question.

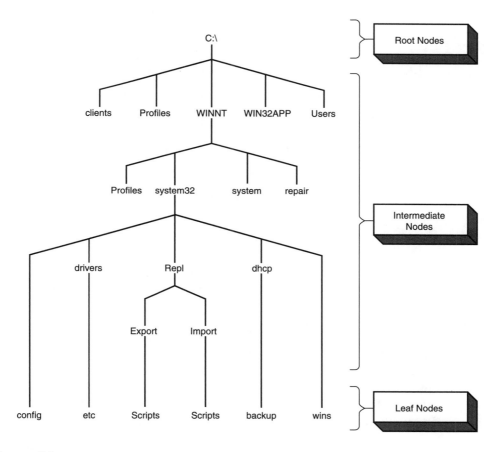

FIGURE 6.1

Example of a file system directory tree.

A fully qualified name can uniquely identify any node in the tree. The names \WINNT\clients and \WINNT\system describe separate nodes (subdirectories) in the directory tree.

Figure 6.2 illustrates an important rule of hierarchies: Siblings might not have identical node names. Thus, the \WINNT directory cannot have two subdirectories named system. Having two nodes named clients is perfectly all right, however, if their fully qualified names differ. Naming directories \clients and \WINNT\clients on the same file system, for example, is permissible.

FIGURE 6.2

Each node in a hierarchy must have a unique fully qualified name.

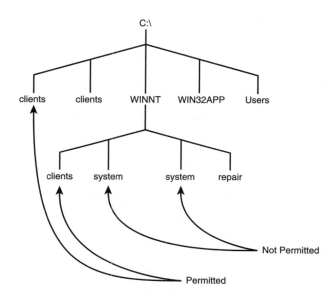

The Domain Name Space

The DNS hierarchical database is called the *domain name space*. Each host in the domain name space has a unique fully qualified name. Figure 6.3 shows a simple DNS hierarchy that an organization might use. The root node of a DNS tree is called either "root" or the "root domain." The root domain often is designated with empty quotation marks (" ").

Each node in the tree has a name, which can contain up to 63 characters.

The fully qualified name for a DNS node is called the *fully qualified domain name (FQDN)*. Unlike fully qualified path names in file systems, which start from the root, the FQDN convention in DNS starts with the node being described and proceeds to the root. Figure 6.3 illustrates bob.sw.eng as an example of a FQDN. The convention with DNS names is to separate node names with a period (referred to as "dot"). The root node might be represented by a trailing dot (as in bob.sw.eng.), but the trailing dot ordinarily is omitted.

DNS trees can be viewed in terms of domains, which are simply subtrees of the entire database. Figure 6.3 illustrates how subdomains can be defined within domains. The eng domain has two subdomains: sw.eng and hw.eng. The name of a subdomain is simply the FQDN of the topmost node in the domain. Subdomains always consist of complete subtrees of the tree, a node and all its child nodes. A subdomain cannot be designated to include both eng and mkt, which are located at the same level of the tree.

FIGURE 6.3

DNS tree for an organization.

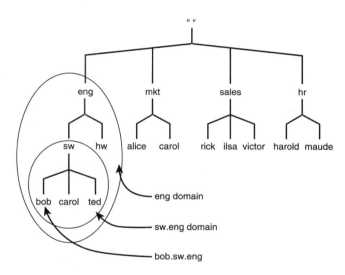

Subdomains are DNS management structures. Delegating management of any subdomain to distribute management responsibility for the complete name space is possible.

Figure 6.4 shows that DNS trees obey the same naming rules as directory trees: Siblings must have unique node names. Nodes that are children of different parents might have the same node names.

NOTE

Domain names can be assigned aliases, pointers from one domain name to another. The domain to which the alias points is called the *canonical* domain name.

FIGURE 6.4

Naming rules for DNS nodes.

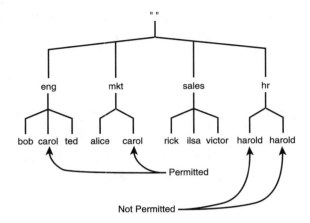

Domain and subdomain are relative terms and are used somewhat interchangeably. Technically speaking, every domain except root literally is a subdomain. When discussion focuses on a particular node, however, that node generally is referred to as a domain. Use of the terms *domain* and *subdomain* is primarily a function of perspective. DNS domains typically are referred to in terms of levels:

- **First-level domain.** A child of root; the more commonly used name for a first-level domain is *top-level domain*

- **Second-level domain.** A child of a first-level domain

- **Third-level domain.** A child of a second-level domain and so forth

Notice that eng.widgets might have two functions: it might serve as a name of a host in the DNS hierarchy and point to a particular IP address. However, eng.widgets also is a structure in the DNS database that is used to organize its children in the database hierarchy. (This works much like a file system. A directory can contain files but can also contain other directories.)

NOTE

Note that the term *domains,* as used with regard to DNS, has no relationship to Windows NT Server domains. Windows NT Server domains provide a way to organize Windows NT computers into manageable groups that share a common security database. DNS domains are related only to the Internet naming service. A Windows NT computer quite certainly can participate in a Windows NT domain under one name and in a DNS domain with another name.

Domain Administration

DNS was designed to handle the Internet, which is too vast to be centrally administered as a single name space. Therefore, being able to delegate administration of subdomains was essential.

Name servers are programs that store data about the domain name space and provide that information in response to DNS queries. The complete name space can be organized into *zones*, which simply are subsets of the DNS tree. A given name server has authority for one or more zones. Figure 6.5 shows a sample tree as it might be organized into three zones. Notice that zones do not require regular boundaries. In the example, eng is maintained in a separate zone on its own name server. Notice that zones, unlike domains, need not be a simple slice of the DNS tree but can incorporate different levels of different branches.

FIGURE 6.5

Zones and delegation of domain authority.

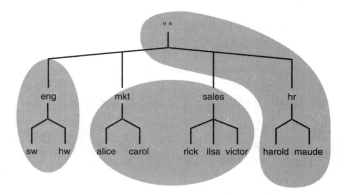

Administration for zones can be delegated to name servers as required. If administration for a domain is delegated to a name server, that name server becomes responsible for the domain's subdomains as well, unless administration for those subdomains is delegated away.

Each zone must be serviced by a *primary master name server*, which obtains the data for the zone from files on its host. Secondary master domain servers obtain zone data by performing *zone transfers* from the primary master name server for the zone. Secondary masters periodically update their databases from the primary to keep the various name servers for the zone synchronized.

DNS is very flexible in the way name servers and zones can be related. Recall that name servers might be authoritative for more than one zone. Beyond that, a name server can be a primary on some zone(s) and a secondary for other zone(s).

The provision for multiple name servers provides a level of redundancy that enables the network DNS to continue to function with secondaries even in the event of a failure of the primary master name server.

Organization of the Internet Domain Name Space

All of the discussed DNS capabilities come into play on the Internet, certainly the largest name space on any network.

The critical nature of root name servers, along with the volume of DNS queries on the Internet, dictates the need for a large, broadly distributed base of root name servers. At this time, the Internet is supported by nine root name servers, including systems on NSFNET, MILNET, SPAN (NASA's network), and in Europe.

The root name servers are authoritative for the top-level domains in the Internet DNS database. On the Internet, no actual organization has a first-level domain name. *Top-level domains (TLDs)* organize the name space in terms of categories.

The only domains the Internet authorities administer are top-level domains. Administration of secondary and lower-level domains is delegated. Domain name registration is under the authority of the Internet Assigned Numbers Authority (IANA), and is administered by the *Internet Registry (IR)*. The central IR is INTERNIC.NET.

The Internet name space evolves too quickly to be centrally administered, and it has been shown how the DNS name space can be organized into subdomains and zones to enable administration to be flexible, efficient, and local. After establishing a new domain, a management authority for the domain is designated. In many cases, second- and lower-level domains are administered by the entities that requested establishment to them. Organizations such as universities, companies, and government agencies maintain name servers that support the DNS database for their portions of the DNS tree.

RFC 1591, "Domain Name System Structure and Delegation," describes the domain name structure for the Internet, as well as guidelines for administration of delegated domains. TLDs fall into the following three categories:

■ Generic worldwide domains

■ Generic domains for only the United States

■ Country domains

Figure 6.6 shows the overall organization of the Internet DNS name space.

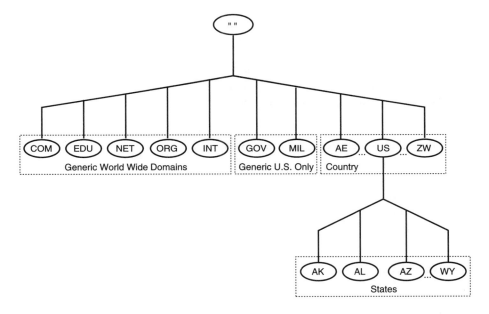

FIGURE 6.6
Organization of the DNS name space.

Generic World Wide Domains

If you have spent any time on the Internet, you have encountered these top-level domains, which organize the majority of Internet DNS names into five categories:

■ **COM.** Identifies commercial entities. Because this domain covers virtually every company that has a presence on the Internet, the COM name space is getting quite large, and consideration is being given to organizing it in subdomains. Example: `microsoft.com`.

- **EDU.** Originally embracing all educational institutions, this domain also is becoming quite extensive. Registration in this domain now is limited to four-year colleges and universities. Other schools and two-year colleges are registered under their respective country domains. Example: `berkeley.edu`.

- **NET.** Includes network providers and Internet administrative computers. Example: `internic.net`.

- **ORG.** Anything that does not fit in the other generic categories. Example: `ietf.org`.

- **INT.** Organizations established by international treaties. Example: `nato.int`.

Registering second-level domains in these categories is the responsibility of the InterNIC (contact `hostmaster@internic.net`). InterNIC also is responsible for registering all new top-level domains.

Generic, United States Only Domains

Two top-level domains are reserved for the United States government:

- **GOV.** At one time, applied to any government office or agency, it has since been decided that new registrations will include only agencies of the U.S. federal government. State and local government entities are registered under country domains. Example: `nsf.gov`.

- **MIL.** The U.S. military. Example: `dca.mil`.

Registration of second-level domains in GOV is the responsibility of the InterNIC (contact `hostmaster@internic.net`).

Second-level domains under MIL are registered by the DDN registry at `nic.ddn.mil`.

Country Domains

Country TLDs are derived from ISO 3166. IANA recognizes the ISO as an international organization with mechanisms in place to identify bona fide countries.

The regional registry for Europe is the RIPE NCC (contact `ncc@ripe.net`). The registry for the Asia-Pacific region is APNIC (contact `hostmaster@apnic.net`). The InterNIC administers North America and other undelegated regions.

Table 6.1 lists the Internet top-level domains as of this writing. The information was obtained from the WHOIS server at `rs.internic.net`. Later in this chapter, the section "Obtaining Domain Information with WHOIS" explains how to conduct WHOIS searches. (The search command was whois root-dom.)

TABLE 6.1

Internet Top-Level Domains

Domain	
AD	Andorra
AE	United Arab Emirates
AG	Antigua and Barbuda
AI	Anguilla
AL	Albania (Republic of)
AM	Armenia top-level Domain
AN	Netherlands Antilles
AO	Angola (Republic of)
AQ	Antarctica
AR	Argentina (Argentine Republic)
ARPA	Advanced Research Projects Agency Domain
AT	Austria (Republic of)
AU	Australia
AW	Aruba
AZ	Azerbaijan
BA	Bosnia-Herzegovina
BB	Barbados
BE	Belgium (Kingdom of)

continues

TABLE 6.1, CONTINUED

Internet Top-Level Domains

Domain	
BF	Burkina Faso
BG	Bulgaria top-level domain
BH	Bahrain (State of)
BI	Burundi (Republic of)
BJ	Benin (Republic of)
BM	Bermuda
BN	Brunei
BO	Bolivia (Republic of)
BR	Brazil (Federative Republic of)
BS	Bahamas (Commonwealth of the)
BW	Botswana (Republic of)
BY	Belarus
BZ	Belize
CA	Canada
CF	Central African Republic
CH	Switzerland (Swiss Confederation)
CI	Cote d'Ivoire (Republic of)
CK	Cook Islands
CL	Chile (Republic of)
CM	Cameroon
CN	China (People's Republic of)
CO	Colombia (Republic of)
COM	Commercial
CR	Costa Rica (Republic of)
CU	Cuba (Republic of)

Domain	
CV	Cape Verde
CY	Cyprus (Republic of)
CZ	Czech Republic
DE	Germany (Federal Republic of)
DJ	Djibouti
DK	Denmark (Kingdom of)
DM	Dominica (Commonwealth of)
DO	Dominican Republic
DZ	Algeria (People's Democratic Republic of)
EC	Ecuador (Republic of)
EDU	Education
EE	Estonia (Republic of)
EG	Egypt (Arab Republic of)
ER	Eritrea
ES	Centro de Comunicaciones CSIC RedIRIS (ES-NIC)
ET	Ethiopia (Democratic Federal Republic of)
FI	EUnet Finland Oy
FJ	Fiji (Republic of)
FM	Micronesia (Federated States of)
FO	Faroe Islands
FR	France
GB	Great Britain (United Kingdom of)
GD	Grenada (Republic of)
GE	Georgia (Republic of)
GF	French Guiana
GG	Guernsey (Channel Islands, Bailiwick of)
GH	Ghana

continues

TABLE 6.1, CONTINUED

Internet Top-Level Domains

Domain	
GI	Gibraltar
GL	Greenland
GN	Guinea (Republic of)
GOV	Government
GP	Guadaloupe
GR	Greece (Hellenic Republic)
GT	Guatemala (Republic of)
GU	Guam
GY	Guyana
HK	Hong Kong (Hisiangkang, Xianggang)
HN	Honduras (Republic of)
HR	Croatia/Hrvatska (Republic of)
HU	Hungary (Republic of)
ID	Indonesia
IE	Ireland
IL	Israel (State of)
IM	Isle of Man
IN	India (Republic of)
INT	International
IR	Iran (Islamic Republic of)
IS	Iceland (Republic of)
IT	Italy (Italian Republic)
JE	Jersey (Channel Islands, Bailiwick of)
JM	Jamaica
JO	Jordan (The Hashemite Kingdom of)

Domain	
JP	Japan
KE	Kenya (Republic of)
KH	Cambodia
KI	Kiribati
KN	Saint Kitts & Nevis
KR	Korea (Republic of)
KW	Kuwait (State of)
KY	Cayman Islands
KZ	Kazakhstan
LA	Lao People's Democratic Republic
LB	Lebanon (Lebanese Republic)
LC	Saint Lucia
LI	Liechtenstein (Principality of)
LK	Sri Lanka (Democratic Socialist Republic of)
LS	Lesotho (Kingdom of)
LT	Lithuania (Republic of)
LU	Luxembourg (Grand Duchy of)
LV	Latvia (Republic of)
MA	Morocco (Kingdom of)
MC	Monaco (Principality of)
MD	Moldova (Republic of)
MG	Madagascar
MH	Marshall Islands (Republic of the)
MIL	Military
MK	Macedonia (The former Yugoslav Republic of)
ML	Mali (Republic of)
MN	Mongolia

continues

TABLE 6.1, CONTINUED

Internet Top-Level Domains

Domain	
MO	Macau
MP	Northern Mariana Islands
MR	Mauritania Top-Level Domain
MT	Malta (Republic of)
MU	Mauritius
MV	Maldives (Republic of)
MX	Mexico (United Mexican States)
MY	Malaysia top level domain
MZ	Mozambique (People's Republic of)
NA	Namibia (Republic of)
NC	New Caledonia (Nouvelle Caledonie)
NE	Niger
NET	Network
NF	Norfolk Island
NG	Nigeria
NI	Nicaragua (Republic of)
NL	Netherlands
NO	Norway (Kingdom of)
NP	Nepal
NZ	New Zealand
OM	Oman (Sultanate of)
ORG	Organization
PA	Panama (Republic of)
PE	Peru (Republic of)
PF	French Polynesia

Domain	
PG	Papua New Guinea
PH	Philippines (Republic of the)
PK	Pakistan (Islamic Republic of)
PL	Poland (Republic of)
PR	Puerto Rico
PT	Portugal (Portuguese Republic)
PY	Paraguay (Republic of)
QA	Qatar
RO	Romania
RU	Russia (Russian Federation)
RW	Rwanda (Republic of)
SA	Saudi Arabia (Kingdom of)
SB	Solomon Islands
SE	Sweden (Kingdom of)
SG	Singapore (Republic of)
SI	ARNES
SK	Slovakia
SM	San Marino (Republic of)
SN	Senegal (Republic of)
SR	Telesur
SU	Soviet Union (Union of Soviet Socialist Republics)
SV	El Salvador
SY	Syria (Syrian Arab Republic)
SZ	Swaziland (Kingdom of)
TG	Togo (Republic of)
TH	Thailand (Kingdom of)
TN	Tunisia

continues

TABLE 6.1, CONTINUED
Internet Top-Level Domains

Domain	
TO	Tonga
TR	Turkey (Republic of)
TT	Trinidad & Tobago (Republic of)
TV	Tuvalu
TW	Taiwan
TZ	Tanzania (United Republic of)
UA	Ukraine
UG	Uganda (Republic of)
UK	United Kingdom of Great Britain
US	United States of America
UY	Uruguay (Eastern Republic of)
UZ	Uzbekistan
VA	Vatican City State
VC	Saint Vincent & the Grenadines
VE	Venezuela (Republic of)
VI	Virgin Islands (US)
VN	Vietnam (Socialist Republic of)
VU	Vanuatu
WS	Samoa
YE	Yemen
YU	Yugoslavia (Federal Republic of)
ZA	South Africa (Republic of)
ZM	Zambia (Republic of)
ZR	Zaire (Republic of)
ZW	Zimbabwe (Republic of)

Subdomains in the US Domain

Within the US domain, second-level domains have been established for each state, using the standard postal abbreviations for the state domain names, for example, NY.US for New York.

RFC 1480 describes some conventions for establishing subdomains within the states (examples are taken from the RFC):

- **Locality codes.** Cities, counties, parishes, and townships. Example: `Los-Angeles.CA.US` or `PORTLAND.OR.US`

- **CI.** City government agencies, used as a subdomain under a locality. Example: `Fire-Dept.CI.Los-Angeles.CA.US`

- **CO.** County government agencies, used as a subdomain under a locality. Example: `Fire-Dept.CO.San-Diego.CA.US`

- **K12.** For public school districts. Example: `John-Muir.Middle.Santa-Monica.K12.CA.US`

- **CC.** All state-wide community colleges

- **PVT.** Private schools, used as a subdomain of K12. Example: `St-Michaels.PVT.K12.CA.US`

- **TEC.** Technical and vocational schools

- **LIB.** Libraries. Example: `<library-name>.LIB.<state>.US`

- **STATE.** State government agencies. Example: `State-Police.STATE.<state>.US`

- **GEN.** Things that don't fit comfortably in other categories

Parallel to the state names, some special names have been designated under US:

- **FED.** Agencies of the federal government

- **DNI.** Distributed national institutes, organizations with a presence in more than one state or region

Figure 6.7 describes the structure of the US domain, including its use of state and lower-level codes.

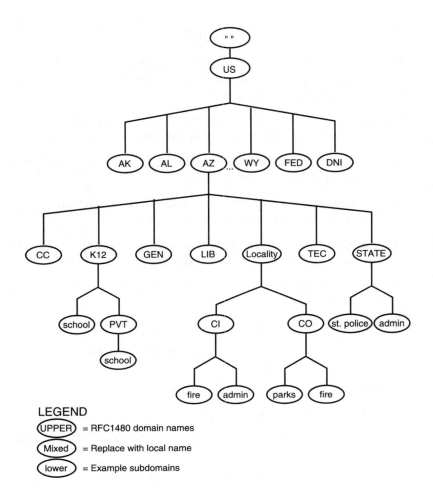

FIGURE 6.7

Organization of the US domain.

Administration of subdomains of US has been extensively delegated to local contacts. To obtain a list of contacts for the US subdomains via anonymous FTP, retrieve the file in-notes/us-domain-delegated.txt from venera.isi.edu. Other useful files are located on this host, and you should find browsing around worthwhile.

Another way to receive this list is to send an email message to RFC-INFO@ISI.EDU. Put the following message in the body of the message:

```
Help: us_domain_delegated_domains
```

The RFC-INFO service is yet another way to obtain Internet documents, including RFCs, FYIs, STDs, and IMRs. To obtain instructions, send email to RFC-INFO@ISI.EDU with the text Help in the body of the message.

Subdomains in Nongovernment Organizations

Below the second-level domain name assigned by InterNIC Registration, the organization that obtains the name is responsible for subdomain administration and has complete freedom to establish the subdomain structure. Any organization that wants to establish a subdomain must arrange for a name server to support the subdomain name space.

DNS services usually are supported on a DNS server operated by the domain's organization. Because a given DNS server can support several zones, however, establishing a new domain on an existing DNS server is possible, such as on one an Internet provider operates.

Earlier examples of an organization's name space (as in Figure 6.3) indicated the top-most node as the root of the tree. When an organization joins the Internet, that can no longer be the case. An organization must apply for a domain name, to be a subdomain of one of the standard domains. If the organization in Figure 6.3 is named Widgets, Inc., it might apply for the domain name widgets.com. In that case, their portion of the Internet name space would look like Figure 6.8. It would be the responsibility of Widgets, Inc. to administer their portion of the name space, starting from the widgets domain.

In this manner, every host on the Internet might be assigned a unique FQDN. Bob's desktop workstation would now have the FQDN bob.sw.eng.widgets.com.

Obtaining Domain Information with WHOIS

WHOIS is a "white pages" directory of people and organizations on the Internet. One way to use WHOIS is for obtaining information about top-level domains, including the contacts.

WHOIS searches are based on keywords. Each top-level domain is keyword-indexed with the domain name concatenated to "-DOM". To search for the COM domain, for example, you would search for COM-DOM.

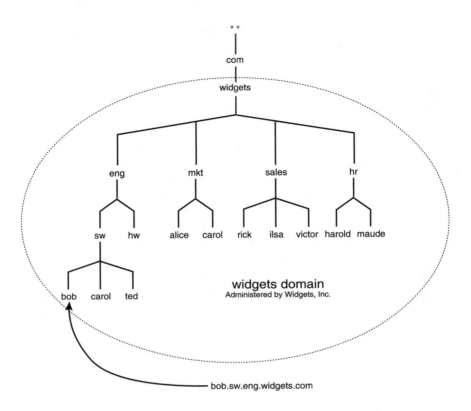

FIGURE 6.8

An organization in the Internet name space.

If your host is on the Internet and has WHOIS client software, you can query WHOIS directly. To find the contact person for the EDU top-level domain, enter the following WHOIS query:

```
whois -h rs.internic.net edu-dom
```

This command directs a WHOIS query using the keyword `edu-dom` to the host `rs.internic.net`. To search for top-level domains, query `whois root-dom`.

On the World Wide Web, use the URL `http://www.internic.net` to access the InterNIC Web site. Enter the AT&T Directory and Databases Services, and select the InterNIC Directory Services ("White Pages"). From there, you can obtain information or search the world-wide directories that are available. You can use this query page to obtain information from two WHOIS servers:

■ DISA NIC for the MIL domain

■ InterNIC Registration Services (rs.internic.net) for point-of-contact information

An excellent way to access the InterNIC WHOIS database is to telnet to rs.internic.net. No login is required. Enter the command whois to start a WHOIS client. The following dialog shows the results of querying for EDU-DOM:

```
Whois: edu-dom
Education top-level domain (EDU-DOM)
    Network Solutions, Inc.
    505 Huntmar park Dr.
    Herndon, VA 22070

    Domain Name: EDU

    Administrative Contact, Technical Contact, Zone Contact:
        Network Solutions, Inc. (HOSTMASTER)   HOSTMASTER@INTERNIC.NET
        (703) 742-4777 (FAX) (703) 742-4811

    Record last updated on 02-Sep-94.

    Domain servers in listed order:

    A.ROOT-SERVERS.NET          198.41.0.4
    H.ROOT-SERVERS.NET          128.63.2.53
    B.ROOT-SERVERS.NET          128.9.0.107
    C.ROOT-SERVERS.NET          192.33.4.12
    D.ROOT-SERVERS.NET          128.8.10.90
    E.ROOT-SERVERS.NET          192.203.230.10
    I.ROOT-SERVERS.NET          192.36.148.17
    F.ROOT-SERVERS.NET          39.13.229.241
    G.ROOT-SERVERS.NET          192.112.36.4
Would you like to see the known domains under this top-level
domain? n
```

As can be seen, it is sometimes possible to drill down to lower-level domains, although the number of subdomains frequently exceeds reporting capacity.

The preceding list contains the names and addresses of the nine name servers that service the Internet root domain. If you want to know more about one of these hosts, you can query WHOIS as follows:

```
Whois: 128.63.2.53
Army Research Laboratory (BRL-AOS)
    Aberdeen Proving Ground, MD  21005-5066
```

```
Hostname: H.ROOT-SERVERS.NET
Address: 128.63.2.53
System: SUN running UNIX

Host Administrator:
    Fielding, James L. (JLF)  jamesf@ARL.MIL
    (410)278-8929 (DSN) 298-8929 (410)278-6664 (FAX) (410)278-
5077

domain server

Record last updated on 17-Aug-95.

Would you like to see the registered users of this host? n
Whois:
```

Mapping Addresses to Names

As described to this point, DNS is adept at resolving domain names to IP addresses. Sometimes, however, exactly the opposite is required. Given an IP address, it might be necessary to determine the domain name associated with the address. To support reverse mapping, a special domain is maintained on the Internet: the in-addr.arpa domain.

Figure 6.9 illustrates in-addr.arpa's structure. Nodes in the domain are named after IP addresses. The in-addr.arpa domain can have 256 subdomains, each corresponding to the first octet an IP address. Each subdomain of in-addr.arpa can in turn have 256 subdomains, corresponding to the possible values of the second octets of IP addresses. Similarly, the next subdomain down the hierarchy can have 256 subdomains corresponding to the third octets of IP addresses. Finally, the last subdomain contains records associated with the fourth octets of IP addresses.

The value of a fourth-octet resource record is the full domain name of the IP address that defines the resource record.

Figure 6.9 shows how a record can be stored in the IN-ADDR.ARPA hierarchy. The domain name mcp.com is associated with the IP address 198.70.148.1. To locate the domain name, DNS searches down the tree beginning with 198.in-addr.arpa. The search continues until reaching the resource record 1.148.70.198.in-addr.arpa. The value of that resource record is mcp.com.

FIGURE 6.9

Resolving an address to a domain name in in-addr.arpa.

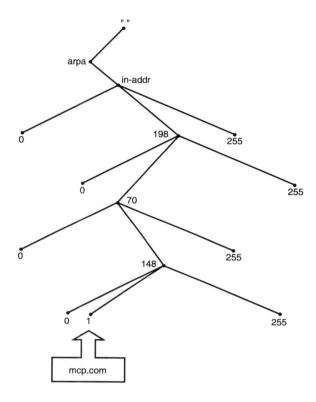

TCP/IP Applications

This section examines several common TCP/IP applications. Some, such as FTP and Telnet, are tools that end users frequently access. Others, although not often seen by users, are mainstays of TCP/IP networking. Specifically, this section examines the following applications:

- File Transfer Protocol (FTP)
- Trivial File Transfer Protocol (TFTP)
- Telnet
- Simple Mail Transport Protocol (SMTP)
- Simple Network Management Protocol (SNMP)
- Network file system (NFS)

Incidentally, DNS name servers also function at the process/application level. Operation of DNS, previously described, will not be considered further.

File Transfer Protocol

FTP is both a protocol and a program that can be used to perform basic file operations on remote hosts and to transfer files between hosts. As a program, FTP can be operated by users to do file tasks manually. FTP also can be used as a protocol by applications that require its file services. FTP is a secure, reliable application. To ensure reliability, FTP operates over TCP. Users who access a host through FTP undergo an authentication login that might be secured with usernames and passwords. These usernames and passwords can be tied into the host's security, enabling administrators to restrict access as required.

Although secure, FTP sends passwords as CLEARTEXT, which can pose problems.

Anatomy of FTP

As Figure 6.10 shows, FTP includes client and server components. A host that makes its file system available to users must run an application that operates as an FTP *server*. Users who access the FTP server must run FTP *client* software on their computers.

When the FTP client opens a connection to an FTP server, a logical pipeline (a virtual circuit defined by two sockets) is established between the client and server hosts. This pipeline enables the FTP components to communicate. The end result is very much like mounting the remote file system for limited local file access. You cannot execute remote files as programs, but you can list directories, type file contents, manipulate local directories, and copy files between the hosts.

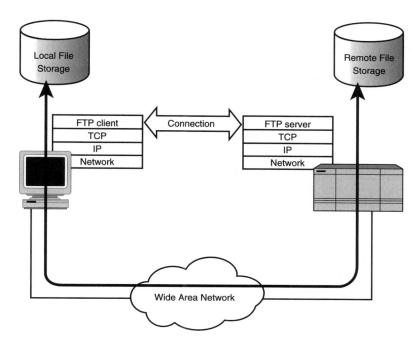

FIGURE 6.10
Anatomy of an FTP session.

NOTE

A word about capitalization is in order. UNIX commands, directories, and filenames are case-sensitive, and the command GET is not interchangeable with get. Therefore, authors of UNIX books conventionally typeset this and other commands entirely in lowercase.

Windows NT recognizes upper- and lowercase characters in filenames, but NT commands are not case-sensitive. It does not matter whether you type ftp, FTP, or fTp. However, when you are interacting with a remote host, you must adhere to the case conventions on that host. Because UNIX hosts expect FTP commands and options to be in lowercase, I have stuck to lowercase in this chapter.

Using FTP

Chances are high that you connect your Windows NT computers to the Internet in some way. When that happens, you leave the realm of Microsoft networking and need to use FTP to perform remote file operations.

Until fairly recently, FTP has been a text-only application, used from the command line. The new popularity of the Internet, combined with the wide availability of graphical user interfaces, has lead to the development of Windows-based applications that provide a point-and-click interface to FTP.

Windows NT, however, ships with a command-line ftp utility only. Fortunately, that is all you need. Chapter 17, "Enabling a Secure Connection to the Internet," tells you everything you need to know to connect Windows NT computers to the Internet. After doing so, you can use ftp as it ships with Windows NT to access FTP sites that can supply you all the tools you need to set up your Windows NT Internet environment, including the previously mentioned graphical interface to ftp.

NOTE

A World Wide Web browser can be used to retrieve files from FTP sites. Specify ftp as the protocol in the URL, for example:

```
ftp://ds.internic.net
```

Example of an FTP Session

This section presents an example of an FTP session. The example is designed to show you how to retrieve an RFC document from the InterNIC server DS.INTERNIC.NET.

Before beginning, you must establish an Internet connection, using either a dial-in service or a direct network connection.

Starting FTP

You can start an FTP session by simply opening a command prompt and typing the command **ftp** as in this dialog (text entered by the user is in bold):

```
C:\ftp
ftp>
```

The prompt changes from C:\ to ftp>. At this point, only ftp commands are accepted.

Getting Help

To obtain a list of ftp commands, use the ? command:

```
ftp> ?
Commands may be abbreviated. Commands are:
!          delete     literal   prompt     send
?          debug      ls        put        status
append     dir        mdelete   pwd        trace
ascii      disconnect mdir      quit       type
bell       get        mget      quote      user
binary     glob       mkdir     recv       verbose
bye        hash       mls       remotehelp
cd         help       mput      rename
close      lcd        open      rmdir
ftp>
```

FTP betrays its UNIX origins in many ways. Many of the file and directory management commands originated in the UNIX environment. Some will be familiar to DOS and Windows users (no points for guessing which OS originated the commands). Others, such as pwd (print working directory) and ls (list files) are unfamiliar to DOS users, but quite understandable after they are explained.

You can obtain brief help on any of these commands by typing **help** followed by the command for which you seek advice. The descriptions aren't very elaborate, but they can help, as in this example:

```
ftp> help ls
ls                 nlist contents of remote directory
```

Opening a Session

After starting FTP, you can open a session with an FTP server by using the open command, as follows:

```
ftp> open ds.internic.net
Connected to ds.internic.net
220-              InterNIC Directory and Database Services
220-
220-Welcome to InterNIC Directory and Database Services provided by
AT&T
220-These services are partially supported through a cooperative
agreement
```

```
220-with the National Science Foundation.
220-
220-Your comments and suggestions for improvement are welcome, and
can be
220-mailed to admin@ds.internic.net.
220-
220-AT&T MAKES NO WARRANTY OR GUARANTEE, OR PROMISE, EXPRESS OR
IMPLIED,
220-CONCERNING THE CONTENT OR ACCURACY OF THE INTERNIC DIRECTORY
ENTRIES
220-AND DATABASE FILES STORED AND MAINTAINED BY AT&T. AT&T
EXPRESSLY
220-DISCLAIMS AND EXCLUDES ALL EXPRESS WARRANTIES AND IMPLIED
WARRANTIES
220-OF MERCHANTABILITY AND FITNESS FOR A PARTICULAR PURPOSE.
220-
220-                    ****************************
220-
220-DS0 will be rebooted every Monday morning between 8:00AM and
8:30AM est.
220-            Please use DS1 or DS2 during this period
220-
220-                    ****************************
220-
User (ds.internic.net:(none)):
```

NOTE

You can start `ftp` and open a session with an FTP server by including the domain name for the server as a command-line parameter. The session with InterNIC could also have started using this command:

```
C:\ ftp ds.internic.net
```

Logging in to Anonymous FTP

Like many FTP servers, ds.internic.net accepts anonymous logins. Any user might log in with limited access rights by using the username anonymous and entering a password. By convention, most systems request that users enter their email addresses as their passwords. The login process is shown here:

```
User (ds.internic.net:(none)): anonymous
331 Guest login ok, send ident as password.
Password: (password does not echo)
230 Guest login ok, access restrictions apply.
ftp>
```

Changing Directories

You now are logged in to the root directory of ds.internic.net. At any given time, you will be working with two working directories: one on the FTP server and one on your local computer. You can change these directories if you need to determine where to copy files from and to.

Two commands are available for changing directories:

- `cd`. Changes your working directory on the FTP server

- `lcd`. Changes your current directory on your local computer

At any time, you can view your current directory on the FTP server by using the `pwd` (print working directory) command:

```
ftp> pwd
257 "/" is the current directory
```

NOTE

When you complete a login to an FTP server, you enter the realm of that server's operating system. ds.internic.net is a Sun system running on SunOS UNIX—the majority of FTP servers run UNIX—and you must apply UNIX conventions to the names of files and directories.

Remember that case is significant in UNIX. You cannot retrieve the file rfc1800.txt with the command parameter RFC1800.TXT. Also, UNIX subdirectories are delimited with forward slashes (/) rather than the back slashes (\) with which DOS and Windows users are familiar.

Similarly, in UNIX, case matters in directory names. If a directory is named /pub/Libraries/Programs, you must be sure to match case when you enter the subdirectory names.

RFC files are stored in the `/rfc` directory. You can access files by specifying the filename with a directory path, or you can change your working directory to `/rfc`. To change your working directory on the server, use the `cd` (change directory) command:

```
ftp> cd /rfc
250 CWD command successful
ftp> pwd
257 "/rfc" is the current directory
```

To change the current directory on your local computer, use the `lcd` command. To store files in \docs, enter this command:

```
ftp> lcd \docs
Local directory now c:\docs
```

Figure 6.11 illustrates a directory tree along with some examples of commands for moving around:

- To move up the directory tree (to the parent directory of the current one) enter the command **cd ..** or **cdup**. The symbol .. simply means "one directory up."

- To change to a subdirectory of the current directory, use a *relative* reference. If your working directory is /ietf, you can change to /ietf/95jul simply by typing **cd 95jul**. A directory specification that does not begin with a / is a relative reference that begins with the current directory.

- You can change to any directory on the system by using an absolute reference that begins with the root directory. The command **cd /ietf/95apr** changes you to the 95apr directory, no matter what your current directory is.

FIGURE 6.11
Navigating a UNIX directory tree.

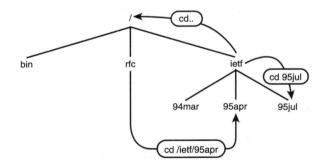

Listing Directory Contents

This directory contains nearly 2,000 files. You could see them all by typing the `ls` command, but you probably want to use wildcards to delimit the file list.

Directory contents might be shown as filenames alone or as detailed file lists. The `ls` (list) command shows only file and directory names. You can use the familiar * and ? wildcards with ls. The following example was chosen to highlight several important documents that you should retrieve during your first session with InterNIC.

```
ftp> ls rfc-*.txt
200 PORT command successful.
150 Opening ASCII mode data connection for file list.
rfc-index.txt
rfc-instructions.txt
rfc-retrieval.txt
226 Transfer complete.
56 bytes received in 0.01 seconds (5.60 Kbytes/sec)
ftp>
```

Processing wildcard characters is called *globbing*. When globbing is turned on, ? and * are treated as wildcards. If required, you can turn globbing off by issuing the glob command. Enter the command again to turn globbing on.

NOTE

Even though some of the commands resemble UNIX commands, you cannot freely use UNIX commands while in an FTP session. The commands are processed by ftp, not by a UNIX shell.

When you know you are working on a UNIX host, however, some command options are supported. The ls command accepts the following parameters (note the use of uppercase in some options):

-a	Lists all files, including hidden ones
-C	Produces a column listing (similar to the DOS /W switch)
-d	Lists directory names only
-F	Displays the file type (directory or executable)
-l	Produces a long listing
-R	Specifies a recursive (continuous) listing

To display more detail, use the dir command. The details you see depend on the OS running on the FTP server. This list originates on a UNIX computer and includes UNIX security information (called *permissions*) in the left-most column. Because this server permits unsecured anonymous logins, you are unlikely to see any files that are not secured with read-only (r) permissions. (Consult NRP's *Inside UNIX Second Edition* if you are

interested in more information about UNIX.) In the following example, a ?
wildcard was used as a single-character placeholder to display all files starting with the characters rfc170.

```
ftp> dir rfc170?.txt
200 PORT command successful.
150 Opening ASCII mode data connection for /bin/ls.
-r—r—r—  1 welcome  ftpguest   458860 Oct 19  1994 rfc1700.txt
-r—r—r—  1 welcome  ftpguest    15460 Oct 20  1994 rfc1701.txt
-r—r—r—  1 welcome  ftpguest     7288 Oct 20  1994 rfc1702.txt
-r—r—r—  1 welcome  ftpguest    17985 Oct 21  1994 rfc1703.txt
-r—r—r—  1 welcome  ftpguest    42335 Nov  1  1994 rfc1704.txt
-r—r—r—  1 welcome  ftpguest    65222 Oct 25  1994 rfc1705.txt
-r—r—r—  1 welcome  ftpguest    19721 Oct 21  1994 rfc1706.txt
-r—r—r—  1 welcome  ftpguest    37568 Oct 28  1994 rfc1707.txt
-r—r—r—  1 welcome  ftpguest    26523 Oct 25  1994 rfc1708.txt
-r—r—r—  1 welcome  ftpguest    66659 Nov 22  1994 rfc1709.txt
226 Transfer complete.
670 bytes received in 0.54 seconds (1.24 Kbytes/sec)
ftp>
```

If the directory contains subdirectories, you see an entry similar to the following. The d at the beginning of the permissions indicates that the entry is
a directory.

```
drwxr-xr-x  3 welcome  1          25600 Sep 20 04:07 rfc
```

Retrieving Files

To retrieve an RFC file, use the get command. Keep in mind as you do that
filenames in UNIX are case-sensitive. The following example gets the file
rfc1700.txt from the working directory on the FTP host and retrieves it to
the working directory on the local computer:

```
ftp> get rfc1700.txt
200 PORT command successful.
150 Opening ASCII mode data connection for rfc1700.txt (458860
bytes).
226 Transfer complete.
471743 bytes received in 92.04 seconds (5.13 Kbytes/sec)
ftp>
```

You do not have permissions to copy files to DS.INTERNIC.NET. For
hosts on which you have file write permissions, the put command works
very similarly to get.

NOTE

As disclosed in the `ftp` dialog, the preceding example was of an ASCII transfer, which generally is preferable for text documents. UNIX and DOS/Windows have different conventions for indicating the ends of lines in text files. UNIX uses the linefeed character alone, whereas DOS/Windows uses a carriage return/linefeed combination. When `ftp` transfers in ASCII mode between different host environments, the proper character translations take place.

To turn off end-of-line character translation, enter the `cr` command. Enter `cr` again to restore translation. You use the `cr` command if the file's ultimate destination is a DOS or Windows computer.

If you transfer program or data files, you do not want any character translation or format changes to take place. Before getting the file, enter the command `binary` to instruct `ftp` not to convert file contents.

Enter the command `ASCII` to restore ASCII-mode file transfers.

`ftp` supports a variety of commands that determine how files transfer and display the information. If you want to know what settings currently are in effect, enter the `status` command, as in this example:

```
ftp> status
Connected to ds.internic.net.
Type: ascii; Verbose: On; Bell: Off; Prompting: On
Globbing: On; Debugging: Off; Hash mark printing: Off
ftp>
```

Ending an FTP Session

After you finish your operations on the FTP server, you need to close your connection by entering the `close` command:

```
ftp> close
221 Goodbye.
ftp>
```

You can then exit `ftp` by using the command **bye**. Typing **bye** while in session with an FTP host both closes the connection and exits `ftp`.

```
ftp> bye
C:\
```

ftp Command Reference

You probably will use `ftp` to obtain files to set up your Internet host or server, and you probably will need to become familiar with command-mode `ftp`. You might find the command-mode approach preferable to a graphical one. A graphical FTP front-end must transfer entire directory contents to make the file names available for mouse actions. This is unnecessary in command mode, and you can connect to a familiar FTP server and retrieve files with a very few commands whereas a graphical front-end would still be transferring directory lists.

Table 6.2 includes an alphabetical listing of `ftp` commands supported on Windows NT with brief explanations of their functions. Many commands are toggles. Each time these commands are executed, they reverse the status of the current function (on-to-off or off-to-on).

TABLE 6.2

***ftp* Commands**

Name	Function
append *local remote*	Appends the contents of the local file *local* to the end of the remote file *remote*.
ASCII	Specifies that file transfers should be performed in 7-bit ASCII text mode. End-of-line characters will be translated as appropriate for the destination host.
binary	Specifies that no translations should be performed when files are transferred between hosts. This mode should be used for data, program, and 8-bit ASCII text files.
bye	Stops `ftp`. If a host connection is active, the connection is closed first.
case	Toggles conversion of upper- to lowercase characters when using the `mget` command.
cd *path*	Changes the working directory on the FTP server to the directory specified in *path*.
cdup	Changes the working directory on the FTP server to the parent of the current working directory.

Name	Function
close	Closes the host connection but leaves FTP running.
cr	Toggles the translation of carriage return characters when transferring text files.
delete *file*	Deletes the file named *file* from the FTP server.
dir	Obtains a detailed directory of files in the working directory on the FTP server.
dir *path*	Obtains a detailed directory of files in the working directory specified by *path*.
get *remote local*	Retrieves the file *remote* from the FTP server and stores it with the name *local* on the local host. Omit *local* to retain the original filename.
glob	Toggles use of filename expansion.
help ?	Lists the names of available commands.
help *command*	Displays a brief message about *command*.
lcd *path*	Changes the working directory on the local computer.
ls	Lists files in the working directory on the FTP server. On a UNIX host accepts UNIX ls options.
mdelete *name*	Deletes all files on the FTP server that match *name*, which might include ? and * wildcards.
mget *name*	Retrieves files from the FTP server that match *name*, which might include ? and * wildcards.
mkdir *directory*	Creates a subdirectory named *directory* on the FTP server.
mput *name*	Copies to the FTP server all local files that match *name*, which might include ? and * wildcards.
open *hostname*	Opens a connection to the specified hostname, which must be running FTP server software to accept the connection.

continues

Table 6.2, Continued

ftp Commands

Name	Function
prompt	Switches prompting on or off during operations on multiple files (wildcards are used). You might find prompting irritating for routine operations such as mput and mget but might prefer to have prompting active for deleting files with mdelete.
put *local remote*	Copies the local file *local* to the FTP host with the name *remote*.
pwd	Prints the working (current) directory on the FTP server.
rename *old new*	Renames a file on the FTP host from the name *old* to the name *new*.
rmdir *directory*	Removes a directory named *directory* from the FTP server.
runique	Toggles unique file mode when receiving files. To ensure that all received files have unique names, an extension from .1 through .99 will be appended to each successive filename. One use is to ensure unique file names when copying many files with long names to a system that supports short filenames such as the DOS 8.3 format.
status	Shows current session settings.
sunique	Toggles unique file mode when sending files. To ensure that all received files have unique names, an extension from .1 through .99 will be appended to each successive filename.
user *username*	Initiates a login to the FTP host with the username specified. ftp prompts for a password.
verbose	Switches verbose mode on or off. Verbose mode provides information you might not care about, such as file transfer statistics.

Trivial File Transfer Protocol

FTP was designed to provide robust and secure file operations over unreliable networks and uses TCP as a transport protocol to provide reliable delivery. To operate over TCP virtual circuits, FTP requires hosts to establish a connection before file operations can commence. Part of FTP connection establishment incorporates logins for security.

When the network is reliable, as on a local area network, the overhead of FTP might not be desirable. Consequently, a simpler protocol was developed, Trivial File Transfer Protocol (TFTP; RFC 1350). TFTP uses the unreliable UDP protocol as a transport and does not require establishing a connection or logging on before file transfer requests are possible.

TFTP's lack of security makes offering TFTP services a bit risky for a computer on a public network because it provides an entrée to the computer that can allow an outsider to gain unsecured access. Therefore, system administrators quite commonly disable TFTP on publicly available computers. File access available to TFTP must be carefully secured.

TFTP is a small and efficient protocol easily embedded in a computer's boot ROM. Sun UNIX workstations, for example, use TFTP to download a central operating system image when booting the system on a network.

Telnet

Remote terminal access is a critical feature on many computers. One way to provide remote terminal access is through dial-in telecommunications. But when you have a network as widespread and functional as the Internet, does having to dial California to gain access to a computer at Berkeley make much sense? Why not communicate through the Internet? Telnet is a program that makes possible remote terminal access through a network.

How Telnet Works

Figure 6.12 illustrates the architecture of Telnet, which like FTP is based on client and server processes. A Telnet server process on the remote host maintains a virtual terminal, an image running entirely in software of a terminal that can interact with the remote host. A user initiates a Telnet session by running Telnet client software and logging on to the Telnet server.

The Telnet server receives keystrokes from the client and applies them to the virtual terminal, which in turn interacts with other processes on the host. The Telnet server also receives screen display data directed to the virtual terminal and communicates the data to the Telnet client. To the user, it appears that the terminal session is taking place on the local computer, whereas the remote host has the viewpoint that it is interacting with a local terminal.

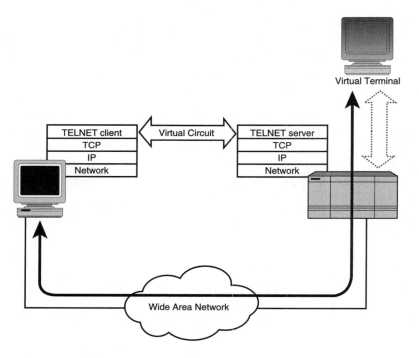

FIGURE 6.12
Telnet operation.

There is nothing terribly fancy about Telnet, which is based on emulation of one of several models of text-mode terminals, most commonly the Digital VT220, VT100/VT102, or the VT52. These terminals can perform sophisticated text-based operations, such as displaying menus that permit option selection using arrow keys. But they remain text-based.

Another limitation of Telnet is that it does not enable the local computer to participate in processing. All processing takes place on the remote Telnet server, and the local host functions as a "dumb" terminal. Therefore, Telnet cannot be used as a foundation for sophisticated network operations, such as file sharing. In fact, Telnet offers no mechanism for file transfer, which must take place under a separate FTP session.

Telnet can be used to access services such as archie, gopher, and veronica, but these services have gradually been eclipsed in popularity by the World Wide Web. In the LAN environment, you are most likely to use Telnet to configure remotely manageable devices such as routers and hubs.

Simple Mail Transfer Protocol

Electronic mail probably is the single most important application on the Internet. The protocol that supports Internet email is SMTP (RFC 821; RFC 822 defines the message format), which is the protocol used to transfer email messages between different TCP/IP hosts. Although a knowledgeable user quite possibly can communicate directly using the SMTP protocol, doing so is not the standard way of working. Usually, several communication layers are involved.

Architecture of SMTP Mail

Figure 6.13 illustrates the architecture of an SMTP-based mail system. Hosts that support email use a *mail transfer agent (MTA)* to manage the process. The most popular MTA in the UNIX community is sendmail. Broadly speaking, the MTA has two responsibilities:

- Sending messages to and receiving messages from other mail servers

- Providing an interface that enables user applications to access the mail system

The MTA is responsible for providing users with addressable mailboxes. When email is addressed to frodo@bagend.org, bagend.org is the domain name that identifies the host running the MTA. The MTA is responsible for ensuring that messages to frodo arrive in the correct mailbox.

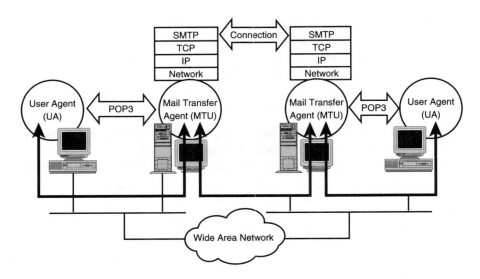

FIGURE 6.13

Architecture of SMTP-based messaging.

End users interface with the MTA, using one of the many available *user agents (UAs)*. The UA puts a friendly face on the network email, shielding the user from a fairly complicated process. UAs use a mail protocol to communicate with the MTA, such as Post Office Protocol, Version 3 (POP3; RFC 1460).

A common UA in the UNIX world is the text-based program named mail. In the Windows environment, a popular program is Eudora, available in both shareware and commercial versions for a variety of platforms. But email is so ubiquitous on the Internet that large numbers of Internet applications, such as Web browsers and newsgroup viewers, now provide at least a rudimentary email front end.

Delivering Electronic Mail

Electronic mail systems are not designed to provide real-time message interchange. For that, users can employ tools such as chat programs. Instead, email systems are designed to route large volumes of messages in a reasonable (but not necessarily short) amount of time with as little network overhead as possible. If every mail message were rushed through the Internet via packet switching, the Internet would quickly be bogged down.

So email is implemented with the understanding that limited message transit time is permissible if it reduces network loading.

Email servers use a store-and-forward method for delivering messages. Figure 6.14 illustrates an example of an email system in which B must forward messages between A and C. B would need to work very hard if it had to route IP datagrams in real-time. However, B takes a more relaxed approach. When B receives a message from A, B receives the entire message, storing it on a local hard drive. If B has other priorities, such as receiving other incoming messages, B might wait until things quiet down before forwarding the message to C. B might even be configured to send to C only when several messages are queued or after a time interval has expired. It is more efficient for B to transfer several messages with one connection than to open a connection for every message. These techniques can slow transit time for a message to minutes or hours but greatly increase overall efficiency.

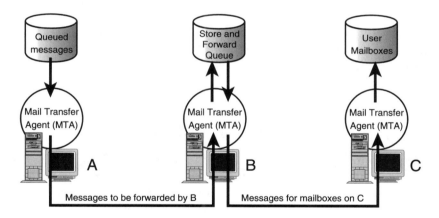

FIGURE 6.14

Forwarding electronic mail messages.

Characteristics of SMTP

SMTP is a fairly old protocol that predates widespread use of graphic terminals. Many of the data types being transported on modern messaging systems were undreamt of in 1982 when RFC 821 was published. Who could have imagined that we would be emailing pictures, voice messages, even video clips? In keeping with then-current technology, SMTP was designed to transfer messages consisting of 7-bit ASCII text.

When binary data must be sent through SMTP mail systems, the data must be encoded to a format compatible with 7-bit character transmission. The receiving site then decodes the message to retrieve the binary data. Many user agents now perform these translations automatically for attached binary files.

The most common encoding scheme in the UNIX community is implemented in the program uuencode (UNIX-UNIX encode), which has a companion program named uudecode. Programs are available to perform uuencodes and uudecodes on DOS, Windows, and Macintosh computers.

The Multipurpose Internet Mail Extensions (MIME; RFC 1521) is an Internet elective protocol that supports transfer of nontext messages via SMTP.

NOTE

SMTP was developed to handle nonsensitive messages in a fairly close-knit Internet community that operated with a high level of trust. Consequently, SMTP has weak security and does not encrypt messages. A knowledgeable person can readily extract messages from the raw protocol data that travels through the public network. Sensitive data, therefore, should be encrypted before transmission through SMTP mail.

Simple Network Management Protocol

A wide variety of activities can fairly be described as "network management." With regard to SNMP, network management means collecting, analyzing, and reporting data about the performance of network components. Data collected by SNMP include performance statistics and other routine reports, as well as alerts that report potential or existing network problems.

SNMP is one of a family of protocols that comprise the Internet network management strategy:

- **SNMP.** The protocol that enables network management stations to communicate with managed devices.

- **MIB.** The *management information base* is the database that stores system management information.

- **SMI.** *Structure and identification of management information*, describes how each object looks in the MIB.

Before looking at these protocols, you should understand how an SNMP-based network management system is organized.

Organization of SNMP Management

As Figure 6.15 illustrates, SNMP is organized around two types of devices:

- *Network management stations* serve as central repositories for the collection and analysis of network management data.

- *Managed devices run an SNMP agent*, which is a background process that monitors the device and communicates with the network management station. Often, devices that cannot support an SNMP agent can be monitored by a *proxy* device that communicates with the network management station.

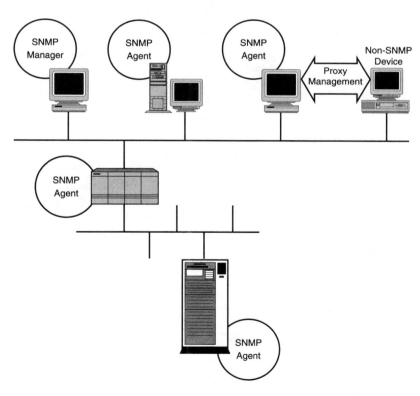

FIGURE 6.15

Organization of an SNMP-managed network.

Information is obtained from managed devices in two ways: polling and interrupts. These methods support different network management goals.

One goal of network management is to maintain a history of network performance that consists of "snapshots" of various characteristics of the network. These snapshots can be used to analyze trends, anticipate future demand, and isolate problems by comparing the current state of the network to prior conditions. The most efficient way to obtain snapshots is to have the management station *poll* managed devices, requesting that they provide the required information. Polling (see Figure 6.16) occurs only at defined intervals, rather than continually, to reduce network traffic. A snapshot of the performance characteristics of a healthy network is called a *baseline*.

FIGURE 6.16

Polling an agent for information.

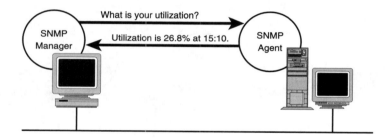

Another goal is to quickly notify managers of sudden changes in the network. When operational conditions for a device alter abruptly, waiting for the next poll from the management station is not timely. Managed devices can be configured to send *alerts* (also called *traps*) under predefined conditions. Network managers define thresholds for specific network performance characteristics. When a threshold is exceeded, the agent on a managed device immediately sends a trap to the management station (see Figure 6.17).

Essentially, a network management station and an agent can perform the following tasks:

- The network management station can poll agents for network information.

- The network management station can update, add, or remove entries in an agent's database. A router's router tables, for example, might be updated from the management console.

FIGURE 6.17
Network management agent sending a trap.

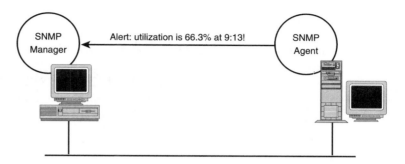

- The network management station can set thresholds for traps.

- The agent on a managed device can send traps to the network management station.

The Management Information Base

A MIB is a set of objects (types of network entities) that are included in the network management database. The MIB specification states the nature of the objects, whereas the SMI describes the appearances of the objects.

Three Internet MIB standards have been associated with SNMP.

- MIB-I (RFC 1156). This was the first MIB specification, initially published as RFC 1066 in 1988. MIB-I defined eight object groups.

- MIB-II (RFC 1213). This is the current recommended standard, defining ten object groups and 171 objects.

- RMON-MIB (RFC 1513/1217). The Remote Monitoring MIB is oriented around monitoring network media rather than network devices.

Additionally, a number of experimental and private (or *enterprises)* MIBs are available. Some enterprises MIBS are provided by vendors to support unique features of their products.

Experimental MIBs are undergoing trial as they are considered as possible extensions to the MIB standards. MIBs that are proven of value during experimentation might be considered for inclusion in the standard MIB space.

SNMP

Although SNMP (RFC 1157) was designed for the Internet, SNMP is not dependent on the TCP/IP protocols and can operate above a variety of lower-level protocols such as Novell's IPX/SPX. With TCP/IP, SNMP runs over the UDP datagram protocol to reduce network overhead.

SNMP requests are identified by a *community name,* a 32-character, case-sensitive identification that serves somewhat as a password. SNMP implementations might impose limitations on the characters that can appear in community names. Community names serve to identify SNMP messages but are transmitted as open text and, therefore, are not secure. The three types of community names are as follows:

- **Monitor Community.** This community name grants read access to MIBs and must be included with each MIB query. The default monitor community name is "public."

- **Control Community.** This community name grants read and write access to MIBs.

- **Trap Community.** This community name must accompany trap messages. An SNMP console rejects trap messages that do not match its configured trap community name. The default trap community name is "public."

SNMP entities operate asynchronously. A device need not wait for responses before it can send another message. A response is generated for any message except a trap, but network management stations and managed devices communicate fairly informally.

The current SNMP standard, version 1, can perform four operations:

- get. Retrieves a single object from the MIB.

- get-next. Traverses tables in the MIB.

- set. Manipulates MIB objects.

- trap. Reports an alarm.

get, get-next, and set commands originate from the network management station. If a managed device receives the command, a response is generated that is essentially the command message with filled-in blanks.

SNMP v1 has several shortcomings, most particularly in the area of security. SNMP names are sent as clear text, which can be observed by anyone who can observe raw network traffic. SNMP v2 (RFC 1441-1452) is a proposed standard that improves security by encrypting messages. SNMP v2 also improves efficiency, for example, by enabling a management console to retrieve an entire table in one request, rather than record-by-record with `get-next`.

Network Management Stations

Network management is of little value if the management data is not available for report, analysis, and action. Among the available network management console products are the following:

- Hewlett-Packard OpenView (DOS, Windows, and UNIX)
- Sun Microsystems SunNet Manager (UNIX)
- Novell Network Management System (NMS) (Windows)
- Synoptics Optivity (Windows)
- Cabletron Spectrum (Windows, UNIX)

Functions of the network management station include receiving and responding to traps, maintaining a trap history database, and getting object data from managed devices. More sophisticated—and costly—management consoles provide a graphic interface to the network and can construct a logical picture of the network structure. High-end management consoles generally are costly and require fairly powerful hardware.

The record-keeping capability of a management console is critical. It enables you to record baseline measurements of the network when it operates normally. These baseline measurements can be used to set thresholds for traps, which alert you to changes in network operation. They also provide a point of comparison that you can use to identify causes of network performance problems.

Network File System

Examination of the limitations of FTP and Telnet shows that they leave much to be desired where network computing is concerned. FTP can be used to transfer files, and Telnet can be used to run terminal sessions on a remote computer. But what if you want to run an application on your computer when some or all the application files are stored on another computer? What if you want, for example, to open a spreadsheet program on your computer and update a spreadsheet on another computer? With FTP, you need to transfer the file to your computer for work and back to the original computer when changes are complete. To complicate the matter further, what if the spreadsheet program itself is located on the remote computer? Must you FTP all the application files as well? FTP just isn't up to the job.

Network file system (NFS) provides the TCP/IP equivalent of Microsoft products' file-sharing capability. NFS was developed by Sun Microsystems and is widely licensed to other vendors who have implemented NFS on most platforms.

An NFS server can export a portion of its directory tree for use by NFS clients. Clients can mount the exported directories as if they are part of the clients' native file systems. DOS users, for example, access the exported directory as if it is a drive letter in the local DOS file structure. Figure 6.18 furnishes an example of exporting an NFS directory.

NFS is a sophisticated, reliable protocol that does not use TCP as a transport. For efficiency, NFS operates over UDP. NFS performs any required security, message fragmentation, and error recovery.

Microsoft does not offer an NFS product for Windows NT, but NFS is available from third-party vendors. Sources of NFS for Windows NT include the following:

- Chameleon32NFS from NetManage (408) 973-7171

- Connect NFS for NT from Beame & Whiteside (919) 831-8989

That Completes the Tour

And so we arrive at the end of our examination of the theory of TCP/IP. You might have wondered whether all this background information was needed, but as you will see, the concepts from these chapters appear many times in the second part of this book where we delve into the details of implementing the TCP/IP protocols on Microsoft operating systems. Let's begin, then, to put theory into practice. One more short—I promise—chapter to introduce you to Microsoft's TCP/IP architecture and we will get to work building your TCP/IP network.

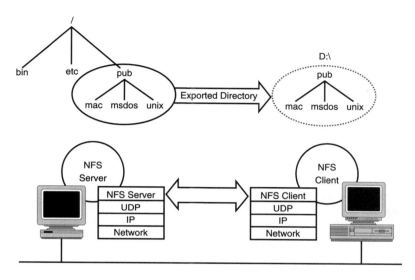

FIGURE 6.18

Exporting a directory with NFS.

Part II

PART II: IMPLEMENTING MICROSOFT TCP/IP

Chapter 7

INTRODUCING MICROSOFT TCP/IP

The preceding chapters provide a thorough introduction to the technologies and protocols in the TCP/IP protocol suite. This chapter begins by putting TCP/IP to work with Microsoft networking products. Microsoft has long included TCP/IP in its network-ready operating systems, beginning with the LAN Manager server product, because the native Microsoft network protocol NetBEUI cannot function on a routed network. TCP/IP was included to support networks that required routing and to provide compatibility with other vendors' networks.

Discussion in this chapter focuses on Windows NT because NT serves as the backbone technology for any extensive Microsoft TCP/IP network. Yes, Windows 3.1 and Windows 95 can function in a TCP/IP network, but you need at least one Windows NT computer if you want to provide services such as automatic IP address assignment or a Windows naming service. Also, the most robust Microsoft networks are based on Windows NT Server, which provides central file and security services.

These chapters assume that you are reasonably comfortable with Windows, particularly with Windows NT. You see all the steps for accomplishing a procedure but not all the operations of Windows management. If you need more information about Windows NT Workstation or Server, please consult the author's book, *Inside Windows NT Server*, published by New Riders. New Riders also offers thorough books about Windows 3.1x and Windows 95: *Inside Windows 3.11* and *Inside Windows 95*.

TCP/IP Features in Windows NT 4

This edition of the book focuses on the features and operation of Windows NT version 4.0. If you are serious about supporting TCP/IP in a Windows NT environment, consider upgrading to version 4.0. Although version 3.5x provided excellent protocol support, many of Microsoft's new TCP/IP tools require version 4.

The most prominent example is the Internet Information Server (IIS), which is included with and requires Windows NT Server 4. IIS is becoming a very popular Internet server, supporting World Wide Web, FTP, and Gopher server functionality. A steady flow of new products is emerging from Redmond, most of which are dependent on NT 4.

It is entirely possible to construct Internet servers using NT version 3.5x. A variety of third-party WWW servers are available, for example, and NT Server 3.5x includes FTP server capability. If you are pursuing a Microsoft-centric TCP/IP strategy, however, you have little choice but to follow Microsoft's lead and upgrade to Windows NT version 4.

DNS services have improved significantly with Windows NT 4. The *Windows NT Resource Kit* for Windows NT 3.5x included a DNS server that was compatible with BIND. It was configured using static files and had no graphic interface. Windows NT Server 4 includes a DNS server with the product. The new DNS server can be configured using static,

BIND-compatible files, but it also provides a Windows interface that supports on-the-fly management. Under NT Server 4, you can manage DNS using the familiar Windows interface, and you can avoid the need to restart the DNS server to make changes in the DNS name space.

Another prominent new feature supported by Windows NT 4 is the Multiprotocol Router, which supports RIP on Windows NT routers. If your network is at all complex, you will find that RIP can greatly simplify routing management.

Since the introduction of NT 4, Microsoft has significantly enhanced NT's capabilities, often with free add-in products. Routing and Remote Access Service, available for download from Microsoft's Web site, beef up RAS and greatly improve NT's routing capability. The Microsoft Proxy Server can be used to configure a proxy firewall between your network and the Internet. IIS has been enhanced twice and is now at version 4. These three upgrades are addressed in their own chapters later in this book.

Now that we have taken a high-level look at Windows NT 4, let's move on to a discussion of NT's support for network protocols.

Microsoft Network Protocols

Current Microsoft operating systems support three network transport protocols: NetBIOS Frame protocol (NBF), NWLink, and TCP/IP. (A standard protocol not discussed in this book, DLC, supports network-attached printers.) These protocols are integrated using two technologies: the *Network Driver Interface Specification (NDIS)* and the *Transport Driver Interface (TDI)*. Before launching into the network protocols, the next section examines the overall architecture of Microsoft protocol stacks, including NDIS and TDI.

NOTE

You will most commonly see NBF referred to by the older name NetBEUI (NetBIOS Extended User Interface). When you want to install NBF, for example, you install NetBEUI in the Network Control Panel applet. Apart from some arguments on the technical correctness of the names, NBF and NetBEUI are different names for the same protocol.

The Microsoft Network Protocol Architecture

As shown in Figure 7.1, NDIS and TDI act as the unifying layers that enable Microsoft workstations to support multiple protocol stacks over a single network interface.

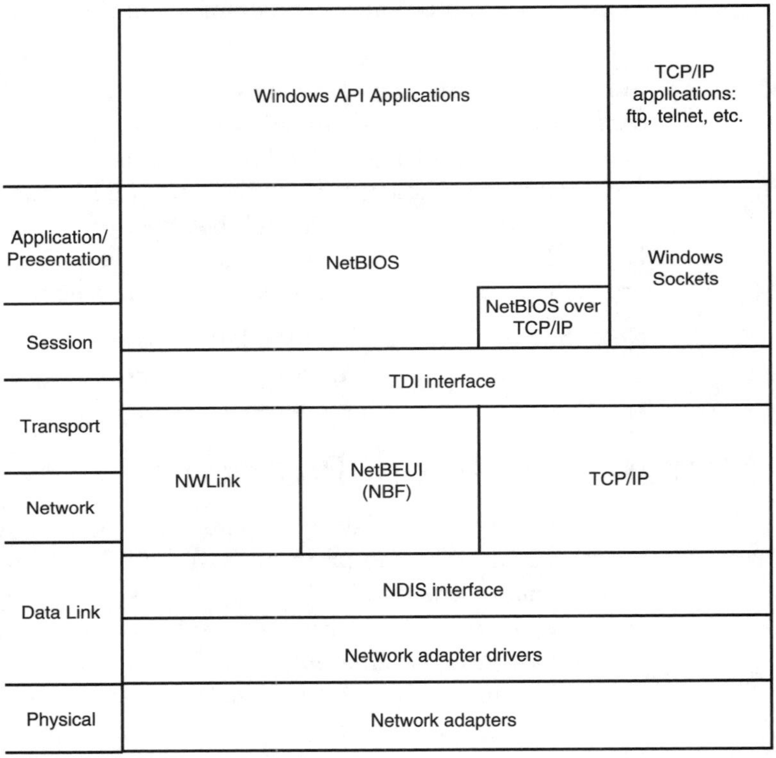

FIGURE 7.1

The Microsoft Network Protocol Architecture.

At the lowest levels of the protocol model are network interface adapters and the driver software that enables them to connect with upper layers. NDIS, developed jointly by Microsoft and 3Com, is a standard interface between MAC-layer protocols and the network layer. At the MAC layer, NDIS provides a well-defined interface that enables vendors to write drivers for their network interface products. NDIS also provides a standard protocol layer that upper-layer protocols can use, enabling multiple NDIS-compliant network-layer protocols to interface with any NDIS-compliant network adapter. Windows NT 3.5x supports drivers written to NDIS version 3.0.

NDIS enables a computer to support multiple network adapters, which might be of the same or mixed types. These adapters communicate with the same upper-layer protocol stacks, mediated by the NDIS interface. This arrangement could permit a computer to access the following environments through a single network adapter: a Windows 3.1 workgroup using NBF, a Novell NetWare 3.12 server using NWLink, and a UNIX host using TCP/IP.

The Transport Driver Interface defines a protocol interface between session layer protocols and the transport layer. Transport protocols, therefore, can be written to standard interfaces both above (TDI) and below (NDIS) in the protocol stack.

Application Programming Interfaces

Application programming interfaces provide a uniform method that enables applications to interface with the operating system and take advantage of operating system features. Above the TDI, Microsoft provides support for two application programming interfaces (APIs):

- NetBIOS over TCP/IP
- Windows Sockets

NetBIOS over TCP/IP

NetBIOS is the historic API for Microsoft network products. The majority of network-ready programs written for the Microsoft environment are written to the NetBIOS interface. NetBIOS over TCP/IP (abbreviated NBT or NetBT) enables NetBIOS applications to operate over the TCP/IP transport. The Workstation, Server, Messenger, NetLogon, and Browser services all rely on NBT.

The most distinct feature of NetBIOS is the NetBIOS namespace. NetBIOS names are 16 characters in length and are registered automatically when computers or services are started. Fifteen characters of the NetBIOS name are human-readable text, consisting of names specified by the network administrator. The sixteenth character is a hexadecimal code (00h-FFh) that indicates a resource type. A computer that supports multiple resources will be associated with multiple NetBIOS names. Table 7.1 lists the sixteenth-byte values that establish NetBIOS unique names.

Table 7.1

Sixteenth-Byte Characters for NetBIOS Unique Names

16th Byte	Identifies
00	The Workstation service. Typically, this name is referred to as the NetBIOS computer name.
03	The Messenger service, used to send and receive messages.
06	The RAS server service.
1B	The domain master browser name. Each domain has one master browser identified by this name.
1F	The NetDDE service.
20	The Server service, the service that provides share points for resource sharing.
21	The RAS client.
BE	The Network Monitor agent.
BF	The Network Monitor utility.

As you can see, these names distinguish various services that a Windows computer can advertise on the network. A Windows NT Server computer named WIDGET that is sharing resources would be visible with several NetBIOS names, including at least the following:

- WIDGET<00>

- WIDGET<03>

- WIDGET<20>

Thanks to the sixteenth character, each of these names is globally unique on the network. This satisfies a requirement of the NetBIOS name space, which is flat. Unlike the hierarchical DNS name space, all NetBIOS names are lumped together. Therefore, each NetBIOS name on the network must be unique on the entire network.

NetBIOS naming on TCP/IP networks is fairly complex. This edition includes an expanded discussion of naming; see Chapter 11, "Host Naming in the Microsoft TCP/IP World," for all the details.

Windows Sockets

The standard API for TCP/IP applications is Berkeley sockets, which Microsoft has implemented as Windows Sockets (WinSock). For environments that choose to implement TCP/IP without NetBEUI and to support the nonroutable NetBIOS protocol over internetworks, Microsoft has provided a NetBIOS over TCP/IP feature (NBT) that enables NetBIOS applications to access the TCP/IP transport.

Windows NT 4 implements the latest version of Windows Sockets (WinSock), version 2.0. Windows 98 includes support for WinSock 2.0, and WinSock 2.0 support is available for Windows 95. Windows NT 3.x supports only Windows Sockets 1.1. Windows Sockets 2.0 has a number of features that reflect the growing sophistication of applications on the Internet. Here are some of the new features:

- Network-based multimedia support

- Internet security

- IP multicast support

- IP version 6 and directory services support

- The ability to talk directly to ATM networks

NetBIOS Frame Protocol

Starting with MS-Net in the mid-1980s, Microsoft's traditional networking protocol has been NetBEUI, an efficient protocol that functions well in local networks. Although still often referred to as NetBEUI, the protocol was updated for Windows NT and is now more properly called the NetBIOS Frame protocol (NBF). NBF is compatible with the earlier NetBEUI implementations found in LAN Manager and Windows 3.x.

NBF provides two service modes (reliable connectionless mode is unavailable):

- Unreliable connectionless communication (datagram)

- Reliable connection-oriented communication (virtual circuit)

Connection-oriented communication is used in many situations on peer-to-peer networks. When a station uses a shared directory, the NET USE command initiates a dialog that establishes a connection between the two computers.

NBF depends extensively on broadcast messages to advertise network names. When a NetBIOS computer enters a network, it broadcasts a message announcing its name to ensure that no other computer on the network already has the same name. This essential NetBIOS mechanism fails in internetworks because broadcasts do not cross routers.

NBF does not include network identification addresses in transmitted frames, making it impossible to use conventional routing to forward the frames through internetworks. Ordinarily, therefore, NBF is restricted to nonrouted networks.

NWLink

NWLink is a Microsoft implementation of the two protocols that are the standard transport on NetWare networks: IPX and SPX. Beginning with Windows NT 3.5, NWLink became the standard Microsoft transport protocol, replacing NetBEUI, now optional. Then starting with version 3.51, NT's default network protocol shifted to TCP/IP.

Internetwork Packet Exchange (IPX) is a datagram network-layer protocol that serves as the primary workhorse on NetWare LANs. The majority of NetWare services operate over IPX. Sequenced Packet Exchange (SPX) is an optional transport-layer protocol that provides the connection-oriented, reliable message delivery that is required in more demanding situations.

IPX is a routable protocol, and NWLink can be used to construct routed networks using Microsoft products. The network/hardware address mechanism differs significantly from the mechanism used for IP.

Usually, nodes on IPX networks utilize their burned-in hardware addresses as node addresses. For networks based on standards that maintain a centralized address registration process, such as the IEEE 802 names described in Chapter 3, "The Network Access Layer," this approach guarantees unique hardware addresses throughout any conceivable internetwork without the need for manually configuring host IDs.

Network logical addresses are maintained as part of the server configuration. Each server connection must be configured using a 64-bit network address shared by all computers using a given protocol on that cabling segment. Stations that insert themselves on a network segment undergo a "get nearest server" dialog that, among other things, determines the network address of the local cabling segment. As a result, the network address must be specified at relatively few points, limited to the servers that connect directly to the network. All other nodes can discover the network address locally or through routing protocols. Novell provides a network address registry service that enables organizations to obtain a unique IPX network number for use on a public data network. Figure 7.2 illustrates the IPX addressing scheme.

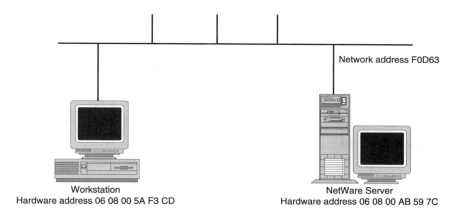

Network address F0D63

Workstation
Hardware address 06 08 00 5A F3 CD

NetWare Server
Hardware address 06 08 00 AB 59 7C

FIGURE 7.2
Addressing on IPX networks.

IPX uses sockets (similar to TCP/UDP ports) to direct messages to and from the correct upper-layer processes. In most cases, upper-layer functions are performed by the *NetWare Core Protocols (NCP)*, which provide network services at the session, presentation, and application layers. NCP is not part of NWLink, although Microsoft has implemented a NetWare client requester that implements the client side of NCP.

The IPX/SPX protocols offer high performance and—because node IDs need not be maintained manually—great ease of administration. Use of IPX/SPX, however, has been confined primarily to the NetWare environment.

In part, this has resulted from the proprietary nature of the protocols. Novell maintains control of the protocols, and IPX/SPX are not as accessible for public input or extension. Many network planners have developed a strong distaste for anything proprietary.

The primary reason, however, probably is the Internet, which functions quite well with TCP/IP. Although cracks have appeared, most notably the limitations on IPv4 address space, mechanisms are in place to enable TCP/IP to evolve on the Internet, and there has been no need to replace the Internet protocols. Now that the Internet is evolving into the fabled Information Superhighway, everyone needs TCP/IP connectivity and the Internet protocols seem to be here to stay.

TCP/IP

Microsoft has been including TCP/IP support in network products since LAN Manager. TCP/IP was Microsoft's choice as a routable protocol for use when the nonroutable NetBEUI was not functional. TCP/IP is available on Windows NT and on Windows 3.x and Windows 95 clients.

Table 7.2 summarizes the RFCs that Microsoft NT TCP/IP supports. Many are recognized from discussion in the foregoing chapters.

TABLE 7.2

RFCs Supported by Microsoft NT TCP/IP

RFC	Title
768	User Datagram Protocol (UDP)
783	Trivial File Transfer Protocol revision 2 (TFTP)
791	Internet Protocol (IP)
792	Internet Control Message Protocol (ICMP)
793	Transmission Control Protocol (TCP)
816	Fault Isolation and Recovery
826	Ethernet Address Resolution Protocol (ARP)
854	Telnet Protocol (TELNET)
862	Echo Protocol (ECHO)

RFC	Title
863	Discard Protocol (DISCARD)
864	Character Generator Protocol (CHARGEN)
865	Quote of the Day Protocol (QUOTE)
867	Daytime Protocol (DAYTIME)
894	Transmission of IP Datagrams over Ethernet
919	Broadcasting Internet Datagrams
922	Broadcasting Internet Datagrams in the Presence of Subnets
959	File Transfer Protocol (FTP)
1001, 1002	NetBIOS Service on a TCP/UDP Transport: Concepts, Methods, and Specifications
1034, 1035	Domain Name System
1042	Transmission of IP Datagrams over IEEE 802 Networks (SNAP)
1055	Transmission of IP Datagrams over Serial Lines: SLIP
1112	Host Extensions for IP Multicasting
1122	Requirements for Internet Host Communication Layers
1123	Requirements for Internet Host Application and Support
1134	Point-to-Point Protocol (PPP)
1144	Compressing TCP/IP Headers for Low-Speed Serial Links
1157	Simple Network Management Protocol (SNMP)
1179	Line Printer Daemon Protocol
1188	Transmission of IP Datagrams over FDDI
1191	Path MDU Discovery
1201	Transmitting IP Traffic over ARCNET Networks
1231	IEEE 802.5 Token Ring MIB
1332	PPP Internet Protocol Control Protocol (IPCP)
1334	PPP Authentication Protocols
1518	An Architecture for IP Address Allocation with CIDR

continues

RFCs Supported by Microsoft NT TCP/IP

RFC	Title
1519	Classless Inter-Domain Routing CIDR: An Address Assignment and Aggregation Strategy
1533	DHCP Options and BOOTP Vendor Extensions
1534	Interoperation between DHCP and BOOTP
1541	Dynamic Host Configuration Protocol (DHCP)
1542	Clarifications and Extensions for the Bootstrap Protocol (BOOTP)
1547	Requirements for an Internet Standard Point-to-Point Protocol (PPP)
1548	Point-to-Point Protocol (PPP)
1549	PPP in High-Level Data Link Control (HDLC) Framing
1552	PPP Internetwork Packet Exchange Control Protocol (IPXCP)
1553	Compressing IPX Headers over WAN Media
1570	PPP Link Control Protocol (LCP) Extensions
Draft	NetBIOS Frame Control Protocol (NBFCP)
Draft	PPP over ISDN
Draft	PPP over X.25
Draft	Compression Control Protocol

As implemented, Microsoft NT offers a solid implementation of the majority of core Internet protocols. Some notable omissions include the following:

- **Native support for SMTP.** Windows NT does not include an SMTP message transfer unit similar to the UNIX `sendmail` MTU.

- **Dynamic routing.** The new Multiprotocol Router supports RIP-1 only. Support for RIP-2 and OSPF are lacking, as is any strategy for routing to other autonomous systems via exterior gateway protocols. Third-party routers remain essential in many situations.

- **Network File Service (NFS).** Although not an Internet standard, NFS is used extensively in the TCP/IP networking community. NFS is available as an option from third-party vendors.

The remainder of this chapter examines some Microsoft TCP/IP features in greater detail.

Dynamic Host Configuration Protocol (DHCP)

Chapter 4, "The Internet Layer," takes a close look at IP addressing. Clearly, maintaining IP addresses in a changing network can pose a significant challenge. DHCP can help.

Very few hosts require fixed IP addresses. Routers and DNS servers are examples of hosts to which you should assign fixed IP addresses because those addresses frequently are entered into the configurations of hosts. But the garden variety host does not require a fixed IP address and can be assigned any valid IP address from the network address space.

When using DHCP, it is unnecessary to assign fixed IP addresses to the majority of hosts. DHCP enables administrators to specify groups of IP addresses, called scopes. When a host is configured to obtain its IP address from DHCP, it is automatically assigned an address from a DHCP scope.

DHCP even permits a network to support more hosts than the number of available addresses. If users require only infrequent TCP/IP protocol support, they can lease an IP address when they need it. When the host no longer needs to use the address, the address is returned to the address pool.

DHCP also enables administrators to specify numerous parameters that tune the operation of IP, TCP, and other protocols. Because DHCP is managed centrally, administrators can manage many characteristics of the hosts for which they are responsible without having to physically visit the hosts.

Chapter 10, "Managing DHCP," includes an examination of the details of DHCP.

Windows Internet Name Service (WINS)

Chapter 6, "The Process-Application Layer," explores naming services in general and DNS in particular. Clearly, a naming service makes it considerably easier for users to access network services. In the Microsoft TCP/IP environment, the standard naming service is WINS. Microsoft networks traditionally have used a naming system based on NetBIOS, and Microsoft

TCP/IP networks can continue to use NetBIOS names, as long as routers are not involved. However, NetBIOS does not maintain a central database of names. Instead, a computer seeking to enter the network makes its presence known by broadcasting messages on the network. If no computer challenges the name, the computer establishes itself on the network and announces itself. This mechanism works on a local network but fails on an internetwork because broadcast messages do not cross routers.

WINS provides a way to integrate NetBIOS with TCP/IP. Under WINS, NetBIOS computer configurations continue to specify names. No central management is required (or, if you prefer, available).

NetBIOS over TCP/IP provides a way to disseminate NetBIOS names throughout an internetwork. A WINS server must be supported on each network segment that requires NetBIOS name support. The WINS servers exchange information via directed host-to-host messages rather than broadcasts, enabling NetBIOS names to cross routers and be advertised on other network segments.

WINS is a Microsoft-only technology and cannot, unfortunately, work in conjunction with DNS. Therefore, a company cannot put itself on the Internet and use WINS to manage its local domain name space. To advertise host names on the Internet, a DNS name server still is required.

Consequently, WINS is only one of several name resolution methods supported. Others include the following:

- **LMHOSTS.** A static file-based naming convention that was used with LAN Manager. LMHOSTS files are still supported on WINS networks.

- **Hosts.** A static file-based naming convention for TCP/IP networks.

- **DNS.** The dynamic naming service used on the Internet. A Windows NT implementation of the DNS program `bind` is included with the Windows NT Resource Kit.

Windows NT host naming strategies are elaborate, and it takes three chapters to cover all the details. Chapter 11, "Host Naming in the Microsoft TCP/IP World," covers the theory. Then Chapter 12, "Managing WINS," discusses management of WINS and Chapter 13, "Managing the Microsoft DNS Server," covers DNS.

Windows NT Routing

In TCP/IP terminology, hosts equipped with two or more network adapters on different network segments are called multihomed hosts. Any multi-homed Windows NT computer can provide IP routing.

A new feature for Windows NT Server 4 is the Multiprotocol Router, which supports dynamic TCP/IP routing using RIP version 1.

NT also supports routing using static tables, which you manage by using the `route` utility. This approach offers the benefits of being efficient, producing little or no network overhead traffic. Networks of substantial scope can be routed using static tables.

Chapter 9, "Routing Basics," covers the fundamentals of Windows NT routing.

Chapter 18, "Routing and Remote Access Service," covers a free add-on product that significantly enhances Windows NT routing with more advanced routing protocols such as RIP version 2 and OSPF.

SNMP

Windows NT supports SNMP, including MIB II, as well as MIBs for LAN Manager, DHCP, and WINS. Chapter 15, "Managing TCP/IP with SNMP," includes a discussion of SNMP.

Enough Orientation, Already!

I promised you this chapter would be brief, with the simple goal of showing how the various pieces of Microsoft TCP/IP fit together. Without further ado, let's get down to work. Chapter 8, "Installing TCP/IP on Windows NT Computers," shows you everything you need to enable TCP/IP protocol support on a basic network. If you understand IP addressing, you will find that installing TCP/IP on NT is no big deal. So, let's get to work.

Chapter 8

INSTALLING TCP/IP ON WINDOWS NT COMPUTERS

If you have installed Windows NT, you already appreciate the general simplicity of the Windows NT installation process. That simplicity carries over to the procedures for installing TCP/IP. All procedures are performed from the graphic interface using the Network utility in the Control Panel.

This chapter examines the basics of installing and configuring TCP/IP on Windows NT computers, including some troubleshooting procedures. After this chapter covers the fundamentals, subsequent chapters examine more advanced topics, including implementing DHCP, WINS, internetworking, DNS, and SNMP.

Discussion assumes familiarity with Windows NT operations and does not delve into procedures that don't relate directly to TCP/IP.

Planning the Installation

Before you install TCP/IP, you must obtain information that defines the computer's TCP/IP configuration. The following list delineates the items you need to determine before you begin installing

- **Must network adapters be installed?** First you must install and configure the hardware. Then you must record the settings for each card in the computer, including the manufacturer and model as well as the card's settings, such as IRQ, DMA, and I/O memory address.

- **Will IP addresses be assigned manually or via DHCP?** With manual addressing you must know the IP address to be assigned for each network adapter that supports TCP/IP. This chapter assumes manual addressing. DHCP is discussed in Chapter 10, "Managing DHCP."

- **What are the addresses of any default IP gateways the computer uses?** This chapter assumes a single network without routing.

- **How will the computer obtain NetBIOS host names?** This chapter assumes NetBIOS names are automatically supported on local segments. NetBIOS names for routed segments can come from WINS or from LMHOSTS files, both of which are discussed in Chapter 12, "Managing WINS."

- **Will the computer obtain TCP/IP host names from DNS?** If so, you need to know the IP address of the DNS server. See Chapter 13, "Managing the Microsoft DNS Server," for more information about running a domain name service. This chapter assumes DNS naming is not active.

- **Will the computer be managed by SNMP?** You need to determine the SNMP community names, traps, and the IP addresses of SNMP management hosts (see Chapter 15, "Managing TCP/IP with SNMP").

On a basic single-segment network, the only essential information is the IP address and subnet mask to be assigned to the computer.

All the required files are included on the Windows NT Workstation and Windows NT Server distribution disks or CD-ROM. You need to have the appropriate disks on hand.

WARNING

When selecting your networking hardware, you are highly advised to choose hardware that appears in the Windows NT Hardware Compatibility List (HCL). When moving from Windows NT 3.51 to 4, I found that some network features did not work. The problem was traced to the generic NE2000-compatible adapters I had been using successfully under NT 3.51. Although NT 4 includes a Novell NE2000 Compatible Adapter driver, evidently the adapter hardware wasn't up to specs for NT version 4. When I changed to approved hardware, the problems cleared up.

Installing and Reconfiguring TCP/IP

If this is a first-time installation, you need to install the adapter hardware and software. After you install the network adapter card, record its settings. Also, if you add the computer to a Windows NT Server domain, you need to create the appropriate computer and user accounts in the domain before login attempts can be successful. Consult *Inside Windows NT Server 4* for detailed information about setting up computer and user accounts.

TCP/IP installation and configuration is performed by using the Network utility, which is one of the tools in the Control Panel. Because this utility is so important in configuring TCP/IP on Windows NT, let's take the time to examine it in detail.

Figure 8.1 shows the Network applet, which displays the Identification tab when it is first started. Take the time to examine each of the tabs, following the order in which you will use the tabs to configure networking.

Figure 8.1

The Network applet in the Control Panel is used to configure all network connectivity settings.

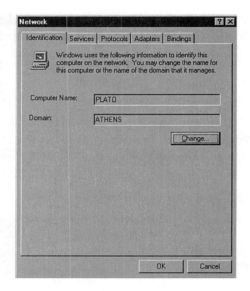

Note

You must restart the computer to activate any changes made to the network configuration in the Network applet.

The Adapters Tab

The Adapters tab is used to add, remove, and configure any network interface devices on the computer. Although only one adapter appears in Figure 8.2, a computer can be equipped with multiple adapters if required. A computer that operates as an IP router, for example, must be configured with at least two adapters.

Note

Install and configure the network card hardware before you start NT. The vast majority of network cards now being made are configured using a software utility. Because NT prevents programs from directly manipulating hardware, the configuration utilities must usually be executed under DOS. Therefore, you cannot change the settings after NT is started. Unfortunately, we must wait for a future version of NT to get support for Plug and Play configuration.

FIGURE 8.2

The Adapters tab.

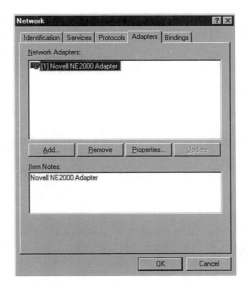

Adding a Network Adapter

To add an adapter:

1. Click **Add** in the Adapters tab to open the Select Network Adapter dialog box.

2. Select an adapter in the Network Adapter list and choose **OK**.

   or

   If your adapter is not listed and you have a driver diskette provided by the vendor for the adapter, choose **Have Disk** and follow the prompts to install the drivers.

3. If an adapter is already installed that uses the same driver you are installing, a Setup Message box prompts you A network card of this type is already installed in the system. Do you want to continue? Choose **OK** to confirm addition of the second adapter.

4. Next, a Network Card Setup dialog box is provided in which you specify the hardware settings for the adapter you are installing. NT does not detect these settings for you and cannot confirm that the settings you enter are correct. Nor can NT confirm that the settings you enter do not conflict with other devices in the computer.

5. If your computer is equipped with more than one expansion bus (ISA and PCI, for example), an Adapter Bus Location dialog box prompts you to specify the bus in which the adapter is installed. First select a bus type. Then, if the computer has more than one bus of that type, select a bus number.

6. When prompted, supply the path where Setup can locate the driver files. For an Intel x86 computer, the files would be located in the \I386 directory on the installation medium, for example, D:\I386.

7. Restart the computer to activate the adapter drivers.

If you are installing PCI network adapters, the installation details will probably differ from the preceding generic procedure described. For one thing, PCI adapters are typically configured automatically, and there is no need to specify hardware settings. Also, in many cases, the driver setup routines have unique features. The setup software for Intel EtherExpress Pro/100B adapters, for example, detects and displays all installed adapters, permitting you to select which hardware adapter you want to configure. Consult the product documentation for your hardware for the details.

Changing Properties for a Network Adapter

To change the settings for an installed adapter:

1. Select the adapter in the Network Adapters list.

2. Choose **Properties** to open a Network Card Setup dialog box in which you can alter the hardware settings for the adapter.

3. Restart the computer to complete the change.

Removing a Network Adapter

To remove an adapter, select the adapter and choose **Remove**. Restart the computer to complete the change. Before removing an adapter, be sure that you will not be disrupting any vital network communication.

The Protocols Tab

Recall from Chapter 7, "Introducing Microsoft TCP/IP," that the Windows NT architecture permits multiple protocols to be installed on the same computer. The Protocols tab is used to install, remove, and configure network protocols, and is operated much like the Adapters tab. Figure 8.3 shows the Protocols tab after TCP/IP has been installed.

FIGURE 8.3

The Protocols tab.

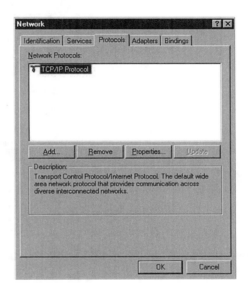

Installing TCP/IP Protocols

To install TCP/IP protocol support:

1. Click **Add** in the Protocols tab to open the Select Network Protocol dialog box.

2. Select **TCP/IP Protocol** in the Network Protocol list and choose **OK**.

3. The next prompt asks, Do you wish to use DHCP? If this computer will obtain its IP address from DHCP, choose **Yes**. If this computer will be configured with a static IP address, choose **No**.

4. When prompted, supply the path where Setup can locate the driver files.

5. Choose **Close** to exit the Network applet. After some fiddling with the configuration, Setup will show you a Microsoft TCP/IP Properties dialog box that will, at first, be blank. Figure 8.4 shows the dialog box after address information has been entered.

FIGURE 8.4

Specifying addresses for TCP/IP protocols.

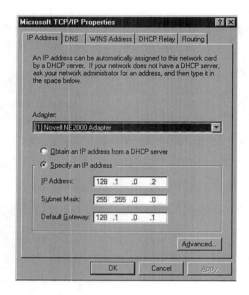

6. If more than one adapter has been installed, select the adapter to be configured in the Adapter list.

7. If this computer will obtain its address configuration from DHCP, click the **Obtain an IP address from a DHCP server** radio button.

8. If this computer will be configured with static addresses, click the **Specify and IP address** radio button and complete the following fields:

   - **IP Address** (Required.)

   - **Subnet Mask** (Required. Setup will suggest the default subnet mask appropriate for the IP address you enter.)

   - **Default Gateway** (Optional.)

 NOTE

Later chapters will examine settings that are reached via the Advanced button.

9. Choose **OK** and restart the computer to activate the settings.

NOTE

Besides installing the TCP/IP protocol stack, adding TCP/IP Protocol also installs a group of TCP/IP utilities such as FTP, TFTP, ARP, and Telnet.

Because duplicate IP addresses can cause havoc on the network, Microsoft TCP/IP clients automatically detect duplicate addresses. If you attempt to add a client to the network using an IP address that is already present on the network, you will receive an error and TCP/IP will be disabled on the client you are adding. The client that is currently using the IP address also receives an error message, although it continues to function.

Reconfiguring TCP/IP Protocol Settings

To reconfigure TCP/IP settings:

1. Select **TCP/IP Protocol** in the Protocols tab of the Networks applet.

2. Choose **Properties** to open the Microsoft TCP/IP Protocols dialog box.

3. Make any required changes, and choose **OK**.

4. Restart the computer to activate the changes.

Removing TCP/IP Protocols

To remove TCP/IP protocols, select **TCP/IP Protocol** in the Protocols tab of the Networks applet and choose **Remove**. Restart the computer to activate the changes. Before removing a protocol, ensure that doing so will not disrupt any vital network communication.

The Identification Tab

The Identification tab (refer to Figure 8.1) contains two vital bits of information that must be established before the computer can successfully log on to a Windows NT domain.

The Computer Name field declares the NetBIOS name of the computer. The NetBIOS name is the native name of the computer on the Windows NT network and is the name used to advertise the computer, advertise any shares the computer might offer, and enable the computer to log on to a network domain.

The Domain field declares the domain to which this computer attempts to connect when it logs on to the network.

The Change button opens the Identification Changes dialog box shown in Figure 8.5. You can change the computer name and domain, but there are many caveats:

- A Windows NT computer cannot log on to a domain unless a computer account has been created in the domain for that specific computer. If you change the computer name, the computer can no longer log on in the domain until a new computer account has been created.

- Changing the name of a computer disrupts any sharing links that have been established with the computer. If you change a computer name, clients will no longer be able to use connections that have been established to shared directories or printers on that server.

- If you change the domain name of a primary domain controller (PDC), you establish the computer as the PDC of a new domain. This leaves the original domain without a PDC.

- If you want to change the domain name of a backup domain controller (BDC), you must first change the domain name for the PDC and restart the PDC. Then, use the Identification tab to change the domain for the BDC. This works only if the PDC and BDC initially belong to the same domain and only if a PDC has not been established for the original domain.

- Except as described in the previous point, you cannot change the domain name of a BDC without installing Windows NT Server on the computer.

NOTE

You must restart a computer to put any computer or domain name changes into effect.

FIGURE 8.5

Changing a computer name or domain name.

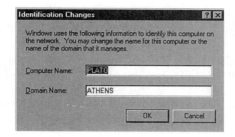

The Bindings Tab

A relationship that establishes communication between two network drivers is a *binding*. When TCP/IP is configured to communicate with a specific network adapter, a binding is established between TCP/IP and that adapter.

Bindings are reviewed and managed in the Bindings tab of the Networks applet, shown in Figure 8.6. The bindings that are displayed are determined by the Show Bindings for field, which can have the following values: all services, all protocols, or all adapters.

FIGURE 8.6

Displaying bindings for all services. In this case, the bindings under the Server service have been expanded.

To prepare this figure, I installed all available transport protocols in the following order: NetBEUI, TCP/IP, and NWLink. The order in which the protocols are installed determines their initial positions in the Bindings list.

I have expanded the entries fully under the Server service heading. In the first entry, you can see that the Server service is bound to the NetBEUI Protocol, which in turn is bound to the [1]Novell NE2000 Adapter. The Server service is also bound to the WINS Client(TCP/IP) protocol, which is bound to the [1]Novell NE2000 Adapter.

The order in which protocols appear is important because it determines the order in which NT will consult the available protocols to search for information on the network. Of particular significance is the sequence in which browsers will be consulted. Suppose that your network consists of a mix of configurations—some computers are configured with NetBEUI, some with TCP/IP, and some with both—in which case separate browser environments are maintained in the NetBEUI and TCP/IP environments. If you are working on a computer configured with both NetBEUI and TCP/IP, the bindings order determines whether your attempts to browse the network will consult NetBEUI or TCP/IP browsers first. If the protocol you use most frequently is raised to the top of the bindings list, your average connection time will decrease. If you use both TCP/IP and NetBEUI, however, but access TCP/IP services infrequently, move NetBEUI to the top of the list. Improperly adjusted bindings orders can degrade performance. In extreme cases, if the bindings order is configured incorrectly, your browsing attempts might time out before an appropriate browser is located.

If TCP/IP is the primary protocol on your network, you probably want tasks such as name resolution to be performed via TCP/IP in preference to NetBEUI or NWLink. To raise the binding priority for TCP/IP, open the bindings under the Workstation service and select a protocol. Then click **Move Up** or **Move Down** to adjust the position of the protocol in the bindings order.

NOTE

Why would you want to maintain multiple protocols on a network? There aren't a lot of good reasons. TCP/IP client software is available for any workstation operating system you could deploy on your network, and multiple protocol stacks eat up memory, particularly on MS-DOS/Windows 3.x computers. If you are going to the trouble of deploying TCP/IP on your network, you should do a thorough job of it and purge other protocols whenever possible.

You can use the Bindings tab to disable bindings that are not currently required. If, for example, you have installed multiple network adapter cards but are not using one of them at present, you can reduce memory requirements by disabling the unused adapter. Select the adapter entry and choose **Disable**. Use the **Enable** button to enable a disabled adapter. In Figure 8.7 the NWLink protocol has been disabled.

FIGURE 8.7

In this bindings list, the NWLink protocol has been disabled.

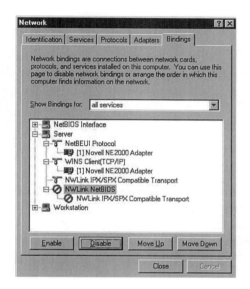

The Services Tab

Network services extend the capability of Windows NT in a variety of ways. In later chapters, you will use the Services tab (see Figure 8.8) to add and manage a variety of services, including DHCP, WINS, and the Internet Information Server. Services are managed much like protocols, and the procedures will be covered in the appropriate chapters.

Testing the TCP/IP Configuration

Installing the TCP/IP connectivity utilities adds several useful troubleshooting tools to the computer. Some, such as ARP, are discussed in Chapter 16, which examines troubleshooting. Chapter 6, "The Process-Application Layer," sufficiently examines FTP and Telnet.

Figure 8.8

The Services tab.

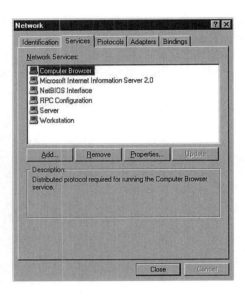

Two of the utilities, `ping` and `ipconfig`, are useful for checking out the network connections of TCP/IP hosts. They are illustrated in the context of the simple network shown in Figure 8.9, consisting of two hosts with IP addresses 128.1.0.1 and 128.1.0.2.

Figure 8.9

An example of a TCP/IP network.

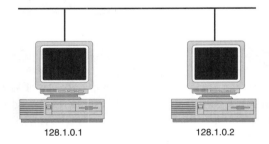

Using *ping*

`ping` is used to verify connections between hosts by sending ICMP echo packets to the specified IP address. `ping` waits up to one second for each packet it sends and reports the numbers of packets sent and received. By default, `ping` sends four echo packets that consist of 32 bytes of data. (The Microsoft documentation indicates that `ping` defaults to 64-byte packets, but the example seems to indicate an actual size of 32 bytes.)

Figure 8.10 illustrates the results of successfully and unsuccessfully pinging a host. When a host does not respond, `ping` displays the message `Request timed out`.

FIGURE 8.10

The results of successfully and unsuccessfully pinging an IP address.

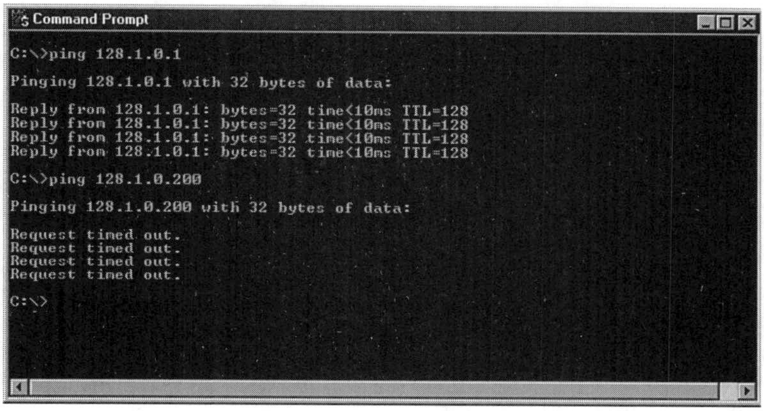

```
Command Prompt                                              _ □ ×

C:\>ping 128.1.0.1

Pinging 128.1.0.1 with 32 bytes of data:

Reply from 128.1.0.1: bytes=32 time<10ms TTL=128
Reply from 128.1.0.1: bytes=32 time<10ms TTL=128
Reply from 128.1.0.1: bytes=32 time<10ms TTL=128
Reply from 128.1.0.1: bytes=32 time<10ms TTL=128

C:\>ping 128.1.0.200

Pinging 128.1.0.200 with 32 bytes of data:

Request timed out.
Request timed out.
Request timed out.
Request timed out.

C:\>
```

During Chapter 4's examination of IP addresses, you encountered a special address, called the *loopback address*, which refers to any valid address that has a netid of 127. The network adapter reflects back any packet sent to the loopback address without letting it enter the network. Pinging the loopback address tests the configuration of the local TCP/IP interface. Figure 8.11 shows an example of pinging the loopback address.

FIGURE 8.11

Pinging the loopback address.

```
Command Prompt                                              _ □ ×

C:\>ping 127.0.0.1

Pinging 127.0.0.1 with 32 bytes of data:

Reply from 127.0.0.1: bytes=32 time=10ms TTL=128
Reply from 127.0.0.1: bytes=32 time<10ms TTL=128
Reply from 127.0.0.1: bytes=32 time<10ms TTL=128
Reply from 127.0.0.1: bytes=32 time<10ms TTL=128

C:\>
```

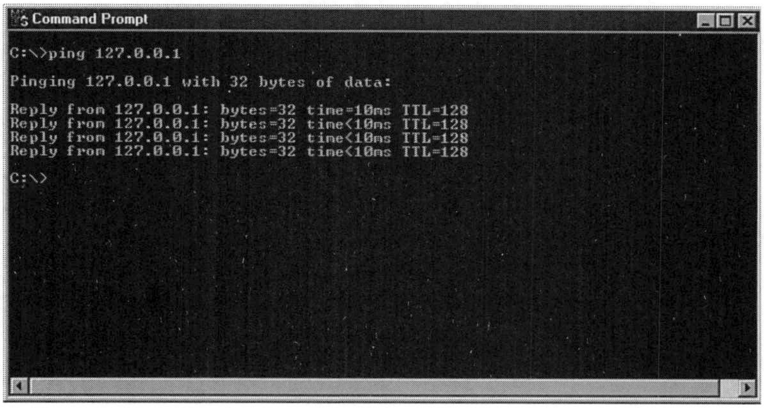

When you add a TCP/IP computer to the network, using ping to test it is a good idea.

1. First, ping the loopback address 127.0.0.1.

2. Then, ping the host's own IP address.

3. Finally, ping other hosts on the network, particularly servers to which the host will connect.

ping can accept IP addresses or DNS host names. If you can ping a host by its IP address but not by its host name, a name resolution problem exists. ping does not recognize NetBIOS host names, however.

Table 8.1 lists options that can be used with ping. The syntax of the ping command is as follows (where square brackets enclose optional parameters):

```
ping [-a][-f][-i ttl][-j host-list][-k host-list][-l length][-n count][-r count]
     [-s count] [-t][-v tos][-w timeout] hosts
```

TABLE 8.1

ping Options

Option	Function
hosts	Specifies one or more hosts to ping.
-a	Addresses should be resolved to hostnames.
-f	Sets the Do Not Fragment flag in the packet so that it will not be fragmented by routers on an internet.
-i ttl	Sets the Time to Live field to the value *ttl*.
-j host-list	Specifies a list of hosts through which the packet is to be routed. Hosts might be separated by routers. The maximum number of hosts is 9.
-k host-list	Specifies a list of hosts through which the packet is to be routed. Hosts *might not* be separated by routers. The maximum number of hosts is 9.
-l length	The *length* parameter specifies the number of data bytes in the echo packets. Maximum is 8192.

Option	Function
-n *count*	The *count* parameter specifies the number of packets to be sent. Default is 4.
-r *count*	Records the route of the outgoing and returning packet in the Record Route field. The *count* parameter specifies a minimum of 1 and a maximum of 9 hosts.
-s *count*	Instructs ping to report time stamps for the number of hops specified by *count*.
-t	Pings the host until interrupted.
-v *tos*	Sets the value of the Type of Service field to *tos*.
-w *timeout*	Specifies a timeout interval in milliseconds.

Using *ipconfig*

The ipconfig utility displays TCP/IP configuration settings for a host. Figure 8.12 illustrates the output from the command ipconfig /all, which displays complete details about a host's TCP/IP configuration. This utility is particularly useful when the host obtains address information dynamically from DHCP or a host name from WINS. Consequently, Chapters 10 and 11 revisit ipconfig.

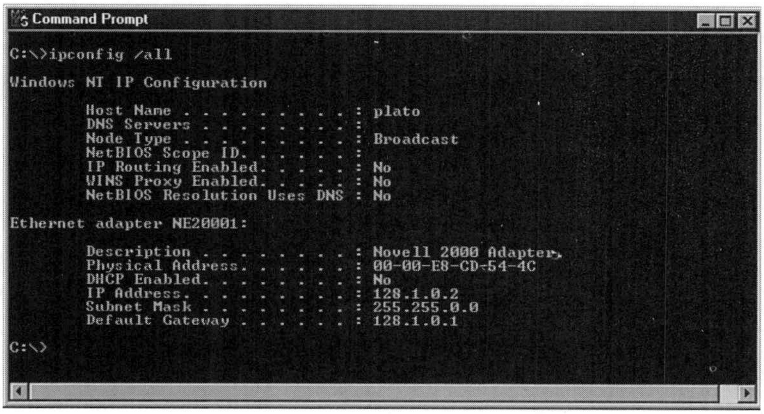

FIGURE 8.12

The ipconfig /all *command displays details about a host's TCP/IP configuration.*

```
Command Prompt

C:\>ipconfig /all

Windows NT IP Configuration

        Host Name . . . . . . . . . : plato
        DNS Servers . . . . . . . . :
        Node Type . . . . . . . . . : Broadcast
        NetBIOS Scope ID. . . . . . :
        IP Routing Enabled. . . . . : No
        WINS Proxy Enabled. . . . . : No
        NetBIOS Resolution Uses DNS : No

Ethernet adapter NE20001:

        Description . . . . . . . . : Novell 2000 Adapter
        Physical Address. . . . . . : 00-00-E8-CD-54-4C
        DHCP Enabled. . . . . . . . : No
        IP Address. . . . . . . . . : 128.1.0.2
        Subnet Mask . . . . . . . . : 255.255.0.0
        Default Gateway . . . . . . : 128.1.0.1

C:\>
```

TABLE 8.2

ipconfig **Options**

Option	Function
/all	Specifies display of all data. Without this option, ipconfig displays only the IP address, subnet mask, and default gateway values for each network card.
renew [*adapter*]	On systems that run the DHCP Client service, this option renews DHCP configuration parameters. To specify a specific adapter, use the optional *adapter* parameter. For adapter, specify the name that appears when **ipconfig** is entered without parameters.
release [*adapter*]	On systems running the DHCP Client service, this option releases the DHCP configuration and disables TCP/IP on the host. To specify a specific adapter, use the optional *adapter* parameter. For adapter, specify the name that appears when **ipconfig** is entered without parameters.

NOTE

In place of ipconfig, Windows 95 substitutes a GUI utility named WINIPCFG. (Don't ask me why Microsoft didn't port WINIPCFG to NT 4 with the rest of the Windows 95 interface!) To run WINIPCFG, open the Start menu, select the Run command, and enter **WINIPCFG** in the Open field of the Run dialog box.

Microsoft TCP/IP Properties Overview

You have already examined some of the TCP/IP protocol properties, such as IP addresses and subnet masks. And you will examine others in later chapters. But it would be a good idea at this time to briefly flip through the options.

To access the Microsoft TCP/IP Properties, start the Network applet, select the **Protocols tab**, select **TCP/IP Protocol** in the Network Protocols list, and choose **Properties**.

IP Address Properties

The first tab you see is IP Address, shown in Figure 8.13. The entries on this tab are as follows:

- **Adapter.** On multihomed hosts, this field enables you to select the interface that is currently being configured.

- **Obtain an IP address from DHCP server.** This radio button enables this host as a DHCP client. Chapter 10 discusses DHCP.

- **Specify an IP address.** This radio button enables manual addressing and activates the three address fields.

- **IP Address.** If manual addressing is active, the host IP address must be specified in this field.

- **Subnet Mask.** If manual addressing is active, the network subnet mask must be specified in this field. All hosts attached to the same IP network segment must be configured with the same subnet mask.

- **Default Gateway.** This field is optional and specifies a default router address. See Chapter 9 for more about configuring default gateways.

FIGURE 8.13

TCP/IP host IP address properties.

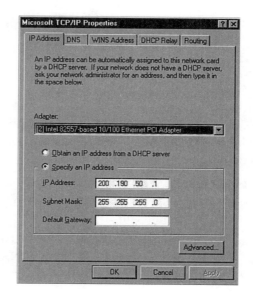

DNS Properties

The DNS tab is shown in Figure 8.14. You only need to be concerned with this tab if your network uses DNS to resolve host names. All the fields in this tab are examined in Chapter 13.

FIGURE 8.14
TCP/IP host DNS properties.

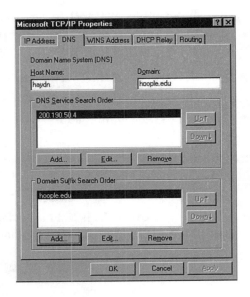

WINS Address Properties

The WINS Address tab (see Figure 8.15) is really a general-purpose tab for configuring name resolution options. Most of the fields will be discussed in Chapter 12, when WINS is examined in detail, but let's review them here and look at some specialized options.

- **Primary WINS Server.** WINS servers are identified by their IP addresses. To enable a host as a WINS client, enter the IP address of a WINS server in this field.

- **Secondary WINS Server.** Any network that uses WINS should be configured with at least two WINS servers. You can specify the IP address of a fallback WINS server in this field.

- **Enable DNS for Windows Resolution.** If you check this box, DNS becomes the host's preferred means of resolving host names.

- **Ena̲ble LMHOSTS Lookup.** If you check this box, the host will consult LMHOSTS files if other resources cannot resolve a name.

- **I̲mport LMHOSTS.** If you have already created an LMHOSTS file that is correct for this network, you can use this button to open a browse box where the file can be selected for import. The default location for the LMHOSTS file is `C:\winnt\system32\drivers\etc`.

- **Scope I̲D.** This field is usually left blank. If desired, you can enter a scope name in this box.

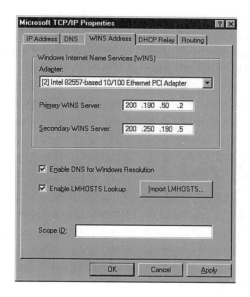

FIGURE 8.15
TCP/IP name resolution properties.

Scope IDs

Scope IDs are seldom used. Scope IDs establish groups of computers that can communicate, and only hosts that have the same scope ID can communicate. By default, the Scope I̲D field is left blank, and all hosts with a blank scope ID can communicate.

In rare instances, it might be desirable to establish computers that are isolated from other hosts on the network. Suppose you want to establish a FINANCE group that will not communicate with any other hosts. To establish the group, you could enter **FINANCE**, or some other scope name, in the Scope I̲D field for each host in the group.

One catch with scope IDs is that a host can have but one scope ID. In the previous example, the FINANCE group would be completely isolated from other hosts on the network. It could not send mail or share files with outside users.

Another catch with scope IDs is that they are not secure. The scope ID is displayed in clear text and travels through the network without encryption. Therefore, scope IDs don't buy any guarantees of privacy.

I'm sure that if I tell you there is no reason to use scope IDs, a dozen readers will write giving me a dozen tasks that can only be performed with scope IDs. So I won't tell you that, and there's no need to write. But, because the primary goal of scope IDs seems to be to insulate some users from others, it seems that other Windows NT Server security tools might be more effective. File security, for example, prevents users from abusing each other's resources without preventing those users from exchanging email. And besides that, Microsoft recommends that whenever possible you avoid using scope IDs. 'Nuff said!

DHCP Relay

The DHCP Relay tab is used to configure routers to enable them to forward DHCP traffic. You can read about the options on this tab in Chapter 10 when DHCP is examined.

Routing

The Routing tab contains one option, the Enable IP Forwarding check box. Checking this box enables a multihomed host to function as a router. You can read all about NT routing in Chapter 9.

NOTE

Registry parameters enable administrators to fine-tune many operational characteristics of Microsoft TCP/IP and NBT.

It's Installed. Now What?

Now you know the basics of installing TCP/IP and testing a host's TCP/IP configuration. As you can see, most of the work is in the preparation, planning the addressing and routing scheme for your network. After that is done, it is a relatively simple matter to put TCP/IP in place. That takes care of the basics, so it's time to move on to more involved topics. In the next chapter, you take up the topic of internetworks and see how Windows NT computers can be configured as routers.

Chapter 9

ROUTING BASICS

Chapter 4, "The Internet Layer," pays considerable attention to routing, and by now, you should have a good grasp of basic routing concepts, including how IP delivers datagrams through an internetwork. You have yet to learn how Windows NT computers can be configured as routers and how to configure a large, routed network. This chapter examines configuration of Windows NT routers in simple and complex internetworks.

Rules of Routing

Before you examine the procedures for configuring routers, take a moment to review some basic rules of routing.

When subnetting is not in effect, two hosts attached to the same network segment can communicate directly only if they have matching netids. In Figure 9.1, hosts A and B can communicate directly. However, neither A nor B can communicate with C, because they have different netids (assuming a subnet mask of at least 255.255.255.0).

FIGURE 9.1

Host communication on a local network.

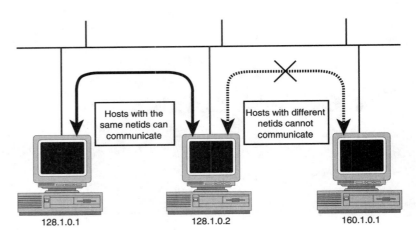

When subnetting is in effect, two hosts attached to the same network segment can communicate only if both their netids and subnetids match. If either the netids or the subnetids differ, a router must be employed. In Figure 9.2, hosts A and B can communicate directly. C has the same netid as A and B, but has a different subnet ID. Therefore, C cannot communicate directly with A or B.

Finally, all hosts that occupy different networks must communicate through a router.

NOTE

As Figures 9.1 and 9.2 illustrate, hosts on the same network segment do not have to share common network IDs. Even though these hosts share a common cable, an IP router is required to enable them to communicate.

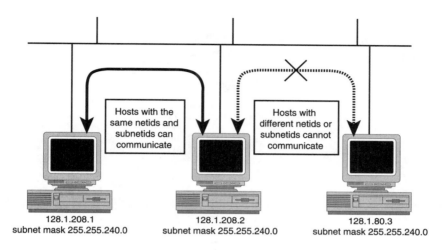

128.1.208.1
subnet mask 255.255.240.0

128.1.208.2
subnet mask 255.255.240.0

128.1.80.3
subnet mask 255.255.240.0

FIGURE 9.2
Host communication with subnetting.

Routing with Two Networks

Figure 9.3 illustrates a basic Internet with two networks: 128.1.0.0 and 128.2.0.0. The common element that connects the two networks is Windows NT host A, which is equipped with a network adapter on each of the two networks. A host that connects to two or more networks is called a *multihomed* host. To turn a multihomed Windows NT computer into an IP router, the IP Routing feature must be turned on.

After routing is activated on a multihomed Windows NT computer, the computer forwards IP datagrams from one of its connected networks to another connected network. Here is an example of what happens:

1. Host 1 needs to send a datagram to host 2, which is not on the local network. Host 1 does not know how to reach 2, and therefore sends the frame to its default gateway, 128.1.0.1.

2. Router A receives the frame on interface 128.1.0.1. The frame is identified by the physical address of A, but the destination IP address is 128.2.0.2. Router A knows that it is not the ultimate destination and proceeds to forward the datagram.

FIGURE 9.3
Routing between adjacent networks.

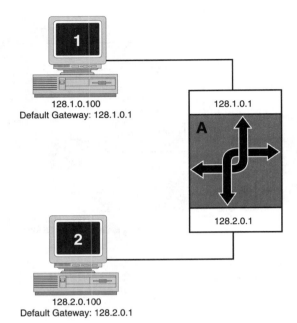

3. Router A consults its routing table and determines that it has a route to network 128.2.0.0.

4. Router A resends the datagram from its interface 128.2.0.1. The frame is addressed with the physical address and the IP address of host 2.

5. Host 2 receives the frame and recovers the datagram.

Two things must be done to enable this simple routing system to work:

■ A router (A in the example) must be installed between the networks, configured with network adapters on each network, and have its routing function enabled.

■ Other hosts must be configured with a default gateway.

Those tasks are performed in the following sections.

Configuring a Windows NT Router

An IP router is a multihomed host that has its routing function turned on. Three steps are involved in setting up a Windows NT router:

1. Install a second network adapter and configure it for TCP/IP.

2. Activate routing.

3. Test the routing configuration.

The following discussion adds a second adapter to router A in Figure 9.3.

Adding a Second Network Adapter

After installing the network adapter hardware, you need to add it to the Windows NT configuration. Here is the generic procedure, although some details might differ depending on the brand and model of the network adapter:

1. Start the Network applet in the Control Panel.

2. In the Adapters tab, choose **Add**.

3. In the Select Network Adapter dialog box, select an adapter from the list in the Network Adapter box. (Or choose **Have Disk** to install a nonlisted card.) Choose **Continue** after specifying a card.

4. If the new adapter is the same type as the one already installed, you will see a Setup Message box that states A network card of this type is already installed in the system. Do you want to continue?. Choose **OK** to confirm your selection.

5. Specify the card settings in the Network Card Setup dialog box and choose **OK**.

6. If the computer has more than one expansion bus, specify the bus that contains the adapter and choose **OK**.

7. If files must be copied, specify the source path. When the adapter installation is complete, the Adapters tab now shows two adapters, as in Figure 9.4. If you have installed more than one adapter of a given type, the adapters are numbered. In the figure, the new adapter is identified as adapter [2].

FIGURE 9.4

The Adapters tab after adding a second network adapter.

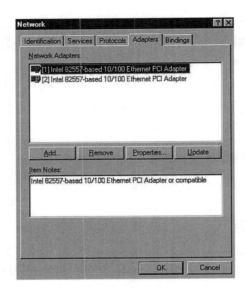

9. Choose **Close** to exit the Network applet.

10. After bindings are configured, the Microsoft TCP/IP Properties dialog box is presented.

11. The new adapter must be configured. Select it in the Adapter list. Then specify the IP address, subnet mask, and default gateway. Figure 9.5 shows the address settings for the second adapter.

12. Review the address settings for each adapter in the computer by selecting each entry in the Adapter list. In most cases, you should specify a default gateway for each adapter. Figure 9.6 shows the address settings for the first adapter.

13. Choose **OK** to close the TCP/IP Properties window, and restart the computer to activate the changes.

NOTE

If the network is simple and this router is directly attached to all network segments, a default gateway is not required. For that reason, no default gateway addresses were entered in this example.

If any network segments are remote, however, you should specify a default gateway. Although you can specify a default gateway for each adapter in the computer, only one default gateway will be added to the routing table. To avoid route confusion, you should specify a default gateway address for only one adapter in the computer.

FIGURE 9.5

Configuration of adapter [2] in the example gateway.

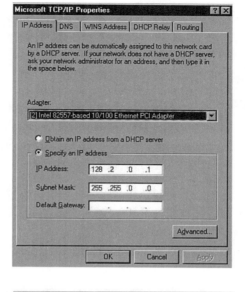

FIGURE 9.6

Configuration of adapter [1] in the example gateway.

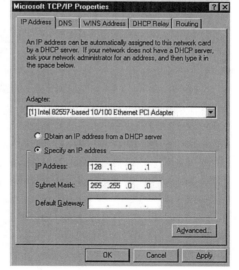

Enabling Routing

After at least two network adapters have been installed, enable routing support as follows:

1. Open the Networks applet.

2. Select the **Protocols** tab.

3. Select **TCP/IP Protocol** and choose **Properties.**

4. Select the **Routing tab**, shown in Figure 9.7. Check the **Enable IP Forwarding** check box.

5. Choose **OK**. Then close the Networks applet and restart the computer to activate the change.

NOTE

Actually, routing is enabled by default in a multihomed computer, but I wanted to show you the procedure so you could check your settings and make changes when needed.

FIGURE 9.7

Enabling routing for a multihomed host.

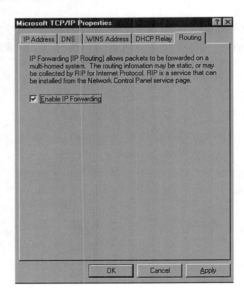

Testing the Routing Configuration

After routing is enabled, it is valuable to test things out using `ping`. When pinging through routers, the `-r` parameter can be handy. This parameter configures `ping` to report the route through which the test packets are directed. Figure 9.8 shows an example in which host 2 in Figure 9.3 pings host 1. Notice that `ping` reports a route via router 128.1.0.1.

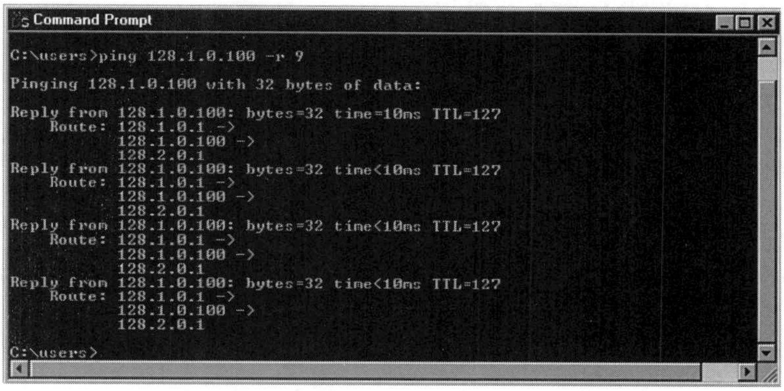

FIGURE 9.8

Pinging through a router using the `-r` parameter.

```
 Command Prompt                                               _ □ X

C:\users>ping 128.1.0.100 -r 9

Pinging 128.1.0.100 with 32 bytes of data:

Reply from 128.1.0.100: bytes=32 time=10ms TTL=127
    Route: 128.1.0.1 ->
           128.1.0.100 ->
           128.2.0.1
Reply from 128.1.0.100: bytes=32 time<10ms TTL=127
    Route: 128.1.0.1 ->
           128.1.0.100 ->
           128.2.0.1
Reply from 128.1.0.100: bytes=32 time<10ms TTL=127
    Route: 128.1.0.1 ->
           128.1.0.100 ->
           128.2.0.1
Reply from 128.1.0.100: bytes=32 time<10ms TTL=127
    Route: 128.1.0.1 ->
           128.1.0.100 ->
           128.2.0.1

C:\users>
```

Adding Default Gateways to Hosts

The TCP/IP Configuration dialog box also serves to configure default gateway addresses on Windows NT hosts. A default gateway must be configured for any host that must communicate with hosts which do not reside on the same subnet.

To configure a default router for a Windows NT computer:

1. Open the **Protocols** tab in the Network applet.

2. Select **TCP/IP Protocol** and choose **Properties.**

3. In the Microsoft TCP/IP Properties dialog box select the **IP Address** tab.

4. Specify the IP address of the default gateway in the **Default Gateway** field.

6. Choose **OK**.

7. Exit the Network applet and restart the computer.

It is possible to configure more than one default gateway for a host. To see how and why you might add more than one default gateway to the host configuration, see the section "Routing with Multiple Default Gateways" near the end of this chapter.

Configuring Default Gateways on Internets with Three Networks

Figure 9.9 illustrates an internet that consists of three networks connected by two gateways. On this network, all required routing can be performed using default gateways. Arrows on the figure illustrate the paths that are followed when datagrams are routed from host 1 to host 2 and from host 1 to host 3.

FIGURE 9.9

Routing in an internet with three networks and two routers.

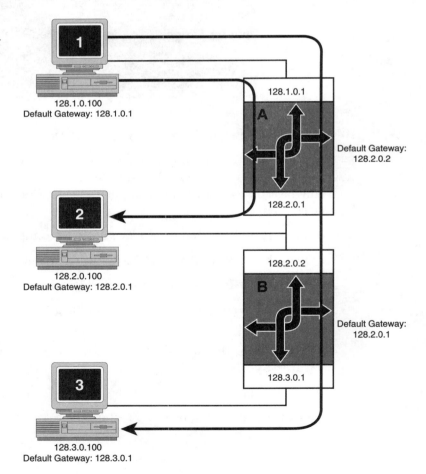

128.1.0.100
Default Gateway: 128.1.0.1

128.1.0.1

A

Default Gateway:
128.2.0.2

128.2.0.1

128.2.0.100
Default Gateway: 128.2.0.1

128.2.0.2

B

Default Gateway:
128.2.0.1

128.3.0.1

128.3.0.100
Default Gateway: 128.3.0.1

Consider the behavior of router A when it receives a datagram to be delivered from host 1 to host 2. Router A has direct knowledge of network 128.2.0.0, on which host 2 resides, and uses that knowledge to address the datagram to host 2 and route it to network 128.2.0.0.

Now consider what happens when host 1 needs to send a datagram to host 3. Router A examines the destination IP address and determines that 128.3.0.100 does not reside on either of the subnets to which A is connected. Therefore, A uses its default gateway and routes the datagram to 128.2.0.2 on router B. Router B can deliver the datagram to network 128.3.0.0.

A mirror of this process occurs when 3 sends a datagram to 1. Host 3 sends the datagram to its default gateway, 128.3.0.1 on B. B sends the datagram to its default gateway, 128.2.0.1 on A, and A can deliver the datagram.

Finally, the case of routing datagrams from host 2 must be examined. When 2 sends a datagram to 1, 2 sends the datagram to its default gateway on A, and A can deliver the datagram.

The route to 3 is a bit more indirect (see Figure 9.10). Host 2 sends to its default gateway on A. A is not aware of the network 128.3.0.0 and sends the datagram to its default gateway on B, from which the datagram can be delivered. Therefore, routing from 2 to 3 requires an extra hop.

NOTE

The route taken from 2 to 3 in Figure 9.10 is clearly not the most efficient route possible, but it is the best you can do if 2 routes by default route only. Later in this chapter, you will learn how to add static routes to a host's routing table. Clearly, efficiency could be improved if you added a static route to host 2's routing table, instructing it to send route datagrams destined for network 128.3.0.0 through 128.2.0.2. The question is, should you use static routes in this case?

The question is one of administrative versus routing efficiency. In all likelihood, 128.2.0.100 is but one of several dozen hosts on network 128.2.0.0. You could easily add a static route to each host on the network during initial configuration, enabling the hosts to route directly to 128.3.0.0. But suppose the route changes. You would be required to visit each host to reconfigure its routing table. On networks that change with any regularity, the administrative burden would soon become overwhelming. In such cases, the default gateway is a simple mechanism that reduces administrative complexity. Only the routers must be reconfigured when a change is made in the network.

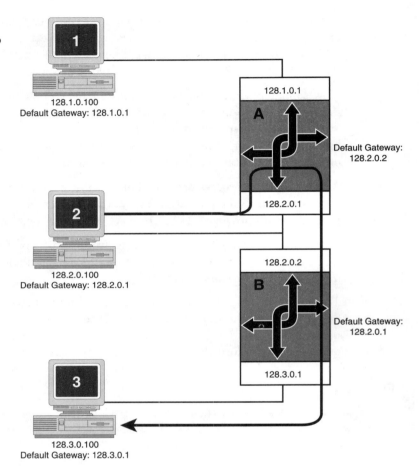

FIGURE 9.10

Routing from host 2 to host 3 on a three-network internet.

Routing with More Than Three Networks

Can default gateways be used to route datagrams to networks of any size? To see, it is necessary to examine a network such as the one illustrated in Figure 9.11.

As Figure 9.11 illustrates, routing datagrams to network 128.4.0.0 can be performed using default routers. If you trace the routes, you will find that the following situations all are covered:

■   1 can route to 2, 3, and 4

■   2 can route to 1, 3, and 4

■   3 can route to 2 and 4

FIGURE 9.11

Routing on an internet with four networks.

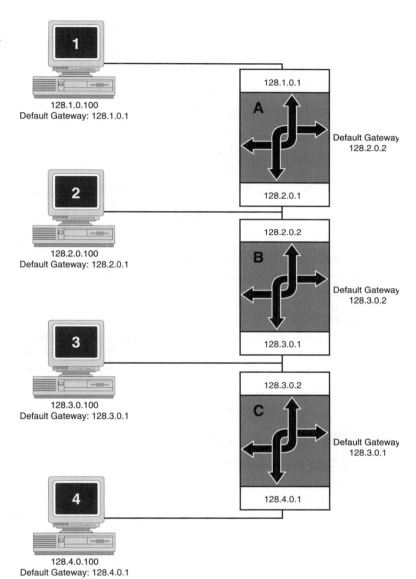

1

128.1.0.100
Default Gateway: 128.1.0.1

128.1.0.1

A

Default Gateway
128.2.0.2

128.2.0.1

2

128.2.0.100
Default Gateway: 128.2.0.1

128.2.0.2

B

Default Gateway
128.3.0.2

128.3.0.1

3

128.3.0.100
Default Gateway: 128.3.0.1

128.3.0.2

C

Default Gateway
128.3.0.1

128.4.0.1

4

128.4.0.100
Default Gateway: 128.4.0.1

The sting in the tail of this diagram is apparent when 3 attempts to route a datagram to 1. Here is the sequence, which is illustrated in Figure 9.12:

1. Host 3 sends the datagram to its default router, 128.3.0.1.

2. Router B has no direct knowledge of network 128.1.0.0. Router B, therefore, routes the datagram to B's default router, 128.3.0.2.

3. Router C has no direct knowledge of network 128.1.0.0. Router C, therefore, routes the datagram to C's default router, 128.3.0.1. The datagram has now arrived back at router B.

4. B routes the datagram to its default router, C.

5. C routes the datagram to its default router, B.

The datagram cannot be delivered to network 128.1.0.0 because it never reaches a router that is aware of the destination network. A loop has developed between B and C that could continue indefinitely.

NOTE

Loops are the reason for including the Time To Live parameter in the IP header. Time To Live is decremented by some amount each time it passes through a router. For any datagram not delivered, Time To Live eventually reaches 0 and the datagram is removed from the network.

Building Static Routing Tables

The default router mechanism is extremely limited. Although hosts can be configured with default routers, backup default routers are used only when the primary default router is unavailable. In other words, any given host is limited to a single default route at any given time, which is why the network shown in Figure 9.11 occasionally fails to deliver datagrams properly.

To solve problems such as the one shown in Figure 9.12, you need to improve the knowledge that hosts and routers possess of possible routes to remote networks. You do so by adding entries to the computer's routing tables.

The problem in Figure 9.12 is that router B is unaware of the existence of network 128.1.0.0. To eliminate the problem, B's routing table is updated with a path to network 128.1.0.0.

FIGURE 9.12

A routing loop.

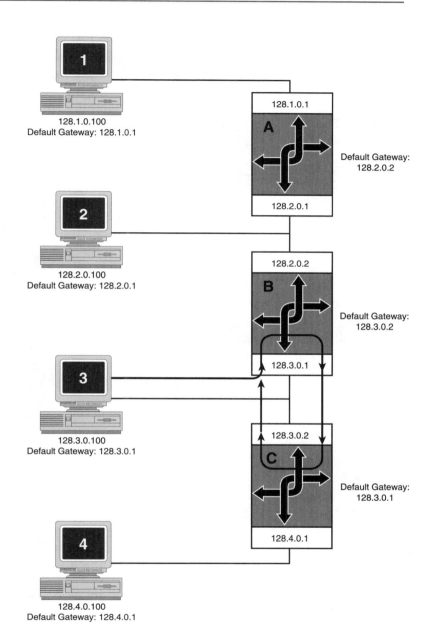

Figure 9.13 shows the same network. This time, router B has been configured with a routing table that supplements the default gateway specifications. The routing table describes the next hop on the route to network 128.1.0.0 on the internet.

FIGURE 9.13

Routing with routing tables.

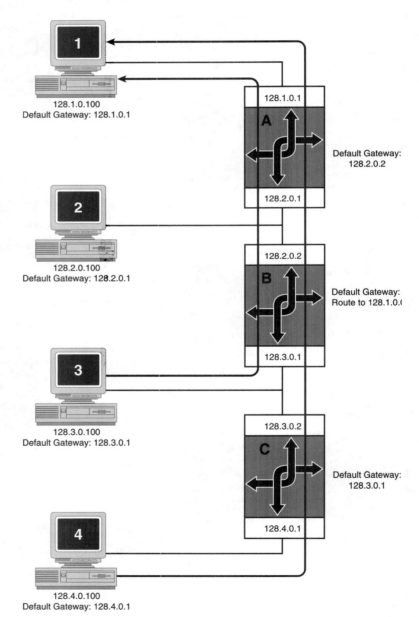

Returning to the problem of routing a datagram from host 3 to host 1, now the sequence of events is as follows:

1. Host 3 sends the datagram to its default router, 128.3.0.1.

2. Router B has an entry in its routing table for network 128.1.0.0. Any datagram directed to 128.1.0.0 will be routed to 128.2.0.1 on router A.

3. Router A is attached to the destination network and can deliver the frame.

Figure 9.13 illustrates the routes from hosts 3 and 4 to host 1, showing how the routing table entry in router B also enables host 4 to reach any network.

The tool used to maintain static routing tables is route, a command-line utility. Figure 9.14 shows a router table for router A in Figure 9.13. The table includes information about default routers and routing to adjacent networks.

FIGURE 9.14

A routing table with adjacent routing entries only.

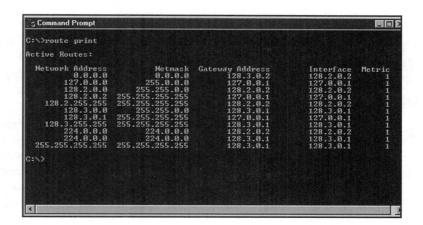

All of the entries shown in Figure 9.14 were created within the Network applet. When installing TCP/IP, IP addresses were declared for each adapter in the host. It is worth examining the entries in the table:

■ **0.0.0.0.** Specifies the default router, address 128.3.0.2.

■ **127.0.0.0.** The loopback network. Any datagrams sent to 127.0.0.0 are routed to 127.0.0.1 and reflected back.

■ **128.2.0.0.** A network address. Datagrams destined for that network are routed through adapter 128.2.0.2.

- **128.2.0.2.** A network adapter on the router. Notice that datagrams sent to that address are routed through the loopback address.

- **128.2.255.255.** A broadcast address for network 128.2.0.0. Broadcasts are routed to the network through adapter 128.2.0.2. Entries such as this should be added if broadcast messages are to be routed to remote networks.

- **128.3.0.0.** The other attached network. The routing table includes entries for 128.3.0.0 that are similar to the entries discussed for 128.2.0.0.

- **128.3.0.1.** The second network adapter on the router. Notice that datagrams sent to this address are routed through the loopback address.

- **128.3.255.255.** A broadcast address for network 128.3.0.0.

- **224.0.0.0.** A multicast address used by IP. Entries are included for each network attached to the computer.

- **255.255.255.255.** The local broadcast address. (Routers do not forward broadcasts to other networks.)

NOTE

In the routing table of Figure 9.14, entries in the Netmask determine the number of bits in the corresponding network address that must match the destination address. In the case of the network address 128.2.0.0, a netmask of 255.255.0.0 indicates that only the first 16 bits are matched against the destination IP address; in other words, it is only necessary for the netid portion to match the destination address for the route to apply. For the host 128.2.0.2, however, a netmask of 255.255.255.255 indicates that all bits must match between the destination address and the network address in the routing table entry.

When IP consults the routing table, it looks for entries in the following order:

1. First IP looks for a host address entry that matches the destination host address.

2. Second IP looks for a network address entry that matches the destination netid.

3. Finally, IP looks for a default route.

4. If none of the above routes are identified, IP reports an error.

NOTE

Notice that the router attempts routes in a definite sequence. It is, therefore, not necessary to specify metrics that make the preferences explicit. You might think, for example, that it is necessary to specify a higher metric for the default router to ensure that it will be used only if all else fails. But the default router can have a metric of 1, as with other standard routes, because it will be used only if an explicit route entry has not been made for the destination host or network.

Figure 9.15 illustrates two routing attempts using ping, both performed on router B. In the first attempt, it proves possible to ping 128.2.0.1, which is not surprising because that host is attached to a network that is directly attached to B.

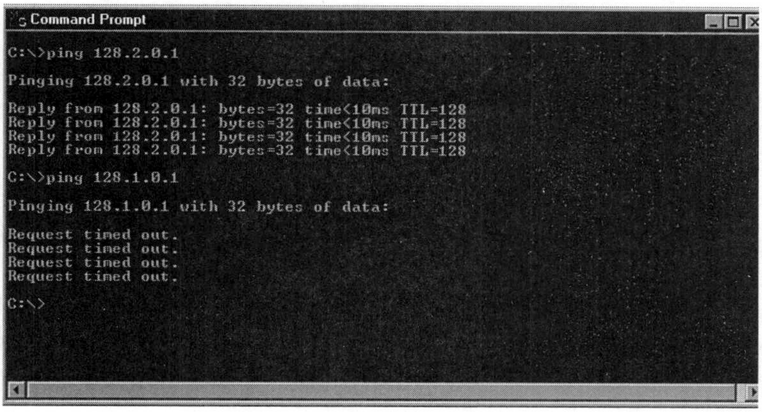

FIGURE 9.15

Pinging routed and nonrouted addresses.

```
Command Prompt                                                          _ □ x

C:\>ping 128.2.0.1

Pinging 128.2.0.1 with 32 bytes of data:

Reply from 128.2.0.1: bytes=32 time<10ms TTL=128
Reply from 128.2.0.1: bytes=32 time<10ms TTL=128
Reply from 128.2.0.1: bytes=32 time<10ms TTL=128
Reply from 128.2.0.1: bytes=32 time<10ms TTL=128

C:\>ping 128.1.0.1

Pinging 128.1.0.1 with 32 bytes of data:

Request timed out.
Request timed out.
Request timed out.
Request timed out.

C:\>
```

An attempt to ping 128.1.0.1 fails, however. B attempts to reach 128.1.0.1 via its default router, 128.3.0.2. This attempt does not succeed and times out.

To solve the problem, an entry must be added to the router table for B. This entry must specify that network 128.1.0.0 can be reached via router 128.2.0.1. Figure 9.16 was made on router B. First, an attempt to ping 128.1.0.1 fails. Then a route command is entered, after which the ping succeeds. Figure 9.17 shows the updated routing table for B. The third entry in the table reflects the route command that was entered.

FIGURE 9.16

Example of using the route *command.*

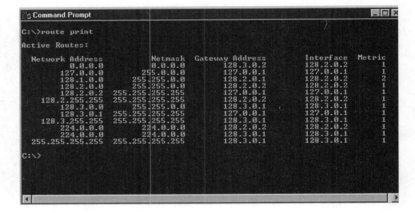

FIGURE 9.17

The routing table after execution of the sample route *command.*

The syntax for route is as follows:

```
route [-f][-p]
      [command]
      [destination]
      [mask netmask]
      [gateway]
      metric metric
```

route accepts four command options:

- **add** adds a route to a table.

- **delete** removes a route from a table.

- **change** modifies the routing for a table entry.

- **print** displays the router table.

destination is an optional parameter that specifies the network address that is the destination to be specified in the routing table entry. It must be supplied with the add, delete, and change options.

mask is an optional parameter. When mask appears, it specifies that the following IP address is an address mask. The default value for netmask is 255.255.255.255. Other values must be fully specified.

gateway is an optional parameter that specifies the IP address of the gateway that is to be used when routing datagrams to the destination.

metric is an optional parameter. When metric appears then *metric* is a number that specifies the cost metric for the route being specified. If the metric parameter is omitted, a cost of 1 is assumed. The metric parameter is required only when multiple routes exist to the destination network, in which case the lowest metric identifies the preferred route.

-f is an optional parameter that specifies the routing table is to be cleared of all entries. It can be included with routes to clear the table before the routes are entered.

-p is an optional parameter that is used with the add option to make an entry persistent. Persistent entries remain in effect after the router restarts. If this parameter is not specified, the table entry does not appear after the router restarts.

NOTE

The -p option is available beginning with Windows NT version 3.51. With earlier versions, the route commands must be reentered when the computer restarts. Persistent routes are stored in the Registry under the key:

```
HKEY_LOCAL_COMPUTER\SYSTEM\CurrentControlSet\Services\
Tcpip\Parameters\PersistenRoutes
```

The metric parameter is new in Windows NT version 4.

The example command is:

```
route add 128.1.0.0 mask 255.255.0.0 128.2.0.1 metric 2
```

This command adds a table entry for network 128.1.0.0 with a network mask of 255.255.0.0. The router to be used to reach 128.1.0.0 is 128.2.0.1, and the cost for the route is 2. (A metric of 2 was used in this example to illustrate use of the metric parameter. Because only one route exists to the destination network, however, any metric would have the same effect, and the default metric would work just as well.)

Effective Use of a Default Router

In many cases, nonrouting hosts need to be configured only with the address of a default router. Consider the network in Figure 9.18. If routers A, B, and C are configured with a routing protocol with RIP, they are busily exchanging routing information. Host 1 can use any of the routers as a default router, because any router has the information required to route messages appropriately.

You might question the efficiency of such a configuration. Host 1's default router is A, but suppose that host 1 needs to route a message to the Internet. Isn't it inefficient to bounce the message around the local network when it could be sent directly to router C? Perhaps a bit. Let's investigate some strategies for reducing traffic that results from routing.

What is the primary communication destination for host 1? Will it be communicating locally, or with the Internet? If locally, then routers A or B are the best choices as default routers. If host 1 spends most of its time connected with the Internet, its default router should be C.

But routing protocols generate traffic. Suppose that we want to eliminate routing protocols and excessive routing from our network. What's the best way to configure routing on host 1?

It wouldn't be practical to configure host 1 with a static route to every destination on the Internet, so router C is the only choice for a default router. We'll assume that router C has been configured appropriately so that it can route messages to the Internet.

That decided, the remaining step is to configure host 1 with static routes to all local networks. The following route statements would be executed to configure host 1:

```
route add 128.2.0.0 mask 255.255.0.0 128.1.0.1 metric 1 -p
route add 128.3.0.0 mask 255.255.0.0 128.1.0.2 metric 1 -p
```

FIGURE 9.18

Host 1 requires only a default route to reach all destinations.

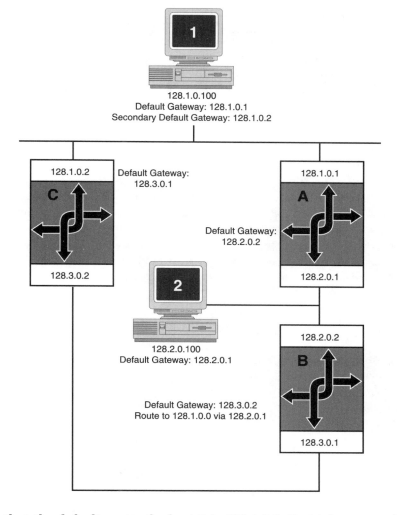

Assuming that the default router for host 1 is 128.1.0.3, that takes care of all possibilities. It is no longer necessary to run RIP (or another routing protocol) on routers A and B, so routing traffic is eliminated. And host 1 will now route messages directly to the appropriate router.

Should you go to this much trouble to set up routing? It depends on whether your network changes frequently. If your network relies on static routes, you need to visit each host every time the network is reconfigured. That can mean a lot of one-on-one sessions with your hosts and may be an inefficient use of your time. In most cases, you'll make better use of resources by running RIP or OSPF, however.

Routing with Multiple Default Gateways

Any TCP/IP computer can be configured with more than one default gateway. Unfortunately, only the first configured gateway will be used for routing. The additional gateways are used only if the primary gateway becomes unavailable. Consequently, multiple gateways cannot be used to take better advantage of network bandwidth. However, they do provide a greater degree of network fault tolerance.

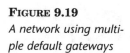

NOTE

Besides configuring multiple default gateways, ICMP provides another mechanism that enables hosts to learn new routes. The Windows NT router uses the ICMP Router Discovery Protocol to notify hosts that a router knows of a better route to a given destination. The router sends an ICMP *redirect* message to the host that originated the datagram.

Unfortunately, ICMP redirection is effective only for the first-hop gateway. ICMP redirect messages from later gateways are ignored. Therefore, a dynamic routing protocol is still a superior solution to the problem of automatically configuring the network.

Figure 9.19 shows an example of a network that can take advantage of multiple default gateways. Host 1 offers two possible routes to host 2:

FIGURE 9.19

A network using multiple default gateways

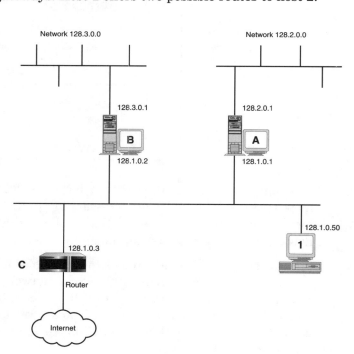

- Via router A

- Via routers C and B

Assuming that routing through A is more efficient, the primary default gateway for host 1 should be 128.1.0.1. Host 1 can have a second route to host 128.1.0.2, however, which enables 1 to reach 2 should router A fail.

Microsoft TCP/IP detects dead routers by sending packets to the default gateway until an acknowledgment is received or until it exceeds one-half of the `TcpMaxDataRetransmissions` parameter. If the default gateway is unresponsive and the host is configured with multiple default gateways, the next default gateway is used.

Additional default gateways are configured using Advanced TCP/IP Configuration. To add a default gateway:

1. Start the Network applet in the Control Panel.

2. In the Protocols tab, select **TCP/IP Protocol** and choose **Properties**.

3. If a default gateway has not been entered, add the gateway in the Default Gateway field of the TCP/IP Configuration dialog box. Remember that you should specify a default gateway for one adapter only on a multihomed host.

4. Choose the **Advanced** button to open the Advanced IP Addressing dialog box for the selected adapter, as shown in Figure 9.20.

FIGURE 9.20

Entering additional addresses for an adapter.

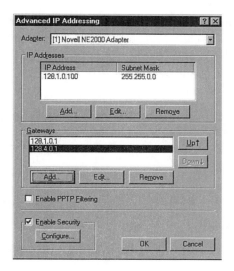

The box to the right of Default Gateway contains two entries. 128.1.0.1 is the default gateway address specified in the TCP/IP Configuration dialog box. 128.4.0.1 was added with the following steps.

5. To add a default gateway, enter the address in the Default Gateway address fields. Then choose Add to move the entry to the default gateway list.

6. Choose **OK**, exit the Network utility, and restart the computer to activate the new address.

The Advanced IP Addressing box is used for a variety of TCP/IP configuration entries. If necessary, for example, you can add more than one IP address to an adapter. Chapter 17, "Enabling a Secure Conncetion to the Internet," shows how to use the Point-to-Point Tunneling Protocol (PPTP), which also has a setting in this window. Chapter 17 also discusses use of the security settings, which enable you to filter the ports and protocols that an adapter will accept.

Testing Routing with Tracert

Tracert (trace route) is included with Windows NT as a tool for debugging routing, using ICMP messages to report the routes between two hosts on an internetwork. When you query a destination with tracert, it will report the route taken together with a variety of statistics. If the destination cannot be reached, tracert reports which router failed.

The following is an example of tracert output, showing the route to ds.internic.net.

```
C:\>tracert ds.internic.net
Tracing route to ds.internic.net [198.49.45.10] over a maximum of
30 hops:
1   <10 ms <10 ms  *                              [134.107.1.100]
2   10 ms  <10 ms  10 ms  serv1-gw.nnet.net       [182.80.12.82]
3   10 ms          10 ms  ssnet.nnet.net          [182.35.180.2]
4   20 ms          10 ms  t3.cnss8.t3.ns.net      [141.222.88.4]
5   30 ms  30 ms   20 ms  losangeles.gans.net     [141.222.8.1]
6   70 ms  70 ms   80 ms  new-york.t3.gans.net    [141.222.24.1]
7   80 ms  81 ms   80 ms  t3.denver.gans.net      [141.222.40.1]
8   100 ms 91 ms   90 ms  t3.new-york.t3.gans.net [141.222.32.2]
```

```
 9  90 ms   90 ms   91 ms  new-york.t3.gans.net    [141.222.32.196]
10 100 ms   90 ms   91 ms  serv3.gans.net          [141.222.222.1]
11 140 ms  191 ms  100 ms  ds.internic.net         [198.49.45.10]
Trace complete.
```

The route is determined by sending ICMP echo packets with varying time-to-live values to the destination. Each router that forwards the packet must decrement the TTL before forwarding it. The result serves as a hop count to the destination. When the TTL times out, the router is required to return an ICMP time exceeded packet.

Tracert determines the route by sending the first echo packet with a TTL of 1 and incrementing the TTL with each packet sent. Consequently, each time tracert sends an echo packet the TTL expires at the router that is next in line to the destination. This enables tracert to reconstruct the route path from the ICMP time-exceeded packets that are returned.

Tracert will fail to determine the route when it encounters some older routers that simply drop packets whose TTL has expired.

Enabling the Multiprotocol Router

Static routing requires some thought, effort, and troubleshooting to ensure that all datagrams can be routed properly to all required destinations. It might appear, therefore, that network administrators would be better served by dedicated, commercial routers that maintain routing tables automatically.

Dynamic routing with a routing protocol, such as RIP or OSPF, is certainly preferable when networks are dynamic or incorporate large numbers of routers. Maintaining routing for a large, evolving organization using static routing would be difficult or impossible.

Dynamic routing also is often preferable when networks provide multiple paths to destinations. Dynamic routing can adapt to failed segments, selecting the optimum path available on the changed network. This again argues for dynamic routing on large networks.

Static routing, however, might be just the thing for networks of moderate size or that change infrequently. Static routing is free in the sense that it generates no network traffic. Dynamic routing protocols require routers to communicate to exchange routing data. With protocols such as RIP, routing messages can utilize a significant portion of available bandwidth.

Should you feel that your network requires a dynamic routing protocol, RIP-1 is supported by the Multiprotocol Router included with Windows NT version 4.

NOTE

Regrettably, the Windows NT Multiprotocol Router is a fairly elementary piece of software that supports only RIP-1 and only in a LAN environment. You cannot use the Multiprotocol Router to route to a WAN (such as X.25 or frame relay) unless the WAN network interface appears to Windows NT as a LAN adapter.

It could not be much simpler to enable the MultiProtocol Router. Do the following:

1. Configure a host with two or more network adapters, as described in the section, "Configuring a Windows NT Router."

2. Enable IP forwarding by checking **Enable IP Forwarding** in the Routing tab of the Microsoft TCP/IP Properties window.

3. In the Networks applet, select the **Services** tab.

4. Choose **Add.**

5. In the Network Service list, select RIP for Internet Protocol and choose OK.

6. When prompted, supply the path where the installation files can be found.

7. Close the Network applet.

8. Restart the computer to activate routing.

When to Configure Default Gateways

When should you configure a host with a default gateway, when should you manually add additional static routes, and when should you enable RIP? Your choice should be guided by two factors: a need to maintain the network with a reasonable level of effort and a need to control network traffic generated by the routing process.

On a typical internetwork user workstations will greatly outnumber routers. Suppose that each workstation is configured with a complete static routing table, providing routes to every destination on the internet. Imagine the drudgery of updating all those routing tables each time the network is reconfigured! You would need to carefully plan the route changes for each network segment, and then you would need to visit each workstation and enter the appropriate `route` commands.

Clearly, it is the better part of valor to configure all single-homed hosts with default gateway addresses only. Provided the addresses of the routers on the networks remain constant, it will be unnecessary to visit the workstations on the network when a routing change takes place. The reduced labor required to maintain the network will repay the fact that default gateway addresses might not always result in routing by the most efficient path.

Now for the routers. Should you select static or dynamic routing? If the routers are few or the internet is reasonably stable, static routing is a good choice because no network traffic will be generated to support routing.

But dynamic routing adapts to network changes—planned or accidental—automatically. On a network of any complexity, a dynamic routing protocol can greatly reduce administrative effort and can easily pay for itself despite the network traffic that it generates. If traffic overhead becomes a concern, consider using third-party routers that support OSPF.

Things are Getting Pretty Complicated

In Chapter 8 "Installing TCP/IP on Windows NT Computers" and this chapter, you learned how to establish the infrastructure of your TCP/IP network, first installing the TCP/IP protocol stack and then establishing the routing required to enable communication throughout your internetwork. At this point, communication is enabled, but several tasks remain to be accomplished.

The next task is to make the network easier to manage. If you have more than a few hosts, you probably don't want to manually administer IP addresses. To simplify your life you need to automate IP address assignment. With that in mind, the next chapter turns its attention to DHCP.

Chapter 10

MANAGING DHCP

The Dynamic Host Configuration Protocol (DHCP) can make TCP/IP network administration much more efficient by dynamically assigning IP addresses to hosts, practically eliminating the need to configure host addresses manually. A DHCP client can even move to a new network without any need for manual reconfiguration.

DHCP also provides a mechanism for local management of the majority of TCP/IP clients on the internetwork. Parameters such as default routers can be configured centrally without visiting each host and making changes manually.

Microsoft DHCP clients and servers are implemented under RFCs 1533, 1534, 1541, and 1542.

This chapter provides an overview of DHCP, defines it, and explains how it works. This chapter then proceeds to examine DHCP beginning with installation, configuration, and management issues.

DHCP Concepts and Operation

DHCP is based on DHCP servers, which assign IP addresses, and DHCP clients, to which addresses are assigned. Figure 10.1 illustrates a simple network that consists of a single DHCP server and a few clients. As shown, a single DHCP server can supply addresses for more than one network. To support DHCP on an internetwork, routers must be configured with BOOTP forwarding (see RFCs 1533, 1534, and 1542). DHCP clients and hosts communicate using BOOTP, an older, less versatile protocol also used to assign IP addresses.

FIGURE 10.1

Example of a network running DHCP.

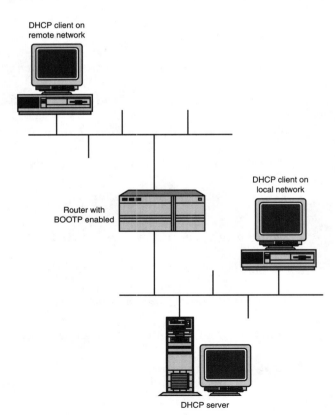

DHCP client on remote network

Router with BOOTP enabled

DHCP client on local network

DHCP server

The DHCP server maintains pools of IP addresses, called scopes. When a DHCP client enters a network, it requests and is granted a lease to use an address from an appropriate scope. BOOTP tags each request for an IP address with the address of the network from which the request originates. This information enables the DHCP server to assign an address that is appropriate for that network.

The concept of leasing is important because DHCP clients are not ordinarily granted permanent use of an address. Instead, they receive a lease of limited duration. When the lease expires, it must be renegotiated. This approach ensures that unused addresses become available for use by other clients.

As shown in Figure 10.1, a single DHCP server can support clients on several networks in an internetwork. Clients moved to different networks are assigned IP addresses appropriate to the new network. (As will be explained later, routers must support a BOOTP forwarding feature for a DHCP server to support hosts on remote networks.)

Figure 10.2 shows the dialog that takes place when a DHCP client obtains a lease from a DHCP server. Figure 10.3 depicts the life cycle of a lease. The stages in the life cycle are as follows:

FIGURE 10.2
A DHCP client obtaining a lease.

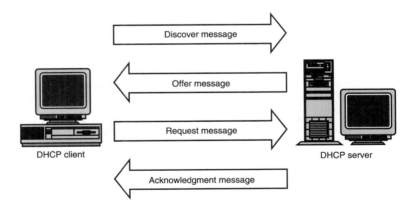

Figure 10.3

The life cycle of a DHCP address lease.

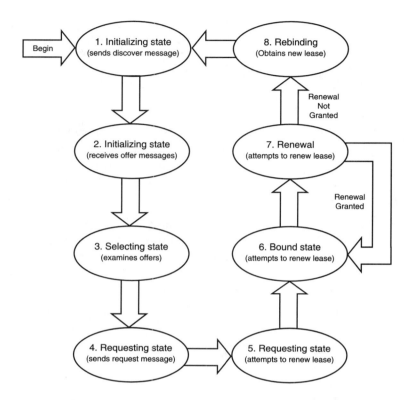

1. A DHCP client host that enters a network enters an initializing state and broadcasts a *Dhcpdiscover* message on the local network. To enable DHCP servers to reply to the discover message, the message includes the MAC address of the DHCP client. This message might be relayed to other networks to deliver it to DHCP servers in the internet. (Routers do not ordinarily forward broadcast messages and must be configured using the BOOTP protocol, RFC 1542, to support DHCP forwarding.)

2. Each DHCP server that receives the discover message and can service the request responds with a *Dhcpoffer* message that consists of an IP address and associated configuration information.

NOTE

If the client does not receive a *Dhcpoffer* message, it repeats the request four times at 2-, 4-, 8-, and 16-second intervals, varying the intervals by a random amount between 0 and 1,000 milliseconds. If it still fails to receive a *Dhcpoffer* message, the client stops trying and waits for five minutes before renewing its attempt. If a DHCP server is unavailable, the client is unable to bind to TCP/IP and cannot enter the network.

3. The DHCP client enters a selecting state and examines the offer messages that it receives. If all offers are equally acceptable, the client will select the first offer that is received.

4. When the DHCP client selects an offer, it enters a requesting state and broadcasts a *Dhcprequest* message to the appropriate DHCP server, requesting the offered configuration. Because the message is broadcast, other DHCP servers will receive the message as well, notifying them that their offered addresses will not be accepted.

5. The DHCP server grants the configuration with a *Dhcpack* (DHCP acknowledgment) message that consists of the IP address and configuration along with a lease to use the configuration for a specific time. The local network administrator establishes lease policies.

6. The DHCP client receives the acknowledgment and enters a bound state in which the IP configuration is applied to the local TCP/IP protocols. Client computers retain the configuration for the duration of the lease and can be restarted without negotiating a new lease.

7. When the lease has been active for 50 percent of the permitted lease duration, the client attempts to renew its lease with the DHCP server. The interval at which a client will begin attempting to renew its lease is the DHCP renewal time (T1).

8. If the lease cannot be renewed by the time it is 87.5 percent expired, the DHCP server sends a *Dhcpnack* (DHCP negative acknowledgment) to the client, which reenters the binding process. It then requests and is assigned a lease to a new address. Non-renewed addresses return to the available address pool. The interval at which the client assumes it cannot renew its current license and initiates an attempt to obtain a new license is the DHCP Rebinding (T2) time.

NOTE

Notice that all DHCP activity is initiated by the client. A client can pull configuration changes in from a DHCP server, but a DHCP server cannot push changes out to a client. For this reason, all leases should have a limited duration. Only when all leases have expired can you be sure that changes made to the DHCP configuration have been distributed to all clients.

Unless errors are encountered, the process of requesting, assigning, and renewing is completely transparent to the client and requires little ongoing maintenance on the part of the network administrator.

When a DHCP client restarts and logs on to the network, it attempts to reestablish its existing lease by broadcasting a *Dhcprequest* rather than a *Dhcpdiscover* packet. The request packet contains a request for DHCP address most recently assigned. The DHCP server responds with a *Dhcpack* and attempts to grant the request. If the request cannot be granted, the server sends a *Dhcpnack* message and the client must enter an initializing state and request a new address lease.

Although the majority of clients will be assigned an IP address that is selected from a pool, DHCP can be configured to assign specific addresses to specific hosts, which enables administrators to use DHCP to set host protocol options while retaining fixed address assignments.

Several types of hosts must be assigned fixed manual addresses so that other hosts can enter the addresses into their configurations, including, among others, the following examples:

- Routers (gateways)
- WINS servers
- DNS servers

Installing DHCP Servers

DHCP Server services can be installed on computers running Windows NT Server. To install DHCP services, follow these steps:

1. Install TCP/IP on the DHCP server computer. DHCP servers must be configured with static IP addresses. All other computers can, if desired, obtain their IP addresses from DHCP. If installing TCP/IP for the first time, restart the computer.

2. Open the Network utility in the Control Panel.

3. Select the Services tab.

4. Choose **Add**.

5. In the _N_etwork Service list, select Microsoft DHCP Server and choose OK.

6. Supply the path to the installation files when prompted.

7. Close the Network utility. This will open the Microsoft TCP/IP Properties dialog box.

8. If necessary, edit the properties. Ensure that the interface adapters are configured with static IP addresses. (Don't select **Obtain IP address from DHCP server**.)

9. Open the Services utility in the Control Panel.

10. In the Ser_v_ice list, select **Microsoft DHCP Server**.

11. Choose **Start**. Before exiting the Services utility, verify that the status of the Microsoft DHCP Server service is Started. If an error prevents the service from starting, consult the Event Viewer to determine the source of the error. (For more information, see the section "Starting and Stopping the DHCP Server" later in this chapter.)

The DHCP Server service is configured to start automatically when the server is started. Therefore, you could also start the service by restarting the server.

NOTE

If you are upgrading to Windows NT Server 4.0 from Windows NT Server 3.51, the DHCP database must be converted. The first time the DHCP service starts, it detects the old database and attempts to convert it using jetconv.exe. The user is informed that conversion must take place, and the user must confirm the procedure.

Before upgrading from Windows NT Server 3.51 to 4.0, bring the DHCP database into a consistent state by using the Service applet in the Control Panel to stop the DHCP Server service.

Setting Up DHCP Scopes

Before DHCP clients can obtain IP addresses from a DHCP server, at least one scope must be created. A scope is a range of IP addresses along with a set of configuration options that apply to clients that receive IP addresses assigned from the scope. All scopes have the following properties:

- A scope name
- A subnet mask
- A lease duration

DHCP is administered using the DHCP Manager utility. An icon for DHCP Manager is created in the Network Administration program group when DHCP Server services are installed. DHCP Manager can also be started from a command prompt by entering the command start dhcpadmn.

Figure 10.4 shows the DHCP Manager dialog box. As yet no scopes have been defined. Before defining a scope, determine the following:

- The starting IP address of the range to be assigned to the scope
- The ending IP address to be assigned
- The subnet mask to be in effect
- Any addresses in the range that are not to be made available to clients obtaining addresses from the scope
- The duration of the lease (default value is three days)

FIGURE 10.4

DHCP Manager prior to creating scope.

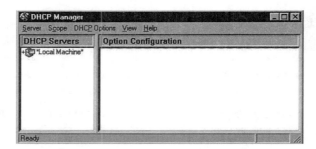

To create a scope, perform the following steps:

1. Start DHCP Manager, which is installed in the Administrative Tools (Common) group of the Start menu. The display in Figure 10.4 shows DHCP Manager before defining any scopes. If a DHCP Server service is running on this computer, it is identified as `Local Machine`.

2. Select a DHCP server in the DHCP Servers list. The example will create a scope on `Local Machine`. A scope is always created on a specific DHCP server.

3. In the DHCP Manager dialog box, choose **Create** in the Scope menu, which opens the Create Scope dialog box (see Figure 10.5). Data fields in the figure have been filled to reflect typical scope properties.

FIGURE 10.5

Creating a scope.

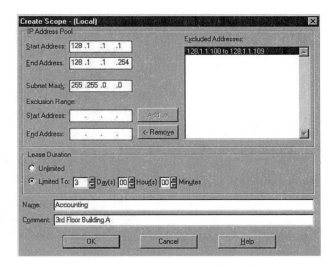

4. Enter the appropriate addresses in the Start Address, End Address, and Subnet Mask input boxes.

5. To exclude an address or range of addresses, under Exclusion Range enter the appropriate addresses in the Start Address and End Address boxes. (An end address is not required when you exclude a single address.) Then choose **Add** to move the addresses to the Excluded Addresses list.

6. To remove an excluded address range, select the range in the Excluded Addresses list. Then choose **Remove**.

7. Choose **Unlimited** if leases for this scope are to be unlimited in duration. Choose **Limited To** and enter a period in days, hours, and minutes to set a lease duration for the scope. Limiting lease duration, even when plenty of addresses are available, is best so that unused leases are eventually released.

NOTE

I strongly recommend against using scopes with unlimited duration. When a client lease has unlimited duration, the client will never check back in with the DHCP server to retrieve changes made to its scope configuration.

8. Optionally, enter a name and comment for the scope in the Name and Comment boxes. This information helps identify the scope in the DHCP Manager.

9. Choose **OK** to return to the DHCP Manager main dialog box. For a new scope, you receive the message shown in Figure 10.6. To activate the scope, choose **Yes**.

FIGURE 10.6
The scope activation message.

10. As Figure 10.7 reveals, the scope you have defined appears under the DHCP server for which the scope was defined. Because it was activated, the light bulb icon is illuminated.

NOTE

To modify a scope, select the scope in the DHCP Servers box and choose **Properties** in the Scope menu, which opens a Scope Properties dialog box in which you can change scope properties. Choose **OK** after you make the necessary changes.

FIGURE 10.7
DHCP Manager after a scope has been defined.

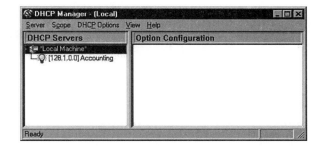

WARNING

Notice in Figure 10.5 that the address range is from 128.1.1.1 through 128.1.1.254, so that the scope range does not contain invalid hostID values. This is, strictly speaking, unnecessary. DHCP understands that network and broadcast addresses should not be assigned. For clarity, however, I typically exclude network and broadcast addresses from the scope.

Be sure that the scope address range does not include the IP addresses of any hosts for which addresses have been manually assigned. This includes all DHCP and WINS servers, which must have fixed addresses. Fixed addresses are also assigned to router interfaces and to many servers. Fixed IP addresses must be outside the scope address range or must be excluded from the scope. The next step explains how to exclude addresses from scopes. Figure 10.8 shows an error message that DHCP Manager displays when it determines that an address it has assigned conflicts with an address already in use.

FIGURE 10.8
Message resulting from an address conflict.

Enabling DHCP Clients

After DHCP has been configured, DHCP clients can be activated. Microsoft operating systems that can be DHCP clients are as follows:

- All versions of Windows NT
- Windows 95 and 98

- Windows 3.11 with the 32-bit TCP/IP client

- MS-DOS workgroup connection 3.0, which is the DOS client included with Windows NT

Configuration of Windows 95/98 and 3.11 is covered in Chapter 14, "Installing TCP/IP on Microsoft Clients."

To enable a Windows NT computer as a DHCP client, perform the following steps:

1. Open the Network utility in the Control Panel.

2. Select **TCP/IP Protocol** in the **Protocols** tab and choose **Properties** to open the Microsoft TCP/IP Properties dialog box.

3. Select the adapter to be configured in the Adapter list.

4. Select **Obtain an IP Address from a DHCP server**.

5. Choose **Apply**.

6. Exit the Network utility and restart the computer.

NOTE

The option **Obtain an IP Address from a DHCP Server** is not available if DHCP Server services or WINS Server services are installed on the computer. DHCP or WINS servers must be configured using fixed IP addresses.

7. Choose **OK** twice to exit Network Settings. Then restart the computer.

NOTE

When a DHCP client obtains an address lease from a DHCP server, you can determine the address assignment by entering the command ipconfig /all at a command prompt on the client.

Windows 95/98 users can run the winipcfg command at a Run prompt. WINIPCFG is a GUI program that performs most of the same functions as ipconfig. The More Info button shows all other DHCP configured information.

Viewing and Managing Active Leases

DHCP clients can obtain addresses after the following have been accomplished:

- DHCP Server services have been installed on at least one Windows NT Server computer.

- At least one scope has been defined that applies to the network on which the DHCP client resides, or a reservation has been established for the client.

- **Obtain an IP Address from a DHCP Server** has been selected in the client's TCP/IP Protocol configuration.

After those steps are accomplished, restarting a DHCP client causes it to obtain a lease for an IP address from a DHCP server. To view active leases, select a scope in the DHCP Servers box. Then choose **Active Leases** in the Scope menu. Figure 10.9 shows a scope with two active leases.

FIGURE 10.9

Active leases for a scope.

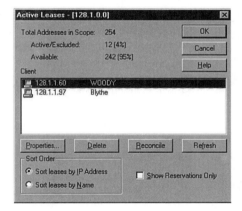

The following information is available in the Active Leases dialog box:

- The NetBIOS name of the computer that has obtained each lease.

- The total number of addresses in the scope.

- The number of addresses currently unavailable for leasing. This number is the total number of active leases, excluded addresses, and reserved addresses.

NOTE

No direct way exists for determining the number of active leases. To determine the number of active leases, record the total number of active/excluded addresses. Then check the **Show Reservations Only** box to determine the number of reserved addresses. Subtract the number of reservations from the total of active/excluded addresses to determine the number of non-reserved leases. Then subtract the number of excluded addresses, which must be determined from the scope properties.

- Whether leases should be sorted by IP address or by name.

- Whether leases should be displayed with reservations.

When a DHCP client restarts, what events take place depend on whether the client holds a lease to an IP address.

- If the DHCP client does not hold an address lease, it enters an initializing state in which it attempts to obtain an address lease.

- If the DHCP client holds a lease to an address, it sends a message to DHCP declaring its configuration. A DHCP server must confirm this information if the client is to continue using the lease. If the DHCP server sends a negative reply, the client must enter an initializing state and acquire a new lease.

Usually, a client is permitted to retain its IP address assignment and can use the same address indefinitely. Changes in scope properties can force the DHCP client to accept a new IP address lease when it restarts.

NOTE

When a client starts TCP/IP with an address obtained from DHCP, it transmits an ARP request frame to determine whether the IP address is active on the network. If it is discovered that another host is using the IP address, TCP/IP is not started and the client reports an error message. Resolve the conflict before attempting to restart the client.

Viewing and Modifying Properties for an Active Lease

To view or modify the properties for a lease, select the lease in the Active Leases dialog box and choose **Properties** to display the Client Properties dialog box (see Figure 10.10).

FIGURE 10.10

Properties for an active lease.

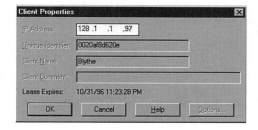

For leases assigned from a scope address pool, no fields in the Client Properties box can be modified.

If the lease has been assigned a reserved address, three fields can be modified: Unique Identifier, Client Name, and Client Comment. The IP Address field cannot be modified. To change the IP address reserved for the client, you must delete the current reservation and create a new one. You also must force the client to release its old address, which you do by executing the command ipconfig /release at a command prompt on the client computer. Windows 95/98 users can run the winipcfg command at a Run prompt and choose the **Release** button to accomplish the same result.

Deleting Active Leases

Deleting an active lease is not quite what it appears. Selecting a lease in the Active Leases dialog box and choosing **Delete** removes the lease from the display but leaves the client free to use the lease for the duration of the current session.

When an active lease is deleted, the result is identical to what happens when the client's lease has expired. The client is not forced off the network but continues to use the IP address until the client is restarted. The next time it reconnects to the network, the client enters a renewing state. DHCP denies the client's request to renew the lease on its old address. This forces the DHCP client into a rebinding state, in which the client requests a new address lease from DHCP.

NOTE

Do not delete an active lease when a client is logged on using that lease. The client can continue to use the IP address until it logs off the network. The IP address, on the other hand, is returned to the pool of available addresses and can be leased by other DHCP clients. As a result, two active clients might find themselves sharing the same IP address.

To force a client to release its current lease and free up its IP address, enter the command `ipconfig /release` at the command prompt of the client. Windows 95/98 users should run the `winipcfg` program at a Run prompt and choose **Release**. Doing so forfeits the client's IP address and effectively disconnects it from the network. Restarting the client and logging back in to the network to obtain a new IP address is necessary.

Establishing Reservations

In some cases, it is important that a client always obtain the same IP address, but it remains advantageous to manage the IP address and its properties through DHCP. To support clients that require fixed addresses, reservations can be specified in DHCP Manager. A reservation consists of an IP address and associated properties, keyed to the physical (MAC) address of a specific computer. Only that computer can obtain a lease for the IP address.

NOTE

All computers can be configured to obtain their addresses from DHCP, except for computers running DHCP Server services or WINS Server services. Here are some examples of situations that might require reserved IP addresses:

- A constant address is required, such as the address of a default gateway or a DNS server.

- A domain controller obtains its address from an LMHOSTS file. (See Chapter 12, "Managing WINS.")

- A host does not obtain its address from DHCP and address conflicts must be prevented.

To define a reservation, the physical address of the client must be determined. After TCP/IP protocols are installed on a computer, either of the following procedures can be used to identify the physical address:

- Enable the computer as a DHCP client and have it obtain a lease to an address in any active scope. Then view the properties for the client as described in the section "Viewing and Managing Active Leases," earlier in this chapter. One of those properties is the host's physical address. You can copy this address to the Clipboard by selecting it and pressing **Ctrl+C**. You can then press **Ctrl+V** to paste the address into the reservation properties.

- At the client host, open an MS-DOS prompt and enter the command `ipconfig /all`, discussed in Chapter 9, "Routing Basics." One of the items in the listing produced reports the physical address of the computer. The Windows 95/98 `winipcfg` utility displays similar data in a GUI format. Run `winipcfg` from the Run command in the Start menu.

On a Windows NT computer, another method is to open a command prompt and enter the command `net config wksta`. Look for the address following the heading "Workstation active on." You can use this command without having to install TCP/IP protocols. (Unfortunately `net config` does not provide this information on Windows 3.1x or Windows 95/98 computers.)

To create a reservation:

1. Start DHCP Manager.

2. In the DHCP Servers box, select the scope in which to define the reservation.

3. Choose **Add Reservations** in the Scope menu to open the Add Reserved Clients dialog box (see Figure 10.11).

4. In the IP Address box, enter the IP address to be reserved. This address must fall within the range of available addresses of the scope chosen in step 2 and must not have been excluded from the available address range.

FIGURE 10.11

Adding a DHCP reservation.

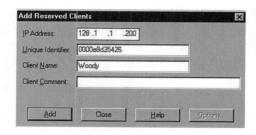

5. In the Unique Identifier box, enter the physical address of the client for which the address is being reserved. This address is often reported with punctuation such as, 00-00-6e-44-9f-4f. Do not include any punctuation in the Unique Identifier box. If you copied the address of the computer to the Clipboard, you can paste it by selecting the **Unique Identifier** box and pressing **Ctrl+V**.

6. Enter the client's name in the Client Name box.

7. If you want, enter a description in the Client Comment box.

8. Choose **Add** to store the reservation.

Reservations are listed in the Active Leases dialog box. As Figure 10.12 shows, reserved leases are identified with the label Reservation in use and state the IP address that has been reserved.

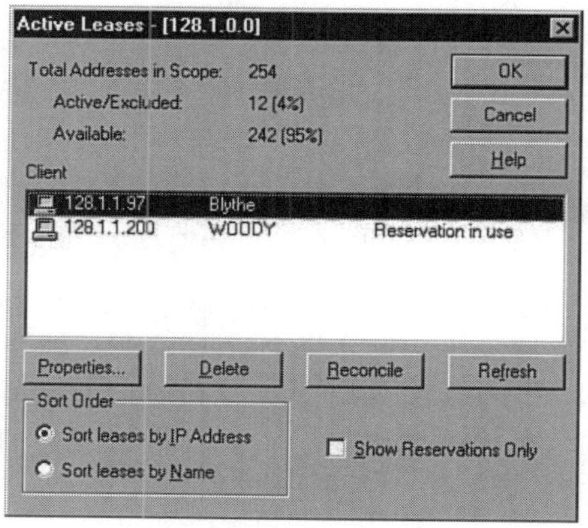

FIGURE 10.12

Active leases showing an IP address reservation.

NOTE

Assigning a reservation to a client currently connected using an address leased from a scope does not force the client to release its current lease and obtain the reserved IP address. The client's current lease is deleted (expired), forcing the client to obtain a new address lease the next time it connects with the network. At that time, the client obtains the IP address that is reserved for it.

As with deleting active leases, therefore, a reservation should be added only when the client has released its current lease. Otherwise duplicate IP addresses can be assigned to the original client and to a new client that leases the address.

Activating, Deactivating, and Deleting Scopes

Scopes can be active or inactive. An active scope services DHCP requests and is indicated in DHCP Manager by an illuminated (yellow) light bulb icon to the left of the scope name. An inactive scope does not service DHCP requests and is indicated by a darkened (gray) light bulb icon to the left of the scope name.

To deactivate an active scope, select the scope in DHCP Manager and choose **Deactivate** in the Scope menu.

To activate an inactive scope, select the scope in DHCP Manager and choose **Activate** in the Scope menu.

To delete a scope, first deactivate the scope. Then choose **Delete** in the Scope menu.

After a scope is deactivated or deleted, currently logged-in clients can continue to utilize the address leases assigned to them. When a client restarts or must renew an expired lease, it must obtain a lease from a different scope.

After deactivating or deleting a scope, you can force a DHCP client to obtain a lease from another scope by entering the command `ipconfig /renew` in a command prompt on the client. It might be necessary to restart the client. The Windows 95/98 `winipcfg` application provides a **Renew** button that accomplishes the same task.

Managing Leases

The duration of leases must be determined by the needs of the network.

- If the available address pool is larger than the number of hosts needing addresses, the lease duration can be fairly long. Indefinite leases are not recommended; all networks experience change to some degree and assigning a lease duration ensures that old leases are eventually purged. A lease duration between three and five days will probably prove most practical.

- If the network configuration changes frequently, choose fairly short lease times so that addresses that become available can be reassigned quickly.

- If the number of TCP/IP users approaches the size of the address pool, a short lease duration might be in order.

When a client lease expires, it remains in the DHCP database for approximately one day. The DHCP client can attempt to renew its old lease within that period. The delay accommodates DHCP clients and servers that are in different time zones or that have unsynchronized clocks.

The Active Leases dialog box reports the sum of active and excluded addresses for the scope selected.

Managing Multiple DHCP Servers

A network can support any desired number of DHCP servers. Multiple DHCP servers reduce the workload on any one server and enable DHCP address assignment to continue if one of the DHCP servers fails.

Unfortunately, having redundant DHCP servers for the same scope is impossible. DHCP does not provide a mechanism that enables DHCP servers to exchange lease information. If any IP addresses appear in the scope definitions for two DHCP servers, therefore, duplicate IP addresses might be assigned. This lack of fault tolerance is a serious defect in the DHCP architecture.

You can build in some fault tolerance by configuring two DHCP servers for each subnet. Divide the address range for the subnet between scopes on the two servers. It's not a perfect solution because half your IP addresses are unavailable when one of the DHCP servers is down. But at least clients can obtain leases from one server when the other fails.

WARNING

You might encounter another suggested method for achieving DHCP fault tolerance, in which you configure two DHCP servers with the exact same scopes. Under this plan, one DHCP server remains shut down while the other actively provides leases. If the active server fails, the backup server would be started.

The problem with this strategy is that the newly activated DHCP server does not have a copy of the database from the failed one. Consequently the new server has no understanding of the IP addresses that are active on the network. It might, therefore, issue new leases that conflict with active workstations. It might also deny existing clients when they attempt to renew leases they hold from the old server. Things can get very messy. The one thing you might be able to do is to copy the database from the inactive server and use the procedures described in the section "Repairing a Corrupted DHCP Database" to restore the database on another server. But that assumes that for some reason the old DHCP server is down but you can still read files from the computer on which it was running.

It doesn't appear that you can improve on two servers that share a subnet address space. Be alert for DHCP server failures and be prepared to restore their proper function as promptly as possible.

All DHCP servers can be managed centrally by a manager who has Administrator permissions for the servers. To add a DHCP server to the DHCP Manager, perform the following steps:

1. Start DHCP Manager.

2. Choose **Add** in the Server menu.

3. In the Add DHCP Server to Server List dialog box, enter the IP address of the DHCP server that is to be added.

4. Choose **OK**.

Managing the DHCP Database

The key DHCP database files are stored by default in `C:\winnt\system32\dhcp`. (If your system files are stored in a directory other than `C:\winnt`, substitute the appropriate directory path.) The files are as follows:

- **DHCP.MDB.** The DHCP database file.

- **DHCP.TMP.** A file used by DHCP to store temporary working data.

- **JET.LOG and JET*.LOG.** These files record transactions performed on the database. This data can be used to recover the DHCP database in the event of damage.

- **SYSTEM.MDB.** Holds information about the structure of the DHCP database.

Windows NT Server periodically backs up the DHCP database and Registry entries. The default backup interval is 15 minutes, configurable using a Registry key.

Compacting the DHCP Database

Windows NT 4.0 will automatically compact the DHCP database from time to time, and it will seldom be necessary to compact the database manually. If you are running DHCP on Windows NT Server 3.51 or earlier, however, you must compact the database manually. Microsoft recommends compacting `DHCP.MDB` when it reaches 10 MB in size. To compact the database, follow this procedure:

1. Open a command prompt.

2. Enter the command `net stop dhcpserver` to stop the DHCP Server service on the computer. Users cannot obtain or renew DHCP leases while the DHCP Server service is stopped.

3. Change to the DHCP directory. If the directory is in the default location, enter the command `cd \winnt\system32\dhcp`.

4. Enter the command `jetpack dhcp.mdb temp.mdb` to compact the database. `dhcp.mdb` is the file to be compacted, whereas `temp.mdb` is a name for a temporary file that jetpack uses during the compacting process.

5. After receiving the message `jetpack completed successfully`, restart DHCP with the command `net start dhcpserver`.

To close the command prompt, enter the command `exit`.

WARNING

jetpack should be used to compact only the `DHCP.MDB` file. Do not compact the `SYSTEM.MDB` file, period, per Microsoft.

Starting and Stopping the DHCP Server

You might need to periodically stop and restart the DHCP Server. You also might need to determine whether DHCP Server services are started. If users experience difficulty obtaining addresses from DHCP, the first troubleshooting step is to make sure that the DHCP Server service is started.

As explained in the previous section, you can start and stop the DHCP Server service from the command prompt. You also can use the Services tool in the Control Panel to start and stop it. To start, stop, or ascertain the status of the DHCP Server service, follow these steps:

1. Open the Services tool in the Control Panel. Figure 10.13 shows the Services dialog box.

2. Scroll through the list of services to locate the entry Microsoft DHCP Server. The status of the server is described by entries in two columns:

   ■ The Status column states whether the service is `Started`. If no entry is found, the service is not started.

   ■ The Startup column indicates whether the service starts automatically when the system restarts. `Automatic` and `Manual` indicate whether manual intervention is required to start the service. A service labeled `Disabled` cannot be started from the Services dialog box.

FIGURE 10.13

The Services applet displaying the status of the DHCP Server service.

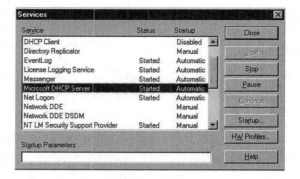

3. To change the startup mode for a service, choose **Sta_r_tup** and change the Startup Type in the Services dialog box.

4. To stop a started service, select the service and choose **S_t_op**.

   To start a stopped service, select the service and choose **Start**.

   A disabled service cannot be started.

5. Choose **Close** to exit the Services tool.

NOTE

The information in this section is sufficient for the purpose of managing the DHCP Server service, but much more can be said about the Services tool. Consult NRP's *Inside Windows NT Server* for a complete discussion of the Services tool.

Repairing a Corrupted DHCP Database

The DHCP database files are backed up at sixty-minute intervals. The default location for the backup copies of the database files is the directory `C:\winnt\system32\dhcp\backup\jet\new`.

NOTE

You can adjust the intervals at which the DHCP database is backed up by creating a BackupInterval Registry value entry. This value entry is described toward the end of this chapter in the section, "Configuring DHCP in the Registry."

If the DHCP Server service is started but users still cannot obtain leases from DHCP, the DHCP database might have become corrupted, which would make DHCP unavailable. Restoring the DHCP database from the backup copy might be possible. To force DHCP to restore its database from the backup, stop and restart the DHCP Server service, using the techniques described in the previous two sections. If the DHCP Server service identifies a corrupted database during startup, it automatically attempts to restore from the backup database.

The section "Configuring DHCP in the Registry," later in this chapter, discusses the RestoreFlag key in the Registry, which can be set to force DHCP to restore its database when the computer is restarted.

If neither procedure restores the database satisfactorily, stop the DHCP Server service. Then copy all files in `C:\winnt\system32\dhcp\backup` to `C:\winnt\system32\dhcp`. Finally, restart the DHCP Server service.

After you restore the database, you need to bring the database up to date on active leases not recorded in the backup copy of the database. This procedure is called reconciling the DHCP database. To reconcile the DHCP database:

1. Start DHCP Manager.

2. Select a scope in the DHCP Scopes box.

3. Choose **Active Leases** in the Scope menu.

4. Choose the **Reconcile** button in the Active Leases dialog box.

NOTE

The DHCP database is not fault tolerant, even though it is periodically backed up. A system crash during the backup process could corrupt both the database and the backup database.

To provide a greater degree of fault tolerance, you can use the Windows NT Replicator service to automatically copy the backup database to another Windows NT computer. After the server is restored to operation, the replicated copy of the backup database could be retrieved and used to restart DHCP.

NRP's *Inside Windows NT Server* offers a thorough discussion of the Replicator service.

Creating a New DHCP Database

If the database is corrupted and a valid backup is unavailable, you can force DHCP to create a new database with the following procedure:

1. Stop the DHCP Server service.

2. Copy the file `C:\winnt\system32\dhcp\dhcp.mdb` to another directory.

3. Delete all files in the directory `C:\winnt\system32\dhcp` (the default primary directory).

4. Delete all files in the directory `C:\winnt\system32\dhcp\backup\jet` (the default backup directory).

5. Copy the file `System.mdb` from the installation CD-ROM to the directory `C:\winnt\system32\dhcp`.

6. Restart the DHCP Server service. The following four steps reconcile the new DHCP database with active leases.

7. Start DHCP Manager.

8. Select a scope in the DHCP Scopes box.

9. Choose **Active Leases** in the Scope menu.

10. Choose the **Reconcile** button in the Active Leases dialog box. When they renew their leases, clients are matched with active leases to complete rebuilding the database.

NOTE

You can force a client to renew its DHCP lease by entering the command `ipconfig /renew` at a command prompt on the client computer. With Windows 95/98, choose the **Renew** button in the `winipcfg` utility, which you can start by entering the command `winipcfg` in a Run dialog box.

DHCP Configuration Options

Your organization might choose to implement DHCP even though IP addresses are not assigned dynamically. DHCP options enable network administrators to configure many settings that affect the TCP/IP protocols.

These DHCP options can be applied to any computer that obtains its address from DHCP, whether the address is dynamically allocated or reserved.

As shown in Figure 10.14, DHCP options are applied in layers:

- **Global** options apply to all scopes on a given DHCP server unless overwritten by scope or client options.

- **Scope** options apply to all clients within the scope unless overridden by client options. Scope properties might be used to set options for a department or for hosts on a specific network.

- **Client** options supersede scope and global options for a specific client. Client-specific options can be configured for clients having DHCP reservations.

FIGURE 10.14

Priority of DHCP options.

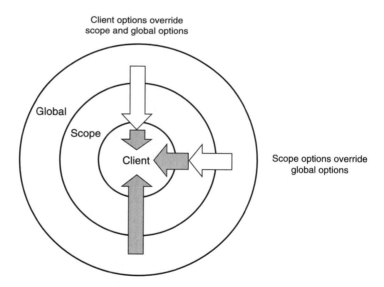

Specifying default options is another possibility. Specifying a default option establishes default values for any parameters associated with the option but does not put the option into effect. Options go into effect only when specified as global, scope, or client options.

A Microsoft DHCP packet can support a DHCP data payload of 312 bytes, which is generally sufficient. If too many DHCP options are configured, some can exceed the 312-byte capacity, making it necessary to trim options of lower priority.

NOTE

DHCP configuration options do not override settings that are made locally on the workstation. If a DNS server, WINS server, or default router has been locally configured, they take
precedence over any options specified in the DHCP scope that is used to configure the client.

Managing Default, Global, and Scope DHCP Options

Options are added, configured, and removed within DHCP Manager.
Default, global, and scope options are managed from the DHCP Manager
dialog box. To change options, follow these steps:

1. Start DHCP Manager.

2. Select an existing scope.

3. To set default parameter values for an option, choose the **Default**
   command in the DHCP Options menu.

   To set options for all scopes on the DHCP server, choose the **Global**
   command in the DHCP Options menu.

   To set options for the selected scope, choose the **Scope** command in
   the DHCP Options menu.

4. The DHCP Options dialog box (see Figure 10.15) is used to add and
   delete options. The legend for the dialog box specifies whether default,
   global, or scope options are being configured. In this example, two
   options have been added.

FIGURE 10.15

*Adding options to a
scope.*

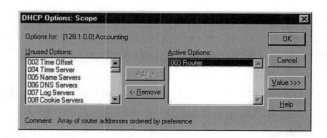

5. To add an option, select an option in the Unused Options box and choose **Add**.

6. To remove an option, select an option in the Active Options box and choose **Remove**.

7. Many options accept or require configuration values. To change the values of an option, select the option in the Active Options box and choose **Value**. The DHCP Options dialog box expands to display the currently assigned value or values (see Figure 10.16).

FIGURE 10.16

Expanding the DHCP Options dialog box to show option values.

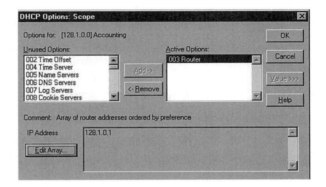

8. To edit values assigned to the option, choose **Edit Array**. An appropriate editor opens. Figure 10.17 shows the IP Address Array Editor dialog box. In this box, values can be added or removed from the array of addresses. (The order of the options determines their priority, and values should be added in order of priority. Unfortunately, no direct way exists for modifying the order of the values.)

FIGURE 10.17

Editing an IP address array.

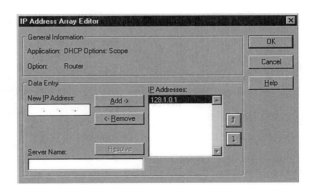

Managing Client-Specific Options for Reservations

Client-specific options can be assigned to reservations only. Options can be assigned to leases only by assigning default, global, and scope options.

To assign options to a reservation:

1. Select the scope supporting the reservation in the DHCP Manager dialog box.

2. Choose the **Active Leases** command in the Scope menu.

3. Select the reservation in the Active Leases dialog box and choose the **Properties** button to open the Client Properties dialog box.

4. For reservations, the **Options** button in the Client Properties dialog box will be active. Choose **Options** to open the DHCP Options: Reservation dialog box, which is similar to the dialog box shown in Figure 10.15. Use this dialog box to add and configure options for the reservation.

5. Choose **OK** to exit the DHCP Options dialog box.

DHCP Options for Microsoft TCP/IP

Table 10.1 summarizes the predefined DHCP options that apply to Microsoft TCP/IP clients. The table includes only options that can be configured using the DHCP Options dialog box.

Several RFC 1533 DHCP options are configured in the Create Scope or Scope Properties dialog box. These options are as follows:

- 1. Subnet mask
- 51. DHCP Lease time
- 58. DHCP Renewal (T1) time
- 59. DHCP Rebinding (T2) time

Options 51, 58, and 59 are all functions of the lease duration specified in the Create Scope or Scope Properties dialog box.

NOTE

RFC 1533 specifies many other options not applicable to Microsoft TCP/IP clients. If non-Microsoft clients will be obtaining addresses from the Microsoft DHCP Server, you can include non-Microsoft options in the properties of the appropriate scopes and reservations.

TABLE **10.1**

DHCP Options for Microsoft Clients

Code	Name	Description
1	Subnet Mask	Specifies the client subnet mask. This option is configured in the Create Scope or Scope Properties dialog box and cannot be directly configured as a scope option.
3	Router	Specifies a list of IP addresses for routers on the client's network.
6	DNS servers	Specifies a list of IP addresses for available DNS servers.
15	Domain name	Specifies the domain name to be used when resolving DNS host names.
44	WINS/NBNS servers	Specifies a list of IP addresses for NetBIOS name servers (NBNS). (See Chapter 11.)
46	WINS/NBT node type	Specifies the NetBIOS over TCP/IP node type. Values: 1=b-node, 2=p-node, 4=m-node, 8=h-node. (See RFC 1001/1002 and Chapter 11.)
47	NetBIOS ID scope	Specifies a string to be used as the NetBIOS over TCP/IP scope ID. (See RFC 1001/1002.)

Configuring DHCP in the Registry

The Registry is the fault-tolerant database in which configuration data are stored for Windows NT computers. Several Registry parameters are related to DHCP and can, like other Registry parameters, be modified using the Registry Editor. The Registry and Registry Editor are discussed more thoroughly in my book *Inside Windows NT Server 4* also published by New Riders Publishing.

WARNING

The Registry includes configuration data for virtually every Windows NT system. Obviously, a great deal of damage can be done if errors are introduced into the Registry. Therefore, when browsing the Registry with the Registry Editor, you should choose Read Only Mode in the Options menu to prevent accidental changes.

The Registry is organized into four subtrees. Each of the subtrees has a window within Registry Editor (refer to Figure 10.18). The subtrees are delineated in the following list:

- **HKEY_LOCAL_MACHINE.** Current configuration parameters for the computer.

- **HKEY_CURRENT_USER.** The profile for the current user.

- **HKEY_USERS.** Stores user profiles.

- **HKEY_CLASSES_ROOT.** Object linking and embedding (OLE) and file-class associations.

Data associated with DHCP are stored in the HKEY_LOCAL_MACHINE subtree. The window for this subtree has been expanded in Figure 10.18 to show the database structure. Note the similarity between the structure of the Registry and of the DOS/NT hierarchical file system. The equivalent of a directory in the Registry database is called a key. *Value entries*, also referred to simply as *values*, contain data that is stored in the Registry.

Keys can contain other keys. In the figure, for example, *SYSTEM* is a key that contains several subkeys such as ControlSet001 and CurrentControlSet.

In Figure 10.18, the *CurrentControlSet* key has been opened for several levels, revealing the *ComputerName* subkey. This subkey contains one value describing the NetBIOS name assigned to this computer. Keys can contain an indefinite number of values. All value entries have three components:

- **Name.** In this example, the name is ComputerName.

- **Data type.** This component describes the characteristics of the data. Here the data type is REG_SZ.

- **Data value.** This consists of one or more data items that are stored in the value. In this example, the data value is KEYSTONE2.

FIGURE 10.18

A value in the Registry.

Registry data have one of five data types:

- **REG_BINARY.** Raw binary data, the form used to store most hardware data.

- **REG_DWORD.** Numeric data up to 4 bytes in length, in decimal, hexadecimal, or binary form.

- **REG_EXPAND_SZ.** Expandable data strings that contain system variables. An example of this variable type would be %SystemRoot\system32.

- **REG_MULTI_SZ.** Data consisting of multiple strings in lists. Often used to store lists of human-readable values.

- **REG_SZ.** Character data, usually human-readable text.

The data types that apply to DHCP Registry entries are discussed along with the associated values. See the section "DHCP-Related Registry Values" later in this chapter.

Viewing and Editing DHCP-related Values in the Registry

DHCP-related Registry values are stored in the HKEY_LOCAL_MACHINE subtree in the following subkey:

    SYSTEM\CurrentControlSet\Services\DHCPServer\Parameters

To observe or modify the DHCP Registry values:

1. To start the Registry Editor, choose the **Run** command in the Program Manager File menu. In the Command Line box for the Run command, enter the command `regedt32` and choose **OK**.

2. If no subtrees are shown, choose the **Open Local** command in the Registry menu.

3. Expand the window for the HKEY_LOCAL_MACHINE subtree.

    Click on the following keys to expand the appropriate branch of the tree:

    ■ SYSTEM

    ■ CurrentControlSet

    ■ Services

    ■ DHCPServer

    ■ Parameters

When that is done, the window resembles Figure 10.19.

FIGURE 10.19

Registry values associated with DHCP.

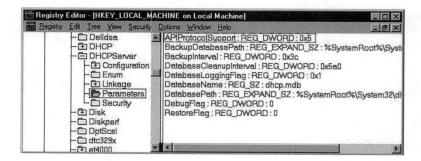

4. To change a value, double-click on the value entry to open the appropriate editor. The editor that appears supports entry only of data that conform to the data type associated with this value. The example shown in Figure 10.20 shows the DWORD editor, which accepts only a binary, decimal, or hexadecimal value. A String Editor is used to enter string-type values.

FIGURE 10.20
Editing a DWORD-type value in the Registry.

Edit the value and, if necessary, click on the button associated with the data format. Then choose **OK** to save the value to the Registry.

5. To save changes, choose <u>C</u>**lose** in the <u>R</u>egistry menu.

DHCP-Related Registry Values

The following Registry values can be viewed and edited using the procedure described in the previous section:

APIProtocolSupport

Data Type:	*REG_DWORD*
Range:	0x1, 0x2, 0x4, 0x5, 0x7
Default:	0x7

Specifies the protocols supported by the DHCP server. Edit this parameter to enable different computers to access the DHCP server. Available values are as follows:

0x1 RPC over TCP/IP

0x2 RPC over named pipes

0x4 RPC over local procedure call (LPC)

0x5 RPC over TCP/IP and RPC over LPC

0x7 RPC over TCP/IP, named pipes, and LPC

BackupDatabasePath

Data Type:	*REG_EXPAND_SZ*
Range:	pathname
Default:	%SystemRoot%\system32\dhcp\ backup

Specifies the directory in which DHCP backup files are stored. The default value places the backup files on the same hard drive as the primary files, making both vulnerable to a single hardware failure. If the system has more than one hard drive, locating the backup directory on an alternative hard drive is preferable. This directory must be on a local hard drive because DHCP Manager cannot access a network drive.

BackupInterval

Data Type:	*REG_DWORD*
Range:	no limit
Default:	15 minutes (see discussion)

Specifies the interval in minutes between DHCP database backups. The official default backup interval, as documented in the *Windows NT Resource Kit,* is 15 minutes. In practice, however, the default backup interval is sixty minutes. I recommend that you add this Registry value and adjust the backup interval to the original 15 minutes.

DatabaseCleanupInterval

Data Type:	*REG_DWORD*
Range:	no limit
Default:	0x15180

DHCP periodically cleans up the database, removing expired records. This parameter specifies the interval in minutes between DHCP cleanup operations. The default value sets an interval of one day (0x15180 is 864,000 minutes, equivalent to 24 hours).

DatabaseLoggingFlag

Data Type:	*REG_DWORD*
Range:	0 or 1
Default:	1

If the value of this parameter is 1, database changes are recorded in the JET.LOG file. If the value is 0, changes are not recorded. The JET.LOG file is used to recover changes that have not been made to the database file. It might be desirable to turn off logging to improve system performance.

DatabaseName

Data Type:	*REG_SZ*
Range:	filename
Default:	dhcp.mdb

The name of the DHCP database file.

DatabasePath

Data Type:	*REG_EXPAND_SZ*
Range:	pathname
Default:	%SystemRoot%\System32\dhcp

The directory in which DHCP database files are created and opened.

RestoreFlag

Data Type:	*REG_DWORD*
Range:	0 or 1
Default:	0

If this value is 0, the database is not restored from the backup database when the DHCP Server service is started. Set this value to 1 to force DHCP to retrieve the backup database. This parameter is automatically set to 0 after a successful database restoration.

DHCP Makes Things a Lot Easier

Although setting up DHCP can at first be more complicated than manually entering IP addresses in client configurations, the effort will be amply repaid by the labor you will avoid when the network is reconfigured or clients are moved.

In view of the fact that DHCP does not coordinate scopes between DHCP servers, it can be a bit difficult to enable multiple DHCP servers, but that's just what you want to do to provide a measure of fault tolerance. Properly configuring DHCP, particularly when multiple DHCP servers are being implemented, takes a bit of planning. So take the time and ensure that scopes are properly assigned.

Remember that DHCP clients pull changes. DHCP servers cannot push changes out to the clients. This forces you to manage your lease duration and to plan for those times when network configurations will take place.

DHCP takes care of IP addresses, but there is another administrative chore: providing users with host names. As with IP addresses, you can choose to specify names by the time-consuming task of manually creating static files, in this case called LMHOSTS files. Or you can learn to use WINS to make naming automatic. And that brings us to the next chapter, where you will learn to add WINS to your network configuration.

Chapter 11

HOST NAMING IN THE MICROSOFT TCP/IP WORLD

To make networks friendly to users, it is common practice to maintain naming services that enable users to identify computers by names rather than numbers. The name serves as an alias for the computer so that the user doesn't need to remember an IP address such as 10.1.55.88 or an Ethernet address such as 00 6A 4B 30 2E 7F.

Traditionally, Microsoft networks have identified computers with names based on NetBIOS. NetBIOS makes it easy to develop applications that interact with the network by providing an application programming interface (API) that enables the applications to access the network without worrying about the folderol of network communication. NetBIOS naming is simple, efficient, and works so smoothly that it is practically invisible.

But when Microsoft began to move their network products toward TCP/IP, they were faced with a problem, because TCP/IP networks do not use NetBIOS names. The result has been a long evolution of technologies that have gradually simplified the process of supporting a naming service on a Microsoft TCP/IP network. That evolution will be complete when Windows NT version 5 is released, finally enabling administrators to configure networks that rely entirely on DNS for host name resolution.

Until NT 5 emerges, however, we're stuck with two systems for naming computers. This complicates our lives as Microsoft network administrators, and you need to understand the complications to deal with the problems that inevitably arise. First we'll focus on NetBIOS names, after which we'll see how TCP/IP host names are supported. Finally, we'll see how naming works on networks that support both naming technologies.

NetBIOS Names

Every computer on a Microsoft network is associated with a NetBIOS name. These NetBIOS names appear in browse lists. For example, if you open Network Neighborhood, computers are identified by their NetBIOS names.

NetBIOS names also can be used in native NetBIOS applications, such as the NET command. For example, you might map a network share with the command **net use m:** \\drew\docs to map network drive m: to the docs share on the computer named drew.

Expressions such as \\drew\docs are UNC (universal naming convention) names. A UNC name consists of a NetBIOS name followed by a share name. Backslashes must appear as shown in the example.

NetBIOS names comprise the backbone of native Microsoft network communication. Even on TCP/IP networks, NetBIOS remain the way most network resources are identified. Unfortunately, NetBIOS doesn't mate naturally with TCP/IP, and the naming architecture gets pretty involved. To understand the techniques Microsoft has devised to support NetBIOS over TCP/IP, we need to look at NetBIOS naming in some depth.

Structure of NetBIOS Names

You might think you know all about NetBIOS names. After all, isn't a NetBIOS name simply the computer name you specify when you install the operating system? Not quite. The name you enter during setup is only part of the NetBIOS naming picture.

At any given time, a Microsoft computer will be known by as many as 16 NetBIOS names. Why so many? Well, a NetBIOS name identifies more than the physical computer. It also identifies a specific service running on that computer. Let's look at two examples for a computer named WOODY. Like every networked Microsoft computer, WOODY is running a Workstation service, the service that enables the computer to interact with network resources. WOODY also is sharing resources and is therefore running a Server service. Suppose that WOODY is communicating with a computer named BLYTHE. If BLYTHE wants to send a message to WOODY's Server service, BLYTHE must address the message so that the message doesn't go to the Workstation service instead.

To differentiate between services, each service is given a different NetBIOS name, which is generated by adding a byte (usually expressed as a number in the range 00 through FF hexadecimal) to the end of the computer's basic machine name. This byte is typically referred to as "the sixteenth byte character" of the NetBIOS name. The Workstation service on the computer named WOODY has the NetBIOS name WOODY[00h] where [00h] is the 16th byte, the hexadecimal digit 00.

A computer registers the NetBIOS names it is using with the network. You can view the NetBIOS names that have been registered by a computer by entering the command **nbtstat -n** at a command prompt. Here is an example of the output:

```
Node IpAddress: [209.51.67.15] Scope Id: []

          NetBIOS Local Name Table

     Name               Type          Status
    ---------------------------------------------

     WOODY        <00>  UNIQUE       Registered
     PSEUDO       <00>  GROUP        Registered
     WOODY        <03>  UNIQUE       Registered
     WOODY        <20>  UNIQUE       Registered
```

The output of nbtstat reports the 16th byte in angle braces (such as <03>). As you can see the computer WOODY is known by three NetBIOS names. WOODY<00> identifies the computer's Workstation service, WOODY<03> is associated with the Messenger service, and WOODY<20> identifies the Server service. These names are identified as UNIQUE because they are uniquely identified with a specific computer.

As you can see in the output of nbtstat, NetBIOS names are padded with spaces if the computer name portion contains fewer than 15 characters. Thus, all NetBIOS names have exactly 16 characters.

Notice that another NetBIOS name appears in the list. PSEUDO<00> is the name of the domain the computer is logged on to. A domain is a GROUP NetBIOS name because it can be associated with more than one computer.

The NetBIOS Name Space

The NetBIOS name space (the totality of NetBIOS names being used on a network) is flat, meaning that all the names are registered in a single name pool. This has some perplexing consequences.

For example, two computers cannot share a computer name, even if the computers log on to different domains. Also a computer cannot share its name with a domain (or workgroup). Let's emphasize that point:

- If a computer named BLYTHE logs on to the PSEUDO domain, there cannot be another computer named BLYTHE that simultaneously logs on to the WIDGETS domain. All computers in all domains are recorded in the same NetBIOS name space.

- If your network has a domain (or workgroup) named PSEUDO, you cannot create a computer with the machine name PSEUDO.

- A network cannot have a domain and a workgroup that have the same name.

The flat nature of the NetBIOS name space has a number of liabilities. Perhaps the most inconvenient arises when the Microsoft DNS server is configured to obtain NetBIOS names from WINS. Because the WINS name space is flat and all names are mushed together, all names obtained from WINS must be registered in a single DNS domain. Chapter 13, "Managing the Microsoft DNS Server," explains the Microsoft DNS server. See the section "WINS Lookup Properties" for more details on the integration of WINS with DNS.

Components of NetBIOS Names

A NetBIOS name consists of up to 16 characters. The first 15 characters are the computer name, as defined in the computer's network configuration. The final character, the 16th byte, is a byte (usually expressed as an 8-bit hexadecimal number) that defines the specific type of the name.

Computer names can consist of up to 15 characters, and must conform to the following rules:

- The following characters are allowed: A–Z, a–z, 0–9, and the dash (-)

- the first and last characters must be alphanumeric (A–Z, a–z, or 0–9)

The 16th byte is assigned by the operating system. NetBIOS names are categorized in three groups:

- Computer names

- Domain/workgroup names

- Other and special names

NetBIOS names can be categorized in another way as well:

- *Unique names* associated with a specific machine

- *Group names* associated with groups of machines

Let's look at some examples of the NetBIOS names you are likely to encounter.

NetBIOS Computer Names

Computer names are associated with processes and services running on the computer that has registered the names. Here are some examples of NetBIOS computer names:

- ***<computername>*[00h]** This unique name registers the computer's Workstation service. This is the basic client NetBIOS name, registered by every NetBIOS client computer.

- ***<computername>*[03h]** This unique name registers the computer's Messenger service, enabling the client to receive and send messages.

- ***<computername>*[06h]** This unique name registers the RAS server service if that service is running.

■ *<computername>*[1Fh] This name is registered for the Network Dynamic Data Exchange (NetDDE) service and appears when NetDDE is started. By default, NetDDE is not started.

■ *<computername>*[20h] This name is registered for the Server service, which is active on all computers that are configured to share resources, and provides a sharepoint for share access.

■ *<computername>*[21h] This name is registered if an RAS server service is running on the computer.

■ *<computername>*[BEh] This name is registered if the Network Monitor is running on the computer. (See Chapter 16, "Troubleshooting," for information about the Network Monitor.)

■ *<computername>*[BFh] This name is registered if the Network Monitoring Agent is running on the computer.

NetBIOS Domain Names

NetBIOS names are also used to register domains. Here are some Domain NetBIOS names you are likely to encounter:

■ *<domainname>*[00h] The Workstation service registers this name, enabling it to receive browser broadcasts.

■ *<domainname>*[1Bh] This unique name is registered by the computer that is the domain master browser, which is always the PDC if the PDC is available. The domain master browser is explained later in this chapter.

■ *<domainname>*[1Ch] This group name registers the IP addresses of up to 25 computers that are domain controllers for the domain. One IP address will be the PDC, and an IP address will be included for each BDC in the domain. The [1Ch] domain name enables BDCs to locate the PDC and enables pass-through logon validation to take place.

■ *<domainname>*[1Dh] This group name registers a master browser. On NWLink or NetBEUI networks, there will be a single master browser for the domain. On TCP/IP networks there will be a master browser for each subnet.

■ **<*domainname*>[1Eh]** This group name is registered by all browser servers and potential browser servers in a domain or workgroup. The master browser uses this name to address requests to fill up its browse lists. This name is also used in election request packets used to force an election.

Special NetBIOS Names

A few NetBIOS names don't fit neatly into categories. The ones you are most likely to encounter are:

■ **<*username*>[03h]** The currently logged-on user is registered with this name, enabling the user to receive messages. If a user logs on to more than one computer, only the first computer will register the name.

■ **_MSBROWSE_[01h]** The master browser registers this name, which is used to broadcast and receive domain announcements on the local subnet. This name enables master browsers of different domains to learn the names of different domains and the names of other domains' master browsers.

NetBIOS Name Resolution Modes

Name resolution is the process of associating host names with addresses. On NBF and NWLink networks, NetBIOS names must be resolved to machine physical addresses, such as the Ethernet MAC address, before communication can take place. On TCP/IP networks, NetBIOS names must be resolved to IP addresses. (IP addresses will be resolved to MAC addresses at a later time by using the ARP protocol.)

Resolution of NetBIOS names on TCP/IP environments is the responsibility of the NetBIOS over TCP/IP (abbreviated NetBT or NBT) service. NBT name resolution can be accomplished in three ways:

■ By broadcasting name resolution requests to computers that maintain name databases. These name databases are called *browse databases* because they support the activity of browsing on the network, and the computers that store copies of the browse database are called *browsers*.

- By querying an LMHOSTS file, a text database file that contains name-to-IP address name mappings.

- By querying a NetBIOS Name Server (NBNS) such as WINS, which maintains a dynamic database of registered NetBIOS names.

Clients can be configured to use any or all of these methods. The resolution method a client uses depends on its *node type*. Three node types, b-node, p-node, and m-node are defined in RFCs 1001 and 1002. The newer h-node type is currently an Internet Draft. Microsoft supports an extension to b-node called *enhanced b-node*, which will also be discussed.

B-Node

Name resolution using broadcast messages (b-node) is the oldest method employed on Microsoft networks. Figure 11.1 illustrates b-node name resolution. When HOSTA needs to communicate with HOSTB, the sequence of events is as follows:

1. HOSTA consults a local cache, maintained in its memory, of recently resolved names. If the required name is found there, name resolution stops. A local cache is maintained to reduce the amount of network traffic that will be caused by name resolution requests.

2. HOSTA sends a broadcast message that interrogates the network for the presence of HOSTB. The broadcast is received by all hosts on the local network.

3. If HOSTB receives the broadcast, it sends a response to HOSTA that includes its IP address. If HOSTA does not receive a response within a preset period of time, it "times out" and the attempt fails.

4. If a browser receives the broadcast and can supply the required information, the browser replies to HOSTA with the IP address of HOSTB. Browser name resolution works somewhat differently under different network protocols. A separate section in this chapter describes the operation of browsers.

B-node name resolution works well in small, local networks, but poses two disadvantages that become critical as networks grow:

FIGURE 11.1

B-node name resolution.

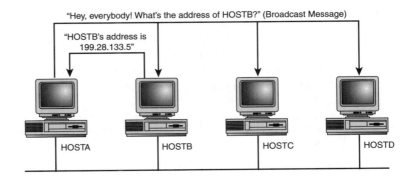

- As the number of hosts on the network increases, the amount of broadcast traffic can consume significant network bandwidth.

- IP routers do not ordinarily forward broadcasts, and the b-node technique cannot propagate names through an internetwork. As Figure 11.2 illustrates, b-node broadcasts cannot resolve the NetBIOS names of computers that reside on remote subnets.

FIGURE 11.2

B-node name resolution is blocked by routers.

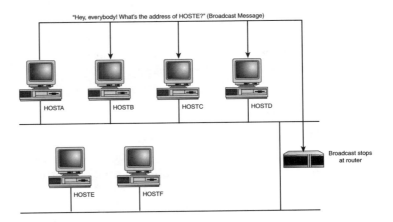

Broadcast messages are necessary when the IP address of the destination host is not known. But high levels of broadcast messages are undesirable, because every host that sees the message must expend some processing power decoding the message to see if that host is the intended destination for the message. So every broadcast message generates some activity on every computer and the overall processing cost of many broadcasts can be significant. Therefore, b-node is not the most desirable name resolution method and is best used only on small networks.

NOTE

The utility nbtstat is useful for diagnosing broadcast mode name resolution and is discussed later in this chapter. The command nbtstat -r is particularly useful, reporting the number of b-node broadcasts that are occurring on the network. This information is useful if you suspect that b-node broadcasts are degrading network performance.

Enhanced B-Node

In its own implementations, Microsoft provides an extension to b-node name resolution. If an enhanced b-node host cannot resolve a NetBIOS name through b-node broadcasts, it will consult a local LMHOSTS file if one has been configured. LMHOSTS files are text database files that map NetBIOS names to IP addresses. The format of the LMHOSTS file is described later in this chapter.

B-node is the default name resolution mode for Microsoft hosts not configured to use WINS for name resolution. In pure b-node environments, hosts can be configured to use LMHOSTS files to resolve names on remote networks. Enhanced b-node is enabled by checking the **Enable LMHOSTS Lookup** check box on the WINS tab of the TCP/IP Properties dialog box. (If WINS server addresses are specified on the WINS tab, the computer will be configured for h-node name resolution, even if the **Enable LMHOSTS Lookup** check box is checked.)

P-Node

Hosts configured for p-node (point-to-point) use only WINS for name resolution. All p-node communication is via point-to-point messages, and no broadcast traffic is generated. P-node computers register themselves with a WINS server, which functions as a NetBIOS name server. The WINS server maintains a database of NetBIOS names, ensures that duplicate names do not exist, and makes the database available to WINS clients. Figure 11.3 illustrates how WINS clients resolve names.

FIGURE 11.3

P-node name resolution.

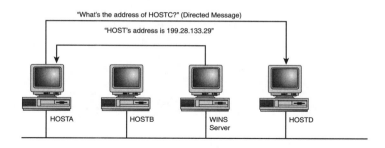

Notice in Figure 11.4 that routers are not barriers to WINS operation. Each WINS client is configured with the address of a WINS server, which might reside on the local network or on a remote network. WINS clients and servers communicate via directed messages that can be routed. No broadcast messages are required for p-node name resolution.

FIGURE 11.4

P-node name resolution is unaffected by routers.

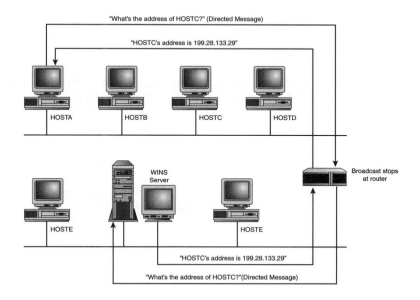

Two liabilities of p-node name resolution are that:

- All computers must be configured using the address of a WINS server, even when communicating hosts reside on the same network.

- If a WINS server is unavailable, name resolution fails for p-node clients.

Because both b-node and p-node address resolution present disadvantages, two address modes have been developed that form hybrids of b-node and p-node. These hybrid modes are called m-node and h-node.

Microsoft network clients can be configured to use p-node or m-node only if they obtain their configuration settings from DHCP. See the section "Configuring DHCP Clients as WINS Clients" in Chapter 12, "Managing WINS," for details.

M-Node

M-node (mixed) computers first attempt to use b-node (broadcast) name resolution, which succeeds if the desired host resides on the local network. If b-node resolution fails and LHHOSTS lookup (enhanced b-node) is configured, an attempt is made to resolve the name through a local LMHOSTS file. If b-node fails, m-node hosts then attempt to use p-node to resolve the name.

M-node enables name resolution to continue on the local network when WINS services are down. B-node resolution is attempted first on the assumption that in most environments, hosts communicate most often with hosts on their local networks. When this assumption holds, performance of b-node resolution is superior to p-node. Recall, however, that b-node can result in high levels of broadcast traffic.

Microsoft warns that m-node can cause problems when network logons are attempted in a routed environment.

H-Node

Like m-node, h-node is a hybrid of broadcast (b-node) and directed (p-node) name resolution modes. Nodes configured with m-node, however, first attempt to resolve addresses using WINS. Only after an attempt to resolve the name using a name server fails does an h-node computer attempt to use b-node, with LMHOSTS lookup if that option is configured. M-node computers, therefore, can continue to resolve local addresses when WINS is unavailable. When operating in b-node mode, m-node computers continue to poll the WINS server and revert to h-node when WINS services are restored.

H-node is the default mode for Microsoft TCP/IP clients configured using the addresses of WINS servers. As a fallback, Windows TCP/IP clients can be configured to use LMHOSTS files for name resolution.

NOTE

Although networks can be configured using mixtures of b-node and p-node computers, Microsoft recommends this only as an interim measure. P-node hosts ignore b-node broadcast messages, and b-node hosts ignore p-node directed messages. Two hosts, therefore, conceivably could be established using the same NetBIOS name.

Name Resolution with LMHOSTS Files

Although a complete name resolution system can be based on LMHOSTS files, static naming files (called "static" because they are not automatically updated as the network evolves) can be a nightmare to administer, particularly when they must be distributed to several hosts on the network. Nevertheless, LMHOSTS files might be necessary if WINS will not be run on a network or if it is desirable to have a backup plan in case the WINS service fails.

Although LAN Manager LMHOSTS files support little more than mappings of NetBIOS names to IP addresses, Windows NT offers several options that make LMHOSTS considerably more versatile.

Format of LMHOSTS Files

A sample LMHOSTS file named LMHOSTS.SAM is installed in the directory `C:\Winnt\system32\drivers\etc`. You can consult this file for formatting examples, but should create your LMHOSTS file from scratch. The LMHOSTS file is processed line-by-line, and the sample file contains numerous comments and extraneous lines that slow name resolution. When you create your own LMHOSTS file, it must be named LMHOSTS (no filename extension) and it must be stored in `C:\Winnt\system32\drivers\etc`.

NOTE

Most Windows-based editors automatically append an extension to the filename when they save a file. If you save a file named LMHOSTS in Notepad, for example, the .txt extension is automatically added to the saved file.

In Notepad, you can override this behavior by enclosing the filename in quotation marks when you save it.

In any case, if LMHOSTS name resolution doesn't appear to work, use Windows NT Explorer to examine the filenames. To see filename extensions, you need to open the Options dialog box (choose **Options** in the **View** menu) and clear the check box **Hide file extensions for known file types.**

The basic format of an LMHOSTS entry is as follows:

```
ip address      name
```

The IP address must begin in column one of the line. Here is an example of a basic LMHOSTS file:

```
128.2.0.100     LAUREN
128.1.0.101     BLYTHE
128.2.0.10      WOODY
```

Windows NT LMHOSTS files can be enhanced by a variety of keywords, discussed in the next section.

NOTE

The entries in the LMHOSTS file are examined sequentially. To speed the name resolution process, place the most-used names toward the beginning of the LMHOSTS file.

LMHOSTS Keywords

Here is an example of an LMHOSTS file augmented using keywords:

```
128.2.0.100     LAUREN
128.2.0.101     BLYTHE
128.2.0.155     WOODY
128.2.0.2       PSEUDO1   #PRE  #DOM:PSEUDO    #Primary DC
128.2.0.3       PSEUDO2   #PRE  #DOM:PSEUDO    #Backup DC
#BEGIN_ALTERNATE
```

```
#INCLUDE \\PSEUDO1\PUBLIC\LMHOSTS       #Primary source for file
#INCLUDE \\PSEUDO2\PUBLIC\LMHOSTS       #Backup source for file
#END_ALTERNATE
```

The #PRE keyword specifies that the entry should be preloaded into the name cache. Ordinarily, LMHOSTS is consulted for name resolution only after WINS and b-node broadcasts have failed. Preloading the entry ensures that the mapping will be available at the start of the name resolution process. #PRE is often used to ensure that domain names loaded with the #DOM keyword will be cached.

The #DOM keyword identifies domain controllers, information that is often used to determine how browsers and logon services behave on a routed TCP/IP network. #DOM entries can be preloaded in cache by including the #PRE keyword. Later in this chapter, the section "Browsing on TCP/IP" illustrates a use of the #DOM keyword.

The #INCLUDE keyword makes loading mappings from a remote file possible. One use for #INCLUDE is to support a master LMHOSTS file stored on logon servers and accessed by TCP/IP clients during startup. Entries in the remote LMHOSTS file are examined only when TCP/IP is started. Entries in the remote LMHOSTS file, therefore, must be tagged with the #PRE keyword to force them to be loaded into cache. There's a trick to using #INCLUDE that is explained later in this chapter.

If several copies of the included LMHOSTS file are available on different servers, you can force the computer to search several locations until a file is successfully loaded. This is accomplished by bracketing #INCLUDE keywords between the keywords #BEGIN_ALTERNATE and #END_ALTERNATE, as was done in the example file just presented. Any successful #INCLUDE causes the group to succeed.

NOTE

In the sample listing, note that the hosts PSEUDO1 and PSEUDO2 are explicitly defined so that the names can be used in the parameters of the #INCLUDE keywords.

It is useful to have copies of the master LMHOSTS file on several computers so that computers can obtain a backup copy if the primary server is down. But maintaining multiple copies of a file gets you back into the task of distributing changed files, an administrative job we prefer to avoid. You can reduce the complexity of maintaining redundant copies of the LMHOSTS by using the Windows NT Replicator service to distribute updated files. The Replicator service is fully described in my book *Inside Windows NT Server 4* (also from New Riders). After configuring replication, share the appropriate import directory to enable the #INCLUDE statements to retrieve the files.

Organizing Entries in LMHOSTS

When the LMHOSTS file is consulted, NT reads entries sequentially starting from the beginning of the file. NT stops when it encounters the first entry that matches the NetBIOS name it is searching for. Because of this behavior, the arrangement of entries in the LMHOSTS file has an effect on the speed of LMHOSTS name resolution. Here are some recommendations:

- Place the entries that will be needed most often at the beginning of the LMHOSTS file.

- Place entries tagged with the #PRE keyword after standard entries. #PRE entries are loaded into cache when LMHOSTS is processed during logon (or when you enter the command nbtstat -R) and there is no need to process them again.

- Place #INCLUDE entries at the end of LMHOSTS, following #PRE statements that they depend on. #INCLUDE statements are processed only during logon or when you enter the command nbtstat -R.

In large LMHOSTS files it is possible to have two entries for the same NetBIOS name. In such cases, only the first entry will be processed. You need to be aware of this behavior when editing the file. If you add an entry for a host while an entry already exists in the LMHOSTS file, only the first entry in the file will be effective.

Enabling #INCLUDE Statements to Succeed During Logon

When a user fires up a network computer, the LMHOSTS file is processed before the user logs on to the network. The #INCLUDE statement must process a file in a shared directory but cannot connect with the share because the user has not been authenticated and therefore does not have security access.

To enable the user to access a share before logon authentication has been accomplished, it is necessary to configure NT to support *null sessions* that enable users to connect to specified shares with null credentials. Windows versions later than 3.1 do not, by default, support null sessions and null sessions must be explicitly enabled. This can be done on a per-share basis, and properly configured null sessions do not jeopardize security.

To enable null sessions support add a Registry value named NullSessionShares of type REG_MULTI_SZ to the following Registry key:

```
HKEY_LOCAL_MACHINE
  \System
    \CurrentControlSet
      \Services
        \LanmanServer
          \Parameters
```

Registry values of type REG_MULTI_SZ accept multiple data entries. To enable null session support for a share, open the NullSessionShares value entry and add the name of the share, for example PUBLIC as in the sample LMHOSTS file. You must restart the server to activate any changes made to the Registry.

Alternatively, you can load the LMHOSTS file after the user has logged on by executing the command nbtstat -R (the -R parameter must be upper-case). The #INCLUDE statement can now succeed because the user has been authenticated to the network. If desired, the nbtstat -R statement can be executed in a logon script. Logon scripts are explained in my book *Inside Windows NT Server 4*.

Enabling Clients to Use LMHOSTS Files

Generally speaking, LMHOSTS files are unnecessary on networks that have a properly functioning WINS name service. If an internetwork does not use WINS, LMHOSTS lookups should be enabled and LMHOSTS files should be configured to enable computers to find critical hosts.

Any TCP/IP client can be enabled to use LMHOSTS files by checking the **Enable LMHOSTS Lookup** check box. On Windows NT Server 4, the check box is found in the WINS Address tab of the Microsoft TCP/IP Properties dialog box.

Guidelines for Establishing LMHOSTS Name Resolution

B-node computers not configured to use WINS name resolution can use LMHOSTS to resolve names on remote networks. If the majority of name queries are on the local network, it is generally not necessary to preload mappings in the LMHOSTS file. Frequently accessed hosts on remote networks can be preloaded using the #PRE keyword.

#DOM keywords should be used to enable non-WINS clients to locate domain controllers on remote networks. The LMHOSTS file for every computer in the domain should include #DOM entries for all domain controllers that do not reside on the local network. This ensures that domain activities, such as logon authentication, continue to function.

To browse a domain other than the logon domain, LMHOSTS must include a #DOM entry that defines the name and IP address of the primary domain controller of the domain to be browsed. Include backup domain controllers in case the primary fails or a backup domain controller is promoted to primary.

LMHOSTS files on backup domain controllers should include mappings to the primary domain controller name and IP address, as well as mappings to all other backup domain controllers.

All domain controllers in trusted domains should be included in the local LMHOSTS file.

NetBIOS Naming with WINS

WINS, the Windows Internet Name Service, is Microsoft's implementation of the NetBIOS Name Service (NBNS) defined in RFCs 1001 and 1002. To appreciate the need for WINS, we need to look at what happens when a user attempts to resolve names on a non-WINS network.

Figure 11.5 illustrates the internet that will be used to demonstrate a non-WINS operation. The internet consists of two networks, 128.1.0.0 and 128.2.0.0, connected by a multihomed Windows NT Server computer on which routing is enabled.

FIGURE 11.5

An internetwork without a WINS server.

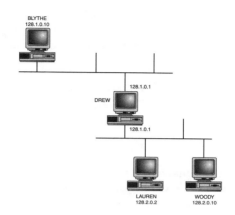

Four computers are attached to the internetwork:

- **BLYTHE**. A Windows NT Workstation computer attached to network 128.1.0.0. BLYTHE has been assigned IP address 128.1.0.10.

- **WOODY**. A Windows 3.11 computer attached to network 128.2.0.0. WOODY's IP address 128.2.0.10.

- **DREW**. A Windows NT Server computer that is backup domain controller for the domain. DREW is statically configured with IP addresses 128.1.0.1 and 128.2.0.1.

- **LAUREN**. A Windows NT Server computer configured as the primary domain controller. LAUREN has been statically configured with IP address 128.2.0.2.

To access a shared resource, a computer must obtain the IP address of the server that shares the resource. BLYTHE could obtain the IP address of DREW without difficulty by sending a broadcast on the local network. But, what happens when BLYTHE attempts to access a share on WOODY?

BLYTHE might be able to see an entry for WOODY in a browse window, or BLYTHE could attempt to access a resource on WOODY by entering the UNC name of the resource, for example by entering the command net use m:\\woody\docs to access the docs share on WOODY. When BLYTHE attempts to connect with WOODY, the attempt fails with a message similar to \\Woody is not accessible. The computer or sharename could not be found. BLYTHE attempted to identify WOODY using b-node broadcasts, which cannot succeed because WOODY is on a separate network from BLYTHE.

So, b-node name resolution has two liabilities. It ordinarily will not resolve names across routers, and it generates broadcast traffic. As we have seen, high levels of broadcast messages are to be avoided whenever possible.

This chapter will examine WINS architecture and operation so that you understand how WINS works and how to use WINS effectively. Chapter 12 delves into the details of WINS administration.

Architecture of WINS

WINS uses one or more WINS servers to maintain a database that provides name-to-address mappings in response to queries from WINS clients. The WINS database can be distributed across multiple WINS servers to provide fault tolerance and better service on local networks. A replication mechanism enables WINS servers to share their data on a periodic basis.

WINS is a particularly good fit when IP addresses are assigned by DHCP. Although the DHCP lease renewal process results in a certain stability of IP address assignments, IP addresses can change if hosts are moved to different networks or if a host is inactive for a time sufficient to cause its address to be reassigned. WINS automatically updates its database to respond to such changes.

Because WINS clients communicate with WINS servers via point-to-point messages (no broadcasts), no problems are encountered when operating in a routed environment. Figure 11.6 shows an internet with three networks. WINS servers are configured on two of the networks. The WINS servers can both resolve name queries and are configured to periodically replicate their databases. WINS clients on all three networks can communicate with a WINS server to resolve names to addresses.

WINS proxies enable non-WINS clients to resolve names on the internetwork. When a WINS proxy receives a b-node broadcast attempting to resolve a name on a remote network, the WINS proxy directs a p-node (point-to-point) name query to a WINS server and returns the response to the non-WINS client.

FIGURE 11.6

Architecture of a WINS name service.

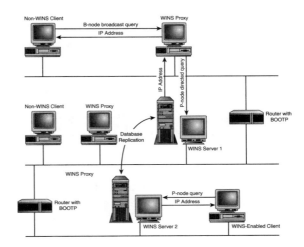

NOTE

WINS will not detect NetBIOS names that are already in use on the network by non-WINS clients, giving rise to a potential source of conflict because the same name could be used by a WINS and a non-WINS client. WINS proxy agents enable non-WINS client names to be registered with WINS and prevent such conflicts.

WINS makes it possible to maintain unique NetBIOS names throughout the internet. When a WINS client computer attempts to register a NetBIOS name with WINS, it is permitted to do so only if the name is not currently reserved in the WINS database. Without WINS, unique names are enforced only through the broadcast b-node mechanism on local networks, and it becomes possible to have the same NetBIOS name on two or more subnets.

When a WINS client is shut down in an orderly manner, it releases its name reservation in the WINS database and the name is marked as released. After a certain time, a released name is marked as extinct. Extinct names are maintained for a period of time sufficient to propagate the information to all WINS servers, after which the extinct name is removed from the WINS database.

If a computer has released its name through an orderly shutdown, WINS knows that the name is available and the client can immediately reobtain the name when it reenters the network. If the client has changed network addresses (by moving to a different network segment, for example), a released name can also be reassigned.

If a computer is not shut down in an orderly fashion, its name reservation remains active in the WINS database. When the computer attempts to reregister the name, the WINS server challenges the registration attempt. If the computer has changed IP addresses, the challenge fails and the client is permitted to reregister the name with its new address. If no other computer is actively using the name, the client is also permitted to reregister with the name.

All names in the WINS database bear a timestamp that indicates when the reservation will expire. If a client fails to reregister the name when the reservation expires, the name is released. WINS also supports definition of static name assignments that do not expire.

WINS Name Registration

WINS is an extension of RFC 1001 and RFC 1002, which relate to the NetBIOS Service Protocols. These specifications have been published and accepted as an Internet Official Protocol Standard (STD 19) by the NetBIOS Working Group of the Internet Engineering Task Force (IETF).

WINS accomplishes NetBT to IP address resolution through a four-step process of:

- NetBIOS name registration
- NetBIOS name renewal
- NetBIOS name release
- NetBIOS name query and resolution

Each of these processes are examined in the following sections.

NetBIOS Name Registration

When a WINS client initializes, NetBIOS over TCP/IP (NBT) sends a *name registration query* (called a NAMEREGISTRATIONREQUEST) message directly to the primary WINS server for that client. The name registration query includes the source (WINS client) IP address, the destination (WINS server) IP address, and the NetBIOS name to be registered.

If the WINS server is available and the NetBIOS name is not already registered in the database, the server replies to the client with a *positive name registration response* message (also called a NAMEREGISTRATIONRESPONSE). This response includes the IP address of the WINS client and WINS server, in order to route the message to the WINS client; the NetBIOS name that has been registered; and the renewal interval, which is a Time To Live (TTL) duration for the NetBIOS name registration. After the renewal interval expires, the NetBIOS name is removed from the database unless the WINS client renews the registration and is given a new renewal interval.

If the WINS server is available and the database already contains a duplicate of the NetBIOS name that was requested to be registered by the WINS client, the WINS server sends a challenge to the currently registered owner of the NetBIOS name. The challenge is sent as a *name query request* (NAMEQUERYREQUEST) three times at intervals of 500 milliseconds. The purpose of the challenge is to see whether the original owner of the NetBIOS name is still using that NetBIOS name. For example, if a computer tries to register its computer name in a WINS server that already has that computer name registered, the WINS server sends a message to the original owner of the computer name to see whether that computer name is still in use on the network.

A multihomed computer in TCP/IP terminology has more than one network interface installed that is bound to TCP/IP. If the registered owner of a NetBIOS name is a multihomed computer the WINS server sends up to three challenges to each network interface on the multihomed computer to ensure that the challenge message reaches the multihomed host.

If the current owner of a registered NetBIOS name responds to the name query challenge from the WINS server, the WINS server sends a *negative name query response* (NAMEQUERYRESPONSE) to the WINS client that is attempting to register the duplicate NetBIOS name. The offending WINS client is not allowed to register that name, and an error message is displayed or recorded at the offending WINS client.

If the WINS server does not respond to the first name registration request, the WINS client sends two more requests, then sends up to three requests to the secondary WINS server if one has been configured for the WINS client. If neither WINS server responds, the WINS client initiates a b-node broadcast to register its NetBIOS names on the local network. If a router on the network is configured to forward b-node broadcasts, then the registrations can be relayed to remote networks as well.

NOTE

LAN Manager 2.2c for MS-DOS and Microsoft Network Client 3.0 WINS clients do not register NetBIOS names with a WINS server, although they can use the WINS server database for NetBIOS name resolution.

NetBIOS Name Renewal

To continue using a registered NetBIOS name, a WINS client must periodically renew its WINS name registrations in the WINS server database. If the client does not renew its registrations before the renewal interval (TTL) of the name registration expires, that NetBIOS name to IP address mapping is marked as *released* (no longer registered) in the WINS server database. The renewal interval is set on the WINS server in the WINS Server Configuration dialog box of the WINS Manager tool found in the Network Administration program group on the WINS server. By default, the renewal interval is 96 hours (four days).

TIP

The renewal interval normally should not be changed from the default duration of 96 hours. If the interval is shortened, network traffic will increase, and performance will likely decrease. The interval can be lengthened, but then the database might be less likely to remain accurate. You should always ensure that the renewal interval is the same for primary and backup WINS servers so that the backup WINS server is not utilized until necessary.

When a WINS client first registers its names on a WINS server, the client is not given a renewal interval to use. Instead it will attempt to renew or refresh the registrations every one-eighth (1/8) of the initial refresh timeout, a value set in the Windows NT Registry. By default, the initial refresh timeout is 16 minutes, and thus the initial registration refresh will be attempted 2 minutes after the initial registration.

The WINS client sends a *name refresh request* directly to its primary WINS server. The name refresh request contains the source (WINS client) and destination (WINS server) IP addresses and the NetBIOS name to be refreshed. If the WINS client gets no response, it tries again every one-eighth of the initial refresh timeout until one-half, or 50 percent, of the initial refresh timeout has expired. After 50 percent of the initial refresh timeout has expired, the WINS client begins again with a new renewal interval, acting as if 0 percent of the renewal interval has expired. This time, however, it starts sending name refresh requests to the secondary WINS server, if configured, every one-eighth of the renewal interval until 50 percent of the renewal interval has expired again. Then the WINS client goes back to trying to register with the primary WINS server.

NOTE

The WINS client continuously attempts to renew its name registrations every one-eighth of the initial refresh timeout until it gets a response from the primary or secondary WINS server. Regardless of this fact, the WINS servers will still mark the registration as released when the first renewal interval has expired if it does not receive the renewal request from the WINS client.

When a WINS server receives a name refresh request, it sends a *name refresh response* directly to the WINS client. The name refresh response contains the WINS client IP address as the destination; the WINS server IP address as the source; the NetBIOS name registered; and the new renewal interval, which by default is 96 hours.

After a WINS client has received its first renewal from the WINS server, it from then on attempts to renew its registration only after 50 percent of the renewal interval has expired, or until the WINS client is restarted.

NOTE

A WINS client registration is not assigned a renewal interval or TTL until after it has renewed its initial registration. Until that point, it will attempt to renew its registrations every one-eighth of the initial refresh timeout, or every two minutes, by default.

NetBIOS Name Release

When a WINS client initiates a normal shutdown of the host, meaning that the operating system is shut down before rebooting, the WINS client sends one *name release request* directly to the WINS server for each of its registered NetBIOS names. The NetBIOS name release request contains the WINS client and WINS server IP addresses, as well as the NetBIOS name to be released in the WINS database.

When the WINS server receives a name release request, it consults the local WINS database to ensure that the name exists and is registered to the WINS client that sent the name release request. If the name requested to be released is found in the database and is mapped to the IP address of the client sending the name release request, the WINS server marks that database entry as *released* and sends a *positive name release response* to the WINS client that sent the name release request. The positive name release response is directed to the WINS client IP address. It contains the released NetBIOS name and a renewal interval or TTL of zero.

If the NetBIOS name requested to be released was not registered in the WINS database, or was registered with a different IP address, the WINS server replies with a *negative name release response* to the WINS client that sent the name release request.

The WINS client treats a negative name release response the same as a positive name release response. After the WINS client receives either type of name release response from the WINS server, it no longer responds to name request registration challenges sent from the WINS server when another host wants to register the same NetBIOS name.

If the WINS client does not receive a name release response from the primary WINS server, it sends up to three b-node broadcasts of the name release request to the local network and any remote networks attached by b-node broadcast forwarding routers. All b-node–enabled clients, including WINS clients, receiving the name release request then ensure that the NetBIOS name is removed from their local NetBIOS name cache.

NetBIOS Name Query and Resolution

When a host running NetBIOS over TCP/IP (NBT) attempts to execute a command containing a NetBIOS name, that NetBIOS name must be resolved to an IP address. For example, if the command `net use p: \\SERVER01\PUBLIC` is executed, NBT must make a connection to the computer SERVER01 in order to map the drive p: to the PUBLIC share on SERVER01. To make this connection, NBT must know the IP address of the computer SERVER01. In other words, NBT must *resolve* the NetBIOS name to an IP address.

The process of NetBIOS name resolution involves checking the NetBIOS name mapping tables in various places until an entry is found that maps the NetBIOS name to an IP address. The NetBIOS name to IP address mappings can be found in some or all of the following places, depending on which components are implemented on the internetwork:

- the local NetBIOS name cache, found in memory on the local or source host

- a WINS server database

- an LMHOSTS file, which is a text file on the local host containing the NetBIOS name to IP address mappings

- a HOSTS file, which is a text file on the local host containing host name to IP address mappings—the host name is often the same as the NetBIOS computer name

- a Domain Name Service (DNS) database, which will also contain host name to IP address mappings and might be used if the client is configured to use DNS for NetBIOS name resolution

- the host that owns the particular NetBIOS name can respond to a b-node broadcast name query if that host is on the same subnet as the source host or on a subnet connected by a b-node broadcast forwarding router

Depending on the configuration of the NBT implementation, any number of the preceding methods of resolving NetBIOS names can be used in an order determined by the NetBIOS node type.

NOTE

If a host is configured to use WINS for NetBIOS name resolution, by default the host uses the h-node (hybrid) NetBIOS name resolution order.

To verify which NetBIOS name resolution node type is being used by a host, enter **ipconfig /all** from a command prompt. For example:

```
C:\>ipconfig/all
Windows NT IP Configuration
        Host Name . . . . . . . . . : frodo.middle_earth.com
        DNS Servers . . . . . . . . : 200.20.16.122
        Node Type . . . . . . . . . : Hybrid
        NetBIOS Scope ID. . . . . . :
        IP Routing Enabled. . . . . : No
        WINS Proxy Enabled. . . . . : No
        NetBIOS Resolution Uses DNS : Yes
```

In the preceding sample output, the NetBIOS node type is "Hybrid" or h-node, meaning that it uses a NetBIOS name server (WINS) first, followed by b-node broadcasts, to resolve NetBIOS names.

After the NetBIOS name has been resolved to an IP address, NBT adds the NetBIOS name and IP address mapping to the local NetBIOS name cache and does not need to query by using any of the other methods. The NetBIOS names are periodically cleared from the NetBIOS name cache.

The NetBIOS name cache contains several names registered by the local host—including the computer name, user name, and domain name—plus any other names that have been recently resolved and added to the NetBIOS name cache. To view the current contents of the NetBIOS name cache, enter the command **nbtstat -n** from a command prompt. Sample output is shown here:

```
C:\>nbtstat -n
Node IpAddress: [200.20.1.30] Scope Id: []
                NetBIOS Local Name Table
        Name              Type        Status
        ---------------------------------------------
        FRODO         <00>  UNIQUE    Registered
        FRODO         <20>  UNIQUE    Registered
        HOBBITS       <00>  GROUP     Registered
        HOBBITS       <1C>  GROUP     Registered
        HOBBITS       <1B>  UNIQUE    Registered
        BILBO         <03>  UNIQUE    Registered
        ADMINISTRATOR <03>  UNIQUE    Registered
```

When the NetBIOS node type is h-node (hybrid), a NetBIOS name query is performed in the following order (see Figure 11.7):

1. The local name cache is consulted for a NetBIOS name to IP address mapping.

2. If no mapping is found, a *name query request* is sent directly to the configured primary WINS server. The name query request contains the NetBIOS name to be resolved as well as the source (WINS client) and destination (WINS server) IP addresses.

   If the primary WINS server does not respond to the name query request, the WINS client resends the request two more times to the primary WINS server. If the primary WINS server still does not respond, the WINS client then sends up to three name query requests to the secondary WINS server, if one is configured on the WINS client.

   If either WINS server resolves the name, a *name query response* is sent to the WINS client along with the requested NetBIOS name and IP address mapping. The name is added to the local cache, and name resolution is complete.

   If a WINS server receives the name query request but the name does not exist in the WINS database, the WINS server sends a *requested name does not exist response* to the WINS client that initiated the request.

3. If no WINS server can satisfy the name query request, or the WINS client receives the response *requested name does not exist*, the WINS client then sends three b-node broadcasts of the name request query to the local network and to any networks attached by b-node broadcast forwarding routers. If the required name is reported, the name and IP address are recorded in the local name cache and name resolution is complete.

4. If b-node broadcasts do not succeed, the WINS client checks its local LMHOSTS file. If the required name is found, the name and IP address are recorded in the local name cache and name resolution is complete.

5. Next the computer consults its HOSTS file.

6. In a final effort to resolve the name the client queries a DNS server. If the computer's DNS server does not respond, several attempts are made to contact the DNS server. It takes a minute or more for a failed DNS name resolution to time out and report an error.

7. If no methods can resolve the name, an error is reported.

NOTE

In my tests, examining DNS queries using the Microsoft Network Monitor, a client attempts to contact its DNS server eight times, at intervals of 5, 10, 15, 20, 5, 10, and 15 seconds. Thus, if a DNS server is unavailable, 80 seconds elapse before the client determines that name resolution has failed.

FIGURE 11.7
Resolving a NetBIOS name on an h-node client.

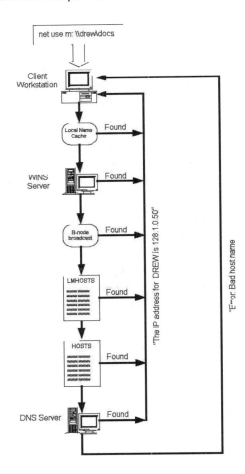

After the WINS client has received a mapping for the NetBIOS name, it adds the mapping to its local NetBIOS name cache. It can then use the Internet Protocol (IP) to route datagrams to the destination NetBIOS host.

If the requested NetBIOS name cannot be resolved to an address, NetBIOS cannot use TCP/IP to communicate with that host. If TCP/IP is the only protocol capable of reaching that host—for example, if the NetBEUI protocol is not being used—the requested NetBIOS command fails, and the host might report an error message such as `The network path was not found`.

TCP/IP Host Names

Chapter 6 describes TCP/IP host names and explains the hierarchical DNS name space. If you are running a Microsoft network with DNS, you must make provisions to resolve TCP/IP host names. These names are used by WinSock applications such as FTP, WWW browsers, and Telnet.

Two methods are available for resolving TCP/IP host names, HOSTS files and DNS. You will want to implement one or both of these methods on your network.

HOSTS Files

Before DNS, name resolution was accomplished using files named HOSTS that, on UNIX computers, were conventionally stored with the filename \etc\hosts. On Windows NT computers, HOSTS files are stored in the directory C:\Winnt\system32\drivers\etc.

A HOSTS file is a text file that contains entries such as the following:

```
127.0.0.1        loopback localhost lb      #this host
128.1.0.100      lauren.pseudo.com lauren
128.1.0.101      blythe.pseudo.com blythe
128.1.0.155      woody.pseudo.com woody
```

Each entry consists of an IP address followed by one or more spaces or a tab character. The next field consists of one or more names that serve as aliases for the host. In this case, each host has been supplied with aliases for its FQDN and its simple host name. Comments can be included in the file. Any text following a # character is ignored when the file is processed.

Supporting a naming service is a simple matter of editing a master HOSTS file and distributing it to all computers. This can be accomplished by copying the file when a user logs on to a domain, or it can be done using a software distribution system such as Microsoft's System Management Server.

Basically, the same tasks are involved in maintaining a master HOSTS file and maintaining DNS database files. DNS saves labor because DNS database files need not be copied to all hosts, but rather need only be installed on the primary and backup DNS servers. So DNS begins to pay off when your network becomes so large that keeping everyone's HOSTS file up-to-date becomes too labor-intensive.

The Domain Name Service

DNS name resolution is performed by *name servers*, which are programs running on network hosts. Because the Internet is so extensive, DNS was designed so that many name servers could share the responsibility for resolving names. This is accomplished by dividing the complete name space into *zones*. Each zone can be serviced by its own name servers.

DNS is an involved technology. This book should contain enough information for you to be able to configure and administer a basic DNS implementation. If you require more extensive information, I recommend the book *DNS and BIND,* by Paul Albitz and Cricket Liu (O'Reilly & Associates Inc., 1997).

Organization of DNS Name Servers

A name server that manages data for a zone is said to have *authority* for that zone. A name server will have authority for at least one zone, but a single name server can have authority for many zones if required. Figure 11.8 illustrates a name space that has been organized into zones. Notice that zones need not follow domain structures. Although a domain must consist of a connected subtree of the overall name space, zones need not consist of contiguous nodes. This flexibility enables a single name server to provide name resolution for multiple domains.

FIGURE 11.8

A name space divided into three zones

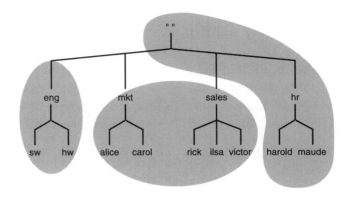

The principal name server for a zone is the *primary master name server*, which collects data for the zone from its configuration files. *Secondary master name servers* are redundant backups to primary servers and obtain data for the zones they service by performing *zone transfers* from the primary master name server for the zone. Secondary masters perform periodic zone transfers to keep up-to-date with changes in the zone. Configuration of two or more name servers for a zone provides fault tolerance and improves performance by distributing name-resolution processing across several hosts.

Assignment of primary and secondary master name servers is quite flexible. A name server can be authoritative for one or for several zones, and a given name server can function as a primary master for one zone and as a secondary master for another.

Because many name resolution attempts must begin with the root domain, the Internet root domain is serviced by nine root name servers, which include systems on NSFNET, MILNET, SPAN (NASA), and in Europe. These root-domain servers are authoritative for all top-level domains on the Internet. Authority for secondary- and lower-level domains is distributed across many name servers operated by the organizations that inhabit the Internet.

When an organization obtains a domain name and establishes a presence on the Internet, a name server must be designated that is authoritative for the domain. In most cases, the name server will be maintained on a host that is operated by the owner of the domain. It is not necessary for an organization to operate its own name server, however. Most Internet connections are now obtained from commercial Internet access providers. Many of these providers will maintain their clients' zones on the provider's name servers.

Contracting an Internet access provider to manage your domain name space is particularly desirable if your organization is small and cannot justify the labor costs to have DNS experts on staff or the hardware required to maintain a primary and a backup name server.

The complete Internet domain name space is maintained by many distributed name servers that have some degree of awareness of each other. This distributed network of name servers cooperates to provide name resolution for the complete Internet.

DNS Name Resolution

The client side of the name service is provided by *resolvers*, which are components of TCP/IP processes and applications that make use of DNS host names. The resolver is embedded in the software of each application, such as FTP or Telnet, enabling the application to contact one name server to initiate a name resolution query. The resolver in the application can construct a DNS query, but resolution of the query is the responsibility of the network name servers.

Figure 11.9 illustrates the process of resolving a query. The configuration of a TCP/IP host will include the IP address of at least one DNS name server. When an application requires name resolution service, it constructs a name service query and sends the query to a known name server, identified in the figure as the "Local Name Server." If the local name server that is queried cannot resolve the name, it initiates a search starting with one of the available root name servers. The root name server provides the address of a name server that is authoritative for the first-level domain in the query. The search proceeds from first- to second- to lower-level domain name servers until a server is found that can respond to the query.

The name search process depends on access to an intact hierarchy of name servers. If a functioning name server is unavailable at any level, name resolution will fail. That is why it is so important to have primary and secondary name servers available and why the Internet is serviced by nine servers at the root domain. Although lower-level servers reduce name resolution traffic by maintaining a cache of recently resolved names, if all root name servers on the Internet were to fail, all name resolution would eventually cease.

FIGURE 11.9

Resolution of a name query

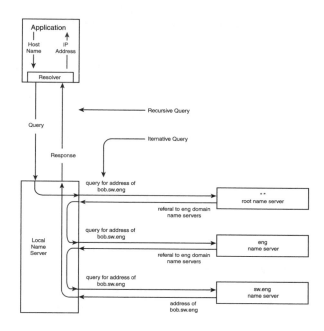

The query illustrated in Figure 11.9 actually shows two different query mechanisms, referred to as *iterative* and *recursive*. You will run into references to these two types of queries in product literature, so let's take a moment to examine their characteristics.

Iterative Queries

In Figure 11.9 the various name servers have significantly different responsibilities. The local name server bears the greatest responsibility for satisfying the query. It must repeatedly query remote name servers to obtain bits of the final answer. The remote name servers perform one of two actions: either returning the required data or returning a reference to a name server that can perform the next step. It is up to the local name server to initiate the next step of the query.

This type of name query performed by the local name server is called *iterative resolution* (or *non-recursive resolution*). The term iteration is a fancy computer term for "repetition." A single process simply repeats, usually with input from the last repetition, until the desired result is obtained or an error is encountered. Ideally, each iteration should generate a response that is a bit closer to the desired goal.

Because most of the work of resolving a name is performed by the local name server, name resolution can be supported by a simple stub resolver at the application end. And, although iterative queries result in higher numbers of dialogs between name servers, iterative queries are relatively easy to perform. Consequently, most name queries are performed iteratively.

Recursive Queries

Another flavor of name query is *recursion* or *recursive resolution*. When a name server receives a recursive query it must either provide the desired data or it must return an error. If a name server is not authoritative for a domain that is requested, it must query another name server for the desired data.

In Figure 11.9, the client's local name server receives a recursive query from the client. The local name server cannot simply respond to the client with a referral to another name server; it must provide the required name resolution or respond with an error.

In Figure 11.9, the local name server fulfills the client's request by making iterative queries of other name servers that provide referrals until the authoritative name server is encountered.

Types of DNS Name Servers

The most commonly used implementation of DNS is BIND (Berkeley Internet Name Domain), which is included in 4.3BSD UNIX. Now at version 4.8.3, BIND has been ported to a variety of UNIX and other platforms. BIND supports tree depths up to 127 levels, sufficient even for the Internet. In fact, all Internet root name servers are running an implementation of BIND.

The Microsoft DNS Server is included with Windows NT Server 4. It is compatible with BIND database files and can perform zone transfers with BIND DNS servers. Therefore the Microsoft DNS server can interoperate in a conventional UNIX DNS environment.

In the Windows environment, however, the Microsoft DNS Server has two particular advantages. It can obtain names from WINS, enabling the DNS database to keep pace as clients make changes to the WINS name database. Also, the Microsoft DNS Server provides a Windows graphic user interface that greatly simplifies administration of the DNS database.

WinSock Name Query and Resolution

When WinSock applications are used, it is necessary to resolve the host's TCP/IP name to obtain its IP address. Under Microsoft TCP/IP, the sequence of resolving a TCP/IP host name, illustrated in Figure 11.10, is as follows:

1. The host checks its own name to see if it matches the name specified in the command. If the local name matches, the command is performed locally and no network traffic is generated.

2. Next the host checks its local HOSTS file. If a match is found the name is resolved.

3. Next the host queries its DNS server. If multiple DNS servers are listed in the computer's TCP/IP configuration, the DNS servers are tried in the order specified. The host makes eight attempts to contact its DNS server after which DNS name resolution times out.

NOTE

Several attempts might be made to contact a DNS server with different names, as determined by settings on the DNS tab of the Microsoft TCP/IP Properties dialog box. In Chapter 14, "Installing TCP/IP on Microsoft Clients" see the section "Enabling DNS Clients" for a discussion of the properties that affect the client's relationship with DNS.

4. If the DNS server cannot resolve the name, the host checks its NetBIOS cache.

5. Assuming that the host is configured for h-node operation, the next step is to check WINS.

6. If WINS cannot resolve the name, three b-node broadcasts are transmitted.

7. Finally, the client examines its LMHOSTS file.

8. If all these name resolution steps fail, an error is reported.

Chapter 13 explains how to set up and manage the Microsoft DNS Server.

FIGURE 11.10

Resolving a TCP/IP host name.

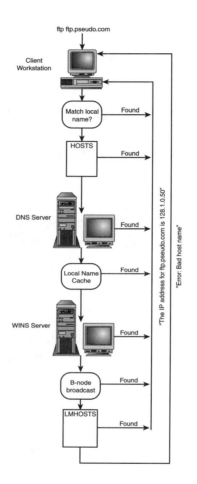

Browsing on Microsoft TCP/IP Networks

Browsing is a peculiarity of Microsoft networks. Computers cooperate to build a database of server NetBIOS names that is somehow magically made available to users who browse the list using Network Neighborhood, Explorer, or other tools. The entire process works so invisibly that we take it for granted while using the network. Browsing just happens.

Except when it doesn't happen, of course. You might encounter times when two users' browsers show completely different views of the network. And WINS was invented because browsing encounters difficulties on a routed

TCP/IP internetwork. Because browsing can break down, you need to know how it works so that you can deal with the fallout and correct the problems.

Browser Roles

Several types of computers participate in maintenance of the browser database. Computers can have six roles, sometimes holding several roles at one time. For example, a master browser can also be a server, and it can be a browser client for another domain. The computer browser roles are:

- Domain master browser (TCP/IP networks only)
- Master browser
- Backup browser
- Potential browser
- Servers
- Browser client, or non-browser

There are subtle differences in the ways computers are assigned browser roles, depending on the underlying network protocol. Let's start with some definitions and general discussion and then look at the specifics for NetBEUI, NWLink, and TCP/IP.

Yes, I know this is a book about TCP/IP, but you will understand TCP/IP browsing better if you comprehend the simpler mechanisms used on NetBEUI and NWLink networks. There are also some differences depending on whether the user is browsing a domain or a workgroup. We'll look at those differences as well.

The Master Browser

Each domain has a *master browser* (also sometimes referred to as a *browse master*). The master browser collects browser announcements for the entire domain, including all network segments, and provides a master browser list for the domain. The master browser list contains information about all servers in the domain.

Any Windows NT computer that is running the Server service (or its equivalent on non-NT Windows versions) will be advertised via the browser mechanism. When a server comes onto the network, it announces itself to the master browser. Periodically, the server checks in with the master browser, decreasing the frequency until it is checking in about every 12 minutes.

The master browser is selected in an election process. For a domain, the election process is highly biased and guarantees that the primary domain controller, if active, is always the master browser. If the PDC is not running, an election takes place and a BDC will be selected from among the list of backup and potential browsers.

If a master browser announces that it is shutting down, other computers hold an election to determine which is best capable of becoming the domain master browser. If a client cannot find a browser, it can force an election of a new master browser.

Backup Browsers

As additional computers are added to the network, they might become backup browsers. By default, Windows NT computers become backup browsers, although computers also can be configured as standby browsers. The master browser can instruct standby browsers to become backup browsers, attempting to maintain about one backup browser per 31 computers. Backup browsers spread the work of browsing around because browse clients can access the browse database through any backup browser.

Backup browsers check in every 15 minutes with the master browser to update their databases. Consequently, it can be up to 15 minutes before a backup browser learns of a change to the backup browser's database.

Backup browsers serve two functions: They contain backup copies of the browser database and can also be consulted by non-browsers to browse the domain server database.

When a master browser fails, it might be 15 minutes before backup browsers detect the failure. The first backup browser to detect the failure forces an election to select a new master browser.

Potential Browsers

Many servers can become browsers when they are called on to do so by the master browser. Potential browsers include Windows NT, Windows 95/98, and Windows for Workgroups computers. A computer must be configured as a server to be a potential, backup, or master browser.

Servers

A server is a computer that can potentially share file and printer resources. Servers can function as master browsers, backup browsers, potential browsers, or they can be configured to always be non-browsers.

On Windows NT, a server is a computer that is running the Server service. Windows 95/98 and Windows for Workgroups computers can also function as servers and have functionality similar to the Windows NT Server service.

When a server enters the network, it transmits a broadcast message that announces its presence. These announcements are repeated periodically to inform browsers that the server remains available. The server announces its presence at increasing intervals of 1, 2, 4, 8, and 12 minutes. Thereafter, the server announces itself at 12 minute intervals.

If the master browser has not heard from a server in three announcement intervals, the master browser removes the server from its browse list. In the worst case, the master browser will not remove a server from its browse list for 36 minutes. Because backup browsers obtain browse lists from the master browser at 15 minutes, it can take up to 51 minutes for backup browsers to learn that a server has been removed from the network. This delay is one reason different backup browsers can have different browse lists.

Browser Clients

When clients browse the network they use a browser client such as Explorer or Network Neighborhood, which uses an API call to identify browsers on the network, to select a browser, and to browse the database in the browser.

Determining Computers' Browser Roles

You might want to configure the browser behavior of specific computers. The following sections describe the configuration procedures for Windows NT, Windows 95/98, and Windows for Workgroups.

Windows NT

A Windows NT computer's browser behavior is determined by a value under the following Registry key:

```
HKEY_LOCAL_MACHINE\
  SYSTEM\
  CurrentControlSet\
  Services\
  Browser\
  Parameters.
```

Under that key, the MaintainServerList value entry can have three values:

- **No**. Indicates that the computer will never be a browser.

- **Yes**. Indicates that the computer will be a browser. It will attempt to contact the master browser and become a backup browser. If no master browser is found, the computer forces an election for a master browser. Yes is the default value for Windows NT computers.

- **Auto**. Indicates that the computer is a standby browser and can become a backup browser if a master browser notifies it to do so.

In rare instances, you might have a Windows NT computer that is configured as a server (it is running the Server service) but that you don't want to be advertised in browser lists. To prevent the server from appearing in browser lists, use the Registry editor to add a value to the key HKEY_LOCAL_MACHINE\System\CurrentControlSet\Services\LanManServer\ Parameters. Add a value entry with the name Hidden of type REG_ DWORD. Set the value to 1 to remove the computer from browse lists. Set the value to 0 to enable the computer to appear in browse lists.

Windows 95/98

Windows 95/98 computers are configured through the Network applet in the Control Panel. A Windows 95/98 computer can only function as a browser if file or print sharing is enabled, because only then does the computer appear as a server on the network.

To configure the browser role of a Windows 95/98 computer do the following:

1. Open the Network applet.

2. Examine the network components list. If the list does not contain the entry File and printer sharing for Microsoft Networks, click **File and Print Sharing** and check either or both of the following check boxes:

■ **I want to be able to give others access to my files**

■ **I want to allow others to print to my printer(s)**

Click **OK** to return to the Network applet.

3. Select `File and printer sharing for Microsoft Networks`.

4. Click **Properties** to open the Advanced dialog box shown in Figure 11.11.

FIGURE 11.11

Configuring the browser behavior for a Window 95/98 computer.

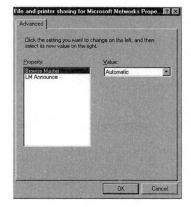

5. Select the **Browse Master** entry in the Property list.

6. Select one of the following browser behaviors in the Value list:

■ **Automatic**. The computer is a potential browser.

■ **Enabled.** The computer will be a browser for its domain or workgroup.

■ **Disabled.** The computer will never be a browser.

7. Exit the Network applet. If you are configuring file and printer sharing for the first time, you will need to specify a directory path so that the required files can be installed.

8. Restart the computer to activate the changes.

Windows for Workgroups

With a Windows for Workgroups computer, you can control the computer's browser behavior by adding a line to the [network] section of the system.ini file. To prevent the computer from functioning as a browser, add the following line:

```
MaintainServerList=No
```

Domain and Workgroup Size Limitations

Prior to Windows NT Server version 4, the list of servers maintained by a master browser is limited to 64KB of data. As a result, a domain or workgroup is limited to about 2,000–3,000 computers.

Browser Protocol Dependencies

Browser operation differs significantly depending on the underlying network protocol. You need to be aware of the protocol dependencies so that you can troubleshoot the browser environment. Although this book focuses on TCP/IP, you might have other protocols running and it will be useful to briefly review the browsing mechanisms for NetBEUI and NWLink as well.

Browsing and NetBEUI

NetBEUI messages are not routable. Therefore, every subnetwork functions as an independent browsing environment. Figure 11.12 shows a NetBEUI network that includes two subnets. The router is deceiving, because the computers function as though they are on completely separate networks.

FIGURE 11.12

Browsing on a NetBEUI network.

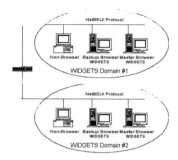

Notice that each subnet has a master browser and a backup browser for the WIDGETS domain. In point of fact, there are *two* WIDGETS domains on this network and they are completely isolated from each other.

Browsing with NWLink

NWLink is a routable protocol, and NetBIOS broadcast forwarding is enabled on Windows NT routers that are configured with the NWLink protocol. As a consequence, the browsing mechanism is not fragmented when routers are introduced to the network. Figure 11.13 illustrates browsing on a routed NWLink network.

FIGURE 11.13

Browsing on an NWLink network.

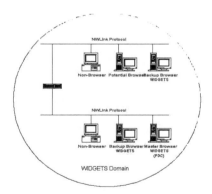

Notice that a single master browser services the entire network. This master browser receives service announcements from all servers and creates a master browse database for the domain. Backup browsers contact the master browser at 15 minute intervals to obtain copies of the domain browse database.

Browsing with TCP/IP

Although TCP/IP is a routable protocol, we have seen that IP routers do not forward NetBEUI broadcasts. Consequently, routers fragment browsing on TCP/IP networks. As Figure 11.14 shows, each subnet is configured with a master browser.

FIGURE 11.14

Browsing on TCP/IP networks.

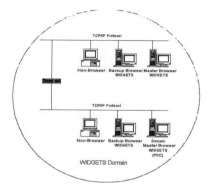

On TCP/IP networks, a new twist is added to the browser mechanism. The PDC for a domain functions as a *domain master browser* for the domain. Each client registers with the domain master browser, which constructs a master domain browse database. Master browsers periodically contact the domain master browser to obtain copies of the master domain browse database. To enable non-browsers to browse the entire domain, each subnet must be configured with at least one computer that can function as a master browser.

To enable the domain master browser mechanism to work, routers must be configured to forward broadcasts sent to UDP port 137. UDP is a protocol in the TCP/IP protocol suite, and port 137 is the service address for the NetBT Name Service. Routers based on Windows NT computers meet this requirement as do some routers from other vendors. If all routers meet this specification, you can configure a naming service without resorting to WINS.

Unfortunately, router configuration isn't enough to enable the master browsers on the segments to communicate with the domain master browser. Although the master browsers can identify and communicate with the PDC, they don't know that the PDC is the domain master browser unless you explicitly inform them through an LMHOSTS file entry. Each master browser must be configured with an LMHOSTS file that contains an entry similar to the following:

```
128.2.0.10      WIDGETS1      #PRE      #DOM:WIDGETS
```

The computer that reads this LMHOSTS file is informed that WIDGETS1 is the PDC for the WIDGETS domain. This LMHOSTS entry enables master browsers to find the domain master browser because the PDC is always selected as the domain master browser.

Although TCP/IP browsing can function without WINS, Microsoft recommends that WINS be configured to support TCP/IP browsing on internetworks. WINS reduces or eliminates broadcast traffic required for NetBIOS name resolution and can be configured for fault tolerance. On a non-WINS network, even though a failed domain master browser might be replaced in an election, master browsers might be unable to communicate with the domain master browser because they still rely on static configuration information in their LMHOSTS files.

Browsing on Multiprotocol Networks

When multiple protocols are installed on a network, a separate browsing environment is maintained for each protocol. If, for example, a subnet is running NWLink and TCP/IP, the subnet will have an NWLink master browser and a TCP/IP master browser, which might or might not be the same computer.

Browsing Domains and Workgroups

Nearly everything I have said applies to browsing domains and workgroups alike. There is a restriction, however, in that workgroups cannot span routers. If computers on a routed network are configured to use the same workgroup name, each subnet has a separate workgroup. Those workgroups might share names, but they do not share browse databases. If you require a browsing strategy that spans routers, you must implement a domain.

Monitoring Browser Status

The Windows NT Resource Kit includes a Browser Monitor that can be used to monitor the status of browsers on a network. The icon for this program is installed in the Resource Kit program group.

When you start the Browser Monitor utility, you must tell it which domain or domains to display. Choose the **Add Domain** command in the **Domain** menu. Then select a domain from the Select Domain list. Workgroups count as well as Windows NT domains; you can add either or both. After you have added domains, you should have a list similar to the one in Figure 11.15. A blue icon in the Domain column identifies a network that has a functioning browser environment. A red icon in the Domain column identifies a network that does not support browsing.

FIGURE 11.15

Browser Monitor.

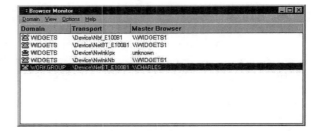

Figure 11.15 depicts a contrived situation in which I have installed all three network protocols. Each protocol that supports browsing should show a master browser. This figure shows master browsers for each of the following protocols:

- **NetBT.** NetBIOS over TCP/IP.
- **Nbf.** NetBIOS Frame protocol (NetBEUI).
- **NWLinkNB.** NetBIOS over NWLink.

The Raw NWLink Network in Browser Monitor

If your network is running NWLink, there will also be a network entry for NWLinkIpx, the raw IPX network. Because the raw IPX network does not support NetBEUI, it does not have a master browser. You can remove this entry by selecting it and using the **Remove Domain** command in the **Domain** menu.

You can determine from this window which computer is functioning as the master browser for each domain. WIDGETS1 is the master browser for the WIDGETS domain, which isn't surprising, since it is the primary domain controller. The Windows 95 computer named Charles is the master browser for WORKGROUP.

Each of these entries can be used to access a separate browser status window, which you can examine by selecting an entry and choosing the **Properties** command in the Domain menu. Figure 11.16 shows the browser status display for the WIDGETS domain NetBT protocol. From this window, you can determine that WIDGETS1 is the master browser for the domain (its icon contains a little red dot at the top, which doesn't carry over very well to a black-and-white illustration. WIDGETS2 server is a backup domain controller for the WIDGETS domain.

The Servers on \\WIDGETS list announces the servers that are known to the selected browser. You can compare this list on different browsers to ensure that server information is being distributed to the various browsers in a domain.

FIGURE 11.16

Browser status for the NetBT protocol on the WIDGETS domain.

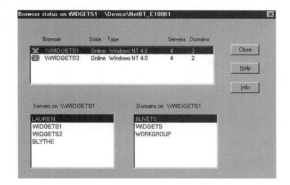

Remember that it takes some time for backup browsers and servers to register their presence with the master browser. If you are running Browser Manager immediately after starting computers on the network, it might take a while before the data catches up with your expectations.

If you want to see details about one of the browsers, double-click its entry in the Browser list. You are rewarded with a list containing more statistics than you care to have. Figure 11.17 offers an example.

FIGURE 11.17

Details about
a browser.

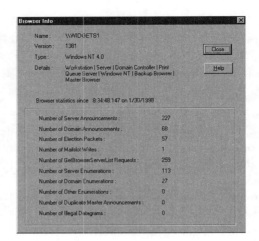

Chapter 12

MANAGING WINS

As we saw in Chapter 11, NetBIOS Name Servers are vital components of a strategy to support NetBIOS name resolution on a Microsoft TCP/IP network. Microsoft's NBNS implementation is the Windows Internet Name Service (WINS). In this chapter, we put theory into practice by examining the implementation of a WINS name service.

Architecture of the Windows Internet Name Service

WINS uses one or more WINS servers to maintain a database that provides name-to-address mappings in response to queries from WINS clients. The WINS database can be distributed across multiple servers to provide fault tolerance and better service on local networks. A replication mechanism enables WINS servers to share their data on a periodic basis.

WINS is a particularly good fit when IP addresses are assigned by DHCP. Although the DHCP lease renewal process results in a certain stability of IP address assignments, IP addresses can change if hosts are moved to different networks or if a host is inactive for a time sufficient to cause its address to be reassigned. WINS automatically updates its database to respond to such changes.

Because WINS clients communicate with WINS servers via directed messages, no problems are encountered when operating in a routed environment. Figure 12.1 shows an internet with three networks. WINS servers are configured on two of the networks. The WINS servers can resolve name queries and are configured to periodically replicate their databases. WINS clients on all three networks can communicate with a WINS server to resolve names to addresses.

FIGURE 12.1

Architecture of a WINS name service.

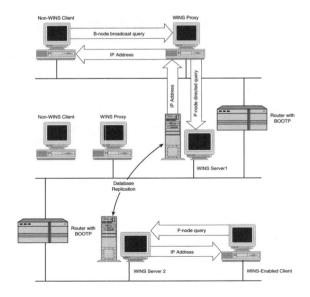

WINS proxies enable non-WINS clients to resolve names on the internetwork. When a WINS proxy receives a b-node broadcast attempting to resolve a name on a remote network, the WINS proxy directs a name query to a WINS server and returns the response to the non-WINS client.

Note

WINS will not detect NetBIOS names that are already in use on the network by non-WINS clients, giving rise to a potential source of conflict because the same name could be used by a WINS and a non-WINS client. WINS proxy agents enable non-WINS client names to be registered with WINS and prevent such conflicts.

WINS makes maintaining unique NetBIOS names throughout the internet possible. When a computer attempts to register a NetBIOS name with WINS, it is permitted to do so only if the name is not currently reserved in the WINS database. Without WINS, unique names are enforced only through the broadcast b-node mechanism on local networks.

When a WINS client is shut down in an orderly manner, it releases its name reservation in the WINS database, and the name is marked as released. After a certain time, a released name is marked as extinct. Extinct names are maintained for a period of time sufficient to propagate the information to all WINS servers, after which the extinct name is removed from the WINS database.

If a computer has released its name through an orderly shutdown, WINS knows that the name is available, and the client can immediately reobtain the name when it reenters the network. If the client has changed network addresses (by moving to a different network segment, for example), a released name can also be reassigned.

If a computer is not shut down in an orderly fashion, its name reservation remains active in the WINS database. When the computer attempts to reregister the name, the WINS server challenges the registration attempt. If the computer has changed IP addresses, the challenge fails, and the client is permitted to reregister the name with its new address. If no other computer is actively using the name, the client is also permitted to reregister with the name.

All names in the WINS database bear a timestamp that indicates when the reservation will expire. If a client fails to reregister the name when the reservation expires, the name is released. WINS supports definition of static name assignments that do not expire.

Naming on a Non-WINS Internetwork

Figure 12.2 illustrates the internet that will be used to demonstrate WINS operation. The internet consists of two networks, 128.1.0.0 and 128.2.0.0, connected by a multihomed Windows NT Server computer on which routing is enabled.

FIGURE 12.2

An internetwork without a WINS server.

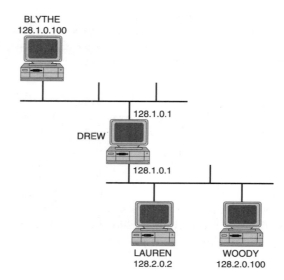

Four computers are attached to the internetwork:

- **BLYTHE.** A Windows NT Workstation computer attached to network 128.1.0.0. BLYTHE has been assigned IP address 128.1.0.10.

- **WOODY.** A Windows 3.11 computer attached to network 128.2.0.0. WOODY's IP address is 128.2.0.10.

- **DREW.** A Windows NT Server computer that is backup domain controller for the domain. DREW is statically configured with IP addresses 128.1.0.1 and 128.2.0.1.

- **LAUREN.** A Windows NT Server computer configured as the primary domain controller. LAUREN has been statically configured with IP address 128.2.0.2.

To access a shared resource, a computer must obtain the IP address of the server that shares the resource. BLYTHE could obtain the IP address of

DREW without difficulty by sending a broadcast on the local network. But what happens when BLYTHE attempts to access a share on WOODY?

BLYTHE might be capable of seeing an entry for WOODY in a browse window, or BLYTHE could attempt to access a resource on WOODY by entering the UNC name of the resource. When BLYTHE attempts to connect with WOODY, the attempt fails with a message similar to \\Woody is not accessible. The computer or sharename could not be found. BLYTHE attempted to identify WOODY using b-node broadcasts, which cannot succeed because WOODY is on a separate network from BLYTHE.

The following sections examine the procedures for configuring WINS servers and clients. Then discussion returns to this example network to see how WINS solves the problem experienced by BLYTHE.

Planning for WINS Installation

The chief question when planning for WINS is, how many WINS servers does the network require? According to Microsoft guidelines, a dedicated WINS server can support up to 10,000 computers.

However, WINS resolution increases network traffic, and you should consider distributing WINS servers throughout the network. Consider placing a WINS server on each network segment, for example, to reduce the WINS traffic that must be routed, particularly through slow WAN links.

At a minimum, you should have two WINS servers, configured to mutually replicate their databases. This provides a measure of fault tolerance in case a WINS server fails. Be sure that your clients are configured with the IP addresses of each of the WINS servers on the network. The easiest way to do that is to configure the clients using DHCP.

When a WINS client is turned off, it releases its WINS registration. When the client restarts, it registers its name with the WINS server, receiving a new version ID. This re-registration results in entries in the WINS database that must be replicated with other WINS servers. Recall from Chapter 7 that a given NetBIOS computer can be associated with multiple NetBIOS names that are associated with the services running on the client. Each NetBIOS name that is registered with WINS increases the WINS replication traffic.

Roving WINS clients generate traffic in a different way. When a client moves to a different network and is restarted, it attempts to register its name with WINS. A registration already exists for that client on the old network. WINS must challenge the existing name registration before it can be released for use by the client on the new network. This challenge is another source of increased traffic generated by WINS.

All of this is to say that you must be sensitive to WINS traffic demands when planning and monitoring your network. On small networks, WINS traffic will probably be insignificant. As networks grow to many hosts, however, WINS traffic can become significant. Proper placement of WINS servers can reduce routed WINS traffic. Additionally, scheduling WINS replication for periods of low network demand can reduce WINS bandwidth requirements.

WINS servers that are separated by WAN links should be replicated infrequently whenever possible. Consider a WAN consisting of sites in New York and San Francisco. Typically, clients will be configured so that their primary services are provided by local servers, and WINS servers would be located at each site. Each site should have at least two WINS servers, which should be synchronized frequently, perhaps at 15 minute intervals. With proper planning, it should be sufficient to synchronize the WINS servers between New York and San Francisco at longer intervals, such as six to 12 hours. Remember, however, that with long replication intervals, the time required to converge the entire network on a change is extended as well. It might be necessary to force replication to take place when significant changes take place.

Installing the WINS Server Service

Any Windows NT Server computer can be configured as a WINS server, but WINS servers cannot receive their IP address assignments from DHCP. WINS clients communicate with WINS servers via directed datagrams, and you do not have to locate a WINS server on each network segment. However, non-WINS clients are supported only if at least one WINS proxy is installed on each network or subnetwork.

NOTE

Multihomed computers should not be configured as WINS servers. A WINS server can register its name with only one network. The name of a multihomed WINS server, therefore, cannot be registered with all attached networks. Also, some client connection attempts fail with multihomed WINS servers.

Multihomed computers can be configured as WINS clients.

To install the WINS Server service, follow these steps:

1. Install TCP/IP on the WINS server computer. DHCP servers must be configured with static IP addresses. All other computers can, if desired, obtain their IP addresses from DHCP. If installing TCP/IP for the first time, restart the computer.

2. Open the Network utility in the Control Panel.

3. Select the **Services** tab.

4. Choose **A**dd.

5. In the **N**etwork Service list, select **Windows Internet Name Service** and choose **OK.**

6. Supply the path to the installation files when prompted.

7. Close the Network utility. This opens the Microsoft TCP/IP Properties dialog box.

8. If necessary, edit the properties. Ensure that the interface adapters are configured with static IP addresses. (Don't select **O**btain IP address from DHCP server.)

9. Close the Network applet and restart the computer.

Configuring a Statically Addressed WINS Client

Clients configured using static IP addresses are enabled as WINS clients by supplying one or more WINS server addresses for the client's TCP/IP configuration. Figure 12.3 shows the TCP/IP configuration of a computer that includes an address for a primary WINS Server. If you are configuring a multihomed computer, be sure to add at least one WINS server address for each network adapter.

FIGURE 12.3

Configuring a TCP/IP host as a WINS client.

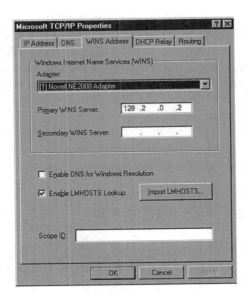

Configuring WINS Proxies

Windows NT, Windows 95, and Windows for Workgroups computers can be configured as WINS proxies, enabling them to receive broadcast b-node name requests from non-WINS clients and resolve them using directed h-node queries to WINS servers. WINS proxies enable b-node computers to obtain name resolutions from WINS.

For WfW computers, the WINS proxy feature is enabled in the Advanced Microsoft TCP/IP Configuration dialog box by checking the box labeled Enable WINS Proxy Agent.

For Windows NT computers, you must edit the Registry. Change the value of the **EnableProxy** entry to 1 (type REG_DWORD). This value entry is found under the following Registry key:

```
HKEY_LOCAL_MACHINE\SYSTEM\CurrentControlSet\Services\Netbt\
Parameters
```

Configuring DHCP Clients As WINS Clients

To enable DHCP clients to make use of WINS, the clients must be assigned the following two DHCP options:

- **44 WINS/NBNS Servers.** This option specifies the WINS servers that the computers will attempt to use. Because hosts in different scopes will probably access different scopes, this option should probably be assigned at the scope level.

- **46 WINS/NBT Node Type.** This option specifies the address resolution mode the WINS client will employ. In the vast majority of cases, all hosts should be configured in h-node mode, and it might be appropriate to assign this as a global option that applies to all scopes on a DHCP server.

To add option 44 to a scope, follow these steps:

1. Start DHCP Manager.

2. Select a scope in the DHCP Servers box.

3. Choose **Scope** in the **D**HCP Options menu.

4. In the DHCP Options dialog box (see Figure 12.4) select **044 WINS/NBNS Servers** in the **U**nused Options box and choose **Add**. Before the option is added to the **A**ctive Options box, you receive a warning, Warning: In order for WINS to function properly, you must now set option 46(WINS/NBT Node Type), and set it to either 0x02(P-Node), 0x04(M-Node) or 0x08(H-Node). Choose **OK** to continue.

5. Choose **Value** to expand the dialog box and display the current values of the option, as shown in Figure 12.4. At first, of course, the IP address list will be empty. Your next task is to add the addresses of WINS servers.

FIGURE 12.4

*The DHCP Options window, choosing **Value** to display the values for the selected option.*

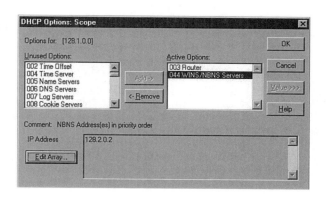

6. Option 44 accepts one or more addresses of WINS servers. To change the values, choose the **Edit Array** button to open the IP Address Array Editor, shown in Figure 12.5.

FIGURE 12.5

Adding an entry to the IP address array.

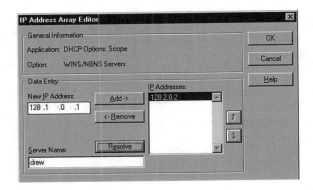

7. To add the address of a WINS server to the array, enter the address in the New IP Address box and choose **Add** to copy the address to the IP Address box. In the figure address, 128.2.0.1 is being added to the array.

    You can also start by entering a WINS server name in the **Server Name** field. Then choose **Resolve** to generate the IP address associated with the name you have entered. After the IP address is added to the New IP Address box, choose **A**dd to copy the address to the IP Address list.

    To remove an address, select the address in the IP Address box and choose **Remove**. In the figure address, 0.0.0.0 has been removed.

8. After addresses have been configured, choose **OK** and return to the DHCP Manager main window.

Global options apply to all scopes unless overridden by a scope option. Because all WINS clients will be configured to use h-node name resolution, option 46 will be added as a global option as follows:

1. Start DHCP Manager.

2. Select a scope in the DHCP Servers box.

3. Choose **Global** in the **D**HCP Options menu.

4. In the DHCP Options: Global dialog box, select **046 WINS/NBT Node Type** in the **U**nused Options box and choose **A**dd.

5. Choose **Value** to expand the dialog box and display the current values of the option (see Figure 12.6). Option 46 requires one of four values that specifies an NBT node type. In general option 0x8, h-node is the preferred choice. Enter the desired value and choose **OK**.

FIGURE 12.6

Editing the value of WINS option 46.

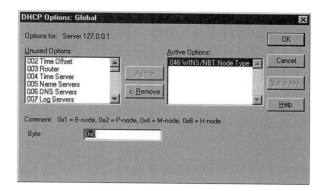

After the required options have been entered, they appear in the DHCP Server Manager main window (see Figure 12.7). Notice that option 046, which was entered as a global option, is identified by a global icon. This option applies to all scopes defined on this DHCP server unless overridden by a scope-level option.

FIGURE 12.7

DHCP options configured for WINS.

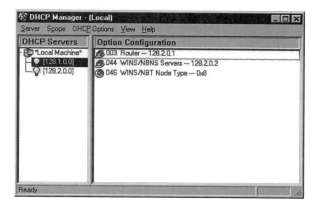

After the WINS options have been added to the appropriate DHCP scopes, it is necessary to force the DHCP clients to release their leases so they can acquire new leases with the WINS options. You can delete the leases in the Active Leases dialog box, but clients cannot acquire new leases until their current leases expire.

NOTE

To force Windows NT and Windows 3.1x DHCP clients to release their current leases, enter the command `ipconfig /release` at a command prompt on the client computer. When the computer is restarted, the DHCP client acquires a new DHCP lease with the WINS options in effect.

To force Windows 95 to release its DHCP lease, enter the command `winipcfg` at a command prompt and choose the **Release** button.

Naming on a WINS Network

After WINS has been configured and all hosts have been registered with the WINS database, attempts to connect with remote hosts will succeed. Consider again now the example of BLYTHE attempting to connect to WOODY on a separate network. Under WINS, BLYTHE generates a p-node request for address information that is directed to BLYTHE's primary WINS server. The WINS server responds with the required address information that BLYTHE uses to establish a connection.

Naming Versus Browsing

Users of Windows products in network environments become so familiar with browsing network resources that mistaking the Windows Browser for a name service becomes rather easy. Browsers, however, maintain databases only of host names. Addresses must still be derived from a name resolution process.

Browsing works somewhat differently on TCP/IP networks than on networks running NetBIOS and NWLink, although the difference becomes apparent only when routing is involved. Windows browsing is based on browse lists, which catalog all available domains and servers. When a user opens a Connect Network Drive dialog box (in Windows for Workgroups) or a Network Neighborhood dialog box (Windows 95 and NT), the information that appears has been retrieved from a browse list.

Browse lists are maintained by browsers. By default, all Windows NT Server computers are browsers. Windows NT Workstation computers are potential browsers and can become browsers if required. Windows 95 and WfW computers also are potential browsers.

Each domain has one master browser that serves as the primary point for collecting the browse database for the domain. Servers (any computer that offers shared resources) that enter the network transmit server announcements to the master browser to announce their presence. The master browser uses these server announcements to maintain its browse list.

Backup browsers receive copies of the browse list from the master browser at periodic intervals. Backup browsers introduce redundancy to the browsing mechanism and distribute browsing queries across several computers. An election process among the various browsers determines the master browser. In domains, the election is biased in favor of making the primary domain controller (PDC) the master browser, which always is the master browser if it is operational.

All Windows NT Server computers function as master or backup browsers. Windows NT Workstation computers can function as browsers. In the presence of sufficient Windows NT Server computers, no Windows NT Workstation computers will be configured as browsers. When no Windows NT Server computers are available, at least two Windows NT Workstation computers will be activated as browsers. An additional browser will be activated for every 32 Windows NT Workstation computers in the domain.

Servers must announce their presence to the master browser at periodic intervals, starting at one minute intervals and increasing to 12 minutes. If a server fails to announce itself for three announcement periods, it is removed from the browse list. Therefore, up to 36 minutes might be required before a failed server is removed from the browse list.

Domains are also maintained in the browse list. Every fifteen minutes, a master browser broadcasts a message announcing its presence to master browsers in other domains. If a master browser is not heard from for three 15-minute periods, other master browsers remove the domain from their browse lists. Thus, 45 minutes might be required to remove information about another domain from a browse list.

Internetworks based on NetBIOS and NWLink protocols can route broadcast name queries across routers. Maintaining a single master browser for each domain, therefore, is necessary.

Internetworks based on TCP/IP cannot forward broadcast name queries between networks. Therefore, Microsoft TCP/IP networks maintain a master browser for each network or subnetwork. If a domain spans more than one network or subnetwork, the domain master browser running on the

PDC has a special responsibility of collecting browse lists from the master browser on each network and subnetwork. The domain master browser periodically rebroadcasts the complete domain browse list to the master browsers, which in turn update backup browsers on their networks.

NOTE

To enable browsing on a TCP/IP internetwork, at least one Windows NT Server computer must be present on each network (or subnetwork if subnetting is used). If WINS is not enabled for the network, each browser must be configured with an LMHOSTS file that contains entries for domain controllers on the internetwork.

Therefore, significant time might be required to disseminate browsing data through a domain on a large TCP/IP internetwork.

The browsing service is a convenience but is not required to enable clients to access servers on the internetwork. Client processes still can use shared resources by connecting directly with the UNC (Universal Naming Convention) name of the resource. If host BLYTHE shares its CD-ROM drive with the share name cd-rom, you can specify the resource as \\blythe\cd-rom in the Path box of a Map Network Drive dialog box (see Figure 12.8). In NT 4, this dialog box is produced when you choose the **Map Network Drive** command in the Tools menu of Windows NT Explorer.

FIGURE 12.8

Entering a UNC path to connect to a resource.

Alternatively, you can connect the resource using a net use command at a command prompt, for example:

```
net use f: \\blythe\cd-rom
```

It is unnecessary to be able to browse WOODY to connect using the UNC name. It is, however, necessary to be able to obtain the IP address for WOODY. On a TCP/IP internetwork, that makes WINS a near necessity. Browsing, however, is convenient but is not essential.

Note

Multihomed hosts often present an ambiguous face to the network community. Different hosts can use different IP addresses to access services running on the host, with unpredictable results. One case in which this unpredictability seems to appear is browsing when the PDC for a domain is multihomed. Clients are not hard-wired with the addresses of browsers, and a multihomed master browser appears to confuse things, causing various clients to see different browse lists. More consistent results seem to be obtained when the PDC has a single IP address. In any case, the PDC cannot serve as a master browser for more than one network or subnetwork.

Managing WINS Servers

WINS functions are managed using WINS Server Manager. The icon for WINS Server Manager is installed in the Network Administration program group. WINS Server Manager is used to monitor WINS servers, establish static address mappings, and manage database replication. A few WINS database management tasks, such as compacting the database, are initiated from the command line.

Adding WINS Servers to WINS Server Manager

Figure 12.9 shows the main window for WINS Server Manager: WINS Manager has been configured to manage two WINS servers. A single WINS Service Manager can be used to monitor all WINS Servers on the internet.

FIGURE 12.9

The WINS Server Manager main window.

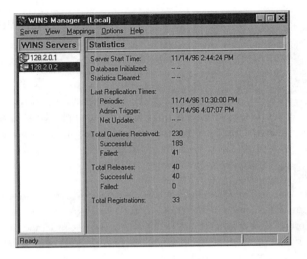

If WINS Server Manager is run on a computer running the WINS Server service, the computer is listed in the WINS Servers list. To add a WINS server to the list of managed servers:

1. Choose the **Add WINS Server** command in the <u>S</u>erver menu to open an Add WINS Server dialog box.

2. Enter the IP address of the new WINS server in the WINS Server entry box and choose **OK**. The server is added to those in the WINS Servers box.

To remove a WINS server from the list, select the server and choose the **Delete WINS Server** command in the <u>S</u>erver menu.

Monitoring WINS

The main window of WINS Server Manager displays several statistics about the WINS server selected in the WINS Servers box. The statistics are as follows:

- **Server Start Time.** The date and time when the WINS Server was started. This is the time the computer was started. Stopping and starting the WINS Server service does not reset this value.

- **Database Initialized.** Static mappings can be imported from LMHOSTS files. This value indicates when static mappings were last imported.

- **Statistics Cleared.** The date and time when the server's statistics were cleared with the Clear Statistics command in the View menu.

- **Last Replication Time: Periodic.** The last time the WINS database was updated by a scheduled replication.

- **Last Replication Time: Admin Trigger.** The last time a WINS database replication was forced by an administrator.

- **Last Replication Time: Net Update.** The last time the WINS database was updated in response to a push request from another WINS server.

- **Total Queries Received.** The number of name queries this WINS server has received from WINS clients. Statistics indicate the number of queries that succeeded and failed.

- **Total Releases.** The number of messages indicating an orderly shutdown of a NetBIOS application. Statistics indicate the number of names the WINS server released successfully and the number that it failed to release.

- **Total Registrations.** The number of registration messages received from clients.

To refresh the statistics, choose the **Refresh Statistics** command in the View menu or press **F5**.

To clear the statistics, choose the **Clear Statistics** command in the View menu.

Setting WINS Manager Preferences

The **Preferences** command in the Options menu can be used to set a variety of optional features for WINS Manager. Figure 12.10 shows the Preferences dialog box. (In the figure, the **Partners** button has been clicked to open the push and pull partner configuration options.) Options in this dialog box are as follows:

- **Address Display.** Contains four options that determine how WINS servers are listed in the WINS Servers list. The options are Computer Name Only, IP Address Only, Computer Name (IP Address), and IP Address (Computer Name).

- **Server Statistics: Auto Refresh.** Check this box to specify that statistics in the WINS Manager be automatically updated. Enter an update interval in the Interval (Seconds) box.

- **Computer Names: LAN Manager-Compatible.** Generally, this box should be checked to force computer names to conform to LAN Manager rules, which limit names to 15 characters. (Some NetBIOS environments use 16 character names.) LAN Manager uses the 16th byte to indicate the computer role (server, workstation, messenger, and so on). All Windows network products follow LAN Manager naming conventions.

- **Validate Cache of "Known" WINS Servers at Startup Time.** Check this option if the system should query all known servers when starting up to determine if the servers are available.

- **Confirm Deletion of Static Mappings & Cached WINS servers.** Check this option if a warning message should be displayed when static mappings or cached names are deleted.

- **New Pull Partner Default Configuration: Start Time.** This value specifies a default start time that will be applied to newly created pull partners. Specify a default replication interval in the Replication Interval fields. This value should be equal to or less than the lowest replication interval that is set for any active WINS replication partners.

- **New Push Partner Default Configuration: Update Count.** This value specifies the default for the number of registrations and changes that will cause a push partner to send a replication trigger. The minimum value is 20.

FIGURE 12.10

*WINS Manager
Preferences.*

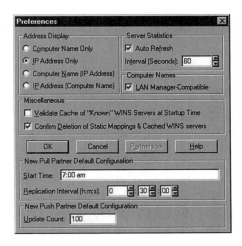

Configuring WINS Server Properties

A number of properties can be adjusted for each WINS server. These properties are configured by selecting a WINS Server in the WINS Server Manager and choosing the **Configuration** command in the Servers menu. Figure 12.11 shows the WINS Server Configuration dialog box. (In Figure 12.11, the **Advanced** button was clicked to open the Advanced WINS Server Configuration box.) The options in this dialog box are as follows:

- **Renewal Interval.** This option determines how frequently a client must reregister its name. A name not reregistered within the renewal interval is marked as released. Forcing clients to reregister frequently increases network traffic. A value of 32 hours enables a client to retain a registration from day to day, while ensuring that the registration is released in a reasonable period of time if it is not used. The maximum value for this field is 96 hours (4 days).

- **Extinction Interval.** This option determines how long a released name is to remain in the database before it is marked extinct and is eligible to be purged. Try setting this value to three or four times the renewal interval.

- **Extinction Timeout.** Specifies the interval between the time a record is marked extinct and the time when the record is actually purged from the database. The minimum value is one day.

- **Verify Interval.** Specifies how frequently the WINS server must verify the correctness of names it does not own. The maximum value is 24 days.

NOTE

Setting renewal and extinction intervals is a balancing act between the needs of your users, keeping the WINS database up-to-date, and generation of network traffic. If you force renewal and extinction to occur at frequent intervals, network traffic increases and users can lose their name reservations if they are away from the office for a few days. However, if these intervals are too long, the database becomes cluttered with obsolete entries.

- **Pull Parameters: Initial Replication.** Check this box to have this server pull new data from its pull partners when it is initialized or when replication parameters change. Then specify a value in the Retry Count field to specify the number of times the server should attempt replication. If the server is unsuccessful, replication is retried according to the server's replication configuration.

- **Push Parameters: Initial Replication.** Check this box if the server should inform its push partners when it is initialized. If push partners should be notified when an address changes in a mapping record, check the **Replicate on Address Change** box.

- **Logging Enabled.** Check this box if database changes should be logged to the JET.LOG file.

- **Log Detailed Events.** Checking this box enables verbose logging. Due to the demand on system resources, this option should be used only when tuning WINS performance.

- **Replicate Only With Partners.** If this option is checked, an administrator cannot force a WINS server to push or pull from a WINS server that is not listed as a replication partner.

- **Backup On Termination.** If this option is checked, the database is backed up upon shutdown of WINS Manager, unless the system is being stopped.

- **Migrate On/Off.** Check this option if you are upgrading to Windows NT from a non-NT system. When checked, this option enables static records to be treated as dynamic so that they can be overwritten.

- **Starting Version Count (hex).** This value must be adjusted only if the WINS database is corrupted and must be restarted. In that case, set the value higher than the version number for this WINS server as it appears on all of the server's replication partners, to force replication of records for this server. The maximum value of this parameter is $2^{31}-1$. Version counts are visible in the View Database dialog box.

- **Database Backup Path.** Specifies the directory in which the database backup files are to be stored. If a path is specified, a backup is performed automatically at 24-hour intervals. This backup can be used to restore the main database if it becomes corrupted. Do not specify a network directory.

FIGURE 12.11

The WINS Server Configuration dialog box.

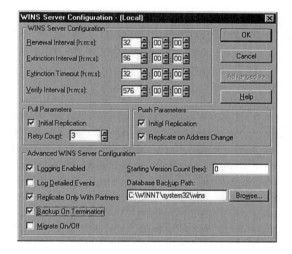

Viewing WINS Server Details

Detailed information for each WINS server can be displayed by selecting the server and choosing the **Detailed Information** command in the Servers menu. Figure 12.12 shows an example Detailed Information box. The fields in this box are as follows:

- **Computer Name.** The NetBIOS name of the computer supporting the WINS server.

- **IP Address.** The IP address of the WINS server.

- **Connected Via.** The connection protocol.

- **Connected Since.** The time when the WINS Server service was last activated. Unlike the Server Start Time statistic in the main window, Connected Since is reset when the WINS Server service is stopped or started.

- **Last Address Change.** The time when the last database change was replicated.

- **Last Scavenging Times.** The last time the database was scavenged to remove old data. Times are reported for the following scavenging events:

  - **Periodic.** Timed scavenging.

  - **Admin Trigger.** Manually initiated scavenging.

  - **Extinction.** Scavenging of released records which were scavenged because they had aged past the extinction time.

  - **Verification.** Last scavenging based on the Verify interval in the WINS server configuration.

- **Unique Registrations.** The number of name registrations for groups that the WINS server has accepted. The Conflicts statistic indicates the number of conflicts encountered when registering names that are already registered. The Renewals statistic indicates the number of renewals that have been received for unique names.

- **Group Registrations.** The number of requests for groups that the WINS server has accepted. The Conflicts statistic indicates the number of conflicts encountered when registering group names. The Renewals statistic indicates the number of group name renewals that have been received.

FIGURE 12.12

Detailed information about a WINS server.

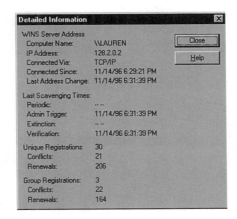

Configuring Static Mappings

Sometimes dynamic name-address mappings are not desirable. At such times, creating static mappings in the WINS database proves useful. A static mapping is a permanent mapping of a computer name to an IP address. Static mappings cannot be challenged and are removed only when they are explicitly deleted.

NOTE

Reserved IP addresses assigned to DHCP clients override any static mappings assigned by WINS.

To add static mappings in WINS Manager, use the following procedure:

1. Choose **Static Mappings** in the Mappings menu to open the Static Mappings dialog box (see Figure 12.13), which lists all active static mappings. The mappings for LAUREN are tagged with an individual icon because LAUREN was entered as a unique address mapping. The mappings for DREW are tagged by a group icon because DREW was entered as a multihomed mapping. Figure 12.14 shows how the static mapping for DREW was entered.

FIGURE 12.13
Static mappings.

FIGURE 12.14
*Adding static
mappings.*

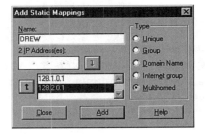

2. To add static mapping, choose **Add Mappings** to open the Add Static Mappings dialog box (see Figure 12.14).

3. Type the computer name in the Name box. WINS Manager supplies the \\ characters to complete the UNC name.

4. Enter the address in the IP Address box.

5. Choose one of the buttons in the Type box. (Group, internet group, and multihomed names are discussed further in the next section, "Special Names.") The following choices are available:

   ■ **Unique.** The name will be unique in the WINS database and will have a single IP address.

   ■ **Group.** Groups are targets of broadcast messages and are not associated with IP addresses. If the WINS server receives a query for the group, it returns FFFFFFFF, the IP broadcast address. The client then broadcasts on the local network.

- **Internet Group.** A group associated with the IP addresses of up to 24 Windows NT Servers plus the address of the primary domain controller, for a total of 25.

- **Multihomed.** A name that can be associated with up to 25 addresses, corresponding to the IP addresses of a multihomed computer.

6. Choose **Add**.

To edit static mapping, perform the following steps:

1. Choose **Static Mappings** in the **M**appings menu.

2. Select the mapping to be modified in the Static Mappings dialog box and choose **Edit Mapping**.

3. In the Edit Static Mapping dialog box, make any required changes.

4. Choose **OK** to save the changes.

Static mappings for unique and special group names can be imported from files that conform to the format of LMHOSTS files, described in Chapter 11 in the section "Managing LMHOSTS Files." Choose **Import Mappings** in the Static Mappings dialog box to import mappings.

NOTE

You will seldom need to add group, internet group, or multihomed static mappings, but several situations might call for unique static mappings. Here are two examples:

- Your network includes non-Microsoft hosts, such as UNIX hosts, that do not announce NetBIOS names. You can advertise the names of these hosts in the NetBIOS name space by adding a static mapping.

- You are configuring an IIS WWW server that will support multiple virtual sites. You can assign a NetBIOS name to each site by adding a static mapping to WINS, enabling NetBIOS clients to access these sites without relying on DNS for name resolution.

Special Names

WINS recognizes a variety of special names, identified by the value of the 16th byte of LAN Manager-compatible names. Special names are encountered when setting up static mappings and when examining entries in the WINS database. The special names recognized by WINS are discussed here.

Normal Group Names

Normal group names are tagged with the value 0x1E in the 16th byte. Browsers broadcast to this name and respond to it when electing a master browser. In response to queries to this name, WINS always returns the broadcast address FFFFFFFF.

Multihomed Names

A multihomed name is a single computer name that stores multiple IP addresses, which are associated with multiple network adapters on a multihomed computer. Each multihomed name can be associated with up to 25 IP addresses. This information is established when TCP/IP configuration is used to specify IP addresses for the computer.

When the WINS Server service is running on a multihomed computer, the WINS service is always associated with the first network adapter in the computer configuration. All WINS messages on the computer, therefore, originate from the same adapter.

Multihomed computers with connections to two or more networks should not be configured as WINS servers. If a client attempts a connection with a multihomed WINS server, the server might supply an IP address on the wrong network, causing the connection attempt to fail.

Internet Group Names

An internet group is used to register Windows NT Server computers in internet groups, principally Windows NT Server domains. If the internet group is not configured statically, member computers are registered dynamically as they enter and leave the group. Internet group names are identified by the value 0x1C in the 16th byte of the NetBIOS name. An internet group can contain up to 25 members, preference being given to the nearest Windows NT Server computers. On a large internetwork, the internet group registers the 24 nearest Windows NT Server computers plus the primary domain controller. Windows NT Server v3.1 computers are not registered to this group dynamically and must be added manually in WINS Manager. Manually adding computers to the group makes the group static—it no longer accepts dynamic updates.

Other Special Names

Several other special names are identified by byte 16:

- 0x0 identifies the redirector name that is associated with the Workstation service of a computer. This is the name that is usually referred to as the NetBIOS computer name.

- 0x1 identifies _MSBROWSE_, the name to which master browsers broadcast to announce their domains to other master browsers on the local subnet. WINS responds to queries to _MSBROWSE_ with the broadcast address FFFFFFFF.

- 0x3 identifies the Messenger service name used to send messages.

- 0x6 identifies the RAS server service.

- 0x1B identifies the domain master browser, which WINS assumes is the primary domain controller. If it is not, the domain master browser should be statically configured in WINS.

- 0x1F identifies the NetDDE service.

- 0x20 identifies the Server service that provides access to file shares.

- 0x21 identifies a RAS client.

- 0xBE identifies a Network Monitor agent.

- 0xBF identifies the Network Monitor utility.

Replicating the WINS Database

Having two or more WINS servers on any network is desirable. A second server can be used to maintain a replica of the WINS database that can be used if the primary server fails. On large internetworks, multiple WINS servers result in less routed traffic and spread the name resolution workload across several computers.

Pairs of WINS servers can be configured as replication partners. WINS servers can perform two types of replication actions: *pushing* and *pulling*. And a member of a replication pair functions as either a *push partner* or a *pull partner*.

All database replication takes place by transferring data from a push partner to a pull partner. But a push partner cannot unilaterally push data. Data transfers can be initiated in two ways.

A pull partner can initiate replication by requesting replication from a push partner. All records in a WINS database are stamped with a version number. When a pull partner sends a pull request, it specifies the highest version number that is associated with data received from the push partner. The push partner then sends any new data in its database that has a higher version number than was specified in the pull request.

A push partner can initiate replication by notifying a pull partner that the push partner has data to send. The pull partner indicates its readiness to receive the data by sending a pull replication request that enables the push partner to push the data.

In summary:

- Replication cannot take place until a pull partner indicates it is ready to receive data. A pull request indicates a readiness to receive data as well as the data the pull partner is prepared to receive. Therefore, the pull partners really control the replication process.

- All data are transferred from a push partner to a pull partner. Data are pushed only in response to pull requests.

Pulls generally are scheduled events that occur at regular intervals. *Pushes* generally are triggered when the number of changes to be replicated exceeds a specified threshold. An administrator, however, can manually trigger both pushes and pulls.

Figure 12.15 illustrates a network that incorporates five WINS servers. In general, replication partners are configured for two-way record transfer. Each member of the partnership is configured as a push partner and a pull partner, enabling both servers to pull updated data from each other.

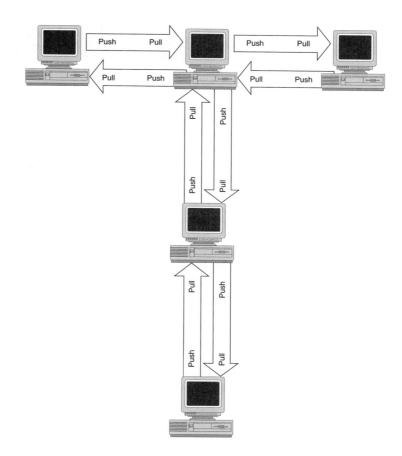

FIGURE 12.15
A network with several WINS replication partnerships.

Adding Replication Partners

To configure replication on a WINS server:

1. Select a WINS server in the WINS Manager main window.

2. Choose the **Replication Partners** command in the Server menu to open the Replication Partners dialog box (see Figure 12.16).

FIGURE 12.16

Configuring replication partners.

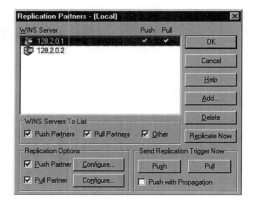

3. The Replication Partners dialog box lists all WINS servers that have been added to the configuration of this WINS Manager.

4. To add a replication partner, choose **Add** and enter the name or the address of a WINS server in the Add WINS Server dialog box.

5. To specify a replication partner, choose a WINS server in the WINS Server box of the Replication Partners dialog box.

6a. To configure the selected server as a push partner:

    a. Check the **Push Partner** check box under Replication Options.

    b. Choose **Configure** to open the Push Partner Properties dialog box (see Figure 12.17).

    c. Enter a value in the Update Count field that indicates the number of updates that should trigger a push. The minimum value is 20. Choose **Set Default Value** to enter the value you selected as a default in the Preferences dialog box.

    d. Choose **OK** to return to the Replication Partners dialog box.

FIGURE 12.17

Configuring a push partner.

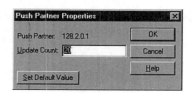

6b. To configure the selected server as a pull partner:

    a. Check the **Pull Partner** box under **Replication Options**.

    b. Choose **Configure** to open the Pull Partner Properties dialog box (see Figure 12.18).

    c. Enter a value in the Start Time field that specifies when in the day replication should begin. The time format must conform to the setting in the International option in the Control Panel. Also, specify a time in the Replication Interval fields to determine the frequency of replication. Choose **Set Default Values** to enter the value you selected as a default in the Preferences dialog box.

    d. Choose **OK** to return to the Replication Partners dialog box.

FIGURE 12.18
Configuring a pull partner.

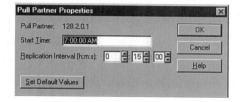

7. Configure other replication partners as required. A WINS server can be configured simultaneously as a push and a pull partner, which is required if two-way replication is to take place.

8. Choose **OK** after replication partners are configured for this WINS server.

Manually Triggering Replication

After adding a WINS server, updating static mappings, or bringing a WINS server back online after shutting it down for a period of time, forcing the server to replicate its data with its replication partners might be advisable. WINS Manager enables administrators to manually trigger both push and pull replications.

To trigger a replication, follow these steps:

1. Choose a WINS server in the WINS Manager main window.

2. Choose the **Replication Partners** command in the Server menu.

3. Choose a replication partner in the WINS Server list of the Replication Partners dialog box.

4. Check the **Push with Propagation** box if you want to trigger a push replication to be propagated to all WINS servers on the internetwork. If you do not check this box, only the immediate push partner receives the replicated data.

5a. To send a replication trigger, in the Send Replication Trigger Now box, choose **Push** or **Pull**.

   A push trigger notifies the pull partner that the push partner has data to transmit but does not force the pull partner to accept a push. Data is not transferred until the pull partner sends a pull request to the push partner that originated the trigger.

   A pull trigger requests updated data from a push partner.

5b. To start immediate replication, select a replication partner and choose the **Replicate Now** button.

Maintaining the WINS Database

When configured, WINS generally requires little maintenance. Some tasks should be performed periodically, however, to improve the efficiency of WINS and to reduce the size of WINS database files. Additionally, when clients experience name resolution problems, you might need to view the contents of the WINS database to diagnose problems.

Viewing the Database

To view the database for a WINS server, select the server in the WINS Manager main window and choose the **Show Database** command in the **Mappings** menu to open the Show Database dialog box (see Figure 12.19).

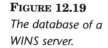

FIGURE 12.19

The database of a WINS server.

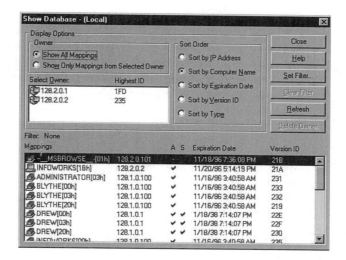

To display all database records for all managed WINS servers, select **Show All Mappings**.

To restrict the display to database records owned by a specific WINS server, select **Show Only Mappings from Select Owner** and select a WINS server in the Select Owner box. The owner of a WINS mapping record is the WINS server that first recorded the mapping.

Each record in the Mappings box includes the following data fields:

- **Icon.** A single terminal icon indicates a unique name. A multiterminal icon indicates a group, internet group, or multihomed name. (See the section "Special Names," earlier in this chapter.)

- **Computer Name.** Some computer names, such as _MSBROWSE_, are special names. User names also are shown in this listing. All are tagged with the hex number stored in byte 16 to identify the NetBIOS name type. See the previous discussion in the section "Special Names."

- **IP address.** The IP address associated with the computer name. Notice that several names can be associated with a single IP address.

- **A and/or S.** Indicates whether the name is established dynamically or statically. A name that was established dynamically and then entered as static can show checks in both columns.

- **Timestamp.** The day and time when the record will expire.

- **Version ID.** A stamp indicating the sequence in which the entries were established. When a pull replication partner requests new data, it requests entries with a revision number higher than the last record revision received from the push partner.

The database display does not update dynamically. Choose **Refresh** to update the display.

The Sort Order box offers several options for sorting database records. You can also restrict displayed records by establishing a filter. Choose **Set Filter** and enter a computer name or IP address in the Set Filter dialog box to restrict the display to a specific computer.

To clear the database of entries for a specific WINS server, select the server in the Select Owner box. Then choose **Delete Owner**.

As discussed in the section "Special Names," NetBIOS names fall into several categories, identified by byte 16 of a LAN Manager-compliant NetBIOS name. Each name in the Mappings box of the Show Database dialog box is tagged with the value assigned to byte 16 of its name. (The WINS Show Database window uses the letter h to identify hex values. The value 01h is equivalent to 0x1.) Figure 12.19 illustrates several categories of NetBIOS names:

- **_MSBROWSE_ (tagged 01h).** The name browsers broadcast to on the local network.

- **INFOWORKS (tagged 1Bh).** The master browser for the domain INFOWORKS.

- **BLYTHE.** Identified by three special name tags: 00h identifies the BLYTHE redirector, 03h identifies the BLYTHE messenger service, and 20h identifies BLYTHE as a server. Multiple names are associated with the same network adapter to respond to different network dialogs.

In Figure 12.20, the display has been scrolled to show entries for the domain name INFOWORKS. Notice that the three entries for this name are identified by a group icon rather than an icon for each individual name. One of these entries, INFOWORKS[1Ch], is an internet group name. Double-clicking that entry opens the View Mapping dialog box (see Figure 12.21). Figure 12.21 shows how the name INFOWORKS[1Ch] is associated with three IP addresses of Windows NT Servers running in the domain: 128.2.0.2 is singly homed and 128.1.0.1/128.2.0.1 is multihomed.

FIGURE 12.20

An internet group in the Mappings list.

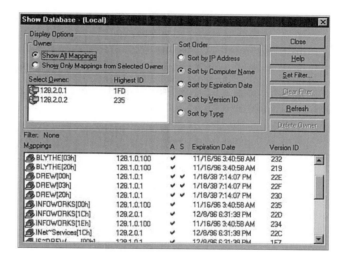

FIGURE 12.21

Mappings for the internet group INFOWORKS.

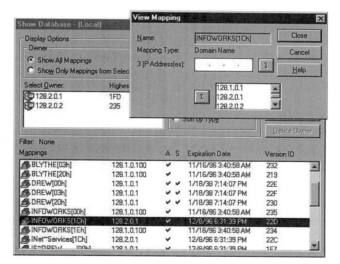

Adding static mappings to the internet group in the View Mapping dialog box is possible. Doing so alters the internet group so that it no longer can be updated dynamically, but might be necessary if Windows NT Server v3.1 computers are included in the domain as domain controllers.

Backing Up the Database

WINS performs a complete backup of its database every 24 hours. The filename and path are specified by registry parameters, as discussed in the section "WINS Registry Parameters." On occasion, you might want to execute an unscheduled backup. The procedure, which must be performed on the computer running the WINS Server service, is as follows:

1. Choose the **Backup Database** command in the Mappings menu to open a Select Backup Directory dialog box (see Figure 12.22).

2. If desired, select a disk drive in the Drives box. The best location is another hard disk so that the database files remain available if the primary hard disk fails.

3. Specify the directory in which backup files should be stored. WINS Manager proposes a default directory.

4. If desired, specify a new directory name to be created in the directory chosen in step 3. By default a subdirectory named wins_bak is created to store the backup files.

5. To back up only records that have changed since the last backup, check the **Perform Incremental Backup** box. This option is meaningful only if a full backup has been previously performed.

6. Choose **OK** to make the backup.

FIGURE 12.22

Selecting a backup directory for WINS.

You also should back up the Registry entries related to WINS. To back up the WINS Registry entries, perform the following steps:

1. Run the REGEDT32.EXE program from a <u>R</u>un prompt in the Startup menu.

2. Select the **HKEY_LOCAL_MACHINE** window.

3. Select the key SYSTEM\CurrentControlSet\Services\WINS.

4. Choose the **Sa<u>v</u>e Key** command in the <u>R</u>egistry menu.

5. Specify a directory and filename in which to store the backup files.

6. Choose **OK**.

Restoring the WINS Database

If users cannot connect to a server running the WINS Server service, the WINS database probably has become corrupted. In that case, you might need to restore the database from a backup copy. This can be done using menu commands or manually. The procedure must be performed on the computer running the WINS service.

To restore the WINS database using menu commands:

1. Stop the WINS Service using one of these methods:

   - Stop the Windows Internet Server Service using the Ser<u>v</u>ices tool in the Control Panel.

   - Open a command prompt and enter the command **net stop wins**.

2. Start the WINS Manager. Ignore any warning message that The Windows Internet Naming Service is not running on the target machine, or the target machine is not accessible.

3. Choose the **<u>R</u>estore Local Database** command in the <u>M</u>appings menu.

4. In the Select Directory To Restore From dialog box, specify the directory from which to restore.

5. Choose **OK** to restore the database.

6. Start the WINS service using one of the following methods:

■ Start the Windows Internet Server Service using the Services tool in the Control Panel.

■ Open a command prompt and enter the command `net start wins`.

To restore the database manually:

1. Stop the WINS Server service.

2. Delete all files in the directory C:\WINNT\SYSTEM32\WINS.

3. Copy the file SYSTEM.MDB from the installation disks to the C:\WINNT\SYSTEM32\WINS directory.

4. Make a backup copy of the file WINS.MDB to the C:\WINNT\SYSTEM32\WINS directory.

5. Restart the WINS Server service.

Scavenging and Compacting the Database

The key WINS database files are stored by default in the directory C:\winnt\system32\wins. (If your system files are stored in a directory other than C:\winnt35, substitute the appropriate directory path.) The files are as follows:

■ **WINS.MDB.** The WINS database file.

■ **WINSTMP.MDB.** Used by WINS to store temporary working data.

■ **J50.LOG.** Records transactions performed on the database. (This was called JET.LOG under Windows NT Server 3.5x.)

WARNING

Never remove or modify the WINS files.

Windows NT Server periodically backs up the WINS database and Registry entries. The default backup interval is three hours, configurable through a Registry key.

Over time, the WINS database becomes cluttered with released and old entries from other WINS servers. Scavenging the WINS database clears these old records. After scavenging, compacting the database to reduce the size of the data file is a good idea.

Scavenging is performed periodically, as determined by parameters in the Registry, but you can choose to initiate scavenging manually—before compacting the database, for example. (Under Windows NT Server 3.51 or earlier, scavenging must be performed manually.)

To scavenge the database, choose the **Initiate Scavenging** command in the Mappings menu.

The WINS database is stored in the file named WINS.MDB, which is stored by default in the directory \WINNT35\SYSTEM32\WINS. To compact the WINS database, do the following:

1. Open a command prompt.

2. Enter the command `net stop wins` to stop the WINS Server service on the computer. Users cannot resolve names on this server while the WINS Server service is stopped.

3. Change to the WINS directory. If the directory is in the default location, enter the command `cd \winnt\system32\wins`.

4. Enter the command `jetpack wins.mdb temp.mdb` to compact the database. `wins.mdb` is the file to be compacted, whereas `temp.mdb` is a name for a temporary file that jetpack uses during the compacting process.

5. After receiving the message `jetpack completed successfully`, restart WINS using the command `net start wins`.

6. To close the command prompt, enter the command `exit`.

WARNING

jetpack should be used to compact the WINS.MDB file only. Do not compact the SYSTEM.MDB file.

Using WINSCHK

The WINS Consistency Check Tool (winschk.exe) is a command-line utility included with the *Windows NT Server Resource Kit*. Winschk can be used to check for name and version number inconsistencies in WINS databases. It can also monitor replication activity and verify the replication configuration.

Winschk is executed at the command prompt and accepts the following options:

0   **Enables or disables interactive mode.** Use this option to toggle between interactive and noninteractive mode. In interactive mode, status messages are displayed in the command prompt window and are recorded in the file Winstst.log. Interactive is the default mode.

1   **Tests for names on WINS servers.** This option runs a quick check for consistency between WINS servers. The check is configured by editing two text files with a text editor.

Names.txt must contain the NetBIOS names of WINS servers to be checked, with one name per line; the format of the NetBIOS names is *name*16th_byte*, for example, BLYTHE*20. Names must be entered in uppercase.

Servers.txt must contain the IP address of a source WINS server from which a list of all replicating WINS servers can be identified.

Winschk queries each WINS server with the list of NetBIOS names. It checks for consistency of IP addresses and reports any mismatched IP addresses or occurrences of "name not found". It also reports nonresponsive WINS servers.

2   **Checks for version number consistencies.** With this option, Winschk uses an RPC function to obtain mappings between owner addresses and version numbers, constructing mapping tables based on data obtained from various WINS servers.

`Winschk` checks consistency by assuming that a WINS server always has the highest version number among the network of WINS servers for the records that it owns. Here is a sample matrix, taken from Microsoft documentation:

```
        A       B       C       List of owners
A       100     80      79      Mapping table retrieved from A
B       95      75*     65      Mapping table retrieved from B
C       78      45      110     Mapping table retrieved from C
```

Each record is a mapping table retrieved from a WINS server. Each diagonal element (for example, the intersection of A with A) should have the highest version number among all the numbers in its column. In this example, the intersection of B with B indicates a problem that needs to be addressed.

3 **Monitors WINS servers and detects communication failures**. This option periodically monitors WINS servers to ensure that both the primary and backup WINS servers are not down at the same time. WINS server activity is recorded in `Monitor.log`. Alerts are sent to the administrator as required.

This option also periodically obtains statistics from the WINS servers to ensure that replication is taking place.

You can run `Winschk` with this option continually if desired. The continual version runs at three-hour intervals by default. Avoid running this option too frequently to avoid excessive network usage.

4 **Verifies replication configuration**. This option checks the Registry of a WINS server to ensure that each replication partner is configured as both a pull and push partner and that a pull interval is properly defined. `Winschk` brings any asymmetric partner relationships to the attention of the administrator.

99 Exits `Winschk`.

NOTE

The *Windows NT Server Resource Kit* includes two other WINS-related tools:

- **Winsdmp.** This utility dumps a copy of a WINS database to a file in comma-delimited form. These files can be analyzed in most databases or spreadsheets.

- **Winscl.** This is another utility for monitoring WINS servers and databases. It can also used as a command-line interface for managing WINS to initiate activities such as database replication, record registration or query, and database backup or restoration. See the online help for documentation of the available commands. Some of the available options are very powerful and should be used with caution.

Managing Remote WINS Servers

You can manage remote WINS servers by adding the remote server to WINS Manager using the **Add WINS Server** command in the Server menu. When managing a WINS server through the Internet, you might encounter difficulty because firewalls or routers can block ports that are required.

WINS Administrator uses "dynamic endpoints" in remote procedure call (RPC) communication. When opening a remote WINS session, an initial session is set up on port 135. Then a second session is set up on a randomly selected port above 1024. Because the second port is not consistent, it is difficult to configure a firewall to pass traffic for the required port.

To enable remote administration of WINS to take place through a firewall, you must supply WINS with a list of all ports that are supported by the firewall. This is done by configuring the Registry.

The required parameters are stored in the following Registry key:

```
HKEY_LOCAL_MACHINE
  \Software
    \Microsoft
      \Rpc
        \Internet
```

The following Registry value entries contain RPC configuration parameters:

Ports

Data Type:	REG_MULTI_SZ
Range:	Valid port ranges (0–65535 inclusive)

Specifies a set of IP port ranges describing either all ports that are available from the Internet or all ports that are not available. Each string represents a single port or a range of ports (for example: `"1030-1055""1068"`). If any ports are outside the range 0–65535, or if any errors are encountered, the RPC runtime ignores the entire value entry.

PortsInternetAvailable

Data Type:	REG_SZ
Range:	Y or N (not case-sensitive)

If `Y`, the ports specified in the `Ports` value entry are Internet-available ports. If `N`, the ports specified in the `Ports` value entry are not Internet-available ports.

UseInternetPorts

Data Type:	REG_SZ
Range:	Y or N (not case-sensitive)

Specifies the default policy. If `Y`, the processes using the default will be assigned ports from the ports defined in the `Ports` and `PortsInternetAvailable` value entries. If `N`, processes using the default will be assigned ports from the set of intranet-only ports.

Managing WINS Consistency Checking

It can be useful to periodically check the distributed WINS database for consistency. Be aware, however, that a consistency check is both network and processor intensive. When performing a consistency check, a WINS server attempts to replicate all its records for an owner that is being checked to determine whether its database is consistent with the database of the record owner. To reduce the impact of WINS consistency checking, carefully configure the relevant Registry parameters, which are located under the following Registry key:

```
HKEY_LOCAL_MACHINE
    \SYSTEM
        \CurrentControlSet
            \Services
                \Wins
                    \Parameters
                        \ConsistencyCheck
```

The value entries are as follows:

TimeInterval

Data Type:	*REG_DWORD*
Range:	Number of Seconds
Default:	86400 (24 hours)

Specifies the time interval between WINS consistency checks.

SpTime

Data Type:	*REG_SZ*
Range:	*hh:mm:ss* (valid time in 24-hour format)
Default:	2:00:00 (2 AM)

Specifies the time at which the first consistency check will be performed, after which consistency checks are performed periodically as specified by TimeInterval.

MaxRecsAtATime

Data Type:	*REG_DWORD*
Range:	Number of Records
Default:	30000

Specifies the maximum number of records that are replicated in one consistency check cycle. WINS performs consistency checks on the records owned by one owner at a time. After checking one owner it goes on to the next owner or stops based on the MaxRecsAtATime value entry.

UseRplPnrs

Data Type:	DWORD
Range:	0 or any nonzero value

If this value entry has a nonzero value, WINS contacts its pull partners when performing a consistency check on records in its local database. If the owner of records to be checked is a pull partner, it will be used. If the owner of the records is not a pull partner, another pull partner will be selected at random.

Because WINS does not know which database is more current, when performing consistency checks, WINS will not delete records in a local database if it is not verifying records with the owner of the records.

WINS Registry Parameters

The Registry was discussed briefly in Chapter 10, "Managing DHCP." Please review that discussion if necessary, or refer to NRP's *Inside Windows NT Server* for greater detail.

Unless otherwise specified, the Registry parameters related to WINS are stored in the key:

```
HKEY_LOCAL_MACHINE
  \SYSTEM
    \CurrentControlSet
      \Services
        \Wins
          \Parameters
```

Not all parameters are inserted in the Registry during WINS installation. If you require the features associated with a parameter, use the Registry Editor to add the value to the Registry.

The Parameters key includes the subkey Datafiles, which specifies the files for WINS to use when it initializes the WINS database. The Registry values in the WINS Parameters key are as follows:

DbFileNm

Data Type:	REG_SZ or REG_EXPAND_SZ
Range:	pathname
Default:	%SystemRoot%\system32\ wins\wins.mdb

Specifies the complete path name for the WINS database file.

DoStaticDataInit

Data Type:	REG_DWORD
Range:	0 or 1
Default:	0

If this parameter is 1, the WINS database is initialized from files specified in the Datafiles subkey. Initialization takes place whenever WINS is started or when changes are made to parameters in the Parameters or Datafiles subkeys. If this parameter is 0, WINS does not initialize its database.

InitTimePause

Data Type:	REG_DWORD
Range:	0 or 1
Default:	0

If this parameter is 1, the WINS Server service starts in a paused state until it has been replicated from one of its replication partners or until replication has failed at least once. If this parameter is 1, the \WINS\Partners\Pull\InitTimeReplication parameter should be set to 1 or removed from the Registry.

LogDetailedEvents

Data Type:	REG_DWORD
Range:	0 or 1
Default:	0

This value ordinarily is set using the Log Detailed Events check box in the WINS Server Configuration dialog box. If 1, verbose logging is enabled. If 0, standard logging is enabled.

LogFilePath

Data Type:	REG_SZ or REG_EXPAND_SZ
Range:	pathname
Default:	%SystemRoot%\system32\wins

Specifies the directory in which to store WINS log files.

LoggingOn

Data Type:	REG_DWORD
Range:	0 or 1
Default:	0

If the value of this parameter is 1, logging takes place using the logging file specified by the LogFilePath parameter. This value ordinarily is set by checking the **Logging Enabled** check box in the WINS Server Configuration dialog box.

McastIntvl

Data Type:	REG_DWORD
Range:	2400 minimum
Default:	400

Specifies the interval in seconds at which the WINS server sends a multicast message to announce its presence to other WINS servers. The minimum value of 2400 sets an interval of 40 minutes.

McastTtl

Data Type:	REG_DWORD
Range:	1–32
Default:	6

Specifies the number of times a multicast announcement can cross a router.

NoOfWrkThds

Data Type:	REG_DWORD
Range:	1–40
Defaults:	Number of processors on the computer.

Specifies the number of worker threads available to WINS. Can be changed without restarting the WINS server computer.

PriorityClassHigh

Data Type:	REG_DWORD
Range:	0 or 1
Defaults:	0

If this parameter is 1, WINS runs at a high priority, ensuring that it is not preempted by other processes on the computer. Use this parameter to emphasize WINS performance on a computer that functions primarily as a WINS name server. A value of 0 sets the WINS priority as normal.

RefreshInterval

Data Type:	REG_DWORD
Range:	Hex value for time in seconds, up to 96 hours, 59 minutes, 59 seconds.
Default:	96 hours

This parameter is a hex value that specifies the interval in seconds at which WINS names must be renewed on the server. The value is ordinarily set by specifying the Renewal Interval in the WINS Server Configuration dialog box.

TombstoneInterval

Data Type:	REG_DWORD
Range:	Hex value for time in seconds, up to 96 hours, 59 minutes, 59 seconds.
Default:	variable

This parameter is a hex value that specifies the interval after which nonrenewed names are marked as extinct. The value is ordinarily set by specifying the Extinction Interval in the WINS Server Configuration dialog box.

TombstoneTimeout

Data Type:	REG_DWORD
Range:	Hex value for time in seconds, up to 96 hours, 59 minutes, 59 seconds.
Default:	variable

This parameter is a hex value that specifies the interval after which extinct names are removed from the WINS database. The value is ordinarily set by specifying the Extinction Timeout in the WINS Server Configuration dialog box.

UseSelfFndPntrs

Data Type:	REG_DWORD
Range:	0 or 1
Default:	0

If this parameter is 1 and the network routers support multicasting, a WINS server can automatically identify other WINS servers and identify push and pull replication partners. If routers do not support multicasting, WINS servers can automatically identify only those WINS servers that are on the same network or subnet. WINS server automatic identification adjusts automatically as WINS servers are started or gracefully shut down.

WINS server automatic identification is overridden if WINS Manager is used to establish replication.

VerifyInterval

Data Type:	REG_DWORD
Range:	Hex value for time in seconds, up to 96 hours, 59 minutes, 59 seconds
Default:	variable

This parameter is a hex value that specifies the interval after which the WINS server must verify entries in its database that it does not own. The value is ordinarily set by specifying the Verify Interval in the WINS Server Configuration dialog box.

What's in a Name?

Naming on Microsoft networks isn't a problem unless TCP/IP is involved. With NetBEUI or NWLink, computer names are propagated automatically, with no need for administrative intervention. Under TCP/IP, however, automatic name propagation stops at routers. Therefore, special medicine is required to provide naming throughout an internetwork.

This chapter explored two methods of providing friendly names for computers on Microsoft TCP/IP networks. Although LMHOSTS can do the job, static LMHOSTS files have the disadvantage of being difficult to manage on large networks. When set up, however, WINS has the virtue of being dynamic. Names are registered automatically, and the database is updated without hands-on intervention. Yes, WINS demands some knowledge of the administrator, and a bit of effort to keep things working smoothly, but WINS remains easier than LMHOSTS on a large network.

A significant disadvantage of WINS is that it is a Microsoft-specific technology. Non-Microsoft TCP/IP hosts cannot query WINS for naming information. Instead, the standard naming tool on TCP/IP networks is the Domain Name Service. And that is where the next chapter takes us, on an investigation of the DNS server that is one of the new components on Windows NT Server 4.

Chapter 13

MANAGING THE MICROSOFT DNS SERVER

Domain Name Service (DNS) is the standard naming service used on the Internet and on most TCP/IP networks. Chapter 6, "The Process-Application Layer," describes DNS fairly thoroughly. This chapter focuses on two issues: whether you need to implement DNS on your network and, if so, how to implement a DNS server on Windows NT computers.

Prior to Windows NT version 4.0, NT's support for DNS was rather anemic. A beta DNS server, compatible with BIND, was included with the Windows NT Resource Kit for NT Server version 3.5. This software was not particularly harmonious with the management style promoted by NT. It was configured entirely by editing BIND-compatible database files and lacked a graphic interface. And it had a reputation for instability, not surprising because it was, after all, a beta.

But now, shipping with Windows NT Server 4.0, a GUI-based DNS Server service is available. Still compatible with BIND, and in fact capable of reading BIND database files, the new DNS Server adds a familiar graphic interface with wizards that greatly simplify the task of maintaining the many entries that make up a DNS name space.

Additionally, the DNS server supports a feature unique to the Microsoft network environment, the capability to capture NetBIOS names to identify computers on the network and add the NetBIOS names to the DNS name space. The DNS Server supports hooks into WINS that enable DNS to offer name resolution for names that it learns from WINS. So far as your Microsoft network clients are concerned, you can add DNS to the network without the necessity of manually entering your Microsoft computer names to the static DNS database. All your Microsoft hosts will be maintained dynamically by the link between the DNS Server and WINS.

NOTE

With Windows NT Server version 5.0, it will become possible to entirely eliminate WINS from your Microsoft TCP/IP network. A new feature dubbed *dynamic DNS* can supply all required naming services, whether on Microsoft-only networks or on TCP/IP networks that use DNS as the standard name service.

Deciding Whether to Implement DNS

If your Windows TCP/IP network is not connected to non-Microsoft TCP/IP networks, you do not need DNS. WINS can provide all the naming services required on a Microsoft Windows network. And because WINS configures name-address mappings dynamically, it requires little or no maintenance to cope with network equipment changes. A user can move a portable computer from one network on the private internet to another network and have no requirement for changes in WINS. WINS recognizes the new location of the host and adjusts its database accordingly.

You need DNS if you want to connect your TCP/IP hosts to the Internet or to a UNIX-based TCP/IP network, but only if you want to enable users outside the Windows network to access your TCP/IP hosts by name. If outside users do not use services hosted on your computers, or if identifying your computers by IP address is acceptable, identifying your network hosts in DNS is not necessary.

In other words, if your network is attached to the Internet, you do not need to include your hosts in the Internet DNS tree to enable your users to connect to outside resources. You need DNS name support only if outsiders connect to resources on your network.

If you decide that hosts on your network must be identified in DNS, ask the following questions:

- Must all hosts be added to DNS or only a select few?

- How often will host name address information change?

- Should the names of local hosts be provided by WINS?

- Will you be obtaining a domain name on the Internet?

- Will hosts under your domain name be dispersed geographically or located in a single location?

The right answers to these questions might indicate that you can hire an Internet service provider to manage your portion of the DNS tree. Recall from Chapter 6, "The Process-Application Layer," that a single DNS server can manage multiple zones in the DNS tree. Many commercial Internet providers will manage your zone for a fee that often is considerably less than the cost of maintaining two private DNS servers. (To provide fault tolerance, two are generally considered to be a minimum.)

Consider contracting the management of your portion of the DNS tree if any or all of the following circumstances apply:

- You obtain your Internet access through an Internet provider which offers DNS management as a service.

- You do not want to have local names of Windows TCP/IP hosts provided by WINS. The majority of Internet access providers run DNS on UNIX computers, which do not support links to WINS.

- Your network is too small to justify training two DNS administrators, allocating a portion of their work time, and maintaining two computers with the capacity to provide DNS services.

- Your network is fairly stable and you do not need immediate posting of changes.

Consider managing your own DNS server if any, some, or all of the following are true:

- You want to use WINS to provide host names of your Windows computers.

- You want local control of your organization's part of the DNS tree.

- Your network changes frequently.

- Your organization can justify the expense of administrative labor and DNS server hardware.

- Your network is local and changes infrequently so that HOSTS files might be used.

Local networks that include UNIX hosts cannot use WINS for name resolution. Although DNS might seem to be the best solution for providing a local database, HOSTS files remain an option under some circumstances. Naming using HOSTS files generates no network traffic for name resolution, and HOSTS files can be maintained easily on a stable network. If the network changes frequently, maintaining DNS is easier than frequently distributing HOSTS files to all computers on the network.

Name Resolution with HOSTS Files

Before DNS, name resolution was accomplished using files named HOSTS that, on UNIX computers, were conventionally stored with the filename \etc\hosts. On Windows NT computers, HOSTS files are stored in the directory C:\WINNT\SYSTEM32\DRIVERS\ETC.

Supporting a naming service is a simple matter of editing a master HOSTS file and distributing it to all computers. This can be accomplished by copying the file when a user logs on to a domain, or it can be done using a software distribution system such as Microsoft's System Management Server.

Basically, the same tasks are involved in maintaining a master HOSTS file and maintaining DNS database files. DNS saves labor because DNS database files need not be copied to all hosts, but rather need only be installed on the primary and backup DNS servers. So DNS begins to pay off when your network becomes so large that keeping everyone's HOSTS files up-to-date becomes too labor-intensive.

Getting Ready for DNS

If your network will never be on the Internet, you can use any naming conventions for DNS. If an Internet connection is a present or future requirement, however, you must do several things:

- Obtain one or more Internet IP network addresses.

- Obtain an Internet connection.

- Obtain a domain name in the appropriate top-level Internet domain.

If an organization already connected to the Internet agrees to let you connect to the Internet by connecting to their network, you are responsible for obtaining IP addresses and domain names. Chapter 6 provides guidelines for identifying and contacting the authority for your parent domain. In these cases, IP addresses are assigned by the InterNIC Registration Service.

Increasingly, however, the principal way to connect to the Internet is to subscribe using an Internet access provider. IAPs are assigned blocks of IP addresses. You need to obtain an address from your IAP, which probably also would be willing to help you obtain a domain name. A good IAP can simplify setting up an Internet connection.

Somewhere along the line, you need to coordinate with the contact for your domain's parent domain and for in-addr.arpa to obtain authority for your domain in the DNS tree. Before you attempt to hook into Internet DNS, however, you should have your DNS system in operation.

Managing Microsoft DNS Server

Figure 13.1 illustrates an internetwork to be used as an example for configuring DNS. The University of Southern North Dakota at Hoople, a school of music (domain name hoople.edu), operates the network. Hosts have been named after the faculty's favorite composers.

FIGURE 13.1

The sample network.

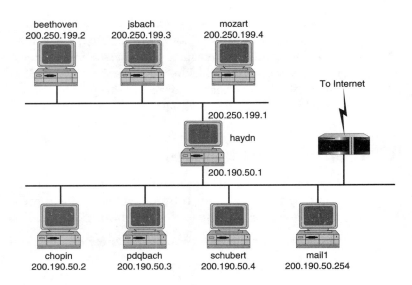

The internetwork consists of two networks, connected by a multihomed host serving as an IP router. The internetwork connects to the Internet via a Cisco router. The primary DNS server will be mozart. The files configured for mozart will assume a secondary name server and will be set up on schubert. The details of configuring the secondary name server are discussed later in this chapter.

Only three computers require fixed IP addresses:

- **mozart** is the primary DNS server.

- **schubert** is the secondary DNS server and also will be the WINS server.

- **mail1** is the mail server.

The HOSTS file for this internetwork is as follows:

```
127.0.0.1          localhost
200.250.199.1      haydn.hoople.edu haydn papa1
200.190.50.1       haydn.hoople.edu haydn papa2
200.250.199.2      beethoven.hoople.edu beethoven
200.250.199.3      jsbach.hoople.edu jsbach jsb
200.250.199.4      mozart.hoople.edu mozart
200.190.50.2       chopin.hoople.edu chopin
200.190.50.3       pdqbach.hoople.edu pdqbach pdq
200.190.50.4       schubert.hoople.edu schubert
```

Much of the information in the HOSTS file shows up in the configuration files for DNS.

NOTE

HOSTS files can be created and modified with any text editor, but caution is required under Windows. Most Windows-based editors automatically append an extension to the filename when they save a file. If you save a file named HOSTS in Notepad, for example, the .txt extension is automatically added to the saved file.

In Notepad, you can override this behavior by enclosing the filename in quotation marks when you save it.

In any case, if HOSTS name resolution doesn't appear to work, use Windows NT Explorer to examine the filenames. To see filename extensions, you need to open the Options dialog box (choose **Options** in the <u>V</u>iew menu) and check **Hide file <u>e</u>xtensions for known file types.**

DNS Configuration Options

The Windows NT Server 4 DNS Server can be configured in two ways:

- Using database files; text files that are maintained using any text editor. The DNS Server accepts database files that are compatible with BIND, which is the most widely used DNS service on the Internet.

- Using the graphic interface, you can manage any feature of the DNS server. If desired, you do not even need to concern yourself with the formats of the BIND database files.

I think it is a good idea to be familiar with both techniques. If you understand how to create and maintain the BIND files, you gain several advantages. If your network is currently running a BIND DNS server, the entries in the existing server database can be imported into the Windows NT Server 4 DNS Server. Similarly, you can generate BIND database files from the DNS Server if you want to export data to a BIND-based DNS server. Another significant advantage is that BIND is well documented, and you will find it easy to obtain support from other DNS managers.

On the other hand, the graphic interface has peculiar advantages that BIND lacks. Instead of creating database files in a text editor, a process that is prone to human error, you use familiar dialog boxes and wizards to add entries to the database. Some operations are greatly simplified by using drag-and-drop. And you can update the database dynamically, without the need to reboot the name server. BIND servers must be stopped and restarted to load new entries to the database.

While planning this chapter, I spent considerable time debating whether to start out showing you the graphic configuration approach or the method for creating BIND database files. In the end, I decided to start by showing you the BIND database files. You will encounter several eccentricities when you enter data in the DNS Manager GUI, such as the use of trailing periods after fully qualified host names. I think it is much easier to understand these eccentricities if you have seen the data in the context of the BIND database files. Knowledge of the BIND data files also comes in handy if there is a need to copy the configuration of an existing BIND DNS server to the Microsoft DNS Server.

So even though the graphic approach is the one you will use for nearly all your management of the Microsoft DNS Server, I'm going to start by showing you how to create the BIND database files. In the process, you will learn about the structure of the DNS databases, knowledge that you can apply when working with the graphic interface as well. With that background in place, I'll show you how to manage the DNS Server graphically, creating the entire database through the GUI interface should you want to do so.

Creating BIND Database Files

When configuring DNS Server using BIND database files, the files are located in the directory %systemroot%\SYSTEM32\DNS, which by default is C:\WINNT\SYSTEM32\DNS. (Note that this directory is different from the directory used in the Windows NT 3.51 beta, which was %systemroot%\SYSTEM32\DRIVERS\ETC. If you are upgrading, you will need to move the files to the new location.) You need to maintain the following DNS files:

- **boot.** This file is the master configuration file. It declares all the various files used to initialize the DNS server.

- **cache.dns.** This file contains host information that establishes basic DNS connectivity. Principally, this file defines the addresses of the root name servers for the DNS.

- **127.0.0.dns.** This file includes reverse lookup data for IP numbers on the 127 (loopback) network, such as localhost.

- ***reverse-netid*.in-addr.arpa.dns.** For each network netid managed by the DNS server, a reverse lookup file is required to specify address-to-name mappings.

- ***domain*.dns.** For each domain managed by the DNS server, a forward lookup file is required to specify name-to-address mappings.

NOTE

BIND servers use these same files without the .dns filename extension. The Microsoft DNS Manager adds the .dns extension to all data files that it creates, and I have adhered to that convention throughout this chapter.

The Windows NT DNS server software includes example files for each file type. Most files require considerable editing to customize the file for local use. The following sections examine each of these files in turn.

NOTE

The information in this chapter should be sufficient to enable you to configure a DNS name server in most situations. If you want to know DNS and BIND in more intimate detail, consult the book, *DNS and BIND*, by Paul Albitz and Cricket Liu, from O'Reilly & Associates, Inc.

The BOOT File

The BOOT file is responsible for the following tasks:

- Specifying the location of the directory that contains the DNS configuration files, if the location differs from the default directory.

- Declaring the domains for which the server is authoritative, and the data file that describes each domain.

- Specifying the name and location of the file that identifies the DNS root name servers.

NOTE

Here is a possible BOOT file for the sample network:

```
;  DNS BOOT FILE

cache    .                              cache.dns

primary  hoople.edu                     hoople.edu.dns
primary  199.250.200.in-adr.arpa        199.250.200.in-addr.arpa.dns
primary  50.190.200.in-adr.arpa         50.190.200.in-addr.arpa.dns
primary  0.0.127.in-adr.arpa            127.in-addr.arpa.dns
```

The BOOT file has two directives: primary and cache. (A secondary directive appears in BOOT files for secondary DNS servers.)

The primary directives declare the domains for which this server is authoritative, as well as the data file that contains data for each domain. This server is authoritative for four domains:

- **hoople.edu.** The file hoople.edu.dns contains the name-to-address mappings for the domain.

- **199.250.200.in-adr.arpa.** The file 199.250.200.in-addr.arpa.dns contains address-to-name mappings for this reverse-lookup domain.

- **50.190.200.in-adr.arpa.** Another reverse-lookup domain serviced by the file 50.190.200.in-addr.arpa.dns.

- **127.in-adr.arpa.** This is a reverse-lookup domain associated with the loopback address, supported by the file 127.in-addr.arpa.dns.

A primary directive is required for each of these domains. Each DNS server is authoritative for the loopback domain (127.0.0) so that attempts to resolve loopback addresses are not propagated beyond the local DNS server.

The cache directive specifies the file that is authoritative for the root domain. Unlike files specified by primary directives, which are searched during the name resolution process, entries in the cache file are held in memory to make them immediately available.

NOTE

The example has stayed with the filename convention established by the Windows NT version of DNS: `domain.dns` files are for name domains and *reverse-address*.`in-addr.arpa.dns` files are for `reverse-matching` domains (in-addr.arpa).

You might encounter two other directives in BOOT files. The `forwarders` directive defines one or more servers at your site that serve as *forwarders*, DNS servers that can be delegated to take responsibility for DNS queries. One use for forwarders is to concentrate your off-site DNS queries in specific DNS servers. By concentrating off-site queries in a few servers, the forwarding servers are capable of building up a rich cache of DNS names, enabling them to resolve a greater proportion of DNS queries locally without using bandwidth of the WAN link to the Internet. You can designate another DNS server as a forwarder for the one being configured by adding a statement such as the following to the BOOT file:

```
forwarders 172.16.32.10 192.168.8.5
```

If you have set up forwarders, you might want to restrict other DNS servers so that they won't even try to connect with the Internet. You do that by configuring the server as a slave. A slave server answers queries from its authoritative data and cache, but relies entirely on forwarders to resolve unknown names. To configure the DNS server as a slave, add the `slave` directive, as in this example:

```
forwarders 172.16.32.10 192.168.8.5
slave
```

The operations of forwarders and slaves are discussed in greater detail later in this chapter in the section "Configuring Forwarders and Slaves."

Domain Database Files

A DNS server is responsible for portions of the overall domain name space. Each portion is called a *zone*. Typically a zone will consist of a specific domain, either in the forward naming domain name space or in the reverse-naming in-addr.arpa name space. The database files shown in this chapter were generated by DNS Manager but could have been created manually as well.

Each zone for which the server is authoritative must be described in a database file. By default, DNS Manager assigns the filename extension .dns to these database files. The hoople.edu.dns database file for hoople.edu is as follows:

```
;   Database file hoople.edu.dns for hoople.edu zone.
;

@                       IN   SOA   haydn.hoople.edu.   peters.hoople.edu.
(
                        10              ; serial number
                        3600            ; refresh
                        600             ; retry
                        86400           ; expire
                        3600       )  ; minimum TTL


;
;   Zone NS records
;
@                       IN   NS   haydn


;
;   WINS lookup record
;
@                       0    IN   WINS   200.250.199.4


;
;   Zone records
;
@                       IN   MX   10   mail1.
ftp                     IN   CNAME   jsbach.
haydn                   IN   A   200.250.199.1
jsbach                  IN   A   200.250.199.3
mail1                   IN   A   200.190.50.254
mozart                  IN   A   200.190.199.4
papa                    IN   CNAME   haydn.
papa190                 IN   A   200.190.50.1
papa250                 IN   A   200.250.199.1
schubert                IN   A   200.190.50.4
```

The following sections examine each of the sections in the domain database. Only a few of the possible resource record types appear in this example. Table 13.1 provides a complete listing of the resource record types supported by the Microsoft DNS Server.

TABLE 13.1

Resource Record Types

Resource Record	Description
A	An address record maps a host name to an IP address.
AAAA	Also an address record, an AAAA record maps a host name to an IPv6 address.
AFSDB	An Andrew File System (AFS) database record provides the location of an AFS cell's database server or the location of a Distributed Computing Environment (DCE) cell's authenticated name server.
CNAME	A canonical name record establishes an alias, a synonym for a host name.
HINFO	A host information record provides information about the name, operating system, and CPU type of a host. RFC 1700 provides standard computer and system names for use in this record.
ISDN	An Integrated Services Digital Network (ISDN) record maps a host name to an ISDN address, a phone number for the specified ISDN resource.
MB	A mailbox record is an experimental record that identifies a DNS host with a specified mailbox. The MB record is used in association with the MG and MINFO records.
MG	A mail group record is an experimental record used to identify a mailbox that is a member of a specified mailing group, a mailing list that is identified by a DNS name.
MINFO	A mailbox information record is an experimental record type that specifies the mailbox responsible for a specific mail group or mailbox.
MR	A mailbox rename record is an experimental record that identifies a mailbox that is the proper name of a specified mailbox.
MX	A mail exchanger record identifies the mail server for a specified DNS domain.

continues

Table 13.1, Continued

Resource Record Types

Resource Record	Description
NS	A name server record identifies a name server for a specified DNS domain.
PTR	A pointer record associates an IP address with a host in a DNS reverse-naming database.
RP	A responsible person record identifies the person responsible for a DNS domain or host. The record includes the email address and a DNS domain name that points to additional information about the responsible person.
RT	A route record identifies an intermediate host that is used to route datagrams to a specified destination host. The RT record is used in conjunction with the ISDN and X.25 resource records.
SOA	A start of authority record specifies the domain for which a DNS server is responsible. It also specifies a variety of parameters that regulate operation of the DNS server.
TXT	A text record associates text information with a record in the DNS database. TXT records could, for example, provide additional information about a host.
WINS	A Windows Internet Name Server record identifies a WINS server that can be consulted to obtain names that are not recorded in the DNS name space.
WINS_R	A reverse WINS record causes Microsoft DNS to use the nbstat command to resolve reverse-lookup (address-to-name) client queries.
WKS	A well-known service record describes services provided by a specific protocol on a specific adapter. Any protocol specified in the %systemroot%\system32\drivers\etc\protocols file can be specified in this record type.
X.25	An X.25 record maps a name to an X.121 address, the address format used on X.25 networks.

The Start of Authority Record

A Start of Authority (SOA) resource record is found at the beginning of each mapping database file. This block of information declares the host that is most authoritative for the domain, contact information, and some DNS server parameters.

An @ symbol at the beginning of the SOA header declares that this file defines members of the domain that were associated with the file in the BOOT file. Recall this entry in BOOT:

```
primary  hoople.edu                     hoople.edu.dns
```

As a result of that declaration, @ refers to the domain hoople.edu. Consequently, when the hoople.edu.dns file declares an entry for the host haydn, the directive is defining information for haydn in the hoople.edu domain. That is, the directive is defining haydn.hoople.edu. Because the domain is implied by the context established by the boot file, the structure of the database file is simplified, requiring less administrative effort. The IN A entry for haydn could have been entered as follows with exactly the same effect:

```
haydn.hoople.edu.        IN  A  200.250.199.4
```

Notice that `haydn.hoople.edu.` is terminated with a period, indicating that its origin is the root domain. Without the period indicating the origin in the root domain, DNS would understand the name as `haydn.hoople.edu.hoople.edu`, because it would be understood in the context of the hoople.edu domain.

WARNING

Improper use of trailing periods is a common cause of error in DNS database files, and it is worth emphasizing the point:

- Omit the trailing period if the host name falls within the domain defined by this database file (which is nearly always the case).

- Include the trailing period if the record fully specifies the domain name of the host being defined, that is, the record specifies the fully-qualified domain name of the host.

The IN directive not surprisingly stands for Internet, one class of data that can appear in the database files. Following IN, the SOA directive declares this as a Start of Authority header.

Following the SOA directive are two internet names:

- The first, `haydn.hoople.edu.`, is the domain name of the name server host that is most authoritative for this domain.

- The second, `peters.hoople.edu.`, is the email address of the primary contact for this name server. The actual email address is "peters@hoople.edu." The @ has been replaced with a period. This email name enables people to send messages when they have trouble with the name server.

Following the email name are five parameters that set the operational characteristics of the DNS server, enclosed in parentheses to enable the parameters to span several lines, thereby permitting a comment to label each parameter. A comment begins with a semicolon (;) and extends to the end of the line. All comment text is for human consumption and ignored by the computer.

Note that the closing parenthesis immediately follows the final parameter, not the comment for the parameter. A parenthesis in the body of the comment would be ignored.

Without comments, the SOA record could have been entered like this:

```
@  IN  SOA  haydn.hoople.edu. peters.hoople.edu.(8 3600 600 86400
3600)
```

You probably agree that the comments make interpreting the record much easier. The five numeric parameters are as follows:

- **Serial.** A serial number that indicates the revision level of the file. The DNS administrator increments this value each time the file is modified. (DNS Manager increments this value automatically when changes are made.)

- **Refresh.** The interval in seconds at which a secondary name server checks in to download a copy of the zone data in the primary name server. The default value for DNS Server is 3600, resulting in a refresh interval of one hour.

- **Retry.** The time in seconds a secondary name server waits after a failed download before it tries to download the zone database again. The default value for DNS Server is 600, resulting in a retry interval of 10 minutes.

- **Expire.** The period of time in seconds that a secondary name server continues to try to download a zone database. After this time expires, the secondary name server discards data for the zone. The default value for DNS Server is 86400, equivalent to 24 hours.

- **Minimum.** The minimum Time To Live in seconds for a resource record. This parameter determines how long a DNS server retains an address mapping in cache. After the TTL expires for a record, the record is discarded. Short TTL values enable DNS to adjust to network changes more adroitly, but increase network traffic and loading on the DNS server. A short TTL might be appropriate in the early days, while a network evolves, but you might want to extend the TTL as the network stabilizes. The default value for DNS Server is 3600, resulting in a TTL of one hour.

The *WINS* Record

The WINS record is specific to the version of DNS that ships with Windows NT Server 4.0. If an outside host queries a name from your DNS server, the server will first attempt to resolve the name from DNS database files. If that is unsuccessful, the DNS server attempts to resolve the name through WINS. If a name is resolved through WINS, an address record is added to the domain database for future use.

The WINS record enables DNS, WINS, and DHCP to cooperate. DNS name resolution is ordinarily static, based on manually maintained database files. With the WINS record, it is possible to assign IP addresses dynamically with DHCP, resolve NetBIOS names to dynamic addresses with WINS, and make the name-to-address mappings available to DNS. In other words, you need not give up the advantages of DHCP dynamic address assignment to enable your network to support DNS name resolution.

The WINS record accepts one or more IP addresses that specify the WINS servers that DNS is to consult when unable to resolve an address. The following WINS record specifies two WINS servers:

```
  @                   IN WINS  200.190.50.2  200.190.50.201
```

As in the SOA record, the @ refers to the domain defined by this data file. This WINS directive states, "If DNS cannot find a host in the keystone.com domain in its database, DNS should query the following WINS servers for name entries."

When DNS learns about a host from WINS, a resource record is created in the DNS database. Records created in this way are not permanent and are not archived when the database files are updated from the active DNS database. However, DNS will no longer consult WINS regarding that name until the resource record is removed.

NOTE

The Windows name space is a "flat" name space, unlike the hierarchical structure supported by DNS. Consequently, all names in the name space supported by a WINS server (or group of servers that replicate a common database) must be unique.

Because the WINS database does not record DNS domain names along with host names, you cannot use a given WINS name space to resolve names in multiple DNS domains. You cannot, for example, include 200.190.50.2 as a WINS server for the domains alpha.com and beta.com.

Name Server Records

A name server (NS) record must declare each primary and secondary name server that is authoritative for the zone. Name servers are declared by IN NS records. Notice that the domain servers terminate with periods, indicating that the name originates with the root.

NS records might begin with the @ specifying "the domain for this database" or the @ might be omitted, in which case the domain is implied. If the @ is omitted, the IN should not occupy the first column of the line. In other words, the following declarations are equivalent in this context:

```
hoople.edu. IN NS  mozart.hoople.edu.
@           IN NS  mozart.hoople.edu.
            IN NS  mozart.hoople.edu.
```

Address Records

Each host name that DNS resolves must be specified using an address (A) resource record—unless the name will be resolved through WINS. One example from the hoople.edu.dns database file is the following:

```
haydn      IN  A  200.250.199.1
```

Multihomed hosts require an address declaration for each network adapter, as with the host haydn in the sample database file.

NOTE

Most host names will be learned from WINS. Only essential hosts, such as the DNS servers, are configured with hard-coded address records. The mappings for these hosts must be available when the DNS server is booted, and therefore cannot be learned from WINS after the server is running.

Aliases

Many networks employ aliases. In most cases, aliases are declared using CNAME (canonical name) resource records. On the hoople.edu network, host jsbach will be configured as an FTP server. So users can access this server with the name ftp.hoople.edu, it is necessary to establish an alias as follows:

```
ftp             IN  CNAME  jsbach
```

A more complex case is presented by multihomed computers. The aliases section of the sample database file includes three declarations related to the host haydn.edu:

```
papa            IN  CNAME  haydn
papa250         IN  A      200.250.199.1
papa190         IN  A      200.190.50.1
```

The CNAME declaration defines papa as an alias for the multihomed host haydn. DNS queries for papa or haydn are resolved to the first IP address in the configuration of haydn. A CNAME declaration maps to a canonical name, however, not to a specific network interface of the multihomed host.

Usually, applications don't care which address of a host they resolve to. When troubleshooting a network, however, you might prefer to be able to diagnose a specific interface, which is why two IN A declarations are included. papa250 and papa190 enable an administrator to, for example, ping by name a specific network attachment of haydn.

The advantage of coding aliases using CNAME is that the actual IP address of the host appears in one place only. If the IP address changes, a single edit updates both the primary address map and the alias. A CNAME record does not specify a particular interface. On a multihomed host, you must use A records to establish a name for a specific interface. If the address for haydn changes, however, it is also necessary to manually edit the A records for papa250 and papa190 as well as the A record for haydn.

Email Server Records

The most popular electronic mail environment in the TCP/IP world is based on a program called *sendmail*. If your network incorporates an electronic mail system that uses sendmail, you should add appropriate records to the zone database file.

In the sample network, sendmail is running on the host mail1.keystone.com. The following resource records support this host:

```
@                    IN  MX 10  mail1.
mail1                IN  A  200.190.50.254
```

The A record specifies the IP address for mail1.keystone.com.

The MX record specifies that mail1 is an email server for the keystone.com domain (specified by the @ character). If the domain is supported by more than one email server, each is specified in an MX record:

```
@    fillin "Enter figure caption" \* Mergeformat           IN
MX  10  mail1
@                    IN  MX  20  mail2
```

The numbers following the MX keywords specify the priority for each mail server. Email will be routed to the server with the lowest priority number that is active, that is, 1 indicates the most preferred server. In other words, if mail1 and mail2 are both active, email will be routed to mail1. The number parameter simply specifies the priority order. Priorities of 2 and 7 will have exactly the same result as priorities of 10 and 20.

By including MX resource records, you make it easier for outsiders to send email into your domain. Email can be addressed to peters@hoople.edu, for example. There's no need to address the message to peters@mail1.hoople.edu. Incoming mail is routed to the available server that has the highest priority.

Reverse-Matching Database Files

A reverse-matching (address-to-name matching) database file is required for each network ID for which the DNS server is authoritative. Recall that the file named 200.250.199 is the database for network 200.250.199, which appears in the reverse database tree as 199.250.200.in-adr.arpa.

The 200.250.199.in-addr.arpa.dns file is constructed as follows:

```
;  Database file arpa-200.250.199 for 199.250.200.in-addr.arpa.
;  Zone version:  5
@ IN SOA mozart.hoople.edu.  peters.hoople.edu. (
              1       ;serial
```

```
                       10800   ;refresh after 3 hours
                       3600    ;retry after 1 hour
                       691200 ;expire in 8 days
                       86400)  ;minimum TTL 1 day

;name servers
@                      IN   NS   mozart.hoople.edu.


;addresses mapped to canonical names
1                      IN   PTR  haydn.hoople.edu.
3                      IN   PTR  jsbach.hoople.edu.
4                      IN   PTR  mozart.hoople.edu.
```

Similarly, the 200.190.50.in-addr.arpa.dns file is constructed as follows:

```
;   Database file arpa-200.190.50 for 50.190.200.in-addr.arpa.
;   Zone version:  5
@ IN SOA mozart.hoople.edu.  peters.hoople.edu. (
                       1       ;serial
                       10800   ;refresh after 3 hours
                       3600    ;retry after 1 hour
                       691200 ;expire in 8 days
                       86400)  ;minimum TTL 1 day

;name servers
@                      IN   NS   mozart.hoople.edu.


;addresses mapped to canonical names
4                      IN   PTR  schubert.hoople.edu.
254                    IN   PTR  mail1.hoople.edu.
```

The reverse-naming files use the same Start of Authority header as the domain database file. As before, @ means "the domain specified in the BOOT file." Also, all host names are to be understood in the context of the domain name. Therefore 4 in the IN PTR record refers to host 200.250.199.4 (which is 4.199.250.200.in-addr.arpa. in the reverse-naming database tree).

NS records declare the name servers that are authoritative for this domain.

PTR (pointer) records provide reverse mappings between IP addresses and host names. Notice that host names must be fully specified from the root domain.

The Localhost Database File

The 127.0.0.in-addr.arpa.dns file includes a reverse mapping for the local-host host name. It resembles the formats of the other reverse-mapping files:

```
@ IN SOA mozart.hoople.edu.  peters.hoople.edu. (
                    1       ;serial
                    10800   ;refresh after 3 hours
                    3600    ;retry after 1 hour
                    691200 ;expire in 8 days
                    86400) ;minimum TTL 1 day


;name servers
@                        IN  NS  mozart.hoople.edu.

;addresses mapped to canonical names
1                        IN  PTR localhost.
```

The Cache File

The cache.dns file declares name-to-address mappings to be cached in the DNS server. Essentially, cached entries define the DNS servers that are authoritative for the root domain.

If you are establishing a private TCP/IP network then the root domain will be supported by DNS servers running on your network. The records in cache.dns will reflect this and will declare entries for local DNS servers authoritative for the root domain.

In the case of hoople.edu, however, the network will be connected to the Internet, and the cache.dns file will identify the Internet root name servers. These root name servers change from time to time, and a DNS administrator should periodically check the related information files and ensure that the local cache database is kept up to date. The official root name server list can be obtained in the following three ways:

- **FTP.** FTP the file /domain/named.root from FTP.RS.INTERNIC.NET.

- **Gopher.** Obtain the file named.root from RS.INTERNIC.NET under menu **InterNIC Registration Services (NSI)**, submenu **InterNIC Registration Archives**.

- **Email.** Send email to service@nic.ddn.mil, using the subject netinfo root-servers.txt.

The NAMED.ROOT file can be used unmodified as the cache database file, although you might want to rename the file based on local database file-naming conventions. At the time this book was being written, the NAMED.ROOT file had the following contents:

```
;          This file holds the information on root name servers
➥needed to
;          initialize cache of Internet domain name servers
;          (e.g. reference this file in the "cache  .  <file>"
;          configuration file of BIND domain name servers).
;
;          This file is made available by InterNIC registration
➥services
;          under anonymous FTP as
;              file                 /domain/named.root
;              on server            FTP.RS.INTERNIC.NET
;          -OR- under Gopher at     RS.INTERNIC.NET
;              under menu           InterNIC Registration Services
➥(NSI)
;              submenu              InterNIC Registration Archives
;              file                 named.root
;
;          last update:  Sep 1, 1995
;          related version of root zone:   1995090100
;
;
; formerly NS.INTERNIC.NET
;
.                          3600000   IN  NS   A.ROOT-SERVERS.NET.
A.ROOT-SERVERS.NET.        3600000       A    198.41.0.4
;
; formerly NS1.ISI.EDU
;
.                          3600000       NS   B.ROOT-SERVERS.NET.
B.ROOT-SERVERS.NET.        3600000       A    128.9.0.107
;
; formerly C.PSI.NET
;
.                          3600000       NS   C.ROOT-SERVERS.NET.
C.ROOT-SERVERS.NET.        3600000       A    192.33.4.12
;
; formerly TERP.UMD.EDU
;
.                          3600000       NS   D.ROOT-SERVERS.NET.
D.ROOT-SERVERS.NET.        3600000       A    128.8.10.90
;
```

```
; formerly NS.NASA.GOV
;
.                         3600000        NS     E.ROOT-SERVERS.NET.
E.ROOT-SERVERS.NET.       3600000        A      192.203.230.10
;
; formerly NS.ISC.ORG
;
.                         3600000        NS     F.ROOT-SERVERS.NET.
F.ROOT-SERVERS.NET.       3600000        A      39.13.229.241
;
; formerly NS.NIC.DDN.MIL
;
.                         3600000        NS     G.ROOT-SERVERS.NET.
G.ROOT-SERVERS.NET.       3600000        A      192.112.36.4
;
; formerly AOS.ARL.ARMY.MIL
;
.                         3600000        NS     H.ROOT-SERVERS.NET.
H.ROOT-SERVERS.NET.       3600000        A      128.63.2.53
;
; formerly NIC.NORDU.NET
;
.                         3600000        NS     I.ROOT-SERVERS.NET.
I.ROOT-SERVERS.NET.       3600000        A      192.36.148.17
; End of File
```

Notice that the names of the root name servers have been changed. You will still encounter the old names of the servers in some TCP/IP literature. The structure of the file is more clearly apparent if the comments are removed as follows:

```
.                         3600000   IN   NS   A.ROOT-SERVERS.NET.
A.ROOT-SERVERS.NET.       3600000         A    198.41.0.4
.                         3600000         NS   B.ROOT-SERVERS.NET.
B.ROOT-SERVERS.NET.       3600000         A    128.9.0.107
.                         3600000         NS   C.ROOT-SERVERS.NET.
C.ROOT-SERVERS.NET.       3600000         A    192.33.4.12
.                         3600000         NS   D.ROOT-SERVERS.NET.
D.ROOT-SERVERS.NET.       3600000         A    128.8.10.90
.                         3600000         NS   E.ROOT-SERVERS.NET.
E.ROOT-SERVERS.NET.       3600000         A    192.203.230.10
.                         3600000         NS   F.ROOT-SERVERS.NET.
F.ROOT-SERVERS.NET.       3600000         A    39.13.229.241
.                         3600000         NS   G.ROOT-SERVERS.NET.
G.ROOT-SERVERS.NET.       3600000         A    192.112.36.4
```

```
.                              3600000    NS    H.ROOT-SERVERS.NET.
H.ROOT-SERVERS.NET.            3600000    A     128.63.2.53
.                              3600000    NS    I.ROOT-SERVERS.NET.
I.ROOT-SERVERS.NET.            3600000    A     192.36.148.17
```

Each host is declared in two directives:

- **NS directive.** Declares the server by name as a name server for the root domain.

- **A directive.** Declares the server name-to-address mapping.

The NS and A directives include an additional parameter in the cache.dns file. In early versions of DNS, a numeric parameter (here 3600000) indicated how long the data should remain in cache. In current versions of DNS, the root name server entries are retained indefinitely. The numeric parameter remains a part of the file syntax but no longer serves a function.

Creating the cache file completes configuration of the DNS database files.

Setting Up a Secondary Name Server

You should consider setting up one or more secondary name servers to prevent failure of a single name server from disrupting name resolution for your domain. The difference between primary and secondary name servers is that secondary name servers obtain their data from other name servers in a process called a *zone transfer*. Secondary name servers might obtain their data from primary or secondary name servers. This capability makes it possible to maintain the data on several name servers with only one set of master database files.

The example files in this chapter have configured the primary name server mozart. They have also anticipated establishment of a secondary name server on schubert, which this section addresses.

Install the DNS software on the secondary name server using the same procedures used to install the primary name server. The distinction between the primary and secondary name servers is found in the structure of the BOOT file.

The DNS directory of the secondary name server needs copies of the following files:

- BOOT
- cache.dns
- 127.in-addr.arpa.dns

The cache.dns and 127.in-addr.arpa.dns files are identical on all DNS servers, and you do not need to create them. A cache.dns file is created on each server when Microsoft DNS Server is installed. The required reverse-look zones such as 127.in-addr.arpa are established when a server is added to the DNS Manager configuration.

The BOOT file would be modified for the secondary server on schubert as follows:

```
;  DNS BOOT FILE

cache     .       cache

secondary  hoople.edu                 200.250.199.4  hoople.edu.dns
secondary  199.250.200.in-adr.arpa    200.250.199.4 200.250.199.in-
↩addr.arpa.dns
secondary  50.190.200.in-adr.arpa     200.250.199.4  200.190.50.in-
↩addr.arpa.dns
primary    0.0.127.in-adr.arpa        arpa-127.0.0.in-addr.arpa
```

schubert is a secondary name server for three zones, specified in the secondary directives. In the three secondary directives, an IP address is added to the syntax. This IP address specifies the computer that serves as the repository for the database file. schubert loads hoople.edu from mozart (IP address 200.250.199.4). During operation, schubert makes backup copies of the database files in its local DNS directory, which enables schubert to start up if mozart goes down.

A name server can be a primary for some zones and a secondary for others. The role of a name server is specified by the use of the primary and secondary directives in the BOOT file.

schubert is a primary only for the reverse-naming 127.0.0.in-addr.arpa zone. Because this information is the same on all servers, there is no sense including the records in the zone transfer.

Because the information in the cache.dns file is identical for all DNS servers, there is no sense in performing zone transfers for root name server data. Each DNS server is configured with a local cache.dns file.

In addition to customizing the BOOT file for the secondary server, you need to add NS records for the secondary server to the database files on the primary DNS server. On the sample network, you would need to add the following resource record to the hoople.edu.dns, 200.190.50.in-addr.arpa.dns, and 200.250.199.in-addr.arpa.dns files:

```
@                          IN  NS  schubert.hoople.edu.
```

Managing the DNS Server

After you complete the configuration files—and check them three or four times for errors, including the correct use of trailing periods in host names—you are ready to start working with the DNS server manager. At this point, you reenter the realm of the GUI interface.

Installing the Microsoft DNS Server

1. Install TCP/IP on the DNS server computer. DNS servers must be configured with static IP addresses so that the addresses can be entered into host configurations.

2. Open the Network applet in the Control Panel.

3. Select the **Services** tab.

4. Choose **Add**.

5. In the Network Service list, select **Microsoft DNS Server** and choose **OK**.

6. Supply the path to the installation files when prompted.

7. Close the Network utility and restart the server.

Initializing the DNS Server

By default, database files for the Microsoft DNS Server are installed in *%systemroot%*\system32\dns. When the DNS Server is installed, only a cache.dns file is installed in this directory.

When DNS Manager is run for the first time, it attempts to initialize using database files in the *%systemroot%*\system32\dns directory. Depending on the contents of this directory, one of two things can happen:

■ If the dns directory contains only the cache.dns file, the DNS Server is initialized with an empty database. This section assumes that only the default files are present in the dns directory.

■ If you have placed a set of BIND data files in this directory, DNS Manager will initialize the server database from those files. The section "Porting Data from BIND Servers" discusses the process of initializing the server from BIND database files.

The icon for the DNS Manager is installed in the Administrative Tools program group. At first, no DNS servers are listed and the display is entirely uninteresting, so I haven't provided you with a picture. The first step is to add one to the DNS Manager configuration. Figure 13.2 shows DNS Manager after a DNS server has been added.

FIGURE 13.2

DNS Manager after a DNS server has been added.

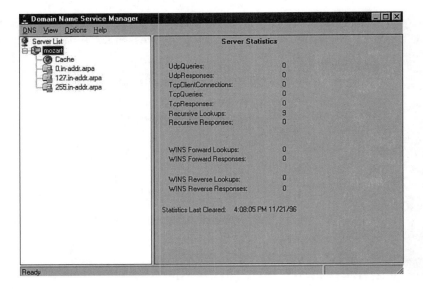

To create a DNS server:

1. Right-click the **Server List** icon and select the **New Server** command from the menu that is displayed.

2. Enter the host name or IP address of the DNS server in the Add DNS Server dialog box, shown in Figure 13.3. If you enter a host name, then Microsoft DNS Server must be installed on the host. Additionally, this host must be capable of resolving the host name to an IP address using WINS or some other means.

FIGURE 13.3

Adding a new DNS name server to DNS Manager.

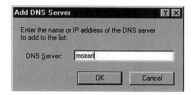

Adding the server creates an icon for the DNS server object, which is assigned a default set of properties. In addition, the following zones are automatically created:

- **Cache.** This zone is filled with records defining the root name servers for the Internet.

- **0.in-addr.arpa.** This zone prevents reverse-lookup queries for the address 0.0.0.0 from being passed to the root name server.

- **127.in-addr.arpa.** This zone supports reverse-lookup queries for the loopback address.

- **255.in-addr.arpa.** This zone prevents broadcast name queries from being passed to the root name server.

NOTE

With the exception of the Cache zone, the automatically created zones are concealed by default. To enable display of these zones, as was done to create Figure 13.2, choose the **Preferences** command in the **O**ptions menu. Then check the **Show Automatically Created Zones** check box. Finally, press **F5** to refresh the display and display the zone icons.

Because these zones require no maintenance on your part, you can safely leave them hidden, as was done in the other figures.

There is no need to create anything resembling the BIND boot file. The information needed to start the DNS server is continually updated as you establish the server's configuration.

Adding the Reverse-Lookup Zones

Before you create a zone for the domain that is to be managed, you should create the zones that support reverse-lookups, the in-addr.arpa zones. If you create these zones first, you can populate them with PTR records automatically, as you add A records to the primary domain zone.

To create a primary reverse-lookup zone:

1. Right-click the icon of the primary DNS server.

2. Select the **New Zone** command from the context menu to open the **Create new zone** Wizard shown in Figure 13.4.

FIGURE 13.4

When creating a new zone, specify whether it is a primary or a secondary zone.

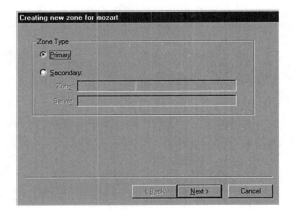

3. Click the **Primary** radio button and choose **Next** to open the Zone Info dialog box shown in Figure 13.5.

4. In the Zone Name field, enter the name of the reverse-lookup zone. Because this is a reverse-lookup zone, adhere to the naming convention (*reverse-netid*.in-addr.arpa). DNS server will realize this is a reverse-naming zone and will configure it accordingly. To create the reverse-lookup zone for network 200.250.199.0, you will enter 199.250.200.in-addr.arpa in the Zone Name field.

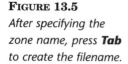

FIGURE 13.5

*After specifying the zone name, press **Tab** to create the filename.*

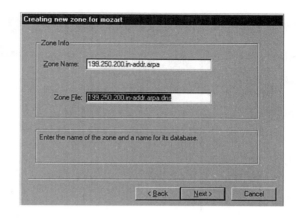

*Always move to the next field by pressing the **Tab** key. Otherwise, the Zone File field will not be automatically completed.*

5. Press **Tab** to automatically generate a filename in the Zone File field. The filename can be anything you want, but the default adheres to the conventions established for the Microsoft DNS Server.

6. Choose **Next**. You will be rewarded with the message: `All of the information for the new zone has been entered.`

7. Press **Finish** to create the zone, or press **Back** to change any information you have entered.

Figure 13.6 shows DNS Manager after entry of the reverse-lookup zones required for the example network. Notice that the NS and SOA resource records have been entered for you. You can probably leave the default values for both records.

Adding a Primary Zone

After the reverse-lookup zones have been created, you can begin to create the name-lookup zones. The procedure is similar to that shown in the preceding section:

1. Right-click the icon of the primary DNS server.

2. Select the **New Zone** command from the object menu to open the Create new zone wizard.

FIGURE 13.6

*A newly created
reverse-naming zone.*

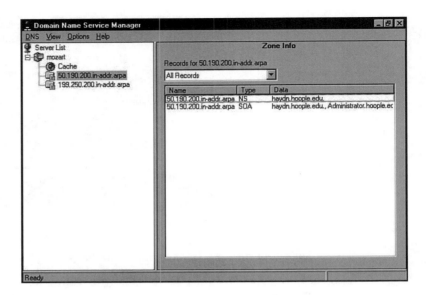

3. Click the **Primary** radio button and choose **Next**.

4. Enter the zone name in the **Z**one Name field and press **Tab** to gener-
    ate the filename. Then press **Next**.

5. Press **Finish** to create the zone, or press **Back** to change any infor-
    mation you have entered.

Figure 13.7 shows the hoople.edu zone after it has been created. Notice that
the NS and SOA resource records have been created for you. You will need to
create any required A records manually.

Adding Resource Records

Figure 13.8 shows DNS Manager after a variety of records have been added
to the hoople.edu domain. This and the following sections will examine the
creation of address, CNAME, MX, and WINS resource records.

FIGURE 13.7

DNS Manager after the hoople.edu name-lookup zone has been created.

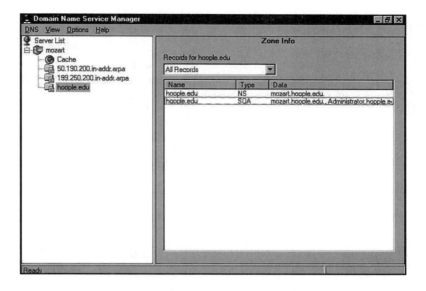

FIGURE 13.8

Various resource records in the hoople.edu domain.

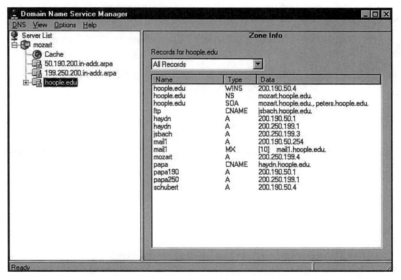

Adding Address Records

Next you must add essential address (A) records to the name-lookup zone. You must add address records only for hosts that are associated with fixed IP addresses or are not registered with WINS. Hosts that are registered with WINS can be entered into the zone database through WINS lookups.

To add an address resource record:

1. Right-click the name-lookup zone icon (in this example, **hoople.edu**) and choose **New Host** from the object menu.

    or

    Right-click in the database area of the **Zone Info** pane and choose **New Host** from the menu.

2. In the New Host dialog box, shown in Figure 13.9, enter the host name in the Host **N**ame field.

NOTE

In most cases, when you are entering a host name, DNS Manager expects only the host name portion of the FQDN. When necessary, the host name will be combined with the domain name to create the FQDN.

3. Enter the host's IP address in the Host IP Address field.

4. If you want to create a record in the appropriate reverse-lookup database, check **Create Associated PTR Record**. The reverse-lookup zone must have been previously created.

5. Choose **A**dd Host to create the database records.

6. Repeat steps 2 through 5 to enter additional address records as required.

7. Choose **D**one when you are finished.

When do you create a PTR record? In most cases, you want to add host addresses to the reverse-lookup zones, but there are some exceptions. In the examples created in this chapter, pointer records were created for all A records except for papa250 and papa190. Because those records were added for administrative convenience and not for public consumption, and because a PTR record for haydn already exists, entries were not added to the reverse-lookup directories. To have done so would have been to create conflicting mappings, where an IP address mapped to two host names.

FIGURE 13.9

Creating an address record.

Adding Other Resource Records

Besides address records, all other types of resource records are entered from the New Resource Record dialog box, shown in Figure 13.10. The fields you see in the Value box depend on the record type that has been selected. This section will examine the procedures for creating CNAME, MX, and PTR resource records.

FIGURE 13.10

Adding a CNAME resource record.

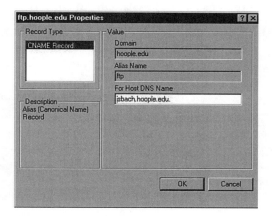

Adding *CNAME* Records

An alias is established by adding a CNAME record. Two aliases are required for the sample network. To add a CNAME resource record:

1. Right-click the zone that is to contain the record.

2. Choose **New Record** from the object menu to open the New Resource Record dialog box shown in Figure 13.10.

3. Select **CNAME Record** in the Record Type list.

4. Enter an alias in the Alias Name field.

5. Enter the FQDN that is the actual name for the host in the For Host DNS Name field. Include the trailing dot when entering the name!

6. Choose **OK** to add the record. The completed records for the example network can be observed in Figure 13.8.

Adding *MX* Records

To add an MX resource record:

1. Right-click the zone that is to contain the record.

2. Choose **New Record** from the object menu to open the New Resource Record dialog box shown in Figure 13.11.

3. Enter the host name only in the Host Name field. (Although the description says the field is optional, I have been unable to get MX records to work without entering the host name here.)

4. Enter the FQDN of the mail exchange server in the Mail Exchange Server DNS Name field (include the trailing dot).

5. Enter a preference number in the Preference Number field.

6. Choose **OK** to add the record. The complete record can be seen in Figure 13.8.

FIGURE 13.11
Creating an MX *resource record.*

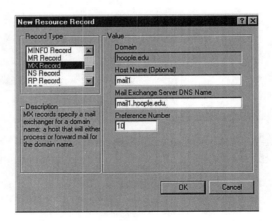

Adding *PTR* Records

To add a PTR resource record to a reverse-lookup zone:

1. Right-click the reverse-lookup zone that is to contain the record. In the New Resource Record dialog box for a reverse-look zone, only three record types can be created, as shown in Figure 13.12.

2. Select **PTR Record** in the Record Type list.

FIGURE 13.12

Creating a PTR resource record for a reverse-lookup zone.

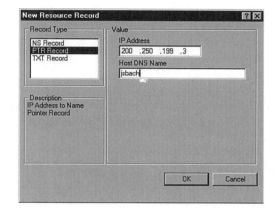

3. In the IP Address field, enter the IP address of the host. Enter the address fields in their conventional order. Do not enter the fields in their reverse order.

4. In the Host DNS Name field, enter the fully qualified host name of the host. Do not enter the host name alone. The reverse-lookup domains are not tied to a particular name domain.

5. Choose **OK** to create the record.

Figure 13.13 shows the records for a reverse-lookup zone after PTR records have been created.

Modifying Resource Records

You can open a dialog box to modify any resource record by double-clicking the resource record in the Zone Info box.

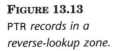

FIGURE 13.13

PTR *records in a reverse-lookup zone.*

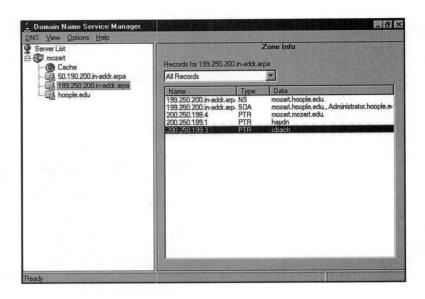

Modifying Zone Properties

When a zone is created, it is assigned a default set of properties and a Start of Authority record is established. You should review the zone properties and the SOA record to ensure that the properties are correct for your network.

To review the zone properties, right-click the zone icon and choose **Properties** from the object menu. The Zone Properties dialog box is shown in Figure 13.14. Four tabs are included in the dialog box and are examined in the following sections.

Zone General Properties

The General properties tab, shown in Figure 13.14, has the following fields:

- **Zone File Name.** This filename specifies the filename that is used to create a server data file for the zone. You can change this filename at any time.

- **Primary.** When the **Primary** radio button is selected, this server is a primary DNS server for the zone. Primary DNS servers maintain a database for the zone locally on the computer on which they are running.

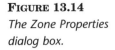

FIGURE 13.14

The Zone Properties dialog box.

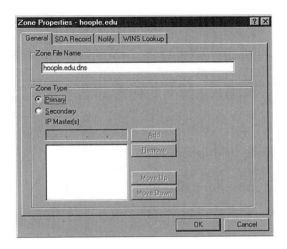

- **Secondary.** When the **Secondary** radio button is selected, this server is a secondary DNS server for the zone. Secondary DNS servers obtain zone data from another DNS server and do not maintain a local database for the zone.

- **IP Masters.** If the **Secondary** radio button is selected, this list is active. You must specify the IP addresses of one or more master DNS servers, servers from which zone transfers will be performed to populate the database of the secondary DNS server.

SOA Record Properties

The SOA Record tab (see Figure 13.15) establishes properties for the SOA record in the zone database. The SOA record was discussed in considerable detail earlier in the chapter, but it is worth listing the fields here as well:

- **Primary Name Server DNS Name.** This field specifies the name server that appears in the SOA record and identifies the name server that is authoritative for the zone defined by this database.

- **Responsible Person Mailbox DNS Name.** This informational field identifies the contact person for this domain, typically by specifying an email address. Because the @ character has a special meaning in BIND database files, a period is substituted for the @ character in the email address. In this case, peters.hoople.edu designates the email address peters@hoople.edu. (The default value for this field is Administrator.domain.)

- **Serial Number.** The serial number is incremented by DNS Manager each time a change is made to the contents of the zone database. Zone transfers take place when a secondary DNS server is made aware that the serial number has changed.

- **Refresh Interval.** This parameter specifies the interval at which a secondary DNS server checks to see whether a zone transfer is required.

- **Retry Interval.** This parameter specifies the time a secondary name server waits after a failed download before it tries to download the zone database again.

- **Expire Time.** This parameter specifies the period of time that a secondary name server continues to try to download a zone database. After this time expires, the secondary name server discards data for the zone.

- **Minimum Default TTL.** This parameter determines how long a DNS server retains an address mapping in cache. After the TTL expires for a record, the record is discarded. Short TTL values enable DNS to adjust to network changes more adroitly, but increase network traffic and loading on the DNS server. A short TTL might be appropriate in the early days, while a network evolves, but you might want to extend the TTL as the network stabilizes.

FIGURE 13.15

The SOA Record properties tab.

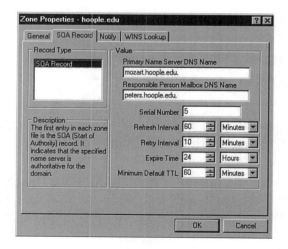

Notify Properties

The Notify tab, shown in Figure 13.16, lists the IP addresses of secondary DNS servers that obtain zone data from this server. A DNS server will notify servers appearing in the <u>N</u>otify List field when changes are made to the zone database.

Zone transfers can be driven by secondary DNS servers, and it is not essential for notification to take place. If, however, you want to restrict the secondary DNS servers that can transfer records from this server, check **<u>O</u>nly Allow Access From Secondaries Included on Notify List**.

FIGURE 13.16

Specifying secondary DNS servers in the Notify List.

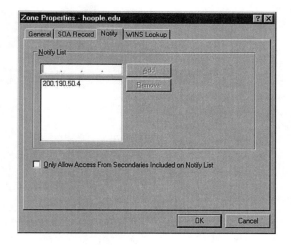

WINS Lookup Properties

This tab (see Figure 13.17) is used to enable DNS Server to use WINS to resolve names that do not appear in the zone database. This tab has three fields:

- **<u>U</u>se WINS Resolution.** When this box is checked, WINS lookup is enabled. A WINS resource record will be added to the zone database, as shown in Figure 13.8.

- **Settings only affect local server.** When WINS resolution is enabled, this field determines how records are handled on secondary DNS servers. Ordinarily, when a record learned from WINS is sent to a secondary DNS server in a zone transfer, the record is flagged as read-only. Such records cannot be modified on the secondary server. When this box is checked, the read-only protection is removed, enabling records to be modified at the secondary DNS server and preventing modified records from being overwritten in a zone transfer.

■ **WINS Servers.** When WINS resolution is enabled, this list must include the IP addresses of one or more WINS servers that will be used to resolve names.

FIGURE 13.17
Establishing WINS lookup properties.

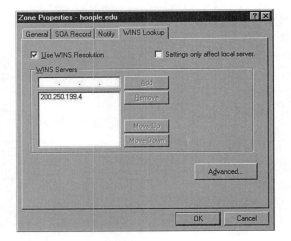

Several advanced WINS properties can be configured by clicking the **Advanced** button to open the Advanced Zone Properties dialog box shown in Figure 13.18. The dialog box has the following fields:

■ **Submit DNS Domain as NetBIOS Scope.** NetBIOS scopes permit administrators to specify a character string (a scope ID) that is appended to NetBIOS and is used for all NetBT (NetBIOS over TCP/IP) names. The effect is that only computers having the same NetBIOS scope can communicate. In the words of the *Windows NT Resource Kit,* "Use of NetBIOS Scope is strongly discouraged if you are not already using it, or if you use Domain Name System (DNS) on your network." Who am I to question Microsoft? Given the many problems that can ensue if NetBIOS scopes are used, I don't recommend them. And, unless they are used, there is no reason to check this box.

- **Cache Timeout Value.** The DNS Server maintains a cache of addresses that have been recently resolved via WINS. These records are retained for a limited time, determined by the settings in these fields. Long timeouts can reduce the number of calls to WINS but can increase memory demand by the DNS Server. By default, this value is 10 minutes.

- **Lookup Timeout Value.** This value determines how long DNS Server will wait for a response from WINS before giving up and returning an error to the sender. By default, this value is 1 second.

FIGURE 13.18
Configuring WINS lookup advanced properties.

Resolving Names with WINS

Very little is required to link Microsoft DNS Server with WINS:

- At least one WINS server must be operating to register hosts in the zone.

- WINS lookup must be enabled in the zone database.

The previous section, "WINS Lookup Properties," shows how to enable WINS lookup. Figure 13.19 shows an example of a database record that has been retrieved from WINS.

Managing Multiple DNS Servers

DNS Manager can manage many DNS servers. Besides consolidating DNS management on a single console, this capability simplifies certain operations by enabling you to use drag-and-drop to copy data. You will see how in the following section, "Creating a Secondary DNS Server."

Figure 13.20 shows DNS manager with two DNS servers appearing in the Server list (no zones have been created for the second server). To add a remote DNS server to the list:

FIGURE 13.19
The resource record for chopin was obtained through a WINS lookup.

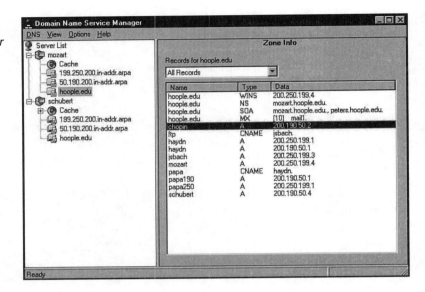

1. Install Microsoft DNS Services on the remote server.

2. Right-click the Server List icon.

3. Choose **New Server** in the object menu.

4. Enter the host name or the IP address of the remote DNS server in the DNS **S**erver field of the Add DNS Server dialog box.

5. Choose **OK**.

NOTE

DNS Managers communicate with remote DNS Servers using RPCs (Remote Procedure Calls). To communicate with DNS Manager, the DNS Service must be running on the computer that is being managed. If DNS Manager cannot communicate with a DNS Service, the icon will be marked with a red X. You will also see an error message in the Server Statistics box stating that The RPC service is unavailable.

FIGURE 13.20

DNS Manager with two managed servers.

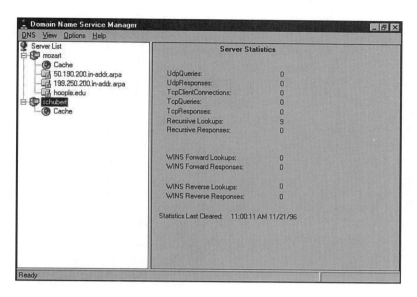

Creating a Secondary DNS Server

On the sample network, schubert will be set up as a secondary DNS sever for the hoople.edu domain. I'll show you two ways to set up a secondary domain: hard and easy.

The hard way is as follows:

1. Right-click the server icon and select **New Zone** from the object menu.

2. Click the **Secondary** check box in the Creating new zone dialog box, shown in Figure 13.21.

3. Enter the zone name in the Zon**e** field.

4. In the Serve**r** field, enter the name of the server from which zone transfers will be made.

5. Choose **Next**.

6. The **Z**one Name field will already be completed with the name of the zone that was specified in step 3. Press the **Tab** key in this field to generate the name for the database file in the Zone **F**ile field.

7. Press **Next**.

8. In the **IP Masters** list, specify the IP address list of at least one DNS server that will be a master server for this secondary.

9. Choose **Next**. Then choose **Finish** to create the zone.

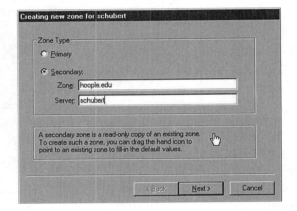

Figure 13.22 shows the schubert server after three secondary zones have been added. Notice that the zone icon consists of two zone icons stacked one on the other, distinguishing a secondary zone from a primary zone.

Now, let's use the easy method to add the secondary zones for the two reverse-lookup zones. For this to work, the primary zone must be displayed in DNS Manager. If necessary, add the server supporting the primary zone and open the server icon to display the icon for the primary zone. After that, here's the procedure:

1. Right-click the server icon and select **New Zone** from the object menu.

2. Click the **Secondary** check box in the **Creating new zone** dialog box.

3. If you examine Figure 13.21, you will notice a hand icon that was ignored in the previous procedure. Use the mouse to drag the hand icon and drop it on the appropriate primary zone. All of the fields in the Create new zone dialog box will be completed as required.

4. Use the **Next** button to review the fields in the Create new zone dialog box.

5. Choose **Finish** to complete creation of the secondary zone.

If every network management task was that easy, network administrators would be out of a job.

FIGURE 13.22

A DNS server after secondary zones have been added.

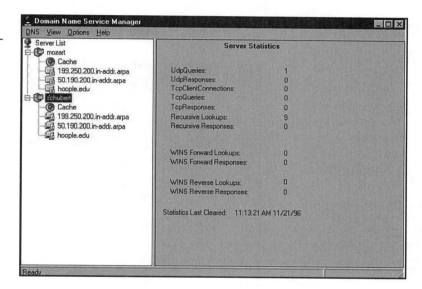

Adding Secondary Zones

As you have learned, the DNS name space is a hierarchy, and you can extend the name space hierarchy by adding domains below existing domains. Although the sample network has only a single domain, it is worth looking at the techniques for adding lower-level domains.

Suppose for example that you want to add domains such as classic.hoople.edu and jazz.hoople.edu to provide subdomains for various departments. Let's examine the procedure.

To create a jazz.hoople.edu subdomain you would do the following:

1. Right-click the icon for the hoople.edu zone.

2. Choose **New Domain** in the object menu.

490 NETWORKING WITH MICROSOFT TCP/IP

3. In the **New Domain** dialog box, enter the domain name in the Domain Name field.

4. Choose **OK**.

Subsequently, you would add address records to the subdomain just as you add them to the primary domain. Figure 13.23 shows DNS Manager after two subdomains have been created. Notice that SOA and NS records are not created. The subdomain uses the same name server and SOA parameters as the primary domain.

FIGURE 13.23

Two subdomains have been added to hoople.edu.

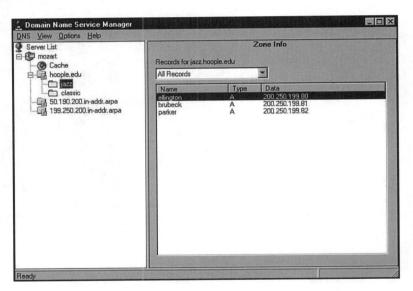

Subdomains have no effect on the reverse-lookup files. The reverse-lookup database is flat and includes all hosts with the same netid, whether or not they are in the same name domain. Figure 13.24 shows how elling-ton.hoople.edu is entered into the reverse-lookup database.

Updating the Database Files

DNS Manager maintains a standard set of BIND data files that can be used to back up the server database or to export the configuration to a BIND name server. To back up the database, choose the **Update Server Data Files** command in the DNS menu.

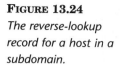

FIGURE 13.24

The reverse-lookup record for a host in a subdomain.

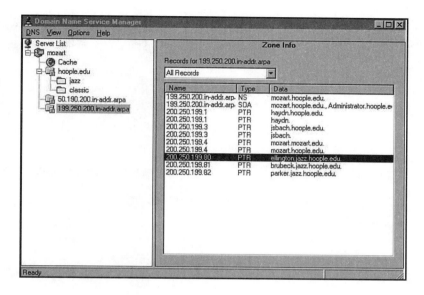

Setting DNS Manager Preferences

Several preferences determine the behavior of DNS Manager. To open the Preferences dialog box, shown in Figure 13.25, choose the **Preferences** command in the Options menu. The options in this dialog box are as follows:

- **Auto Refresh Statistics.** Ordinarily, DNS Manager updates server statistics only when you click a server icon. If you check this check box, statistics will be updated at the interval specified in the Interval field.

- **Show Automatically Created Zones.** Check this box to display the zones that are automatically created when a new DNS server is created.

- **Expose TTL.** Each resource record is assigned a Time To Live. Ordinarily, you don't see the value of the TTL parameter, but you can see and adjust TTL if you check this option. When **Expose TTL** is checked and you open the properties for a record (by double-clicking the record), a TTL field is added to the Properties dialog box, as shown in Figure 13.26. You can change the TTL value if desired.

FIGURE 13.25
Setting DNS Manager preferences.

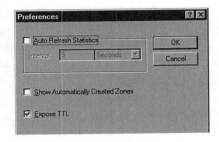

FIGURE 13.26
The TTL parameter can be displayed in a record's properties dialog box.

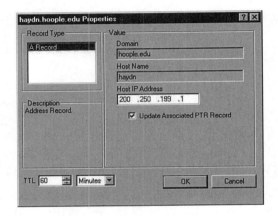

DNS Server Properties

DNS Manager maintains several statistics that describe the operation of the DNS Server. Figure 13.27 shows statistics for the mozart DNS Server. These statistics give you an idea of the activity and health of the DNS server.

Ordinarily, DNS Manager does not dynamically update these statistics. You can update them manually by selecting a server icon and pressing **F5**. Or you can configure DNS Manager preferences so that the statistics are updated at periodic intervals. See the preceding section, "Setting DNS Manager Preferences," for the technique.

The DNS Server statistics are initialized when the Microsoft DNS Server service is started. If you want to reinitialize the statistics without stopping and starting the DNS Server, enter the command dnsstat servername /clear where *servername* is the name of a computer running the DNS Server service. dnsstat is included with the *Windows NT Server Resource Kit*.

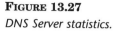

FIGURE 13.27

DNS Server statistics.

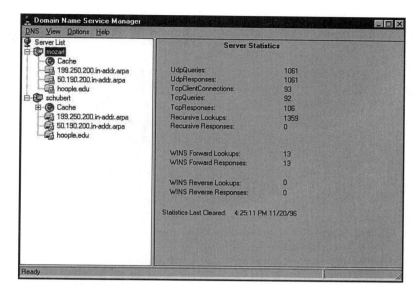

Configuring Forwarders and Slaves

Suppose that your company is connected to the Internet and that you use DNS to resolve both internal host names and host names on the Internet. The Internet connection is through a WAN link that has limited bandwidth, and you want to use that bandwidth as efficiently as possible. Therefore it is advantageous to resolve as many DNS name lookups as possible out of the DNS servers' local name caches. When a name can be resolved locally, no WAN bandwidth is utilized.

If you have four DNS servers and all name servers are used to resolve Internet names, the names that have been resolved will be distributed through the local name caches of all four servers. Consequently, a host that needs to resolve a name has a reduced chance that the name server it is using will have the required name in its cache.

In such cases, it is preferable to designate a limited number of DNS servers to perform Internet name lookups. If all resolved names are concentrated in the name caches of one (or at most two) name servers, the likelihood improves that a DNS client's name resolution request can be resolved locally.

Figure 13.28 illustrates a configuration of DNS servers that is designed to minimize WAN bandwidth used by DNS. Locally, DNS lookups are performed conventionally. Local zones are serviced by a primary (host 1)and a secondary (host 2) DNS server. The primary DNS server is configured to use WINS to identify the names of local hosts. Zone transfers copy static and WINS name-address mappings to the secondary DNS server. Consequently, complete local name records are stored on both the primary and secondary DNS servers. Local hosts (A through D) can use either the primary or secondary DNS server to resolve local names. To balance processing load, half the hosts (A and B) use DNS server 1 as their principal name server, and half (C and D) use DNS server 2 as their principal name server. However, all hosts list both name servers in their configurations, enabling them to use either should their principal name server fail.

FIGURE 13.28

Using forwarding servers to reduce WAN traffic.

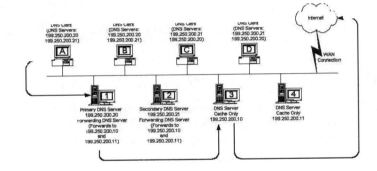

DNS servers 1 and 2 have complete knowledge of local host names through WINS or static resource records. If, however, they are asked to resolve a name that is not stored locally in a zone database or in the DNS server's name cache, they must forward the name resolution request to an outside name server. Ordinarily, they would forward the name request to a root name server and then resolve the name request iteratively through referrals to other name servers. In that case, a name that was resolved from the internet would be cached only on the DNS server that received the name request. Consequently, only half the hosts on the network would have access to the cached name. If the other DNS server must resolve the same request, it must query the internet to resolve the name.

In Figure 13.28, DNS servers 1 and 2 are configured to forward requests they cannot resolve from static data or from cache. They forward requests they cannot resolve to a designated DNS server. Their first choice is to forward all requests to DNS server 3, but DNS server 4 will be used if 3 is not available. DNS servers that receive forwarded DNS name resolution requests from other DNS servers are known as *DNS forwarders*.

Let's see how forwarding works:

1. DNS client A originates a name resolution request, which it sends to its principal DNS server, server 1.

2. DNS server 1 cannot resolve the name locally and forwards the request to DNS server 3.

3. DNS server 3 queries the Internet and stores the response in its local name cache.

4. DNS server 3 returns the response to DNS server 1, which stores the response in its local name cache.

5. DNS server 1 returns the response to DNS client A.

Now the remote name is cached on DNS servers 1 and 3. If the name is required again, one of two things happens:

- If DNS clients A or B query the name again, DNS server can supply the IP address from its local cache.

- If DNS clients C or D query the name, DNS server 2 will forward the request to DNS server 3, which can resolve the name out of its local cache. When the response is passed back to DNS server 2, it also stores the name in its cache.

In either case, the name is resolved without using any WAN bandwidth.

DNS server 4 is included as a backup in case DNS server 3 fails. Unfortunately cached data cannot be zone transferred to another DNS server. Therefore if DNS server 4 must take over, it is starting from scratch, and initially all name resolution requests must go to the internet. With time, however, DNS server 4 will fill in its name cache and increasing numbers of names will be resolved locally.

DNS servers 3 and 4 are *caching only name servers*. They are not authoritative for any zones. The only zones configured on these servers are the Cache zone and the automatically configured (and normally hidden) zones. The presence of a cache zone enables these name servers to resolve names on the internet. But these name servers are specialists and do not participate in local name resolution.

If DNS servers 3 and 4 are both down, name servers 1 and 2 are permitted to query outside name servers themselves. Each is configured with a cache domain and each has the information required to query outside name servers.

In some cases, you might want to prevent local name servers from querying outside name servers. If that is the case, they can be configured as *slave name servers*. A slave name server will forward all name requests that it cannot resolve to a designated forwarder. If none of the designated forwarders are available, the slave name server will not attempt to resolve the name by querying outside name servers. Instead the name resolution request will fail and the slave will return a "bad IP address" response to the DNS client.

NOTE

Although it is possible to configure slave name servers, I can see few if any reasons for doing so. If non-forwarders are configured as slaves they are completely dependent on forwarders to resolve non-local names. If all forwarders fail, then remote names cannot be resolved. In the interest of fault tolerance, don't configure your local name servers as slaves without a clear reason.

To configure a Microsoft DNS server to use forwarders, do the following:

1. In DNS Manager, right-click on the server in the Server List.

2. Choose **Properties** from the context menu to open the Properties dialog box.

3. Select the **Forwarders** tab, which is shown in Figure 13.29.

4. Check the **Use Forwarders** check box. This enables the other fields in this dialog box.

5. Click **Add** and add the IP address of at least one forwarder to the address list. Repeat to add the IP addresses of other forwarders.

6. Forwarders will be accessed in the order they appear in the IP address list. To change the list order, select an IP address and use the **Move Up** and **Move Down** buttons to adjust the position of the address in the list.

7. Specify a timeout value in the Forwarders Time Out field. The DNS server will attempt to contact each forwarder for the time you specify before it moves on to the next server in the IP address list.

8. If the DNS server is unable to contact any of the specified forwarders, it will ordinarily initiate an outside query itself. You can prevent the name server from generating outside name resolution queries by checking **Operate As Slave Server**.

FIGURE 13.29

Configuring a DNS server to use forwarders.

DNS forwarders can significantly improve the efficiency of outside name resolution requests, but you should be careful when you configure them. Do not chain forwarders; in other words, do not configure forwarders to use forwarders. And above all be sure that you don't configure forwarding loops, such as A to B to C to A.

Porting Data from BIND Servers

DNS Manager can import data from BIND database files, a handy feature if you want to move from a BIND name server to Microsoft DNS Server. Before attempting to port the data, assemble all the required BIND configuration files. You will not need a cache file, but you will need a BOOT file as well as the database files for the various domains. Before you first start DNS Manager, place these files in the *%systemroot%*\system32\dns directory. Review the formats of these files carefully, making any changes that are required to make them compatible with Microsoft DNS Server.

The first time you start DNS Manager, it looks for BIND files in the dns directory. If the files are found, DNS Manager will attempt to initialize the DNS Server database from the BIND files. Otherwise DNS Manager will initialize the DNS Server with default settings from the Registry.

Subsequently, when DNS Server is started, it will consult the Registry for DNS Server data. Any BIND files in the dns directory are ignored.

You can force DNS Server to initialize from BIND files in the dns directory by changing a Registry value. Use the Registry Editor to create or modify the following value:

```
\HKEY_LOCAL_MACHINE\SYSTEM\CurrentControlSet\Services\DNS\
Parameters\EnableRegistryBoot
```

If the EnableRegistryBoot value is 1, DNS Server initializes from the Registry. If the EnableRegistryBoot is 0, DNS Server initializes from BIND files.

After changing the value of EnableRegistryBoot to 0, use the Service applet in the Control Panel to stop and restart the Microsoft DNS Server service.

Enabling DNS Clients

Windows NT clients are configured to use DNS by editing the TCP/IP Protocol properties in the Network applet of the Control Panel. On the WINS Address tab check the **Enable DNS for Windows Resolution** check box. Also complete the DNS tab, shown in Figure 13.30, as follows:

- **Host Name.** With Windows NT, the default DNS host name is the same as the NetBIOS computer name after removing the sixteenth hexadecimal character that designates the service type. This default name can be changed by editing the Host Name property. (Permitted characters in host names follow the same rules as with NetBIOS: A–Z, a–z, 0–9, hyphen, and period. Although DNS names can contain upper- and lowercase letters, the names are not case-sensitive.)

- **Domain.** In this field, specify the domain name under which the host appears in the DNS name space.

NOTE

The 15-character NetBIOS name is combined with the specified domain name to establish the FQDN for the host.

- **DNS Service Search Order.** In this list specify the IP addresses of one or more DNS name servers. Resolution attempts will query name servers in the order they appear in the search order list. Use the **Up** and **Down** buttons to adjust the search order.

- **Domain Suffix Search Order.** In this list specify one or more domain names that are to be used as suffixes during attempts to resolve names that are not entered as fully qualified domain names. (A name that includes a period is regarded as an FQDN.) If key-stone.com appears in this list and an attempt is made to resolve the name oliver, the resolver will query DNS with the name oliver.key-stone.com. The suffixes are used in the order they appear in the search order list. Use the **Up** and **Down** buttons to adjust the search order.

NOTE

Always include at least one domain name in the Domain Suffix Search Order list, even if it is the same as the domain specified in the Domain field. Some processes will not work proper-ly with out a domain suffix list.

Understanding Windows NT Name Resolution

As you see in this chapter and in Chapter 11, "Host Naming in the Microsoft TCP/IP World," several mechanisms enable hosts to resolve names in the Microsoft TCP/IP environment:

- NetBIOS broadcasts
- NetBIOS name servers (WINS)
- LMHOSTS Files

- HOSTS files

- DNS servers

It is worth taking a moment to see how these various technologies work together. There are several variables that determine how a Microsoft TCP/IP host will attempt to resolve names. Principally, there are three factors, all of which are enabled under the WINS Address tab of the Microsoft TCP/IP Properties dialog box in the Control Panel Network applet.

FIGURE 13.30

Configuring client DNS properties.

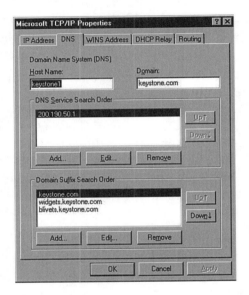

- **Is WINS lookup enabled?** WINS lookup is enabled whenever at least one WINS server is specified in the WINS Address tab. By default, all WINS clients are configured to use h-node name resolution. Non-WINS clients use b-node name resolution by default.

- **Is DNS lookup enabled?** DNS lookup is enabled by checking the **Enable DNS for Windows Resolution** check box. Additionally, at least one DNS server must be specified in the DNS tab.

- **Is LMHOSTS lookup enabled?** LMHOSTS lookup is enabled by checking the **Enable LMHOSTS Lookup** check box.

NOTE

For non-DHCP clients, the node type is determined by whether the computer is configured as a WINS client. By default, all WINS clients are configured to use h-node name resolution. Non-WINS clients use b-node name resolution by default.

For DHCP clients, you can specify the node type using DHCP option 46. Typically, you will use option 0x8 (h-node) for WINS clients and option 0x1 (b-node) for non-WINS clients.

With all of these variables, how are the various name resolution options used? Let's examine the sequence for a Windows NT 4.0 computer.

1. If the host name is greater than 15 characters in length, or if the host name contains a period, and if DNS lookup is enabled, the host will first attempt to use DNS. (The host will not attempt to use DNS first for conventional NetBIOS names of 15 characters or less.)

2. If the name is not resolved by DNS, and if WINS lookup is enabled, the host queries a WINS server.

3. If the name is not resolved by WINS, the host attempts a local broadcast for name resolution.

4. If the local broadcast fails, and if LMHOSTS lookup is enabled, the host checks its LMHOSTS file.

5. At this point, if the name has not been resolved and if DNS lookup is not enabled, name resolution fails and an error is returned.

6. If the LMHOSTS lookup fails and if DNS lookup is enabled, the host checks its HOSTS file.

7. If the HOSTS lookup fails, the host once again queries DNS.

8. If DNS cannot resolve the name, an error message is returned.

In the above sequence, notice that two attempts are made to consult DNS. This behavior is new with Windows NT version 4. Prior to version 4, the sequence began with step 2, and WINS was the first resource consulted to resolve a name. DNS was consulted only when WINS, LMHOSTS, and HOSTS lookups failed.

For NT version 4, however, DNS is the highest priority name service. The second DNS lookup is a result of the older behavior exhibited by Windows NT 3.x.

Using *nslookup*

Windows NT Server 4.0 includes nslookup, a utility borrowed from BIND that can be used to troubleshoot DNS servers. nslookup is a fairly elaborate tool, and this section will only cover the basics. If you want greater detail, consult the Windows NT Help utility.

nslookup is used in a command prompt window and can be used in interactive and noninteractive modes. Let's look at the noninteractive mode first.

Making Noninteractive Queries

The following dialogue shows two nslookup queries. The first is a name-to-address query. The second is an address-to-name query. (If you enter an IP address, nslookup inverts the address, appends in-addr.arpa, and looks up PTR records instead of address records.) Clearly, noninteractive use of nslookup is pretty elementary.

```
C:\>nslookup mozart
Server:    mozart.hoople.edu
Address:   200.250.199.4

Name:      mozart.hoople.edu
Address:   200.250.199.4


C:\>nslookup 200.190.50.4
Server:    mozart.hoople.edu
Address:   200.250.199.4

*** mozart.hoople.edu can't find 200.190.50.4: Non-existent domain
```

The first thing nslookup must do is locate a name server. It does so by consulting the addresses in the DNS Service Search Order list in the TCP/IP Properties dialog box. If nslookup cannot contact a name server in the list it makes several attempts before moving to the next name server. For the following example, I turned off the DNS Server service and tried an nslookup query. You can see the retry attempts as they time out.

```
C:\>nslookup mozart
DNS request timed out.
    timeout was 2 seconds.
```

```
DNS request timed out.
    timeout was 4 seconds.
DNS request timed out.
    timeout was 8 seconds.
*** Can't find server name for address 200.250.199.4: Timed out
DNS request timed out.
    timeout was 2 seconds.
DNS request timed out.
    timeout was 4 seconds.
DNS request timed out.
    timeout was 8 seconds.
*** Can't find server name for address 200.250.199.4: Timed out
*** Default servers are not available
Server:  UnKnown
Address:  200.250.199.4

DNS request timed out.
    timeout was 2 seconds.
DNS request timed out.
    timeout was 4 seconds.
DNS request timed out.
    timeout was 8 seconds.
*** Request to UnKnown timed-out
```

Making Interactive Queries

nslookup can also be used in interactive mode. The next dialogue shows the beginning of an interactive session. The > character is the nslookup prompt.

```
C:\>nslookup
Default Server:  mozart.hoople.edu
Address:  200.250.199.4

>
```

A number of commands and queries can be entered from the nslookup prompt. The most basic are name and address queries, as in this example:

```
> mozart
Server:  mozart.hoople.edu
Address:  200.250.199.4

Name:     mozart.hoople.edu
Address:  200.250.199.4
```

By default, nslookup searches for entries in address (A) resource records. You can alter the query by specifying different resource record types, or you can search in all records. The target of a search is defined by the value of the querytype set variable (abbreviated q), which by default is set to a, resulting in address record lookups. The next listing shows how you can examine the SOA record for a domain. The first step is to use the command **set q=soa**, which sets the querytype to soa. Then, a query on the domain name returns the contents of the SOA resource record.

```
> set q=soa
> hoople.edu
Server:    mozart.hoople.edu
Address:   200.250.199.4

hoople.edu
        primary name server = mozart.hoople.edu
        responsible mail addr = peters.hoople.edu
        serial  = 15
        refresh = 3600 (1 hour)
        retry   = 600 (10 mins)
        expire  = 86400 (1 day)
        default TTL = 3600 (1 hour)
```

Another record type used in this chapter is MX. Here is an exchange that shows two queries for mail1. Note that when the querytype changes to mx, the contents of the MX record are displayed.

```
> set q=mx
> mail1
Server:    mozart.hoople.edu
Address:   200.250.199.4

mail1.hoople.edu        MX preference = 10, mail exchanger =
mail1.hoople.edu
mail1.hoople.edu        internet address = 200.190.50.254
```

As a final example of using the querytype set variable, you can examine all records for a host by setting the querytype to any, as shown in this dialogue.

```
> set q=any
> mail1
Server:    mozart.hoople.edu
Address:   200.250.199.4
```

```
mail1.hoople.edu          internet address = 200.190.50.254
mail1.hoople.edu          MX preference = 10, mail exchanger =
mail1.hoople.edu
mail1.hoople.edu          internet address = 200.190.50.254
```

Want to directly examine the records in a domain? To do that, use the ls command. ls accepts a variety of arguments that focus or expand the query. In the next example, the -d parameter results in the display of all resource records in the specified domain, as determined by querying the default name server. In this case, the records fit on one screen, but long lists are presented a page at a time.

```
> ls -d hoople.edu
hoople.edu.                      WINS
        WINS lookup info
            flags = 0 ( )
            lookup timeout = 5
            cache TTL      = 600
            server count   = 1
            WINS server = (200.190.50.4)
hoople.edu.               NS      mozart.hoople.edu
ftp                       CNAME   jsbach.hoople.edu
haydn                     A       200.190.50.1
haydn                     A       200.250.199.1
brubeck.jazz              A       200.250.199.81
ellington.jazz            A       200.250.199.80
parker.jazz               A       200.250.199.82
jsbach                    A       200.250.199.3
mail1                     A       200.190.50.254
mail1                     MX      10   mail1.hoople.edu
mozart                    A       200.250.199.4
papa                      CNAME   haydn.hoople.edu
papa190                   A       200.190.50.1
papa250                   A       200.250.199.1
schubert                  A       200.190.50.4
hoople.edu.               SOA     mozart.hoople.edu
➥peters.hoople.edu. (15 3600 600 86400 3600)
```

In the following command, the -t parameter is used with ls. The -t parameter accepts one argument, a resource record name or any, and configures queries much like the querytype variable did in the previous example. In this example, only address records are displayed, but notice that the command found address records in subdomains as well.

```
> ls -t a hoople.edu.
[mozart.hoople.edu]
  hoople.edu.                    NS    server = mozart.hoople.edu
  haydn.hoople.edu.              A     200.190.50.1
  haydn.hoople.edu.              A     200.250.199.1
  brubeck.jazz.hoople.edu.       A     200.250.199.81
  ellington.jazz.hoople.edu.     A     200.250.199.80
  parker.jazz.hoople.edu.        A     200.250.199.82
  jsbach.hoople.edu.             A     200.250.199.3
  mail1.hoople.edu.              A     200.190.50.254
  mozart.hoople.edu.             A     200.250.199.4
  papa190.hoople.edu.            A     200.190.50.1
  papa250.hoople.edu.            A     200.250.199.1
  schubert.hoople.edu.           A     200.190.50.4
```

You can direct the output from ls to a file if desired. nslookup includes a view command that permits you to list file contents without leaving nslookup. If you compare the following results to the previous listing, you will notice that view sorts its output alphabetically.

```
> ls -t a hoople.edu > templist
[mozart.hoople.edu]
Received 18 records.
> view templist
  brubeck.jazz          A     200.250.199.81
  ellington.jazz        A     200.250.199.80
  haydn                 A     200.190.50.1
  haydn                 A     200.250.199.1
  hoople.edu.           NS    server = mozart.hoople.edu
  jsbach                A     200.250.199.3
  mail1                 A     200.190.50.254
  mozart                A     200.250.199.4
  papa190               A     200.190.50.1
  papa250               A     200.250.199.1
  parker.jazz           A     200.250.199.82
  schubert              A     200.190.50.4
[mozart.hoople.edu]
```

nslookup can access only one name server at a time. If you want to query a different name server, enter the server or lserver command at the nslookup prompt, as in the following example:

```
> server schubert.hoople.edu
Server:   schubert.hoople.edu
Address:  200.190.50.4
```

Subsequent queries will be directed to schubert.hoople.edu. The `server` and `lserver` commands accomplish much the same thing but differ in a significant way. `lserver` queries the local server, the server you started the `nslookup` session with, to obtain the address of the server to be switched to. `server`, however, queries the current default name server. If you change to a server that is not responding, `nslookup` is cut off from a working name server. If the current default server is not responding, you can use `lserver` to access the name server that was used to start `nslookup`, putting yourself back in business.

A lot more could be said about `nslookup`, but many of the options are quite advanced or specialized and are beyond the scope of this book. Consult the Help files or the book *DNS and BIND*, written by Paul Albitz and Cricket Liu, from O'Reilly & Associates, Inc., for more information.

You're Ready for Users

Clearly, name resolution is one of the trickiest aspects of Microsoft TCP/IP. NetBIOS name resolution requires help from WINS because NetBIOS broadcasts won't propagate across routers. And if you want to participate in the larger TCP/IP world, you need to implement DNS. DNS is a fairly involved technology, but I think the graphic administration provided by DNS Manager is a significant step in the right direction, reducing the likelihood of syntax errors and greatly simplifying the tasks of creating domains.

This chapter presents the last piece that is required to establish a TCP/IP network infrastructure. Now you can start to add some clients to the network. You have already seen how Windows NT clients are configured for TCP/IP. The next chapter shows you how to configure Windows 95, Windows 3.11, and Windows 3.1/MS-DOS clients.

14

INSTALLING TCP/IP ON MICROSOFT CLIENTS

Chapter 8, "Installing TCP/IP on Windows NT Computers," examines the procedures for setting up Windows NT computers as Microsoft TCP/IP clients. Besides Windows NT, Microsoft provides TCP/IP client software for the following environments:

- Windows 95 and Windows 98

- Windows 3.11

- Windows 3.1 and MS-DOS

This chapter examines installation and configuration of client software in those three environments.

Windows 95 and Windows 98

Windows 95/98 includes TCP/IP protocol support. The easiest way to install network support on Windows 95/98 is to use the Setup Wizard, which identifies most network adapters and simplifies adding network protocols. Therefore, discussion considers only the case of adding TCP/IP support to a Windows 95/98 configuration that already is network enabled.

To add TCP/IP protocols to a Windows 95/98 computer configured with basic network support, follow these steps:

1. Open the Control Panel in the My Computer window.

2. Start the Network tool in the Control Panel. Figure 14.1 shows the Network tool dialog box. The computer depicted in the example has been configured with a network adapter (3COM 3C589) and with the NetBEUI and NWLink protocols. Basic Microsoft network support has also been configured.

FIGURE 14.1

The Windows 95 Network tool before TCP/IP installation.

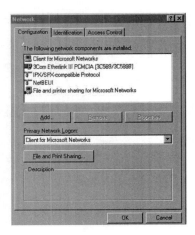

3. To add TCP/IP, choose **Add** in the Network tool dialog box. This will open the Select Network Component Type dialog box (see Figure 14.2). Select **Protocol** and choose **Add** to open the Select Network Protocol dialog box (see Figure 14.3).

FIGURE 14.2

Selecting a network component.

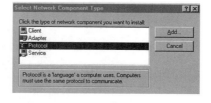

FIGURE 14.3

Selecting a network protocol.

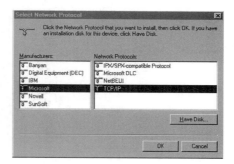

4. In the Manufacturers box, select **Microsoft** to open a list of Microsoft protocols. Then, in the Network Protocols box, select **TCP/IP**. Choose **OK** to continue. The focus returns to the Network tool dialog box. Now TCP/IP is listed as a protocol (see Figure 14.4).

FIGURE 14.4

TCP/IP protocols installed in the network configuration.

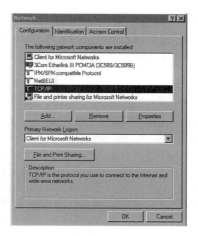

5. The TCP/IP protocols have been installed, but currently are configured with default properties. To review the protocol properties, select **TCP/IP** in the box labeled **The following network components are installed:**. Then choose **Properties** to open the TCP/IP Properties dialog box (see Figure 14.5).

FIGURE 14.5

The TCP/IP Properties dialog box.

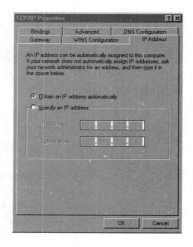

6. The TCP/IP Properties dialog box has several tabs that enable you to configure various aspects of the TCP/IP configuration. The information on these tabs is similar to the information that appears in the Windows NT protocol dialog boxes. After configuring the protocols, choose **OK** to return to the Network tool main dialog box.

7. After you exit the Network applet, you might need to supply diskettes and file paths required to copy files to the computer. After copying the files, restart the computer to activate the new protocols.

NOTE

Windows 98 introduces support for Automatic Private IP Addressing (APIPA). Windows 98 clients that are configured to obtain their IP addresses from a DHCP server can automatically assign themselves a private IP address if the DHCP server is unavailable.

The private IP address is chosen from the range 169.254.0.1 through 169.254.255.254. Addresses in this range are for private use only and cannot be used to communicate with the Internet or with remote IP subnets. Windows 98 clients that obtain private IP addresses through APIPA can communicate only with hosts on the local subnet that are also assigned IP addresses in the private IP address range.

If a DHCP server becomes available while a Windows 98 client is using a private IP address, the client will obtain an IP address from the DHCP server which it will then use to communicate with the network. Clients using private IP addresses can communicate with the Internet through a proxy server, such as Microsoft Proxy Server, described in Chapter 21, "Microsoft Proxy Server."

You might want to disable Automatic Private IP Address assignment if your network uses routers or connects directly to the Internet. To disable this feature, add value entry **IPAutoconfigurationEnabled** to the Registry. Create the value entry with type DWORD and assign it the value 0x0. Place the value entry in the following Registry key:

```
HKEY_LOCAL_MACHINE
    \System
        \CurrentControlSet
            \Services
                \VxD
                    \DHCP
```

Installing TCP/IP for Windows for Workgroups, MS-DOS, and Windows 3.1

Windows NT Server includes TCP/IP client software for Windows for Workgroups 3.11. Also included is client software that supports Microsoft network access for MS-DOS computers, including computers running Windows 3.1. This section describes the procedures for creating client installation disks, and then discusses the procedures for installing TCP/IP support on Windows 3.1x and MS-DOS clients.

Creating Client Disks

Client installation disks must be created to install TCP/IP protocols on Windows for Workgroups 3.11, MS-DOS, or Windows 3.1. The diskettes are created using the Network Client Administrator utility, included with Windows NT Server. The icon for Network Client Administrator is installed in the Network Administration program group.

Network Client Administrator can be used to initiate a variety of client installation procedures. A complete discussion of the possibilities can be found in *Inside Windows NT Server*. The procedures covered in this section describe the process for creating two types of installation disk sets and assume that Windows NT Server was installed from a CD-ROM:

■ TCP/IP 32 for Windows for Workgroups 3.11

■ Network Client v3.0 for MS-DOS and Windows

To create a set of client installation diskettes:

1. Start Network Client Administrator.

2. In the Network Client Administrator dialog box (see Figure 14.6) select the option **Make Installation Disk Set** and choose **Continue**.

FIGURE 14.6

Selecting a Network Client Administrator option.

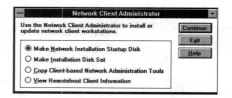

3. In the Share Network Client Installation Files dialog box (see Figure 14.7), select **Use Existing Path**. Then, in the Path box, enter the path to the \CLIENTS directory on your Windows NT Server CD-ROM. You can browse for the appropriate path by clicking the **browse** button (the button with three dots on it) to the right of the Path box.

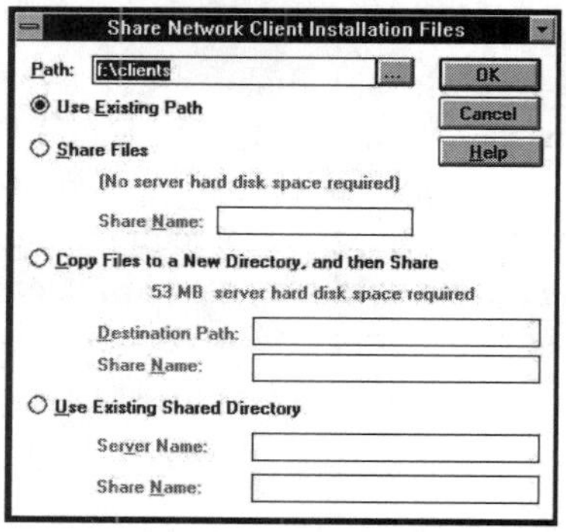

FIGURE 14.7

Setting the network client installation path.

4. The Make Installation Disk Set dialog box that appears next enables you to create five types of client disk sets (see Figure 14.8). To create a disk set, follow steps a through d:

FIGURE 14.8

Selecting a network client.

a. In the Network Client or Service box, select the disk set to create.

b. Select the **Destination Drive** (A: or B:).

c. Obtain the number of disks specified in the dialog box. The disks must be blank and formatted. To have the disks formatted before files are copied, check **Format Disks**.

d. Choose **OK** and supply disks when they are requested.

5. Quit Network Client Administrator.

6. Label the disks you prepared.

The following sections assume that appropriate client installation disks have been created using Network Client Administrator.

Windows for Workgroups 3.11

Windows for Workgroups 3.11 (WfW) is a network-ready implementation of Windows 3.x. Although WfW is network-ready, the standard package does not include TCP/IP protocols. You need to build a TCP/IP 32 for Windows for Workgroups 3.11 client installation disk using the Windows NT Server Client Administrator.

The following procedures assume that WfW has been installed and that a network adapter card has been configured. Only procedures for adding TCP/IP client support are covered.

To add TCP/IP to a WfW network configuration, perform the following steps:

1. Start the Windows Setup utility.

2. In the Windows Setup dialog box, choose the **Change Network Settings** command in the Options menu.

3. The Network Settings dialog box should resemble Figure 14.9. The dialog box should specify support for Microsoft Windows Network (version 3.11). Also, the Network Drivers dialog box should specify the network adapter that is installed in this computer.

FIGURE 14.9

WfW network settings prior to installing TCP/IP.

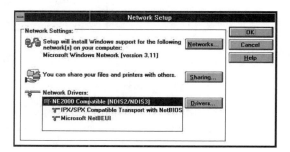

4. To install TCP/IP client support, choose the **Drivers** button to open the Network Drivers dialog box (see Figure 14.10).

FIGURE 14.10

The Network Drivers dialog box.

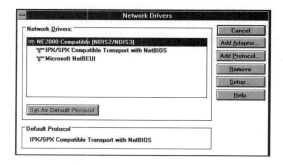

5. In the Network Drivers dialog box, choose the **Add Protocol** button.

6. In the Add Network Protocol dialog box (see Figure 14.11), choose **Unlisted or Updated Protocol** in the protocol box and choose **OK**.

FIGURE 14.11

Selecting the protocol to install.

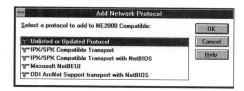

7. When prompted for the location of the protocol files, insert the TCP/IP 32 Client for Windows for Workgroups disk in a disk drive. Specify the drive path, and choose **OK**.

8. After the Unlisted or Updated Protocol dialog box appears, choose **Microsoft TCP/IP-32 3.11** and choose **OK**. Files are copied from the client disk and Setup returns to the Network Drivers dialog box, which now shows Microsoft TCP/IP-32 3.11 as an installed network driver.

9. To configure the TCP/IP protocols, in the Network Drivers dialog box, select **Microsoft TCP/IP-32 3.11** and choose **Setup** to open the Microsoft TCP/IP Configuration dialog box (see Figure 14.12).

FIGURE 14.12

The WfW TCP/IP Configuration dialog box.

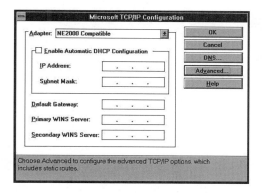

The WfW TCP/IP protocol Configuration dialog boxes are nearly identical to the dialog boxes used for Windows NT. Consult Chapter 8 if you require additional information about these dialog boxes.

10. After entering the TCP/IP configuration, choose **OK**, exit the Windows Setup utility, and restart the computer.

Icons for the TCP/IP utilities ftp and telnet are installed in the newly created Microsoft TCP/IP-32 program group. Also installed in this program group are icons for Microsoft TCP/IP help and for a Release Notes file.

The Windows NT Server installation CD-ROM contains a number of files that upgrade Windows for Workgroups networking capabilities. The files should be copied to WfW from the directory \Clients\Update.wfw on the installation CD-ROM. Copy the files as follows:

- Copy NET.EXE and NET.MSG to the Windows directory, usually C:\WINDOWS.

- Copy all other files (with DLL and 386 extensions) to the SYSTEM directory, usually C:\WINDOWS\SYSTEM.

MS-DOS and Windows 3.1

Unlike Windows for Workgroups 3.11, Windows 3.1 does not include network client software. Windows 3.1 relies on DOS clients to provide the network redirector capability that enables Windows 3.1 to communicate with shared network resources. Therefore, the same client software is used to enable networking for MS-DOS and for Windows 3.1.

NOTE

Windows 3.1 network support is extremely limited. If networking is important to your organization, it is strongly recommended that you upgrade to Windows for Workgroups 3.11 or Windows 95/98.

Follow the instructions in the previous section "Creating Client Disks" to build client disks for Network Client v3.0 for MS-DOS. To install the MS-DOS client, exit to an MS-DOS prompt, insert Disk 1 of the Network Client v3.0 disk set in a disk drive, and do the following:

1. Change to the drive (A: or B:) in which the disk was inserted.

2. Enter the command **setup**.

3. When the Welcome to Setup screen appears, press **Enter**.

4. Next, you are asked to specify the destination directory for the client files. The default directory shown is C:\NET. You can edit the directory. Press **Enter** to continue.

5. The next screen (see Figure 14.13) asks whether you want to optimize the client software for performance at the expense of memory. Buffers are used to store data waiting to be sent to the network or retrieved

by MS-DOS. Increasing the number of buffers improves performance, at the cost of memory. Press **Enter** to optimize the client for performance at the cost of reducing available MS-DOS memory. Press **C** to optimize memory usage at the cost of reduced performance.

FIGURE 14.13

Setting client network buffers.

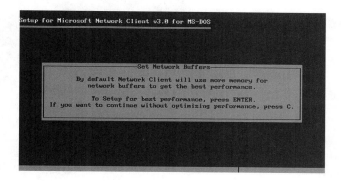

6. Next, Setup requests a username to use as the default username when attempting to log on to the network. The screen (see Figure 14.14) lists the characters that cannot appear in a logon name. After entering a name, press **Enter**.

FIGURE 14.14

Entering a logon username.

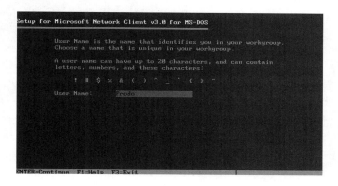

7. The next screen (see Figure 14.15) displays several characteristics of the client configuration and is used to branch to several screens used to specify client options. Highlight **Change Setup Options** and press **Enter**.

Figure 14.15
Primary client configuration menu screen.

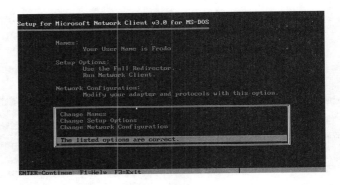

8. As shown in Figure 14.16, the client software has four setup options. Highlight any option and press **Enter** to change the setting.

Figure 14.16
Configuring the client redirector.

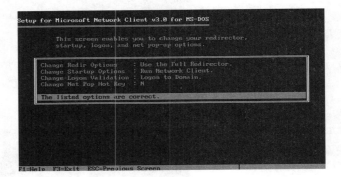

■ **Use the Full Redirector** is the default redirector option that supports all redirector functions, including named pipes. You should probably retain the default setting, because the full redirector is required for Windows and remote access services. You can change this option to **Use the Basic Redirector** if only MS-DOS will be used.

■ **Run Network Client** is the startup option that configures MS-DOS to start the network software when the system boots. In most cases, the default value should be retained. If you will be using the network pop-up utility, change the setting to **Run Network Client and Load Pop-up.** Disable both features by changing the setting to **Do Not Run Network Client**.

■ The default logon validation option is **Do Not Logon to Domain.** If this computer will be logging on to a Windows NT Server domain, change the setting to **Logon to Domain.**

■ The Net Pop-up is a DOS-based pop-up utility that can be used to connect to shared network resources. It loads automatically if **Run Network Client and Load Pop-up** is chosen, or can be started by typing the command **NET** at the command line. The hotkey that pops the utility up can be changed from Ctrl+N.

Choose **The listed options are correct** after options are configured as desired. You return to the primary client configuration menu.

9. To add a network adapter and the TCP/IP protocol, choose **Change Network Configuration.** The network adapter and protocol configuration screen is shown in Figure 14.17.

FIGURE 14.17
Configuring client adapters and protocols.

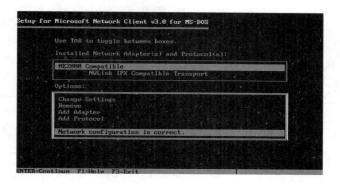

To change a setting on this screen, perform steps a and b:

a. Choose an object in the Installed Network Adapter(s) and Protocol(s) box.

b. Choose an option in the Options box.

If a mouse is active, you can use it to select items in either box. Otherwise, use the Tab key to change boxes and then select an item with the arrow keys.

Press **Enter** to execute an option for the selected adapter or protocol.

10. If the appropriate adapter is not listed in the Installed Network Adapter(s) box, choose **Add Adapter** in the Options box. A series of dialog boxes enables you to select an adapter from those included on the client software disks or from a third-party disk (see Figure 14.18). Supply the third-party disk when it is requested. You are then returned to the adapter and protocol configuration screen.

FIGURE 14.18

Selecting a network adapter.

11. Select the adapter that has been installed and choose **Change Settings** to examine and change the adapter's hardware settings. Figure 14.19 shows example settings. The example shows an entry for Adapter Slot Number, an option that appears only on computers that have an EISA bus. Choose **The listed options are correct** when the adapter has been configured.

FIGURE 14.19

Setting the adapter hardware configuration.

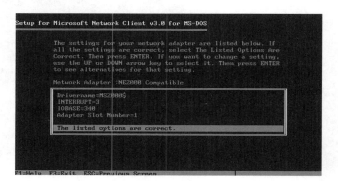

12. By default, adapters are configured with the NWLink protocols. These are not required on a purely TCP/IP network and can be removed. To remove the protocols, select **NWLink IPX Compatible Transport** and then choose **Remove** in the Options box.

13. To add the TCP/IP protocols, select the adapter in the Installed Network Adapter(s) box. Then choose **Add Protocol** in the Options box. Select the **Microsoft TCP/IP** protocol in the list shown in Figure 14.20. You return to the main menu. The TCP/IP protocol is shown in the Installed Network Adapter(s) and Protocol(s) box.

FIGURE 14.20

Selecting a protocol.

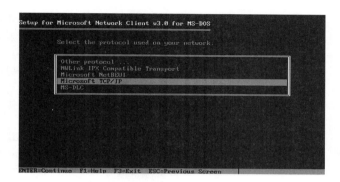

14. TCP/IP must be configured. Select the **TCP/IP** protocol in the Installed Protocol(s) list and choose **Change Settings** in the Options box. Figure 14.21 shows the TCP/IP settings.

FIGURE 14.21

TCP/IP settings for the MS-DOS requestor.

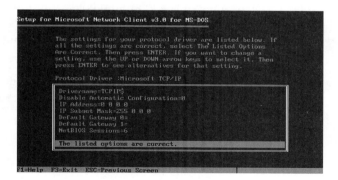

To configure the client to obtain an IP address from DHCP, retain the default setting of **0** for Disable Automatic Configuration. Set this parameter to **1** to manually configure addresses.

If addresses are manually configured, enter appropriate information in the **IP Address**, **IP Subnet Mask**, and **Default Gateway** sessions.

Choose **The listed options are correct** after completing the settings.

15. When adapters and protocols have been configured, select **Network configuration is correct** and press **Enter** to return to the Setup main menu.

16. When all configuration options are as desired, return to the Setup main menu, select **The listed options are correct** and press **Enter.**

    Even if you selected one of the prepackaged network adapter drivers, you are asked to insert an OEM drivers disk. Insert Disk 2 of the client installation set to supply the driver files. For drivers not included with the client disk set, insert the OEM disk.

17. After copying files, restart the computer to activate the client software.

When the MS-DOS client starts up, a logon dialog box opens. If the client can locate the required workgroup or domain, the TCP/IP software has been properly configured. If not, check the settings in the file C:\NET\PROTOCOL.INI and edit them as required. Logon share settings are stored in the file C:\NET\SYSTEM.INI.

The NET utility is installed with the MS-DOS client. You can use the NET command or the pop-up shown in Figure 14.22 to connect to resources. Type **NET HELP** for a list of the available NET commands. Type **NET command /?** for more detail about a particular command. See the Appendix of NRP's *Inside Windows NT Server* for more information about the NET commands.

If the computer uses Windows 3.1, use the Windows 3.1 System Setup utility to enable Windows 3.1 to operate as a Microsoft Network client. The steps are as follows:

1. Start the Windows Setup utility.

2. In the Windows Setup dialog box, choose **Change System Settings** in the Options menu.

3. In the Change System Settings box, (see Figure 14.23), pull down the list for the **Network** box and choose **Microsoft Network (or 100% compatible).**

4. Exit the Windows Setup utility. You are prompted to supply disks from which Windows copies the required network support files. Restart Windows to activate networking.

FIGURE 14.22

The MS-DOS client NET utility.

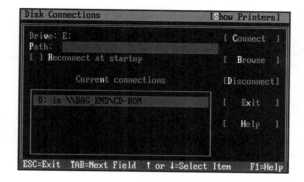

FIGURE 14.23

Activating Microsoft Network support for Windows 3.1.

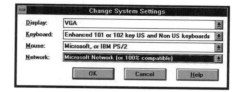

You've Got Users. Now Things Get Really Complex!

You now know how to enable a variety of clients to access your TCP/IP network. The moment you start adding users, seemingly placid networks become turbulent. At the very least, you encounter performance issues as users chew up your network bandwidth. At worst, things start to go seriously wrong. Users can't resolve names; messages aren't routed properly; things just start to go wrong.

You need to take a close look at the management tools Microsoft has provided, and it is to management that we now turn our attention. In the next chapter, you encounter some facilities that can help you diagnose and resolve problems on your network.

Chapter 15

MANAGING TCP/IP WITH SNMP

The SNMP management tools included with Windows NT are fairly limited, not surprising considering the high cost of the best network management tools. This chapter covers configuring SNMP on Microsoft systems.

Although Microsoft includes SNMP agents with Windows, they do not include an SNMP management console. A couple of rudimentary command-line utilities are included in the *Windows NT Server Resource Kit*, but if your network depends on TCP/IP, you should seriously consider obtaining an SNMP management console. Among the best are:

- Microsoft's System Management Server, for Windows NT (limited to monitoring traps).

- Hewlett Packard's Open View, available for DOS, DOS/Windows, or UNIX.

- Sun Microsystem's NetManager, for UNIX.

- Novell's NetWare Management System (NMS), for DOS/Windows.

- SynOptics' (Bay Networks) Optivity, for DOS/Windows, UNIX, or for use in conjunction with Novell's NMS.

- Cabletron's Spectrum, for DOS/Windows, UNIX, or for use in conjunction with Novell's NMS.

SNMP agent support is an option on Windows NT and Windows 95/98. This chapter covers installation of SNMP in these environments. Before you install an SNMP agent, please review the discussion of SNMP in Chapter 6, "The Process-Application Layer".

Any SNMP configuration includes a *community* parameter, which is simply the name of a group of systems that exchange SNMP messages. The community name might be used to limit the extent to which some SNMP messages are propagated through the network. The default community name is *public*.

An SNMP agent also must specify at least one *trap destination*, the address of an SNMP computer to receive SNMP trap messages. Microsoft TCP/IP SNMP can send traps to IP and IPX addresses.

Configuring SNMP on Windows NT

The SNMP service is installed using the Network applet. The procedure is as follows:

1. Open the Network applet in the Control Panel.

2. Select the **Services** tab. Choose **Add Software** in the Network Settings dialog box.

3. Choose **Add** to open the Select Network Service dialog box. Select **TCP/IP Protocol and related components** in the Network Settings box of the Add Network Software dialog box, and then choose **Continue**.

4. Check **SNMP Service** in the Windows NT TCP/IP Installation Options dialog box Network Service list. Then choose **OK to continue**.

5. Supply disks and path information as required to install the software.

6. Choose **OK** to close the Network Settings dialog box.

7. Next, you see the **Microsoft SNMP Properties** dialog box (see Figure 15.1). Specify the following information in the Agent tab:

   a. In the Contact field, specify the name of the person to be contacted for information on this computer. Often this will be a user's email name.

   b. In the **Location** field, provide information about the location of this computer. This might be the computer's DNS domain name.

   c. Check the appropriate SNMP service options in the Service box. The options are as follows:

   - **Physical**. This computer manages a physical layer TCP/IP device such as a repeater.

   - **Applications**. This computer supports applications that use TCP/IP. This option should be selected for all Windows NT computers.

   - **Datalink/Subnetwork**. This computer manages a data link layer such as a bridge or a subnetwork.

   - **Internet**. This computer manages an internet layer device, that is, it functions as an IP gateway (router).

   - **End-to-End**. This computer acts as an IP host. This option should be selected for all Windows NT computers.

FIGURE 15.1

*The Agent tab in the
Microsoft SNMP
Properties dialog box.*

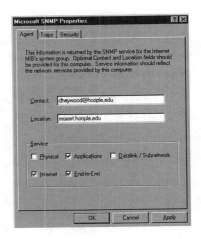

7. Next, select the **Security** tab, shown in Figure 15.2. This tab is used to specify monitor community names and SNMP managers with which this agent will correspond. Complete the fields as follows:

   a. Check the **Send Authentication Trap** check box (the default setting) to generate traps in the event of authentication failures.

   b. In the **Accepted Community Names** box specify at least one SNMP monitor community to which this computer will belong. The default community is **public.** Choose **Add** to add names to the list in the Accepted Community Names box. The agent will accept requests from managers only if both agent and manager are configured with the same community name.

   c. By default, the **Accept SNMP Packets from Any Host** option is checked. If this computer should accept packets only from hosts that have specific IP or IPX addresses, check **Only Accept SNMP Packets from These Hosts** and add the hosts in the associated box.

NOTE

Don't be lulled into a false sense of security. All of the SNMP security options can be circumvented. Community names are not encrypted when sent through the network and can easily be intercepted. Even IP addresses can be faked by a knowledgeable person. If your SNMP-managed network is connected to the Internet or any public internetwork, a firewall should be in place to prevent intrusion from outside SNMP management consoles.

FIGURE 15.2

Specifying the monitor settings.

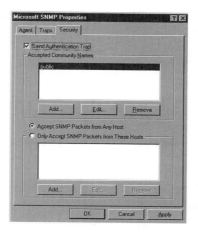

8. The SNMP agent can generate trap messages in response to changes such as host system startup, shutdown, or password violation. If this SNMP agent will generate traps, select the **Traps** tab, shown in Figure 15.3. In this tab, you specify which SNMP managers will receive traps from this agent.

    a. First specify a trap community name in the Community Name field. The agent will identify traps with this community name. Managers will receive the traps only if they are configured with the same trap community name.

    b. In the Trap Destination list, add the name of at least one SNMP manager that will receive traps from this agent.

FIGURE 15.3

Specifying the trap settings.

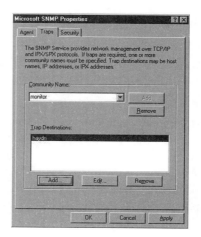

9. When SNMP settings are complete, choose **OK.**

10. Close the Network applet and restart the computer to activate the changes.

Configuring SNMP on Windows 95/98 Computers

Setting up an SNMP agent on a Windows 95/98 computer involves two procedures, and possibly a third:

1. Installing the SNMP software.

2. Configuring the SNMP agent using the System Policy Editor.

3. If more than one community name is required, adding the community names to the Registry.

Installing the SNMP Software

To install the SNMP software:

1. Start the Network applet in the Control Panel.

2. In the Network dialog box, choose **Add**.

3. In the Select Network Component Type dialog box, select **Service** and choose **Add**. A box opens temporarily with the title Building Driver Database. When the box completes its work, the Select Network Service dialog box appears.

4. Choose **Have Disk** to open the **Install From Disk** dialog box. In the Copy manufacturers files from box, specify the path to the \ADMIN\NETTOOLS\SNMP directory on the Windows 95/98 CD-ROM.

   If necessary, choose the **Browse** button to open an **Open** dialog box and browse the local computer for its CD-ROM drive, or browse the Network Neighborhood for a shared CD-ROM drive that contains the Windows 95/98 CD-ROM. After specifying the drive letter of the CD-ROM, return to the Install From Disk dialog box and complete the path to the \ADMIN\NETTOOLS\SNMP directory. After you finish, the Open dialog box should resemble the one shown in Figure 15.4.

FIGURE 15.4

Browsing for the SNMP files on the Windows 95/98 CD-ROM.

5. Choose **OK** to return to the Install from Disk dialog box. The Copy manufacturers files from box should now specify the path to the SNMP files. Choose **OK** to continue.

6. Next, the Select Network Service dialog box appears. Only the Microsoft TCP/IP agent is shown as an installable service, so nothing must be selected. Choose **OK** to continue.

7. Files now are copied from the CD-ROM to the hard drive. You might see messages concerning missing files. The reported files are part of a standard Windows 95/98 network installation and are already in place. You can choose **Skip** to ignore the missing files.

8. After returning to the Network utility, restart the computer to activate the SNMP agent.

Configuring the SNMP Agent

The SNMP agent is configured by editing the Registry using the System Policy Editor, which is not installed in a standard Windows 95/98 configuration. To install the System Policy Editor:

1. Open the Add/Remove Programs tool in the Control Panel. Click the **Windows Setup** tab. Then click **Have Disk**.

2. In the Install From Disk dialog box, specify the path to the \ADMIN\APPTOOLS\POLEDIT directory on the Windows 95/98 CD-ROM. You might browse for a CD-ROM drive as described in the previous section.

3. After specifying the path, choose **OK** to go to the Have Disk dialog box. Two entries appear in the **Components** box. Select **System Policy Editor** and choose **Install**.

4. After files are copied, quit the Add/Remove Programs tool.

To configure the SNMP agent using the System Policy Editor:

1. Choose the **Run** command in the Start menu. Enter the command `poledit` in the <u>O</u>pen data entry field of the Run dialog box and choose **OK.**

2. In the System Policy Editor window choose the **Open <u>R</u>egistry** command in the <u>F</u>ile menu. Two options are presented as icons in the System Policy Editor: **Local User** and **Local Computer** (see Figure 15.5).

FIGURE 15.5

Options in the System Policy Editor.

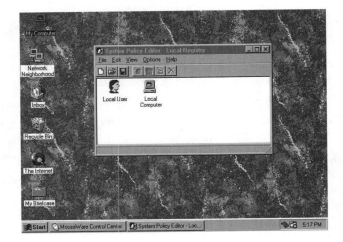

3. Double-click **Local Computer** to establish default SNMP policies for the computer. The next window you see is the Local Computer Properties window. In Figure 15.6, the Network icon was double-clicked on to list the option's subcategories.

4. Double-click on **Network**, and then double-click **SNMP** to reveal the property entries for the SNMP agent, as shown in Figure 15.7.

    Each entry in the policy editor is tagged with a box icon to the left of the option description. The box can be marked with a check mark, or it can be cleared.

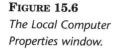

FIGURE 15.6

The Local Computer Properties window.

■ When the box is cleared, the Registry entry is not implemented.

■ When the box is checked, the Registry entry is implemented and is configured using the values specified in the Settings dialog box.

The four SNMP policy options are similar to options that have been discussed for Windows NT SNMP clients:

■ **Communities**. Settings include one or more names of which the computer is a member.

■ **Permitted managers**. Settings include IP or IPX addresses of computers that are permitted to manage this computer.

■ **Traps for 'Public' community**. By default, only the public community is supported. Additional communities must be added to the Registry. Specify addresses of stations in the public community that are to receive traps from this station.

■ **Internet MIB (RFC1156)**. Settings are the contact name and location associated with this computer.

5. To set an SNMP policy:

   a. Click the policy's box until it shows a check mark.

   b. Choose the **Show** button to open a Show Contents dialog box in which you can add and remove values.

   c. Choose **OK** after configuring all policies.

6. To remove a Registry entry along with previous configuration settings, click the policy's box until it is cleared.

7. When the required settings have been entered, choose **OK** to return to the main window of the System Policy Editor.

8. Close the editor, and respond **Yes** when you are prompted, Do you want to save changes to the Registry?

FIGURE 15.7
Policy properties for the SNMP agent.

Adding SNMP Communities

If more than one SNMP community will be active on the network, the community name and traps must be added to the Registry. This is most easily done with the Registry Editor. To add a community to the Registry:

1. Choose the **Run** command in the Start menu. Enter the command **regedit** in the **Open** field of the Run dialog box and choose **OK.**

2. Unlike the Windows NT Registry editor, here you will find all of the Windows 95/98 Registry subtrees merged into a single tree. Double-click on keys to open deeper levels of the Registry tree. In the Registry Editor, open the following key:

```
        Hkey_Local_Machine
  \System
    \CurrentControlSet
      \Services
        \SNMP
          \Parameters
            \TrapConfiguration
```

At first, **Public** will be the only subkey of TrapConfiguration. Additional community names are created as additional subkeys of TrapConfiguration.

3. To create the subkey, be sure that TrapConfiguration is selected in the Registry tree.

   Click the **Edit** menu. Then click **New** to open the New submenu. Choose **Key** in the New submenu (see Figure 15.8).

FIGURE 15.8

Entering the data for a Registry value.

4. A key will be added to the Registry tree with the name New Key #1. The key name is selected for editing. Type a community name for the key to overwrite the default name. Press **Enter** after typing the name.

5. Next, a value must be created for each console that will receive SNMP traps from this computer. These values are named with integers, starting with 1. The data portion of the value is an IP or IPX address.

   To assign a value to the key:

   a. Select the new key.

   b. Click **Edit**, click **New**, and click **String Value** in the New sub menu. A new value will be added to the values pane of the Registry Editor.

   c. The initial name of the new value is New Value #1, which is selected for editing when the value is created. If this is the first value in the community key, its name should be 1. Additional values should be named 2, 3, and so forth.

   d. After renaming the value, click **Edit** and click **Modify** to open the Edit String dialog box (refer to Figure 15.8). In the **Value data** field, enter an IP address or an IPX address. Choose **OK** after finishing.

Figure 15.9 shows the state of the Registry editor after the new key has been added and values in the key have been defined.

6. Exit the Registry Editor to save the changes.

FIGURE 15.9

The Registry Editor after adding community keys.

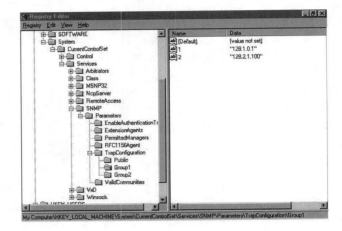

WARNING

Remember, the Registry is critical to proper functioning of Windows 95/98. Make changes with care. You might want to save a copy of the Registry using the Export Registry File command in the File menu. Even if the Registry is damaged so that the system cannot be started, you can start the system using the emergency startup disk that is created during installation. A real-mode Registry editor on the startup disk can be used to import a working Registry from the export file.

The Registry is stored in two files: SYSTEM.DAT, which contains general system information, and USER.DAT, which contains information related to user profiles.

If you are certain that a backup file contains a complete Registry image, you can use the regedit utility on the startup disk to restore the complete registry by entering the command **regedit /c filename.reg** where filename is the name of the export file. Using the /c option with an export file that does not contain a complete Registry image will be disastrous!

That's the SNMP Groundwork

This chapter explained how to configure SNMP agents, but the management picture isn't complete until you add a management console. Because there are so many consoles available, I haven't tried to describe SNMP management in detail.

Although NT is weak on SNMP management tools, it includes many tools that enable you to monitor and troubleshoot network operations. Those tools are the subjects of the next chapter

Chapter 16

TROUBLESHOOTING

This chapter embraces a variety of topics related to the ongoing management of Microsoft TCP/IP networks, starting with instructions on how to remove TCP/IP software components from a Windows NT computer. The chapter then reviews some tools that can be used in addition to ipconfig *to troubleshoot TCP/IP networks.*

This chapter also examines some tools that can be used to troubleshoot basic network problems.

Removing TCP/IP Components

Do not attempt to remove TCP/IP components manually. Most components require a number of files, which are not always installed in the same directories. And installation of all components involves adding keys and values to the Registry. Attempting to back out all of these changes is both trouble-prone and unnecessary.

To remove a network software component:

1. Start the Network applet in the Control Panel.

2. Select the tab in which the component is installed.

3. Select the component to be removed.

4. Choose **Remove** to remove the component.

5. In most cases, you are required to restart the computer to complete removal of the component.

All software is permanently removed. Reinstallation is required to restore the component.

Troubleshooting Utilities

Microsoft TCP/IP includes several utilities that can be used to troubleshoot the network. Chapter 8, "Installing TCP/IP on Windows NT Computers," examines ping and ipconfig. The tools discussed in this chapter are arp, tracert, netstat, and nbtstat.

arp

All TCP/IP computers maintain an ARP cache that stores the results of recent ARP inquiries. The arp utility is used to view and manage the ARP cache. arp accepts three command options with the following syntaxes, where *ip_address* is an Internet IP address, *mac_address* is the physical address of a network interface, and *ip_host_address* is the IP address of the host whose ARP cache is being examined or modified:

```
arp -a ip_address [-N ip_host_address]
arp -d ip_address [ip_host_address]
arp -s ip_address mac_address [ip_host_address]
```

If hosts cannot ping each other, their ARP cache entries could contain incorrect information. To view the ARP cache on a computer, enter the command **arp -a** at a command prompt. The following listing shows the results of an arp inquiry. If the MAC addresses in the ARP table are incorrect, delete the problematic entries.

```
C:\>arp -a
Interface: 128.1.0.1
   Internet Address      Physical Address      Type
   128.1.1.1             00-00-6e-44-9f-4f      dynamic
   128.1.1.60            00-20-af-8d-62-0e      dynamic
C:\>
```

To restrict arp to reporting cache entries for a specific IP address, include the address in the command. The following command lists cache entries on the local computer that relate to IP address 128.1.0.60:

```
arp -a 128.1.0.60
```

By default, arp reports on the cache table for the first network adapter in the computer's configuration. To access other adapters on multihomed hosts you must specify an interface using the **-N** option. This command reports cache entries on the second adapter of the host:

```
arp -a -N 128.2.0.1
```

To delete the cache record associated with an IP address, use the **-d** option. This command removes the entry for host 128.1.0.60 from the cache table for the first network adapter:

```
arp -d 128.1.0.60
```

The cache table for other network adapters can be specified using the -N option.

You can also manually add an entry to the ARP cache. The following example adds a cache entry mapping an IP address to a MAC address:

```
arp -s 128.1.0.60 00-20-af-8d-62-0e
```

As the following listing illustrates, entries added using the -s option are regarded as static, in that they are not determined by dynamic ARP inquiries.

```
C:\>arp -a
Interface: 128.1.0.1
   Internet Address         Physical Address          Type
   128.1.1.1                00-00-6e-44-9f-4f          dynamic
   128.1.1.60               00-20-af-8d-62-0e          dynamic
C:\>arp -s 128.1.1.60 00-20-af-8d-62-0e
C:\>arp -a
Interface: 128.1.0.1
   Internet Address         Physical Address          Type
   128.1.1.1                00-00-6e-44-9f-4f          dynamic
   128.1.1.60               00-20-af-8d-62-0e          static
C:\>
```

tracert

tracert is a route reporting utility that sends ICMP echo requests to an IP address and reports ICMP errors that are returned. Successive attempts are made starting with the Time To Live (TTL) field set to 1 and incrementing TTL by one with each attempt. Thus, each attempt gets one hop closer to the destination. The result is that tracert produces a report that lists all of the routers crossed. Here is an example of a tracert report:

```
C:>tracert ftp.microsoft.com
Tracing route to ftp.microsoft.com [198.105.232.1]
over a maximum of 30 hops:
  1     *        *        *       Request timed out.
  2   132 ms   138 ms   144 ms   iq-ind-gw1-en2.iquest.net
[198.70.144.10]
  3   176 ms   166 ms   168 ms   border2-hssi1-0.KansasCity.mci.net
[204.70.41.5]
  4   316 ms   237 ms   201 ms   core-fddi-1.KansasCity.mci.net
[204.70.3.65]
  5   172 ms   176 ms   164 ms   core2-hssi-2.WillowSprings.mci.net
[204.70.1.82]
  6   175 ms   167 ms   167 ms   core1-aip-4.WillowSprings.mci.net
[204.70.1.61]
  7   189 ms   188 ms   185 ms   core2-hssi-2.Denver.mci.net
[204.70.1.77]
  8   225 ms     *        *       core-hssi-4.Seattle.mci.net
[204.70.1.90]
  9     *      224 ms   229 ms   border1-fddi-0.Seattle.mci.net
[204.70.2.146]
 10   227 ms   220 ms   223 ms   nwnet.Seattle.mci.net [204.70.52.6]
```

```
11    239 ms    232 ms    231 ms    seabr1-gw.nwnet.net [192.147.179.5]
12    227 ms    228 ms    229 ms    microsoft-t3-gw.nwnet.net
[198.104.192.9]
13    238 ms    236 ms    232 ms    131.107.249.3
14    233 ms    240 ms    237 ms    ftp.microsoft.com [198.105.232.1]
Trace complete.
C:\WINDOWS>
```

netstat

The netstat utility reports current TCP/IP connections and protocol statistics. A basic netstat report appears in the following listing:

```
C:\>netstat
Active Connections
   Proto   Local Address        Foreign Address        State
   TCP     bag-end:1028         128.1.0.1:nbsession     ESTABLISHED
   TCP     bag-end:1069         128.1.1.60:nbsession    TIME_WAIT
C:\>
```

netstat reports the following information for each connection:

- Proto. The transport prototype with which the connection is established.

- Local Address. The name or IP address of the local computer, along with the port number the connection is using.

- Foreign Address. The foreign address and the port name or number associated with the connection. Both of the connections shown are NetBIOS resource sharing connections.

- State. For TCP connections only, the state of the connection. Possible values are:

CLOSEDFIN_WAIT_1   LISTEN   TIMED_WAIT

CLOSE_WAIT   FIN_WAIT_2   SYN_RECEIVED

ESTABLISHED   LAST_ACK   SYN_SEND

The syntax of netstat is as follows:

```
netstat [-a] [-e] [-n] [-s] [-p protocol] [-r] [interval]
```

netstat accepts several arguments that produce enhanced reports:

- -a. Displays all connections and listening ports, information not normally reported.

- -e. Displays Ethernet statistics. May be combined with the -s option.

- -n. Displays addresses and ports in numerical rather than name form.

- -p protocol. Shows connections for the specified protocol, which might be tcp or udp. If used with the -s option, *protocol* might be tcp, udp, or ip.

- -r. Displays routing table data.

- -s. Displays statistics separately for each protocol. By default, netstat reports statistics for TCP, UDP, and IP. The -p option can be used to display a subset of the three protocols.

- interval. Include an *interval* parameter to have netstat report repeatedly, with *interval* specifying the number of seconds between reports. Press **Ctrl+C** to stop netstat.

The following listing illustrates use of the -e option:

```
C:\>netstat -e
Interface Statistics

                         Received            Sent
Bytes                     124083           76784
Unicast packets              484             577
Non-unicast packets           95              96
Discards                       0               0
Errors                         0               0
Unknown protocols             62
C:\>
```

The -s option reports statistics for the IP, ICMP, TCP, and UDP protocols, as in this example:

```
C:> netstat -s
IP Statistics
  Packets Received             = 634
```

```
       Received Header Errors                    = 0
       Received Address Errors                   = 0
       Datagrams Forwarded                       = 0
       Unknown Protocols Received                = 0
       Received Packets Discarded                = 0
       Received Packets Delivered                = 634
       Output Requests                           = 658
       Routing Discards                          = 128
       Discarded Output Packets                  = 0
       Output Packet No Route                    = 0
       Reassembly Required                       = 0
       Reassembly Successful                     = 0
       Reassembly Failures                       = 0
       Datagrams Successfully Fragmented         = 0
       Datagrams Failing Fragmentation           = 0
       Fragments Created                         = 0
   ICMP Statistics
                               Received      Sent
       Messages                115           152
       Errors                  0             0
       Destination Unreachable 0             0
       Time Exceeded           109           0
       Parameter Problems      0             0
       Source Quenchs          0             0
       Redirects               0             0
       Echos                   0             152
       Echo Replies            6             0
       Timestamps              0             0
       Timestamp Replies       0             0
       Address Masks           0             0
       Address Mask Replies    0             0
   TCP Statistics
       Active Opens                              = 6
       Passive Opens                             = 0
       Failed Connection Attempts                = 0
       Reset Connections                         = 0
       Current Connections                       = 1
       Segments Received                         = 307
       Segments Sent                             = 374
       Segments Retransmitted                    = 0
   UDP Statistics
       Datagrams Received                        = 211
       No Ports                                  = 1
       Receive Errors                            = 0
       Datagrams Sent                            = 132
```

nbtstat

nbtstat reports statistics and connections for NetBIOS over TCP/IP. The most basic option for nbtstat is -r, which reports complete name resolution statistics for Windows networking. Here is an example, which was generated on a network that did not incorporate a WINS server:

```
C:\>nbtstat -r
NetBIOS Names Resolution and Registration Statistics
----------------------------------------------------
Resolved By Broadcast     = 6
Resolved By Name Server   = 0
Registered By Broadcast   = 11
Registered By Name Server = 0
    NetBIOS Names Resolved By Broadcast
-----------------------------------------
      GANDALF
      GANDALF
      RIVENDELL
      GANDALF
      MIDDLE_EARTH    <1B>
      RIVENDELL
C:\>
```

The syntax of nbtstat is as follows:

```
nbtstat [-a remotename][-A ipaddress][-c][-n][-r][-R][-s][-S]
[interval]
```

The following options are available for nbtstat:

- -a remotename. Lists the name table of a remote computer, specified by *remotename*.

- -A ipaddress. Lists the name table of a remote computer, specified by the computer's IP address.

- -c. Lists the contents of the local computer's NetBIOS name cache.

- -n. Lists local NetBIOS names.

- -r. Lists local Windows name resolution statistics, including broadcast and WINS-based name resolution.

- -R. Purges the name table and reloads it from entries in the computer's LMHOSTS file. (Clearly, the options make a difference when using nbtstat!)

- **-s.** Displays workstation and server sessions, attempting to resolve remote IP addresses based on the HOSTS file.

- **-S.** Displays workstation and servers sessions, listed by IP address only.

- **interval.** Include an *interval* parameter to specify that nbtstat should report repeatedly with *interval* seconds between displays. Press **Ctrl+C** to terminate nbtstat.

The display produced by nbtstat -s illustrates the data that is available from the utility:

```
C:\>nbtstat -s
C:\>
```

Monitoring TCP/IP with Performance Monitor

Performance Monitor is a versatile tool, and it is beyond the scope of this book to exhaustively consider its features. Please consult *Inside Windows NT Server* for thorough coverage. This discussion examines the basics of charting statistics in Performance Monitor, along with some specifics that apply to monitoring TCP/IP objects.

Performance Monitor starts in chart mode. Before any data is displayed, you need to add a chart line using the following procedure:

1. Choose the **Add to Chart** command in the <u>E</u>dit menu. This opens the Add to Chart dialog box (see Figure 16.1).

FIGURE 16.1

Specifying parameters for a chart line.

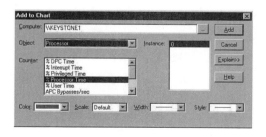

2. In the <u>C</u>omputer box, specify the UNC name of a computer to be monitored. If desired, you can browse for a computer by choosing the **Browse** button (the one with three dots on it).

3. In the Object box, select the object to be monitored. TCP/IP services add the following objects to Performance Monitor:

   ■ ICMP

   ■ IP

   ■ Network Interface

   ■ TCP

   ■ UDP

   ■ FTP (if the FTP Server service is installed)

   ■ WINS (if the WINS Server service is installed)

4. In the Counter box, select a counter to be charted.

5. If the counter you selected has more than one instance (such as two network interface adapters), select one in the Instance box.

6. If desired, customize the chart line by choosing options in the Color, Scale, Width, and Style boxes.

   Scale is an extremely useful option that enables you to adjust the magnitude of the line that will chart this counter. Choose a scale greater than 1 to increase the height of the chart and enhance display of counters reporting small values. Choose a scale less than 1 to reduce the height of the graph for counters reporting large values.

7. Choose **Add** to add the line to the chart.

8. Add other lines to the chart as desired.

9. Double-click the legend for a chart line to edit the line's parameters.

The majority of the available counters should require little explanation. Consult the Windows NT Server TCP/IP manual for descriptions.

Network Monitor

Performance Monitor is limited to reporting statistics related to network performance. You cannot, however, use Performance Monitor to examine the network traffic itself. Although you can, for example, gauge NWLink protocol performance by charting the numbers of frame bytes sent and received and by charting the numbers of errors that are encountered; you cannot examine the frames to determine the nature of the traffic, the types of protocols, or the types of errors that are taking place. To diagnose your network in detail, you need a tool that can perform *protocol analysis*, enabling you to look inside the actual data circulating on your network.

NOTE

Unfortunately, protocol analysis can be very involved, requiring a detailed understanding of the protocols being analyzed. That is the reason Part I devotes so much time to the details of the TCP/IP protocols, including the frame and header formats. Before you read this chapter, you might want to review Part I to refamiliarize yourself with the material.

Network Monitor extends your capability to manage the network by enabling you to capture network data for detailed examination. You can look inside the frames to perform a detailed analysis of the network's operation.

Network Monitor is equipped with a wide variety of *protocol parsers*, which are modules that examine network frames to decode their contents. Among the 62 or so included protocol parsers are many you will recognize from discussion in this book including Ethernet, Token Ring, IPX, IP, TCP, and PPP. However, a complete discussion of the protocol parsers is far beyond the scope of this book. Although it is not a book on protocol analysis, you can find more detailed descriptions of the network standards and protocols supported by Windows NT in the *Windows NT Server Professional Reference*, by Karanjit Siyan, also published by New Riders Publishing.

As shipped with Windows NT 4.0, Network Monitor has one significant limitation: Network Monitor can capture only those frames that originate from or are delivered to the computer on which Network Monitor is running, including broadcast and multicast frames that the computer receives or originates. You cannot use Network Monitor to monitor frames associated with other computers on the network.

NOTE

To monitor the entire network from a single computer, you need Microsoft's Systems Management Server (SMS), which includes a more powerful version of Network Monitor. SMS can monitor network traffic associated with any computer that is running a Network Monitor Agent. (*Agents* are proxy programs that collect data and forward them to another computer for analysis.) The Network Monitor Agent is included with Windows NT 4.0.

continues

Ordinarily, computers on a network are selective and will only receive frames that are addressed to them. As shipped with Windows NT 4.0, Network Monitor is designed to work with standard network adapter cards, which in part accounts for the restriction that Network Monitor can capture only those frames that originate from or are delivered to the computer on which Network Monitor is running. Network Monitor works with NDIS 4.0, new with Windows NT 4.0, to capture network data with little or no degradation in computer performance.

The SMS Network Monitor captures network traffic in *promiscuous mode*, meaning that it can capture all network data regardless of the destination of the frames. This enables SMS to monitor any computer running a Network Monitor Agent. However, capturing data in promiscuous mode is intense work, and performance will suffer on the computer running SMS. Therefore, monitoring the network with SMS Network Monitor is an activity best reserved for a dedicated network management computer. (On some network types, such as Token Ring, special network adapters are required to support promiscuous mode. Because the Network Monitor included with Windows NT 4.0 does not operate in promiscuous mode, special network adapters are not required.)

SMS has other capabilities as well, including hardware inventory management and software management.

Installing Network Monitor

To install Network Monitor, open the Network utility in the Control Panel and open the Services tab. You can add two services related to the Network Monitor:

- **Network Monitor Agent.** Choose this option if this computer will be monitored by another computer running the SMS.

- **Network Monitor Tools and Agent.** Choose this option if this computer will be used to collect and analyze network data. This option also installs the Network Monitor Agent, which enables SMS to monitor this computer remotely.

Network Monitor is added to the Administrative Tools group of the Start menu. Network Monitoring Agent is added to the Control Panel as the Monitoring Agent utility. The computer must be restarted to activate Network Monitor.

Setting Up Network Monitor Security

The data captured by Network Monitor can include very sensitive information. Suppose, for example, that you are logging in to a terminal session with a remote computer that does not use encrypted logins. Data frames sent to the remote computer would include your password in clear text, and the password could be discovered by any user with access to the Network Monitor. You should, therefore, prevent unauthorized users from using Network Monitor by assigning two types of passwords:

- A *capture password* is used to restrict the users who can use Network Monitor to capture and display statistics and data associated with this computer.

- A *display password* is used to determine which users can open previously saved capture files.

A capture password also restricts SMS access to the Network Monitor Agent. SMS can be used to capture data from a given agent only when the capture password is known.

To assign or change the Network Monitor passwords:

1. Open the Monitoring Agent utility in the Control Panel to open the Configure Network Monitoring Agent dialog box shown in Figure 16.2.

FIGURE 16.2

Options used to configure the Monitoring Agent utility.

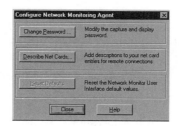

2. Choose **Change Password** to open the Network Monitoring Password Change dialog box shown Figure 16.3.

FIGURE 16.3

*Configuring Network
Monitor Passwords.*

3. To remove all passwords, choose **No Password** followed by **OK.**

4. To change the capture password, first enter the current password in the Old Capture Password box.

5. To specify a display or capture password, complete the appropriate Password field. Then enter the password again in the associated Confirm field to verify the entry.

6. Choose **OK** when passwords have been specified as desired, and then exit the Monitoring Agent utility.

Describing Your Network Cards

When one computer will be monitored by another, you should enter descriptions for each of the network adapters in the Network Monitor Agent. These descriptions enable the administrator who is monitoring the network to more easily identify the computer's network interfaces.

To describe network cards:

1. Open the Monitoring Agent applet in the Control Panel to open the Configure Network Monitoring Agent dialog box shown in Figure 16.4.

2. Choose **Describe Net Cards** to open the Describe Net Cards dialog box shown in Figure 16.4. In the figure, a description has been entered for the E100B1 adapter. The E100B2 adapter has not yet been described.

3. To change the description of a network adapter, select the entry and choose **Edit Description** to open a Change Net Card Description dialog box. Enter a new description and choose **OK**.

FIGURE 16.4

Describing network cards.

4. Repeat step 3 for each network card to be described.

Capturing Network Frames

The Network Monitor Capture window is shown in Figure 16.5. The window contains four panes:

- **Graph Pane.** This pane includes bar charts that dynamically display current activity. The five bars in this pane are % Network Utilization, Frames Per Second, Bytes Per Second, Broadcasts Per Second, and Multicasts Per Second. You can display or hide this pane by clicking the **Toggle Graph Pane** button. (A line in the % Network Utilization bar designates the highest utilization encountered during the current capture. The numbers at the right ends of the other bars describe the highest measurement encountered.)

- **Total Statistics.** This pane displays cumulative network statistics. These statistics summarize network traffic in five areas: Network Statistics, Capture Statistics, Per Second Statistics, Network Card (MAC) Statistics, and Network Card (MAC) Error Statistics. You can display or hide this pane by clicking the **Toggle Total Statistics Pane** button.

- **Session Statistics.** This pane displays statistics about sessions that are currently operating on the network. You can display or hide this pane by clicking the **Toggle Total Session Statistics Pane** button.

- **Station Statistics**. This pane displays statistics about sessions in which this computer is participating. You can display or hide this pane by clicking the **Toggle Total Station Statistics Pane** button.

FIGURE 16.5

Elements of the Network Monitor window.

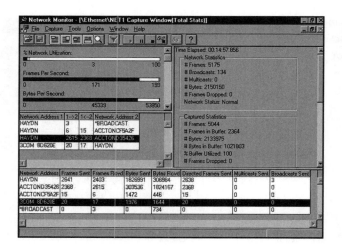

When capturing is active, network frames are captured into a buffer that is limited in size. When the buffer fills, older data is discarded to make room for new entries. Control capture status using the following options in the Capture menu: **Start, Stop**, **Stop and View**, **Pause**, and **Continue.** These functions can also be controlled using buttons in the toolbar, identified in Figure 16.5.

Figure 16.5 was prepared while a capture was taking place. The information in the various panes is updated dynamically while capturing is active.

TIP

If you want, you can focus on the activity in one of the panes. Select the pane and click the **Zoom Pane** button in the toolbar. The pane you select expands to fill the available space. To return to normal display, click the **Zoom Pane** button again.

Saving Captured Data

After you are finished, choose **Stop** in the Capture menu to stop the capture. The data in the capture buffer can now be analyzed as required, or it can be saved for future study.

Creating an Address Database

When you first capture data in Network Monitor, most devices will be identified by their physical network addresses (such as their Ethernet MAC addresses).

Because Microsoft network administrators generally prefer to identify computers by their NetBIOS names, Network Monitor includes a feature that identifies the NetBIOS names of computers from which data is captured.

To build the address database, start capturing data on the network and let Network Monitor continue to collect data for an extended period of time. As traffic is generated, computers will be added to the Session Statistics and Station Statistics panes, identified by their network addresses.

After capturing a large number of frames, stop capturing. Then select the **Find All Names** command in the <u>C</u>apture menu. The frames in the capture buffer will be scanned and the names will be added to the address database. During future capture operations, computers will be identified by name, as shown in Figure 16.6.

FIGURE 16.6

Computers identified by name in Network Monitor.

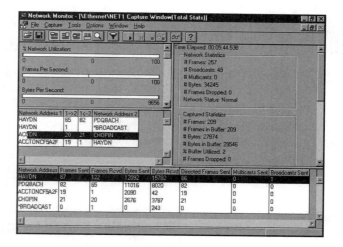

NOTE

A bit of luck is required to capture frames that include computer names. Each time you capture data, collect names and add them to the database until the list is complete.

You can view the address database, shown in Figure 16.7, by choosing the **Addresses** command in the <u>C</u>apture menu. Notice in the figure that a given computer might be represented by multiple entries associated with different protocols and network types.

FIGURE 16.7

Viewing the address database.

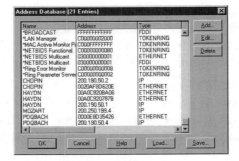

In the Address Database dialog box, you can add, edit, and delete specific entries. You can save the database to a file with an .ADR extension and load existing address files. The default address database, which is used unless you load another, is saved as DEFAULT.ADR.

Selecting the Network to be Monitored

When the Network Monitor computer is attached to two or more networks, it can monitor only one at a time. You can specify which network will be monitored by using the <u>N</u>etworks command in the <u>C</u>apture menu to open the Select Capture Network dialog box, as shown in Figure 16.8. The network that will be monitored is identified by the word CONNECTED in the Connect State column.

To change the connected network, select the network and choose **Connect.**

FIGURE 16.8

Selecting the connected network.

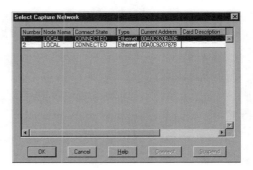

Managing the Capture Buffer

Data captured by Network Monitor is stored in system memory in a *capture buffer*. Due to lower performance of hard disks, disk storage cannot be used without the risk of losing frames during the capture process.

Ideally, the capture buffer should reside entirely in RAM. Virtual memory can be used, but frames might be lost. Therefore, setting the size of the capture buffer involves compromise. If the buffer is too small, it will not be large enough to capture a reasonable sample of network traffic. If the capture buffer is too large, part of it might be swapped into virtual memory and the efficiency of network data capture might be impaired.

To adjust the size of the capture buffer, choose the **Buffer Settings** command in the <u>C</u>apture menu to open the Capture Buffer Settings dialog box shown in Figure 16.9. In the <u>B</u>uffer Size (in MB) field, adjust the size of the capture buffer as desired. By default, the maximum size of the capture buffer is 8MB less than the amount of RAM installed in the computer. To maximize the amount of RAM available for the capture buffer, stop as many applications as possible. Ideally, only Network Monitor should be running.

FIGURE 16.9

Configuring the capture buffer.

On a busy network, captured frames can quickly fill a capture buffer. In many cases, to ensure that the frames you need are captured, you will need to capture more frames than will fit in the capture buffer at one time. Fortunately, the most critical bytes are often found at the beginning of the frame. In many cases, you can use the capture buffer more efficiently by capturing only the frame header to obtain the information you need. In other cases, you need only capture the header and a limited portion of the data field.

The F<u>r</u>ame Size (in bytes) field in the Capture Buffer Settings dialog box specifies the number of bytes to be captured from the start of each frame that is captured. By default, the value of this field is Full, indicating that complete frames are to be captured. Suppose, however, that you are capturing data from an Ethernet network, and that you require only the bytes in the Ethernet frame headers, which make up the first 22 bytes of the frame. In that case, you can set the value of the Frame Size (in bytes) field to **64** (the smallest setting). Other size increments are available.

Avoiding Dropped Frames

When data is being captured, a significant part of the computer's processing capacity is required to dynamically update the Network Monitor display. When the CPU is busy, frames might be lost. You can reduce CPU loading by placing Network Monitor in dedicated capture mode.

Choose the **Dedicated Capture Mode** command in the Capture menu. When capturing is active, the Dedicated Mode dialog box will be displayed, as shown in Figure 16.10. If capturing is currently stopped, the Dedicated Mode box will be displayed when capturing is started.

FIGURE 16.10

Capturing in dedicated mode.

When capturing in dedicated mode, only the number of captured frames is updated in the display. You can stop and pause capturing in the Dedicated Mode dialog box. If you choose **Normal Mode**, capturing will continue while the full Network Monitor window is displayed. If you choose **Stop and View,** capturing will stop and the Capture window is displayed. See the section, "Examining Capture Data," later in this chapter for a discussion of the Capture window.

Using Capture Filters

On a large network, the volume of data can overwhelm you unless you have a way of focusing on specific types of data. *Capture filters* enable you to specify which types of frames will be captured, enabling you to capture data from a specific subset of computers or protocols.

NOTE

Capture filters determine which frames will be stored in the capture buffer, however, all frames are reported in the performance statistics, regardless of any capture filter that might be in effect.

Structures of Capture Filters

Figure 16.11 shows the default Capture filter, which is organized as a *decision tree*. Filters consist of three sets of criteria, connected by AND keywords. Frames will be captured only if they meet all three of the following criteria: SAP/ETYPE, address, and pattern match.

The Capture filter criteria are described in the following sections.

FIGURE 16.11

The default Capture filter.

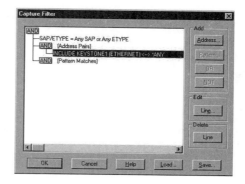

SAP/ETYPE Filters

The frames associated with specific protocols are identified by hexadecimal numbers referred to as SAPs or ETYPEs. By default, Network Monitor captures frames matching all supported protocols, but you can restrict capturing to specific protocols by selecting the SAPs and ETYPEs that will pass through the filter.

ETYPEs (*EtherTypes*) and SAPs (*service access points*) are used to specify the upper layer protocols that are associated with a frame. An EtherType of 800 hex is associated with the IP protocol, for example. An EtherType of 8137 hex is associated with NetWare running on an Ethernet II LAN.

To establish Capture filters for specific SAPs or ETYPES, select the **SAP/ETYPE=** line in the Capture Filter dialog box. Then choose **Line** in the Edit box to open the Capture Filter SAPs and ETYPEs dialog box shown in Figure 16.12. Network Monitor will capture frames matching protocols that are specified in the Enabled Protocols list, and by default all supported ETYPEs and SAPs are listed in this list.

FIGURE 16.12
*Filtering SAPs and
ETYPEs.*

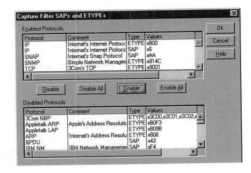

To disable protocols, use the **Disable** and **Disable All** buttons to move protocols to the Disabled Protocols list. In Figure 16.12, several protocols have been disabled in this way.

To enable disabled protocols, use the **Enable** and **Enable All** buttons to move protocols to the Enabled Protocols list.

Address Filters

Every frame is associated with a source-destination address pair. By default, frames will be captured for all source-destination address pairs, but you can limit capturing to specific address pairs if desired.

An address pair consists of the following components:

- A source address (or computer name)

- A destination address (or computer name)

- A direction arrow (—>, <—, or <—>) specifying direction(s) in which traffic should be monitored

- The keyword INCLUDE or EXCLUDE specifying whether frames should or should not be captured for this address pair

Address pairs are established in the Address Expression dialog box shown in Figure 16.13. Open this dialog box as follows:

- To edit an existing address pair, select the entry in the entry under (Address Pairs) and choose **Line** in the **Edit** box, or double-click the entry.

- To create a new address pair, select any line in the (Address Pairs) section and choose **Address** in the Add box, or double-click the (Address Pairs) line.

FIGURE 16.13

Filtering on address pairs.

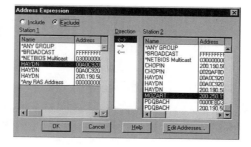

You can specify up to four address pairs. Suppose that you want to display all traffic between the HAYDN server and clients, but that you want to ignore traffic with the MOZART server. The following address pairs establish a filter to accomplish that goal:

```
INCLUDE HAYDN <—> ANY
EXCLUDE HAYDN <—> MOZART
```

Figure 16.13 shows the establishment of the EXCLUDE HAYDN <—> MOZART filter.

TIP

When multiple address pairs are specified, EXCLUDE statements have priority. If a frame matches an EXCLUDE statement, it will not be captured even though it might also match one or more INCLUDE statements.

Data Pattern Filtering

In some cases, you might want to filter frames depending whether they include or do not include a specific pattern of bytes. In that case, you must specify one or more entries in the Pattern Matching section.

A pattern consists of two components:

- The pattern of bytes to be matched, which can be specified as a series of hexadecimal numbers or as a string of ASCII characters.

- An offset, which specifies the position of the bytes in the frame. The offset can specify the position relative to the beginning of the frame or relative to the end of the topology header. (An offset of 0 specifies the first byte, which is 0 bytes from the beginning of the frame. Therefore, an offset of 19 specifies the 20th byte of the frame.) Specify the offset from the beginning of the topology header if the topology protocol permits variable length headers, such as Ethernet or Token Ring MAC frames.

TIP

You don't get much help when constructing capture filters based on data patterns. When you need to analyze frames based on data patterns, you might find it easier to construct data filters instead. As you will see later in this chapter in the "Display Filters" section, considerable expertise is built into the expression editor, which knows the structures of the headers for all the supported protocols.

Clearly, to set up filters you must have a thorough understanding of the structures of the frames on your LAN. It is, unfortunately, beyond the scope of this book to consider the details of the message structures associated with the various protocols supported by Windows NT.

To add a filter, select the **(Pattern Matches)** line and choose **Pattern** in the Add box, or double-click the **(Pattern Matches)** line. This will open the Pattern Match dialog box shown in Figure 16.14.

FIGURE 16.14

Entry form for a pattern match filter.

Using Logical Operators

When two or more patterns have been entered, you can set up complex filtering criteria using AND, OR, and NOT logical operations. Select the line to receive the logic operator and choose **AND, OR,** or **NOT** in the **Add** box. After you add a logical operator, you can drag the operators and expressions around to construct the logic tree that you require.

The logical operators function as follows:

- An AND branch of the tree will be true if all of the expressions under the AND are true. Otherwise, the AND branch will be false.

- An OR branch of the tree will be true if any of the expressions under the OR are true. The OR branch will be false if all of the expressions under the OR are false.

- A NOT will be true if the expression under the NOT is false. A NOT will be false if the expression under the NOT is true.

NOTE

Pattern matching is the one place in this book where we enter the esoteric realm of boolean algebra. The programmers among you will be comfortable enough, but readers new to boolean logic should be wary when setting up complex filters. It is easy to get the logic wrong and establish filters that misbehave in mysterious ways. If you aren't capturing the frames you want, check the logic in your capture filter.

Using Capture Triggers

On occasion, you might want to have an action occur when a particular network situation occurs. A *trigger* describes a set of network conditions and an action that takes place when the conditions are met.

To define a capture trigger, choose the **Trigger** command in the Capture menu to open the Capture Trigger dialog box shown in Figure 16.15. The following trigger types can be selected:

- **Nothing.** No triggers are specified. This is the default setting.

- **Pattern Match.** The trigger is initiated when a specified pattern is identified in a captured frame. Specify the pattern in the Pattern box.

- **Buffer Space.** The trigger is initiated when the free buffer space falls below the threshold specified in the Buffer Space box.

- **Pattern Match Then Buffer Space.** The trigger is initiated when the pattern specified in the Pattern box is identified, followed by a free buffer space that falls below the threshold specified in the Buffer Space box.

- **Buffer Space Then Pattern Match.** The trigger is initiated when the free buffer space that falls below the threshold is specified in the Buffer Space box, followed by the detection of a frame that includes the pattern specified in the Pattern box.

FIGURE 16.15

Establishing a capture trigger.

When the trigger occurs, one of three events can take place, as specified in the Trigger Action box:

- **No Action.** No action is taken when the trigger occurs.

- **Stop Capture.** Capturing will halt when the trigger occurs. This option ensures that the frame that initiated the trigger will remain in the capture buffer.

- **Execute Command Line.** The command specified will be executed when the trigger occurs. Include the path and command to be executed.

Saving Capture Data

After you have stopped capturing data, you can save the contents of the capture buffer for later analysis. Use the **Save** command in the File menu to save the capture buffer in a file with a .CAP name extension. Load previously saved data with the **Open** command in the File menu.

Examining Captured Data

After frames have been captured, you can examine them in considerable detail. To examine captured frames, do one of the following:

- When capturing is active, click the **Stop and View Capture** toolbar button, choose the **Stop and View** option in the Capture menu, or press **Shift-F11**.

- When capturing is stopped, click the **Display Captured Data** toolbar button, choose the **Display Captured Data** option in the Capture menu, or press **F12**.

Any of these actions opens the Capture dialog box shown in Figure 16.16. At first, this dialog box includes one pane, which lists all frames currently in the capture buffer.

The capture consists of a single ping event in which HAYDN (the host running Network Monitor) pinged pdqbach.hoople.edu by name. As you determine from the Description column, the sequence begins with a DNS query to determine the IP address of pdqbach, together with a response from the DNS server. Next, an ARP request and ARP reply establish the physical address of a DNS server. Finally, a series of ICMP Echo and Echo Reply datagrams comprise four repeated pings.

FIGURE 16.16

The Capture window showing captured frames.

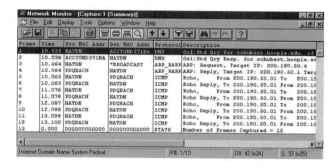

To examine details for a frame, double-click the entry for the frame. In Figure 16.17, an ICMP Echo datagram has been opened. The panes are as follows:

- **Summary Pane.** This pane includes a one-line summary of each frame in the capture buffer.

- **Detail Pane.** This pane displays the contents of the frame, organized by protocol layer.

- **Hex Pane.** This pane displays the data in the pane in hexadecimal and in ASCII characters. The bytes that are highlighted are associated with the protocol section that is highlighted in the Detail Pane.

The following sections discuss the Summary and Detail Panes.

FIGURE 16.17

The Capture window showing all panes.

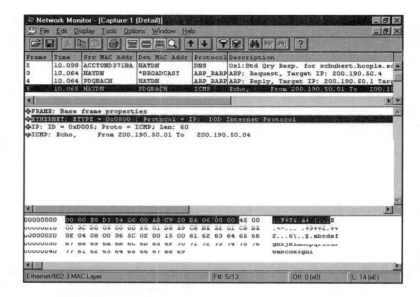

The Summary Pane

The Summary Pane briefly describes each frame that is held in the capture buffer. To open a frame for detailed analysis, select the entry in the Summary Pane.

The source and destination computers are identified by the Src MAC Address and Dst MAC Address fields. If a name database has been created then NetBIOS names will appear in place of hexadecimal physical addresses.

The Protocol field describes the protocol associated with the frame.

As you can see, the entries in the Description column can be reasonably clear (for example, "Echo Reply, To 200.190.50.01"), but they can also be obscure. To decode the descriptions, you will need to learn the operational details of the protocols that are being analyzed.

The Detail Pane

Unless you are knowledgeable enough to undertake a byte-by-byte analysis of the data, the Detail Pane will probably be the pane that occupies most of your analytical effort. This pane translates the data in the various header layers into human-readable form. Network Monitor is configured to parse many protocols so that you don't have to.

In Figure 16.18, the Detail Pane was expanded by selecting the pane and clicking the **Zoom Pane** button.

FIGURE 16.18

The Detail Pane.

The frame that is represented is an ICMP Echo frame. In Figure 16.19, notice that each entry is tagged with a + to the left, indicating that the entry can be expanded by clicking the + to show greater detail. To illustrate the significance of the discussion in Part I, it is worthwhile to open each entry and examine the details.

First, notice the layers of encapsulation:

- **FRAME.** This layer describes the raw characteristics of the frame at the physical layer.

- **ETHERNET.** This layer describes the MAC sublayer characteristics.

- **IP.** This layer describes the IP protocol encapsulation of the ICMP message.

- **ICMP.** Here at last is the ICMP message itself.

Open each of these layers for more detailed examination. (After opening the entry, the + changes to a -, indicating that the entry is fully expanded.) First, the FRAME layer, containing raw frame data, is shown in Figure 16.19. Notice in the decoding that there is no notion of the frame's purpose or type of data at this layer. There is only the notion that the frame consists of a certain number of bytes to be transmitted.

FIGURE 16.19

Example of FRAME layer data.

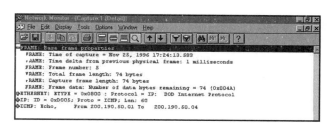

In Figure 16.20, the ETHERNET entry has been expanded. Each entry under the ETHERNET heading corresponds to a field in the Ethernet frame format. Within the example entry you can see how Network Monitor has decoded entries such as the destination and source addresses, the frame length, and the length of the data field.

In this screen shot, I have included the Hex Pane, which shows the data in raw, hexadecimal form. Notice that as each entry is selected in the Detail Pane, the appropriate bytes are illuminated in the Hex Pane. This will give you an appreciation for the way the Detail Pane translates data for easier analysis. Take some time to compare the entries and trace them back to the material in Part I.

When you select a field in the Detail Pane, the legend at the bottom of the window provides some useful information about the field:

- First is shown a brief description of the field.

- F#. This box designation specifies the frame's position in the capture buffer. For example, F# 4/10 designates that this is the fourth of ten frames captured.

- Off. This box specifies the offset of the selected byte from the start of the frame. For example: Off: 74(x4A) specifies that the selected byte is offset 74 (decimal) bytes (4A hex) from the first byte of the frame. The first byte of the frame has an offset of 0. (This field is a valuable guide when setting up Capture and Display filters.)

- L. This box specifies the length of the field in bytes.

FIGURE 16.20
Details of the Ethernet frame.

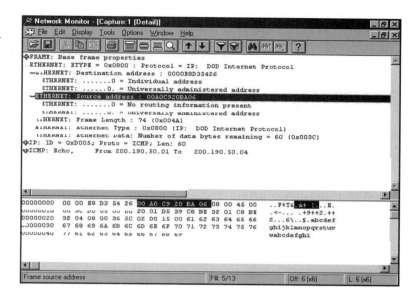

Figure 16.21 expands the data at the IP datagram level. I had to further expand the IP: Service Type and the IP: Flags Summary fields to show their contents. Given your experience reading Part I, you should be able to interpret the contents of this datagram.

FIGURE 16.21
Details of the IP datagram header.

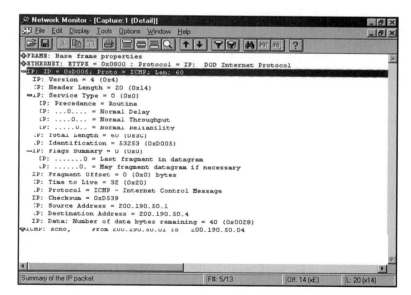

Finally, in Figure 16.22, we come to the ICMP payload.

FIGURE 16.22
Details of the ICMP
Echo message.

Clearly, given the complexity of the data, there is nothing easy about protocol analysis. That's why so much detail was included in Part I. Your understanding of this information can go a long way when it is necessary to troubleshoot your network.

Display Filters

Okay, you've collected a buffer full of frames and you want to focus your attention on just a few without scrolling through the thousands that are available. No problem, just design a display filter. Choose **Filter** in the Display menu to open a dialog box where you can design a Display filter. Display filters are a bit different from Capture filters, so let's take a brief look at the procedure.

Figure 16.23 shows the Display Filter dialog box, showing the default filter that displays frames for all protocols and computer addresses.

FIGURE 16.23
The default Display
filter.

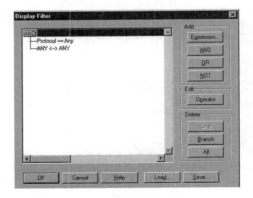

Adding Expressions

To add an expression to the Display filter, select the line that will precede the new expression and choose **Expression** in the Add box to open the Expression dialog box shown in Figure 16.24. This dialog box has three tabs, enabling you to enter expressions based on three types of properties: address, protocol, and property. Figure 16.24 shows the Address tab.

FIGURE 16.24

Constructing an address expression for a Display filter.

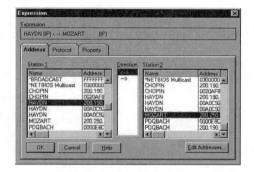

Address expressions specify the addresses of two computers whose frames are to be captured together with a direction specification. As you select entries for **Station 1**, **Direction**, and **Station 2**, the expression you are constructing is displayed in the Expression box.

The Protocol tab (Figure 16.25) allows you to enable and disable filters for specific protocols. If a protocol is listed in the **Disabled Properties** list, frames for that protocol will not be displayed.

FIGURE 16.25

Constructing a protocol expression for a Display filter.

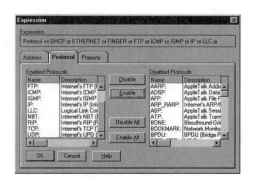

The Property tab (Figure 16.26) is used to construct filters based on data patterns. As you see, you receive no help when establishing data patterns for Capture filters, however, considerable help is available when constructing Display filters.

FIGURE 16.26

The Display filter Property tab.

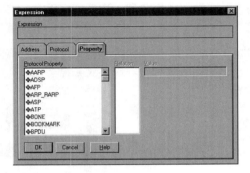

Each of the protocols in the Protocol Property list can be opened to list the data fields in the protocol header. In Figure 16.27, the IP protocol has been expanded to reveal the fields of an IP datagram header. After selecting Destination Address, a list of valid options is revealed in the Relation list. And, while I could have manually entered a hex number in the Value field, I was able to select one of the predefined options based on the IP addresses that Network Monitor has learned. After selecting CHOPIN, the IP address was entered for me.

FIGURE 16.27

Constructing a protocol property expression for a Display filter.

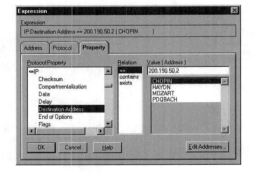

TIP

It is easier to construct Display filters than Capture filters. You might want to filter in two stages. So that you don't have unwanted frames cluttering the capture buffer, construct Capture filters to limit the general categories of frames that are captured, perhaps sorting by protocol (using SAP or ETYPE filters). Then use Display filters to zoom in on the details and isolate specific frames.

Using Logical Operators

You can use AND, OR, and NOT operators to modify the expressions in Display filters. To add a logical operator to an expression, select the expression and choose **AND**, **OR**, or **NOT**. The easiest way to organize the structure of the logic tree is to drag expressions and operators around.

TIP

To change a logical operator in a Display filter, click the Operator icon. The icon will change from AND to OR to NOT with each click.

Management: Not Glamorous, but Essential

TCP/IP management is a very complex endeavor and has been the subject of numerous and quite substantial books. This and the previous chapters focus on getting you started, but it is likely that your network management requirements will go beyond the discussion in this book. You should take the time to examine the various SNMP management consoles that are available.

Network Monitor provides you with basic protocol analysis capabilities. You might find that on very busy networks Network Monitor drops frames. This is due to the limitations of the PC hardware and is one reason dedicated protocol analyzers are so expensive; they need high-powered hardware to keep up with the deluge of data. If you can't afford a dedicated protocol analyzer, the best plan is to obtain the Microsoft System Management Server so that you can monitor the entire network from a single, dedicated console. Network Monitor has a better chance to capture network data if the computer on which it is running is not busy with other network tasks.

Chapter 17

ENABLING A SECURE CONNECTION TO THE INTERNET

How you connect your computers to the Internet depends a great deal on what you want your Internet connection to accomplish. The following list presents just a few of the possibilities:

- A few of your users need light-duty access to services on the Internet.

- You want to enable all users on your LAN to connect to Internet services.

- You want to provide an FTP server to enable outside Internet users to send and receive files. Your users need access to files on the FTP server but don't need Internet access.

- You want to set up a Web server that will be used to provide a presence for your company on the Internet.

- All of your users need to access the Internet. You also want to enable outside Internet users to access services offered on your network and to exchange data with your users via email and file transfer.

After you define your organization's requirements, you can begin to answer several questions, such as the following:

- Do you need permanent access to the Internet, or is dial-up (switched) access sufficient?

- Do you need dedicated computers to provide services such as FTP or World Wide Web, or can you provide the required services on nondedicated systems?

- What are the security risks of the type of connection you intend to use, and what precautions should you take?

This chapter addresses these questions about connection methods and security risks.

Connecting to the Internet

You can connect computers to the Internet in two ways: using a switched (dial-up) connection or using a dedicated communication channel. Switched and dedicated connections are suitable to different sets of Internet connection requirements.

Switched Internet Connections

The Windows Remote Access Server (RAS) can be configured to connect to the Internet in several ways:

- **Analog modems.** Dial-up connections using SLIP and PPP protocols at analog modem speeds.

- **ISDN.** High-performance dial-up connections using PPP.

- **X.25.** Packet switching, up to 56Kbps.

Switched connections, as provided by analog modems and ISDN, are best suited to people who need occasional Internet connections. Although configuring a computer to route TCP/IP between a network and the Internet via an analog modem is possible, anyone who uses a modem to connect to the Internet knows that analog connections are quite slow, even when dedicated to servicing a single user. Several users successfully sharing even a 28.8Kbps modem connection with any comfort is a highly unlikely proposition.

A common misconception about analog modems is that data compression is a reliable means of achieving high data rates. Although the majority of modems sold do support data compression, several factors limit the utility of data compression:

- Poor connection quality frequently prevents modems from using their highest data rates. Modems negotiate a data rate when they first connect, based on the fastest speed they can reliably use with the current connection quality. This data rate frequently is less than the theoretical potential of the modems.

- Poor connection quality can prevent attached modems from using data compression.

- Compressed data cannot be further compressed. Many data-intensive tasks involve downloading and uploading files, which are frequently already compressed. For example, the majority of graphic images on Web pages are stored in compressed form. Modems cannot compress this data further, and the effective data rate is limited to the highest noncompressed rate the modems support.

Analog modems, therefore, should generally be regarded as individual connectivity tools.

Another switched communication method is ISDN. The most popular ISDN service provides two 64Kbps "B" channels, which can be aggregated to support 128Kbps data rates. ISDN data rates can support multiple users, but ISDN remains a switched connectivity option. A connection must be established each time access to the Internet is required. ISDN tariffs typically charge for connect time, and the cost of ISDN can escalate quickly if users connect for substantial periods of time.

The one nonswitched option RAS does support is X.25. Although obtaining a dedicated connection to an X.25 network is possible, data rates for X.25 are limited to 64Kbps—sufficient for a few Internet users, but hardly adequate to accommodate dozens of users transferring files or accessing the Web.

Switched connections should be considered dial-out connections only. If you want a permanent presence on the Internet to offer a Web, FTP, or other server, you need a dedicated, permanent connection.

Permanent Internet Connections

A permanent connection to the Internet typically involves leasing a digital, dedicated line between your site and the site that provides your Internet connection. Dedicated lines are available in a wide variety of data rates, from 56Kbps to several megabits per second. The cost of a dedicated line is high, but you cannot avoid the expense if you intend to maintain a permanent presence on the Internet.

Typically, when setting up a permanent Internet connection you will work with an ISP or a telecommunications service provider which designs and installs the circuit and the required termination equipment. Various WAN options are discussed in Chapter 3, "The Network Access Layer." A router at your end of the connection will include an interface to which you connect your local network. The service provider will be responsible for everything from the WAN interface to the Internet, but you will be responsible for your local network. So, you should ensure that you understand the interface device and any management or configuration tasks you must perform at your end. If necessary, work with your service provider to obtain the training and technical support you require to manage your part of the communication link.

Permanent connections to the Internet are inherently risky. The TCP/IP protocols were not designed with security in mind, and many Internet users have the expertise to crack into your network.

Isolating the Server

If your organization merely wants to offer a service to the Internet community without enabling your users to use the same connection to the Internet, limiting your security risk is easy. Figure 17.1 illustrates a configuration that completely isolates local users' computers from the Internet. If someone breaks into your Internet server, access is limited to the server itself.

Consider this scenario, however. Your organization is a magazine publisher. You want to enable your authors to submit articles via ftp, and you want your editors to be able to retrieve articles from the FTP server through your LAN—this isn't possible if users are isolated from the Internet server, as in Figure 17.1. In this figure, the local network is physically isolated from the Internet. The local network is secure, but communication between local and remote environments is not possible.

FIGURE 17.1

An Internet server isolated from the local network.

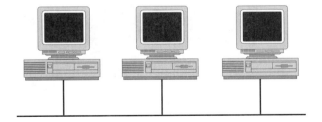

Suppose that you want to enable local users to communicate with the FTP server without enabling users on the Internet to intrude on your local network. Windows supports protocols other than TCP/IP, however, and a possible solution to this problem is to use a different network protocol internally. Figure 17.2 shows an Internet server that connects to the Internet using TCP/IP. The server is connected to the organization's LAN using NWLink (IPX/SPX). Windows NT servers do not route between different protocol stacks, and this approach effectively isolates outside TCP/IP users from inside users connected using NWLink. This protocol isolation approach is very secure, but does not permit local users to access resources on the Internet.

FIGURE 17.2
Isolating local computers using multiple protocols.

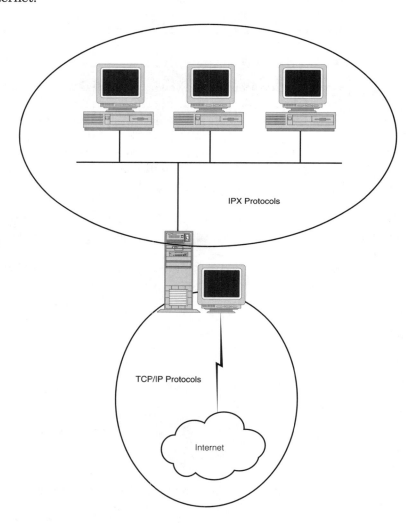

Providing Full Internet Connectivity

Suppose, however, that you want your Internet connection to enable outside users to connect in and inside users to connect out. What is wrong with the network shown in Figure 17.3? If an outsider attempts to violate security, you'll know it, won't you? After all, the intruder can be readily identified because he will be using a nonlocal netid.

FIGURE 17.3

An insecure Internet connection.

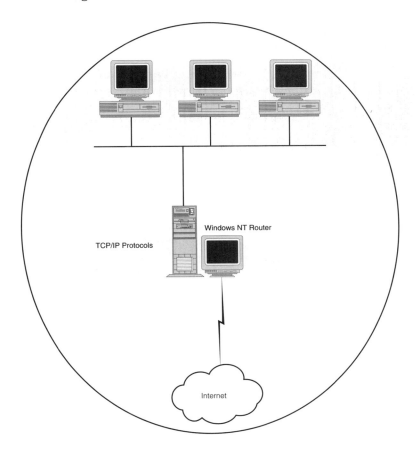

Unfortunately, IP addresses aren't secure. Any reasonably knowledgeable Internet snoop can use a technique known as *IP spoofing* to make his packets appear to have originated on your local network. All the intruder needs to do is listen into your network for awhile, pick up a few usernames and passwords (which FTP transmits in the clear), spoof an IP address, and break in. After he's in, an intruder can gain entry to dozens of TCP/IP systems. If the intruder can "spoof in" using the address of a user logged on to a server, the intruder might be able to impersonate the logged-on user and access files using that user's security permissions.

A basic rule of TCP/IP security is as follows: *Never base security on IP addresses*. Security must always be based on a secure login procedure that authenticates all users who are given access to critical systems.

Another basic rule is to isolate your Internet servers from your LAN clients. And isolation brings us to the subject of firewalls.

A *firewall* is a filter that can be configured to block certain types of network traffic. Traffic can be filtered in various ways:

- Restricting certain protocols

- Permitting inside traffic out, while preventing outside traffic from entering

- Restricting certain types of packets

A firewall is essentially an IP router that has had its routing function replaced by a more secure method of forwarding messages. Some firewalls are specialized pieces of hardware, while other firewalls might consist of software running on a multihomed TCP/IP host.

This is not the place to discuss the details of firewalls, which are quite technical. A look at some options for deploying firewalls, however, is worth taking. Figure 17.4 illustrates a firewall configuration in which one Internet host provides all Internet services *and* runs firewall software. The Internet server/firewall combination is configured to enable inside users to connect out to the Internet. Outside users, however, are not permitted to connect to the LAN. Microsoft Proxy Server is a product with many firewall capabilities; you learn about it in Chapter 21, "Microsoft Proxy Server."

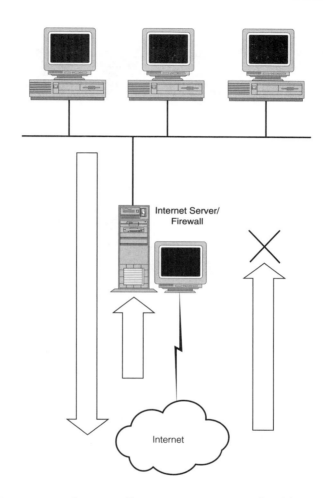

FIGURE 17.4
*A basic
firewall/Internet server
combination.*

If you must configure more than one Internet server, you should avoid the configuration shown in Figure 17.5. No matter how tightly the firewall is configured to restrict outside users from accessing specific hosts, an intruder still could circumvent the firewall and gain access to other LAN-based hosts.

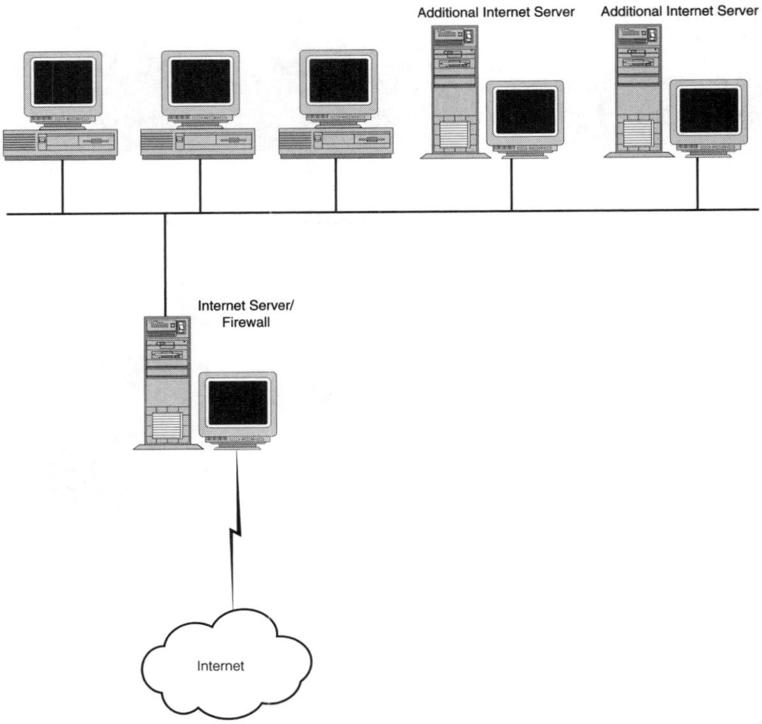

FIGURE 17.5
A firewall configuration that poses potential problems.

Instead, you should isolate the servers on a separate network segment and configure the firewall to route traffic appropriately. Figure 17.6 illustrates such an approach. The firewall permits outside users to access designated servers on one network segment but prevents access to systems on the other segment.

The techniques for cracking into TCP/IP networks are advancing at least as quickly as the techniques for building firewalls, and putting too much faith in the security you implement is unwise. For many, a secure network is merely an inspiration to try harder. For that reason, physical isolation of critical computers remains the one certain way to prevent intrusion.

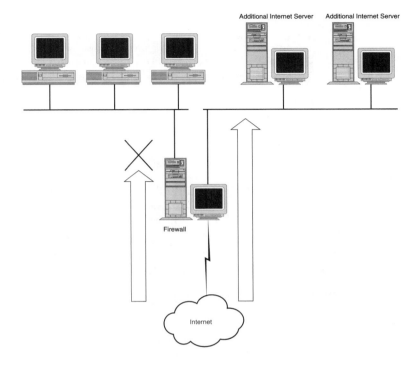

FIGURE 17.6
A more secure firewall configuration.

> ## NOTE
>
> Using the Windows NT router capability to make an Internet connection is possible, but the Windows NT router has limited performance. Nor can the Windows NT router provide any firewall capabilities. In most cases a commercial hardware router, preferably one that possesses firewall capabilities, is the most satisfactory way to connect to the Internet.

Connecting Through Proxy Servers

A *proxy server* offers yet another approach to controlling traffic between your local network and the Internet. A proxy substitutes for local hosts when they are interacting with outside networks, using the following process:

1. A client that needs to access a host examines a table to determine whether the IP address of the host is on the local network or must be accessed remotely.

2. If the IP address is remote, the client directs the request to the proxy server.

3. The proxy server replaces the host's IP address with the IP address of the proxy server. It then routes the request to the remote host.

4. The remote host responds to the request and returns the result to the proxy server.

5. The proxy server replaces the IP address with the IP address of the originating host and forwards the response to the originator.

Figure 17.7 shows how a proxy server isolates local hosts from outside networks. In fact, the only host that is visible to the outside is the proxy server. The anonymity that the proxy server provides for local hosts goes a long way toward reducing the damage an intruder can wreck on your network. In this way, a proxy server serves as a firewall of sorts, restricting the kinds of traffic that can flow between the local and remote networks.

Chapter 21 discusses Microsoft's Proxy Server product.

FIGURE 17.7

Use of a proxy server.

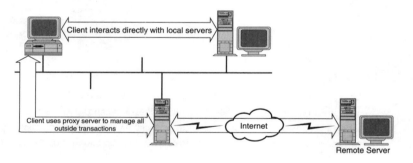

Using RAS to Connect to the Internet

For individuals and small LANs, connecting to a dial-up account using RAS might be an acceptable way to reach the Internet. This section covers installation, configuration, and use of RAS to access the Internet by dialing in to an Internet access provider. This section shows how to install RAS, configure modem connections for the SLIP and PPP protocols, and access the Internet. It also shows you how to configure RAS to enable it to function as a router between LAN users and the Internet.

Two remote access protocols are used with TCP/IP dial-in accounts. SLIP is an older protocol that offers high performance but provides nothing in the way of creature comforts or error checking. PPP is an improved protocol that is more reliable than SLIP and provides some management advantages but operates somewhat more slowly than SLIP. The majority of Internet dial-in accounts are configured to use PPP.

To connect to the Internet, you need the following:

- A SLIP or PPP dial-in account with an Internet access provider. You need the following account information:

  - Access telephone number

  - Username

  - Host name

  - Password

- Unless these IP addresses are assigned dynamically when a connection is made, you need:

  - IP address

  - Subnet mask

  - Default gateway address

  - Primary and backup DNS server IP addresses

- You also need to know if Van Jacobsen (VJ) header compression should be on or off.

Installing and Configuring Dial-Up Networking

Dial-Up Networking is the dial-out component of the remote access service, the service that provides dial-in and dial-out connectivity for Windows NT. In this chapter, you will focus on the capabilities of RAS that enable Windows NT computers to connect with the Internet. You can read about the full range of RAS capabilities in my book *Inside Windows NT Server 4*, published by New Riders.

RAS is configured as a network service. In many ways, installation and configuration procedures resemble the procedures used with a network adapter card, and many of the procedures will be familiar to you from earlier chapters. In this section, you will concentrate on the procedures used to enable RAS to dial in to an Internet access provider and act as an Internet gateway. RAS can also function as a dial-in remote access server and as a general-purpose dial-out client.

NOTE

Before attempting to use Dial-Up Networking, you should install the latest Windows NT 4 Service Pack. Some features do not appear to work without the service pack update. Obtain the service pack from the Microsoft Web site at the following URL:

```
http://www.microsoft.com/ntserversupport
```

Dial-Up Networking installation and configuration has the following stages:

1. Hardware installation

2. Configuration of serial ports

3. Installation of the Dial-Up Networking software

4. Creating a dial-out account

Because hardware installation is highly varied, it won't be addressed here.

Adding Serial Ports

Before you can install modems or X.25, you must install serial ports to support the hardware. (RAS also supports ISDN. Consult the manufacturer's literature if you are installing an ISDN device.) Serial ports are added using the Ports applet in the Control Panel.

Figure 17.8 shows the Ports window. In this example, COM1 is dedicated to the computer's mouse and is not available for configuration. COM2 was present when Windows NT was installed.

FIGURE 17.8

The Control Panel Ports applet.

NOTE

Under the PC architecture, for interrupts 1 though 8, lower-number interrupts have the highest priority. COM2, typically serviced by interrupt 3, has a higher priority than COM1, which is ordinarily serviced by interrupt 4. Consequently, for the best performance, a modem should be connected to COM2 whenever possible.

To add a serial port, click **Add** to open a dialog box in which you enter the following information:

- **COM Port Number**
- **Base I/O Port Address**
- **Interrupt Request Line (IRQ)**
- **FIFO Enabled**

To change the settings for a port, select the port and click **Settings**. From the Settings dialog box, you can configure the following settings:

- **Baud Rate**
- **Data Bits**
- **Parity**
- **Stop Bits**
- **Flow Control**

You can click the **Advanced** button in the Settings dialog box to reconfigure the port number, port address, interrupt request line, and FIFO-enabled settings for the port.

After one or more serial ports are available, you can install modems on the ports.

Installing Modems

Before installing Dial-Up Networking, you should configure at least one communications device (although devices can also be configured during the installation of Dial-Up Networking). Modems are installed using the Modem utility on the Control Panel as follows:

1. Open the Modem applet in the Control Panel.

2. If no modem is installed, the Install New Modem Wizard is invoked automatically.

3. Windows NT is adept at detecting modem hardware. In the majority of cases, you should *not* check Don't detect my modem; I will select it from a list.

4. Choose **Next**. The Wizard will scan your COM ports and attempt to identify a modem. The modem might not be identified by brand. A standard Hayes compatible modem is identified as a Standard Modem.

NOTE

Even though your modem might qualify as a generic Standard Modem, you should attempt whenever possible to purchase modems that are on the approved equipment list for Windows NT. Subtle differences between modems might make nonapproved modems interact poorly with RAS. In any case, if you have a problem with RAS and call Microsoft for support, they won't be very willing to assist if your modem isn't approved.

5. If you don't like the modem choice, choose **Change.** You can then select a specific make and model.

6. Choose **Next** when you are satisfied with the modem choice.

7. When you are informed Your modem has been set up successfully, choose **Finish**.

If at least one modem has been installed, the Modem applet looks like Figure 17.9. You can use this window to add, remove, and change the properties of modems. Choosing **Add** starts the Install New Modem Wizard.

FIGURE 17.9
*The Modem applet
after a modem has
been installed.*

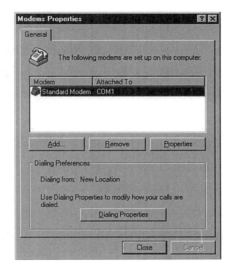

To change the properties of a modem, select the modem in the Modem applet and choose **Properties.** The modem Properties dialog box has two tabs that enable you to configure the modem.

The General properties tab has three settings:

- **Port.** Describes the COM port to which the modem is connected.

- **Speaker volume.** Determines the loudness of the modem speaker.

- **Maximum speed.** Specifies the maximum speed at which software should attempt to operate the modem.

The Connection properties tab enables you to configure the following modem properties:

- **Data bits**. Specifies the size of the data character to be used, with 8 bits being the most common and the default setting.

- **Parity**. Specifies the type of parity to be used. The most common, and the default, setting is None.

- **Stop bits**. Specifies the stop bits to be sent after a data character is sent. 1 is the most common setting and is the default.

- **Wait for dial tone before dialing**. When checked (the default), the modem will not commence dialing until a dial tone is detected.

- **Cancel the call if not connected within ... Secs**. Check this option if calls should time out if a specified number of seconds elapse before a call is connected, and specify a time in seconds.

- **Disconnect a call if idle for more than ... mins.** Check this option if connections should be terminated if no traffic is generated within a specified period of time, and specify a time in minutes.

The Advanced button on the Connection tab opens a dialog box in which several advanced properties can be configured:

- **Use error control**. Check this box if error control protocols will be in use. If error control is enabled, select one or more of the following error control protocols:

  - **Required to connect**. If this option is checked, error control should be used. Modems at either end of the connection must agree on an error control protocol. If this option is not checked, connections can be established without error control in effect.

  - **Compress data**. Checking this option enables modems to compress data. The modems must be able to communicate using a common data compression protocol.

  - **Use cellular protocol**. Check this option if the modem will communicate through a cellular telephone link.

- **Use flow control**. Check this option if flow control will be used to regulate data transfer between the modems. Select one of the following flow control methods:

  - **Hardware (RTS/CTS)**. Hardware flow control uses wires in the serial interface cable to signal when the modem is ready to receive data. Hardware flow control is more efficient than software flow control because extra traffic is not generated.

  - **Software (XON/XOFF)**. Software flow control consists of sending special XON and XOFF characters to start and stop data transmission. Software flow control is generally used only when hardware flow control is not supported.

- **Modulation type**. Under some circumstances, this field is used to configure nonstandard modulating techniques.

- **Extra settings**. This field accepts setup codes in addition to the codes specified by the modem's standard settings.

■ **Record a log file**. Check this field to log events related to this modem. The log file can be useful for troubleshooting communication problems.

Installing Dial-Up Networking

RAS and Dial-Up Networking are closely related and are installed together. If you have installed RAS, Dial-Up Networking is already installed. In this section, you will see one procedure for installing Dial-Up Networking.

The icon for Dial-Up Networking is installed in the My Computer window. If Dial-Up Networking has not been used, the first time you use it a message box prompts you, `Dial-Up Networking is currently uninstalled. Press 'Install' to install and configure.` Click **Install** to start a wizard that takes you through the installation process as follows:

1. First the required files are copied from the installation disk.

2. If no RAS hardware (a modem or other communications device) has been installed, you will see the message `There are no RAS capable devices to add. Do you want RAS setup to invoke the Modem installer to enable you to add a modem?` If you respond **Yes** to the prompt, the Install New Modem Wizard supervises the installation of a new modem. This wizard was examined in the preceding section "Installing Modems."

3. Next, the Location Information dialog box prompts you for the following:

   ■ **What country are you in now?** If you are not in the United States of America, pull down the list and select your country.

   ■ **What area (or city) code are you in now?** Enter the appropriate area or city code.

   ■ **If you dial a number to access an outside line, what is it?** If you dial out through a private telephone system, enter the number required to obtain an outside line.

   ■ **Tone dialing or Pulse dialing**. Select the appropriate dialing mode.

   Choose **Next** to continue.

4. Next, you will be shown the Add RAS Device dialog box, shown in Figure 17.10. Review the current configurations by pulling down the **RAS Capable Devices** list. In this dialog box, you have the following options:

- **Install Modem**. Click this button to add a modem to the configuration by starting the Install New Modem Wizard.

- **Install X.25 Pad**. Click this button to add an X.25 packet assembler-disassembler.

FIGURE 17.10

Adding an RAS device.

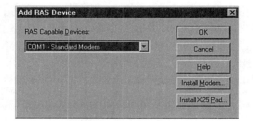

5. Choose **OK** when the RAS capable devices have been configured.

6. The next dialog box is the Remote Access Setup dialog box, shown in Figure 17.11. This dialog box is used to add ports and devices to the RAS configuration and can be used to configure any ports that have been previously installed.

FIGURE 17.11

The Remote Access Setup dialog box.

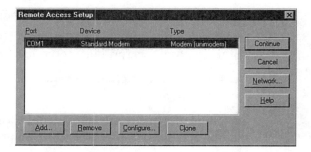

7. Select a port and choose **Configure** to open the Configure Port Usage dialog box. Each port can be configured for one of the following usages:

- **Dial out only**

- **Receive calls only**

- **Dial out and Receive calls**

If you are configuring the port for RAS to use as an Internet router, the most appropriate setting is **Dial out only.**

Choose **OK** when the port is configured.

8. Next, you must select the protocols that will be supported by RAS. In the Remote Access Setup dialog box, choose **Network** to open the Network Configuration dialog box. The dialog box you see depends on your selections instep 7:

   ■ If you selected **Dial out only** you will see the dialog box shown in Figure 17.12.

   ■ If you selected **Receive calls only**, you will see the dialog box shown in Figure 17.13, but the entries in the **Dial Out Properties** box will be deactivated.

   ■ If you selected **Dial out and Receive calls**, you will see the dialog box shown in Figure 17.13 with all options active.

9. In the **Dial out Protocols** box, check the protocols that should be available when dialing out to a dial-in server. Although you can check protocols that are not supported by the dial-in server, it is preferable to check only the protocols that are required.

10. In the Server Settings box, complete the dialog box as follows:

   ■ **Allow remote clients running**. Check the protocols that this server will support. When you check a protocol, the corresponding Configure button is activated. These buttons are used to configure protocol-specific settings.

   ■ **Encryption settings**. The radio buttons under this heading offer four choices:

      ■ **Allow any authentication including clear text**. This choice allows the broadest range of encryption options, including clear text. This setting is useful with clients that do not support logon data encryption.

      ■ **Require encrypted authentication**. This option enables a wide variety of clients to connect using MS-CHAP, MD5-CHAP, and SPAP encryption.

      ■ **Require Microsoft encrypted authentication**. This option requires clients to support MS-CHAP, the most secure authentication supported by RAS. If this option is selected and you check **Require data encryption**, all data transferred between the client and the server are encrypted using the RSA Data Security Incorporated RC4 algorithm.

■ **Enable Multilink**. If this option is checked, RAS can aggregate multiple physical links into a logical bundle. Bundling is a common technique used with ISDN links.

Choose **OK** to return to the Remote Access Setup dialog box.

Note

CHAP, *Challenge Handshake Authentication Protocol,* adds considerable security to the RAS session. When a connection is being established, the CHAP server sends a random challenge to the client. The challenge is used to encrypt the user's password, which is returned to the server. This has two advantages: The password is encrypted in transit, and an eavesdropper cannot forge the authentication and play it back to the server at a later time because the challenge is different for each call.

MS-CHAP is the most secure protocol supported by RAS. MS-CHAP, also known as RSA Message Digest 4 (MD4), uses the RC4 algorithm to encrypt all user data during the RAS session.

PAP, the *Password Authentication Protocol*, is a clear-text authentication protocol that is associated with PPP. PAP authentication should be used only when dialing in to servers that do not support authentication, such as SLIP and PPP servers.

SPAP, the *Shiva Password Authentication Protocol*, is supported on the RAS server only and is an implementation of PAP on Shiva remote client software.

Figure 17.12
Selecting protocols for port that supports dial-out only.

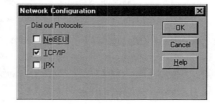

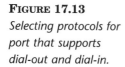

FIGURE 17.13
Selecting protocols for port that supports dial-out and dial-in.

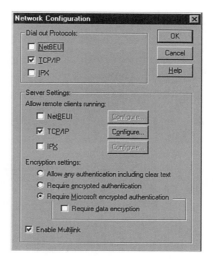

11. If you are configuring a server to support TCP/IP, choose **Configure** to open the RAS Server TCP/IP Configuration dialog box shown in Figure 17.14. Complete this dialog box as follows:

   ■ **Entire network**. If this button is selected, dial-in clients use this server as a router that enables the client to access the entire network.

   ■ **This computer only**. If this button is selected, dial-in clients can access only those resources that reside on the RAS server. This obviously has fewer security risks than allowing dial-in users to access the entire network.

   ■ **Use DHCP to assign remote TCP/IP client addresses**. If the Dynamic Host Configuration Protocol (DHCP) is running on your network, this is the most satisfactory approach because no further address configuration is required.

   ■ **Use static address pool**. When this option is selected, you can specify a range of addresses from which addresses will be assigned for dial-in users. You will need to specify the address range in the **Begin** and **End** fields.

   ■ **Excluded ranges**. If a static address pool is being used, you can exclude ranges of addresses in the pool so that they will not be assigned to clients. Specify the ranges in the **From** and **To** fields and use the **Add** button to add the range to the E**x**cluded ranges list.

- **A**l**low remote clients to request a predetermined IP address.** In rare instances, it might be desirable to permit the client to specify the IP address. Check this button if that behavior is permitted.

Choose **OK** to exit the dialog box when the desired settings have been entered.

Figure 17.14
RAS server TCP/IP configuration.

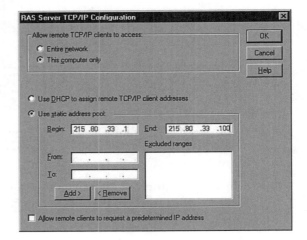

12. Exit the TCP/IP Network Configuration dialog box when the required settings have been established.

13. In the Remote Access Setup dialog box, choose **Continue** when all ports have been configured. The settings will be checked and the RAS bindings will be established.

14. Restart the computer to activate the RAS settings.

NOTE

You can reconfigure any RAS settings through the Network applet. Select **Remote Access Server** in the Services tab. Then choose **Properties** to open the configuration dialog boxes.

Managing the Remote Access Server

When RAS is installed, two new programs are installed:

- **Dial-Up Monitor**. This utility echoes status lights for several of the modems' most critical lines. It is especially useful with internal modems. The icon is installed in the Control Panel.

- **Remote Access Admin**. This utility is used to configure an RAS server. You can also use it to start the RAS server. It is located in the Administrative Tools submenu of the Start menu.

This section examines the tasks required to manage the RAS server after it is installed.

Configuring RAS User Accounts

Before users can use an RAS server, you must use Remote Access Admin to set up user permissions. Figure 17.15 shows the main window for Remote Access Admin. The window displays the status of each RAS communication channel and is used to access RAS administration functions.

FIGURE 17.15

The main window for Remote Access Admin.

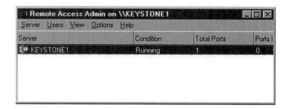

To administer RAS user permissions, choose the **Permissions** command in the Users menu to open the Remote Access Permissions dialog box shown in Figure 17.16. In this dialog box, you administer remote access permissions for individuals or for all network users.

FIGURE 17.16
Granting remote
access permissions.

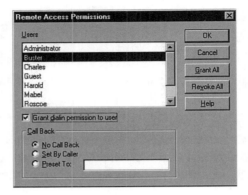

To revoke RAS permissions from all users, choose **Revoke All.**

To grant permissions to an individual user, select the user account name in the Users box. Then set the permissions that apply to that user.

Check the **Grant dialin permission to user** box to grant RAS dial-in access to the selected user.

Three options are available in the Call Back box:

- **No Call Back**. This option enables users to call in and connect with the network on the same call.

- **Set By Caller**. With this option, the caller will be asked to enter a telephone number. RAS will disconnect, call the user at the number specified, and connect the user to the network.

- **Preset To**. This option requires you to specify a number that RAS will use to connect the user. Using a specified number enhances security because a user must have physical access to a particular telephone to enter a remote session.

After making the required settings, choose **OK.**

WARNING

Because the Guest account does not ordinarily have a password, you should avoid giving this account dial-in permissions. If you intend to grant guests dial-in access, either strictly restrict permissions assigned to this account or assign a password.

Starting and Stopping the Server

The Server menu in the Remote Access Admin has four options for starting, stopping, and pausing the RAS server:

- **Start Remote Access Service.** Starts the remote access server service.

- **Stop Remote Access Service.** Stops the remote access server service.

- **Pause Remote Access Service.** Prevents users from accessing the service but leaves it enabled for administrators and server operators.

- **Continue Remote Access Service.** Changes the status of the service from Paused to Started.

These same actions can be performed using the Services applet in the Control Panel. When RAS is installed, the remote access service is configured to start automatically when Windows NT is started.

Monitoring the RAS Server

To monitor RAS server activity, open RAS Server Admin and choose the **Communication Ports** command in the Server menu. This command is available only when the RAS server has been started.

The Communication Ports dialog box shown in Figure 17.17 indicates session information for each connected port, including the user and when the session started. You can also use this dialog box to disconnect users and to send messages to individual users or to all users.

FIGURE 17.17

Monitoring RAS server port status.

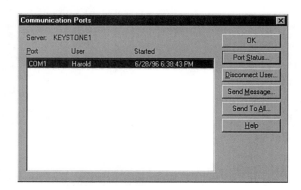

Dialing Out with Dial-Up Networking

Dial-Up Networking can dial out to an Internet access provider using either the Point-to-Point (PPP) or the Serial Line Interface Protocol (SLIP). SLIP is an older, very simple protocol that performs well but provides few amenities. PPP is a more recent protocol that provides more reliable communication and a number of options that automate session configuration and login. As a result of the advantages of PPP, it is the preferred protocol for the majority of Internet access providers.

RAS dial-out has changed dramatically in Windows NT version 4, using the Telephony Services and Dial-Up Networking features that were introduced with Windows 95. Configuration of both these features is covered in this section.

Configuring Telephony Services

Telephony Services are optional but very useful. Use them to establish contexts for dialing out from various locations. To manage your dialing locations:

1. Open the Telephony applet in the Control Panel, shown in Figure 17.18.

FIGURE 17.18

Adding a location to Telephony Services.

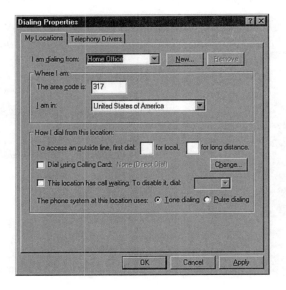

2. In the **I am dialing from** field, enter a name for a new location or choose an existing location to be modified.

3. In the **The area code is** field, enter the local area code. An area code will not be added to phone numbers of calls placed in this area code.

4. In the **I am in** field, select the country for this location.

5. In the **To access an outside line, 1st dial: ... for local, ... for long dist**. fields, enter any dialing prefixes that are required to obtain a local and a long-distance outside line.

6. If your long-distance charges are to go on a calling card, check **Dial using Calling Card** to open the Charge Calling Card dialog box. Select the service in the **Calling Card to use** field and enter your PIN in the **Calling Card number** field. Choose **OK** to save the entry.

7. If your location has call waiting, disable the feature by checking **This location has call waiting. To disable it, dial**. Then enter the code to disable call waiting in the field provided.

8. Specify the dialing mode by selecting **Tone dialing** or **Pulse dialing**.

9. Choose **Apply** to save the entry. Then choose **OK** to exit.

Adding Phonebook Entries to Dial-Up Networking

The Dial-Up Networking Application is used to manage your dial-up configurations and to connect to remote locations. After you learn how to manage phonebook entries, you are ready to dial out to RAS and other servers.

The first time you start Dial-Up Networking, you see the message `The phonebook is empty. Press OK to add an entry`. When you choose **OK**, you are shown the New Phonebook Entry Wizard. You need to configure at least one phonebook entry to use Dial-Up Networking. The following information is required by the wizard:

- A name for the new phonebook entry

- Whether you are calling the Internet

- Whether it is okay to send your password in plaintext if requested by the server

- If you are calling a non-Windows NT server, whether the server expects you to enter login information after connecting

- The phone number (and alternate phone numbers if available)

- Whether the phonebook entry will use telephony dialing properties.

When the phonebook entry is completed, it will resemble Figure 17.19.

FIGURE 17.19

A completed phone-book entry.

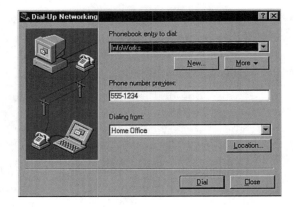

To edit a phonebook entry, choose **More** and select **Edit** from the menu that is displayed to open the Edit Phonebook Entry dialog box shown in Figure 17.20. This dialog box has five tabs. Only the tabs relevant to this chapter will be examined.

FIGURE 17.20

Basic properties of a phonebook entry.

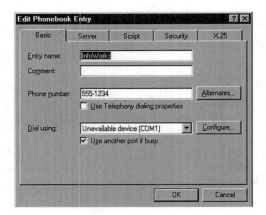

Basic Dialing Properties

The Basic tab, shown in Figure 17.20, defines the basic dial-out configuration. If you want to use settings established in your Telephony configuration, check **Use Telephony dialing properties.** The entries in this tab should require no explanation.

Choose **Configure** to open a dialog box in which the following check boxes are available.

- **Initial speed (bps).** Enter the highest speed supported by your modem. Modems will negotiate down from that speed when a connection is established.

- **Enable hardware flow control.** Typically hardware flow control should be enabled.

- **Enable modem error control.** Modem error control can be used if modems at both ends support the same error control protocol.

- **Enable modem compression.** In most cases, software compression performs better and modem compression should be disabled.

- **Disable modem speaker.** If you don't want to hear the beeps, disable the speaker. In most cases, you will want to enable the speaker during early testing phases, but might want to disable it after things are running smoothly.

Server Protocol Properties

The Server tab (see Figure 17.21) defines the protocols that will be used to communicate with the server. Options in this tab are as follows:

- **Dial-up server type.** In this field you have three choices:

  - **PPP: Windows NT, Windows 95 Plus, Internet.** The Point-to-Point Protocol (PPP) is the most commonly used protocol for TCP/IP dial-up services. This is the default and the best all-around choice. PPP can be used with all supported protocols.

  - **SLIP: Internet.** The Serial-Line Internet Protocol (SLIP) is an older Internet protocol that is losing popularity. SLIP is less reliable and has fewer features than PPP, but is more efficient and provides somewhat better performance. When SLIP is selected, only TCP/IP is available as a protocol option.

■ **Windows NT 3.1, Windows for Workgroups 3.11.** This option selects an older RAS protocol that is not usable on the Internet.

■ **Network protocols.** You must check **TCP/IP** in this box to enable TCP/IP support.

■ **Enable software compression.** This option is checked by default and configures the communication software to compress and decompress communications data. It is unproductive and unnecessary to enable both hardware (modem) and software (protocol) compression. Typically, software compression is more efficient, particularly on higher-end computers. Software compression is not supported by the SLIP protocol.

■ **Enable PPP LCP extensions.** LCP is a component of newer PPP implementations but is not supported by older PPP servers. Try deselecting this box if problems occur when using PPP.

FIGURE 17.21
Configuring RAS server protocols.

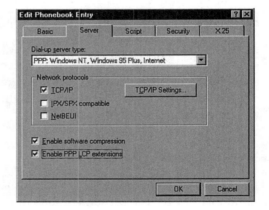

After **TCP/IP** has been checked, the TCP/IP Settings button can be used to access the TCP/IP Settings dialog box. The contents of the dialog box depend on whether you have selected PPP or SLIP. Figure 17.22 shows the PPP TCP/IP Settings dialog box, which has the following options:

■ **Server assigned IP address.** Check this option if the PPP dial-in server will assign an IP address to you. This is the most common situation.

■ **Specify an IP address.** Select this option and specify an IP address in the IP address field if the PPP server does not assign an IP address.

- **Server assigned name server addresses.** Select this option if the PPP dial-in server adds the address of a DNS server to your configuration when you dial in. This is less commonly done than automatic IP address assignment.

- **Specify name server addresses.** Select this option to manually specify the IP addresses of DNS and WINS name servers.

- **Use IP header compression.** Header compression—also known as Van Jacobson IP header compression, or VJ header compression—is almost always used to reduce the amount of traffic. Check with the manager of the dial-in server to determine if header compression is used.

- **Use default gateway on remote network.** This option applies to computers that are connected to local networks at the same time they are dialing remotely. When this option is checked, packets that cannot be routed to the local network are routed to the default gateway on the remote network.

FIGURE 17.22
TCP/IP protocol configuration options for PPP.

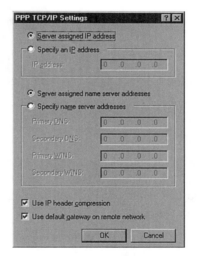

Figure 17.23 shows the SLIP TCP/IP Settings dialog box. When connecting to an Internet access provider, you must complete the following fields:

- **IP address.** SLIP cannot supply an IP address.

- **Primary DNS.** SLIP cannot supply a DNS server address. Optionally, you can supply a secondary DNS server address.

- **Force IP header compression.** Check this option if the SLIP server uses header compression.

- **Use default gateway on remote network.** This option applies to computers that are connected to a local network at the same time they are dialing remotely. When this option is checked, packets that cannot be routed to the local network are routed to the default gateway on the remote network.

- **Frame size.** This value determines the size of frames that will be used. Adjust this value if required for the SLIP server. Frame sizes of 1006 and 1700 can be selected.

FIGURE 17.23

TCP/IP protocol configuration options for SLIP.

Script Properties

Figure 17.24 shows the Script tab. *Scripts* are text files that contain commands that automate dial-in events such as logon. The details of scripts are beyond the scope of this book and are discussed in the Windows NT Server documentation.

Scripts are typically unnecessary when dialing in to PPP servers. PPP includes the Password Authentication Protocol (PAP), which automates the acceptance of user IDs and passwords. Because no automation is available for SLIP, however, scripts might be of benefit.

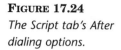

FIGURE 17.24

The Script tab's After dialing options.

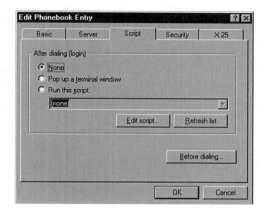

The Script tab provides options for scripts to be executed after dialing. The options are:

- **None.** No script will be executed. This is the default and will work with most PPP servers.

- **Pop up a terminal window.** If this option is selected, a terminal window will be opened when a connection is established. The terminal will be used to accept the user's password and other required logon information.

- **Run this script.** If this option is selected, enter the path name for a script file. You can choose **Edit scripts** to create and modify script files.

You can also specify scripting to take place before dialing. Choose **Before dialing** to open the Before Dialing Script dialog box, which is practically identical to the After dialing box shown in Figure 17.24.

Security Properties

The Security tab, shown in Figure 17.25, determines the types of encryption that will be used. The option chosen must match the requirements of the server. These choices were discussed in the section about RAS server configuration. Refer to the discussion accompanying Figure 17.11.

If you select **Accept only Microsoft encrypted authentication**, you can check **Use current username and password.** Checking this box instructs Dial-Up Networking to automatically use your Windows NT username and password when dialing out.

FIGURE 17.25

The Security Tab.

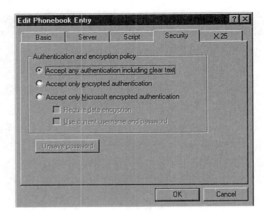

X.25 Properties

If you are connecting to an X.25 network, select the X.25 tab, shown in Figure 17.26. Entries on this tab are as follows:

- **Network.** Select the name of the X.25 network you are calling.

- **Address.** Specify the X.25 address supplied by the X.25 network provider.

- **User Data.** Enter additional connection data supplied by the X.25 network provider. This field might be left blank.

- **Facilities.** Enter parameters to request facilities from your X.25 provider. Consult the provider for appropriate parameters. This field is optional.

FIGURE 17.26

The X.25 tab.

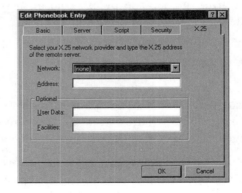

Unfortunately, X.25 configuration can be quite involved and is beyond the scope of this book. When obtaining an X.25 connection, consult with your service provider for the appropriate setup procedures.

Dialing with a Phonebook Entry

After you have entered a phonebook entry, choose OK in the New Phonebook Entry window to open the Dial-Up Networking window, shown in Figure 17.19. The events that take place when dialing depend on two factors:

■ Whether the host is an RAS server or a TCP/IP network.

■ Whether the host is configured for dial-back operation.

Here is the sequence of events that take place when you use Dial-Up Networking to call an RAS server:

1. Select a phonebook entry in the Phonebook entry to dial field.

2. Verify the entry in the Dialing from field. You can select another location by choosing **Location.** New locations must be entered using the Telephony utility in the Control Panel.

3. Verify the number in the Phone number preview field. If the number is not complete and correct, check the configuration for the location.

Choose **Dial** to open the Connect to InfoWorks dialog box (Figure 17.27).

FIGURE 17.27

Entering connection information for a dial-out connection.

5. Complete the fields in the Connect to InfoWorks dialog box as follows:

   ■ **User name.** Enter your username on the destination network. This field and the **Password** field will be completed with your Windows network username if you checked **Use current username and password** in the Security tab when configuring this phonebook entry.

   ■ **Password.** Enter your password on the destination network.

   ■ **Domain.** If you are dialing to a RAS server, enter the domain you want to log on to. If you are dialing a non-RAS server, clear this field.

   ■ **Save password.** Check this field if you want to have your password saved with the phonebook entry. This can be hazardous. Saving your password enables any user who has access to your computer to dial your remote account without entering a password.

   Choose **OK** when you have configured the Connect dialog box.

6. The client dials and enters a conversation with the RAS server.

7. The RAS server sends a challenge to the client.

8. The client sends an encrypted response.

9. The server checks the response against its database.

10. If the response is valid, the server checks for remote access permissions.

11. If callback is enabled, the server disconnects, calls the client, and completes steps 6 through 10 again.

12. Next, a message box informs you that the connection is complete. At this point, you can specify two actions that will take place when you make future connections:

    ■ **Close on dial.** If this box is checked, the Dial-Up Network application will be closed when a connection is established.

    ■ **Do not display this message again.** If this box is checked, you will not see this message in the future when a connection is completed.

13. When the session is complete, choose the **Hang Up** button in the Dial-Up Networking application. You will need to reopen the application if you checked **Close on dial** in step 12.

You are now connected. The connection mimics a direct network connection, and you can use any applications that are appropriate to the environment. For example, you can use Windows NT applications to access files on a remote RAS server. Or you can use Winsock-compatible applications to access remote TCP/IP services such as those on the Internet.

More Options in the Dial-Up Networking Application

If you click the **More** button in the Dial-Up Networking application, a menu opens with the following options:

- **Edit entry and modem properties.** Choose this option to use the phonebook editor to modify a phonebook entry.

- **Clone entry and modem properties.** Use this option as a shortcut for creating a new phonebook entry that has settings similar to an existing entry.

- **Delete entry.** Use this option to remove the entry shown in the Phonebook entry to dial field.

- **Create shortcut to entry.** This option opens a dialog box you can use to create a shortcut. To place the shortcut on your desktop, store it in C:\Winnt\Profiles*username*\Desktop\Start Menu\Programs*folder* where *username* is your Windows NT username and *folder* is the submenu that should contain the shortcut.

- **Monitor status.** This option opens the Dial-Up Networking Monitor dialog box shown in Figure 17.28. This utility, which can also be started from the Control Panel, displays a variety of information about the dial-up session and enables you to configure certain options. In the Preferences tab, you can determine whether status lights will be displayed as a Taskbar icon or as a window on the desktop.

- **Operator assisted or manual dialing.** Use this option if the phone number must be entered manually or by an operator.

- **Logon preferences.** This option opens the Logon preferences utility shown in Figure 17.29. Use this utility to configure a variety of options that affect the dial-up process. Of particular interest is the Callback tab shown in the figure. Use this tab to enable callback operation.

FIGURE 17.28

*The Dial-Up
Networking Monitor.*

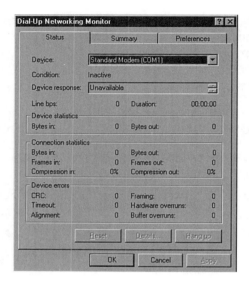

FIGURE 17.29

*The Logon Preferences
utility.*

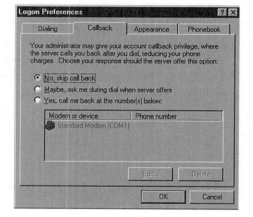

Using Automatic Dialing

With Windows NT 4, an automatic dialing feature has been added to Dial-Up Networking. When a connection is established, automatic dialing associates a network address with a phonebook entry. AutoDial also learns about every connection that is established over an RAS link.

If you are not connected to a dial-up network, whenever the address is referenced, RAS will automatically be invoked and will attempt to connect using the appropriate phonebook entry.

Under certain circumstances, you might want to disable the AutoDial feature. To do so:

1. Choose **More** in the Dial-Up Networking dialog box and select the Logon Preferences option in the menu.

2. Select the **Appearances** tab.

3. Deselect the entry **Always prompt before auto-dialing.**

Using RAS as an Internet Router

After RAS has been configured and tested, you can configure RAS as a router that enables other users on your network to access the Internet. Performance is limited by the slow bit rates supported by analog modems, but routing through RAS is one possible way to connect multiple users to the Internet.

To configure RAS as an Internet router, you need the following:

- A PPP connection to the Internet.

- An Internet class C network address or a valid IP subnet and subnet mask, assigned by your Internet access provider.

- A domain name and name server if you want to have your local computers identified through DNS.

- A Windows NT computer configured with a high-speed modem and serial card.

WARNING

You cannot perform this procedure if your Internet service provider (ISP) uses Windows NT computers to provide dial-in connections.

Figure 17.30 illustrates a Windows network that uses RAS to route traffic to the Internet. To configure a network with an RAS Internet router:

1. Configure your local TCP/IP hosts with IP addresses that have been assigned to your site. The RAS gateway connects your local network to the Internet through a router, and it is essential that your network be configured with legitimate Internet addresses.

2. Configure the default gateway for all TCP/IP computers to the IP address that matches the LAN adapter card in the RAS server.

3. On the RAS server, use `regedt32` to add a value to the Registry in the following key:

```
\HKEY_LOCAL_MACHINE
    \System
        \CurrentControlSet
            \Services
                \RasArp
                    \Parameters
```

The value to add is:

- Name: DisableOtherSrcPackets

- Data Type: REG_DWORD

- Value: `0`

This value ensures that packets routed through the RAS server retain the IP addresses of the clients that originated the packets.

4. In the Network applet, examine the TCP/IP properties to ensure that routing is enabled.

5. Obtain the IP address of your Internet default router from your ISP. Add a static route to the RAS gateway's routing table that defines the router as a default gateway for the RAS server. See Chapter 9, "Routing Basics" for instructions on using the `route` command to add a static route. The command will resemble the following:

```
route -p add 0.0.0.0 mask 0.0.0.0 ipaddress
```

Establish a phonebook entry on the gateway RAS server for your ISP. When you connect with this phonebook entry, the RAS server is established as an Internet gateway.

FIGURE 17.30

*Using RAS as an
Internet router.*

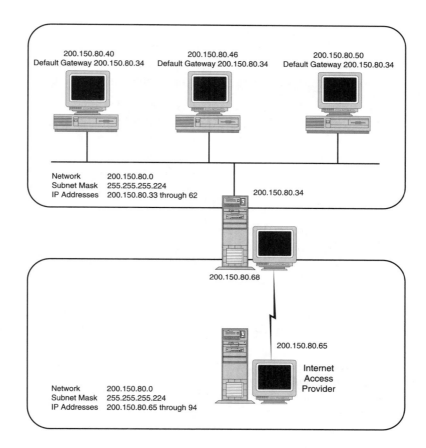

FIGURE 17.30

*Using RAS as an
Internet router.*

Using the Point-to-Point Tunneling Protocol

Using RAS, you can construct a dial-in server that enables clients to access your network from anyplace in the world. RAS works well and provides a high level of security. What more could you want?

Lower cost, for one thing. If you have dozens of users calling in via RAS, you can run up a lot of long-distance charges. If your network is connected to the Internet, you might begin to wonder whether your users could connect to your network by dialing into the Internet. They would be making a local call to an ISP, and their traffic would be routed to your RAS server for free through the global Internet. Nice and cheap!

Unfortunately, the Internet is not a very secure place. The majority of traffic is unencrypted and is vulnerable to eavesdropping. Sensitive communication should always be secured when it passes through the public Internet, but until recently, RAS has not had that capability.

The Point-to-Point Tunneling Protocol (PPTP) is a new feature in Windows NT version 4. PPTP uses *tunneling* to enable packets for one protocol to be carried over networks running another protocol. For example, NWLink packets can be encapsulated inside IP packets, enabling the IPX packets to be transported through the TCP/IP world of the Internet. PPTP has the added benefit of enhancing security, because it works hand-in-hand with the encryption capability of RAS.

Let's look at two scenarios for using PPTP. In Figure 17.31, both the RAS client and the RAS server are directly connected to the Internet. A PPTP tunnel between the client and the server establishes a secure communication channel between them. The use of PPTP enables the client and server to connect via the Internet, without a need for the client to dial in to RAS through a switched connection. While communicating, RAS encrypts traffic between the client and server, providing a secure communications data stream.

FIGURE 17.31

Client and server can communicate through the Internet using PPTP.

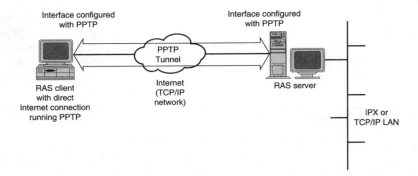

A slightly more elaborate example is shown in Figure 17.32. The RAS server is connected to a LAN running NWlink. By establishing a PPTP tunnel through the Internet, the client can connect with the NWLink network even though it is communicating through the TCP/IP Internet. This is accomplished by loading the NWLink protocols on the client together with PPTP. The client dials in to the Internet and opens a PPTP tunnel with the RAS server. From that point, the NWLink packets are encapsulated in PPP packets for transfer through the Internet. The RAS server decapsulates the PPP packets to recover the NWLink messages, which are forwarded to the LAN.

FIGURE 17.32

A dial-up client can communicate with an NWLink or TCP/IP LAN through the Internet using PPTP.

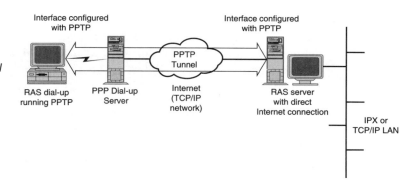

Microsoft refers to PPTP tunnels as *virtual private networks* (VPNs) because they establish a logical private network that runs over the public network infrastructure.

PPTP configuration is not difficult. The following sections show how to configure PPTP support on the RAS server and client.

Configuring PPTP

PPTP must be enabled for each RAS server or client that will use PPTP. To enable PPTP:

1. Using the Network applet in the Control Panel, install the Point-to-Point Tunneling Protocol in the Protocols tab.

2. After the protocol is copied from the installation disks, the PPTP Configuration dialog box is displayed (see Figure 17.33). The Number of Virtual Private Networks specifies the number of PPTP connections that will be supported. In the example, two VPNs will be established.

FIGURE 17.33

Specifying the number of connections PPTP will support.

3. Next, the RAS setup utility is started. Here, you will add the virtual ports that support the Virtual Private Networks you want to establish.

4. Choose **Add** to open the Add RAS Device dialog box shown in Figure 17.34. In the example, I have opened the RAS Capable Devices list to show you the two virtual ports that correspond to the two VPNs that were specified in step 2. Select an entry (for example VPN1 - RASPPTPM) and choose **OK**.

5. In the Remote Access Setup dialog box, select each new entry and choose **Configure** to open the Configure Port Usage. Select one of the following options to define how the port will be used: **Dial out only**, **Receive calls only**, or **Dial out and Receive Calls.**

For a PPTP client, at least one VPN port must be configured to permit dial-out.

For a PPTP server, at least one VPN port must be configured to permit receiving calls.

FIGURE 17.34

Adding VPN virtual devices.

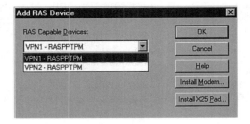

6. Repeat steps 4 and 5 for each VPN virtual device you want to add. Figure 17.35 shows Remote Access Setup after both VPNs have been added.

FIGURE 17.35

Remote Access Setup after VPN devices have been added.

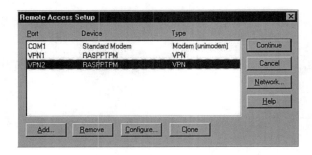

7. When all virtual devices have been added, choose **Continue.**

8. When you return to the Protocols tab, choose **Close.**

9. Restart the computer.

Enabling PPTP Filtering

After PPTP is installed, the RAS server will support both PPTP and non-PPTP connections, a potential security hole. If you want, you can enable PPTP filtering, disabling support for any traffic except PPTP.

To enable PPTP filtering:

1. Select the **Protocols** tab in the Network applet.

2. Select **TCP/IP Protocol** and choose **Properties.**

3. Select the **IP Address** tab.

4. Select a network adapter for which PPTP filtering is to be enabled.

5. Click **Advanced.**

6. Check **Enable PPTP Filtering.**

7. Repeat steps 4 through 6 for each interface that will support PPTP filtering.

8. Restart the computer to activate the changes.

Monitoring Server PPTP Support

You can monitor the PPTP ports in the RAS Server Admin utility by choosing the **Communication Ports** command in the Server menu. As shown in Figure 17.36, VPN ports are listed with modem ports and can be managed in the same way. Ports will only appear if they are configured to receive calls. Dial-out only ports will not be listed.

FIGURE 17.36
VPN ports being monitored in RAS Server Admin.

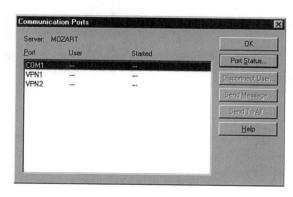

Enabling Client PPTP Support

When a client is dialing in to the Internet, as in Figure 17.27, establishing a PPTP tunnel to the RAS server has two steps:

■ The client establishes a dial-up connection to the Internet through an Internet access provider.

■ The client establishes a PPTP connection to the RAS server.

When a client is directly connected to the Internet, it is unnecessary to establish a dial-up connection. The procedure for starting a PPTP connection to the RAS server remains the same, however.

To establish a PPTP connection, you need to create a special entry in the Dial-Up Networking phonebook. This entry, an example of which appears in Figure 17.37, has two distinguishing characteristics:

■ The **Dial using** field is configured with one of the VPN virtual devices that was added to the RAS configuration when PPTP was installed. In Figure 17.37, the field has been pulled down to show the available ports. VPNs will appear in this list only if they have been configured to support dial-out.

■ The **Phone number preview** field is completed with the DNS name or the IP address of the PPTP server.

FIGURE 17.37

Configuring a PPTP client phonebook entry.

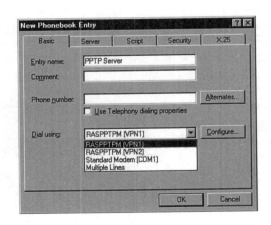

Creating a dial-up connection to PPTP has two steps:

- In Dial-Up Networking, run the phonebook entry that connects to your IAP using a telephone number and a modem.

- After the connection is established, run the phonebook entry that connects to the PPTP tunnel using a DNS hostname or IP address.

If the client is directly connected to the Internet, it is only necessary to run the phonebook entry that creates the PPTP tunnel.

Now You're Connected

Now that you know how to connect your LAN to the Internet, you are probably wondering how you can join the world of Internet content providers. Microsoft has made the task incredibly simple by bundling the Internet Information Server (IIS) with Windows NT Server 4. IIS is an easily administered way to provide World Wide Web, FTP, and Gopher services on your private intranet or on the Internet. So, without further ado, let's move on to IIS.

Chapter 18

ROUTING AND REMOTE ACCESS SERVER

As it ships, the routing capabilities of Windows NT Server are pretty basic. You can configure static routing for IP, and you can install a basic Multiprotocol Router that supports IP routing with version 1 of the RIP protocol. You can route IPX (NWLink) but can't do much to configure the IPX router. These features are better than nothing and they might be enough for your network. But networks have a tendency to grow, both in size and complexity, and eventually the services built into NT Server 4.0 run out of steam.

Microsoft has risen to the challenge of providing a richer and more robust routing service by introducing Routing and Remote Access Server, an optional service for Windows NT 4.0 that extends NT's routing capabilities. The product name Routing and Remote Access Server is just too big a handle to repeat throughout this chapter, and Microsoft hasn't provided an official acronym, so I'll refer to the product as RRAS. (This is one of those times I wish Microsoft had stuck with the product's development code name, "Steelhead," certainly a catchier name than Routing and Remote Access Server.)

RRAS replaces both the Multiprotocol Router and RAS. Although the most significant enhancements are to Windows NT's routing capabilities, RRAS also improves on RAS in some key areas. Here are some of the salient features of RRAS:

- IP routing includes RIP version 1, RIP version 2, and Open Shortest Path First (OSPF).

- IPX routing can be managed, as can the IPX Service Advertising Protocol (SAP).

- Demand-dial routing enables your LAN to connect to a remote network such as the Internet through dial-up modem or ISDN connections.

- Routing and RAS Admin is a GUI management utility that simplifies router management.

- Packet filtering improves network security and performance.

The multiprotocol router included with Windows NT Server 4.0 is pretty rudimentary. But RRAS is in a whole different league, and you won't get the most out of it unless you ground yourself in some routing theory. So this chapter starts out by looking at routing protocols, and then proceeds to show you how to install and manage RRAS.

RRAS supports two routing protocols:

- Routing Information Protocol (with versions for IPX and IP)

- Open Shortest Path First (for IP only)

The essential characteristics of these protocols were reviewed in Chapter 4, "The Internet Layer," and you were introduced to RIP in Chapter 9, "Routing Basics."

NOTE

Routing is complex enough to be considered a networking specialty, and there are many massive books on the topic. RRAS is a very sophisticated piece of software, and one chapter is insufficient to make you an expert on its capabilities. If your network demands the advanced routing capabilities of RRAS, you will want to extend your knowledge by reading some books that are devoted to routing.

NOTE

In this chapter, I am assuming that you are familiar with the features and operation of the standard Remote Access Server. If you need to brush up your skills on RAS, may I recommend my book, *Inside Windows NT Server 4*, also from New Riders.

Installing RRAS

Routing and Remote Access is a free update for Windows NT Server 4.0. As I am writing, it can be downloaded from the following URL:

```
http://www.microsoft.com/msdownload/
```

After downloading the installation file, install RRAS as follows:

1. If it is installed, remove the Multiprotocol Router by removing it from the Services tab of the Network applet in the Control Panel.

2. If it is installed, remove the Remote Access Service, also by removing it form the Services tab in the Network applet.

3. Verify that Service Pack 3 (or later) is installed on the server.

4. Install and configure the network adapters, modems, and other devices that are required for your RRAS configuration.

5. Execute the file that is downloaded from Microsoft, which is currently named mpri386.exe for the I386 platform.

6. Specify a location for the RRAS files, which by default is C:\Program Files\Routing.

7. Select which of the following services are to be installed:

   ■ **Remote access service.** The replacement for standard RAS.

- **LAN routing.** Support for IPX and IP routing.

- **Demand–dial routing.** Support for on-demand dial-up connections to remote networks.

8. Add RAS devices to the configuration and configure network protocol support.

9. Restart the server.

Managing RRAS Routing Services

RRAS installation adds an icon for the Routing and RAS Admin utility to the Administrative Tools (Common) program group in the Start Menu. Figure 18.1 shows the RRAS Admin utility. Notice that RRAS setup configures routing protocol support for IPX.

Assuming it is installed on a computer that has two or more network interfaces, RRAS begins to route packets when the routing service is started. RRAS is automatically configured to recognize the interfaces installed on the computer, and packet forwarding is activated for IP and for IPX if those protocols are installed.

At this point, the routing table can be maintained by adding static routes. No dynamic routing protocols are configured for IP during setup, however, and you must add RIP or OSPF to the RRAS configuration if you require dynamic routing.

FIGURE 18.1
Routing and RAS Admin.

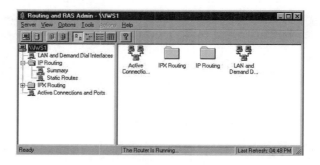

Adding Protocols to RRAS

RRAS is designed to accept add-in protocols from Microsoft and potentially from other vendors as well. To enable RRAS to support RIP, OSPF, or DHCP forwarding, you must add those protocols to RRAS using the following procedure:

1. Under the IP Routing icon in the service tree, right-click **Summary** to open its context menu.

2. Select **Add routing protocol** from the Summary context menu to open the routing protocol list shown in Figure 18.2.

3. Select the protocol to be added and choose **OK**.

4. Configure the protocol as described in the following sections.

Configuring RIP

Figure 18.2 shows RRAS Admin after RIP has been installed and configured. Two distinct procedures are required to configure RIP: you must configure the protocol parameters that apply to all RIP network interfaces and you must add and configure individual interfaces. (Figure 18.2 was prepared after interfaces had been added.) These tasks are performed from separate dialog boxes.

FIGURE 18.2
RRAS Admin after RIP has been configured.

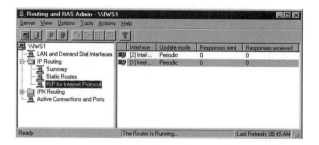

Configuring General RIP Properties

Figure 18.3 shows the dialog box used to configure RIP protocol properties. This dialog box is presented when RIP is added to the RRAS configuration. You can also access the RIP Configuration dialog box by right-clicking the RIP for Internet Protocol icon in the RRAS protocol tree and selecting Configure RIP from the context menu.

FIGURE 18.3

The RIP for Internet Protocol Configuration dialog box: the General tab.

Minimum seconds between triggered updates. Selecting a shorter triggered update interval speeds network convergence while potentially increasing network traffic. A longer interval enables the router to collect more network changes before sending a triggered update.

Event Logging. The radio buttons in this box determine the types of messages RRAS will record in the Event Viewer.

- **Disable error logging.** RRAS will not log RIP events.

- **Log errors only.** Only errors will be recorded. Errors record routing failures. This is probably the best compromise setting.

- **Log errors and warnings.** Errors and warnings will be recorded. Warnings record problems that do not necessarily result in routing failures.

- **Log the maximum amount of information.** Verbose logging information will be recorded, resulting in high levels of messages to the Event Log. Depending on the Event Log settings, this can result in the loss of other messages. Consequently, this setting should be used only when testing or troubleshooting the router configuration.

The Security tab is shown in Figure 18.4. Settings on this tab enable you to specify which routers are permitted to communicate with this router. The options are as follows:

- **Process announcements from all routers.** This router will process all RIP announcements it receives. This is the default setting.

- **Process only announcements from the routers listed.**
Announcements will be processed only if they originate from a router
whose IP address appears in the Routers list.

- **Discard all announcements from the routers listed.**
Announcements will not be processed if they originate from a router
whose IP address appears in the Routers list.

FIGURE 18.4

*The RIP for Internet
Protocol Configuration
dialog box: the
Security tab.*

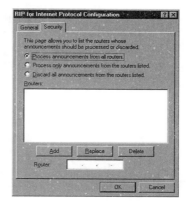

Adding RIP Interfaces

RIP does not automatically recognize the interfaces that are installed in the
computer. You must add interfaces to the RIP configuration before RIP will
handle routing for the attached networks. Interfaces can be individually
configured with a variety of parameters.

To add an interface to RIP:

1. Right-click **RIP for Internet Protocol** in the protocol tree.

2. Choose **Add interface** from the context menu.

3. Select an interface from the list and click **OK**.

4. Configure the interface as described in the next section.

5. Repeat steps 1–4 for each interface to be added.

Configuring RIP Interfaces

Figure 18.5 shows the RIP interface configuration dialog box. This dialog
box appears when the interface is installed. To open the dialog box at a later
time, do the following:

1. Select **RIP for Internet Protocol** in the protocol tree. The right pane of RRAS Admin displays the interfaces that have been added to RIP.

2. Right-click an interface.

3. Choose **<u>C</u>onfigure interface** in the context menu.

FIGURE 18.5

RIP interface configuration: the General tab.

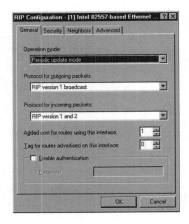

The following sections review the parameters on the tabs of the interface configuration dialog box.

RIP Interface Configuration: The General Tab

Figure 18.5 shows the General tab of the RIP Interface configuration dialog box. Parameters on this tab determine the general operational characteristics for RIP.

NOTE

Remember that each interface is configured individually.

Operation <u>m</u>ode. This field offers two options:

- **Periodic update mode.** If this mode is selected, the router sends RIP route advertisements periodically, at intervals specified in the Periodic announcement timer field of the Advanced tab. Routes learned while RIP is running in this mode are marked as dynamic RIP routes and are lost if the router is stopped and restarted. This is the default setting for interfaces connected to LANs.

- **Auto-static update mode.** If this mode is selected, RIP sends route advertisements through this interface only when they are requested by other routers. Routes learned while in auto-static update mode are marked as static and remain in the routing table when the router is stopped and restarted. This is the default setting for demand-dial interfaces.

Protocol for outgoing packets. This field determines how RIP communicates through the interface. The options are as follows:

- **RIP version 1 broadcasts.** Select this option if routers on the attached network are running only version 1 of RIP.

- **RIP version 2 broadcasts.** Select this option if the attached network includes a mixture of RIP-1 and RIP-2 routers.

- **RIP version 2 multicasts.** Select this if the attached network includes only RIP-2 routers. RIP-1 routers will not receive RIP-2 multicasts. Only RIP-2 routers process the RIP-2 multicasts, reducing the processing load for non-routers.

- **Silent RIP.** If this option is selected, the router listens for incoming RIP broadcasts but outgoing RIP broadcasts are disabled. This option is ideal for a single-homed RIP router, such as a router on a Windows NT Server computer. The computer will update its local routing table from the RIP broadcasts it receives but will not generate additional network traffic.

Added cost for routes using this interface. RIP routes are advertised individually for each interface. When an interface advertises a route, it typically advertises the route with a cost of 1, however it might be desirable to assign a different cost in order to define network route preferences. The value of this field represents the cost that is advertised for routes using this interface. Figure 18.6 shows how costs can be used to configure route preferences.

NOTE

Each interface on the router can be assigned a different cost. The cost is advertised to routers on the network attached to the interface and represents the cost of routing packets that arrive at the router through the interface. The cost for routing a packet is determined by the cost assigned to the incoming interface, not by the combined costs of the incoming and outgoing interfaces.

FIGURE 18.6
*Using interface cost
to establish route
preferences.*

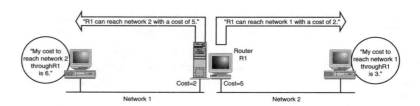

Tag for routes advertised on this interface. The route tag is an option-al attribute that might be assigned to a route. The intended purpose is to provide a method of separating routes learned from within the RIP routing domain from routes learned from external routing domains. Other uses for the route tag are permitted. (This parameter is not supported by RIP-1 routers.)

Enable authentication. RIP-2 routers can exchange an authentication password. When a password is assigned, routers will exchange routing mes-sages only if they share the same password. The password, between 8 and 16 characters, is sent in clear text and therefore provides minimal security.

RIP Interface Configuration: The Security Tab

By default, RIP accepts all routes that it receives through an interface and announces all routes that it learns. The Security tab, shown in Figure 18.7, can be used to alter that behavior. Settings on this tab determine which routes will be processed when accepting and announcing routes through the interface.

You can configure two classes of route security by selecting each of the fol-lowing settings:

- **When accepting routes.** Parameters you select for this option spec-ify which routes RIP accepts from outside routers.

- **When announcing routes.** Parameters you select for this option specify which routes RIP announces to outside routers.

For each security class, the following options are available:

- **Process all routes.** This interface processes all RIP announcements it accepts or announces. This is the default setting.

- **Process only routes in the ranges listed.** This interface accepts or announces only routes that correspond to a range that appears in the Ranges list.

- **Discard all routes in the ranges listed.** This interface does not accept or announce routes that correspond to a range that appears in the Ranges list.

FIGURE 18.7

RIP interface configuration: the Security tab.

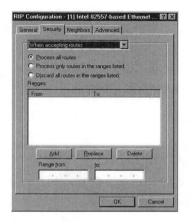

RIP Interface Configuration: The Neighbors Tab

Some types of networks do not support broadcast and multicast messaging. Examples are X.25 and ATM. To communicate on these networks, computers must establish one-to-one connections between each other. But as we have seen so far, RIP relies on broadcast or multicast messages to communicate between routers.

The Neighbors tab (Figure 18.8) provides a mechanism that enables RIP routers to communicate on non-broadcast networks. This tab establishes explicit lists of routers with which this router communicates RIP routing messages. The options on the Neighbors tab are as follows:

- **Disable neighbors list.** This is the default setting. The router communicates through this interface using the method defined on the General tab.

- **Use neighbor-list in addition to broadcast or multicast.** The router supplements broadcast or multicast messages (as configured on the General tab) with messages directed to routers listed in the Neighbors list.

- **Use neighbor-list instead of broadcast or multicast.** Routing information is communicated only through messages directed to routers listed in the Neighbors list.

FIGURE 18.8

*RIP interface
configuration: the
Neighbors tab.*

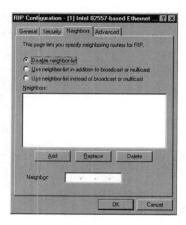

RIP Interface Configuration: The Advanced Tab

The Advanced tab, shown in Figure 18.9, is used to configure a variety of RIP settings. In the majority of cases, the default settings can be used, but here is an explanation of the settings on this tab in case you have the knowledge to tinker with them:

- **Periodic-announcement timer.** This timer determines the frequency with which the router will advertise routes through this interface. The default for IP RIP is 30 seconds. This parameter is effective only if Periodic update mode is selected on the General tab.

- **Route-expiration timer.** Routes learned from other routers must be refreshed periodically. External routes that are not refreshed within the period specified by the route expiration timer are marked as expired in the routing table. The default value of this field is 180 seconds. This parameter is effective only if Periodic update mode is selected on the General tab.

- **Route-removal timer.** This parameter specifies the interval between the expiration of a route and the time the route is removed from the routing table. This parameter is effective only if Periodic update mode is selected on the General tab.

- **Enable split-horizon processing.** When this option is checked, split-horizon processing is used to determine which interfaces will be used to advertise routes learned from outside routers. When split-horizon is in effect, a route will not be advertised through the interface from which the route was learned.

- **Enable poison-reverse processing.** This option is available when split-horizon processing is enabled. When poison-reverse processing is in effect, a route is advertised through the interface from which the route was learned, but it is advertised with a cost of 16.

- **Enable triggered updates.** When triggered updates are enabled, if the router learns a route or metric change it advertises the change immediately without waiting for the interval specified by the periodic announcement timer. The minimum interval for triggered updates is specified on the General tab of the RIP for Internet Protocol Configuration dialog box, described earlier in this chapter. Triggered updates are enabled by default. Although triggered updates speed network convergence, they result in higher levels of router traffic.

- **Send clean-up updates when stopping.** When this option is selected, a router that is shutting down announces its entire routing table with all metrics set to 15, thereby informing other routers that all its routes are unreachable. Other routers can immediately update their routing tables without waiting to discover the change in periodic router announcements. This option is enabled by default.

- **Override non-RIP routes with RIP-learned routes.** If this option is enabled, the router discards routes learned from outside routing protocols (for example OSPF or static routes) if a route to the destination is learned from RIP. This option is disabled by default.

- **Process host routes in packets received.** By default, RIP updates its routing table with network routes learned from other routers' route advertisements. Host routes, however, are ignored. Enable this option if RIP should process host routes that are learned from other routers.

- **Include host routes in packets sent.** By default, RIP advertises only the network routes in its routing table. Host routes are not advertised. Check this option if RIP should advertise the host routes in its routing table.

- **Process default routes in packets received.** By default, default routes in incoming route advertisements are not recorded in the local routing table. Enable this option if incoming default routes should be processed for addition to the local routing table.

- **Include default routes in packets sent.** By default the router does not advertise default routes in its own routing table. Enable this option if default routes should be advertised.

FIGURE 18.9

RIP interface configuration: the Advanced tab.

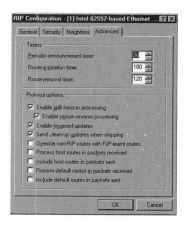

Monitoring the Router

It is easy to monitor RRAS activity. Let's see how RRAS Admin displays statistics for interface, routing table, and RIP activity.

Monitoring Interfaces

Interface activity is displayed by selecting **Summary** in the routing service tree. Figure 18.10 shows sample summary statistics. If you examine the horizontal scrollbar, you see that the additional columns are scrolled off the right side of the statistics pane.

To reduce CPU loading, statistics are updated at periodic intervals, not continually. You can manually update the statistics for all interfaces by pressing **F5**. To refresh an individual interface, right-click the interface and choose **Refresh** from the context menu.

FIGURE 18.10

RRAS interface summary statistics.

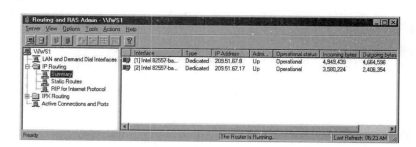

You can customize the columns that are displayed in the summary statistics. Right-click any of the column headers and choose **Customize** to open the Customize Columns dialog box shown in Figure 18.11. To customize a column:

1. Check the entry in the **Columns** list so that the column is displayed.

2. Select an entry and click **Move up** to move the column to the left in the summary statistics pane.

3. Select an entry and click **Move down** to move the column to the right in the summary statistics pane.

4. Select an entry and adjust the **Column width** slider to adjust the display width for the column.

FIGURE 18.11
Customizing the statistics display.

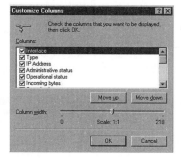

TIP

You can customize other statistics displays, such as RIP statistics, in a similar manner.

Monitoring the Routing Table

An example of a RRAS routing table is shown in Figure 18.12. To examine the IP routing table:

1. Right-click **Static Routes** in the routing services tree.

2. Choose **View IP routing table** from the context menu.

Many of the routes shown in Figure 18.12 will be familiar to you from the discussion in Chapter 9:

- Most of the routes designated as Local are routes learned from the computer's TCP/IP configuration.

- The route to network 10.1.0.0 was entered as a static route but is designated as Local because it was not learned from another router.

- Some of the routes were learned from another RIP router and are designated as such in the Protocol column.

Information in the routing table can provide vital clues when troubleshooting routing errors. You might find for example that routes known to one router are not known to another. In such cases, you need to check the routers' configurations to ensure that they communicate correctly. Some factors to consider follow:

- Are both routers using the same version of RIP?

- Are all routers using the same communications mode (broadcast or multicast)?

- Is either router configured to use silent RIP?

FIGURE 18.12

Example of an IP routing table.

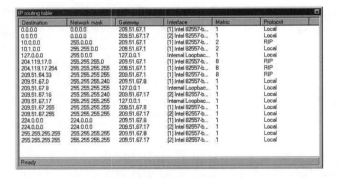

Configuring OSPF

Like RIP, OSPF configuration has two procedural components: configuration of the OSPF router's general parameters and configuration of the interfaces. You can learn how OSPF works in Chapter 4. Before you actually implement an OSPF network, you need to know how to configure OSPF routing areas.

Configuring OSPF Routing Areas

Figure 18.13 shows a diagram of a network that uses OSPF routing. The diagram focuses on routers and, of course, many more TCP/IP hosts will appear on the networks that the routers join. Now, let's review the components of the network with an emphasis on concepts that you must consider when configuring OSPF routers.

FIGURE 18.13

Diagram of an OSPF network.

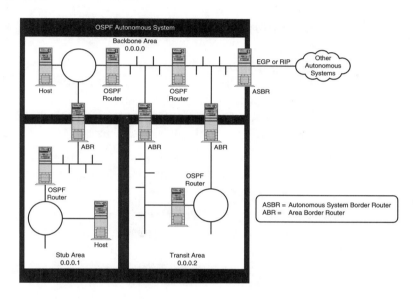

An *autonomous system* (AS) is a collection of networks that share a common routing protocol. Figure 18.13 includes one OSPF AS.

Areas define groups of OSPF routers that share a common link-state database. OSPF advertises routes using link-state advertisements (LSAs), which are flooded throughout an area. *Flooding* describes the process of distributing LSAs to all OSPF routers in an area. On small- to medium-size networks the entire AS can be configured as a single area.

One router in an area is identified as the *designated router* through an election process that can be configured by setting priorities for individual routers. The designated router is responsible for preparing LSAs for the area.

Within an area, OSPF routers communicate with *neighbors*, which are peer OSPF routers. On broadcast networks, OSPF routers can discover their peers using Hello packets. Only routers that exchange Hello packets establish themselves as neighbors. On non-broadcast networks, such as X.25 and frame relay, the addresses of neighbors must be added manually to the routers' configurations.

A *designated router* is established for each network that attaches through two or more routers. The designated router is selected through an election process and becomes adjacent to all other routers on the network. All link-state advertisements for the network are originated by the designated router.

As areas grow in size, OSPF performance diminishes in two areas: It takes longer to recompute the new routes that result from link-state changes, and increasing amounts of network traffic are devoted to distributing link-state advertisements. Consequently, the design of OSPF accommodates partitioning the AS into multiple areas. This has two advantages:

- Areas can be configured around organizational or geographical relationships, limiting the sharing of routing information and making the network more secure.

- The number of LSAs in the areas is reduced, and they are limited to the information users require most often.

NOTE

A good rule of thumb is to limit the size of an AS to 200 routers.

Areas must be organized hierarchically, with one area designated as a backbone area. All other areas must connect to the backbone area. Each area is identified by an area ID, a four-byte number that is usually expressed in dotted-decimal notation. These area IDs are not IP addresses and don't need to follow IP address restrictions. The backbone area is always assigned the area ID 0.0.0.0.

Areas must be configured out of contiguous groups of routers and networks. In other words, parts of an area should not be separated by another area. Because most areas typically support a localized subset of hosts, it is seldom a problem to configure areas out of contiguous components. Because only one backbone is permitted, however, it might be difficult to configure a backbone contiguously on a geographically dispersed network.

It is possible to partition the backbone area into multiple physical areas and to enable the backbone partitions to communicate using a virtual link through another area. The area that supports the virtual link is called a *virtual-link transit area*. Figure 18.14 illustrates a backbone that is partitioned to span a large area. In such cases a virtual link must be established to extend the backbone partition to the New York area. This approach enables Chicago and New York to share the same leased circuit between Chicago and Los Angeles. Because virtual links are complex and trouble-prone, I regard them as advanced tools that are beyond the scope of this chapter.

FIGURE 18.14

Partitions of a back-bone connected through a virtual link.

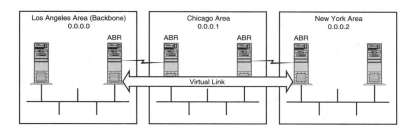

Area border routers (ABRs) connect areas and advertise destinations across area boundaries in the form of *summary link advertisements*.

Two types of areas can connect to the backbone area:

■ *Stub areas* connect to the backbone through a single ABR. The ABR of a stub area does not advertise external routes. Instead, because all external traffic must go through the ABR, a single default route is advertised. Configuration of stub areas reduces the memory, processing, and bandwidth requirements of the ABR but obviously makes the area subject to a single point of failure.

■ *Transit areas* connect to the backbone with more than one ABR. Processing, memory, and bandwidth requirements are higher for ABRs than for support transit areas.

Routing within an area, called *intra-area routing* can take place without knowledge of external routes. Routing between areas, or inter-area routing, requires ABRs to exchange routing information about their areas.

Autonomous system border routers (ASBRs) are responsible for routing traffic between the OSPF AS and ASs based on other routing protocols such as RIP. External routes are advertised through *external link advertisements*.

NOTE

OSPF gives different preferences to routes that are obtained from the local AS (internal routes) and from remote ASs (external routes). On a network that includes OSPF and RIP routers, for example, an OSPF router prefers a route that it learns internally from another OSPF router over a route that it learns externally from a RIP router.

If your network includes multiple brands of routers, you need to ensure that all routers employ the same preferences. Consult the TCP/IP Reference manual for more information about OSPF protocol preferences.

Configuring OSPF Router General Properties

When you add OSPF by Bay Networks, the dialog box shown in Figure 18.15 enables you to configure general OSPF parameters. The OSPF Configuration dialog box can also be opened by right-clicking **OSPF by Bay Networks** in the protocols tree and selecting **Configure OSPF** from the context menu.

FIGURE 18.15

OSPF Configuration: the General tab.

Router Identification. In this field, enter a 32-bit number in dotted-decimal notation that uniquely identifies this OSPF router. One approach to selecting the route identification is to select the IP address that is assigned to one of the router's interfaces. You are not restricted to using IP addresses, however, and can devise your own standards for identifying routers if you want.

Enable autonomous system boundary router. Check this field if this router functions as an ASBR.

Event logging. The radio buttons in this box determine the types of messages that will be recorded in the Event Viewer. Options are the same as for the RIP protocol and are explained earlier in this chapter.

Configuring Areas

The Areas tab is shown in Figure 18.16. The Areas box is configured with a list of all areas that are connected to by interfaces on this router. The first area in an OSPF autonomous system is designated as the backbone area and is assigned area number 0.0.0.0.

FIGURE 18.16

OSPF Configuration: The Areas tab lists areas supported by all interfaces installed in the router.

After an area has been added to the Areas list, select the area and choose **Configure** to open the OSPF Area Configuration dialog box shown in Figure 18.17. The General tab has the following fields:

- **Enable clear text passwords**. If this field is checked, passwords will be used to determine which OSPF routers will communicate with one another. When passwords are used, each interface must be configured with a password.

- **Stub area.** Check this box if this router is an area border router servicing a stub area. The backbone (area 0.0.0.0) cannot be configured as a stub area. Virtual links cannot be configured as stub areas.

- **Stub metric.** If Stub area is checked, this field specifies the routing cost that the ABR will advertise to outside areas.

- **Import summary advertisements.** By default, routing within a stub area (*intra-area routing*) makes use of default routes. If this option is checked, the ABR will import routes learned from outside areas (non–intra-area routes) and will advertise non–intra-area routes within the area.

FIGURE 18.17

OSPF Area Configuration: the General tab.

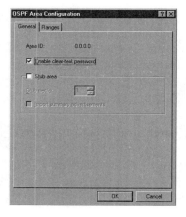

Areas are explicitly configured to service ranges of IP addresses. This is done in the OSPF Area Configuration Ranges tab, shown in Figure 18.18. To add an IP address range to an area:

1. Enter an IP subnet address in the Address field

2. Enter the subnet mask in the Mask field.

3. Choose **Add**.

Enter all of the address ranges that are encompassed by the area being defined.

FIGURE 18.18

Defining address ranges for an area.

NOTE

Typically, a given area will be serviced by two or more OSPF routers. There is no mechanism that enables OSPF routers to exchange information about the configuration of an area. It is up to the administrator to manually review the area configurations on each router to ensure consistency.

Configuring OSPF Interfaces

As with RIP, OSPF interfaces must be individually added to the router configuration and configured. The procedure for adding the routers is the same as for RIP, but as you would expect, the interface configuration parameters are considerably different. The following sections explain OSPF interface configuration parameters.

OSPF Interface Configuration: The General Tab

The OSPF interface configuration General tab is shown in Figure 18.19. The settings on this tab are as follows:

- **Enable OSPF on this interface.** This box is checked by default, enabling OSPF support on the interface.

- **Area ID.** Select the OSPF area associated with the network that connects to this interface. Before areas can be selected in this field they must be defined in the OSPF router general configuration.

- **Router priority.** The router priority establishes preferences for the election of the designated router for a network. In general, the router that has the highest router priority is selected as the designated router.

- **Cost.** This parameter defines the cost for sending a packet out through this interface. Lower-cost interfaces will be preferred over higher-cost interfaces. The default cost is 1 for a broadcast interface and 4 for a point-to-point interface. The maximum cost is 32,767.

- **Password.** If passwords are enabled for an area (**Enable clear text passwords** is checked on the Area Configuration dialog box), all routers that communicate to that area must be configured to use the same area password.

- **Type.** This box offers the following three options that specify the type of interface:

  - **Broadcast.** Select this option for a broadcast interface, such as Ethernet, token ring, FDDI, or another LAN protocol.

  - **Point-to-point.** Select this option for a point-to-point link such as a T1, T3, or dial-up connection.

  - **NBMA.** Select this option for a *non-broadcast multiaccess* (NBMA) network such as X.25 or frame relay. Use the Neighbors tab to define neighbors for this router.

FIGURE 18.19

Defining general parameters for an OSPF interface.

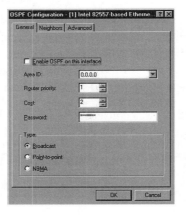

OSPF Interface Configuration: The Neighbors Tab

OSPF routers use the Hello protocol to establish adjacencies and neighbor relationships. The Hello protocol relies on broadcast messages that are not supported on non-broadcast networks such as X.25 and frame relay. On non-broadcast networks, neighbors must be explicitly defined. This is done on the Neighbors tab, shown in Figure 18.20. A neighbor definition has two fields:

- **Address.** Enter the neighbor's IP address.

- **Priority.** Specify a priority in the Priority field. The router with the highest priority on a given network will be preferred in elections to determine the designated router for the network.

FIGURE 18.20

Defining neighbors for an OSPF router on a non-broadcast network.

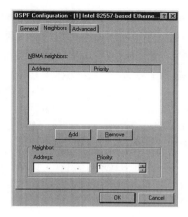

OSPF Interface Configurations: The Advanced Tab

The Advanced tab is shown in Figure 18.21. In most cases, you will not need to adjust the parameters on this tab. The following parameters are available:

- **Transit delay (seconds).** This parameter is an estimate of the time in seconds required to deliver a link state advertisement through this interface. The default value is 1 second.

- **Re-transmit interval (seconds).** This parameter specifies the number of seconds between retransmission of LSAs and should exceed the round-trip time between this router and its adjacencies. This parameter should be adjusted to reflect the type of network and must be increased for slow networks and virtual links. If the retransmit interval is too short, LSAs might be needlessly retransmitted.

- **Hello interval (seconds).** This parameter specifies the interval between transmission of Hello packets, and must be the same for all routers on a given network. A shorter interval results in faster propagation of network changes but also results in greater levels of network traffic. A Hello interval of 30 seconds might be used on a low-bandwidth network such as X.25, while 10 seconds might be used on a LAN.

- **Dead interval (seconds).** This parameter determines how long this router will wait before declaring a silent router to be dead. A silent router is a router that fails to respond to Hello packets. Typically this parameter should be several multiples of the Hello interval. If the

Hello interval is 10 seconds and the Dead interval is 40 seconds, the router transmits four unacknowledged Hello packets before declaring a given router to be dead.

- **Poll interval (seconds).** On non-broadcast networks, routers cannot use broadcast Hello packets to determine that a dead router has been reactivated. This parameter is specified on MBMA networks to establish the interval between attempts to contact the dead router. The poll interval should be at least twice the dead interval.

- **MTU size (bytes).** This parameter specifies the *maximum transfer unit* (MTU), which is the maximum packet size to be used when sending OSPF packets from this interface. The default value of 1500 is appropriate for 10Mbps Ethernet. The standard MTU for FDDI networks is 4096. Adjust this parameter to reflect the maximum packet size and reliability of the attached network.

Figure 18.21

Configuring advanced OSPF parameters.

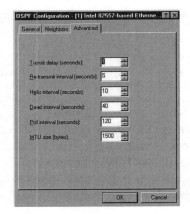

Configuring the DHCP Relay Agent

When RRAS is installed, the standard DHCP relay agent is disabled. If DHCP forwarding is required on your network, you must configure the DHCP relay agent on computers running RRAS.

The DHCP Relay Agent protocol has a single configuration dialog box, shown in Figure 18.22. As with the standard DHCP relay agent, add the IP addresses of DHCP servers to the DHCP Servers list.

FIGURE 18.22

Configuring the DHCP relay agent.

After installing the protocol, you must also add interfaces to the DHCP Relay Agent. Figure 18.23 shows the DHCP Relay Agent interface configuration dialog box, which has the following fields:

- **Relay DHCP packets across this interface.** Check this box if this interface should be used to forward packets to DHCP servers.

- **Hop count threshold.** This field specifies the maximum hop count allowed for DHCP packets originating at this router. The maximum value is 16 hops.

- **Seconds-since-boot threshold.** This parameter specifies the period of time the relay agent will wait before forwarding DHCP requests. This delay provides a time interval in which a local DHCP server can respond before an attempt is made to contact a remote DHCP server. The default value is 4 seconds.

FIGURE 18.23

Configuring a DHCP Relay Agent interface.

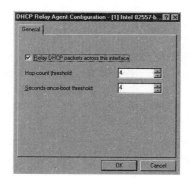

Configuring Static Routes

Even if you don't configure a routing protocol, RRAS makes it easier to configure static routes. Instead of using the esoteric route command, you can configure static routes using a graphic interface. Static routes are managed using the Static Routes entry that appears under the IP Routing header in the protocols tree.

Adding Static Routes

To add a static route:

1. Right-click the **Static Route** entry in the routing services tree.

2. Select **Add static route** in the context menu to open the Static Route dialog box shown in Figure 18.24.

FIGURE 18.24

Adding a static route.

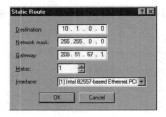

3. In the Interface field, select the interface that routes traffic for this route.

4. Complete the Destination, Network mask, Gateway, and Metric fields appropriately. See Chapter 9 for descriptions of these fields.

5. Choose **OK** to save the entry.

Completed static routes are listed in the routes pane when you select **Static Routes** in the routing services tree.

Other Static Route Operations

Right-click an existing static route to open a context menu with the following options:

- **View routing table.** This option displays the complete routing table for this router. Refer to Figure 18.22 for an example. Notice that the source of each route is identified.

- **Customize.** This option opens a dialog box where you can customize the columns appearing in the static route list. Refer to the discussion associated with Figure 18.21 for procedures used to customize RRAS lists.

- **Refresh.** This option manually refreshes the routing table display to reflect recent changes. Refresh options can be specified in the Options menu.

- **New.** This option provides an alternative way to start a new static route entry.

- **Edit.** This option opens a dialog box where existing routes can be modified.

- **Remove.** Finally, here is the option for deleting a route from the routing table.

As you can see, the hardest part about managing static routes under RRAS is understanding how routing works. After you determine the routes that are required for your network, it is extremely easy to maintain them in the routing table.

Demand-Dial Connections

Many organizations that have multiple sites face a dilemma. They need to enable computers to communicate with remote locations, but they don't have enough traffic to justify the expense of full-time leased lines. In many such cases, a demand-dial router can be an ideal solution.

Demand-dial routers can use modem or ISDN connections. Modem connections, of course, use conventional voice phone lines. ISDN connections might use the Internet as a communications backbone with local ISPs providing the local interfaces. When a node needs to communicate with a remote network, RRAS dials up the connection and keeps it active only while it is required. When communication ceases, the connection is closed.

Depending on the needs of your organization, demand-dial can save you money. Here are some factors to consider:

- Modem connections are limited to 56Kbps under ideal situations. More typically, modems connect at 28.8Kbps to about 50Kbps. This limited bandwidth clearly will not support the level of traffic that is typical on a LAN.

- Typically, ISDN connections are limited to 128Kbps when two 56Kbps channels are aggregated. Base ISDN costs only marginally less than a dedicated frame relay connection, about 25 percent in my experience, and in many cases ISDN accumulates charges depending on the amount of time the circuit is active.

- Modem long-distance charges and ISDN connections are taxed based on the amount of time they are active. If the dial-up connection will be activated frequently, it can easily cost more than a dedicated frame relay connection. Discuss costs carefully with your communications providers to ensure you know what to expect.

In summary, demand-dial connections make the most sense when they are lightly used or when modems are used to communicate using local connections. Figure 18.25 shows an example that uses dial-up connections to enable two local sites to communicate.

FIGURE 18.25

Using a dial-up connection.

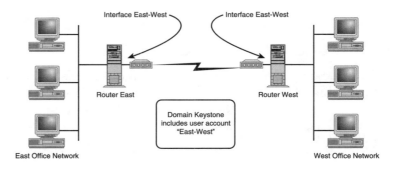

Setting up a dial-up connection requires four steps:

1. Enabling demand-dial routing support on the RAS ports.

2. Adding demand-dial interfaces to the routers.

3. Setting credentials on the routers.

4. Setting up user accounts to make the connections.

In Figure 18.25, the demand-dial setup parameters are as follows:

- The interface router interface is named "East-West." The same name is used on both routers.

- The user account that dials in to demand-dial interfaces is named "East-West" from domain Keystone. One account can be used regardless of the direction in which the demand-dial connection is established.

The following sections discuss the procedures for setting up the demand-dial connections.

Enabling Demand-Dial Routing on a RAS Port

To enable a RAS port to support demand-dial routing, do the following:

1. Open the **Services** tab of the Network applet in the Control Panel.

2. Select **Routing and Remote Access Service** and choose **Properties** to open the Remote Access Setup dialog box.

3. If the desired port is not present, add it. (See *Inside Windows NT Server 4* if you are unfamiliar with the procedure.)

4. Select a port and choose **Configure** to open the Configure Port Usage dialog box shown in Figure 18.26.

5. To enable demand-dial router support for this port, check **Dial out and receive calls as a demand-dial router.** This parameter is added to RAS when RRAS is installed.

6. Close the Network applet and restart the computer to activate changes.

Perform this procedure on each router that supports the demand-dial connection.

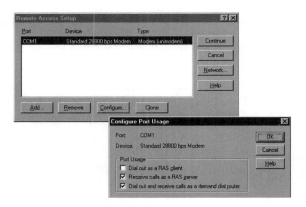

Adding Demand-Dial Interfaces to Routers

After demand-dial support has been added to at least one port, a demand-dial interface can be added to the router. This procedure must be performed on each router that participates in a demand-dial connection.

Although a setup wizard is available to walk you through the setup procedure, you won't need the wizard if you are familiar with RAS. The following procedure does not use the setup wizard. The procedure is as follows:

1. In Routing and RAS Admin, right click **LAN and Demand-Dial Interfaces.**

TIP

When using a wizard to set up the demand-dial interface, if **Use demand-dial wizard** is not checked, select that option to enable it. Then begin again at step 1 and follow the prompts in the wizard.

2. Choose **Add Interface** in the context menu to open the New Phonebook Entry dialog box.

3. The General tab is shown in Figure 18.27. This tab is nearly identical to the corresponding tab in RAS (refer to Figure 16.23), and should require no discussion. The Interface Name and Comment fields should clearly identify this entry as a remote router.

FIGURE 18.27

Configuring a demand-dial interface: the General tab.

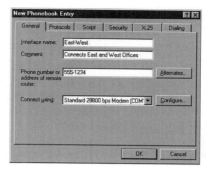

4. The Protocols tab is shown in Figure 18.28. As you can see, only IPX and TCP/IP are supported for demand-dial routing. (NetBEUI is not routable.) Configure the protocols as for a RAS port, as described for the RAS Server tab in Chapter 17. (Refer to the discussion related to Figure 17.21.)

FIGURE 18.28

Configuring a demand-dial interface: the Protocols tab.

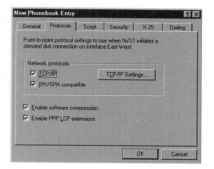

5. Configure the Script tab as described in Chapter 17 (refer to the discussion related to Figure 17.24). The option Pop up a terminal window is not found and would clearly be inappropriate for a connection that is intended to be automatic. No script will be required when connecting to another RRAS router.

6. The Security tab is shown in Figure 18.29. Parameters are similar to those discussed with Figure 17.25, with the following exceptions:

■ **Require strong data encryption.** When **Require data encryption** is checked, all data traveling through the connection is encrypted. If this box is checked, RRAS will use the strongest encryption method available on this computer (different data encryption strengths are available in versions of NT sold for domestic U.S. and international use). If strong encryption is activated, it must be selected for routers on both ends of the demand-dial connection.

■ **Use two-way authentication.** By default, the dial-in router authenticates the dial-out router, but authentication is one-way only. Check this option if you want the dial-out router to authenticate the dial-in router as well.

FIGURE 18.29

Configuring a demand-dial interface: the Security tab.

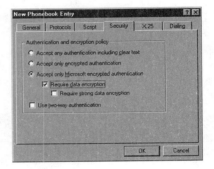

7. The **X.25** tab is described in Chapter 17 (refer to the discussion accompanying Figure 17.26).

8. The Dialing tab is shown in Figure 18.30. This tab has the following parameters:

   ■ **Number of redial attempts.** Specifies the number of times the router will attempt to establish a dial-out connection.

   ■ **Seconds between redial attempts.** Specifies the interval in seconds between redial attempts.

   ■ **Demand dial connection.** When this option is selected, the dial-up connection will be closed when the connection is idle for the number of seconds specified.

   ■ **Persistent connection.** When this option is selected, the connection is established when the routing service is started and remains active until the service is stopped.

FIGURE 18.30

Configuring a demand-dial interface: the Dialing tab.

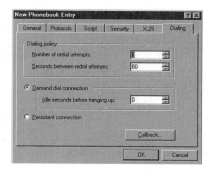

9. If you want the receiving router to call back and establish the connection, click **Callback** in the Dialing tab to open the Callback dialog box shown in Figure 18.31. Options in this dialog box are as follows:

   ■ **No, skip call back.** This is the default setting.

   ■ **Yes, call me back at the number(s) below.** If the remote router supports callback, you can select this option and specify a list of phone numbers that can be used to dial in to this router.

FIGURE 18.31

Configuring a demand-dial interface: Callback options.

10. Close the New Phone Book Entry dialog box by clicking **OK**. This will open the Selecting Routing Protocols dialog box shown in Figure 18.32. Check the protocols to be supported on this routing interface.

FIGURE 18.32

Configuring a demand-dial interface: selecting routing protocols.

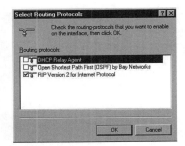

11. Close the Selecting Routing Protocols dialog box by clicking **OK**. If the interface supports TCP/IP, the next dialog box will be the IP Configuration dialog box shown in Figure 18.33. Options in this dialog box are as follows:

   ■ **Enable IP router manager on this interface.** Check this option if IP routing is to be supported on this interface.

   ■ **Enable router-discovery advertisements.** Router-discovery announcements enable hosts to update their default gateway settings. Check this option to support router-discovery advertisements. The **Level of Preference** determines which router on a network will receive the most traffic, where the router with the highest level of preference receives the most traffic. Adjust the **Advertisement rate** and **Advertisement lifetime** fields appropriately. (The default values are usually appropriate.)

   ■ **Input Filters** and **Output Filters.** These buttons open dialog boxes where you can establish input and output filters based on IP and network addresses. Filtering is beyond the scope of this chapter.

FIGURE 18.33

Configuring a demand-dial interface: configuring IP routing.

12. If the interface supports IPX, the next dialog box will be IPX Configuration, shown in Figure 18.34. Options in this dialog box are as follows:

- **Enable IPX on this interface.** Check this option if IPX routing is to be supported on this interface.

- **IPX CP.** Select this option if the remote router and clients are using Windows NT.

- **IPX WAN.** Select this option if the remote router and clients are using Novell products.

- **Input Filters** and **Output Filters.** Filtering is beyond the scope of this chapter.

FIGURE 18.34

Configuring a demand-dial interface: configuring IPX.

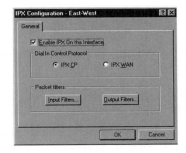

13. If the interface supports IPX, the next three dialog boxes will be:

- **NB Broadcast Configuration.** By default, demand-dial interfaces do not accept NetBIOS broadcasts.

- **RIP for IPX Configuration.** Use this dialog box to modify RIP for IPX settings.

- **SAP for IPX Configuration**. Use this dialog box to modify settings for the Service Advertising Protocol.

14. Depending on the protocols that were selected in step 10, the following dialog boxes might appear:

- DHCP Relay Configuration

- OSPF Configuration

- RIP Configuration

Configuration parameters for these protocols are discussed earlier in this chapter.

Figure 18.35 shows Routing and RAS Admin after a demand-dial interface has been added. After the demand-dial interface is created, you can proceed to set the router credentials.

FIGURE 18.35

A demand-dial interface has been added to the RRAS configuration.

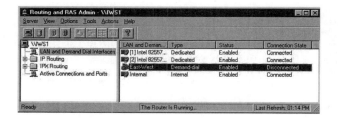

Setting Credentials on Routers

You must set credentials on all routers that will be receiving dial-in connection requests. To set credentials on a router:

1. Right-click the interface and select **Set Credentials** from the context menu.

2. Complete the Interface Credentials dialog box, shown in Figure 18.36. Specify the username, domain, and password of the user account that will be permitted to establish a demand-dial connection with this interface.

FIGURE 18.36

Configuring a demand-dial interface: entering interface credentials.

Creating Users on Routers

A dedicated user account is used to make the dial-up connection. With User Manager for Domains, create a user account that matches the interface credentials entered in the previous step.

RAS Changes

RRAS replaces the standard RAS service that ships with NT. You won't notice many changes, and you continue to manage the RAS component of RAS pretty much as you are used to. Consequently, in this section I'm going to focus on some significant differences that you might encounter.

Serial Ports and Modems

RRAS does not introduce any new features or management considerations for serial ports and modems, which are managed as described in Chapter 17.

Configuring RAS Ports

RRAS adds a few configuration parameters to the Network Configuration dialog box shown in Figure 18.37. To open this dialog box:

1. Open the Network applet in the Control Panel.

2. Select the **Services** tab.

3. Select the **Routing and Remote Access** Service and choose **Properties** to open the Network Configuration dialog box.

4. Select a port and choose **Network.**

The following new parameters are found in the Network Configuration dialog box:

■ **Require strong data encryption.** If this option is selected, RRAS will communicate using Microsoft strong encryption (128-bit encryption) only. When this option is selected, both the server and the clients must be configured to support the same level of data encryption or communication will not be permitted.

When this option is selected, clients must be running Windows NT 4.0 with Service Pack 3 or later. All routers must be Windows NT RRAS routers. After Microsoft strong encryption is enabled on the client, the client can communicate only with servers that support Microsoft strong encryption.

- **Authentication Provider: Windows NT.** Select this check box when Windows NT provides client authentication services for dial-in clients.

- **Authentication Provider: Radius.** Select this option if your network uses the Remote Authentication Dial-In User Service (RADIUS) to authenticate dial-in clients.

FIGURE 18.37

The RRAS Network Configuration dialog box.

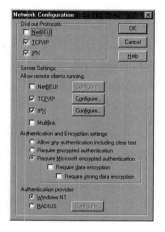

Building a High-Performance Routing Infrastructure

With RRAS, Microsoft has made it possible to implement sophisticated routing at moderate cost by taking advantage of Windows NT running on a microcomputer. If you are running a large busy network, however, a software-based router such as RRAS will probably not provide the routing throughput that you require, and you might experience slow traffic throughput or dropped frames. Better performance is available with dedicated hardware-based routers such as those offered by Cisco and other vendors. If you are networking on a budget, however, RRAS is a significant improvement on the capabilities that ship with Windows NT Server 4.

Chapter 19

EMAIL AND MICROSOFT EXCHANGE SERVER

If there's a killer application for TCP/IP, it's clearly the World Wide Web. However, email is a close second! The ability to asynchronously communicate with others around the globe, quickly and efficiently, enables new standards for personal and organizational efficiency.

In this chapter you learn about email over TCP/IP, and more specifically about Microsoft's standard email system for TCP/IP: Microsoft Exchange Server. You will learn the following topics:

- Basic email concepts

- Email protocols and standards

- Different ways of connecting email systems

- Microsoft Exchange Server features and capabilities

Understanding the rudiments of email can help round out your knowledge of TCP/IP networks and how they support this important application area.

Exchange Server is an elaborate product that we can't possibly cover in a chapter. My purpose here will be to cover the basic concepts of Internet mail protocols, to introduce you to Exchange, and to show you how Exchange integrates with TCP/IP email systems.

Understanding Internet Email

When you talk about email over TCP/IP, you're really talking about Internet email, which uses a number of different protocols and standards that are carried through a TCP/IP network connection.

In this section of the chapter, you learn about Internet email concepts, protocols, and standards.

Basic Internet Email Concepts

Internet email was originally found on ARPAnet, using a variety of informal standards for the sending of text messages from user to user. Initially codified in RFC 733, which was supplanted by the present RFC 822 Internet email at its most basic level, is the sending of text-only messages from user to user, when each user might be located on the same or different computer networks.

You should be familiar with basic email terms and concepts, as follows:

- **Message.** A message is a collection of data sent from one email user to another. The message is made up of different types of data, such as sender email address, recipient email address, Internet routing information, subject line, and message body.

- **Address**. Internet email addresses are in the form *user@host.domain*. For example, `fred_flintstone@bedrock.gov` is a valid email address. A message must have at least one recipient address and one sender address.

- **Message body.** The actual text of an email message. A number of additional protocols describe how binary data, including multiobject binary data, can be included into a message body.

- **Attachment.** Binary data encoded within a message body.

- **Mailbox.** A mailbox is a location designed for the storage of messages, usually for a particular individual who uses and has access to the mailbox.

- **Distribution List.** Some email systems allow the definition of distribution lists, which are made up of a number of email recipient addresses. For instance, a message might be sent to `actors@flint-stones.com` and be automatically distributed to the individual recipients who make up the distribution list.

- **Mail Host.** A system that stores and forwards email messages.

- **Message Transfer Agent (MTA).** An MTA is a program running on a computer that is responsible for sending a message from one system (or subsystem) to another. Often, an MTA transfers mail from one host to another.

These are the basic concepts of email. In the following sections you learn about the actual standards that make email work and enrich its capabilities.

Protocols and Standards

The protocols and standards used for email are crucial to its success. Although some email systems improve on the technologies described here to enable additional features within a particular organization, the following sections describe the *lingua franca* of email communications.

SMTP

The Simple Mail Transfer Protocol (SMTP) describes a protocol for the delivery of email from one site to another over the Internet. Details of the protocol can be found in RFC 821. Basically, SMTP defines a dialogue between a sending system and a receiving system, along with different error messages and so forth. SMTP traffic is carried over TCP/IP port 25.

NOTE

How are SMTP mail hosts on the Internet located by other SMTP mail hosts? When a mail host wants to send mail to another mail host, it looks up the receiving mail host's address using the Domain Name System (DNS). Within the DNS database are records that define Internet servers generally (A Records) and records that define the mail servers for a domain (MX Records or Mail Exchangers). An MX record looks something like this:

```
bedrock.gov     IN     MX     10     smtp.bedrock.gov
```

The first portion of the MX record defines the domain that is being described by the rest of the record. In this example, the MX record is showing the DNS name for the server that handles mail for the bedrock.gov domain. The MX defines that this is an MX record, whereas the 10 indicates the cost for the connection (more on this in a bit). Finally, smtp.bedrock.gov shows the DNS name of the mail server. MX records are linked to A records to find the actual address, and most DNS servers send this information back automatically on receipt of an MX request. So, for instance, when querying for the MX record for bedrock.gov, the DNS server will return the record listed earlier, as well as the A record for smtp.bedrock.gov, which will contain the actual IP address of the server. Alternatively, the requester can request the A record after the MX record is received to resolve the address of smtp.bedrock.gov.

Domains can have multiple mail servers defined with multiple MX records. Doing so provides two benefits: load balancing and redundancy. When two or more MX records are defined (pointing to different mail hosts) and one mail server is down, mail can still be sent to the mail host described by the second (or successive) MX record.

The cost field (shown as a 10 in the preceding example) defines the cost for the mail route. If two MX records both use a cost of 10 the sender will randomly choose between the two hosts, splitting the load between them roughly in half. Alternatively, raising the cost for one MX record will cause that mail host to be used less often, proportional to the various costs in the MX records. So, with two mail hosts with costs of 20 and 10, the mail host with a cost of 20 will get roughly a third as much mail as the one with a cost of 10.

A basic SMTP dialogue begins with the sending system connecting to port 25 of the receiving system using the TCP/IP address resolved by the DNS. The dialogue is carried out in 7-bit plain ASCII text. After the connection is established, the sending system sends a HELO command followed by its DNS address. The receiving system responds with an acknowledgement along with its own address. For example, the following shows an example of this portion of the dialogue. Note that the Sender: and Receiver: labels are for your reference; they are not part of dialogue.

Sender: HELO smtp.road-runner.org

Receiver: 250 smtp.coyote.com

The reply 250 is a general acknowledgement code that basically means okay. It can be appended by other information, such as the receiver's address in the preceding example.

The next part of the dialogue is a request to send mail to the receiver system using the MAIL command. The MAIL command is typically appended with the term FROM: and then the address of the message sender. The following shows this second stage of the dialogue:

Sender: MAIL FROM:<roadie@road-runner.org>

Receiver: 250 OK

At this point, the receiving system knows what host is communicating with it, that it wants to send a message, and who the sender of the message is. The next piece of the dialogue defines to whom the message is being sent using the RCPT (recipient) command. Note that multiple recipients can be defined; the following example shows two, with the second being an invalid recipient.

Sender: RCPT TO:<charles@coyote.com>

Receiver: 250 OK

Sender: RCPT TO:<chuck@coyote.com>

Receiver: 550 No such user

Now the sending system will start to send the message body, which it requests to start with the DATA command. After sending the DATA command, the receiving system acknowledges that it is ready to receive the data. The data is sent in a stream of 8-bit ASCII characters (with the eighth bit cleared so that it is effectively 7 bits) with each line terminated with a Carriage Return/Line Feed (CR/LF) combination. The sender indicates that it is done sending the message body by sending CR/LF.CR/LF (CR/LF, a period, and another CR/LF combination). Following is an example of this portion of the dialogue.

Sender: DATA

Receiver: 354 Start sending your mail; terminate with <CR/LF>.<CR/LF>

Sender: (Stream of data lines sent)

Sender: <CR/LF>.<CR/LF>

Receiver: 250 OK

At this point several options exist for the sending system. It can terminate the connection with the QUIT command; request to send another message in the current session with the MAIL command; or offer to receive mail in the other direction with the TURN command, which is typically not used over TCP/IP networks. Usually, you will see the following:

Sender: QUIT

Receiver: 221 Terminating connection

T IP

Most email that supports SMTP communications offers logging options that enable you to see the actual SMTP dialogue being carried out between systems.

UUENCODE, MIME and S/MIME

As you have seen earlier in this chapter, Internet email is sent using only 7 bits of the available 8 bits. Because of this, you cannot send binary attachments within a typical email message. To get around this limitation, several standards have been developed that can take 8-bit binary data and encode it into 7 bits, and then decode it back into its original 8-bit form on the receiving side. The early standard for doing this was called UUEN-CODE, while the present standard is called MIME.

In the earlier days of Internet email you would run a program called UUENCODE to process a binary file. The UUENCODE program would produce 7-bit ASCII text in a text file, which could then be included within an email message body. The recipient could then save the encoded text out to a text file, and run UUDECODE to return it to its original binary format. In this way, program files, graphics files, and so forth could be sent through email messages.

The newer—and more ubiquitous—standard is called Multipurpose Internet Mail Extensions protocol, or MIME for short. MIME does fundamentally the same thing as UUENCODE and UUDECODE, but it is more sophisticated in that it can handle different types of binary data and multiple binary files within a single MIME stream of data. Each file within the MIME data can have a file type, which can be automatically associated with a viewer application on the receiving side. For instance, a MIME attachment with a *jpeg* type can be automatically loaded into an installed graphics program that understands JPEG files.

Because of concerns about security of information transmitted over the Internet, a standard called S/MIME (Secure-MIME) is taking hold. It allows an entire message to be encoded using one of several encryption schemes, with public key crypto used for decrypting the messages. S/MIME is supported by most large email systems vendors.

Most current email programs automatically decode attachments in UUENCODE or MIME formats (and more commonly S/MIME) and present them to the user as an attached file within a message. However, on occasion an attachment might not properly decode. For instance, it might have been created using some other binary email attachment technology (such as BinHex, which tends to be used by Macintosh computers). When this happens, you have to download a decoder for the type of file you received and process it as described at the beginning of this section.

POP and IMAP

Post Office Protocol (POP) and Internet Message Access Protocol (IMAP) are protocols that let a remote client retrieve email stored on an email host server. POP, the older of the two protocols, connects to the host server and downloads any new messages from the server completely. IMAP, however, makes a connection to the remote host, downloads message headers, and only retrieves the messages as they are requested by the user.

By far the more sophisticated of the two protocols is IMAP. Because it is designed to leave messages stored on the host server (it is a client/server protocol), it includes capabilities to display and work with remote folders, even hierarchical folders on the server. Moreover, IMAP can be used for reading Usenet newsgroups and is often used for this purpose by some email clients, such as Outlook Express.

When choosing to set up a connection to a remote email system using either POP or IMAP, keep these considerations in mind:

- If someone uses a single computer accessing a single email mailbox, POP is the simpler protocol to use and is probably the best choice. Message management can be easily accomplished on the client, although bandwidth requirements can be higher because you generally have to download all the messages, even those you might not want.

- If someone accesses email from many different computers, perhaps on different networks, IMAP might be the best choice. Because messages are stored and managed on the email server, the client becomes independent; all the messages are available no matter the location from which the user connects to his or her mailbox.

- If there are requirements for several users to access a common pool of messages in a single mailbox or mail folder, IMAP will be the required protocol.

HTTP

Many email systems now allow interaction with the email host through Web pages using the HTTP protocol. Examples include Microsoft Exchange Server, as well as many free email servers available on the Internet (such as HotMail or Yahoo! Mail).

X.500 and LDAP

One of the roles of an email system is to provide a directory of the users of the system. Such directories can be public, private (to users of the system only), or both. However, in order to make such a directory work globally across the Internet, it needs to be standardized so that all clients and servers can be sure of exchanging the correct data.

X.500 is an ISO standard for defining a global database of email addresses, which are made up of local databases stored on each email host participating in the global directory database. Part of X.500 is its Directory Access Protocol (DAP), which defines how the database is administered and operates with client computers. Unfortunately, X.500 is significantly more complex than anyone actually needs, at least at present, and it is beyond the capabilities of most email servers to manage.

To resolve these problems with X.500 DAP, a simpler version was introduced called Lightweight Directory Access Protocol (LDAP). This newer protocol requires much fewer resources to work properly; is a subset of the X.500 DAP, making it easier to evolve into full X.500 DAP when it makes sense); and operates correctly over TCP/IP networks—something that is problematic with X.500 DAP.

MAPI

Microsoft Messaging Application Programming Interface (MAPI) is a set of services that runs on a computer running Windows 9x or NT. MAPI services provide underlying connectivity to email systems from various email applications running on a system, which can include general applications, such as those in Microsoft Office. The main purpose for an interface such as MAPI is this: Applications want to use messaging in some fashion have a much easier time using the MAPI services in the operating system than having to write their own messaging interface routines into their application. MAPI enables more applications to make use of integral messaging and therefore helps improve the utility of email systems.

X.400

X.400 is a protocol for both a directory service and a mail transfer protocol. It was designed jointly by ISO and CCITT and is used fundamentally in Exchange Server to identify its own recipients and mail objects. However, its use is generally declining; it's more complicated than is needed and is not an elegant design.

X.400 defines recipients using a number of fields. The minimum fields are as follows:

- g=Given name (first name)
- s=Surname (last name)
- o=Organization name
- a=Administrative management domain
- c=Container name

These address fields are usually listed on a single line, each one separated from the next with a semicolon. So for example, the following is a valid X.400 address:

```
g=Fred;s=Flintstone;o=Bedrock;a=CityHall;c=Recipients
```

X.400 also defines a protocol for transmitting email between X.400-compliant email systems, somewhat similar to SMTP in concept. In Exchange Server, you use the X.400 connector to connect to other X.400 mail hosts and also to other Exchange Servers when you need to exert strict control over how often transmissions take place between the servers; otherwise you use the more generic Exchange Site Connector.

Connection Types

Both server to server connections and server to client TCP/IP connections require some sort of underlying physical connection. The following are the most common connections:

- **WAN/dedicated.** A dedicated connection is often used for site to site message transfer. Often, this might be through a T1 (DS-1) connection through which each network is connected to the Internet or to a private network. The main advantages to this type of connection are high bandwidth and 100 percent availability.

  T1 connections are made up of 28 normal (DS-0) telephone lines, each one capable of handling up to 56Kbps of bandwidth (when connecting to a digital line on the other end, such as another T1). Many companies also employ *fractional T1* lines, which are made up of 2 to 27 DS-0 lines and are somewhat more economical if lower bandwidths are required.

- **Dial-up/asynchronous.** Smaller sites and most clients will use a dial-up modem connection, also known as Plain Old Telephone Service or POTS to transfer messages. The main drawbacks to dial-up connections are slow modem speeds (33.6Kbps, typically) and slow connect times (30–60 seconds). Moreover, international connections are especially problematic due to delays and poorer line conditions when connecting outside of your country. However, POTS dial-up connections are by far the most economical if the other limitations are not a great concern.

■ **ISDN.** Some smaller networks use dial-up ISDN routers to connect to the Internet, through which they can then transfer messages. ISDN is relatively low-cost (particularly if it's not being used often) and also offers very fast connect times (1–2 seconds). Also, there are quite a few remote offices and home offices that use ISDN connections to connect to the Internet or to a company network. ISDN lines are made up of one *D channel* and two or more *B channels*. The D channel carries 16Kbps of bandwidth and is used for call setup and control information. Each B channel, also called a *bearer channel*, carries 64Kbps of bandwidth. There are two main types of ISDN lines in use: BRI and PRI. A BRI ISDN line (Basic Rate Interface) is composed of two B channels and one D channel and can carry up to 128Kbps of bandwidth if both B channels are in use simultaneously. A PRI ISDN line (Primary Rate Interface) is 24 B channels and is equivalent in bandwidth to a T1 connection (1.54Kbps).

■ **xDSL.** A newer technology than ISDN that is gaining rapid popularity, DSL (Digital Subscriber Lines) are digital network connections from a location, such as an office or home, to the local telephone company's central office (CO). DSL lines require that the remote location be within a certain distance of the nearest CO, generally about three miles. DSL lines make use of much greater bandwidth than traditional DS-0 telephone lines. Because a DS-0 line is limited to 8KHz of data (4KHz in each direction), a vast amount of data that could otherwise be carried over the telephone wires is never used. DSL addresses this by using newer interfaces in the telephone company's CO, which can access over 1MHz of bandwidth.

DSL lines come in many flavors, but the two most popular are SDSL (synchronous DSL) and ADSL (asynchronous DSL). An SDSL connection offers the same bandwidth in both directions of the connection, often 768Kbps of bandwidth. An ADSL connection, however, offers much higher speeds from the CO to the remote location (downstream) than from the remote location to the CO (upstream); typically 1.5Mbps downstream and 256Kbps upstream. Other implementations of ADSL offer less bandwidth, such as 256Kbps downstream and 56Kbps upstream. Which DSL services are available in your area is dependent on the installed capabilities of your local telephone carrier.

■ **Cable.** Many cable television carriers are trying to get into the business of carrying data and are starting to offer Internet access over special cable modems. Depending on the cable carrier in your location, service can be subscribed to for as little as $100 per month, with bandwidth of about 1Mbps. This technology is not yet implemented widely enough to know how successful it will be over the long run, although the cost per Mbps is extremely competitive and attractive.

Right now the industry of carrying data from one place to another is in a time of transition. Modem speeds are running at the theoretical limits of the 8KHz of available bandwidth. ISDN, while widely implemented, offers relatively poor cost per Mbps and has high implementation costs relative to modems and dial-up lines (and isn't really that much faster). DSL and cable modems seem to be the wave of the future and have garnered lots of industry support, but fundamentally it takes a long time to roll out services like these; they are capital-intensive for the carriers and labor-intensive to centrally install. Your best bet is to make the best short-term decision for connection types given your different requirements, and keep a close eye on the implementation of the newer technologies in your specific area. Contacting your local cable company and your Regional Bell Operating Company (RBOC) are good ideas; most have now laid firm plans for implementing these technologies and might have some idea of how they'll price them for your locality.

Understanding Exchange Server

Microsoft Exchange Server is a complete, soup-to-nuts messaging system that also provides substantial functionality for various groupware applications. Now shipping for several years, Exchange Server is reliable and is packed with features. It is the only email server (host) provided by Microsoft and the one they recommend for TCP/IP-based networks.

Microsoft initially entered the messaging business with two products: Microsoft Mail for AppleTalk networks and a product they acquired that was first called Network Courier and was then renamed to Microsoft Mail for PC networks. The names of both of these products shouldn't confuse the issue: They were not similar and were not even compatible (you couldn't even get the Macintosh AppleTalk product to exchange messages with the PC version). Microsoft Mail for PC networks (called simply MS Mail from now on) quickly became the dominant product, and continued to gain popularity. However, there were quite a few fundamental flaws with its design:

- MS Mail was a file-based email system in which each client had to access a shared set of folders located on a fileserver and was responsible for manipulating the messaging files for all messaging operations. There was no email server that carried out any tasks, just a fileserver that was the repository for the email database.

- MS Mail could be connected to other MS Mail sites and the Internet through the use of gateway software, which typically ran on a dedicated PC and had the necessary physical connection. For instance, you can connect two MS Mail sites to one another through a program called EXTERNAL.EXE, which used either a WAN connection or a dial-up modem to transfer mail between sites. Also available was a gateway to the Internet (SMTP) that was renowned for its instability; many sites connected the MS Mail SMTP gateway to timers to regularly power off and back on the gateway computer, because it was virtually guaranteed to crash *at least* once a day.

- MS Mail had relatively poor security; a knowledgeable user could wreak havoc with the shared email database. Whereas messages stored in the shared database were encrypted, because of the way in which clients had to access the database, each user had to have full read/write/delete privileges to most of the database files.

Before long it became obvious to Microsoft that MS Mail was not a solution that would carry it very far into the future. Starting approximately in 1993 Microsoft began work on an entirely new messaging server: Microsoft Exchange Server. Whereas Exchange Server offers an upgrade path from current MS Mail users and includes software for connecting to existing MS Mail sites, Exchange Server is an entirely new product and one that was written to be extensible for many years to come.

In this section you learn about Exchange Server, most particularly version 5.5, the latest version, running on Windows NT Server 4. If you are deploying a Microsoft TCP/IP network, you'll find that there is virtually no messaging need that Exchange Server cannot meet.

Overview of Exchange Server

Microsoft Exchange Server is a client/server messaging system that runs exclusively on Windows NT Server. Using an object-oriented approach, Exchange Server runs entirely as a collection of Windows NT services, making it easy to manage on a Windows NT network.

NOTE

Object-oriented refers to a programming model in which software components are treated as separate objects in the system. Communication takes place between the different objects to accomplish work. Object-oriented systems tend to be good frameworks when you want to retain the capability to plug in new or updated modules over time without disturbing the other parts of the system.

Broadly, Exchange Server offers the following features:

- **Client/server messaging.** Clients do not have direct access to the Exchange Server messaging databases, but rather access them through various available protocols that insulate the server and maintain the system's security and reliability.

- **Integration with Windows NT.** Because Exchange Server was written exclusively for use on Windows NT, it became possible to integrate Exchange Server with existing Windows NT Server advantages, such as security and manageability. Exchange Server participates seamlessly within the Windows NT domain security model, and was designed to be administered like any other Windows NT Server service. For example, when you add a new user to a Windows NT Server on which Exchange Server is installed, you can also automatically create his or her mailbox and set its parameters. Similarly, Exchange Server includes a slightly modified version of Windows NT Backup so that backup tasks for both the messaging stores and other files on the NT Server can be backed up simultaneously.

- **Transaction-based Database.** Exchange Server uses a sophisticated transaction-based database system in which messaging transactions are committed to the database similar to how SQL databases such as Oracle or SQL Server operate. If the server crashes, any unfinished messaging transactions are automatically rolled back out of the database, preventing corruption of the messaging stores. Moreover, transactions are first written to a sequential log file and are then updated into the main database. In the case of a server crash, those transactions—if they are complete—are automatically applied to the database. In this way, the system increases its performance and still maintains database reliability and integrity.

■ **Public Folders.** Exchange Server can host folders that can be accessed by multiple people. These public folders can contain messages of interest to many people; or other messaging *items* such as calendar entries, contact entries, or other entries containing programmed information. Access to these public folders can be easily controlled. Moreover, they can be made available to local Exchange Server users, to remote Exchange Server users (either replicated to their own Exchange Server or as remote users), or Internet users. If desired, anonymous access can even be granted to these folders.

■ **Network News Capabilities.** Exchange Server fully supports Network News Transfer Protocol (NNTP) for Usenet newgroups. Usenet newsgroups can be automatically downloaded into Exchange Server public folders and made more easily available for local Exchange Server users. Other public folders can be published as if they were Usenet newsgroups, provided the remote Usenet newsreader connects to the Exchange Server as its news server.

■ **HTTP Access.** One of the most interesting features in Exchange Server is the capability to access mailboxes, public folders, and calendar data through a Web browser. Using Internet Information Server along with special Exchange Server services, users can connect to Exchange Server over the World Wide Web and access their email, calendar, and public folders to which they have access. Domain security can be maintained for this access. Also, you can choose to publish the Exchange Server directory information to anonymous Web users.

■ **Unlimited Messaging Stores.** Exchange Server versions up to 5.0 are limited to 16GB for the public information store and the private information store. Starting with Exchange Server 5.5, both information stores now support unlimited amounts of data.

■ **Custom Applications.** Custom messaging-based applications can easily be designed and deployed using the Exchange Forms Designer (EFD), which generates Visual Basic-based forms in which you can enter your own program logic. Using this, for example, you could design intelligent purchase orders, marketing applications, or just about any type of messaging-based application you want. Basic, but still powerful, forms can be built using just the EFD and you can then extend them using Visual Basic for unlimited design possibilities.

■ **Server-based Scripting.** New with Exchange Server 5.5, the server can now execute scripts based on messaging activities, typically within public folders.

■ **Server-based Attachment Encoding and Decoding.** Exchange Server automatically decodes message attachments encoded using most of the standard attachment protocols, including UUENCODE, MIME, and S/MIME. Local users can also control which method is used to encode outgoing mail attachments, with the default being MIME encoding.

■ **Multiple Server Model.** Exchange Server is designed to support extremely large sites with tens of thousands of users. Doing this on a single messaging server is virtually impossible, particularly with growing message-size requirements such as all those .AVI files users keep getting sent. Exchange Server allows messaging services to be deployed on any number of servers within a site, with various features that enable the system administrator to balance the load between the various servers. Impressively, this can be handled so that it is transparent to the users. For example, a system administrator can move a user's mailbox from one Exchange Server to another within the same site, and the user will not be able to tell the difference. The same features apply to other Exchange Server services, such as public folders and different gateway components (called *connectors* in Exchange Server parlance).

■ **Central Administration.** An Exchange Server site, whether composed of one Exchange Server or many, can be easily administered from a single administrative program, which can be run either on a Windows NT Server or Workstation system.

■ **Scalable Architecture.** Exchange Server is not only scalable because you can deploy as many messaging servers within a site as you need, but also because it benefits from Windows NT Server's scalability. Exchange Server runs nicely on NT systems with multiple processors and is programmed to benefit from multiprocessing when it is available.

■ **Full Internet Standards Support.** Microsoft has done a good job of building Exchange Server to support not only Microsoft-sponsored protocols and standards, but more importantly to support generally accepted Internet protocols and standards. All the standards discussed in the beginning of this chapter are supported by Exchange Server. Also, because Exchange Server is so modular, it will be easy to add support for future standards that might emerge.

■ **POP and IMAP Client Connectivity.** In addition to supporting client connections using the native Exchange Server connector, clients can also connect to an Exchange Server using both POP3 (POP, version 3) and IMAP4 (IMAP, version 4), which are supported by a wide variety of client messaging applications. You can, for instance, easily access a mailbox and public folders stored on Exchange Server using Netscape Mail or Eudora Pro.

■ **Connectivity to Other Systems.** Exchange Server connects to the Internet using the standard SMTP protocol. However, often a large organization has many different messaging platforms deployed, and it is advantageous to be able to connect Exchange Server directly to those systems instead of having to use Internet mail as a backbone. For example, a direct connection to a cc:Mail system can enable directory synchronization between Exchange Server and the cc:Mail system. Exchange Server connectors are available for MS Mail, Lotus cc:Mail, Lotus Notes, OfficeVision/VM, X.400-based systems, and SNADS-based messaging systems.

■ **Highly Secure.** Exchange Server supports Microsoft Key Management Server, allowing public-key cryptography for extremely sensitive messaging.

■ **Easy Migration.** Microsoft made it fairly easy (as easy as possible, anyway) to migrate from most messaging systems to Exchange Server, making Exchange Server an excellent platform to consolidate the activities of an organization that has deployed many different messaging systems. Migration tools are included for MS Mail, cc:Mail, IBM PROFS and OfficeVision, Verimation MEMO, Collabra Share, Novell GroupWise, and DEC All-In-1.

■ **Good Client Support.** Clients are included with Exchange Server for systems running Windows 9x, NT, MS-DOS (limited to email only) and Macintosh systems. Other systems can easily connect to and make use of Exchange Server through its strong support of standard protocols discussed previously, such as POP and IMAP. For instance, Eudora, Outlook Express, and Netscape Mail will all connect to Exchange Server using one of the standard protocols supported.

As you've seen in the preceding bullets, Microsoft Exchange Server is an extremely powerful and capable messaging server. To date, it has been deployed at thousands of sites encompassing hundreds of thousands of mailboxes. It is a proven solution to virtually any messaging need.

Key Exchange Server Components

It's hoped that the preceding section has whet your appetite so that you'll want to learn more about Exchange Server and how it works. In the remainder of this chapter, certain key Exchange Server features are examined and discussed in more detail.

Exchange Server is extremely flexible. This flexibility is both a boon and a curse. On the one hand, you can configure it to do just about anything an organization might want in terms of messaging. On the other hand, this flexibility makes it sometimes difficult to understand the product in its entirety. When a product can handle everything from a single site with 100 users to a multisite, multientity conglomerate with millions of users, it makes it more difficult to get a handle on which features are important to an individual. Knowing how the features that users need work, without getting bogged down understanding features that they don't need and might never use, can become difficult. When learning Exchange Server in detail, it is important to identify the features and capabilities that matter for a particular implementation.

Exchange Administrator

Most Exchange Server administrative duties are carried out using Exchange Administrator, a tree-based tool that manages most aspects of an Exchange Server site. Figure 19.1 shows Exchange Administrator.

TIP

Exchange Administrator can be run from any Windows NT computer within a domain, including Windows NT Workstation. Access to the Exchange Server configuration information is based on the NT domain security settings and various permissions for each object in Exchange Server set within Exchange Administrator by the administrative account.

To install Exchange Administrator properly, run the Exchange Server installation program, but use the Custom install to only install the Administration program. You cannot install other Exchange Server components onto Windows NT Workstation.

Organization container   Site container

FIGURE 19.1
*The Exchange
Administrator
program.*

Containers —

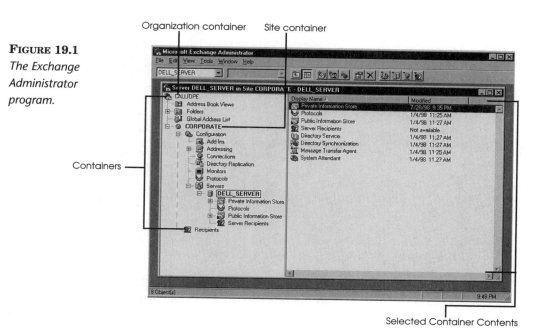

Selected Container Contents

Exchange Server is organized in a tree hierarchy, the top of which is the organization. Usually, the organization is the name of the company using Exchange Server. Beneath the organization are various sites. Usually, each site refers to a collection of LAN-connected resources, and is often geographic in nature. For instance, the New Riders organization might include site names for Indianapolis, West Coast, East Coast, and so forth. Beneath each site name are the server names, which are each server running Exchange Server. Typically, the server names are the names of the Windows NT servers. Finally, within each server can be multiple recipient containers, which are collections of recipients. Usually, only one recipient container is defined per server, although the system allows for multiple recipient containers if a need exists to divide up the local email directory in that way.

The Administrator program is arranged somewhat similarly to Windows Explorer. In the left pane are all of the object containers. Each container contains various configuration objects that you control through property dialog boxes. For example, if you select an actual mailbox in the recipients container and then choose **File**, **Properties**, you see the recipient's Properties dialog box as shown in Figure 19.2.

FIGURE 19.2

*A recipient's Properties
dialog box.*

FIGURE 19.2

*A recipient's Properties
dialog box.*

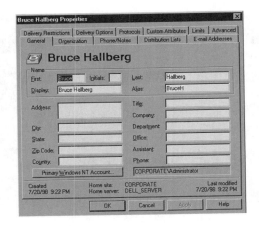

Exchange Administrator Objects

To add new objects to a container, you use the four New commands within
the Administrator's **File** menu. Figure 19.3 shows you this menu with the
New Other submenu open, whereas Table 19.1 describes the different
types of objects you can create.

FIGURE 19.3

*Create new objects
with the New com-
mands in the File
menu.*

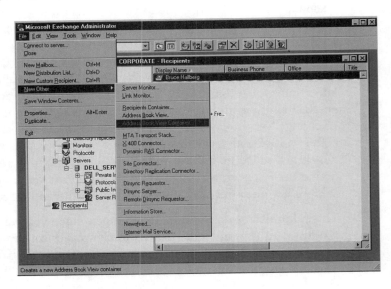

Table 19.1   Object Types in Exchange Administrator

Name	Purpose or Description
Mailbox	Created in the Recipients container, this object creates a standard mailbox for an individual.
Distribution List	Creates a distribution list, a recipient in the directory which actually refers to a number of individuals.
Custom Recipient	Defines a recipient in the Exchange Server directory that is located on another system. Custom recipients can be MS Mail users, Internet mail users, cc:Mail users, or others. The definition for a custom recipient includes information about the host on which they are located. The benefit for custom recipients is that they appear to Exchange Server users as local recipients; the server then takes care of forwarding mail to their actual mailbox on the remote system.
Server Monitor	Server Monitors are processes that monitor the state of a particular Exchange Server. Server Monitors are powerful; you can define exactly what services on the server are monitored, how often they are checked, and what actions the monitor takes when a service stops or reports problems. Actions can include launching a Windows NT process, restarting the process automatically, restarting the entire server automatically, sending an email message, or creating a Windows NT alert.
ink Monitor	A Link Monitor is an object that monitors a server at a remote site. It does this by sending `ping` messages at regular intervals, and then taking defined actions when the `ping` messages are not returned in a specified amount of time. For example, if you are connected to another site and your company regularly messages back and forth to that site, a Link Monitor can be used to alert the administrator to problems before the users are aware of any.

continues

Table 19.1,   CONTINUED

Name	Purpose or Description
Recipients Container	By default an Exchange Server site contains one recipients Container in which all recipients in the site are stored. You can also, however, create additional recipient containers. These additional containers can be used to further segregate directory listings. For example, you can put all customer service personnel in a particular recipients container that is available for public directory lookup over the Internet, but that still maintains the anonymity of other employees in the company.
MTA Transport Stack	A Message Transfer Agent (MTA) stack is required to send and receive messages over different protocols. MTA stacks can be installed for TCP/IP, RAS, X.25, and TP4.
X.400 Connector	If you want to connect Exchange Server to an X.400-based system, the X.400 Connector object should be installed. Note that this connector is among the most robust—in terms of features—of all the available connectors. Also, the X.400 connector can be used to connect two Exchange Server sites together. Often, you choose to connect sites in this way when you want to connect them over a slower WAN link; the X.400 connector allows for scheduling and other bandwidth-budgeting settings, whereas the Exchange Connector does not.
Dynamic RAS Connector	Lets you configure inter-site connections using schedule RAS connections, typically accomplished over dial-up lines using a modem, but sometimes also used over other types of connection types (such as ISDN or xDLC).
Site Connector	To connect two Exchange Server sites you need to create a Site Connector object. Using this object, you can configure message transfer between sites, as well as directory and public folder replication.

Name	Purpose or Description
Directory Replication Connector	This connector, installed after the Site Connector, lets you configure directory replication from one site to another. Directory replication is the process whereby changes in one Exchange Server's directory are automatically updated to other connected Exchange Server sites and vice-versa.
Dirsync Objects	MS Mail allows its directories to be exchanged with other MS Mail systems through a process called *directory synchronization*. These are scheduled updates of directory information sent within the body of a mail message. Exchange Server can function as a Dirsync Requestor to an existing MS Mail Dirsync Server, or as a Dirsync Server, or as a Remote Dirsync Requestor that receives updates from an upstream Dirsync Requestor that is in turn connected to the Dirsync Server. There can be only one Dirsync Server within an MS Mail organization, although it can be hosted on either MS Mail or Exchange Server.
Information Store	The Information Store is a collection of two databases: the Public Information Store and the Private Information Store.
Newsfeed	Newsfeed objects connect to news servers over the Internet and send and receive news articles for the specified newsgroup.
Internet Mail Service	To enable users of Exchange Server to transfer mail to Internet mail users (and vice-versa) you need to install the Internet Mail Service object. This object is also required to connect Exchange Server sites through Internet mail. Essentially, this object gives Exchange Server the capability to handle SMTP traffic with other mail servers.

Exchange Server Services

Microsoft Exchange Server runs through Windows NT Services. This structure makes administration of Exchange Server much easier. For one thing, a user does not have to log in to the Exchange Server computer as it boots in order to start the Exchange Server services; they are started immediately after the system boots, and they log themselves in to the system. For another, these services break down the Exchange Server components into more manageable pieces that can be started and stopped as the system is reconfigured or as problems occur. For example, if an error occurs in a message transfer agent, that service can be stopped and restarted. Or, when certain configuration changes are made, the service that relies on those settings can be stopped and restarted manually in order to apply the changes. Figure 19.4 shows most of the Exchange Server services in the Windows NT Services dialog box.

FIGURE 19.4

Exchange Server services under Windows NT Server.

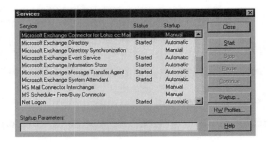

The main Exchange Server services are as follows:

- **Directory.** The Directory service is responsible for maintaining the Exchange Directory, the list of resources available on the Exchange Server, and for fulfilling requests from connected clients.

- **Information Store.** The Information Store (IS) combines the two main repositories of information on Exchange Server: the Public Information Store and the Private Information Store. The Public Store holds information stored in public folders, while the Private Store holds user mailboxes and their private folders, including folders that hold other types of objects, such as calendar entries or contact entries. The IS service handles message transfers for mail within an Exchange Server, manages the databases themselves, and forwards messages to the Message Transfer Agent for processing to other systems.

- **Event Service.** Exchange Server makes use of Windows NT events to log problems, failures, and other critical information. These events are viewed with the Windows NT Event Viewer, just like other events under Windows NT. In order for Exchange Server events to be logged, however, the Microsoft Exchange Event Service must be running. Also, with Exchange Server 5.5, the Event Service handles server-side scripting duties.

- **Message Transfer Agent.** The Message Transfer Agent is the software that handles message routing, translation, address mapping, and actual message transfer between servers. The MTA is engaged when messages are sent from one Exchange Server to another and when they are sent to remote X.400 messaging systems.

- **Connector Services.** Installed connectors for other messaging systems, such as MS Mail or cc:Mail, also run as Windows NT Services. These connectors contain all of the logic required to transfer mail directly to the connected systems. More importantly, they do not make use of the Message Transfer Agent, but instead interface directly with the Information Store.

- **System Attendant.** The core Exchange Server service, the System Attendant (SA), must be running in order for other Exchange Server services to operate. Shutting down the System Attendant will, in fact, automatically shut down all other running Exchange Server services because of this dependency. The SA ensures that the directory is consistent at all times, does the work for any installed server or link monitors, and handles site routing within the Exchange Server site.

Exchange Server Backup and Restore

Email use is growing rapidly in corporate America and the amount, quality, and sensitivity of information stored in email systems is enough to keep an IS manager awake at nights worrying about system crashes. Indeed, many users today are lost when email services aren't working, and you can imagine the horror if the information stored in an email service is lost.

Exchange Server includes sophisticated backup capabilities to maintain high system availability and keep the data in the Information Store safe. Included with Exchange Server is a modified version of Windows NT Backup, which is really all you need to properly back up an Exchange

Server system. Moreover, there are several third-party backup solutions that include special add-ons specifically designed to support Exchange Server backup and restore.

You can perform two types of backups on Exchange Server: offline and online. Offline backups back up the entire Exchange Server, but require that the services be stopped in order to get a good backup. Of more utility, online backups will back up the system while it continues to function normally. The Exchange Server version of Windows NT Backup supports Exchange Server's transaction database and interacts with it in such a way that reliable online backups can be made. As you might recall from earlier in this chapter, Exchange Server writes most messaging traffic to log files as it operates, and it then updates the information in the IS at a lower priority level when the system has time to complete the transactions. This structure also supports online backups; while an online backup is running, the Exchange Server can continue to handle all of its messaging duties using these log files, while the IS files are frozen for the backup process. After the backup is finished, the log file contents are automatically updated into the IS files.

The only drawback in the area of Exchange Server backup and restore is the inability to selectively back up *or* restore individual mailboxes. Instead, to restore an individual mailbox without disturbing others, a second Exchange Server (with the same site name) must be created onto which the backup can be restored. Access to the mailbox of interest can then be gained and the information transferred to the real Exchange Server. To help mitigate this shortcoming in Exchange backup, Microsoft added a message retention feature in Exchange Server 5.5 whereby items a user deletes can be held in the Information Store for a configurable amount of time before they are truly deleted.

TCP/IP and Exchange Server

Exchange Server transfers Internet email using the Internet Mail Connector (IMC). This connector handles SMTP communications for Exchange Server. It is usually installed after Exchange Server itself is installed, through an Internet Mail Connector Wizard that prompts the administrator for the necessary information and then sets up the Properties dialog box for the IMC accordingly.

The main part of the IMC configuration is handled within the Connections tab of its Properties dialog box, shown in Figure 19.5. The following table describes the main settings available in this dialog box.

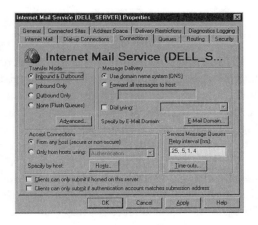

Setting	Description
Transfer Mode	Controls whether the current Exchange Server handles inbound Internet email, outbound, or both. Selecting None disables this connector after flushing any waiting messages.
Message Delivery	This section lets you choose to forward Internet email to a downstream mail host, either another Exchange Server or a mail server at your ISP; or to communicate directly with each mail host as defined in the DNS and based on the address to which mail is being sent. Generally, Exchange Server functions best (and fastest) when it handles message transfer directly with individual mail systems for each messsage; it can handle as many simultaneous SMTP conversations as you want and as much as bandwidth allows.
Accept Connections	Lets you specify the criteria with which Exchange Server accepts inbound mail from outside mail hosts. For sites with extremely high security requirements you can use the settings in this section to define that only messages from secure hosts using some authentication method will be accepted. You can also specify different rules for different mail hosts, if desired.

continues

continued

Setting	Description
Service Message Queues	In this area of the dialog box you specify when message redelivery takes place. The default is to retry in 15 minutes, then 30 minutes, then one hour, and then four hours, before a non-delivery report is generated.

The Internet Mail tab (see Figure 19.6) of the IMC's Properties dialog box lets you define some overall characteristics for the connector. With the Internet Mail tab, you can choose to which mailbox non-delivery reports are sent (usually the system administrator, or the postmaster), and how outgoing message attachments should be encoded (users can choose a specific encoding for a particular message if they want). You can also activate both support for S/MIME attachments and conversion of incoming messages to a fixed-width font (some Internet email relies on having a fixed-width font to preserve formatting; Exchange's default is to use Arial or whatever default font the user has selected). Also, you can set the appropriate character sets to use for MIME and Non-MIME traffic and can further specify these settings by domain. Finally, you can enable Message Tracking, which, while consuming a lot of space on the server, can help in tracking down problems with the IMC connector.

FIGURE 19.6

IMC's Internet Mail tab.

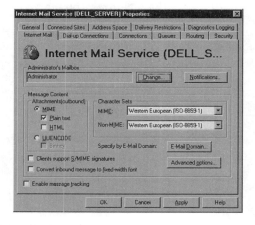

While there are a number of other tabs available in the IMC dialog box, they tend to be used more for other administrative tasks than for connecting Exchange Server to the Internet. All you really need to do to connect Exchange to the Internet is:

- Set up the TCP/IP protocol on Windows NT Server

- Establish an Internet connection on the server

- Install Exchange Server

- Install the Internet Mail Connector, making the appropriate settings as described earlier

- Assert the Exchange Server's A record and MX record to the DNS system

In more complicated environments you can also configure a number of Exchange Servers to fill different tasks. For instance, you can have one Exchange Server handling Internet mail but then forwarding it to another Exchange Server for handling within the site (decoding attachments and delivering to user mailboxes). Or, you can have different Exchange Servers to handle inbound and outbound mail separately. For extremely large sites you can even have multiple Exchange Servers handling inbound mail and outbound mail; inbound mail is balanced between servers using the Route Cost setting in the various MX records in the DNS system.

Internet Email References

The best way to learn about the various technologies that go into Internet mail is to read the RFCs available on the Internet. These RFCs define technologies such as SMTP, MIME, X.400, X.500, LDAP, and so forth. Table 19.2 shows you key RFC documents in this area that you might want to examine for yourself.

Table 19.2   Internet Email RFC Documents

Document	Discusses
RFC 821	SMTP Protocol
RFC 822	Basic SMTP Message Format
RFC 974	Mail Routing and the Domain Name System
RFC 977	NNTP Protocol
RFC 1123	Requirements for Internet Hosts
RFC 1154	Automatic UUENCODING/UUDECODING of Messages

continues

Table 19.2, CONTINUED

Document	Discusses
RFC 1521	MIME Message Format
RFC 1522	MIME Encoding for Headers
RFC 1725	POP3 Protocol
RFC 1777	LDAP Protocol
RFC 1869	Extensions to SMTP (ESMTP)
RFC 1870	SMTP Service Extensions for Message Size
RFC 1891	SMTP Service Extensions for Delivery Status Notification
RFC 1895	SMTP Service Extensions for Remote Message Queue Starting
RFC 1945	HTML for Electronic MIME Messages
RFC 2060	IMAP4 Protocol

Chapter Summary

If messaging over TCP/IP networks is of interest and importance to you, there are many good books available that discuss the topic in far greater detail than the overview in this chapter can provide. Indeed, there are many books on just this one topic alone, and a surprising depth to the information is available if you need it. However, in this chapter Internet messaging is discussed, and you learned about the basic concepts of this important subject.

If you are deciding on a new messaging server, it's hard to go wrong by choosing Exchange Server, particularly if you're already managing a Windows NT domain. As you have seen, Exchange Server is a remarkably robust, reliable, and powerful platform on which to build messaging functionality and custom applications that make use of messaging. It can be connected to every major system available, and includes tools that make upgrading from other systems as easy as possible. However, changing email systems is *always* a difficult task that should not be undertaken lightly. Using Exchange Server, you can build a messaging system that is limited more by your imagination than by any real technical limitations.

Chapter 20

INTERNET INFORMATION SERVER

This chapter introduces you to version 4.0 of the Internet Information Server. In this version of IIS a number of new features have been introduced. When you look at all the component products that comprise IIS it is now quite an extensive product. You will not only learn how to install and configure the product(s) but also how to test and use the various products as a user.

The main feature of IIS is its WWW service. However, there are many additional services within IIS such as FTP, MTS, MMC, NNTP, SMTP, and Certificate server.

If you check the bookstores, you will find entire books devoted to the subject of IIS 4.0. Therefore, a single chapter obviously cannot cover a subject with the same depth as an entire book can. Nonetheless, I think you will find this chapter provides you with a sufficient level of knowledge and the skills required to not only install, but also to configure and use the subcomponents of IIS. In fact several advanced IIS components are covered to a greater depth here than in the books devoted to the subject.

So, read on as you install and implement the features of IIS. I trust that you will want to employ some if not a majority of the features presented here on production NT servers.

Windows NT 4.0 Option Pack Features

Internet Information Server version 4.0 is included in the Microsoft Windows NT 4.0 Option Pack. To install the Option Pack you must first install Service Pack 3 and Internet Explorer 4.01; these products are available for download by choosing **Downloads** at www.microsoft.com/ntserver.

NOTE

In the past Microsoft has included both bug fixes and new features in Service Packs. Microsoft has decided to split these into two separate packages. Service Packs now contain bug fixes only, whereas Option Packs include new features.

In addition to Internet Information Server 4.0, the Option Pack also includes a number of related supportive servers, online documentation, and Web content analysis applications. The major features related to IIS 4.0 and the other products included in the Option Pack are summarized below.

Microsoft Internet Information Server 4.0 Features

In the computer world, change is a given. But few things have changed as much in as short a time as Microsoft's Internet Information Server (IIS). Version 2 of IIS, which shipped on the Windows NT Server 4.0 CD-ROM, was obsolete almost as soon as NT 4 hit the streets. Version 3 was soon available as a free upgrade. And now version 4 is included as part of the Windows NT 4.0 Option Pack, which is available as a free download.

Because IIS is still distributed as a free NT 4 add-on, and because IIS 4.0 is a significantly more robust and capable product, you should not even consider living with the limitations of IIS 2.0 or 3.0.

IIS is a product comprised of other services, such as the WWW, FTP, and MTS services to name a few. The key service is the World Wide Web (WWW) service, which provides Web content to end users by sending files that are typically HTML documents, and either GIF or JPEG graphic files. However, IIS can also send other file types including OCX, CAB, DLL, and EXE files as well. IIS 4.0 now supports HTTP 1.1, which transfers files using a more efficient process.

A typical Web page that a user views is the product of numerous individual files. The first file transferred is the HTML document itself; it contains the text of the Web page. HTML files usually contain addresses to other graphic or sound files that give Web content its richness. Prior versions of IIS supported HTTP 1.0, which for each file transferred established a new session using the TCP three-way handshake, and then dropped the session following the file transfer using a second three-way handshake. In addition to six extra packets for each file, each new TCP session goes through its own slow start process, therefore, not gaining any significant benefit from slow start optimization.

Some of the significant new features found in IIS 4.0 are listed and described below:

Hypertext Transfer Protocol (HTTP 1.1)

Simple Mail Transfer Protocol (SMTP)

Network News Transfer Protocol (NNTP)

Active Web Content

Security Features

Front Page Server Extensions and Posting Acceptor

Hypertext Transfer Protocol (HTTP 1.1)

Version 1.1 is now supported by IIS; if the client's Web browser also supports HTTP 1.1 then the user should experience quicker Web page responses and more importantly, less traffic on the Web. HTTP 1.1 allows the session between the IIS 4.0 server and the Web browser to be "kept alive" from one file to the next. This typically results in dramatically fewer TCP three-way handshakes and sessions that are long enough to benefit from slow start optimization.

Simple Mail Transfer Protocol (SMTP)

This service supports both SMTP and Post Office Protocol (POP3) protocols. This service allows IIS to provide mail services to clients.

Network News Transfer Protocol (NNTP)

Using this service you can now publish news content using the NNTP protocol. The newsgroups you create can be public or private and can also be made read-only or moderated to ensure that inappropriate content is not added to the newsgroup.

Active Web Content

IIS includes support for developers that build active Web-based applications. In addition to traditional CGI, IIS also supports newer methods for developers to enhance Web content. Active server pages (ASPs) are special HTML Web pages. Part of an ASP is ultimately sent to the end user as a standard HTML document, but other portions of an ASP execute VBScript (Visual Basic) or JavaScript on the IIS server first. These scripts can alter what is ultimately sent to the end user. IIS, through ActiveX Data Objects (ADO) or Interactive Database Connector (IDC), can access database servers such as SQL Server and Oracle to include database content in Web pages. Internet Server Application Programming Interface (ISAPI) extensions allow developers to build applications that directly access IIS. Also by using Component Object Model (COM) and Distributed COM (DCOM) IIS is capable of running compiled ActiveX applications that provide business logic. With IIS 4.0 these applications can be run in separate address spaces, thereby protecting IIS and other ActiveX servers in the event of a program failure.

Security Features

IIS has the capability to implement security through several means. IIS security ranges from anonymous access at the low end and can include

Windows NT Challenge Response Logon Authentication, use of Windows NT accounts and Groups, NTFS file permissions, IP address and domain blocking, and Certificated Authentication of users. IIS also supports Secure Sockets Layer (SSL) 3.0 and Private Communication Technology (PCT) 1.0.

Front Page Server Extensions and Posting Acceptor

These features allow Web content developers to post content directly to IIS using FrontPage Visual InterDev or the Web Publishing Wizard.

Microsoft Management Console Features

The Microsoft Management Console (MMC) is the interface Microsoft plans to use for configuring Windows NT and Back Office products. Windows NT 5.0 will use the MMC as its primary interface for configuration changes. By itself the MMC provides a graphical user interface but no functionality. Through the use of *snap-ins* MMC is capable of viewing and configuring various products. In this Option Pack Microsoft includes snap-ins for configuring IIS, MTS, and Index Server.

The concept behind the MMC is that Microsoft wants to provide a single universal interface for configuring any of their products, thereby making it easier on administrators especially when they need to configure a new product. Microsoft is also supplying the MMC specifications to third-party vendors and in the future you should expect to see non-Microsoft applications also use MMC for configuration. Additionally MMC console settings can be saved and optionally marked as read-only, giving administrators a great way to customize task-based interfaces for assistants or send snap-in tools via email.

Microsoft Index Server Features

Microsoft Index Server scans the files that make up your Web site then creates an index of the words found in the HTML, TXT, DOC, XLS, and PPT files. Additional file types can also be scanned if the proper filters are installed. Index server automatically updates the index when new files are added or when existing files are changed. When an end user wants to search for documents that include certain words such as *discount* and *vacation* the Index Server will be capable of providing a list of Web pages or other documents that include the desired words.

Microsoft Transaction Server Features

Microsoft Transaction Server (MTS) makes it easy for application programmers to create applications that perform complex functions. A transaction is a change to two or more pieces of data that you want either performed completely successfully, or not at all. An example of a transaction is a cash withdrawal from your checking account at an ATM. You donít want half of the transaction performed, say a $200 debit from your checking account. Unless of course the other half also completes, that being the ATM giving you the cash. Using MTS a developer can easily develop an application that must update any number of data sources within a single transaction. The programmer writes the program as if it were transacting against a single data source and MTS handles the complexity no matter how many data sources are actually updated.

MTS also performs a second function for ActiveX Code Components. A programmer can write a program (a server) that provides a service (that is, some functionality) to another program such as a Data Entry program. Many end users can run programs that utilize the services of a single server program. However, eventually the number of end user programs will overburden the thread of execution in the server program. MTS again makes it easy on the programmer. Instead of the programmer writing code to determine when additional threads should be created to handle increased workloads, MTS handles the creation of additional threads.

Microsoft Message Queue Server Features

Microsoft Message Queue (MMQ) Server provides an easy, secure, and reliable means for two programs to communicate asynchronously. In todayís business environment many programs need to interact with other programs. For instance, if a customer orders 15 left-handed monkey wrenches the order entry program should inform the inventory program so the quantity on hand can be adjusted. What happens if the inventory program or even the inventory system is down? Do you stop taking orders? If these two systems were tightly coupled through synchronous messaging you might in fact have to stop taking orders if another system is offline. MMQ provides a means for two programs to exchange messages asynchronously. MMQ guarantees to deliver messages sent from one program to the second program when the second program is back online. The messages are delivered in order. If desired, the second program can then respond to the first again through MMQ. MMQ provides reliable program to program communication through network outages, either planned and unplanned system downtime.

Microsoft Certificate Server Features

Microsoft Certificate Server is a service that manages issuing, renewal, and revocation of *Digital Certificates*. Digital Certificates are used to accurately identify the identity of a user, author, or service. Digital Certificates are used as part of public/private key authentication of client and server when using SSL or PCT secure channel technology.

Microsoft Site Server Express Features

Site Server Express includes light versions of Web management application tools found in Site Server. Available separately, Site Server is a Microsoft product for maintaining commercial Web sites. Site Server Express includes the following three utilities:

- Content Analyzer—Content Analyzer *walks* your Web site to see how your Web pages are linked. It then can display a hierarchical or a graphical representation of your Web site. Using this tool makes it easy to see layout, navigation paths, and operational and broken links of a Web site. See Figure 20.1 for an example of Content Analyzer.

- Usage Import—Usage Import imports log files in any of four formats into a database. After the log file information has been imported it can be analyzed with Report Writer. Therefore both Usage Import and Report Writer are predicated on IIS generating log files of their usage.

- Report Writer—Report Writer allows you to generate reports on Web usage. These reports identify high and low traffic pages, bandwidth utilization throughout the day, the location of people who visit your Web site, hit rates per hour, and so on. These reports are beneficial for determining items as different as advertising rates and available capacity for growth.

FIGURE 20.1
Content Analyzer Cyberbolic depiction of the ExAir sample Web site.

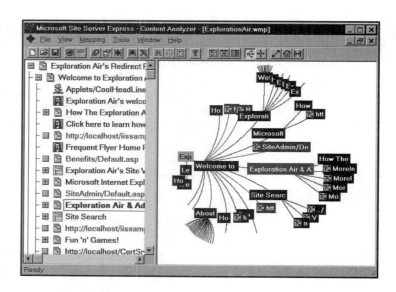

Installing IIS 4.0

Before you can install IIS 4.0 you must first get a copy of the Windows NT 4.0 Option Pack. If you have the Option Pack on CD-ROM, use it. Otherwise you will need to download installation file(s); start by selecting the **Downloads** link at www.microsoft.com/ntserver. During the download process you can choose which components to download. If you download all components for NT Server you are looking at approximately 87MB in downloads! To install the Option Pack you must first install Service Pack 3 and Internet Explorer 4.01; you can also download these updates from the preceding URL.

After you have access to the Windows NT 4.0 Option pack there is very little preparation required. When you load the Windows NT 4.0 Option Pack CD-ROM a Welcome Web page is displayed. Choosing the Install link displays the Web page shown in Figure 20.2. This page summarizes the prerequisites required prior to installing IIS 4.0.

Do the following to get ready:

- Configure TCP/IP on the computers that are participating.

FIGURE 20.2

Windows NT 4.0 Option Pack installation requirements Web page.

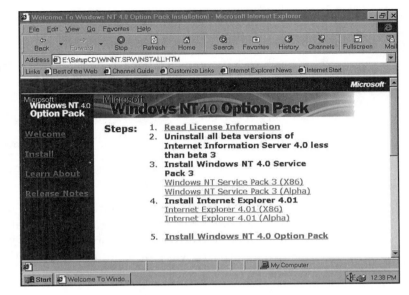

IIS functions properly if the IIS server is a DHCP client. However, because IP addresses can potentially change on DHCP clients I recommend you consider using fixed IP addresses on IIS servers. Moreover if your IIS server is accessible from the Internet then InterNIC requires that you use a fixed IP address.

- Install Windows NT 4.0 Service Pack 3 or the most recent version if there has been a new release. The service pack will probably be included if you obtain IIS on CD-ROM. It is included in TechNet and can be downloaded from www.microsoft.com.

- Install Microsoft Internet Explorer version 4.01 or later. If you obtain IIS on a CD-ROM, IE 4.01 is included. Alternatively you can download an appropriate version of IE from www.microsoft.com.

- Identify a Windows NT Server computer that will host IIS. If you expect IIS to be heavily used, this server should be dedicated to the task of providing IIS services.

- Disable any WWW, FTP, or Gopher servers that might be running on the IIS server. (IIS 4.0 installation will remove earlier versions of IIS from the host system.)

- Just in case, back up any WWW or FTP content directories that are currently on the server.

- Format or convert the volumes to be used by IIS with NTFS. This ensures the highest possible level of security.

- Enable auditing if you feel you need to closely monitor the server for security breaches.

- Set up a name resolution method. You have several choices:

  DNS is best if you are connected to the Internet or if your network includes non-Microsoft hosts.

  WINS is probably easiest to maintain because it copes with network changes automatically, particularly if IP addresses are assigned by DHCP. But WINS cannot supply names to non-Microsoft hosts unless it is configured to work in conjunction with the Windows NT DNS server.

  HOSTS files can be used to support Microsoft and non-Microsoft hosts. But HOSTS files are static, and any change to the network means updating everyone's hosts files. HOSTS files won't enable outsiders to access your Web and FTP servers by name.

  LMHOSTS files can provide static naming for Microsoft hosts.

Start the installation process by choosing option 5, Install Windows NT 4.0 Option Pack (see Figure 20.2). You are then presented with three screens that allow you to select options which govern the installation. The first screen identifies the features of the Option Pack, the second screen is a license acceptance, and the third screen allows you to choose between Upgrade Only and Upgrade Plus. The Upgrade Plus choice allows you to add new features. Following these three screens you should see the screen depicted in Figure 20.3. This screen allows you to choose which components to install.

Depending on how many components you select from the screen depicted in Figure 20.3 you will be presented with a number of screens where you must accept or choose alternative directories for the major services of IIS 4.0; these services use the following directories:

FIGURE 20.3

*Windows NT 4.0
Option Pack
Component Setup
screen.*

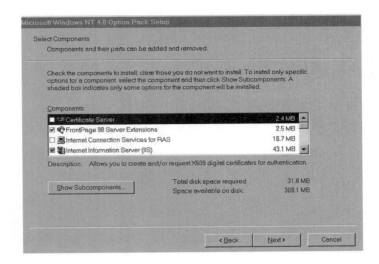

- WWW Service root. This folder is the root directory of the directory tree that is available to the WWW service. The default directory is C:\inetpub\wwwroot.

- FTP Service root. This folder is the root directory of the directory tree that is available to the WWW service. The default directory is C:\inetpub\ftproot.

- NNTP Service root. This folder is the root directory of the directory tree that is available to the NNTP service. The default directory is C:\inetpub\news.

- Mailroot Directory. Directories supporting the SMTP mail server are created in this folder. The default directory is C:\Inetpub\Mailroot.

- Application Installation Point. This is the folder in which directories are created for the installation of IIS. The default directory is C:\Program Files.

The screen shown in Figure 20.4 is for the SMTP Service, however, it is typical of those related to IIS, Transaction Server, Index Server, NNTP Service, and the Certificate Server.

FIGURE 20.4

Select the Directory Location used by the SMTP Service.

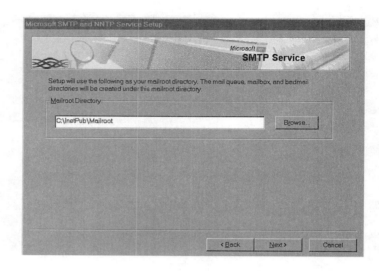

The Certificate Server will prompt you for information relative to the Certificate Authority (CA) that you are establishing; see Figure 20.5 for an example of the information required by the certificate server.

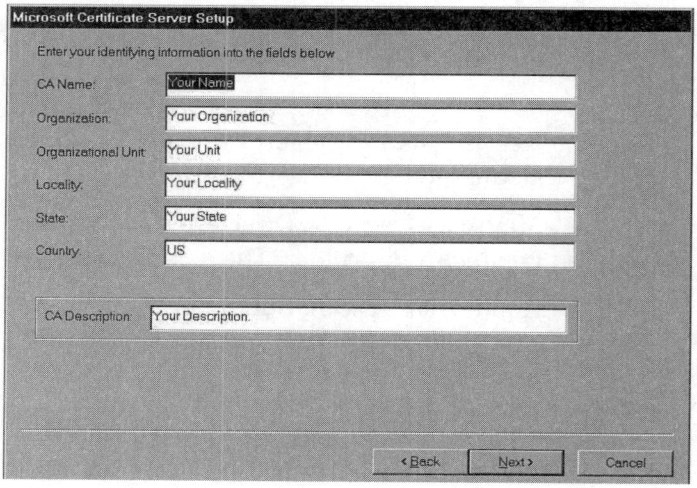

FIGURE 20.5

The certificate server identifying information.

Installing the Microsoft Message Queue Server (MSMQ) requires SQL Server and requires you to choose options on a number of screens. The first installation screen for the Message Queue Server is depicted in Figure 20.6. In a production environment several servers are installed as Message Queue Servers; during installation you choose the role a specific Message Queue Server will play. In order to test MSMQ you only need a single Message Server that must be installed as a Primary Enterprise Controller (PEC).

FIGURE 20.6

MSMQ Message Server Setup role selection.

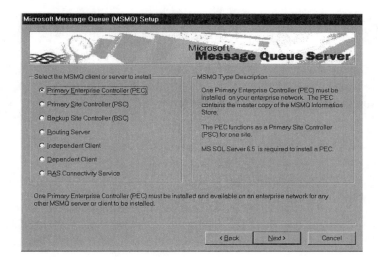

The second MSMQ screen depicted in Figure 20.7 allows you to enter names for the Enterprise and Site to be created. The Enterprise Name might parallel the company or organization name while the Site Name usually parallels where the server is located. A site normally includes the computers from one physical locationsuch as a building for example. Typically, computers within one location are capable of communicating with each other without traversing slow speed networks. However, between sites the line speeds are typically much slower than within a site. For instance if a company has three offices located in Los Angeles, Chicago, and New York, and if your company operates NSMQ servers in these locations then in this case three sites should be established.

FIGURE 20.7

Enter Enterprise and Site Names for MSMQ.

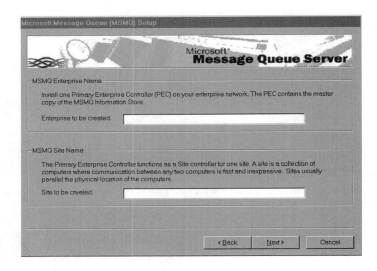

The third MSMQ installation screen allows you to choose which directory to install the MSMQ Administrative Tools in (and SDK if you have chosen to also install it).

The fourth MSMQ installation screen allows you to choose the size and location for two SQL Server database device files. You can accept the prompted values or override with different values. Figure 20.8 is an example of this screen.

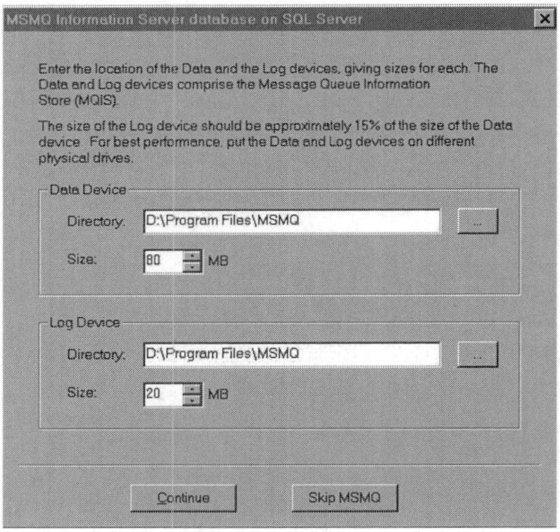

FIGURE 20.8

SQL Server data and Log Device file selection screen.

The fifth MSMQ installation screen, as shown in Figure 20.9, allows you to view and create connected network names. To add new network names choose the **Add** button, which displays another screen where you can choose IP or IPX as a network type and you can also type a new connected network name.

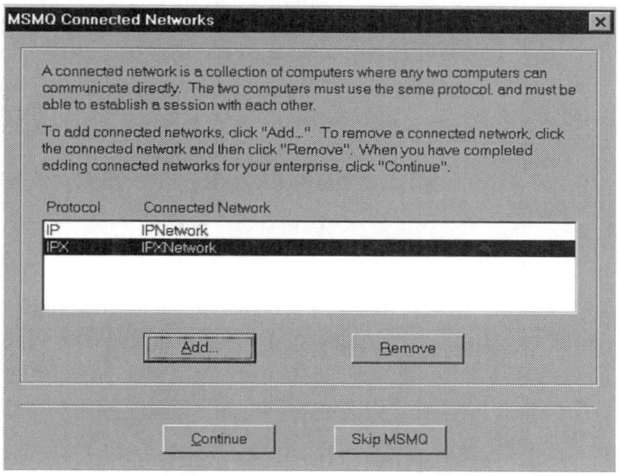

FIGURE 20.9

The MSMQ Connected Networks screen.

Figure 20.10 shows the last MSMQ installation screen; it allows you to associate an IP address with a connected network name.

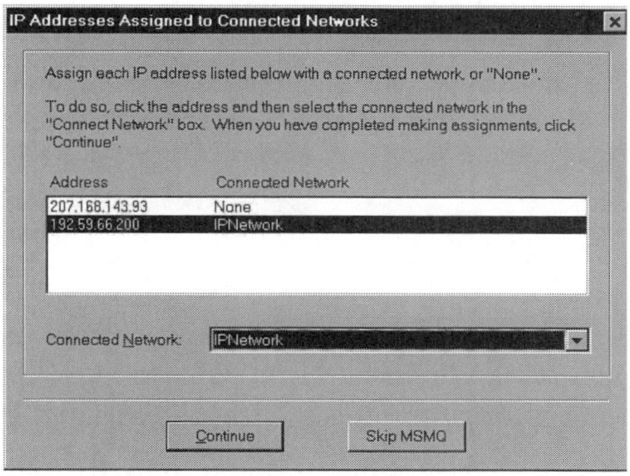

FIGURE 20.10

MSMQ Assign IP address to Connected Network screen.

When you install IIS 4.0 three installation options are presented:

- Minimum Install. This option installs the following IIS components:
  - WWW Service, enables you to provide Web services.
  - Active Server Pages, server scripts that provide dynamic content.
  - Microsoft Data Access components, support connectors to a variety of databases, including ActiveX Data Objects with Remote Data Service and OLE DB.
  - Internet Service Manager Snap-In, supports Web and FTP server management.
- Typical Install. Actually, this is a full installation of IIS that provides the following additional components, although it does not install all components of the Option Pack:
  - FTP Service, the FTP server component of IIS.
  - Internet Service Manager (HTML), enabling you to administer IIS from a Web browser located anywhere on your network.
  - Documentation, the full set of online documentation.
- Custom Install. This option opens a dialog box where you can select individual components for installation. Notice that some components are interdependent. If you select a component for installation, setup automatically selects any other options on which the component depends.

After files are copied, restart the computer to activate IIS.

Using the Product Documentation

Application and documentation icons are installed in the Start Menu under Programs/Windows NT 4.0 Option Pack. To access the documentation from the server running IIS select the Product Documentation option.

The product documentation is actually served up by the WWW server, part of the reason why the WWW server must be installed and running as part of every IIS system. You can access the documentation from a browser on a remote system as well. If the workstation is logged on to the server's NT domain, you can access the documentation using the following URL, where *server* is the server's NetBIOS name:

```
http://server/iisHelp/iis/misc/default.asp
```

If the server is named in DNS, you can also use its domain name in the URL. The following URL assumes the help files are on server www.keystone.com:

```
http://www.keystone.com/iisHelp/iis/misc/default.asp
```

Figure 20.11 shows the product documentation viewed from IE. If the documentation displays correctly then your Web server is presumed to be functioning.

FIGURE 20.11

Viewing the Product Documentation in Internet Explorer.

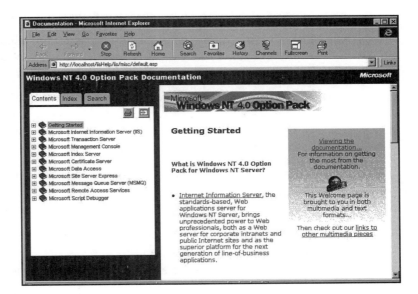

NOTE

The product documentation makes heavy use of ActiveX controls, which are currently supported only on Microsoft's Internet Explorer browser, versions 3.0 and later. Some features in the documentation will be unavailable if you are using another brand of browser.

Uniform Resource Locators

Uniform resource locators (URLs) are used to request access to directories, files, and services on the World Wide Web. A URL specifies three categories of information:

- The *protocol* to be used. The protocol name is followed by the characters `://`. Protocol specifiers you encounter in this chapter are:

  `http://`—Hypertext Transport Protocol, the protocol used to display WWW documents formatted with Hypertext Markup Language.

  `ftp://`—File Transfer Protocol, a protocol that enables users to receive files from and send files to the server.

  `nntp://`—Network News Transfer Protocol, the protocol that enables users to retrieve news messages from a news server.

- The *domain name* or *IP address* that the user wants to access. Typically users specify a domain name. If a WWW server is running on the local computer, you can refer to it as `localhost`.

- The *path* to the information the user wants to retrieve. A path specifies directories and subdirectories and specifies a file to be accessed. The path is optional. If a path is not specified then the WWW server opens its root directory.

The following URL accesses the root directory of the WWW server at www.microsoft.com.

    http://www.microsoft.com

Here is an example that opens a specific subdirectory for FTP transfer:

    ftp://www.widgets.com/public

Finally, this example opens a specific file on a Web server:

    www://www.keystone.com/public/information/goodstuf.htm

For more information on URLs, check out:

    www.w3.org/hypertext/WWW/addressing/addressing.html

Introducing the Microsoft Management Console

IIS 4.0 will probably provide your first exposure to the Microsoft Management Console (MMC), which is inexplicably named the Internet Service Manager in the Start Menu. The MMC will be the focus for nearly all management activities on Windows NT Server 5.0. The MMC accepts snap-in components that extend its capability and has built-in links to some commonly used administrative tools. In fact, the Internet Service Manager, formerly a standalone utility, is now a snap-in to the MMC.

What Is the Microsoft Management Console?

MMC uses snap-ins to add functionality and provide the capability to view and change configuration settings. Eventually each Microsoft Back Office server configuration tool such as Internet Service Manager or SQL Enterprise Manager will be converted to snap-ins. The MMC basically has a two-pane Explorer look and feel. The left pane is called the Scope pane, and it displays snap-ins and controlled objects in a hierarchical tree. The right pane is called the Results pane, and it displays objects based on the item selected in the left pane. You can right-click an object then choose **Properties** to view, add, or alter configuration items. What is actually displayed within the MMC interface and how the objects appear are all dependent on the snap-in. Therefore you can expect objects to have different properties and often different icons than objects associated with a different snap-in.

IIS, MTS, and Index Server Snap-ins

IIS, MTS, and Index Server are implemented as MMC snap-ins. The IIS snap-in is used to configure IIS including the WWW, FTP, SMTP, and NNTP services. The MTS and Index Server snap-ins are used to configure their respective services. The Microsoft Message Queue Service is currently not supported by a snap-in and is configured by a traditional applet.

Figure 20.12 shows the MMC. In the left pane is a tree-oriented display of the services MMC is configured to manage. I have expanded the tree under Internet Information Server to show you its contents. In this example, IIS is installed on a computer named IW2. As you can see, WWW, FTP, and SMTP servers have been installed. Note that two WWW sites are in place. IIS supports the configuration of virtual servers, enabling a single IIS computer to support multiple WWW, FTP, and SMTP servers. You will learn how to set up virtual servers later in this chapter.

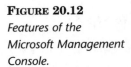

FIGURE 20.12

Features of the Microsoft Management Console.

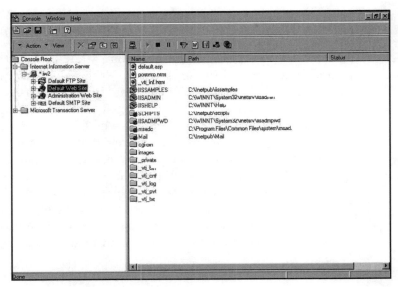

Take a moment to examine the MMC. The scope pane displays a hierarchical tree of node objects that you are able to manage, that is your scope of management authority. The results pane shows those elements that fall within the selected node's domain.

As with many objects in Windows NT 4.0, you can right-click services and folders to open context menus. These menus replace much of the functionality that was found in the drop-down menus used in earlier versions of IIS. Figure 20.13 shows the context menu for the Default Web site. The contents of the context menus will vary depending on the type of the object with which they are associated.

If you dislike right-clicking objects in order to manage them, you can alternatively manage objects by using the drop-down menus from the *Rebar*. The Rebar is the toolbar that changes depending on what node is selected.

You can put any site in one of three states:

- **Running.** A Running site is started and operating normally. Start a stopped or paused site by selecting it in the scope pane and pressing the **Start** button in the toolbar. Alternatively you can right-click the site and select the **Start** command in its context menu.

- **Paused**. A Paused site continues to operate but will not permit new users to connect. To pause a site select the site and press the **Pause** button in the toolbar. Or you can use the Pause command in the site's context menu. When a site is paused, the legend (Paused) will appear after the site's name.

- **Stopped**. A Stopped service is no longer operating. To stop a site, select it and press the **Stop** button in the toolbar, or use the Stop command in the site's context menu. When a site is stopped, the legend (Stopped) will appear after the site's name.

FIGURE 20.13
The context menu for a Web site.

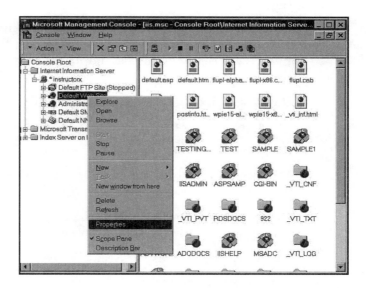

TIP

For a given service, all sites are supported by the same Windows NT service. For example, WWW sites are supported by the World Wide Web Publishing Service. These services can be started, stopped, or paused using the Services applet in the Control Panel.

Figure 20.13 shows the Rebar with its Action and View menus, which is a context-sensitive toolbar. Other additional toolbar buttons perform the following functions:

- **Delete.** Deletes the selected object when deletion is permitted. You cannot delete the default site for an active service, but you can delete secondary sites.

- **Properties**. Opens the properties dialog box for the selected object. (Equivalent to selecting the Properties option in the object's context menu.)

- **Up one level.** Navigates to the next higher level in the scope tree.

- **Hide/Show Scope.** Hides and reveals the scope (left) pane of the MMC.

- **Add a computer to the list.** Connects the Internet Service Manager to a specific IIS server. After it is connected, the services running on that server can be observed and managed by persons with administrative permissions.

- **Pause service**. Pauses the selected service.

- **Start service**. Starts the selected service.

- **Stop service**. Stops the selected service.

- **Key Manager.** Opens the Key Manager, which creates key pair files used by the Secure Sockets Layer (SSL).

- **Performance Monitor.** Opens the Performance Monitor utility. A set of counters is configured and tailored to monitoring IIS.

- **Event Viewer.** Opens the Event Viewer.

- **Server Manager.** Opens the Server Manager.

- **User Manager.** Opens the (Oh, you guessed!) User Manager.

You can open multiple service trees in MMC by using the New option in the Console menu. This feature enables you to display multiple services on the same server or on multiple servers, as your needs require.

In the future, you will be able to extend the capabilities of MMC by installing supplementary modules called snap-ins. As Windows NT Server 5.0 approaches, expect to spend more and more of your NT administration time in the MMC.

Managing Web Sites

The Default Web site is fully configured and running after IIS is installed and the server is restarted. The site is configured with default performance properties. Security assumes that logons will be anonymous, meaning that all users are permitted to access the site without logging on.

NOTE

When installed, each service is configured with a default site. If multiple sites are defined for an IIS service, users will access the default site unless they explicitly request a site.

You cannot delete the default site, but you can rename it. You can delete the original default site if you have added a site and made it the default site.

Although the defaults might be fine, you can do a great deal to configure site security and properties. These topics will be covered in the following sections.

Essential Site Properties

Each site is configured by a series of property sheets. There is also a set of master properties that will be inherited by newly created sites.

Configuring Master Properties

To configure the master properties for the IIS server:

1. In the services tree, select the server to be configured.

2. Click the **Properties** button in the toolbar (or select **Properties** from the server's context menu). This will open the Master Properties page shown in Figure 20.14.

3. In the Master Properties field, select **WWW Service** or **FTP Service**.

4. Choose **Edit** to open the property sheets.

The property sheets are described in the section, "Configuring Web Site Properties," later in this chapter.

The server Properties page has two other options that you should be aware of. These options enable you to activate bandwidth throttling and configure MIME types.

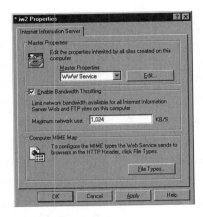

Configuring Bandwidth Throttling

If an IIS server is accessed through a channel that is shared with other servers, it is possible for IIS traffic to grow to levels that prevent other services from receiving sufficient bandwidth. This can be a problem if, for example, outside users are accessing your Web site through the same T1 line that your users depend on to access the Internet. If you want to limit IIS traffic then you can activate bandwidth throttling, setting an upper limit on the amount of outgoing traffic IIS generates.

To configure bandwidth throttling:

1. Open the Master Properties page for the server.

2. Check the Enable Bandwidth Throttling check box.

3. In the Maximize network use field, specify the maximum network bandwidth in kilobytes/second that should be used by all Web and FTP sites running on this server.

Configuring MIME Types

The Multipurpose Internet Mail Extensions (MIME) enable non-text content (binary)—such as video, audio, and non-HTML documents—to be published through Internet services such as the Web and email. To play back multimedia content, client browsers must receive information that specifies which application should be used to handle the data.

When IIS publishes binary data to a Web client, it creates a header for the file that specifies the file's MIME type. This information enables the client's browser to open the appropriate application to process the data. IIS is configured with a default set of MIME file types. If your office is Microsoft-centric, the default file types might be adequate. If you are not using Microsoft Office or Microsoft applications you might need to add or modify MIME type definitions.

In the server Properties page, click **File Types** to open the MIME File Types list, shown in Figure 20.15. You can add and remove MIME file type mappings from this dialog box.

FIGURE 20.15
MIME file types.

Configuring Properties for Web Sites

Each Web site is configured through its own set of property pages. This section examines selective property pages and shows you what you need to know to manage an IIS Web site.

Web Site Properties

The Web Site Properties tab is shown in Figure 20.16. Properties on this page establish the identity, or identities, of the Web site.

Description. This field provides a name for the Web site, which can be changed. The only function of this name is to identify the Web site in the MMC tree of services.

IP Address. The default Web site is assigned the IP address (All unassigned), which associates the site with all IP addresses configured on its server. If you create multiple Web sites on this copy of IIS, you might need to add IP addresses to the server and change this field.

NOTE

The (All unassigned) setting configures a Web site to service all IP addresses that are not explicitly assigned to other Web sites on the same computer. This makes the Web site with the (All unassigned) address the default Web site for its computer. You must have a Web site configured with the (All unassigned) address to have a default Web site.

TCP Port. Each service running on a TCP/IP computer is assigned a port number that enables TCP/IP to deliver messages to the correct service. The default port for the Web is 80, but you can assign different ports if desired. One reason for changing the port is to add a new Web site to the IIS server. If you specify a port other than 80 the user must specify the port in the URL. If the port is 8080, for example, the user would use a URL similar to the following:

```
www://www.widgets.com:8080/
```

Connections. By default, a Web site is configured with the setting Unlimited, permitting unlimited numbers of users to access the site. Now frankly few Web servers are equipped with the server hardware and the network bandwidth to allow unlimited numbers of users, so it is very likely that you will want to limit connections (along with limiting bandwidth by adjusting the bandwidth throttling parameter).

Connection Timeout. This field specifies a time in seconds after which IIS will close an inactive connection. This timeout value ensures that the server's connection allotment is not used up by HTTP connections that have not been properly closed.

Enable Logging. If this box is checked the Web server will maintain administrative logs. The logging file format is specified in the Active log format field. Four file formats are available.

- **W3C Extended Log File Format**. An ASCII log format that can be customized by the administrator. This is the default setting.

- **Microsoft IIS Log Format**. These logs consist of fixed-format ASCII data. This format is available only for the IIS.

- **NCSA Common Log File Format.** An ASCII data file following a format specified by the National Center for Supercomputing Applications.

- **ODBC Logging.** This option generates a fixed-format log that is directed to a database.

If you have enabled logging, first select the desired logging format. Then choose Properties to open a Properties dialog box. Logging properties vary depending on the logging format you have selected. They are described in the next section.

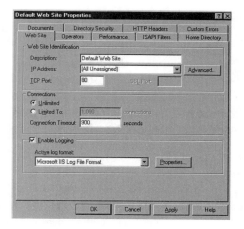

FIGURE 20.16
Default Web site properties.

Logging General Properties

A General Properties tab (see Figure 20.17) is provided for the following log formats:

- W3C Extended Log File Format
- Microsoft IIS Log Format
- NCSA Common Log File Format

The format of this dialog box is similar for those three log file formats.

FIGURE 20.17

*General properties for
W3C, Microsoft, and
NCSA logging.*

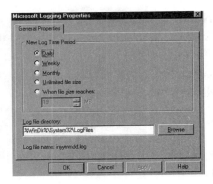

Entries in the New Log Time Period box determine when IIS will close the current log and open a new one. You can choose to create a new log file at fixed time intervals (Daily, Weekly, Monthly). Or you can select **Unlimited** file size, permitting the log file to grow indefinitely, in which case you must manually initiate a new log file. Or you can set a fixed maximum size for the log file by selecting **When the size reaches** and entering a file size in MB, in which case the log file is closed and a new one is started when the specified file size is exceeded.

The Log file directory field specifies the directory in which log files will be created. Filenames consist of a two-letter prefix designating the log file type, followed by the date in yymmdd format and ending with a filename extension of .log. You can review the template for log file names at the bottom of the General Properties dialog box.

W3C Logging Extended Properties

If you select W3C logging, logging properties include the Extended Properties tab shown in Figure 20.18. Check the data that you desire to have recorded in the log file. For descriptions of the options, click **Help**.

ODBC Logging Properties

You can have IIS log messages to any database that supports the Open Database Connectivity model (ODBC), such as Microsoft Access or Microsoft SQL Server. Because database management is a specialized skill not covered in this book, setup of ODBC logging will not be discussed. For users familiar with database administration, the online help provides configuration assistance.

FIGURE 20.18

W3C logging extended properties.

Web Site Operator Properties

Returning to the Web Site Properties, the Operators tab (Figure 20.19) is used to specify which users can administer the Web site. By default the group Administrators is listed in the <u>O</u>perators list. You can add individual users or groups if desired. The Administrators group can be removed if other users have been assigned to the operators list.

FIGURE 20.19

Specifying Web site operators.

Performance Properties

The Performance tab is shown in Figure 20.20. This tab is used to configure several parameters that affect performance of the Web site.

Performance Tuning. This slider control can take three values, based on the number of hits that are anticipated for the Web site, where a hit is the establishment of a connection with the Web server. Connections will be established most rapidly if the setting is greater than the actual number of hits experienced by the Web server. If the Performance Tuning setting is too high, server memory will be wasted.

Enable Bandwidth Throttling. Earlier you saw how to establish bandwidth throttling for the entire IIS server. Properties on the site Performance tab enable you to establish bandwidth throttling for the individual Web site. If the server supports multiple sites, you might need to adjust bandwidth throttling to prevent busy sites from denying bandwidth to less busy sites.

Connection Configuration. If you check **HTTP Keep-Alives Enabled** (it is checked by default) a client is permitted to maintain an open connection with the server so that it is unnecessary to establish a new connection with each request. If you deselect this option, clients must establish a connection for each new request, conserving server connections but resulting in slower response time.

FIGURE 20.20

Specifying Web site performance options.

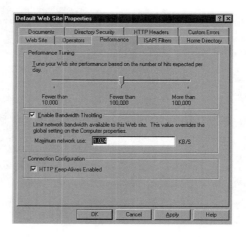

Directory Security Properties

The Directory Security tab, shown in Figure 20.21, accesses security options for the Web server. You can base your security on a combination of anonymous access, password controls, and address controls.

Figure 20.21

The Directory Security tab.

Anonymous Access and Authentication Control

Select the **Edit** button in this box to open the Authentication Methods dialog box shown in Figure 20.22. In this tab you have three options that define the level of security for the Web site. You can use any or all of these authentication control methods.

IIS server security has several levels that give administrators considerable control over access to their Web sites. Here is the process IIS uses to determine whether a user will be given access to a resource:

1. IIS checks to see if any access restriction prevents the user's IP address from connecting with the site. If the IP address is restricted, IIS returns an error.

2. IIS checks to see if anonymous users are permitted to access the resource. If anonymous access is permitted, the user is connected with the resource and is given the permissions established for the anonymous user account.

3. If anonymous users cannot access the resource, IIS uses one of the following methods to authenticate the user:

- Basic (unencrypted) logon if that feature is enabled.

- Microsoft Challenge/Response (encrypted) logon if that feature is enabled.

- A digital certificate if Secure Sockets Layer security has been enabled.

After establishing an authenticated connection, the user is logged on with the permissions assigned to a predefined account.

4. IIS checks the server permissions to determine the type of access that the server will grant (read or read/write).

5. IIS checks NTFS permissions to ensure that the user has access to the desired resource.

6. If the user is authenticated (or has anonymous access), and if the server offers the required access, and the user has the required NTFS permissions then user is given access to the resource.

A nice feature of IIS is that it works closely with standard Windows NT security. Users log on using conventional NT user accounts and are subject to the file permissions established for their accounts. Therefore most of IIS server security uses skills you have already acquired in this book. Now, let's see how to manage the special security features of IIS.

FIGURE 20.22

Selecting IIS authentication methods.

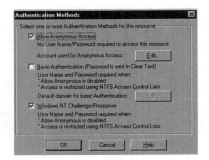

Anonymous Access

By far, the majority of Web sites are available for anonymous access. Users are not required to log on to anonymous sites and typically are limited to Read permissions only. When IIS is installed, setup creates a user account named IUSR_*servername* where *servername* is the name of the computer on which IIS is running. When anonymous users connect with the Web site, they are given the permissions assigned to IUSR_*servername*, which by default is a member of the Domain Users and Guests groups.

The anonymous user account has passwords in two locations. It is assigned a Windows NT user account password, which becomes part of the account's information in the security database. It also has a password that is entered in the IIS Web site configuration that enables IIS to log on to the anonymous user account. These passwords must agree. If the user account exists on the IIS server computer, the passwords can be synchronized automatically. If the user account exists on another computer, the passwords must be synchronized manually. Here is how to tell if the user account exists on the IIS server computer:

■ The anonymous user account exists on the IIS computer if the computer is a domain controller (which has a copy of the domain security database) or if it is a standalone server with its own security database.

■ The user account exists on another computer if IIS is running on a server that belongs to a domain but is not a domain controller.

If **Allow Anonymous Access** is checked, you can click **Edit** to open the Anonymous User Account dialog box shown in Figure 20.23. This dialog box has the following fields:

■ **Username**. This field specifies the name of the Windows NT user account that provides permissions for anonymous users. You can edit this entry or choose **Browse** to select a different user account.

■ **Password**. This field can be modified if Enable Automatic Password Synchronization is not checked. If the anonymous user account does not exist on the local computer, you must enter its password in this field. This makes the password known to IIS so that it can log on to the user account.

■ **Enable Automatic Password Synchronization**. If the anonymous user account exists on this computer, as described earlier, check this field so that IIS will synchronize its password with the password of the Windows NT account.

FIGURE 20.23

*Setting up the anony-
mous user account.*

Basic Authentication

In many cases you will want to authenticate users who need to access Web resources. IIS supports two methods of authenticating users through passwords: Basic and Windows NT Challenge/Response.

NOTE

You can easily mix access requirements on a site. Suppose that your site supports anonymous access but that you want to require a logon for certain material. Simply restrict the permissions for the anonymous account so that it cannot access the secure directories. When the user's browser is linked to the secure directories for the first time during a session the user is presented with a logon dialog box. Either Basic or Challenge/Response authentication can be used to verify the user's account name and password. Alternatively you can use digital certificates to make the security processes transparent to the user.

Basic authentication requires the user to enter the username and password of a Windows NT account. Users are required to authenticate under either of two conditions:

- Anonymous logon is disabled.

- The anonymous user account does not have the permissions required to access a resource.

In either of these cases, if basic authentication is enabled the user's browser displays a dialog box where the user is required to enter a username and password to gain access to the desired resource.

Because the Windows NT user account database is used to authenticate users, you do not need to maintain separate user accounts for IIS. But basic authentication is just that: basic. Passwords are not encrypted as they traverse the network, making them available to anyone equipped with a protocol analyzer. Therefore, you run the risk of compromising your Windows NT passwords when using basic authentication.

You should use basic authentication only if you must support users whose browsers do not support Microsoft Challenge/Response. If that is the case, consider setting up user accounts that are used exclusively with IIS. Edit the permissions assigned to these accounts so that they cannot be used to log on to Windows NT. Then if the passwords of your Web users are discovered they will not provide a means of logging on to your LAN.

If you check **Basic Authentication** you can choose **Edit**. After a warning about the dangers of transmitting passwords in clear text, you will see the Basic Authentication Domain dialog box as shown in Figure 20.24. By default IIS authenticates users with the domain in which the Web server is active. Choose **Use Default** to use the IIS server's domain for user authentication.

If desired, you can authenticate users from another domain. Enter a domain name or choose **Browse** to look for a domain on the network. User accounts in the domain you specify are used to authenticate users who are required to log on to the IIS server.

FIGURE 20.24

Basic authentication can authenticate users from any Windows NT domain.

Windows NT Challenge/Response

Windows NT Challenge/Response supports secure, encrypted logons for clients using Microsoft Internet Explorer version 2.0 or later. At this time, other Web browsers do not support Windows NT Challenge/Response.

Windows NT Challenge/Response authentication uses an encrypted logon dialog box in which the user's actual password is not transmitted through the network. Users are authenticated using Windows NT domain account information and are assigned permissions allocated to their user accounts. Windows NT Challenge/Response authentication is supported only on NTFS volumes.

If Windows NT Challenge/Response is enabled in the Authentication Methods dialog box it will be used to authenticate users under either of the following conditions:

■ Anonymous logon is disabled.

■ The anonymous user account does not have the permissions required to access a resource.

Secure Communications

Windows NT Challenge/Response provides a secure logon process. The logon dialog is encrypted, and the user's password is not sent through the network. But apart from the logon, Challenge/Response does not encrypt data that goes through the wire.

If your Web site is serving up data that requires the ultimate in security, you need to investigate the secure communications option for IIS. IIS supports two technologies that enable you to set up very tight encryption-based security for your Web server.

■ Secure Sockets Layer (SSL)

■ Private Communication Technology (PCT)

The basis of SSL/PCT technology is that the *digital certificate* is an encrypted digital document that identifies an organization. The certificate is encrypted using a *private key* known only to the organization generating the certificate. A *public key* can be freely distributed, enabling outside users to decrypt the digital certificate and establish the identity of the organization. The public key can only decrypt the digital certificate and therefore cannot be used to forge a certificate. Private/public key encryption is a very reliable method of securing data.

Digital certificates can be issued by the organization running an Internet server, and IIS 4.0 includes a certificate manager. When your Web server is in commerce with outside organizations, however, you probably want to use your digital certificate to uniquely identify your Web server so that outside users know that they can trust the identity of your server. In such cases you probably want to obtain your digital certificate from an independent organization that both parties mutually trust.

After the public/private *key pair* is used to initiate a secure connection, all exchanged data can be encrypted. This makes secure communications ideal for supporting Internet commerce and exchanging credit card and other sensitive information. IIS enables you to specify the degree of encryption to vary the security with your requirements. Greater degrees of encryption, measured in terms of the number of bits in the encryption keys, result in slower communication due to the added time required to encrypt and decrypt the data at the communication end-points.

IIS 4.0 includes everything you need to set up secure communication. However the process is a bit involved for this introductory chapter, so I have elected not to cover it. Moreover, you enter the realm of serious legal liability whenever you transmit sensitive data through a public network, and I strongly recommend that you obtain advice from a security consultant if you require secure Web communication.

IP Address and Domain Name Restrictions

You can regulate access to the IIS server based on the IP address or DNS domain name of the user. This is a convenient but not very secure method of restricting users because knowledgeable users can impersonate IP addresses. Consequently, this technique should be viewed as an administrative convenience not as a method of securing access to your Web server.

Three types of address-based restrictions can be entered:

- **IP address**. You can grant or deny access to a user working on a computer with a specific IP address.

- **Group of computers**. You can grant or deny access to a range of IP addresses defined by a network ID and a subnet mask.

- **Domain name.** You can grant or deny access to a user working on a computer with a specified DNS domain name. If this method is used, IIS must perform a DNS domain name lookup for each new user, which can significantly degrade server performance.

To add an entry to the list:

1. Select the **Directory Security** tab in the Web Site Properties dialog box.

2. Click the **Edit** button to open the IP Address and Domain Name Restrictions dialog box shown in Figure 20.25.

FIGURE 20.25
IP address and domain name restrictions.

3. Select the **Granted Access** or the **Denied Access** radio button to establish the default security.

   If you select **Granted Access** as the default security all users are permitted to access the Web server unless they are explicitly denied access. This is the default setting.

   If you select **Denied Access** as the default security all users are denied access to the Web server unless they are explicitly granted access.

4. Choose **Add** to open a dialog box similar to Figure 20.26.

FIGURE 20.26
Selecting an access restriction based on an IP network address.

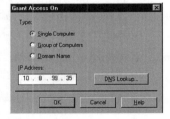

5. Select the radio button for the desired type of access restriction.

6. If you select **Single Computer**, enter the IP address of the computer in the **IP** Address field.

7. If you select **Group of Computers**, the display changes as shown in Figure 20.27. Complete the Network **ID** and Subnet **Mask** fields to define the range of addresses to which the restriction applies.

FIGURE 20.27

Selecting an access restriction based on an IP network address.

8. If you select **Domain Name**, enter a domain name, as shown in Figure 20.28. The first time you access this option you will be shown a warning stating that domain name lookups will degrade server performance.

FIGURE 20.28

Selecting an access restriction based on a domain name.

Document Properties

When a browser accesses a Web server, the browser is attempting to retrieve documents from the server. Browsers can retrieve two types of documents from IIS 4.0 (with the option of configuring additional document types in the future):

■ **HTML documents.** These documents are identified by the .htm filename extension and contain Hypertext Markup Language. HTML is the traditional language used to create Web documents.

■ **Active Server Pages.** These documents are identified by the .asp filename extension. Active Server Pages is a Microsoft technology that enables IIS to provide many content types that cannot be included in HTML documents. Any Web browser should be capable of viewing Active Server Pages because the active portion is executed on the Web server.

Web documents provide different levels of interaction. Simple Web documents have an .htm or .html extension and are basically static. Any browser can view them; the only active elements on a simple Web page are hyperlinks to other Web pages.

Web content can be made more active by including programming code. The code can be designated to run either at the IIS server (Server side script), or at the Web browser (Client side script).

If the code is designated to run at the Web browser (Client side) it is typically coded in either JavaScript or VBScript. However, in order for the browser to use the script the browser must be capable of interpreting and executing the code. Many but not all Web browsers understand JavaScript; IE version 3.0 and higher understands VBScript as well.

If you run the code on the IIS server (Server side) you are not dependent on the capabilities of the browser. ASP allows either JavaScript or VBScript to run at the server. The resulting output is a standard HTML file that can be viewed by any browser.

Another type of document is an ActiveX document. ActiveX documents are actually server applications that execute on the client machine and are comprised of a combination of at least two files. The Web browser acts as a client program that communicates with the server, which is the ActiveX document. One file contains compiled code and has either an .exe or a .dll extension. The other file has a .vbd extension, where vbd stands for Visual Basic Document. ActiveX documents are powerful and fast because their code is compiled rather than interpreted as in the case of VBScript or JavaScript. Unfortunately most browsers do not support ActiveX documents. At this time IE 3.0 and above support ActiveX documents. Often there is an .htm file that points to the .vbd file that in turn accesses the .exe or the .dll file. This allows the user to navigate to an HTML file.

When a Web browser opens a directory on a Web server, one of the following events will take place:

- If the URL specifies a directory on the server and the directory exists, that specified directory opens.

- If the URL specifies a directory on the server and the directory does not exist, an error is returned.

- If the URL does not specify a directory, the home directory for the site opens.

- If the URL specifies a particular .htm or .asp file and that file is contained in the directory that is opened, that file is served to the user's browser.

- If the URL does not specify a particular document file, and a default document exists in the directory, the default document is served to the user's browser. On IIS the default document is typically named either default.htm or default.asp.

- If a default document is not found in the directory that is opened by the user, the server optionally can generate a browsing document, which is an HTML document generated by the server that consists of a graphical listing of the directory contents. Users can use these browsing documents to examine the contents of the directory and to browse the Web site.

To reiterate, when a user opens a directory without specifying a document name, IIS serves up a default document when one is available. Actually, IIS can serve more than one default document; Figure 20.29 shows default.htm and default.asp. However you could add any number of default documents such as default.html, index.htm, or index.html. Assuming that the directory contains a default.htm and a default.asp file, how does IIS know which to serve up?

That is determined by settings on the Documents tab of the Site Property pages, which is shown in Figure 20.29.

FIGURE 20.29.
Configuring default documents for a Web site.

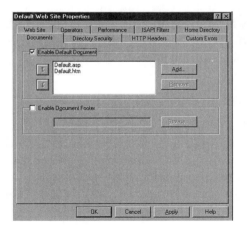

Enable Default Document. By default there is a check mark in this field configuring IIS to serve default documents when a document is not specified in the URL. If the check mark is removed, IIS will not search for default documents. Any attempt to access the server without specifying a filename in the URL will fail.

Default document names are specified in the document list. Use the Add and Remove buttons to add and remove document names from the list. You can name your default documents something besides default.htm, for example. But remember, IIS uses the filename extensions to tag outgoing data so that the browser can process it properly. Files with extensions .htm and .html are recognized as HTML documents. If you stray from this convention, you will need to change the definition in the MIME Types property page for the server.

The order in which entries appear in the default documents list is important because it defines the order in which the server will attempt to search for the documents. IIS searches in the order specified and retrieves the first document it finds. Thus, if the directory contains both default.asp and default.htm files, by default IIS will retrieve the default.asp document.

You can adjust the document search order by selecting a document in the list and clicking the arrow keys to move that document to another position in the search order.

Enable Document Footer. If this option is checked, you can specify a document name that will be inserted as a footer for each Web document that is sent to the user. You must specify the full pathname of the document file, which should not be a complete HTML document but should include only the HTML tags required to produce the desired footer. By default, document footers are disabled.

Home Directory Properties

Each Web site is configured with a home directory, which appears as the root directory for site. Users of the Web site cannot see directories unless they are subdirectories of the home directory. Open the Home Directory tab of the site properties to establish the home directory and its characteristics. The Home Directory tab is shown in Figure 20.30.

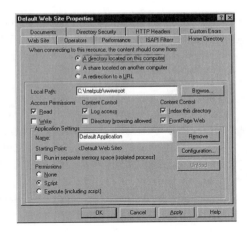

FIGURE 20.30

Home directory options when the home directory is on the local computer.

The home directory does not need to reside on the server that is running IIS. In fact, you can select one of three options to specify the location of the home directory:

- A <u>d</u>irectory located on the IIS computer
- A share located on another computer
- A redirection to a <u>U</u>RL

The remaining options on the home directory property page change to reflect the location of the home directory.

If the home directory is on the local computer, you will see the options shown in Figure 20.30. The options are as follows:

- **Local Pa<u>t</u>h.** First create the home directory using your choice of utility. Then enter the path in this field, browsing for the directory if desired.

- **<u>R</u>ead**. Check this box to grant users the ability to read files in the home directory. By default, the <u>R</u>ead option is checked. Generally speaking users should be given Read access to directories containing HTML files, but should not be given Read access to application directories (such as directories containing CGI applications).

- **<u>W</u>rite.** Check this box to grant users the ability to write files to the home directory or to modify files. Users can write to Web directories using only browsers that support the Put feature of HTTP version 1.1.

- **Log access.** If this box is checked, visits to this directory will be recorded in the log file. Visits will be logged only if logging is enabled as described earlier in this chapter.

- **Directory browsing allowed.** In most cases, when a user accesses a directory on a Web server an HTML document will be sent to the user's browser. In some cases this will be the default document for the directory. In other cases it will be a document specified in the URL sent to the server. If a default document is not available and a valid document is not specified in the URL, the Web server can be configured to generate an HTML document that lists the contents of the directory in browsable format. Users can use these HTML directory documents to navigate the directory tree and browse the file contents. Check this option if you want the Web server to support directory browsing for the home directory. Figure 20.31 shows an example of a browsing document that can be generated by IIS.

- **Index this directory.** IIS includes the Microsoft Index Server, which automatically generates indexes of the contents of documents residing on the server. The home directory will be included in the index if this box is checked. Remove the check mark to exclude the home directory from the index.

- **FrontPage Web**. Check this box to generate a FrontPage Web for this Web site. Consult the documentation for Microsoft FrontPage for information about using FrontPage Webs.

FIGURE 20.31

An example of a browsing document generated by IIS.

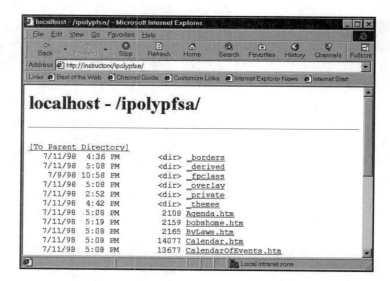

By default the Web site root directory is marked as an application starting point, a concept that is explained in the following sidebar. Consequently, applications starting in the Web site root directory have a scope extending to the entire Web site directory tree, except for branches that are separately designated as application starting points. Settings in the Application Settings box have to do with the application configuration of your Web server and are beyond the scope of this book.

Originally Web servers were in the business of serving up HTML documents and static documents formatted using the Hypertext Markup Language. Those days are long gone, and a Web server now has a much richer set of responsibilities. In many cases, for example, the Web server runs applications to provide dynamic content.

In IIS terms an *application* is a file that is executed within a specified set of directories on the Web site. For each application, the IIS administrator specifies a starting-point directory. Each directory under the starting-point directory is considered to be a part of the application until another starting-point directory is encountered. Consequently, starting-point directories establish the scope of the application.

Applications appear as package icons in the contents of a Web site. Refer to Figure 20.12 to see three applications that are defined for the default Web site (IISSAMPLES, IISADMIN, and IISHELP). A starting-point directory can be specified for each application.

HTTP Header Properties

Entries on the HTTP Headers tab, shown in Figure 20.32, enable you to configure content-related settings for your Web site.

Content Expiration

Browsers conserve network bandwidth by caching recently received Web documents. When the browser needs to access a Web page, it checks first to determine if the page is cached locally. If the page is in cache, the browser can display it without communicating with the Web server. That's great, but it can cause problems with material that is timely in nature. The browser might continue to access expired data in its local cache, rather than retrieving the current version from the Web site.

FIGURE 20.32

Configuring the HTTP Headers properties.

For data that has a known lifetime, check **Enable Content Expiration**. You can then specify an expiration date that notifies the browser when cached data has expired, causing the browser to retrieve updated pages from the Web server. You can choose three expiration settings:

- **Expire immediately.** The browser retrieves the page every time it is read.

- **Expire after.** This setting enables you to specify an interval in minutes, hours, or days after which the page expires.

- **Expire on.** This setting enables you to specify a date and time at which pages expire.

Custom HTTP Headers

You can create pairs of custom header names and custom header values that are appended to all request responses generated by the Web server.

Content Rating

Many Web sites are choosing to rate their sites in terms of language, violence, nudity, and sexual content. These ratings are recognized by a variety of browsing tools such as Internet Explorer and can be used by parents and organizations to limit the material that can be retrieved from the Web.

IIS supports content ratings that are defined by the Recreational Software

Advisory Council (RSAC), a non-profit organization that provides a standardized content-rating scheme for Internet and enables Web sites to register themselves. The Edit Ratings button leads you to Web site links to the RSAC. After you learn about the RSAC rating system, you have the option of registering your site and assigning ratings to your site.

MIME Map

You can use this option to define additional MIME type mappings that might be required for your Web site.

Managing Web Site Directories

As you learned in the previous section, each Web site has a home directory that serves as the site's default directory. When a browser connects with the Web site but does not specify a directory, the browser is sent the default document from the home directory.

But few Web sites consist only of a home directory. You can easily extend the home directory by adding subdirectories. By using *virtual directories* you can even include in your Web site directories that are in other directory trees, on other volumes, or even on other computers.

Directory paths can be quite long, and it would be inconvenient if users always had to include the physical path in a URL. So when you establish a virtual directory you also specify an alias that provides a shortcut for accessing the directory. Table 20.1 shows some examples of virtual directories, aliases, and the URLs that access the directories. The home directory for this server is `C:\wwwroot on server IW2`.

TABLE 20.1

Virtual Directories, Aliases, and Corresponding URLs

Physical Directory	Alias	URL
C:\wwwroot	*none*	`http://www.keystone.com`
C:\wwwroot\widgets	*none*	`http://www.keystone.com/widgets`
D:\Support	support	`http://www.keystone.com/support`
\\iw1\sales	sales	`http://www.keystone.com/sales`

Figure 20.33 shows a Web server named Another Web Server that has the preceding virtual directory structure in MMC. Notice that the folders for the support and sales virtual directories are tagged with a world icon, indicating that they are mapped globally to a directory other than the server home directory.

FIGURE 20.33

Virtual directories in MMC.

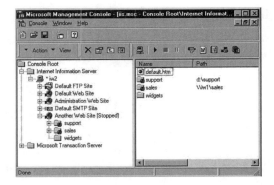

Creating Web Sites

IIS enables you to support multiple Web sites from the same IIS server. When several sites run on the same computer, they are often referred to as *virtual sites* because the sites do not have a unique physical presence on the network but share a single computer. Virtual sites can be used by an Internet service provider to enable two or more clients to have Web sites that share the same server hardware. Or they can be used inside an organization to enable several departments to have independent Web sites without the cost of multiple servers.

Identifying Web Sites

When two or more Web sites are running on the same computer, but both are running on the same operating system and the same copy of IIS, then the question arises: How do you enable those Web sites to coexist without being confused? Clearly, you can't have two Web sites named www.*company*.com.

TCP/IP hosts might be running many services, such as multiple Web sites that are our current concern. So it is reasonable to ask how a client application knows how to communicate with the correct service on the correct server. A communication path is established by two pieces of information:

- The IP address of the server

- The port associated with the service

Port numbers are used by TCP/IP to deliver messages to the correct application. Each service is associated with a port number. In many cases a service will use a "well-known port number" that is reserved for use with that service. The well-known port number for Web servers is 80.

If you want to have multiple distinct Web servers (or FTP or SMTP servers) running on the same server, each must be identified by a unique combination of an IP address and port. You can distinguish the Web server by any of the following means:

- Assigning it an IP address that is different from others in use on the server.

- Assigning it a different port number.

- Assigning both a unique IP address and a unique port.

Any of the preceding options will work, just so long as you establish a unique identity for the Web site.

Figure 20.34 shows MMC with three Web sites. Notice that when the server is selected, the right-hand pane lists the sites that are configured on the server along with their resources. The Web sites on this server are:

- **Default Web Site.** This site has an address of *All Assigned* and a port of 80.

- **Administration Web Site.** This site has an address of *All Assigned* but does not conflict with the Default Web Site because it has a port of 5677.

- **Another Web Site.** This site has a port of 80 but does not conflict with the default Web site because it has an explicit IP address assignment of 209.51.67.7. This host is configured with two IP addresses, and 209.51.67.6 remains available for the default Web site. Therefore, even though both sites use the same port, they avoid conflict by using distinct IP addresses.

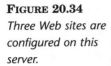

FIGURE 20.34

Three Web sites are configured on this server.

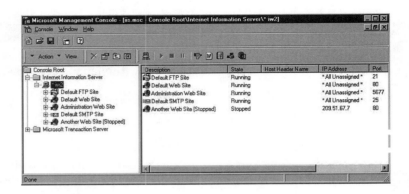

Configuring Multiple IP Addresses

The most commonly used technique for setting up virtual Web sites is to assign each site a unique IP address. This is done in two steps:

- Entering additional IP addresses in the server's TCP/IP properties.

- Adding an A record for each address in DNS, enabling each Web server to be accessed by name.

To assign multiple IP addresses to a computer, do the following:

1. Open the Network applet in the Control Panel.

2. Select the **Protocols** tab.

3. In the <u>N</u>etwork Protocols list select **TCP/IP** and choose <u>P</u>**roperties**.

4. Select the **IP Address** tab of the TCP/IP Properties. This tab is shown in Figure 20.35.

5. If this computer has more than one network adapter, select the adapter to be configured in the Adapter list.

6. Choose **Ad<u>v</u>anced** to open the Advanced IP Addressing dialog box, shown in Figure 20.36. The IP Add<u>r</u>esses list contains all IP addresses assigned to the selected network adapter. Notice that the list includes the IP address that was entered on the TCP/IP Properties tab.

FIGURE 20.35
TCP/IP properties.

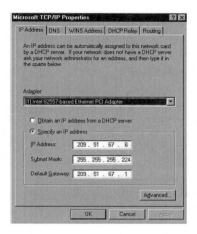

FIGURE 20.36
Configuring TCP/IP advanced properties.

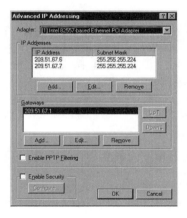

7. Choose **Add** to add an IP address to the list. Remember that each IP address must be unique on the entire network, including the Internet if you are connected to it.

    Use **Edit** to modify an entry or choose **Remove** to delete an entry.

8. Close the Network applet. It is not necessary to restart the computer to activate the IP address changes.

9. Use DNS Manager to add an A record for each address you have added. See Chapter 13, "Managing the Microsoft DNS Server," for information about DNS A records and DNS Manager.

If Web sites are assigned unique IP addresses then users must properly specify the IP addresses in the URLs used to access the Web sites. In most cases each IP address will be mapped to a unique name in DNS.

Using Non-Standard Ports

In most cases, a port number is not specified in the URL that is used to access a Web site. When a port is not included in the URL, a port of 80 is assumed.

When a port other than 80 is used, the port must be specified in the URL. If a Web site was configured with a port of 8080, the URL will resemble the following:

```
http://www.keystone.com:8080/
```

A non-standard port does not provide added security because anyone can specify the port number in a URL. But it does conceal your Web site from casual observation, including utilities that assume Web sites will use port 80. This enables you to set up a Web site on the Internet that is not cataloged by any of the Web indexing services, for example. It also prevents your Web site from experiencing hits from users who are casually browsing the Net.

Configuring a New Web Site

Before you can create a virtual Web site, you must determine how the site will be identified. Here are some guidelines:

- For greatest user convenience, identify the Web site with a unique IP address and DNS domain name. Users can then use conventional URLs to access the site.

- To conceal a site from conventional access, use a distinctive port. Users must know the port number to connect with it.

After you have decided on the method for identifying your Web site, create it as follows:

1. Use your choice of tools to create a home directory for the new virtual server.

2. Use User Manager to create a user account that supports anonymous user access to the Web server. Or, you can use the IUSR_*servername* account.

3. Assign the Web site user account appropriate permissions to the Web site home directory. In most cases anonymous users have Read permissions for Web sites.

4. Open the Microsoft Management Console.

5. In the Scope tree, right-click the server that will support the virtual site.

6. In the server's context menu, select **New/Web Site** to open the New Web Site Wizard.

7. In the **W**eb Site Description field enter a description that identifies the site in the MMC scope tree.

8. The New Web Site Wizard dialog box is shown in Figure 20.37. Here you must specify a combination of an IP address and a port that uniquely belongs to this Web site.

   In this example, an explicit IP address was selected. The original default Web site still has the setting of *All Unassigned* and remains the default Web site.

FIGURE 20.37

Specifying the IP address and port for a Web site.

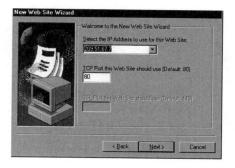

9. In the next dialog box (Figure 20.38), specify the path of the home directory that you created in step 1. Also, if anonymous access is permitted, check **A**llow anonymous access to this web site.

FIGURE 20.38
Specifying the home directory for a new Web site.

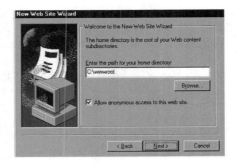

10. In the next dialog box (Figure 20.39) check the access permissions that you want to be available for the home directory.

11. Choose **Finish** to create the Web site.

12. Start the Web site. Either right-click the Web site in the scope pane and choose **Start** from its context menu, or select the Web site and press **Start** on the toolbar.

FIGURE 20.39
Specifying access permissions for a new Web site.

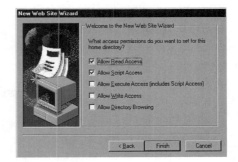

Providing Web Content

The task of adding content to your Web site is much more involved than just managing the server; I can't even scratch the surface in this chapter. Web servers now provide a wide variety of content, including static HTML pages, interactive pages, graphics, video, and sound. Anything I could say here would be the mere beginning.

But here's a simple exercise that will get Web administrator newbies going. Create a new Web site. Then use a text editor to create the following document, being careful to enter all punctuation and spaces as shown:

```
<HTML>
<HEAD>
<TITLE>Hello!</TITLE>
</HEAD>
<BODY>
Hello! Welcome to my Web page.<BR>
<A HREF="http://www.microsoft.com">This is a link to Microsoft's
Web site.</A><BR>
</BODY>
</HTML>
```

Save the document to the Web server's home directory with the name default.htm. (See the following note if you are using Notepad.) Then access the Web server from a browser. You will see something similar to Figure 20.40. This Web page contains a link to Microsoft's Web site. If you have an Internet connection, you can test the link.

Figure 20.40

The sample Web page.

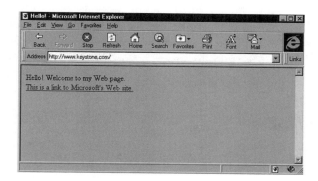

A brief look at the features of the sample document won't hurt, but I won't even scratch the surface of HTML. HTML documents are formatted by *tags* that the browser reads with information about how the text should be formatted. The details about the formatting are up to the browser, and there will probably be differences between the displays produced by any two browser brands.

Some tags come in pairs, such as <HEAD> and </HEAD>, which mark the beginning and end of the section containing the document header, whereas <BODY> and </BODY> mark the body of the document, which is where most of the interesting stuff appears. Some HTML tags can only appear in the header or body of the document.

Other tags appear on their own, such as <BR> which introduces a line break.

Text is reproduced pretty much as it is entered, but it will be formatted based on the width of the browser window and on the fonts the user has selected for the browser display. Lines of text will be formatted as continuous paragraphs unless a tag interrupts the flowing text.
 tags are the most common tools for breaking text into paragraphs.

The Anchor tags <A> and </A> are the keys to much of the magic on the Web. They provide the means of linking to other documents, which can be on this or other servers. The example includes a *hypertext reference*, which is indicated by an HREF attribute that provides the link to http://www.microsoft.com/. This simple entry is all you need to link to an entirely different Web site.

That wasn't hard, but it wasn't very exciting, either. We have grown to expect a lot from the Web: graphics, cool layouts, and exciting content. That's why I can't turn you into a Web content provider in a single chapter. But for a great introduction to Web authoring, visit the following URL:

    http://www.utoronto.ca/webdocs/

NOTE

You don't need a fancy editor to create Web pages, although an HTML-aware editor is an asset if you really get into HTML authoring.

You can use Notepad if you want, but you need to be aware of a quirk. Notepad always adds the extension .txt to saved text files, so if you tell it to save default.htm it will be put on disk as default.htm.txt. To suppress the .txt extension, use the Save As option and place quotation marks around the filename.

Because Web servers make extensive use of filename extensions, I always configure Windows NT Explorer to display filename extensions. To display filename extensions, open **View|Options** and remove the check mark from Hide file extensions to known file types.

Managing an FTP Server

If you have followed the discussion about the Web server, you won't have any trouble at all with the FTP server. It is managed much like the Web server with fewer options to worry about. Also, the FTP service hasn't changed much since IIS version 2.0, so experienced administrators have little new to learn.

There's not much to say about setting up FTP. Simply:

- Review the FTP server properties.

- Set up the directory structure.

- Add files to the directory.

- Verify that the IUSR_*servername* account has Read permissions for the FTP directories. In most cases, directories available for anonymous FTP will give users Read permissions, although FTP clients can also write files to the FTP server if they have Write permissions.

No ongoing maintenance is required. Simply add and remove files from the directories as required.

Setting Up File Permissions

If users log on with a personal username and password, the permissions they have will be determined by the permissions given to their user accounts.

If users log on anonymously, they have the permissions assigned to the IUSR_*servername* account. Typically this account has Read permissions for the FTP directories. Write permissions might be given to specific directories to enable users to upload files. In some cases, an administrator will grant the Write permission but will not grant the Read permission, preventing users from examining files that other users have uploaded until the administrator can review the files.

Configuring FTP Server Properties

The Properties page for the FTP server is similar to what you have seen for the WWW server, but several distinctive features exist.

FTP Site Properties

The FTP Site Properties tab is shown in Figure 20.41. Most of the settings resemble settings for the Web server. A couple of fields deserve discussion:

- **TCP Port.** The standard port for the FTP service is 21. If you change the port, users must specify the non-standard port number when they attempt to connect with the FTP server.

- **Connection Timeout.** Users formally log on to FTP and establish a connection that persists until they log off. Without some mechanism for closing inactive connections, unclosed connections could persist indefinitely. The FTP server will close inactive connections when the connection timeout expires.

FIGURE 20.41

The FTP Site Properties tab.

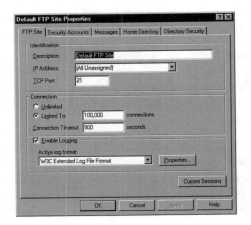

On the Security Accounts tab is the check box Allow Anonymous Connections (see Figure 20.42). FTP does not encrypt passwords when users establish a connecting rendering password susceptible to discovery by anyone who is snooping the network with a protocol analyzer. When users log on to FTP using their regular network usernames and passwords, the passwords become vulnerable. Therefore it is common practice to require anonymous connections from all users. Just be sure to apply proper security to the IUSR_*servername* account to ensure that users are not given inappropriate access to network resources.

If you want to require password logons for users who have Write permissions for the server, I strongly suggest that you create special user accounts for these users so that general-purpose network accounts cannot be compromised if a network snoop discovers their passwords. The FTP user accounts should have no permissions except for the FTP directories. To limit the potential for mischief you could establish Write-only directories in which users could write but not read files. Users would, of course, require some training because they could not catalog the directories.

FIGURE 20.42

Configuring FTP security account properties.

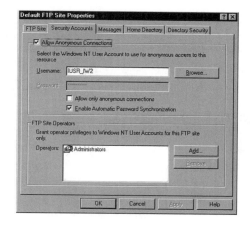

The Messages Tab

The Messages tab (see Figure 20.43) can be used to specify three messages:

- A Welcome message is displayed when users first connect. This message can be quite extensive.

- An Exit message is displayed when users disconnect.

- A Maximum Connections message that appears when the number of users has reached the value specified in the Maximum Connections field of the Service tab.

FIGURE 20.43

Configuring FTP server messages.

The Home Directory Tab

The Home Directory tab is shown in Figure 20.44. Here you can specify the path to the home directory, which can be on a local hard drive or on a network share provided by another computer. As with the Web server, the FTP server home directory appears as the root directory to users who establish FTP connections with the servers. Users cannot use FTP to view higher-level directories or directories in other directory trees.

The users' permissions for the home directory are determined by two things:

- The NTFS permissions assigned to the anonymous user account or to the account used to log on to the FTP server.

- The settings of the Read and Write check boxes on the Home directory tab.

The user must have a required permission both in NTFS and in the Home Directory tab to perform an operation on the home directory.

A setting on this tab determines whether users will see a UNIX-style directory or an MS-DOS–style directory (see Figure. 20.44). Some FTP clients require directories with a UNIX format, and UNIX is the best choice unless you know the MS-DOS format is supported for all your FTP clients. MS-DOS directories are selected by default.

FIGURE 20.44

Configuring home directory properties.

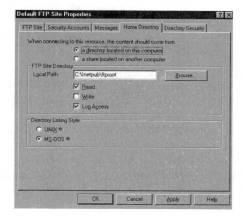

The Directory Security Tab

The Directory Security tab, shown in Figure 20.45, functions similar to the IP Address and Domain Name Restrictions dialog box used to configure directory security for the Web server. Here you can establish access controls based on IP address, network address, or domain.

FIGURE 20.45

Configuring directory security properties.

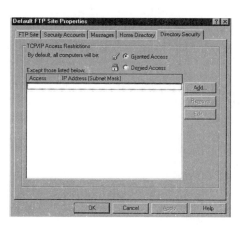

Internet Explorer can access FTP servers using the FTP protocol. Figure 20.46 shows an example. The URL ftp://iw2/ accessed the FTP service on the IW2 server. The FTP root directory contains three files and one directory.

FIGURE 20.46

Right-click a file to open an options menu.

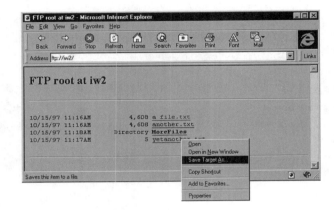

In Figure 20.46 the user has right-clicked the file YETANOTHER.TXT, opening an options menu. To download the file, choose **Save Target As** and specify a download location in the Save As dialog box.

Implement the NNTP Service

New to IIS 4.0 is the capability to provide newsgroup services. Newsgroups allow users to post articles for others to see and also to retrieve articles posted by other users. The collection of articles related to a specific topic form a conversation thread that users can view historically, or that they can participate in as real-time chat sessions. Newsgroups can be moderated to prevent inappropriate material from being made available for retrieval from the news server. The Network News Transfer Protocol (NNTP) is used to post and retrieve news messages from news servers.

Newsgroup articles can be displayed using Outlook Express or other newsreaders. During installation of the NNTP service you select the directory location for files used by this service. The default location is C:\InetPub\nntpfile; this directory contains a directory structure including a *root* directory as well as three other directories. During installation a

Welcome news article is created at the following location: `C:\InetPub\`
`nntpfile\root\microsoft\public\ins\1000000.nws`. Notice that news articles
have an .nws extension. Figure 20.47 shows the default Welcome article
with Outlook Express.

FIGURE 20.47

Outlook Express displays the Welcome news article.

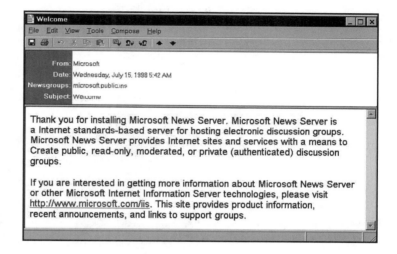

Create a New Newsgroup

Follow these steps below to create a new newsgroup:

1. Start Internet Service Manager then expand the left pane so you can
   see Default NNTP Site.

2. Right-click the **Default NNTP Site** then choose **Properties**.

3. Select the **Groups** property sheet then click the **Create new newsgroup...** button; see Figure 20.48.

4. Enter a name without spaces in the Newsgroup field; see Figure
   20.49.

FIGURE 20.48

NNTP Groups property sheet.

FIGURE 20.49

Newsgroup Properties dialog box for creating new newsgroups.

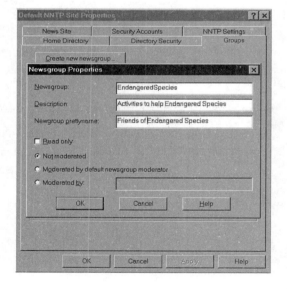

5. Optionally enter or select the other properties listed below:

- Use the <u>D</u>escription field to enter a phrase that more fully describes the focus of this newsgroup.

- Use the Newsgroup <u>p</u>rettyname field to provide a name without spaces or to supply a foreign language name for the newsgroup.

- Select the **Read-only** check box to allow only the moderator to post news articles to this newsgroup.

- Not Moderated is the default moderation choice. This selection allows any user to post articles in an unrestricted fashion.

- The M<u>o</u>derated by default newsgroup moderator selection sends all newly posted articles to *newsgroup@default-domain* for approval. The moderator can approve or reject articles that are not pertinent to the newsgroup.

- Use the Moderated <u>b</u>y selection and enter the mail address of the person who moderates this newsgroup. All new postings are sent to this email account for approval or rejection.

6. Click **OK** twice to complete creating the new newsgroup.

Create a News Server Entry

Use the following steps to create a news server entry in Outlook Express.

1. Launch Outlook Express, choose **<u>T</u>ools** from the menu then choose the <u>A</u>ccounts menu item.

2. Click the **<u>A</u>dd** button followed by the **News...** selection choice.

3. The Internet Connection Wizard appears. On the first page of the wizard enter your name as you want it to appear when you post messages then choose **<u>N</u>ext**.

4. On the second wizard page enter your email address. This allows people to respond to you directly.

5. On the third wizard page enter the domain or computer name of the news server.

6. On the fourth wizard page enter a friendly name for this news server. This is the name that you will see when using Outlook Express.

7. On the fifth screen, choose the connection type. Your choices are to use phone lines, a LAN, or to manually connect to the Internet.

8. The last screen congratulates you for creating a news server entry. You are then prompted to download newsgroups from your new news server entry. You can respond by choosing **Yes** or **No**.

Post Messages to a Newsgroup

Before you can post or retrieve news messages you must first subscribe to the newsgroup. Use the following steps to subscribe and post a message to the news server:

1. In Outlook Express right-click the friendly nameî you created in step 6 then choose the **Ne̲wsgroups...** pop-up menu item.

2. Select the newsgroup that you want to subscribe to then choose the **Subscribed** button, followed by the **OK** button. See Figure 20.50, the newsgroup name ES.InstructorX is selected.

FIGURE 20.50
Subscribe to a newsgroup.

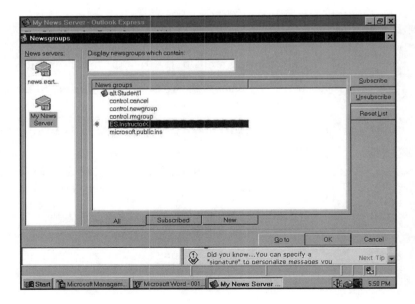

3. Select the newsgroup you just subscribed to then click the **Compose Message** button (see Figure 20.51). A form is displayed that you can use to create your news article. When you are finished creating your message click the **Post** button.

FIGURE 20.51

Post a message to a newsgroup.

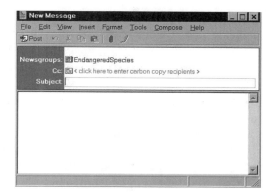

4. Within a few minutes your posted message will appear in the Subject pane. See Figure 20.52.

FIGURE 20.52

A posted message in Newsgroup.

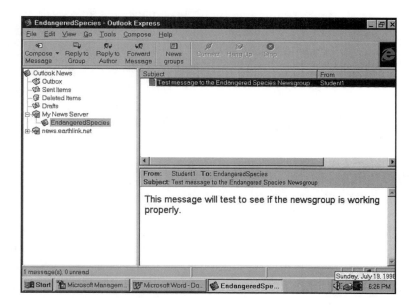

Microsoft Transaction Server

Microsoft Transaction Server (MTS) allows programmers to create application programs as if they were to be used by a single user then have the program scale seamlessly to handle numerous users. MTS performs two different functions. One function allows a server program in the form of a .DLL to scale and handle many users. The second function allows a program to update or add records to multiple databases and to handle those updates as a transaction. A transaction simply means that either all updates are completed successfully and made permanent, or no updates are applied to any database. The code required to reliably ensure that updates performed against multiple databases, from possibly multiple manufacturers located on multiple servers, would be both complex and difficult to debug. MTS is designed to handle these complex transactions for the programmer. The programmer writes the program as if it were transacting a single server.

Install and Use a Sample MTS Application

With MTS you create *packages* that tell MTS which ActiveX code components belong together. These packages are constructed from program modules known as code components. The next several paragraphs address three programming models at a high level to introduce you to terminology and concepts that you should be familiar with.

One programming model is to build standalone monolithic applications. These applications are not designed to work with other programs and are completely self-contained. For instance, the Calculator is an example of such an application.

Another programming model is referred to as client/server. In client/server one program provides a service (the server) while the other program provides a user interface and uses the service provided by the other program (the client). SQL server is an example of a server program, specifically a database program. A program such as an order entry program provides the user interface and allows an order entry clerk to input new orders to the SQL server.

A third programming model that is growing rapidly in popularity is known as a three-tier or often n-tier architecture. This is basically the client/server model but with one or more other programs in the middle. The user interface program is still the client, and the SQL server program for example is still the server. But the program in the middle is both client and server simultaneously. To the client the middle tier appears to be a server. To the SQL server the middle tier appears to be a client.

The middle tier becomes a great location to implement business logic. For instance, the business logic in an order entry program might allow a 3 percent discount on orders over $5,000. However, business often changes the rules. Sales might now allow a 5 percent discount on orders exceeding $5,000 if the customer's account balance is less than 30 days, and 3 percent for accounts 30 to 60 days, and no discount for accounts over 60 days.

Assume you have 300 order entry workstations. If for instance this logic were implemented in the client program of a client/server architecture, technicians would need to install the new program on 300 machines.

However, if this logic resides in the middle tier then the old middle-tier program could be replaced with the new middle-tier program on one server without changing the client UI program or the SQL server program. And when sales decides to change the rules again next week, it will be easy to implement that change as well.

Certificate Server

The Microsoft Certificate Server is used to issue and revoke digital certificates over the Internet. Certificates are used to identify that the Web site or person you are communicating with is actually who you think it is.

Digital certificates are used with encryption software. Data to be transmitted is encrypted using a special private key. The private key is never transmitted and should be well guarded against loss or theft. The data can be decrypted by either of two keys, the original private key or a second public key. The public key is created when the data is encrypted and can be sent to anyone who requests it. Often the public keys are sent within a digital certificate. The certificate identifies who created the public key and whether the public key has been modified in any way since it was created. The key should never be used if it has been modified in any way. An analogy could be the keys to a building. The master key opens any door and should be well guarded, and is analogous to the private key. Individual keys that open a specific door can be given to individuals with a need to access a specific room; this is analogous to a public key.

Certificates are issued from Certificate Authorities (CAs) only after the CA has completed a thorough search to verify that the company or person who is requesting a certificate is actually who they claim to be. It can take weeks or even months for the verification process to be completed. Only then is a certificate issued.

The following is a list of CAs and their sites contacts:

VeriSign	`www.verisign.com`
Shiva Corporation	`ftp.shiva.com`
Entrust Technologies	`www.entrust.com`
Xcert Software Inc	`www.xcert.com`
Digital Signal Trust	`www.digsigtrust.com`
GTE CyberTrust	`www.gte.com/Products/trust.html`

Certificate Server can be used to issue public keys from CAs, but Certificate Server also has the capability to transmit certificates that you create. Obviously these certificates are not considered near as rigorous as those issued by a CA.

Generally speaking you would want to use a certificate purchased from a third party (a CA) when the certificate is applied to executable code that could include viruses or other malicious code. The other caveat is the files being identified with purchased certificates generally do not change; for instance, executable programs don't change from user to user.

You might decide to create certificates locally for changeable files. For example, an insurance company that sends policy coverage statements might want to create a certificate for each document. Another example might be for contracts, as each contract includes unique text.

Configure Certificate Server to Issue Certificates

Use the following steps to create a certificate request file that can be submitted to a CA.

1. Launch Internet Service Manager then right-click the **Default Web Site** and choose **Properties**. When the Property sheets appear choose the **Directory Security** property sheet. Next click the **Edit** button in the Secure Communication frame. Then choose the **Key Manager...** button.

2. The **Key Manager** window appears, as shown in Figure 20.53. Right-click the service you want to create a key for. In this example, right-click the **WWW service**, then choose the **Create New Key...** menu item.

FIGURE 20.53

Use Key Manager to create a new key.

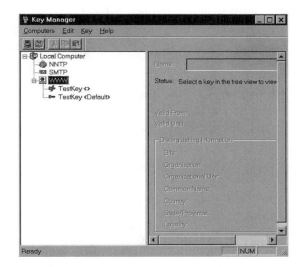

3. The **Create New Key** wizard appears. On the first wizard page choose **Put the request in a file that you will send to an authority** and accept the default name of C:\NewKeyRq.txt. Save the NewKeyRq.txt file in the C:\Certs folder. Then choose the **Next** button.

3a. Alternatively, the process can be shortened by allowing the certificate to be sent directly to the Certificate Server. Using this approach you will not have a file to send to a CA. The Create New Key wizard appears. On the first wizard page choose **Automatically send the request to an Online Authority** and accept the Microsoft Certificate Server selection. Then choose the **Next** button to proceed on to steps 4, 5, and 6. Following step 6 the certificate is completed and installed.

4. On the second Create New Key wizard page enter a name for your new key in the Key Name field. Also enter and confirm a password in the two respective password fields. Finally choose 512, 768, or 1024 bit length. Larger bit lengths equate to additional security. Also, be aware that longer bit lengths correspond to slower use by the system.

5. On the third Create New Key wizard page enter your Organization Name, Organizational Unit, and domain name in the Organization, Organizational Unit, and Common Name fields respectively.

6. On the fourth Create New Key wizard page enter your Country, State, and City in the three appropriate fields.

7. On the fifth Create New Key wizard page enter your Name, Email address, and Phone number in the three appropriate fields.

8. Read the summary then click the **Finish** button to complete creating the request. This text file can be sent to a CA. Based on the information contained within the request the CA will either issue or deny a certificate.

Submit the Request File to Certificate Server

Certificate Server can create a certificate from the request file you created previously. Use the following steps to create and install the certificate.

1. Use Notepad to open the certificate text file you created previously. Highlight and copy all the text including and between the following lines. Be sure to include these two lines in what you copy:

    -----BEGIN NEW CERTIFICATE REQUEST-----

    -----END NEW CERTIFICATE REQUEST-----

2. Launch Internet Explorer and navigate to `http://localhost/certsrv/`. Choose **Certificate Enrollment Tools** then on the next Web page choose **Process a Certificate Request**.

3. Paste your copied text into the text box located on the Web Server Enrollment Page then press **Submit Request**.

4. You should see a new Web page indicating that your request has been successfully processed. Selecting the **Download** button downloads the new certificate to your Web browser. Choose to save the new-cert.cer file to disk in the C:\Certs folder.

5. Install the new certificate by right-clicking the **Default Web Site** in Internet Service Manager. Choose **Properties** then choose the **Directory Security** property page. Next click the **Edit** button in the Secure Communications section.

6. In the Secure Communications window select **Key Manager...** this displays the Key Manager window.

7. Right-click the key icon that you created previously. The key icon should have a red and yellow line through it. Choose **Install Key Certificate...** from the menu.

8. Browse for the certificate name you saved in step 4. Click the **Open** button then enter the password you assigned when creating the certificate request in the dialog box provided.

9. The Server Bindings dialog box appears. Choose the **OK** button. Look for the message that states: **The key is complete and usable**. You can now close Key Manager and save all changes.

Install the Certificate to Internet Explorer

To install the certificate you have created follow these steps:

1. Launch Internet Explorer then navigate to `http://localhost/certsrv/`. On the Web page choose **Certificate Enrollment Tools**; on the second Web page choose **Request a Client Authorization Certificate**.

2. You see a Web-based form that you must complete. See Figure 20.54 for an example of the Web page. When you have entered all information click the **Submit Request** button.

3. The Certificate Download page appears. Choose the Download button. You should receive a confirmation Web page indicating a successful download.

FIGURE 20.54

Submit the Certificate Registration Form.

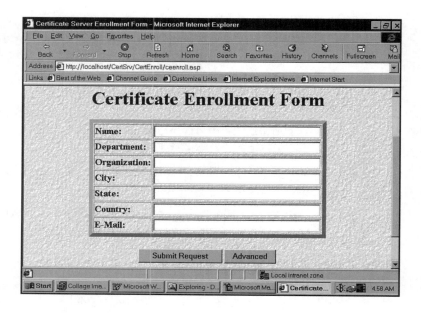

Enable Secure Communications

Now that a certificate is created and installed you can implement secure communication.

1. Launch Internet Service Manager then right-click the **Default Web Site**. Choose **Properties** then choose the **Directory Services** property sheet. Choose **Edit** from the Secure Communications grouping.

2. Choose the **Require secure channel when accessing this resource** check box. Then choose **OK** twice. The **Inheritance Overrides** dialog box appears; choose **OK** to complete.

3. From now on users must use https:// instead of http:// as a protocol when accessing secure Web pages.

Using HTML Administration

When you set up IIS, a special Administration Web site is included in the configuration. This Web site supports an HTML version of the Internet service manager (ISM) that enables you to manage IIS from a remote site using a Web browser. You must use Internet Explorer version 3.0 or later to use the HTML ISM.

You might have noticed that the Administration Web site is configured with the port 5677. To start the HTML administrator, connect to the Web server and specify that port in the URL, similar to this:

```
http://www.keystone.com:5677/
```

Figure 20.55 shows the HTML version of the ISM. The Default Web site has been expanded to illustrate the tree structure of the management interface. Management procedures will be familiar if you have used the MMC. When you are in the Web browser you can't manage IIS objects by right-clicking the way you do in MMC, and there is no taskbar so you need to do things a bit differently. Still you should have no trouble making the transition.

Anonymous connections are disabled for the Administration Web site, and you must have permissions as an IIS administrator to use HTML administration. If you use Internet Explorer to connect from another domain computer and are logged on using an account that is an IIS administrator, and if you are using Internet Explorer, you are given access transparently to the HTML Internet Service Manager. If you log on from a non-domain computer, you will be required to log on. The logon process uses Microsoft Challenge/Response. Therefore you must use Microsoft Internet Explorer to use the HTML version of Internet Service Manager.

FIGURE 20.55

Using the HTML Internet Service Manager.

Chapter 21

MICROSOFT PROXY SERVER

These days, everyone wants to be connected to the Internet. But still many organizations are holding out, often for very good reasons. They might be put off by the complexity, the security risk, or the cost of a high-bandwidth connection. Or they might not want their employees surfing sports Web sites on company time. Well, believe it or not, there is a technology that addresses all those concerns and a few more. It's called a proxy server, and Microsoft offers a good one, with the clever name of Microsoft Proxy Server.

In human terms, a proxy is "a person authorized to act as a substitute." Well, a proxy server acts as a substitute for one or many clients, letting them communicate with the Internet without actually being connected to the Internet. It's a slight-of-hand trick that can make your life as a network administrator a whole lot easier.

A proxy server can provide some firewall protection for your local network. The proxy server handles all communication between your internal network and the proxy server. It is the only host that is visible to the outside world, so your local network is shielded from prying eyes. That's great unless you have internal hosts that need to be accessible to external users, in which case they cannot be behind the proxy server. When internal hosts must be exposed to the outside, you should engage the services of a security consultant to configure a properly designed firewall barrier.

This chapter addresses Microsoft Proxy Server, version 2.0. This version of Proxy Server has many new features, too many to cover in a single chapter. My focus here is to explain Proxy Server to you and to show you how to set up a basic proxy server. After you have implemented your first proxy server, you will find it easy to use the online documentation to expand your understanding of the product.

How Microsoft Proxy Server Works

In part, a proxy server is a heavy-duty translator that acts as an intermediary between your network clients and the Internet (see Figure 21.1). Superficially, the proxy server looks like a router, but it isn't. A router forwards packets more or less intact from one network to another, extending the reach of the computer that originated the packet. A router has a tough, busy life, but it is mostly one of receiving packets and forwarding them to the correct network.

But nothing is simply passed through a proxy server. In Figure 21.1, the client can't actually communicate with the Internet. It communicates with the proxy server, *and the client thinks the proxy server is the Internet.* Similarly, servers on the Internet can't communicate with the clients on the private network. Instead, servers communicate with the proxy server. In between, the proxy server copies, translates, and forwards as required to facilitate communication.

FIGURE 21.1

A proxy server in action.

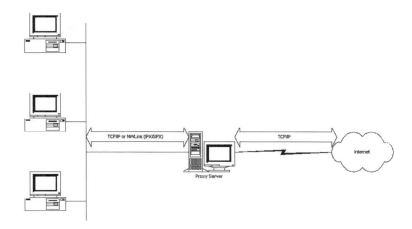

There is something interesting in Figure 21.1. Notice that the private network doesn't even have to be running TCP/IP! The private network can be configured with either TCP/IP or NWLink (IPX/SPX). When local clients are running on NWLink, the proxy server takes on the task of translating data between the local NWLink network and the public TCP/IP Internet.

The ability to configure the private network with NWLink has a couple of advantages:

- You don't need to worry about setting up TCP/IP on the local network, so you avoid the complications of IP addresses, WINS, and DHCP.

- Because the local network is not running TCP/IP it is isolated from the public Internet. It is much more difficult—one never says impossible where security is concerned—for an intruder to break into your private network because inbound requests are not translated or forwarded to the private network.

But you don't need to feel obligated to use NWLink on your private network. Proxy Server functions as an effective firewall even when the private network is running TCP/IP.

NOTE

A proxy server is more than a router. It is an example of a *gateway* device, an interface device that performs heavy-duty translation between two different environments. It really isn't important to know what a gateway is, but Microsoft's documentation occasionally mentions a "Proxy Server gateway service," and I thought you should know about it.

continues

Remember from discussion of TCP/IP in Chapter 4 that TCP/IP terminology often calls routers gateways. In that context they are the same thing, but that isn't the way the term gateway is generally used. So, we're not talking about TCP/IP gateways here. It might help to know that the TCP/IP community is gradually migrating to the term router, so the confusion about usage of the word gateway will eventually fade.

Okay, so the Proxy Server lets your clients connect to the Internet. What's so great about that? Well, several things, for instance:

- The proxy server is the only computer that is visible from the Internet. Your private network is invisible to the outside, and the proxy server can act as a firewall that protects your network from intruders.

- If you want to enable select individuals to access the Internet, the proxy server can be set up to authenticate users. Only users who successfully log on to the proxy server can get to the Internet. You can even individually restrict the services available to each user.

- The proxy server can maintain a cache of recently retrieved data. If a client needs data that is in the cache, the proxy server can provide the data without going to the network. So, a proxy server promotes efficient use of the WAN connection.

- The proxy server can filter outgoing requests. You can install domain filters that prevent access to undesirable Web sites, for example, without blocking users from accessing Web sites that are vital to your organization. So, employees won't be visiting erotica.com on company time.

- The isolation between the private network and the Internet is so complete that the private network doesn't even need to be running TCP/IP! NWLink is much simpler to configure than TCP/IP. If you want, you can run NWLink on your private network while still enabling your clients to access all the Web services they need.

Actually, Microsoft Proxy Server provides three proxy services, one for the Web, one for WinSock clients, and one for clients using the Socks 4.3a API. Let's look how they function.

Proxy Server Arrays

Microsoft Proxy Server version 2.0 offers several new features that enhance the utility and performance of Proxy Server. One enhancement, illustrated in Figure 21.2, is the capability to use arrays of proxy servers. The client is configured to interact with only one of the proxy servers in the arrays, but the proxy servers interact behind the scenes. If any of the proxy servers in the array have cached data being requested by the client, the data will be returned to the client without querying the Internet.

FIGURE 21.2

An array of proxy servers.

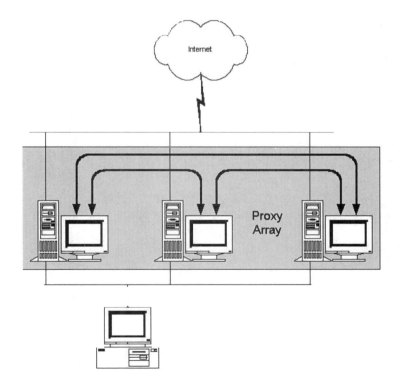

Proxy server arrays have two advantages. They introduce fault tolerance into the configuration. Also, by distributing requests across multiple servers, they improve performance through load balancing.

Proxy Server Chains

Another feature that is new in Proxy Server 2.0 is the capability to configure chains of proxy servers, such as those shown in Figure 21.3. The proxy server nearest to the client is known as the *downstream* proxy server. A proxy server that is closer to the Internet is an *upstream* proxy server. Downstream proxy servers can pass Internet access requests to upstream proxy servers, which return the requested data through the downstream proxy servers to the clients.

FIGURE 21.3

Chaining proxy servers.

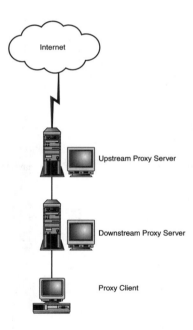

Chains of proxy servers provide another means of distributing proxy server processing. If desired, a proxy chain can be combined with a proxy array, as shown in Figure 21.4. In high-demand environments, proxy chains and arrays can significantly enhance proxy server performance and reliability.

FIGURE 21.4
Combining proxy chains and arrays.

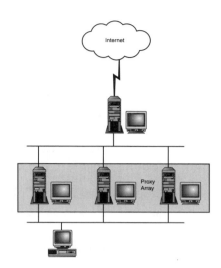

Reverse Proxy

Suppose that your organization operates a Web server that is publicly available to users of the Internet. Ordinarily, Web servers perform a lot of disk access. Every time a user requests an object from your Web server, the Web server must retrieve the object from disk. Think about your organization's home page for a moment. Every user who contacts your Web server retrieves the home page; as a result every new user connection results in disk activity to retrieve the exact same data.

Disk access is slow. That's why so many computer systems cache data in memory in an attempt to limit the amount of disk activity. Well, proxy servers are designed to cache data that is requested on the network, substituting fast cache retrieval for slow network retrieval. Wouldn't it be nice if you could use a proxy cache to take some of the disk retrieval load off your Web servers?

Proxy Server 2.0 has the capability to configure a *reverse proxy cache* as shown in Figure 21.5. Outside users interact with the Proxy Server proxy thinking that it is a Web server. If the Proxy Server's cache contains the data requested by the user, no activity is generated on the Web server. The proxy server will cache all the pages that are most often requested by your users, greatly reducing the processing that the Web server must perform.

FIGURE 21.5
Reverse proxy.

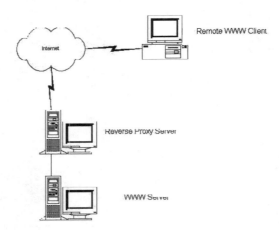

Reverse proxy is one of the techniques that keeps the World Wide Web from grinding to a halt. Busy Web sites have been in a position of having to support arrays of many Web servers in order to provide reasonable response times. Because reverse proxy servers have been introduced, however, many Web sites have found that they can reduce their numbers of Web servers by 75 percent or more.

Proxy Server Firewalls

In some cases, it might be desirable to have the proxy server computer operate as a firewall that selectively passes some protocols to the local network. Proxy Server 2.0 has some firewall capabilities based on packet filtering and can be configured to filter inbound and outbound packets.

Proxy Server Proxy Services

Proxy Server supports three types of proxy services, each answering a different set of requirements:

- **Web Proxy Service.** This service supports Web browsers capable of using the CERN proxy protocol, including Internet Explorer and Netscape Navigator.

- **Winsock Proxy Service.** This service enables nearly all Winsock applications to contact the Internet through a proxy server.

■ **Socks Proxy Service.** This service enables sockets applications on non-Windows platforms to use the proxy server to interact with the Internet.

The Web Proxy Service

As the name says, the Web Proxy service is especially designed to serve as a proxy for Web access. To use the Web Proxy, you must use a Web browser that supports the CERN proxy protocol. Fortunately, most browsers do, including Microsoft Internet Explorer, Netscape Navigator, and the PointCast Network. The browser does not have to run on a Microsoft operating system. In fact, the Web Proxy service can support clients on UNIX, Macintosh, or Windows computers.

The Web Proxy requires TCP/IP on a private network. If your private network is running NWLink, you must configure clients to access the network through the WinSock Proxy.

Although the World Wide Web emphasizes HTTP, several other protocols are commonly used. The Web Proxy service supports the following protocols:

■ HTTP

■ FTP

■ Gopher

■ Secure Sockets Layer (SSL)

The Web Proxy server supports Internet resource caching, domain filtering, and client authentication. When very secure communication is required, it also supports the Secure Sockets Layer (SSL). SSL enables clients to communicate with a server using a secure, encrypted data stream.

To promote efficient use of network bandwidth, the Web Proxy server maintains a cache of recently retrieved objects. When a user requests an object, the proxy server determines whether the object is in its cache, in which case the object can be returned to the user without going to the Internet.

The Web Proxy employs two types of caching:

■ *Passive caching* is used to cache copies of appropriate objects. Some objects are dynamically generated or require authentication for access and are not suitable for caching. Each cached object has a Time

To Live (TTL) that determines how long the object will remain in the cache. After the TTL expires, the object is purged and must be retrieved from the Internet the next time it is requested.

- *Active caching* is used to ensure that the cache has fresh copies of popular objects. If a popular object has expired, the cache manager will generate its own request for a fresh copy. To determine which objects should be cached, the cache manager considers the popularity of objects as well as their rate of change.

The WinSock Proxy Service

Most Web services do not have an equivalent of the CERN proxy protocol, so the Web Proxy server can handle only some of the popular Internet protocols. To enable those services to be managed by Proxy Server, the WinSock Proxy service enables WinSock applications to function in a proxy server environment. The WinSock Proxy server supports an extensive set of Internet protocols. Here's a brief sample:

- FTP
- Gopher
- HTTP
- Microsoft NetShow
- NNTP (news)
- POP3 (email)
- Telnet

To work with the WinSock Proxy server, clients are configured with a modified protocol stack. When an application requests a supported Internet service through WinSock, the request is transparently forwarded to the WinSock Proxy server. This enables unmodified client applications to communicate through the WinSock Proxy server.

An interesting feature of the WinSock proxy redirector is that the local network can use either TCP/IP or IPX/SPX. This enables you to configure network clients with NWLink, Microsoft's implementation of IPX/SPX, and avoid the complications of putting TCP/IP on your private network. Such a configuration also improves the resistance of the local network to outside intrusion. If an attacker coming in through the TCP/IP-based Internet contacts a local IPX/SPX network, it is much more difficult for the attack to penetrate local resources.

A downside of the WinSock Proxy is that it does not maintain a cache of recently retrieved network objects. Given the number of protocols supported by the WinSock Proxy, caching data would probably be unworkably complicated. If your private network is running TCP/IP, configure Web clients to use the Web Proxy so that they can take advantage of caching.

NOTE

Many organizations are using TCP/IP services such as Web servers to improve communication in their company. But prior to proxy servers, deploying a Web server meant converting clients to TCP/IP. Now organizations that have standardized their internal networks on NWLink (IPX/SPX) can easily set up a proxy server and a private TCP/IP network. Any required intranet services can be placed on the TCP/IP network, and clients can access the TCP/IP services with the minor change of installing the Proxy Server client software.

The Socks Proxy Service

Prior to Proxy Server version 2.0, the proxy server could support only CERN Web clients and Winsock clients. Other clients, such as UNIX and Macintosh hosts, were not supported. The Socks proxy service is a new feature of Proxy Server 2.0 that enables non-Windows clients to transparently access the Internet through the proxy server. It enables clients that use SOCKS version 4.3a and greater to access HTTP, Telnet, FTP, and Gopher protocols. Protocols that rely on UDP are not supported.

Installation

Most of the work of installing Proxy Server is preparation. You must plan your network addressing scheme and install and configure network adapters. Then you can install Proxy Server, which is a very straightforward procedure.

Plan Your Server Hardware

Table 21.1 summarizes Microsoft's recommendations for Proxy Server server hardware, based on the size of the installation.

TABLE 21.1

Server Hardware Recommendations for Microsoft Proxy Server

Clients	CPU	Disk for Cache	Minimum RAM
Minimum	Intel 486 or Alpha AXP	100MB + .5MB per client	24MB (Intel) 32MB (Alpha)
0–300	133MHz Pentium	250–2,000 MB	32MB
300–2,000	166MHz Pentium	2–4GB	32MB
2,000+	Proxy Array 1 server per 2,000 clients	2–4GB each array member	32MB each array member

Plan the Local Address Table

When you install Proxy Server, you will define a Local Address Table, referred to as a LAT. The LAT is a list of all the IP addresses that appear on the private network serviced by Proxy Server. As far as Proxy Server is concerned, if an IP address isn't in the LAT, it doesn't exist on your network.

Because Proxy Server completely isolates your private network from the Internet, you can take advantage of an interesting loophole in the Internet address scheme. You don't need to obtain an IP address range from the InterNIC, because you can use specifically designated private IP address ranges. These address ranges have been set aside by the Internet Assigned Numbers Authority (IANA) and cannot be used on the Internet. No hosts can use them, and routers will not route traffic associated with the IP addresses. These private IP addresses are set aside for use on private networks, for testing, and for other purposes that don't require Internet communication.

Three private address ranges have been designated by IANA, one range in each IP address class:

- Class A: 10.0.0.0 through 10.255.255.255

- Class B: 172.16.0.0 through 172.31.255.255

- Class C: 192.168.0.0 through 192.168.255.255

Remember, these addresses are yours to use. They won't step on anyone else's toes, but they can't ever communicate directly with the Internet.

The local address table is stored in a file named Proxy Serverlat.txt in the Proxy Serverclnt directory. When a TCP/IP client installs Proxy Server client software, it receives a copy of the LAT, which it uses to determine whether hosts are on the private network. This information enables the WinSock Proxy client to determine whether a service request should be directed to the local network or to Proxy Server. If the Proxy Serverlat.txt file is updated on the server, the modified version is copied to the clients periodically to keep their local copies up to date.

NOTE

In some cases, the Proxy Serverlat.txt file might not contain complete local address information. You can edit the Proxy Serverlat.txt file manually, and your changes will be replicated to the clients. The following are examples of entries in the Proxy Serverlat.txt file. The first entry is a network address range and the second is an individual IP address:

```
10.100.0.0      10.100.255.255
10.75.83.199    10.75.83.199
```

Under some circumstances, a client might require a custom LAT. You cannot edit the client's local Proxy Serverlat.txt file, because it will be overwritten the next time the Proxy Serverlat.txt file is copied from the server. Instead, place the custom entries in a file named Locallat.txt. The client will combine entries in the Proxy Serverlat.txt and Locallat.txt files to determine its working LAT.

Install Network Adapters

Although Microsoft Proxy Server can be installed on a computer equipped with a single network adapter, it will then function only as a document caching service for local network users and will provide no Internet access service. To take full advantage of Proxy Server, you must equip its computer with two network adapters, one connected to the Internet and one to your private network.

Proxy Server is not a router. In fact, it is intended to provide a high degree of isolation between the external and private networks by controlling every bit of traffic that flows between the internal and external network. To support this isolation, the adapters require some special configuration steps.

Use the Control Panel Network applet to configure the adapters as follows:

1. Install TCP/IP on the computer.

2. If the private network will be using NWLink, install that protocol.

3. Install the network adapters. Take note of the numbers of the adapters so that you can identify which is connected to the external network and which is connected to the private network.

4. Open TCP/IP properties, select the **Routing** tab, and disable IP forwarding.

5. The adapter connected to the internal network must be configured for TCP/IP even though the internal network might be running only NWLink. When you configure TCP/IP on the internal network adapter do the following:

    ■ Do not use DHCP to specify settings. Enter all settings manually. The Proxy Server must have a fixed IP address.

    ■ Do not enter a default gateway for the internal network adapter. Only the external network adapter should be configured with a default gateway address.

6. Open the **Bindings** tab in the Network applet. The next procedure is easiest if you select **all adapters** in Show bindings for, as was done in Figure 21.6. This figure shows bindings for a Proxy Server server that has an internal NWLink network.

7. Select the adapter that is connected to the external network (adapter 1 in the figure) and expand the entries beneath it. Disable any services that are not required. You should, for example, disable the following protocols:

- **Server**

- **NWLink IPX/SPX Compatible Transport**

- **WINS Client (TCP/IP)**

- **NetBEUI Protocol**

Typically, the binding that is active on the external network adapter
is TCP/IP Protocol.

8. Select the adapter that is connected to the external network (adapter
2 in the figure) and expand the entries beneath it. Disable any services that are not required. If the network is running NWLink but is
not running TCP/IP, you can disable the following:

- **TCP/IP Protocol**

- **WINS Client (TCP/IP)**

- **NetBEUI Protocol**

FIGURE 21.6

*Disable unneeded
bindings from the net-
work adapters.*

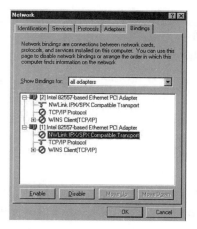

After the network adapters have been configured, take some time to test the
configuration. Don't try to install Proxy Server unless you know the underlying network is working.

Test the TCP/IP configuration by using ping. Then ensure that the Microsoft
network components are functioning. Be sure that network clients can see
shares on the computer. They must be capable of connecting to shares to use
Proxy Server.

Install the Service Pack

Proxy Server requires a Windows NT Service Pack to run. You can install the Service Pack that is included on Proxy Server CD-ROM, or you can obtain the most recent one from www.microsoft.com. Windows NT Service Pack 3 or later is required for Proxy Server 2.0.

Install IIS

Proxy Server makes use of the IIS Web server and is managed from the Internet Service Manager. You will need to install a copy of IIS 3.0 or later to install Proxy Server.

Install Microsoft Proxy Server

1. To install Proxy Server run the setup.exe program from the root directory of the CD-ROM.

2. First you see a preliminary screen with a copyright after which a dialog box requests your CD key.

3. The next dialog box specifies the installation directory, which is C:\Proxy Server by default. Click **Change Folder** to select a different directory. Click **OK** to accept the directory that is shown.

4. Setup examines your system for installed components, after which it displays the dialog box shown in Figure 21.7. You have another chance to change the installation folder by clicking **Change Folder**. Click the **Installation Options** button to continue with the installation.

5. The Installation Options dialog box is shown in Figure 21.8. Here you can check Proxy Server components to be installed. (You also get a third chance to change the Installation folder. Microsoft really doesn't want you to miss that option!)

FIGURE 21.7

If necessary you can change the Installation folder.

You can use a single administration tool to manage several Proxy Servers through the network, so you don't need a copy on each Proxy Server computer. Also, you can probably live with one set of documentation on your network.

After checking components to be installed, choose **Continue**.

FIGURE 21.8

Selecting Proxy Server components for installation.

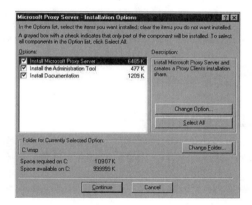

6. The message box in Figure 21.9 appears if the Proxy Server computer is configured with the NWLink protocol but the SAP agent has not been configured. SAP is the Service Advertising Protocol that is used to announce the availability of servers on IPX networks. If you want to configure Proxy Server to work with an IPX internal network, you must abort the installation at this point. Install the SAP agent and then restart the Proxy Server setup program.

FIGURE 21.9

*This message is dis-
played if NWLink is
not installed.*

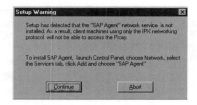

7. The next dialog box, shown in Figure 21.10, is used to configure the disk cache. Although you can configure a cache as small as 5MB, Microsoft recommends a minimum size of 100MB plus 0.5MB for each client. The cache size you specify will be rounded down to the next 5MB interval.

    To obtain the best performance, spread the cache accross multiple hard disks (as in Figure 21.10), or place it on a stripped volume.

    To set up file caching, select a volume in the drive list. Then enter the cache size for that volume in the Maximum Size (MB) field and click **Set**.

    When the cache is configured, choose **OK** to continue.

NOTE

The cache will have the best performance if it is distributed across two or more volumes, each on a separate hard drive. To add a volume to the Proxy Server cache configuration, you must create the volume *before* installing Proxy Server. Only NTFS volumes can be used by the Proxy Server Cache. Windows NT volume management is described in my book *Inside Windows NT Server 4.0* from New Riders Publishing.

7. The next dialog box configures the Local Address Table. The LAT should specify any IP addresses in use on your private network. It can also contain the private Internet address ranges. The private address ranges have been added in Figure 21.11.

8. To manually enter an IP address range, enter the starting and ending IP addresses in the range in the From and To fields. Then click **Add** to copy the address to the LAT Internal IP Address list.

    To specify a single IP address, enter the same address in the From and To boxes.

FIGURE 21.10
Configuring the Proxy Server Cache.

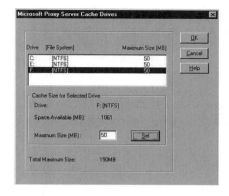

FIGURE 21.11
Configuring the Local Address Table.

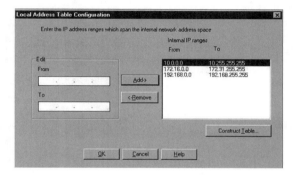

9. To build the table from information Setup provides, choose **Construct Table** to open the Construct Local Address Table dialog box shown in Figure 21.12. This dialog box has two major options:

    ■ **Add the private ranges to the table.** Check this option to include the private Internet address ranges in your LAT. This was done to construct the LAT shown in Figure 21.11.

    ■ **Load from NT internal Routing Table.** Check this option to populate the LAT with IP addresses currently in use on your network. If you want Setup to examine the network and retrieve IP addresses known to all interfaces in the computer, select **Local known address ranges from all IP interface cards**. If Proxy Server is running on a multihomed computer (which is probably the case), you can specify that addresses should be learned from specific interfaces by selecting **Load known address ranges from the following IP interface cards**. Then select the cards that are attached to your private network.

Choose **OK** when you have configured the LAT as required for the network. You can modify the LAT later if required.

NOTE

The LAT should include only IP addresses for your private network. Because one of the interfaces on Proxy Server will be connected to the public Internet side of the server, you should exclude that adapter when building the LAT. Check **Load known address ranges from the following IP interface cards**. Then check only the interface cards that are on your private network.

FIGURE 21.12

Loading the LAT with private address ranges.

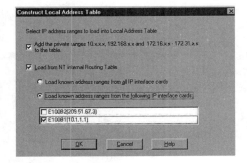

10. Next you will encounter the Client Installation/ Configuration dialog box, shown in Figure 21.13. This dialog box specifies how clients will access the two proxies supported by Proxy Server.

    The options for WinSock Proxy clients are as follows:

    ■ **Computer name.** Select this option if clients will identify the Proxy Server server according to a NetBIOS or DNS name, and specify the name. If clients are working on a NWLink network, they must connect with the Proxy Server server using its NetBIOS name. On a TCP/IP network you can use a name or an IP address.

    If this computer belongs to an array of Proxy Server computers, specify a DNS name that resolves to a member of the array. You must, of course, enter an address (A) record for each member of the array in your DNS server domain database.

    ■ **IP Address.** If the private network is running TCP/IP, you can select this option and specify an IP address that enables clients to connect to the Proxy Server server.

■ **Manual.** Specifies that the `Server IP Addresses` section in the `Proxy Serverclnt.ini` file is not overwritten, enabling the administrator to manually specify the IP addresses of Proxy Server servers by editing the `Proxy Serverclnt.ini` file. This option is unavailable if the `Server IP Addresses` section of the `Proxy Serverclnt.ini` file is empty.

FIGURE 21.13
Specifying proxy server client settings.

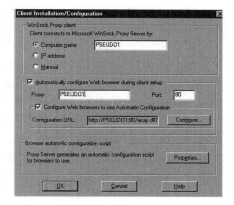

NOTE

In step 10 of the installation procedure, you specify how WinSock clients will identify the Proxy Server server. These settings are copied to Windows clients when the client component of Proxy Server is installed. By default, the setup program enters the NetBIOS name of the Proxy Server server, which is fine if TCP/IP naming is fully configured so that all clients can connect with Proxy Server by its NetBIOS name. On a routed network, you must set up WINS servers to enable NetBIOS names to propagate throughout the network.

Non-Windows clients are not affected by the client configuration entered during setup, and must be manually configured. When you set up a non-Windows browser, you can identify the Proxy Server server by its IP address or, if DNS naming is in use, by its DNS domain name.

11. WinSock clients are configured by running setup scripts that are installed on the Proxy Server server. When the WinSock client is configured, you have the option of automatically configuring how the WinSock client will access the Proxy Server server. Automatic configuration is defined in the remaining options found in the **Client Installation/Configuration** dialog box.

■ **Automatically configure Web browser during client setup.** If this box is checked, the client setup program will attempt to configure the client as a Web Proxy client. The **Proxy**, **Port**, and

Configure Web browsers to use Automatic Configuration fields are active only if this box is checked.

- **Proxy.** This field is active if a check mark appears in the **Automatically configure Web browser during client setup** check box. By default the field is completed with the NetBIOS name of the computer on which Proxy Server is being installed, but another computer can be specified if necessary. DNS names can also be entered in this field.

- **Port.** This port number specifies the port Web clients will use to connect with the IIS Web server. The port number cannot be changed here and is specified as part of the IIS Web server configuration. To change the port, use the Internet Service Manager.

- **Configure Web browsers to use Automatic Configuration.** Newer Web browsers, including Internet Explorer 3.02 and later and Netscape 4.0 and later, can use a JavaScript to specify the proxy server to be used. To enable automatic configuration via a JavaScript, check this box.

- **Configuration URL.** This field is active if you have checked **Configure Web browsers to use Automatic Configuration.** When Proxy Server is installed, a default client configuration JavaScript is created. The default entry in this field specifies the URL of the default JavaScript. To modify the URL, click the **Configure** button.

- **Configure.** Click this button to modify the JavaScript URL and open the **Configuration URL for clients** dialog box. This dialog box has two options:

  - **Use default script supplied by server.** Select this radio button to use the default URL.

  - **Use Custom URL.** Select this radio button to specify a different URL. Enter the URL in the field that is provided.

After completing entries on the dialog box choose **OK** to continue.

12. The **Properties** button in the **Client Installation/Configuration** dialog box opens the Advanced Client Configuration dialog box shown in Figure 21.14. This dialog box enables you to include or exclude

specific IP addresses and domains from those that will be accessed by Proxy Server. The fields in this dialog box are as follows:

- **Use Proxy for local servers.** Check this box if the proxy should service requests for objects from local Web sites. A local Web site is specified by a name that does not contain dots. For example, `http://goofy` is a local Web server name, while `http://www.goofy.com` is an external Web server name.

- **Do not use proxy for the following IP Addresses.** Check this box if you want to specify the IP addresses of Web servers that will not be accessed via this proxy server. If you check this box, use the **Add**, **Edit**, and **Remove** buttons to manage the list of IP Address/Subnet Mask pairs.

- **Do not use proxy for domains ending with.** If this proxy server should not access Web servers in specific domains, check this box. Then enter a list of domains in the box that is provided, separating the domain names with semicolons (;).

- **Backup route.** If this proxy server is down, clients can be configured to access other proxy servers or the Internet directly, enabling them to function should the proxy server fail. Check this box to enable clients to use backup paths in the event of a failure of the proxy server. By default, clients will go directly to the Internet if the proxy server fails.

- **Modify.** If **Backup route** is checked, click this button to open the Configure Backup Route shown in Figure 21.15. This dialog box has the following options:

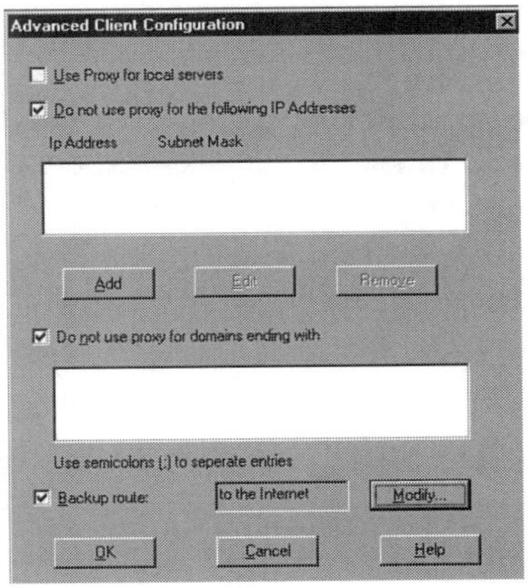

Figure 21.14

WinSock proxy advanced configuration options.

- **Route to the Internet**. Select this radio button if clients should connect directly to the Internet if the proxy server is unavailable.

- **Route to Web Proxy**. Select this radio button to specify a Web proxy server that the client is to use if this proxy server is unavailable. In the Proxy field specify the name of the backup proxy server. In the Port field specify the port that is to be used on the backup proxy server.

13. After completing the client installation configuration dialog boxes, return to the Client Installation/Configuration dialog box (Figure 21.13) and click **OK** to continue Proxy Server installation.

FIGURE 21.15

Configuring a client's proxy server backup route.

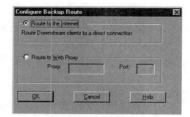

14. The next dialog box is Access Control, shown in Figure 21.16. Access controls enable you to limit access to specific Internet services and protocols. Check the boxes corresponding to the services for which access controls are to be enabled.

WARNING

If you enable access control during installation, you *must* configure access permissions for the proxy services as described in the section "Web Proxy Properties—The Permissions Tab" later in this chapter. (See the discussion related to Figure 21.29).

If users attempt to access a service for which they do not have the required permissions, they do not get a nice, friendly error message. Instead, the proxy server returns an empty object. For example, the user's Web browser says, "Done," but displays a blank Web page.

Consequently, I recommend that you do not enable access control until after you have Proxy Server running. When you are sure that communications are operating properly, you can enable access control, confident that Proxy Server is working. Then your only problem is to establish and debug the access permissions.

FIGURE 21.16

Enabling access controls for the WinSock and Web proxy services.

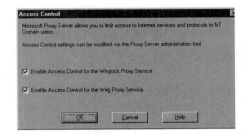

15. Choose **OK** to continue. Files will be copied and services will be started.

Proxy Server is now installed. The default settings for the Web Proxy and WinSock Proxy servers restrict all users, preventing them from accessing the servers. You will need to enable access, as described in the following section, before users can reach the Internet.

Managing Proxy Server

The Proxy Server proxy servers are managed using the same Microsoft Management Console that is used to manage IIS. (If Proxy Server is installed over IIS version 3.0, you will use the Internet Service Manager.) Figure 21.17 shows the MMC after Microsoft Proxy Server has been installed. I have expanded the server tree to expose the entries for the various proxy servers.

The following sections show you how to modify the property settings. As Proxy Server is installed, access is restricted to both the Web Proxy and the WinSock Proxy. You will need to edit the properties for these services to enable users to communicate through the Proxy Server server.

FIGURE 21.17
Proxy Server entries in the MMC.

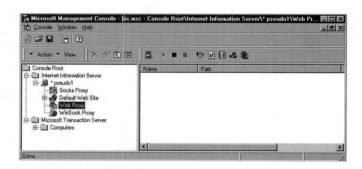

Web Proxy Properties

Figure 21.18 shows the property pages for the Web Proxy server. To access the property page for a service, right-click the service in the service tree. Then choose **Properties** from the context menu. Let's look at the tabs and examine the settings.

FIGURE 21.18
Web Proxy property pages.

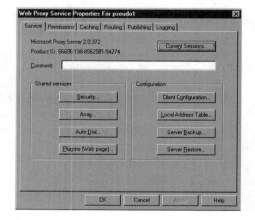

Web Proxy Properties—The Service Tab

Properties on the Service tab (Figure 21.18) configure various characteristics of the Web Proxy service. Microsoft Proxy Server must be installed on a computer that is running IIS 3.0 or later, and hooks into the IIS Web server. When Proxy Server is installed, it configures the IIS Web server so that it no longer listens for incoming requests for Web publishing. Any attempts by outside users to contact the Web server are ignored. This is done to enhance the security that Proxy Server can provide for your private network. Access to FTP and Gopher publishing services is not affected.

The Service property page contains only one data entry field, named **Comment.** This optional field accepts a comment that identifies the Web Proxy service in the MMC.

Otherwise the Service property page consists of several buttons that access subdialogs. We'll review these options one button at a time.

Configuring Web Proxy Service Security

Clicking the **Security** button on the Security property page opens the Security dialog box shown in Figure 21.19. This dialog box has four pages that configure security-related properties.

WARNING

By default, all Proxy Server security features are disabled. You must enable packet filtering, domain filtering, alerts, and logging to activate those security features.

Keep in mind the fact that no security is perfect. There are probably several dozen hackers who have Microsoft Proxy Server in their sights, some for the challenge and some with larceny in mind. Sooner or later someone will discover a chink in Proxy Server's armor. So don't assume that your job is done when you turn on Proxy Server's security features. Pay attention to your audit logs, watch your trade journals, and stay current on announcements posted on Microsoft's Web site.

Microsoft has published a white paper on Proxy Server security. Obtain the white paper at http://www.micorosoft.com/proxy. Click **Product Guide** in the left-hand column and then click **Technical Papers**.

Packet Filtering

Packet filtering intercepts and examines packets sent to or received from the interface. When packet filtering is enabled, a given packet type will not be allowed on the local network unless Proxy Server has been specifically configured to pass that type of packet. Packet filtering can protect the local network from a variety of attacks, such as address spoofing, SYN, and FRAG attacks.

FIGURE 21.19

Proxy Server security properties—packet filtering.

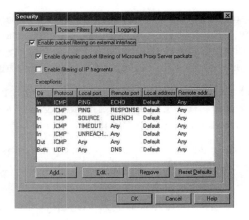

SYN attacks attempt to tie up servers by opening many connections, rapidly consuming server connection resources. (Recall from Chapter 5 that a SYN message is sent when a client attempts to open a TCP connection with another host.) When connection resources have been consumed, new clients cannot connect. Attacks that block access to a server are referred to as "denial of service" attacks.

Address spoofing is an attempt to penetrate a network from the outside by sending packets that contain an address used on the internal network. Such packets might appear to originate on the internal network, and might be capable of circumventing address-based security. Proxy Server packet filtering can help protect against spoofing attacks.

FRAG attacks use message fragments in attempt to tie up a server and result in a denial of service condition.

Packet filtering can be enabled only on Proxy Server computers that have two or more interfaces. If you are using a dial-up interface to connect with the Internet, you must configure an ISDN or modem interface before packet-filtering options are enabled.

The **Packet Filtering** property page (Figure 21.19) has three check box options:

- **Enable packet filtering on external interface.** By default, packet filtering is disabled and this box is not checked. When this box is checked, Proxy Server will filter incoming and outgoing packets that pass through the external network interface.

- **Enable dynamic packet filtering of Microsoft Proxy Server packets.** This option is checked by default if packet filtering is enabled. Dynamic packet filtering enables Proxy Server to create filters as required so that protocol ports are open only when they are needed. Microsoft recommends that you enable dynamic packet filtering.

- **Enable filtering of IP fragments.** Microsoft does not make a specific recommendation on this option, which is disabled by default. Although enabling this option might slow Proxy Server performance somewhat, it seems to make sense to enable it.

The Exceptions list specifies packet types that are not to be filtered by Proxy Server. Add exceptions if you will be running services that are not supported by Proxy Server, such as Microsoft Exchange. See the online help for descriptions of the properties for entries in this list.

Domain Filters

The next tab in the Security dialog box is Domain Filters, shown in Figure 21.20. Domain filtering is disabled by default, but is enabled in the figure by checking **Enable filtering**. Domain filtering can be enabled only if Proxy Server has a connection to the Internet.

FIGURE 21.20

Proxy Server security properties—domain filtering.

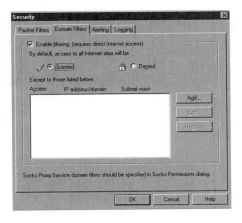

After enabling domain filtering, you must select one of the following options:

- **Granted.** When this option is selected, users can access all domains *except* those you specifically identify.

- **Denied.** When this option is selected, users can access *only* those sites you specifically identify.

After you select a default access setting, you must populate the Access list. Click <u>A</u>dd to open an Deny Access To dialog box like the one shown in Figure 21.21. In this dialog box you can specify Internet hosts in one of three ways:

- **Single Computer.** You will be prompted to enter the IP address of a single host.

- **Group of Computers.** You can restrict access to all computers on a given network. You will be prompted to enter the network ID and subnet mask for the network.

- **Domain.** You can restrict access to computers in a specified DNS domain. The Web Proxy server must query DNS to determine whether a client is attempting to access a restricted domain, and this option can result in high network traffic levels.

FIGURE 21.21

Defining a Web Proxy filter.

The problem with filtering Internet access is that there are too many sites out there for an administrator to ride herd on. At this point, Microsoft doesn't offer preconfigured lists of sites that businesses might want to restrict, so it's up to you. You might find it easier to deny everything and to add specific sites that are required by your organization. Remember that many Web servers call other Web servers, so you might need to add more than one IP address to allow complete access to an organization's Web content.

If your organization maintains a Web server that publishes on the Internet, you should consider running the Web server and Proxy Server on different computers to avoid compromising Proxy Server firewall security. If your budget cannot support separate computers you should enable Internet publishing on the computer running Proxy Server.

NOTE

Cyber Patrol is a highly regarded Internet filtering product that is used by many organizations to limit access to Internet sites. A proxy version of Cyber Patrol can operate with Microsoft Proxy Server. You can obtain information at `http://www.cyberpatrol.com/`.

Alert Options

Proxy Server can be configured to generate alert messages that are sent via email to the server administrator. Alerts are configured using the Alerting tab of the Security dialog box, shown in Figure 21.22.

FIGURE 21.22

Proxy Server security properties—configuring alerts.

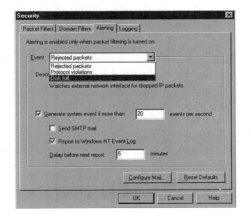

To configure an alert, do the following:

1. In the **Event** field, (which is pulled down in the figure) select one of the following event types:

   ■ **Rejected packets**. Proxy Server generates an alert after a specified number of packets have been rejected. A high frequency of packet rejection might signal an attempt to penetrate the security of your system.

- **Protocol violations.** Proxy Server might identify some rejected packets as potentially malicious. This option configures Proxy Server to send alerts when high numbers of packets are rejected.

- **Disk full.** Generates an alert when the Proxy Server is short on disk space.

NOTE

Besides the alerts, events are recorded in the packet-filtering log, the Proxy Server logs, and optionally in the Windows NT event log.

2. Check **Generate system events if more than...events per second** to configure the event frequency that generates an alert. Specify the frequency in the field that is provided.

3. Check **Send SMTP mail** if the alert should be transmitted via SMTP mail.

4. Check **Report to Windows NT Event Log** if events should be logged in the standard Windows NT Event Log.

5. **Delay before next report** enables you to configure the minimum time period between alert messages so that you aren't driven out of your mind with repeated messages. Configure the message delay in the field that is provided.

6. If alert messages are to be sent via email, click **Configure** to open the Configure Mail Alerting dialog box shown in Figure 21.23. Complete the dialog box as follows:

   - **Mail server.** Enter the IP address or the DNS name of the mail server to be used.

   - **Port.** Enter the port number to be used when communicating with the mail server.

   - **Send mail to.** Enter the email name that is to receive the name.

   - **From address.** Enter the email address that is to appear in the from field of the alert message.

   After entering the email parameters, click the **Test** button to send a test email message.

FIGURE 21.23

Configuring an email recipient for alerts.

Logging Options

If desired, the Web Proxy server will record security activity in a log, which is configured in the Logging tab of the Security dialog box shown in Figure 21.24. Configure settings on this tab are as follows:

1. **Enable Logging using.** Check this field to enable logging. Then select one of the following logging options in the selection field:

   - **Regular.** Select this option to create a sparse log with only essential information, while conserving disk space.

   - **Verbose.** Select this option to create a detailed log. Remember that an active Proxy Server will generate large logs. Don't enable verbose logging unless you intend to actively monitor the server and ensure the log files don't fill free disk space.

2. **Log to File.** Select this radio button to log to a file that you examine in a text editor. If you enable file logging, the following options are active:

   - **Automatically open new log.** If this box is checked, the current log is closed and a new log is opened when the specified event occurs. You can choose to open a new log daily, weekly, or monthly.

   - **Limit number of old log files to.** Check this box if you want to limit the number of old log files that will be retained on the server. If you check this option, specify the number of old logs that are to be retained. I recommend that you limit the number of logs to conserve disk space.

   - **Stop all services if disk full.** Log files can fill up the hard disk and interfere with the proper operation of Proxy Server. Check this option if you want Proxy Server to stop all services if the hard disk is full.

■ **Log file directory**. This field specifies the directory where the log file will be recorded. You can change the directory, but not the name of the log file itself. Log filenames have the format PF*yymmdd*.log where *yymmdd* specifies the date when the log file was created.

3. **Log to SQL/ODBC Database.** Select this radio button to log alerts to a SQL or other ODBC-compatible database. This is perhaps the optimal way to log. By recording log data in a database, you can analyze Proxy Server activity using Microsoft Access, Microsoft SQL Server, or another database application. You must create an appropriate database before database logging is enabled, a topic that is beyond the scope of this book.

FIGURE 21.24

Configuring Web Proxy security logging.

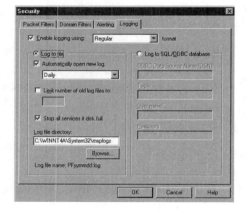

Joining and Leaving Arrays

Clicking the **Array** button on the Security property page opens the Array dialog box shown in Figure 21.25. (Figure 21.25 was prepared after an array had been established.) This dialog box enables you to configure the Proxy Server as a member of an array. Microsoft Proxy Server 2.0 can form arrays only with other Microsoft Proxy Server 2.0 computers.

FIGURE 21.25

A Proxy Server array.

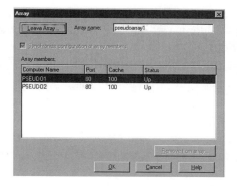

To add a Proxy Server to an array, do the following:

1. Configure at least two proxy servers that will form an array. The computers should be configured with static IP addresses. Create name entries for the proxy servers in DNS.

2. On one of the proxy servers, open the properties for the Web Proxy server. Select the **Array** button to open the Array dialog box. Then click **Join Array** in the Array dialog box to open the Join Array dialog box.

3. In the Join Array dialog box, enter the name of a proxy server you want to form an array with.

4. If the proxy server you specify in step 3 is not a member of an existing array, you will see the dialog box stating The server you are try-ing to join is not part of an existing array. A new array will be created with this server. Specify the name of the array you are creating and choose **OK**.

5. The array will be defined in the Array dialog box (Figure 21.25).

To remove a computer from an array, click the **Leave Array** button in the Array dialog box.

Configuring Auto Dial

Okay, you don't have a direct dedicated connection to the Internet. Instead, you need to dial up using an ISDN line or a modem. Does that mean you can't use Microsoft Proxy Server? No indeed! If only a few users need to contact the Internet, Proxy Server is an ideal intermediary because it uses intelligent caching to minimize traffic to the Internet. In many cases, this enables more than one person to take advantage of a dial-up connection that would ordinarily support but one person at a time.

Before configuring Proxy Server to use automatic dial-up, you must install and configure a Dial-Up Networking connection. (See my book *Inside Windows NT Server 4* from New Riders if you aren't familiar with Remote Access Service and Dial-Up Networking) You can use any Internet dial-up account. All you need is the single IP address that is assigned by your ISP. IP addresses on your private network can be selected from the Internet private address ranges. So, a simple dial-up account is all you need. Of course, you want the fastest connection possible. If your ISP offers 56Kbps dial-up lines, purchase a compatible modem to take advantage of them. Or install an ISDN line to bump bandwidth up to 128Kbps.

After Dial-Up Networking is configured and tested, do the following to set up Proxy Server:

1. In MMC Open the properties for the Web Proxy Server and click **Auto Dial** to open the Microsoft Proxy Auto Dial dialog box shown in Figure 21.26.

2. On the Configuration tab, check the check boxes corresponding to the proxy services for which auto dial is to be enabled.

3. In the Dialing Hours box, mark any hours when dial-out will not be permitted. Drag a frame through the hour block to change its setting. White blocks mark hours when Proxy Server will not dial out.

4. On the Credentials tab, enter the required access information, which will be the same settings you enter for Dial-Up networking (see Figure 21.27).

After the dial-out connection is configured, Proxy Server behaves as follows:

- The Web Proxy will dial out to the Internet whenever it receives a request for an object that it cannot supply from cache.

- The WinSock Proxy and Socks Proxy will dial out for all requests directed to the Internet.

The caching capability of the Web Proxy is particularly advantageous when dial-out connections are used. If an object is found in the Proxy Server's cache, the object can be returned to the client without the need to establish a connection. This saves money on ISDN connections, which usually charge extra for the first minute of a connection, and it saves time when modem dial-up connections are avoided.

FIGURE 21.26

Configuring Proxy Server to dial out for an Internet connection.

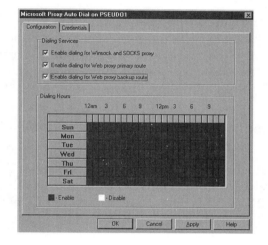

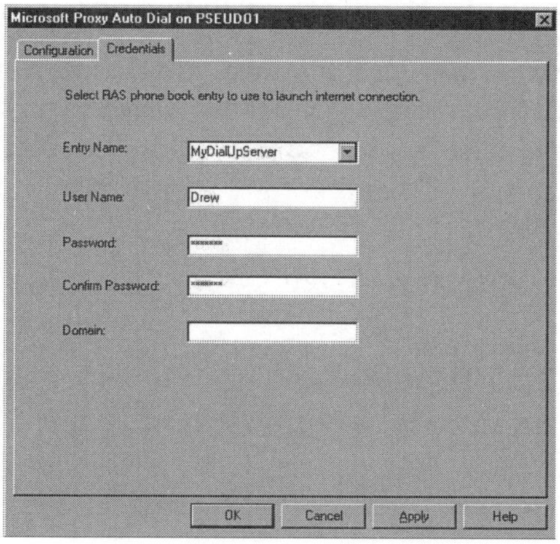

FIGURE 21.27

Entering credentials to enable Proxy Server to dial out for an Internet connection.

Proxy Server Plug-Ins

The **Plug-Ins** button in the properties page opens a connection to a Web page on Microsoft's Web site that is devoted to third-party add-ons for Proxy Server.

Configuring the Client

The **Client Configuration** button in the Web Server properties page (refer to Figure 21.18) opens a Client Installation/Configuration dialog box similar to the one you see when installing Proxy Server (refer to Figure 21.13). This dialog box enables you to modify client installation and configuration settings after Proxy Server has been installed.

Configuring the Local Address Table

The **Local Address Table** button in the Web Server properties page (Figure 21.18) opens a **Local Address Table Configuration** dialog box similar to the one you see when installing Proxy Server (refer to Figure 21.12.) This dialog box enables you to modify the LAT after Proxy Server has been installed.

Specifying the Backup Directory

Proxy Server automatically backs up configuration settings to a directory that you specify. The default directory is `C:\msp\config`. To change the directory, click **Server Backup** in the Web Proxy properties page (refer to Figure 21.18) and enter a new directory path in the Backup dialog box.

Restoring the Proxy Server Configuration

You can restore an earlier configuration for the Proxy Server by clicking the **Server Restore** button on the Web Proxy properties page (refer to Figure 21.18). The Restore Configuration dialog box is shown in Figure 21.28.

FIGURE 21.28

*Restoring an earlier
Proxy Server configura-
tion.*

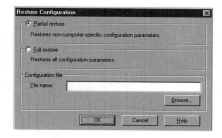

FIGURE 21.28

*Restoring an earlier
Proxy Server configura-
tion.*

Web Proxy Properties—The Permissions Tab

The Web Proxy server supports access to Web, FTP, Gopher, and Secure
Socket Layer services, and you can restrict access to each service. Figure
21.29 shows the Permissions tab, which is accessed from the Web Proxy. To
permit all users to access all services, remove the check from the **Enable
Access Control** check box. To regulate access to Web Proxy services, do the
following:

1. Check the Enable Access Control check box.

2. Select a protocol in the Protocol field, which has been pulled down in
    Figure 21.29.

3. Click **Edit** to open a Permissions dialog box similar to the one in
    Figure 21.30. (The figure was prepared after a group was added to the
    list.)

4. Select the users and groups to be added from the list in the Add Users
    and Groups dialog box.

5. Select an access restriction in the Type of Access list. Some services,
    such as WWW, offer only one type of access.

6. Return to the Permissions tab and define permissions for other ser-
    vices as required.

7. To copy a user or group from one service to another, select the user or
    group. Then click the **Copy To** button and select the service to which
    the user or group is to be copied.

8. To remove a user or group from the access list for a service, select the
    user or group and click **Remove From.**

FIGURE 21.29

Regulating access to Web Proxy services.

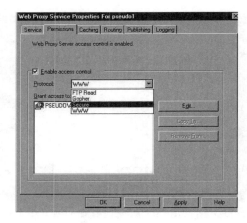

FIGURE 21.30

Specifying groups and users for access control.

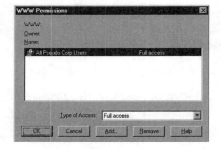

WARNING

If access control is enabled during the installation of Proxy Server, there will be a check in the Enable Access Control check box and no users can reach the Internet. You must either remove this check mark, enabling all users to access all services, or add some permissions to enable users to access the Internet.

Web Proxy Properties—The Caching Tab

The Caching tab is shown in Figure 21.31. Cache configuration is your primary tool for adjusting Web Proxy Server performance and use of resources.

Caching is enabled by placing a check in the **Enable Caching** check box. By default, caching is enabled and in most cases you should leave caching enabled. Caching significantly improves Web Proxy access performance while at the same time economizing WAN traffic. Consider disabling caching if the Web content being accessed changes frequently, in which case caching might result in users receiving outdated Web objects. Also, because caching can use a great deal of disk space, you might want to disable caching on a server with limited resources.

Configuring the Cache Expiration Policy

Settings in the Cache Expiration Policy box determine how long objects will remain in cache. Three options are available:

- **Updates are more important (more update checks).** Select this option if objects change frequently. The Web Proxy server will make frequent checks to detect changes and retrieve updated objects.

- **Equal importance.** Select this option to balance update checks between the other two settings.

- **Fewer network accesses are more important (more cache hits).** Select this option if you want to minimize the WAN traffic generated by the Web Proxy. This setting is appropriate of objects that change infrequently.

FIGURE 21.31

Configuring cache settings.

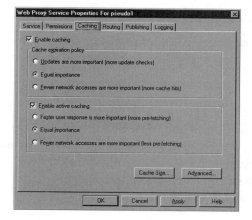

Configuring Active Caching

Active caching enables the Web Proxy to anticipate object retrieval requests. Suppose that a user retrieves a Web page that has links to several other pages. With active caching the Web Proxy might attempt to retrieve some of the linked objects when WAN usage is low so that the objects will be in cache should a user request them. Active caching will also attempt to renew select cache objects if their TTLs approach expiration. Active caching is enabled by checking the **Enable active caching** check box. Three options are available to configure the behavior of active caching:

- **Faster user response is more important (more pre-fetching).** Select this option if active caching should make a concerted effort to anticipate user requests for objects.

- **Equal importance.** Select this option to balance active caching behavior between the other settings.

- **Fewer network accesses are more important (less pre-fetching).** Choose this option to conserve network bandwidth by reducing active cache requests at the cost of a cache that is more stale.

Configuring the Cache Size

To manage the size and configuration of the cache, click **Cache Size** in the Caching tab. This opens the Microsoft Proxy Server Cache Drives dialog box shown in Figure 21.32. In the figure, I have done two things to improve the performance of the cache:

- I disabled caching from the C: volume so that the cache will not compete with access to the system files.

- I distributed the cache across two volumes to improve performance.

These strategies bear fruit only if the volumes are located on separate disk drives, and only if SCSI hard disks are used. Most current SCSI controllers have a *SCSI disconnect* feature that enables disk service requests to be performed on multiple drives simultaneously. IDE disks do not lend themselves to cache distribution because only one disk of an IDE master/slave pair can operate at a given time.

To change the cache size on a volume, select the volume, specify the cache size in the Maximum Size field, and click **Set**.

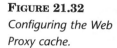

FIGURE 21.32

*Configuring the Web
Proxy cache.*

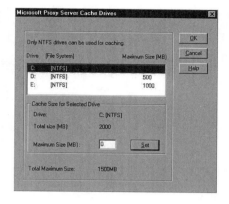

Configuring Advanced Caching Parameters

Click the **Ad_vanced** button on the Caching tab to open the Advanced
Caching Policy dialog box shown in Figure 21.33. This dialog box has several settings that determine which objects will be cached and how long they
will be retained. The following parameters can be configured:

- **Limit si_ze of cached objects to.** If your Proxy Server has limited cache
  space, you might not want to cache large objects. In such cases, you
  should check this option and specify a maximum object size in the field
  provided. Objects larger than the value you specify will not be held in
  cache. (In most cases, however, it makes sense to cache large objects.
  They are, after all, the ones that cost the most in terms of bandwidth.
  Consider buying more disk drive capacity before you enable this option.)

- **R_eturn expired objects for up to...% of original TTL if source
  Web site cannot be contacted.** If the Web Proxy receives a request
  for an object that has expired it will attempt to retrieve a new copy of
  the object from the server that originally supplied it. If that server is
  unavailable, the Web Proxy can exhibit one of two behaviors: It can
  report that the target server is unavailable, or it can return the
  expired object from cache. It's up to you. Is an expired object better
  than no object at all?

FIGURE 21.33

Configuring advanced cache settings.

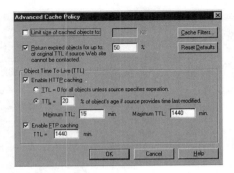

- **Enable HTTP caching.** This check box enables and disables Web server caching. If the box is checked, you have the following options for specifying the TTL of objects held in cache:

  - **TTL = 0 for all objects unless source specifies expiration.** Web servers can specify a TTL for objects they provide. If this option is selected, cached objects are not assigned a TTL unless a TTL is specified by the source Web server.

  - **TTL = ...% of object's age if source provides time last-modified.** Select this option if you want to define a time span between object updates. You must enter values for **Minimum TTL** and **Maximum TTL**.

- **Enable FTP caching.** If you want to cache FTP objects, check this option and specify a TTL for cached FTP objects.

Configuring Cache Filters

Typically, active caching will be permitted to determine which sites will be cached. If desired, you can manually define caching on a site-by-site basis. Click the **Cache Filters** button to open the Cache Filters dialog box shown in Figure 21.34. This figure was prepared after some cache filters were specified.

To add a cache filter, click **Add** to open the Cache Filter Properties dialog box shown in Figure 21.35. Specify a URL (which must contain at least one / character) and select **Always cache** or **Never cache** to determine how objects from that site will be cached.

FIGURE 21.34

Cache filters.

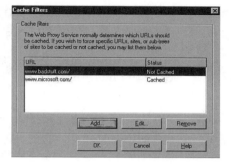

FIGURE 21.35

Specifying a cache filter.

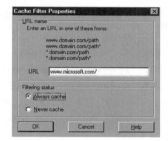

Web Proxy Properties—The Routing Tab

The Routing tab of the Web Proxy dialog box is shown in Figure 21.36. Use this dialog box to configure routing to upstream servers, backup routes, and the relationship of this Proxy Server with its peers in an array. Figure 21.36 does not show the default configuration. I have selected options as required to enable all of the options in the dialog box.

FIGURE 21.36

Configuring Web Proxy routing.

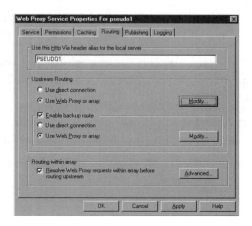

Configuring Upstream Routing and the Backup Route

The Upstream Routing box has two radio buttons:

- **Use direct connection.** When this button is selected, the Proxy Server connects directly with the Internet to obtain all objects that it cannot obtain from cache. This is the default upstream routing option.

- **Use Web Proxy or array.** This button is selected when the Proxy Server cannot provide an object from cache so it forwards the request to an upstream proxy server or array. Upstream proxy servers are not required to use Proxy Server 2.0, and can use Proxy Server 1.0 or a proxy server based on another platform such as UNIX. Click **Modify** to open an Advanced routing options box where you can define the upstream connection.

If the **Use Web Proxy or array** radio button is selected, the **Enable backup route** check box is enabled along with the two related radio buttons. The backup route determines how the client will connect if its primary Proxy Server is down. Configure the backup route options as follows:

- **Enable backup route.** Unless you want to force users to access the Internet through this Proxy Server, check this option so that a backup route can be enabled.

- **Use direct connection.** If this radio button is selected, clients will connect directly with the Internet if this proxy server becomes unavailable.

- **Use Web Proxy or array.** If this radio button is selected, clients will use the proxy server or the proxy array you specify if this proxy server becomes unavailable. Click the **Modify** button to open an Advanced routing options dialog box where you can define the backup route.

The upstream and backup routes are configured in the Advanced routing options dialog box shown in Figure 21.37. The options in this dialog box are as follows:

- **Proxy.** Enter the name of the upstream or backup proxy server. When you complete this field, the name will be used to fill the Array URL field.

- **Port.** The default port is 80, but another port can be specified if necessary.

■ **Auto-poll upstream proxy for array configuration.** If the upstream proxy server is running Proxy Server 2.0, this Proxy Server can poll the upstream server to obtain the upstream server's array configuration. Disable this option if the upstream server is not a member of a Proxy Server 2.0 array.

■ **Array URL.** If auto-poll is enabled, this field specifies the URL of a file that contains the array configuration data for the upstream server. This field is automatically completed with the proxy server name entered in the Proxy field and the default location and filename.

■ **Use credentials to communicate with upstream proxy/array.** Proxy servers can be configured to require downstream proxy servers to authenticate before connecting. If authentication is required on the upstream proxy server, check this box.

■ **Username.** If authentication is required by the upstream proxy/array, enter an authorized username.

■ **Password.** Enter the password associated with the username.

■ **Allow basic/clear text authentication.** If the upstream proxy/array uses clear text authentication, select this radio button. Clear text authentication must be used with most proxy/arrays that do not use Proxy Server 2.0.

■ **Allow encrypted authentication.** Check this option if the upstream proxy/array uses Windows NT encryption.

FIGURE 21.37

Configuring routing for an upstream proxy server or array.

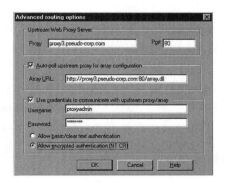

Configuring Array Routing

At the bottom of the Routing tab (Figure 21.36) is the check box **Resolve Web Proxy requests within array before routing upstream.** If this box is checked, the Proxy Server cannot provide a requested Web object from its cache and it will contact its peers in an array to determine whether they have the object in cache. Only if the object cannot be found in the array will the Proxy Server forward the request upstream or to the Internet.

Web Proxy Properties—The Publishing Tab

Microsoft Proxy Server uses IIS to provide its core functionality, and a Web server operates on every Proxy Server. Typically, however, publishing is disabled for the Web Server. Although you can publish Web pages on the Proxy Server, Microsoft recommends against it because Web publishing can weaken the security of the Proxy Server.

You can, however, enable Web publishing by checking the **Enable Web publishing** check box on the Publishing tab shown in Figure 21.38. If Web publishing is enabled, you must determine how incoming Web server requests are handled by selecting one of the following three options:

- **discarded**. Incoming Web requests that cannot be mapped with the mapping table are discarded.

- **sent to the local web server.** Incoming Web requests that cannot be mapped with the mapping table are sent to the Web server operating on this computer.

- **sent to another web server.** Incoming Web requests that cannot be mapped with the mapping table are sent to the Web server you specify. Enter the server name and port in the fields that are provided.

You can map specific incoming requests to specific URLs by adding mappings to the **Except to those listed below** list. These explicit mappings override the radio buttons just discussed. To add a mapping, click **Add** to open the Mapping dialog box shown in Figure 21.39. This dialog box has two fields:

- **Path.** Specifies the URL of the Web server to which the incoming request is directed.

- **URL.** Specifies the URL of the destination to which the incoming request is redirected.

FIGURE 21.38

Configuring Web publishing properties.

FIGURE 21.39

Adding an explicit referral mapping to the Web publishing configuration.

After you specify a referral map and choose **OK** you will see the Default Local Host Name dialog box shown in Figure 21.40. This dialog box accepts a host name, which is required by some older HTTP clients (usually browsers that use HTTP 1.0). These older browsers do not include a host header in their requests. The host header specifies the host name to client Web browsers used to connect to the Proxy Server. If a request does not include a host header, the request is routed to the default local host name that you specify. The default mapping can be entered or modified by clicking the **Default Mapping** button of the Publishing properties tab.

FIGURE 21.40

Specifying a default local host name.

Web Proxy Properties—The Logging Tab

The Logging tab of the Web Server Services Properties dialog box configures logging for the Web server. Shown in Figure 21.41, the settings are similar those for security logging. Refer to the discussion related to Figure 21.24 for an explanation of the available options. Note the name of the log file, which is specified below the Log file directory field. The filename varies depending on the frequency selected for opening new logs.

FIGURE 21.41

Configuring Web Server logging.

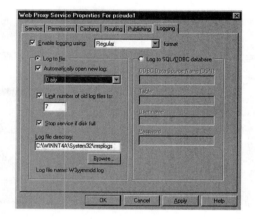

WinSock Proxy Properties

Properties for the WinSock Proxy server are similar in many instances to properties you have seen for the Web Proxy server, so we'll only examine two tabs: Protocols and Permissions.

WinSock Proxy Properties—The Protocols Tab

The WinSock Proxy server enables users to reach the Internet with nearly every popular Internet service protocol. You can, if necessary, disable specific protocols or add new ones. Protocol support is configured in the Protocols tab, shown in Figure 21.42.

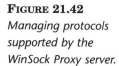

FIGURE 21.42

Managing protocols supported by the WinSock Proxy server.

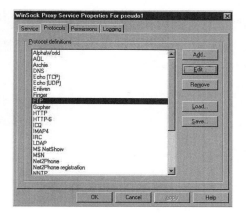

It is easy to remove a protocol from the list. Suppose that you don't want WinSock clients to be able to access outside mail services; remove the POP3 protocol from the protocols list.

TIP

Before you remove a protocol, examine it by selecting the protocol and choosing Edit. Record the settings in the Edit dialog box, or file away a screen shot. That way you can easily add the protocol back at a future time.

Modifying and adding a protocol, on the other hand, requires considerable knowledge of the protocol. Consider, for example, the definition for the FTP protocol shown in Figure 21.43. This dialog box was opened by selecting FTP in the Protocol definitions list and then clicking the **Edit** button. I have not provided you with specific information about the supported protocols in this book, and I consider modification and adding of protocols to be beyond this book's scope.

WinSock Proxy Properties—The Permissions Tab

You can control the services users can access on a protocol-by-protocol basis. Figure 21.44 shows the Permissions tab. Recall that the WinSock Proxy supports only WinSock—and hence Windows—clients. That being the case, you can require all users to log on using valid NT domain accounts, enabling you to restrict protocol access by user and group.

FIGURE 21.43
The definition of a pro-
tocol in the WinSock
Proxy service.

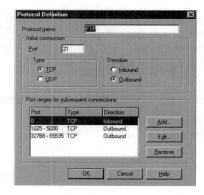

To assign protocol permissions:

1. To disable protocol permissions, clear the **Enable Access Control** check box. This enables all clients to use all protocols, without need for authentication.

2. To enable protocol permissions, check the **Enable Access Control** check box. If you do so, you *must* define specific access permissions or no users can access any services.

3. To define permissions for a specific protocol, select an entry in the **P**rotocol field. Select **Unlimited Access** to define permissions for all protocols.

4. Choose **Edit** to open an Access Permissions dialog box**.** In this dialog box, click **Add** to open an Add Users and Groups dialog box where you can select the user and group accounts that are to have access to the protocol you selected.

WARNING

If you enabled access control for the WinSock Proxy service while installing Proxy Server, there will be a check in the **E**nable Access Control check box and no users can reach the Internet because no permissions have been assigned to any protocol. You must either remove this check mark, enabling all users to access all services, or you must add some permissions to enable users to access the Internet.

FIGURE 21.44

Assigning protocol permissions.

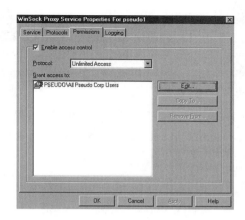

Socks Proxy Properties

Properties for the WinSock Proxy server are similar in many instances to properties you have seen for the Web Proxy server, so we'll only cover the Permissions tab, shown in Figure 21.45.

FIGURE 21.45

The Socks Proxy Permissions tab.

The Permissions tab configures the Socks Proxy to permit or deny packets based on the source, destination, protocol, or some combination of those features. To add a permission to the list click the Add button to open the Socks Permission dialog box shown in Figure 21.46. Most fields in this dialog box are self-explanatory.

To filter traffic based on port or protocol:

1. Complete the **Action, Source,** and **Destination** areas of the dialog box.

2. Check the **Port** check box.

3. Select an operator from the following choices:

    ■ **EQ.** The permission applies to the protocol that matches the specified port number or service name.

    ■ **NEQ.** The permission applies to protocols that do not match the specified port number or service name.

    ■ **GT.** The permission applies to protocols having port numbers greater than the specified port number.

    ■ **LT.** The permission applies to protocols having port numbers less than the specified port number.

    ■ **GE.** The permission applies to protocols having port numbers greater than or equal to the specified port number.

    ■ **LE.** The permission applies to protocols having port numbers less than or equal to the specified port number.

4. After returning to the Permissions tab, use the **Move Up** or **Move Down** buttons to adjust the order of the defined permissions.

When a packet is received, the Socks Proxy service examines permissions in the order they appear and applies the first permission that satisfies the request. Consequently, the order of permissions in the Permissions tab is significant. Suppose that the fifth permission permits a packet to be forwarded, but that the third permission blocks the packet. The third permission will take effect and the fifth permission will not be evaluated.

FIGURE 21.46

Configuring a permission for the Socks Proxy service.

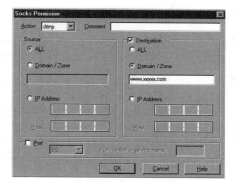

Monitoring Proxy Server Performance

When you install Microsoft Proxy Server, a shortcut named Monitor Proxy Server Performance is added to the start menu in the Microsoft Proxy Server submenu. This shortcut starts Performance Monitor with chart lines defined to monitor Proxy Server operation. See my book *Inside Windows NT Server 4.0* if you need to review the use and features of Performance Monitor.

Configuring and Using Proxy Server Clients

During installation, the Proxy Server setup program creates a shared folder on the server that is given the sharename mspclnt. This folder contains client software for Windows NT, Windows 95/98, and Windows 3.x.

To install the client software:

1. Open the Network Neighborhood and browse for the mspclnt share on Proxy Server's computer.

2. Windows NT and Windows 95/98 clients are set up by running the Setup program in the root directory of the sharename.

3. Windows 3.x clients are set up by running the Setup1.exe program in the Win3x subfolder.

4. The only option during setup is to change the destination folder.

The client installation program makes two changes:

■ It installs a modified WinSock that directs service requests made to non-local IP addresses to the WinSock Proxy server.

■ If a supported browser is present, it modifies the browser configuration to enable it to use the Web Proxy server.

There is nothing more to configure with regard to the WinSock Proxy server, simply start using WinSock applications. Supported browsers should require no further modification, but you can review and modify their settings if necessary.

Configuring Microsoft Internet Explorer

To configure Internet Explorer, open the Internet applet in the Control Panel. (You can also open the applet from within Internet Explorer by choosing View | Options.) The Internet applet is shown in Figure 21.47. I have selected the Connection tab that is used to configure proxy server access. (If Internet Explorer has not been installed, the Internet applet will have only an Advanced tab.)

FIGURE 21.47

Proxy server settings in the Internet applet.

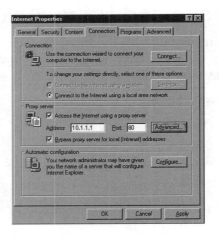

The client's initial settings are determined by options you specified when installing Proxy Server or when managing the properties of the Web and WinSock Proxy services. Recall that in step 10 (Figure 21.13) you specified how clients will identify the Web Proxy server, whether by NebBIOS name, DNS name, or IP address. That setting is copied into the client's configuration.

In most cases you will want IE to automatically load its configuration. The automatic configuration URL is discussed earlier in this chapter in the text associated with Figure 21.13. To examine or modify the automatic configuration URL in the Internet applet, select the **Connection** tab and click **Configure** to open the **Automatic Configuration** dialog box.

NOTE

Because you specified a name in the Proxy Server setup dialog box, you don't need to specify a name in the browser's configuration. In TCP/IP, a name is simply a way to obtain an IP address.

Remember that a Web Proxy client can be any browser that supports the CERN Web proxy protocols. If the browser is running on a non-Windows operating system, specify the Web Proxy server using its DNS domain name or its IP address.

Typically, all services requests—whether for HTTP, FTP, or Gopher—are serviced by the same proxy server on port 80. If you want to specify individual settings for different protocols, click the **Advanced** button on the Connection tab to open the Proxy Settings dialog box shown in Figure 21.48. Then remove the check mark from **Use the same proxy server for all protocols**. Then you can individually modify the protocol settings.

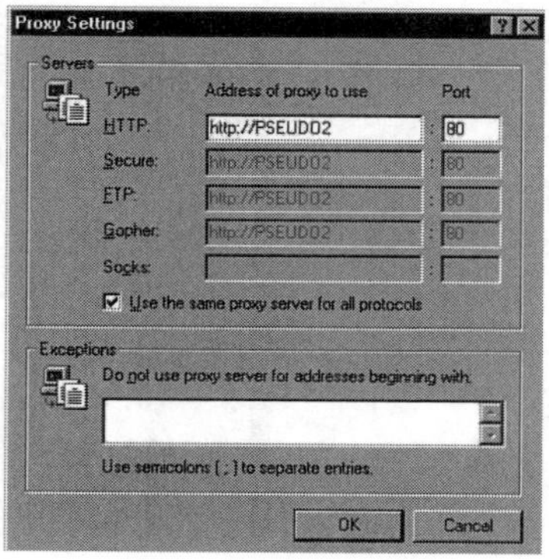

FIGURE 21.48

You can use the Proxy Settings dialog box to individually specify ports for protocols.

NOTE

Internet Explorer maintains a local cache of objects it receives. By default, this cache is cleared only when Internet Explorer is restarted. As a result, IE is operating its own cache in tandem with the Web Proxy server. This can result in stale data, and you might want to turn off IE's cache so that you can take full advantage of the Web Proxy server's active caching.

To turn off the local cache:

1. Open the Internet applet in the Control Panel.

2. Select the **General** tab.

3. Choose **Settings**.

4. Select **Every visit to the page**.

With that setting, IE will obtain a new copy each time a page is requested. That's expensive with a direct Internet connection, but not very costly when using Proxy Server on a LAN. Bear in mind, however, that the Proxy Server cache might contain a fairly recent copy of the object being requested.

Configuring Netscape Navigator

To configure Navigator, select Edit | Preferences to open the Preferences dialog box shown in Figure 21.49. You will need to expand the Advanced subtree to locate the Proxies preferences.

FIGURE 21.49

Proxy server settings for Netscape Navigator.

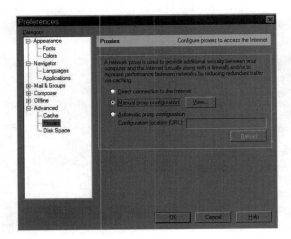

In most cases, you will enable proxy server access as follows:

- Select Automatic proxy configuration

- Enter the URL of the Proxy Server server in the Configuration location field. The automatic configuration URL is discussed earlier in this chapter in the text associated with Figure 21.13.

As configured in Figure 21.49, Netscape will use the same proxy server and port for all services. If you need to manually configure the services, select **Manual proxy configuration**. Then click **View** to open the dialog box shown in Figure 21.50, where settings can be individually entered for each protocol.

FIGURE 21.50

Manual proxy server settings for Netscape Navigator.

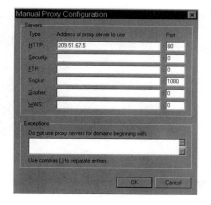

Configuring the WinSock Proxy Client

There isn't much to configure in the WinSock Proxy client, but what there is you do with the WSP Client that is added to the Control Panel when the Proxy Server client software is installed. The WSP Client applet is shown in Figure 21.51.

If you want to use a different Proxy Server:

1. Edit the Configuration Location field with the new server name. This must be a computer name. It cannot be a DNS name that resolves to multiple DNS addresses.

2. Click **Update Now** to download the WinSock Proxy client configuration from the new server.

There might be times when you want to disable the WinSock Proxy server client. To do so, remove the check from **Enable WinSock Proxy Client**.

NOTE

One reason for disabling the WinSock Proxy Client is that it prevents you from using Dial-Up Networking in the client computer. While the WinSock Proxy Client is active, the client consults the LAT to determine whether a service request is local or remote. All remote requests are directed to Proxy Server.

That means that you use an Internet access account while the WinSock Proxy Client is active because all WinSock requests are directed to Proxy Server instead of the dial-up connection. That effectively prevents you from using a private Internet dial-up account when Proxy Server is down or unavailable. So, you must use the Proxy Server Client applet to disable the WinSock Proxy Client before you dial out.

FIGURE 21.51
*Configuring the
WinSock Proxy client.*

Using Proxy Server

Actually, this is a trick section, because after the client is configured there is nothing special about using it with Proxy Server. Users browse as usual, and Proxy Server should work more or less transparently. A couple of things you should tell your users follow, however:

- When you start a browser and enter the first request for a URL, it seems to take an extended period of time to establish the initial connection with the Proxy Server and retrieve the first page.

- Subsequent requests are serviced pretty much as they would be if the client had a direct Internet connection, except that requests that can be filled from Proxy Server's cache are fulfilled almost instantly.

Beyond that, there's not much your users need to know. You should, of course, inform them of any access restrictions you have imposed. Aside from that, however, Proxy Server is unobtrusive.

Monitoring Client Sessions

The Proxy Server property pages have a Current Sessions button that opens the dialog box shown in Figure 21.52. From this dialog box you can view lists of active sessions on each proxy server. Keep in mind that a Web server opens a new TCP connection for each request and does not keep a session constantly open. Consequently, Web clients will appear and disappear from the sessions lists depending on their recent activity.

FIGURE 21.52

Monitoring Proxy Server sessions.

The End of the Trail

Well, that's the end of a very long trail. Starting with communications basics we've worked our way up to some pretty sophisticated TCP/IP tasks. If you've stayed with me through all the discussion, you can consider yourself to be a TCP/IP expert, with enough knowledge that you can probably pass Microsoft's MCSE exam on TCP/IP with little or no trouble.

But that doesn't mean you know everything there is to know about TCP/IP. If you want to delve into greater depth on the TCP/IP protocol suite, I highly recommend *Inside TCP/IP* by Karanjit Siyan, also published by New Riders Publishing. And don't forget to check out the RFCs and Internet Drafts on the IETF Web site. New IETF documents are being published at an amazing pace, and the rate of change appears, if anything, to be accelerating. Your career as a TCP/IP network administrator is certain to remain challenging and exciting.

Appendix

When working with TCP/IP, encountering binary, decimal and hexadecimal number representations is unavoid able. Subnet masks, for example, are written in dotted decimal form, but the workings of subnet masks must be understood in binary. And some computer numbers, such as the contents of large blocks of memory, can comfortably be expressed only in hexadecimal form. It is the purpose of this appendix to simplify these number systems.

All data in computers are represented internally by switches, which are either on or off (or high/low, or some other either/or situation). A single switch that represents a two-state value is called a *bit*, a name which derives from the expression *binary digit*. *Binary* refers to a numbering system in which digits have only two states, making binary a natural match for computer memory.

A single bit is pretty limited in the range of data it can represent. Most data are more complex than the either/or data that can be represented by a single bit, and it usually takes many bits to represent any substantial real-world value. When working with large sequences of bits, engineers need a shorthand method for representing the positions of all those switches. Writing down "on-off-off-on-off-off-off-on" whenever representing the positions of a series of computer switches isn't very convenient.

That is why binary representation was adopted for computers. If 1 represents one state of the switch and 0 the other state, representing a group of switches as something like 10001001 is easy. Binary numbers aren't that hard to understand. Before attempting an explanation, however, reviewing the way everyday decimal numbering works should prove useful. Decimal notation is based on powers of 10, and you probably have no trouble understanding that the decimal number 5,821 is evaluated as follows:

5 represents 5×10^3 ($5 \times 10 \times 10 \times 10 = 5 \times 1,000$)

8 represents 8×10^2 ($8 \times 10 \times 10 = 8 \times 100$)

2 represents 2×10^1 (2×10)

1 represents 1×10^0 (1×1)

This same procedure applies with binary and hexadecimal numbers. Binary numbers are based on powers of 2, and the binary number 1011 evaluates like this:

1 represents 1×2^3 ($1 \times 2 \times 2 \times 2 = 1 \times 8$)

0 represents 0×2^2 ($0 \times 2 \times 2 = 0 \times 4$)

1 represents 1×2^1 (1×2)

1 represents 1×2^0 (1×1)

From the preceding breakdown, you can see that the binary number 1011 is equivalent to the decimal number 11.

Because you encounter binary numbers quite frequently, you should find remembering the powers of 2 through 2^8 useful:

$2^0 = 1$, $2^1 = 2$, $2^2 = 4$, $2^3 = 8$, $2^4 = 16$, $2^5 = 32$, $2^6 = 64$, $2^7 = 128$, $2^8 = 256$

If you were to apply these values to a byte that consists entirely of 1s, you would see that the highest value that eight bits can represent is 11111111, which is 255 decimal.

Long series of binary digits are very difficult for humans to scan, and the networking profession frequently uses two different representations to make long binary numbers more human-friendly.

One form is the dotted-decimal form used to represent IP addresses. In dotted-decimal notation, a 32-bit IP address is broken into four 8-bit groups like this:

01101101 11101101 00010001 11110010

Each 8-bit group is then represented by a decimal number in the range of 0 through 255 like this:

109 237 17 242

The preceding is then represented in dotted-decimal form as 109.237.17.242. Granted, not many of us can convert 8 bits to a decimal value without considerable help, but the end result is much easier to handle.

Apart from IP addresses, however, the most common way to represent large binary numbers is hexadecimal notation, usually called *hex*. Hex notation begins by breaking binary numbers into groups of four bits like this:

0110 1101 1110 1101 0001 0001 1111 0010

Each four-bit group represents a decimal value in the range of 0 through 15. Hex notation uses the digits 0 through 9 for values up to 10. For 10 through 15, hex uses the letters A through F. Table A.1 summarizes the binary, decimal, and hex values through 15.

TABLE A.1

Binary, Decimal, and Hexadecimal Equivalents

Binary	Decimal	Hexadecimal
0000	0	0
0001	1	1
0010	2	2

continues

TABLE A.1, CONTINUED

Binary, Decimal, and Hexadecimal Equivalents

Binary	Decimal	Hexadecimal
0011	3	3
0100	4	4
0101	5	5
0110	6	6
0111	7	7
1000	8	8
1001	9	9
1010	10	A
1011	11	B
1100	12	C
1101	13	D
1110	14	E
1111	15	F

Because each hex digit corresponds to four bits, representing any binary number in hex form is easy. Consider the following example:

0110	1101	1110	1101	0001	0001	1111	0100
6	D	E	D	1	1	F	2

Two common notations are used to identify hexadecimal numbers. One is a trailing h, for example, 29h. Another is the representation used in C programming, which prefixes the hex number with 0x, for example, 0x29. You encounter both notations when working with Microsoft TCP/IP.

NOTE

The Windows Calculator applet is a handy tool for converting numbers among various base representations. Choose **Scientific** in the **View** menu to display the scientific calculator options.

Index

Symbols

N